The Open University

A206
The Enlightenment

Texts, I

Edited by Simon Eliot and Keith Whitlock

First published in 1992 by

The Open University
Walton Hall
Milton Keynes
United Kingdom
MK7 6AA

ISBN 0 7492 1102 4

Acknowledgements

Grateful thanks are due to Professor A. G. Cross and Mr Robert Dimsdale for permission to use documents 16, 31, 41 and 43 in the section on Catherine the Great.

Edited, designed and typeset by The Open University.

This book forms part of an Open University course A206 *The Enlightenment*.

Printed and bound in Great Britain by The Bath Press, Bath
1.7
16496C/A206texti1.7

Contents

Introduction

Michael Bartholomew

The four volumes of *Texts* contain most of the text studied on A206, *The Enlightenment*. Volumes I and II contain printed texts (including a music score and libretti), and of the other two volumes, one, the Illustration Book, contains visual texts and the other is the full English translation of *Nathan the Wise*. In all four volumes, the grouping of the texts follows the pattern established in the two volumes of *Studies*, which contain most of the teaching material associated with the course. Additionally, there is a folder of engravings to accompany the Adam texts and study.

In preparing these texts for publication, a number of compromises have had to be struck. On one hand, we wished to present you with versions which are close to those read, seen or heard at the time of their publication, during the eighteenth century. But on the other hand, we did not wish to encumber you with the unproductive difficulties that can arise from struggles with eighteenth-century typography, punctuation and spelling. It is productive for all readers to go, from time to time, to a good dictionary to look up a word that has fallen out of common usage, or whose meaning has shifted during the past two hundred and fifty years, but the pure doctrine of absolute fidelity to the original text becomes an irritation when it forces readers to keep stumbling over the eighteenth-century letter 's', which, to the modern eye, is hardly distinguishable from the modern 'f'.

Moreover, what ought to be done with the many texts here which are translations, from French, German, Russian or Italian? Should the modern translator attempt a sort of pastiche of eighteenth-century English, or render the text into modern prose?

Or again, how should we handle the problem of abridging lengthy texts down to the selections printed in these volumes? The pure doctrine dictates that every single amendment to the original document ought to be clearly signalled, and that any material that has been cut should be signalled by an ellipsis.

The result is, as we have said, a series of compromises. First, each section is preceded by a headnote which explains what the editor has done with it. In some cases – particularly those in which the text is unabridged – very little, if any modification will have taken place. In other cases, where an abridgement of an extremely long work is being presented, an indication of how the abridgement has been made, will be given. Secondly, the volumes as a whole have a number of conventions running through them. We have tended not to signal every omission of a passage from the original by an ellipsis, on the grounds that they interfere with the flow of the passages. We have modernized some spellings and punctuation, often on marginal, and finally arbitrary grounds: should 'cloaths' be modernized into 'clothes', for instance? In some passages, however, the original spellings have been adhered to, in order to make the useful point that some eighteenth-century writers and printers were inconsistent in their spelling even within one document. Source references are given at the end of each text.

Translations are mostly given in modern English. One text, though, – Rousseau's *Émile* – was translated into English during the eighteenth century. We have based our text on an early translation, with a number of small modifications where the translation does not come up to modern standards of accuracy.

The engravings by Adam in the folder are reproduced to a larger size than the pages of these volumes. They are thus easier to study. None the less, they are still at a scale smaller than the originals, and some of the detail in the captions is hard to read. Consequently, we have added explanatory keys that give the information contained in the original captions. In addition, the original captions to the engravings, written by Adam, are provided in *Texts*, I.

Finally, a word on footnotes. Many of the texts have them, and you will need to be clear about how they work. There are three quite different sorts of footnotes:

1   Footnotes written by the eighteenth-century author of the text. Unless indicated otherwise, footnotes will be of this sort.

2   Footnotes added by a later editor or translator, but not by a member of the A206 Course Team. Often we have used excellent scholarly texts, and we have readily taken over their scholarly apparatuses. We have signified this sort of footnote by giving the scholar's initials, or name, within square brackets.

3   Footnotes added by A206 Course Team editors. These are signified by the term 'eds', within square brackets.

Part A
Varieties of Enlightenment

Contents

The Encyclopédie

Prepared for the Course Team by
Michael Bartholomew, Stephanie Clennell
and Linda Walsh

Contents

The Encyclopédie

The following extracts come from the Encyclopédie, *pub-lished in seventeen volumes of texts and eleven volumes of plates between 1751 and 1772. This vast encyclopedia was edited and overseen by Denis Diderot (1713–84), aided in the early stages by Jean d'Alembert (1717–83). Its thousands of entries, many of them written by the leading philosophes of the period, combine to make the enterprise one of the central achievements of the French Enlightenment.*

The extracts printed here are necessarily short, and each has been edited. The source of the complete passages in the French first edition is given at the foot of each extract. Obscure phrases and words have been glossed in the foot-notes. In some extracts, summaries of passages which have been omitted are given in the text within square brackets.

Section 1   The purpose of Encyclopedias and the role of the **philosophe**

1 ENCYCLOPEDIA by Diderot

ENCYCLOPEDIA (philosophy). This word means interconnection of knowledge; it is made up of the Greek preposition *en*, in, and the nouns *kyklos*, circle, and *paideia*, knowledge.

The aim of an encyclopedia is to bring together the knowledge scattered over the sur-face of the earth, to present its overall structure to our contemporaries and to hand it on to those who will come after us, so that our chil-dren, by becoming more knowledgeable, will become more virtuous and happier; and so that we shall not die without earning the gratitude of the human race.

[Diderot goes on to say that a work on this scale can be done only by many people working together. The Académie Française took sixty years to produce its dictionary. Many specialists are needed for definitions alone, even more for the coverage of all the subjects in an encyclo-pedia.]

A universal and rational dictionary of the sciences and the arts cannot then be the work of a single man. I will go further. I do not think that it can be the work of any of the existing lit-erary or learned societies working either indi-vidually or in co-operation.

[The work of each academy is specialized, but an encyclopedia has to make links between branches of knowledge.]

An encyclopedia which undertakes this project will necessarily include not only the fields covered by our academies, but all branches of human knowledge. Such a work can be car-ried out only by a society of men of letters and artisans, each working in his own field, and bound together by the general interest of humanity and by a feeling of mutual benevo-lence.

I say 'a society of men of letters and artisans' in order to include all the talents.

[Contributions must come from different fields and no one learned society has all the knowledge needed.]

I add 'men united by the general interest of humanity and a feeling of mutual benevolen-ce' because the motives, being the most honest ones which can inspire decent people, are also the most durable. You approve of yourself in what you do; you are enthusiastic; you will do for your colleague or your friend things that you would not undertake for any other reason; and I can confirm from experience that the success of what is undertaken is thereby more certain. The *Encyclopédie* has collected its material in a com-paratively short time. It has not been base self-interest which has united and spurred on the authors. They have seen their efforts supported by the majority of those men of letters from whom they could expect some help; and they have been hindered only by those lacking the talent to contribute even a single good page.

A work like this will not be completed if a government becomes involved. Its influence should be limited to supporting the work under-taken.

[Diderot here gives details of the kind of thing which makes the work drag on: no one is really in charge and there are many conflicts of interest. If the work takes too long it quickly becomes out of date, especially in the sciences and in the mechanical arts.]

But what will make the work seem out of date and bring it into disrepute is above all the revolution which will take place in the minds of men and in the national character. Nowadays philosophy is advancing with great strides; it influences every subject it deals with; its tone is dominant and it is beginning to shake off the yoke of authority and tradition and to follow the laws of reason; but there is no satisfactory basic instructional work to take account of these developments. There are only works based on what has already been written by others: none goes straight to the truth of nature. Such are the effects of progress in reason which will knock down so many statues and restore others which have been knocked down. These will be the statues of those rare men who have been in advance of their time.

[Works become out of date. Esoteric knowledge of one period becomes commonplace in the next. This is reflected in rapid change and development in language. Work on any encyclopedia must be done quickly to keep up with the changes.]

Yet knowledge becomes, and can become common to all only up to a point. In fact we do not know what this limit is. We do not know just how far any individual can go. We know even less how far the human race could go, what it would be capable of, if progress were unhindered. But revolutions are necessary; they have always taken place and always will; the maximum interval between one revolution and the next is fixed. For this reason alone the scope of the work is limited. In the sciences there is a point beyond which it is hardly possible to go. When this point is reached what survives of their achievements will be the marvel of the entire human race for all time. But if the efforts of the human race are limited, how much more so are those of any individual. The capacity of any individual's faculties – both animal and intellectual – is limited; his life is short; he is forced into alternating work and rest; he must satisfy passions and needs and he is subject to an infinite number of distractions.

The most glorious moment for a work like this would come immediately after some great revolution which had cut short progress in science, interrupted work in the arts and plunged part of our hemisphere into darkness. What gratitude the generation which comes after this troubled time will feel for the men who anticipated it long before and who prevented the havoc it would cause by safeguarding the knowledge of past ages.

[Diderot then discusses the nature and role of language, through which all knowledge is conveyed and by which one can estimate the level of cultural development of a nation.]

Above all we should not lose sight of one consideration, which is that if man or some thinking or contemplative being is banished from the face of the earth, the sublime and pathetic spectacle of nature would be no more than a sad, mute scene. The universe would be dumb; night and silence would reign. Everything would turn into a vast solitude, where unobserved phenomena would move dimly and unheard. It is the presence of man which makes creatures interesting and what better way can be found of dealing with the history of these creatures than to accept this view? Why not give man the same place in our work as he has in the universe? Is there any place in infinite space which would give us a better starting point for the infinite number of connecting links which we want to lead to all the other points? That is what made us decide to take the principal faculties of man[1] as the general headings under which we have classified our work.

You may follow any other path you prefer, provided that you do not substitute some mute, insensible, cold creature for man. Man is the only starting point to which you return, if you want to arouse pleasure, interest, involvement in even the most arid matters and the driest details. Take away my existence and the happiness of my fellow men and what does the rest of nature mean to me?

[The different parts of the *Encyclopédie* must be kept in proportion, links made between them and contributions suitably edited. Diderot then discusses at length the use of cross-references: these can link subjects, suggest new ideas, be controversial by suggesting opposing ideas and occasionally be satirical.]

We think we are aware of all the advantages of an enterprise such as the one we are working on. We have been only too frequently aware of the difficulty of achieving some degree of success in a first attempt and of how the talents of any one man, whoever he might be, were not adequate for this project. Long before we started we had some insight into this and had all the

---

[1] Memory, reason, imagination. [eds]

reservations which come from long reflection about it. These expectations have been fully confirmed by experience. As we worked, we found that the subject matter expanded, nomenclature became confused, substances were introduced under an immense number of different names, instruments, machines and processes constantly increased in number and the many paths through an inextricable labyrinth got more and more complicated. We saw what effort was needed to assure ourselves that identical concepts were the same and what was needed to make sure that others which seemed very different were in fact identical. The alphabetical order which was constantly a relief to us and which brought so much variety to our work and which in these respects seemed so advantageous to follow in a long work, equally constantly faced us with difficulties. We saw how important and how difficult it was to find a happy mean. We saw that only several centuries of work could impose a proper order on such a mass of material; make sure that each part was in proportion; reduce each article to a reasonable length; cut out what is bad, supplement what is lacking and complete the plan which was made when the work was started. We saw that the *Encyclopédie* could be undertaken only in a philosophical century; that this century is here; that reputation, which will give immortality to the names of those who carried it out, will perhaps not scorn to include our own.

[Fundamental principles must be clearly set out.]

I said that the *Encyclopédie* can be produced only in a philosophical century and I said so, because the entire work demands a bolder outlook than is usually found in faint-hearted centuries which are preoccupied with good taste. Everything must be brought to light, boldly, without exceptions and unsparingly.

[Diderot finishes the article by saying that the first edition has many imperfections. He gives details of the way in which they have worked (including advice never to send manuscripts to the censor, only printed pages), praises the team work and points out that they have insisted on good writing throughout. It is a work for posterity and will be even more appreciated in years to come.]

Source: Encyclopédie, translated by S. Clennell, volume v, 1755, pp.635–48.

2 PHILOSOPHE *Anonymous*

Other men are impelled to act without feeling or knowing the causes which lead them to do so. The *philosophe* on the contrary works out the causes as far as he can, and often even anticipates them, and accepts them with understanding: he is like a clock which, you might say, sometimes winds itself up. So he avoids objects which can arouse in him feelings which are not conducive to well-being or to being a reasonable person, and seeks those which can give rise to reactions on his part which fit in with his own situation. Reason is, for the *philosophe*, what grace is to the Christian. It is grace which impels the Christian to act; it is reason which impels the *philosophe*.

Other men are swept along by their passions without reflecting before they take action: they are men who walk in darkness; on the other hand the *philosophe*, even in his passions, acts only after reflecting; he is walking at night, but there is a torch in front of him.

The *philosophe* bases his principles on an infinite number of particular observations. The people adopt the principle without thinking about the observations which have led to it: they think that the maxim exists as it were on its own, but the *philosophe* goes back to the sources of the maxim; he examines its origins, he knows its true value, and uses as much of it as suits him.

[From this knowledge that principles are derived only from particular observations the philosophe derives a respect for the science of facts; he likes to learn about details and about all that is not guesswork; so he considers that a mind which concentrates on meditation alone and which holds that man arrives at the truth from within himself is a fundamentally unenlightened mind.]

For the *philosophe* truth is not a mistress who corrupts his imagination and which he believes he can find everywhere; he limits himself to being able to distinguish it when he can perceive it. He does not confuse it with probability; he takes as true what is true, as false what is false, as doubtful what is doubtful and as probable what is only probable. He does more, in that a great strength of the *philosophe* is that, when he has no reason to judge, he can suspend judgement.

So the philosophic mind concentrates on observation and precision, which take everything back to its fundamental principles; but it is not only the mind which the *philosophe* cultivates, his attention and his concerns go further than this.

Man is not a monster who must live only at the bottom of the sea or in the depths of a forest. The needs of everyday life mean that he needs to associate with other people; and whatever his circumstances may be, his own needs and well-being commit him to living in society. Therefore reason requires him to know, study and work to acquire sociable qualities.

Our *philosophe* does not think he is in exile in this world; he does not think he is in a hostile country; as a sensible manager he wants to enjoy the benefits which nature offers him; he wants to find pleasure in the company of others; and to find this he has to give it; so he tries to fit in with those among whom he lives by chance or by his own choice; and at the same time he finds what suits himself: he is a civilized man who wants to give pleasure and make himself useful.

Most people of high rank, whose many activities do not leave them enough time for meditation, are ferocious to those who in their view are not their equals. Ordinary philosophers who meditate too much, or rather who are bad at meditation, are ferocious to everyone; they escape from men and men avoid them. But our *philosophe*, who is able to divide his time between solitude and human society, is full of humanity. He is like Terence's[2] Chremes who feels that he is a man and that his very humanity makes him concerned with the bad or good fortunes of his neighbour. *Homo sum humani a me nihil alienum puto.*[3]

It should be unnecessary to point out here how much concern the *philosophe* has for everything called honour and integrity. Civil society is in a sense a divinity on earth to him; he praises it warmly, honours it with integrity, with exact attention to his duties and by a sincere desire not to be a useless or tiresome member of it. Feeling for integrity plays as great a part in the mechanical constitution of the *philosophe* as the enlightenment of the mind. The more reason you find in a man the more integrity you find. On the other hand where fanaticism and superstition dominate, passions and anger dominate. The *philosophe*'s temperament is to act according to a sense of order or to reason; as he is strongly attached to society, it is much more important for him than for other men to do everything that he can to produce only effects which fit in with the idea of a civilized man. There is no fear that, because no one is keeping an eye on him, he will embark on an action which betrays his integrity. No. Such an action in no way fits the mechanism of a civilized man; you might say he is kneaded with the yeast of order and rules; he is filled with the idea of the good of civil society; he knows the principles of it better than other men. Crime would be too much against his nature, he would have to destroy too many natural and too many acquired ideas. His capacity to act is, as it were, tuned to a certain note like a string of a musical instrument; it cannot produce a different one. He is afraid of being out of tune, of not being in harmony with himself; and that reminds me of what Velleius said of Cato of Utica:[4] 'He never', he said, 'did good actions in order to be seen to be doing them, but because it was not in his nature to act otherwise'.

This love of society, which is so essential to the *philosophe*, shows how true the Emperor Antoninus's[5] remark was: 'How happy peoples will be when kings are philosophers or when philosophers are kings!'.

The true *philosophe*, then, is a civilized man who acts in all things according to reason, and who combines a spirit of reflection and precision with social manners and qualities. Graft a sovereign on to a philosopher of like quality and you will have a perfect sovereign.

Source: Philosophe, translated by S.Clennell, volume xii, 1765, pp.509–11.

---

[2] Publius Terentius Afer (Terence c.190–159 BC), a Roman playwright. Chremes was a character in his play *Heauton timorumenos* (*The self-tormentor*). [eds]

[3] I am a man and nothing which is human is foreign to me. [eds]

[4] Velleius the historian Velleius Paterculus, who lived and wrote at the time of the Emperor Tiberius (AD 14–37). [eds]

[5] Titus Aurelius Fulvus Antoninus Pius (AD 86–161), Roman emperor. [eds]

3 MEN OF LETTERS by Voltaire

MEN OF LETTERS (philosophy and literature). This name corresponds exactly to 'grammarians'. The Greeks and the Romans designated by 'grammarian' not someone who was merely versed in grammar – the basis of all knowledge – but a man familiar with geometry, philosophy, and general and particular history, a man whose special studies were poetry and eloquence. Today that is what our *men of letters* are. This name is not given to a man whose knowledge is limited and who cultivates only one *genre* of literature. No man is considered a *man of letters* if he has read only novels and writes nothing but novels, if without any literary background he happens to have written some plays or if without any knowledge he has composed some sermons. Today the name '*man of letters*' has an even more extended meaning than the 'grammarian' of the Greeks and Romans. The Greeks were only interested in their own language, the Romans learned only Greek, but today a *man of letters* often studies Italian, Spanish, and especially English, as well as Greek and Latin. The scope of history is a hundred times more vast than it was at the time of the ancients and natural history has grown in the same proportion as the history of nations. It is not expected that a man of letters delve deeply into all these subjects: universality of knowledge is no longer within man's grasp, but true *men of letters* acquire the ability to venture into these different fields even if they cannot cultivate them all.

Formerly, in the sixteenth century and well into the seventeenth, *men of letters* devoted much time to grammatical criticism of Greek and Latin authors. To their labours we owe dictionaries, correct editions, and commentaries on the masterpieces of antiquity. Today this criticism is no longer so necessary and has given way to the philosophic spirit. This spirit seems to characterize *men of letters*; and when it is combined with good taste, it produces a perfect literary man.

Our century enjoys a great advantage over former times in having such a great number of educated men who pass from the thorns of mathematics to the flowers of poetry and judge equally well a book of metaphysics and a play. The spirit of the century has made most of them as much at ease in society as in their study. This is the great advantage they hold over *men of letters* of preceding centuries. Up to the time of Balzac and Voiture[6] they were not admitted to society; since that time they have become a necessary part of it. The profound and clear reasoning which many have infused into their books and their conversation has done much to instruct and polish the nation. Their criticism is no longer spent on Greek and Latin works but, with the aid of a sound philosophy, it has destroyed all the prejudices with which society was afflicted: astrologers' predictions, the divinings of magicians, all types of witchcraft, false prodigies, false marvels, and superstitious customs. This philosophy has relegated to the schools thousands of childish disputations which had formerly been dangerous and have now become objects of scorn. In this way *men of letters* have in fact served the state. We are sometimes amazed that matters which formerly disturbed the world no longer trouble it today. We owe this to true *men of letters*.

They are ordinarily more independent of mind than other men. Those who were born poor easily find in the endowments established by Louis XIV the means to strengthen this intellectual independence. We no longer encounter, as formerly, those dedicatory epistles offered to vanity by self-interest and servility.

A *man of letters* is not what we call a wit. One does not need to know philosophy to be a wit, nor does one need to be so learned and cultivated. To be a wit requires above all a brilliant imagination, a mastery of the art of conversation, and wide reading. A wit may well not merit the name of *man of letters*, and a *man of letters* may not be able to aspire to the brilliance of the wit.

There are many *men of letters* who do not publish anything. They are probably the happiest of all. They are spared the humiliations that the profession of author sometimes brings with it, as well as the quarrels occasioned by rivalry, partisan spite, and unfounded opinions. They live in greater concord with each other, they enjoy sociability more, they are the judges while the others suffer judgement.

Source: Gens de lettres, translated by N.Hoyt and T.Cassirer, volume vii, 1757, pp.599–600.

---

[6]   Jean-Louise Guez de Balzac (1595–1654), essayist, and Vincent Voiture (1598–1648), poet and letter-writer, were prominent French authors of their period. [eds]

Section 2   Government and society

4 POLITICAL AUTHORITY by Diderot

No man has received from nature the right to command others. Liberty is a gift from heaven, and each individual of the same species has the right to enjoy it as soon as he enjoys the use of reason. If nature has established any *authority*, it is paternal control; but paternal control has its limits, and in the state of nature it would terminate when the children could take care of themselves. Any other *authority* comes from another origin than nature. If one seriously considers this matter, one will always go back to one of these two sources: either the force and violence of an individual who has seized it, or the consent of those who have submitted to it by a contract made or assumed between them and the individual on whom they have bestowed *authority*.

Power that is acquired by violence is only usurpation and only lasts as long as the force of the individual who commands can prevail over the force of those who obey; in such a way that if the latter become in their turn the strongest party and then shake off the yoke, they do it with as much right and justice as the other who had imposed it upon them. The same law that made *authority* can then destroy it; for this is the law of might.

Sometimes *authority* that is established by violence changes its nature; this is when it continues and is maintained with the express consent of those who have been brought into subjection, but in this case it reverts to the second case about which I am going to speak; and the individual who had arrogated it then becomes a prince, ceasing to be a tyrant.

Power that comes from the consent of the people necessarily presupposes certain conditions that make its use legitimate, useful to society, advantageous to the republic, and set and restrict it between limits: for man must not nor cannot give himself entirely and without reserve to another man, because he has a master superior to everything, to whom he alone belongs in his entire being. It is God, whose power always has a direct bearing on each creature, a master as jealous as absolute, who never

loses his rights and does not transfer them. He permits for the common good and for the maintenance of society that men establish among themselves an order of subordination, that they obey one of them [i.e. one man], but he wishes that it be done with reason and proportion and not by blindness and without reservation, so that the creature does not arrogate the rights of the creator. Any other submission is the veritable crime of idolatry. To bend one's knee before a man or an image is merely an external ceremony about which the true God, who demands the heart and the mind, hardly cares. He leaves, to the institution of men to do with as they please, the tokens of civil and political devotion or of religious worship. Thus it is not these ceremonies in themselves, but the spirit of their establishment that makes their observance innocent or criminal. An Englishman has no scruples about serving the king on one knee; the ceremonial only signifies what people wanted it to signify. But to deliver one's heart, spirit, and conduct without any reservation to the will and caprice of a mere creature, making him the unique and final reason for one's actions, is assuredly a crime of divine *lèse majesté*[7] of the highest degree.

The prince owes to his very subjects the *authority* that he has over them; and this *authority* is limited by the laws of nature and the state. The laws of nature and the state are the conditions under which they have submitted or are supposed to have submitted to its government. One of these conditions is that, not having any power or *authority* over them but by their choice and consent, he can never employ this *authority* to break the act or the contract by which it was transferred to him. From that time on he would work against himself, since his *authority* could only subsist by virtue of the right that established it. Whoever annuls one, destroys the other. The prince cannot therefore dispose of his power and his subjects without the consent of the nation and independently of the option indicated in the contract of allegiance.

Moreover the government, although hereditary in a family and placed in the hands of one person, is not private property, but public property that consequently can never be taken from the people, to whom it belongs exclusively,

---

[7] High treason. [eds]

fundamentally, and as a freehold. Consequently it is always the people who make the lease or the agreement: they always intervene in the contract that adjudges its exercise. It is not the state that belongs to the prince, it is the prince that belongs to the state: but it does rest with the prince to govern in the state, because the state has chosen him for that purpose: he has bound himself to the people and the administration of affairs, and they in their turn are bound to obey him according to the laws. The person who wears the crown can certainly discharge himself of it completely if he wishes, but he cannot replace it on the head of another without the consent of the nation who has placed it on his. In a word, the crown, the government, and the public *authority* are possessions owned by the body of the nation, held as a usufruct[8] by princes and as a trust by ministers. Although heads of state, they are none the less members of it; as a matter of fact the first, the most venerable, and the most powerful allowed everything in order to govern, allowed nothing legitimately to change the established government or to place another head in their place. The sceptre of Louis XV necessarily passes to his eldest son, and there is no power who can oppose this; nor any nation because it is the condition of the contract; nor his father for the same reason.

The depositing of *authority* is sometimes only for a limited time, as in the Roman republic. It is sometimes for the life of only one man, as in Poland; sometimes for all the time a family exists, as in England; sometimes for the time a family exists only through its male descendants, as in France.

This depository[9] is sometimes entrusted to a certain class in society, sometimes to several people chosen by all the classes, and sometimes to one man.

The conditions of this pact are different in different states. But everywhere the nation has a right to maintain against all forces the contract that they have made; no power can change it; and when it is no longer valid, the nation recovers its rights and full freedom to enter into a new one with whomever and however it pleases them. This is what would happen in France if by

the greatest of misfortunes the entire reigning family happened to die out, including the most remote descendants; then the sceptre and the crown would return to the nation.

It seems that only slaves whose minds are as limited as their hearts are debased could think otherwise. Such men are born neither for the glory of the prince nor for the benefit of society; they have neither virtue nor greatness of soul. Fear and self-interest are the motives of their conduct. Nature only produces them to improve by contrast the worth of virtuous men; and Providence uses them to make tyrannical powers, with which it chastises as a rule the people and the sovereigns who offend God; the latter for usurping, the former for granting too much to man of supreme power, that the Creator reserved for Himself over the created being.

The observation of laws, the conservation of liberty, and the love of country are the prolific sources of all great things and of all beautiful actions. Here we can find the happiness of people, and the true lustre of princes who govern them. Here obedience is glorious, and command august. On the contrary, flattery, self-interest, and the spirit of slavery are at the root of all the evils that overpower a state and of all the cowardice that dishonour it. There the subjects are miserable, and the princes hated; there the monarch has never heard himself proclaimed *the beloved*; submission is hateful there, and domination cruel. If I view France and Turkey from the same perspective, I perceive on the one hand a society of men united by reason, activated by virtue, and governed by a head of state equally wise and glorious according to the laws of justice; on the other, a herd of animals assembled by habit, driven by the law of the rod, and led by an absolute master according to his caprice.

Source: Autorité politique, translated by S.J. Gendzier, volume i, 1751, pp.898–900.

5 NATURAL EQUALITY by de Jaucourt

NATURAL EQUALITY (natural law) is that which is found among all men solely by the constitution of their nature. This *equality* is the principle and foundation of liberty.

---

[8] A legal term meaning 'the right of temporary possession'. [eds]

[9] Of authority. [eds]

Natural or *moral equality* is therefore based on the constitution of human nature common to all men, who are born, grow, live and die in the same way.

Since human nature is the same in all men, it is clear according to natural law that each person must value and treat other people as so many individuals who are naturally equal to himself, that is to say, as men like himself.

Several consequences ensue from this principle of the *natural equality of men*. I shall rapidly examine the principal ones.

1   It follows from this principle that all men are naturally free and that the faculty of reason could only make them dependent for their own welfare.

2   That in spite of all the inequalities produced in the political government by the difference in station, by nobility, power, riches, etc., those who have risen the most above others must treat their inferiors as being naturally equal to them by avoiding any insults, by demanding nothing beyond what is required, and by demanding with humanity only what is unquestionably due.

3   That whoever has not acquired a particular right by virtue of which he can demand preferential treatment, must not claim more than others but, on the contrary, allow them to enjoy equally the same rights that he assumes for himself.

4   That anything which is a universal right must be either universally enjoyed or alternately possessed, or divided into equal portions among those who have the same right, or allotted with equitable and regulated compensation; or finally if this is [im]possible, the decision should be made by lot: a quite suitable expedient that removes any suspicion of contempt and partiality without diminishing in any way the esteem of those people not immediately favoured. Finally, to go even further, I base on the incontestable principle of

natural equality, as did the judicious Hooker,[10] all the duties of charity, of humanity, and of justice which all men are obliged to practise towards one another, and it would not be difficult to demonstrate this.

The reader will derive further consequences that arise from the principle of the *natural equality* of men. I shall observe only that it is the violation of this principle that has established political and civil slavery. The result is that in the countries subject to arbitrary power, the princes, the courtiers, the principal ministers, those who control the finances, possess all the riches of the nation, while the rest of the citizens have only the necessaries of life, and the great majority of people groan in poverty.

Nevertheless let no one do me the injustice of supposing that with a sense of fanaticism I approve in a state that chimera, absolute *equality*, which could hardly give birth to an ideal republic. I am only speaking here of the *natural equality* of men. I know too well the necessity of different ranks, grades, honours, distinctions, prerogatives, subordinations that must prevail in all governments. And I would even state that *natural* or *moral equality* are not contrary to this. In the state of nature men are truly born into *equality* but do not know how to remain so. Society forces them to lose it, and they only become equal again by laws. Aristotle[11] relates that Phaleas of Chalcedon had imagined a way to equalize the fortunes of the republic: he would have the rich give dowries to the poor and not receive any in their turn, and the poor receive money for their daughters and not give any to others. 'But,' as the author of the *Spirit of Laws*[12] has observed, 'has any republic ever accommodated itself to such a regulation? It places the citizens in conditions of such striking discrimination that they would hate even that equality that one would attempt to establish, and that would be foolish to try to introduce.'

Source: Égalité naturelle, translated by S. Gendzier, volume v, 1755, p.415.

---

[10]   Richard Hooker (1554–1600), English theologian and jurist, author of *Of Laws of Ecclesiastical Polity* (1594). [eds]

[11]   Aristotle (384–322 BC), Greek philosopher and scientist. [eds]

[12]   Charles de Secondat, Baron de la Brède et de Montesquieu (1689–1755), wrote *De l'esprit des lois* (*The Spirit of the Laws*) (1748). [eds]

6 THE SLAVE TRADE by de Jaucourt

THE SLAVE TRADE (Commerce of Africa) is the buying of unfortunate Negroes by Europeans on the coast of Africa to use as slaves in their colonies. This buying of Negroes, to reduce them to slavery, is one business that violates religion, morality, natural laws, and all the rights of human nature.

Negroes, says a modern Englishman full of enlightenment and humanity, have not become slaves by the right of war; neither do they deliver themselves voluntarily into bondage, and consequently their children are not born slaves. Nobody is unaware that they are bought from their own princes, who claim to have the right to dispose of their liberty, and that traders have them transported in the same way as their other goods, either in their colonies or in America, where they are displayed for sale.

If commerce of this kind can be justified by a moral principle, there is no crime, however atrocious it may be, that cannot be made legitimate. Kings, princes, and magistrates are not the proprietors of their subjects: they do not, therefore, have the right to dispose of their liberty and to sell them as slaves.

On the other hand, no man has the right to buy them or to make himself their master. Men and their liberty are not objects of commerce; they can be neither sold nor bought nor paid for at any price. We must conclude from this that a man whose slave has run away should only blame himself, since he had acquired for money illicit goods whose acquisition is prohibited by all the laws of humanity and equity.

There is not, therefore, a single one of these unfortunate people regarded only as slaves who does not have the right to be declared free, since he has never lost his freedom, which he could not lose and which his prince, his father, and any person whatsoever in the world had not the power to dispose of. Consequently the sale that has been completed is invalid in itself. This Negro does not divest himself and can never divest himself of his natural right; he carries it everywhere with him, and he can demand everywhere that he be allowed to enjoy it. It is, therefore, patent inhumanity on the part of judges in free countries where he is transported, not to emancipate him immediately by declaring him free, since he is their fellow man, having a soul like them.

There are authors who, posing as political jurists, come to tell us confidently that the questions relative to the state of persons must be decided by the laws of the countries in which they belong and that therefore a man who is declared a slave in America and who is transported from there to Europe must be regarded there as a slave. But this is to decide the rights of humanity by the civil laws of a gutter, as Cicero[13] says. Must the magistrates of a nation, out of consideration for another nation, have no regard for their own people? Must their deference to a law that binds them in no way make them trample underfoot the law of nature that binds all men at all times and in all places? Is there any law as obligatory as the eternal laws of equity? What problem is created if a judge is bound to observe them more than to respect the arbitrary and inhuman practices of the colonies?

One will say perhaps that these colonies will soon be ruined if the slavery of Negroes were abolished there. But if this were true, should we conclude from this that the human race must be horribly injured to enrich us and to provide us with luxuries? It is true that the pockets of highwaymen would be empty if robbery were to be entirely suppressed, but do men have the right to enrich themselves by cruel and criminal acts? What right has a bandit to rob travellers: who is allowed to become opulent by making his fellow men unfortunate? Can it be legitimate to rob mankind of its sacred rights solely to satisfy one's avarice, one's vanity, or one's particular passions? No. Therefore let the European colonies be destroyed rather than make so many unfortunate people.

But I believe it is false that the suppression of slavery would entail its ruin. Commerce would suffer for some time, I agree; this is the effect of all new arrangements, because in this case new trade relations could not be readily found to follow another economic system; but out of this suppression other advantages would arise.

It is this *slave trade*, this practice of slavery, that has prevented America from being populated as promptly as it would have been. Let

---

[13] Marcus Tullius Cicero (106–43 BC), Roman writer, orator and statesman. [eds]

them free the Negroes, and in a few generations this vast and fertile country will have innumerable inhabitants. The arts and talent will flourish there, and instead of a land populated almost entirely by savages and wild beasts there will soon be a country of industrious men. It is freedom, it is industry that are the real sources of abundance. As long as a nation conserves this industry and this freedom, it has nothing to fear. Industry as well as necessity is ingenious and inventive: it finds a thousand different ways to procure riches for itself; and if one of the channels to opulence is blocked, a hundred others immediately open up.

Sensible and generous souls will without doubt applaud these reasons in favour of humanity; but avarice and greed which dominate the earth will never wish to hear them.

Source: Traite des nègres, translated by S. Gendzier, volume xvi, 1765, pp.532–3.

7 WOMAN by de Jaucourt (i) and Desmahis (ii)

(i) WOMAN (natural law). The female of man, viewed in relation to her marital union with him. See Marriage and Husband.

The Supreme Being, having judged that it was not good that man should be alone, inspired in him the desire to enter into an intimate relationship with a companion, and this relationship is formed by means of a voluntary agreement between the two parties. As the main purpose of this union is the procreation and care of children, it demands that the father and mother devote great care to feeding and raising these fruits of their love, until they are able to provide for themselves and live independently.

But although the husband and wife share these basic aims within their relationship, it is nevertheless essential that the authority of government belongs to one or the other. Now, positive law in civilized nations, the laws and customs of Europe, attribute this authority unanimously and unquestionably to the males, that is to the sex assumed to possess greater strength of mind and body and therefore to contribute more to the common good in human and sacred affairs. Consequently, *woman* is forced to be a subordinate of her husband and to obey his orders in all domestic matters. This is the view of all jurisconsults, ancient and modern, and the formal judgement of legislators.

Thus the Codex Fridericianus,[14] which appeared in 1750 and which seems to have attempted to introduce a system of fixed and universal laws, declares that the husband is, according to nature itself, the master of the home, the head of the family; and that when a *woman* enters a home of her own free will, she is as it were under the rule of the husband, from which it follows that various prerogatives are granted to him personally. Finally, the Scriptures order *woman* to submit to him as to her master.

However, to the humane, the above claims to marital power are not irrefutable; and the nature of this work allows us to state this boldly.

Firstly (1), it seems that it would be very difficult to prove that the husband's authority comes from nature, because this principle is contrary to the natural equality of men; and from the simple fact that one is fit to command, it does not necessarily follow that one should now have the right to do so. Secondly (2), man does not always possess greater physical strength, wisdom, intellect or strength to act than *woman*. Thirdly (3), as the precept of the Scriptures was established as a form of punishment, this indicates fairly clearly that it relates only to positive law. One could therefore argue that there is no subordination in conjugal union other than that which is sanctioned by civil law and that consequently there is nothing to prevent particular conventions from changing civil law, whenever natural law and religion do not dictate anything to the contrary.

We do not deny that in a relationship involving two people it is necessary that the legislative rights of one or other partner should be given precedence; and since it is normally the case that men are more capable than *women* of effectively managing private business matters, it is very prudent to establish as a general rule that the man's opinion should prevail as long as the parties involved have not come to any contrary arrangement, because the general rule is derived

---

[14]   See the study of Frederick the Great (*Studies*, I). The *Codex Fridericianus* was the document recording Frederick's reform and codification of Prussian law. It was published in 1749 in Prussia and translated into French in 1751. [eds]

from the human institution[15] and not from natural law. It follows then that a *woman* who knows what civil law dictates and who agrees in a straightforward, simple manner to her marriage contract, has thereby submitted tacitly to this civil law.

But if any *woman,* convinced that she is superior in judgement and conduct, or aware that she is of greater wealth or rank than the man who presents himself as her husband, stipulates the opposite of that which is stated by the law, and gains the consent of her husband, should she not enjoy, by virtue of natural law, the same power which the husband holds by virtue of the monarch's laws? The example of a queen who holds sovereignty in her own right and who marries a member of royalty of inferior rank, or even one of her subjects, is sufficient proof that the authority of a *woman* over her husband, even with regard to family government, is in no way incompatible with the nature of conjugal relationships.

[Examples of successful marriages of state in which women have held sovereign power are cited (e.g. Mary Queen of England and Philip II).]

England and Moscow offer examples which demonstrate clearly that *women* can be equally successful in both moderate and despotic systems of government; and if it is not contrary to reason or nature that they should rule an empire, it seems no less reasonable that they should be mistress of a family.

(ii) WOMAN (morality) This very name touches the soul but does not always uplift it. It evokes nothing but pleasing ideas, which instantly turn into anxious sensations or tender sentiments; and the philosopher who believes he is engaged in contemplation is soon no more than a man with desires or a lover with dreams.

A *woman* was having her portrait painted. What she lacked in beauty was precisely what made her pretty. She wanted an increase in her beauty while losing none of her grace; she wanted all at once an unfaithful rendering by the artist and a portrait with a good likeness. That is how they will all appear to the writer who must speak of them.

This half of the human race, compared physically with the other, is superior in charms, inferior in strength. A curviness of physique, fine features, a glowing complexion: these are all distinctive characteristics.

Women are no less different from men in heart and mind than in height and shape; but education has changed their natural disposition in so many ways; dissimulation, which seems to be for them a duty of the sex, has made their souls so secretive; there is such a large number of exceptions which are so difficult to extricate from the generalities, that the more observations one makes, the fewer conclusions one draws.

A *woman*'s soul may be likened to her beauty in that it is only revealed in order to stimulate the imagination. As for general character, this may be compared to a spectrum of colours: some pure, some changing with the light, with an infinite range of nuances in between. *Women* usually possess a complex, ambivalent or variable character, either because education affects their natural disposition more deeply than ours or because their delicate physical constitution turns their soul into a mirror which is sensitive to everything, reflecting brightly but retaining nothing.

Who can define *women*? Every part of them speaks, but it is an ambiguous language. She who appears the most indifferent is sometimes the most sensitive; the most indiscreet among them often passes for the most false. The judgements we make of them are always prejudiced by love or hate and the most liberated thinkers and those who have studied them most closely think they are finding solutions when in fact they raise new questions. There are three things, a wit used to say, that I have always loved without understanding anything about them: painting, music and *women*.

If it is true that weakness gives rise to timidity, timidity to subtlety and subtlety to duplicity, we must conclude that truthfulness is a most estimable virtue in *women*.

If the same physiological delicacy which makes *women*'s imaginations more lively makes them less capable of mental concentration, it could be said that they are more perceptive, see things very clearly, but dwell on them for a shorter time.

---

[15] Of marriage contracts. [eds]

How I admire virtuous *women* when they are as steadfast in their virtue as wicked *women* are intrepid in their vice.

Women's youth is shorter and more dazzling than that of men; their old age is longer and less happy.

Women are vindictive. Vengeance, which is an act of momentary power, is proof of weakness. The weakest and most timid must be cruel: this is a general law of nature which, in all sensitive beings, apportions the keenest feelings to those in most danger.

How could they be discreet? They are inquisitive. And how could they fail to be inquisitive when a mystery is made out of everything for them: they are called upon neither to act nor to advise.

Women are less united than men because they have but one aim.[16]

Distinguished by their inequalities, the two sexes have an almost equal number of favourable qualities. On the one hand nature has placed strength and majesty, courage and reason; on the other there is grace and beauty, subtlety and sentiment. These qualities are not always incompatible; they are sometimes different attributes which serve to balance one another; sometimes the same qualities, of differing degrees of intensity. Whatever is attractive or virtuous in one sex is a defect or deformity in the other. Natural differences should dictate differences in education which, like the sculptor's hand, can turn a lump of clay into an object of value.

For men, who share among themselves the occupations of civil life, the employment for which they are destined determines and differentiates the education they receive. In the case of *women*, the more general their education, the worse it is, and the more useful it is, the more negligent it becomes.[17] We should be surprised that such uncultivated minds are capable of so much virtue and that vice does not germinate in them more frequently.

Source: Femme, translated by L.Walsh, volume vi, 1756, pp.468–81.

Section 3   Morality and Religion

8 PRIESTS by d'Holbach

PRIESTS (religion and politics). With this name one designates all those who perform services for religious worship established among the different nations of the earth.

The outward forms of worship presuppose certain ceremonies whose goal is to strike the senses of men and to inspire reverence for the divinity to whom they pay homage. See WORSHIP. Superstition having multiplied the ceremonies of different forms of worship, the persons destined to perform them were not slow to form a separate order that was solely destined for religious service. One believed that those who were charged with such important offices should be devoted entirely to the divinity. From that time on they shared with the divinity the respect of all human beings; the occupations of the common people appeared beneath them, and the people believed they were obliged to provide for the sustenance of those who were invested with the most saintly and the most important of ministries. The latter, confined within the enclosure of their temples, hardly communicated with each other; this probably increased still more the respect that one had for these isolated men. People became accustomed to regarding them as favourites of the gods, as the depositants and the interpreters of their wills, as mediators between them and mortals.

It is sweet to domineer over one's fellow men. The *priests* knew how to make profitable the high opinion which they cultivated in the minds of their fellow countrymen. They claimed that the gods appeared to them: they announced their decrees; they taught dogmas; they prescribed what was necessary to believe and what was necessary to reject; they determined what pleased or displeased the divinity; they pronounced oracles; they predicted the future to anxious and curious men; they made them tremble for fear of the punishments with which the

---

[16]   i.e. the pursuit of a good marriage partner. [eds]

[17]   Presumably because 'useful' subjects such as needlework and domestic management were studied at the expense ('neglect') of subjects which would prepare women for intellectual and civil responsibilities. You will encounter a more detailed discussion of the education of women in Part E of the course, where the ideas of Rousseau, Laclos and Wollstonecraft are discussed. [eds]

angry gods menaced rash people who would dare their mission or discuss their doctrine.

To establish their empire more securely they painted the gods as cruel, vindictive and implacable. They introduced ceremonies, initiations, and mysteries whose atrocious character could nourish that sombre melancholy, so favourable to the empire of fanaticism. Then human blood flowed with great torrents on the altars; the people, subjugated by fear and intoxicated with superstition, believed they could never pay too dearly for celestial benevolence. Mothers delivered with dry eyes their tender children to the devouring flames; thousands of human victims fell under the knife of sacrificial *priests*. People submitted to a multitude of frivolous and revolting practices that were, however, useful to the *priests*, and the most absurd of superstitions finally extended and consolidated their power.

Free from cares and assured of their empire, these *priests*, with the view to charming away the boredom of their solitude, studied the secrets of nature, mysteries unknown to the average man; hence the highly praised knowledge of Egyptian *priests*. One notices that in general among almost all uncivilized and ignorant people the priesthood and medicine have been practiced by the same men. The *priest*'s usefulness to the people was bound to consolidate their power. Some of them went still further: the study of physics furnished the means to strike the imagination with dazzling works. People considered them supernatural because they were ignorant of the causes; hence that throng of wonders, marvels, and miracles. Astonished human beings believed that their sacrificial *priests* controlled the elements, commanded at pleasure the vengeance and favours of heaven, and had to share with the gods the veneration and fear of mortals. It was difficult for men held in such reverence to remain for a long time within the bounds of subordination necessary for the good order of society. The priesthood, elated with its power, often disputed the rights and privileges of royalty. Sovereigns, amenable themselves, as well as their subjects, to the laws of religion, were not strong enough to protest against the usurpation and tyranny of their ministers. Fanaticism and superstition held a knife suspended over the heads of monarchs; their thrones shook as soon as they wanted to check

or punish some holy men whose interests were combined or confused with those of the divinity. To resist them was a revolt against heaven; to touch their rights was a sacrilege; to want to limit their power was to sap the foundations of religion.

Such were the degrees by which the *priests* of paganism raised their power. Among the Egyptians the kings were subject to the censure of the priesthood; those monarchs who had displeased the gods received from their ministers the order to kill themselves, and such was the force of superstition that the sovereign did not dare disobey that order. The Druids among the Gauls wielded the most absolute power over all the people. Not content to be just the ministers of their form of worship, they were also the arbitrators of the disputes that arose between the two peoples. The Mexicans groaned in silence because of the acts of cruelty that their barbarous *priests* made them commit under cover and in the name of the gods; kings could not refuse to undertake the most unjust wars when the pontiff announced the will of heaven. 'God is hungry,' he said; immediately emperors armed themselves against their neighbours, and each one hastened to capture prisoners for a sacrifice to the idol, or rather to the atrocious and tyrannical superstition of its ministers.

The people would have been too happy if the *priests* of imposture had only abused by themselves the power that their minister gave them over men. In spite of the obedience and kindness advised so strongly by the Gospel, in the centuries of darkness we have seen some *priests* of the God of peace raise the standard of revolt, arm the hands of subjects against their sovereigns, insolently order kings to descend from the throne, arrogate the right to break the sacred ties that unite people to their masters, treat as tyrants the princes who are opposed to their audacious ventures, claim for themselves a chimerical independence of the laws, which were made equally binding on all citizens. These vain pretensions were sometimes cemented with torrents of blood and established by reason of the ignorance of people, the weakness of sovereigns, and the shrewdness of *priests*. The latter often succeeded in holding on to their usurped rights. In the countries where the hideous Inquisition was established, it furnished frequent examples of human sacrifices that were in no way inferior to the barbarism of the Mexican *priests*. It is not the same in countries enlightened by the light of reason and philosophy. There the *priest* never forgets that he is a man, a subject, and a citizen. *See* THEOCRACY.

Source: Prêtres, volume xiii, translated by S. Gendzier, 1765, pp.340–3.

9 ADORE by Diderot

ADORE (theology). This term in its literal and etymological sense means to carry to one's lips, to kiss one's hand, or to kiss something, but with a feeling of reverence or worship.

The three words *adore, honour, revere* are used for both religious and secular forms of worship. In religious worship one *adores* God, one *honours* the saints, one *reveres* relics and images. In secular worship one *adores* a mistress, one *honours* decent people, one *reveres* celebrated people and people of outstanding merit. In religion, *adoring* is devoting oneself to God in a spirit of obedience and dependence; honouring is paying homage to lesser spiritual beings in a spirit of invocation or petition; *revering* is paying external homage, with respect and careful attentiveness, to material existences, in memory of the spiritual existences to which they have belonged.

In the secular sphere one *adores* by devoting oneself entirely to the service of what one loves, even to the extent of admiring its faults; one *honours* by attentions, consideration and politeness; one *reveres* by giving signs of high esteem and a more than ordinary consideration.

The manner in which we *adore* the true God should never part company with Reason, because God is the author of Reason and wants us to use Reason even in how we behave in respect to Himself. People did not perhaps *honour* saints, nor *revere* their images and relics,

to the same extent in the first centuries of the Church as they do now, because of the aversion then felt towards idolatry, and the caution felt about a form of worship not prescribed sufficiently clearly by an explicit commandment.

Beauty only commands *adoration* when accompanied by graces as well; worship of beauty can scarcely ever be justified, because beauty is so often accompanied by capriciousness and injustice.

The education of the common people extends no further than teaching them to live in peace and fellowship with their equals. The common people do not know what it is to *honour* one another; that is a feeling reserved for their superiors. Virtue deserves to be *revered*; but who is actually acquainted with Virtue? Yet for all this, her rightful place is everywhere.

Source: Adorer, translated by P.N. Furbank, volume i, 1751, p.144.

10 AGNUS SCYTHICUS by Diderot

AGNUS SCYTHICUS[18] (botany, natural history). I shall first report what Scaliger[19] said in order to bring to light what the *agnus scythicus* is; then Kaempfer[20] and the physician Hans Sloane[21] will teach us what we must know about it. 'Nothing', says Julius Caesar Scaliger, 'is comparable to the wonderful shrub of Scythia. It grows mainly in the Zaccolham, which is as famous for its antiquity as for the courage of its inhabitants. In this country they sow a seed that is very much like that of a melon, except that it is less oblong in shape. This seed produces a plant about three feet high that is called *boramets*, or a *lamb*, because it looks exactly like this animal with its feet, nails [hooves], ears, and head. It is only missing the horns, but in its place there is a tuft of hair. It is covered with a light skin with which the inhabitants make caps. They say that its pulp

---

[18] Scythian lamb (cf. *Agnus dei* — lamb of God). [eds]

[19] Julius Caesar Scaliger (1484–1558), born in Italy, but settled in France. A physician and a great scholar of the Renaissance who became famous for his treatise on poetics. [Gendzier]

[20] Engelbert Kaempfer (1651–1716), German physician and traveller. [Gendzier]

[21] Sir Hans Sloane (1660–1753), physician and Secretary of the Royal Society, whose private collection was purchased by the government, leading to the foundation of the British Museum. [Gendzier]

resembles the meat of a lobster, that blood flows from it when an incision is made, and that its taste is extremely sweet. The root of the plant extends very deeply into the earth, which adds to its prodigious nature by drawing nourishment from the surrounding shrubbery and perishing when they die or have just been torn out. Chance has no part in this accident of nature, for the shrub died each time it was deprived of the nourishment drawn from the neighbouring plants. Another marvel is that wolves are the only carnivorous animals craving it.' (This was bound to be.) We can see by what follows that Scaliger only lacked knowledge of the manner in which the feet of this plant were produced and came out of the trunk.

This is the history of the *agnus scythicus*, or the marvellous plant of Scaliger, Kircher, Sigismond, Hesberetein, Hayton Arménien, Surius, Chancellor Bacon[22] (*the Chancellor Bacon,* take careful note of this witness), Fortunius Licetus, Andreas Libavius, Eusebius of Nuremberg, Adam Olearius, Olaus Vormius, and an infinite number of other botanists.

Is it possible that after so many authorities have attested to the existence of the lamb of Scythia, after all the details of Scaliger, who only remained ignorant of the way its feet were formed, that the lamb of Scythia could be a fable? What can one believe in natural history, if this is so?

Kaempfer, who was not less versed in natural history than in medicine, took all the trouble possible to find this lamb in Tartary without having been able to succeed. 'Neither the local peasantry nor the botanists here,' says this author, 'know of any zoophytes[23] that graze; and I have derived from my research only the shame of having been too credulous.' He adds that what gave rise to this tale, with which he allowed himself to be deluded like so many others, is the use people made in Tartary of the skin of certain lambs whose births are prevented by killing the mothers before the animals are brought forth, thereby ensuring a finer wool. Coats, gowns, and turbans are edged with these lamb skins. Travellers, either mistaken about the nature of these skins because of their ignorance of the country's language or for some other reason, then proceeded to deceive their compatriots by presenting the skin of an animal for the skin of a plant.

Mr Hans Sloane says that the *agnus scythicus* is a root longer than a foot with some tuberosities, some points from which there protrude several stems about three to four inches in length, quite similar to ferns, and having a large part of its surface covered with a yellowish-black down as shiny as silk, a quarter of an inch in length, which is used for the spitting of blood. He adds that in Jamaica one can find several fern plants that become as large as trees and are covered with a kind of down similar to that which can be observed on our maidenhair ferns; and that moreover it seems as if people made use of their artistic imaginations to give these ferns the shape of a lamb, as the roots resemble the body and the stems the legs of that animal.

So consequently all the wonder of the Scythian lamb is reduced to nothing, or at least to very little, to a villous[24] root which has been given the shape, or approximately the shape, of a lamb by distorting it.

This article will furnish us with reflections that are more useful against superstition and prejudice than the down of the Scythian lamb against the spitting of blood. Kircher, and after Kircher, Julius Caesar Scaliger, wrote a marvellous fable and they wrote it with this tone of gravity and conviction that never fails to inspire respect. They are people whose learning and integrity are not questionable; everything testifies in their favour, so they are believed. And by whom? By the leading minds and geniuses of their time. And that's that, for suddenly a cloud of testimony more powerful than their own supports the tale and creates for those who come later a weight of authority against which they will have neither the force nor the courage to resist; and the Scythian lamb will pass for a real thing.

---

[22] Francis Bacon (1560–1626), Chancellor of England and writer on scientific method. The *philosophes* were generally very respectful towards Bacon's writings. [eds]

[23] Plant-like animals. [eds]

[24] Hair-covered. [eds]

It is necessary to divide facts into two classes: those that are simple and ordinary, and those of an extraordinary and prodigious nature. The testimony of several educated and trustworthy people is sufficient to establish the authenticity of simple facts. The others require, for a man who thinks, much stronger authorities. In general it is necessary for the authorities to be in inverse ratio to the probability of the facts, that is to say, much more numerous and reliable as the probability decreases.

It is necessary to subdivide the facts, the simple as well as the extraordinary, into transitory and permanent. The transitory ones are those that exist only for the moment of the duration, while the permanent ones always exist and can be verified at all times. We can see that the latter type of facts are less difficult to believe than the former and that the ease with which anyone can verify the truth or falsity of testimony must make witnesses cautious and dispose other men to believe them.

It is necessary to distribute transitory facts into those that have taken place in an enlightened century and others that have taken place in times of darkness and ignorance; and permanent facts into those in an accessible place and others in an inaccessible place.

It is necessary to consider the various pieces of testimony separately then to compare them together: to consider them separately to see if they imply any contradiction and are by enlightened and educated people; to compare them together to discover if they are not copied from each other and if all that crowd of authorities with Kircher, Scaliger, Bacon, Libavius, Licetus, Eusebius, etc., could not be reduced by chance to nothing or to the authority of a single man.

It is necessary to consider if the testimony is by eyewitnesses or not; what they have risked to make themselves believed; what fears or hopes they had when announcing to others the facts of which they claim to be eyewitnesses. If they had imperiled their lives to maintain their depositions, we must agree that their testimony would acquire great strength. If they had sacrificed and lost their lives, how would we then regard their evidence?

Neither should we confuse the facts that have taken place before an entire people with those that have had as spectators only a small number of individuals. Clandestine facts, even if they appear marvellous or supernatural, are almost not worth our belief. Public facts, against which people have not protested in the past or against which there have been objections only on the part of a few ill-intentioned or poorly educated people, can almost not be contradicted.

These are a few principles to use when granting or refusing belief, if one does not wish to fall into reveries and if one sincerely loves the truth. *See* CERTAINTY, PROBABILITY, etc..

Source: Agnus scythicus, translated by S. Gendzier, volume i, 1751, pp.179–80.

11 CONSECRATED BREAD by Diderot

CONSECRATED BREAD[25] (ecclesiastical history) is the *bread* that one blesses every Sunday at the parish mass and then distributes to the faithful.

The custom, in the first centuries of Christianity, was that all those who attended the celebration of the holy mysteries participated in the communion of the *bread* that had been consecrated; but the Church, having found an objection to this practice, because Christians could be in a bad mood, restricted the sacramental communion to those who were duly prepared. Nevertheless, in order to preserve the memory of the early communion that was extended to everybody, one continued the distribution of ordinary *bread* that was blessed, as we do today.

Moreover, the taste for luxury and a magnificence onerous to many people having slipped even into the practice of religion, the custom was introduced in the cities to give more or less dainty cake instead of *bread*, and to add some other costly and burdensome trimmings; which gives to poor families an inconvenient expense that would be more profitably used for real needs. If it were not demonstrated by an exact calculation, one would not believe what this single article costs the nation every year.

We know that in the nation there are forty thousand parishes where *consecrated bread* is

---

[25] The wafer, or host, used at the Mass, or communion. [eds]

distributed, sometimes at even two high masses in one day, without counting those of the brotherhood, those of the different art and business groups. I saw twenty-two of them provided for a celebration by new master craftsmen in a Parisian community. We are astonished that there is so much misery [poverty] around us; and I for one, when I see all our extravagance and folly, am even more astonished that there does not exist much more.

However that may be, I believe that all told one can estimate the expense of *consecrated bread*, including paraphernalia and chapels, at about forty sous each time it is offered. If it costs a little less in the country, it costs much more in the city, and many people will find an estimate too low. Nevertheless forty thousand wafers of *bread* at forty sous apiece equals eighty thousand pounds, a sum which, multiplied by fifty-two Sundays, adds up to more than four million per year, or 4,000,000 livres.[26] What prevents us from sparing the public this expense? It has already been said elsewhere: *bread* does not carry more of a blessing than the water used to bless it; and consequently one could be satisfied with just the water, which costs nothing, and do away with the expense of the *bread*, which becomes a real loss.

While we are on the subject, let us say a word about lights.[27] There is hardly any probability that they could be completely done away with; we are still too childish, too much the slaves of custom and prejudice, to realize that there are many more useful and truly religious occupations than those of burning candles in a church. Nevertheless, any enlightened man will agree that one could spare three quarters of the lights which are wasted today, and which are strictly speaking only a pious decoration. This being granted, we have more than forty thousand churches or parishes in the kingdom and we would say an equal number for collegiate churches, convents, communities, etc., which makes eighty thousand churches in all. I estimate the average saving from lights that could be made in each one at fifty pounds a year; this sum, although moderate, multiplied by eighty thousand churches, equals four million a year. We have here consequently, with the four million

above, an annual loss of eight million in the kingdom; and this for small objects and petty expenses about which people have perhaps never thought: a total of 8,000,000 livres.

How many other costly and useless things in superfluous ornaments, in bells, processions, altars for the monstrance, etc.. *Populus hic labiis me honourat, cor autem eorum longe est a me* (Matt. 15:8).[28]

Religion does not consist in decorating temples, in delighting the eyes or the ears, but in paying sincere reverence to the Creator and in making ourselves conform to the example set by Jesus Christ. Let us love God by preference, and let us fear to displease Him by violating His commandments; let us love our neighbour as ourselves, and let us consequently always be careful to do him good, or at least always be on guard not to do him evil; finally, let us fulfill our duties to the state. This is precisely the religion that God has prescribed for us and the very one which men do not practise. But they try to compensate for these failures in another manner: they bear the expenses, for example, of the decorations for the altars and of the pomp for the ceremonies: the ornaments, the lights, the chants, the bells are not spared. Strictly speaking, all of this constitutes the soul of their religion, and most of them know nothing beyond. Vulgar and deceitful piety, so little in accordance with the spirit of Christianity, which inspires only charity and brotherly love!

How many more important deeds of good will must be done that are much more worthy of the followers of Jesus Christ! How many unfortunate, crippled, and infirm people without help and without consolation! How many uncomplaining poor without any chance and without any work! How many poor families overburdened with children! In fact, how many wretched souls of every description, whose relief and comfort should be the great object of Christian commiseration! An object consequently to which we should assign as many sums of money as we fruitlessly and unnecessarily squander elsewhere.

Source: Pain béni, translated by S. Gendzier, volume xi, 1765, p.751.

---

[26] French currency 20 sous = 1 livre. Many people earned little more than a livre in a day. [eds]

[27] Candles. [eds]

[28] This people pays me lipservice, but their heart is far from me. [eds]

12 ENJOYMENT by Diderot

ENJOYMENT (grammar[29] and morality). To enjoy means to know, to experience, to feel the advantages of possession. One often possesses without *enjoyment*. Who owns these magnificent palaces? Who has planted these immense gardens? The sovereign. But who enjoys them? I do.

Let us leave these magnificent palaces, that the sovereign has constructed for other people than himself, these enchanting gardens in which he never walks, and stop to contemplate pleasure that perpetuates the chain of living beings and to which we have consecrated the word *enjoyment*.

Among the objects that nature everywhere offers to our desires, you who have a soul, tell me if there is anything more worthy of your pursuit, anything that can make us happier than the possession and enjoyment of a being who thinks and feels as you do, who has the same ideas, who experiences the same sensations, the same ecstasies, who brings her affectionate and sensitive arms towards yours, who embraces you, whose caresses will be followed with the existence of a new being who will resemble one of you, who will look for you in the first movements of life to hug you, whom you will bring up by your side and love together, who will protect you in old age, who will respect you at all times, and whose happy birth has already strengthened the tie that bound you together?

Crude, insensitive, and unmoved beings who are deprived of life's vital force and who surround us can be useful for our happiness, but without knowing or sharing it; and our sterile and destructive *enjoyment*, which affects all of these people, does not produce any real *enjoyment* in its turn.

If there is a perverse man who could take offence at the praise that I give to the most noble and universal of passions, I would evoke Nature before him, I would make it speak, and Nature would say to him: why do you blush to hear the word pleasure pronounced, when you do not blush to indulge in its temptations under the cover of night? Are you ignorant of its purpose and of what you owe it? Do you believe that your mother would have imperiled her life to

give you yours if I had not attached an inexpressible charm to the embraces of her husband? Be quiet, unhappy man, and consider that pleasure pulled you out of nothingness.

The propagation of beings is the greatest object of nature. It imperiously solicits both sexes as soon as they have been granted their share of strength and beauty. A vague and brooding restlessness warns them of the moment; their condition is mixed with pain and pleasure. At that time they listen to their senses and turn their considered attention to themselves. But if an individual should be presented to another individual of the same species and of a different sex, then the feeling of all other needs is suspended: the heart palpitates; the limbs tremble; voluptuous images wander through the mind; a flood of spirits runs through the nerves, excites them, and proceeds to the seat of a new sense that reveals itself and torments the body. Sight is troubled, delirium is born; reason, the slave of instinct, limits itself to serving the latter, and nature is satisfied.

This is the way things took place at the beginning of the world, and the way they still take place in the back of the savage adult's cave.

But when woman began to discriminate, when she appeared to take care in choosing between several men upon whom passion cast her glances, there was one who stopped them, who could flatter himself that he was preferred, who believed that he brought to the heart he esteemed the very esteem that he had for himself, and who considered pleasure as the recompense for some merit; then, when the veils that modesty cast over the charms of a woman allowed an inflamed imagination the power to dispose of them at will, the most delicate illusions competed with the most exquisite of senses to exaggerate the happiness of the moment; the soul was possessed with an almost divine enthusiasm; two young hearts lost in love vowed themselves to each other forever, and heaven heard the first indiscreet oaths.

Yet how many happy moments existed before the one in which the entire soul sought to spring forth and lose itself in the soul of the person loved! *Enjoyment* began the moment that hope was born.

---

[29] Many of the articles of the *Encyclopédie* were classified as 'grammar', and aimed to provide accurate definitions of words, for one of Diderot's key aims was to rationalize and clarify usage of the French language. In reality, of course, such definitions provided a rich and subtle context for polemic. In this case the definition is exemplified by a reference to the wealth of sovereigns: an opportunity to attack their vanity. [eds]

Nevertheless confidence, time, nature, and the freedom of caresses led to the forgetfulness of self; one swore after experiencing the final ecstasy that there was no other person who could be compared to her (or to him); and this was true in these circumstances each time people had sensitive and young organs, a tender heart and an innocent soul unacquainted with either mistrust or remorse.

Source: Jouissance, translated by S. Gendzier, volume viii, 1765, p.889.

13 EPICUREANISM by *Diderot*

EPICUREANISM (history of philosophy). The Eleatic[30] school gave birth to the Epicurean school.[31] No philosophy has ever been less understood and more slandered than that of Epicurus. People accused this philosopher of atheism although he admitted the existence of the gods, frequented the temples, and was not reluctant to bow down at the foot of an altar. They considered him the apologist of debauchery,[32] he whose life was a continual practice of all the virtues, especially of temperance. This prejudice was so current that we must admit, to the shame of the Stoics[33] who used every possible means to spread it, that the Epicureans were exceptionally honourable people who had the worst kind of reputation.[34] But in order for the reader to have an enlightened judgement of the doctrines of Epicurus, we shall introduce this philosopher himself, surrounded by his disciples, dictating his lessons to them in the shade of some trees that he had planted. It is therefore he who is going to speak in the rest of our article, and we hope that the reader will be fair enough to keep this point in mind. The only thing we shall allow ourselves is to cast between his principles some of the most direct consequences that can be deduced from them.[35]

About philosophy in general. Man is born to think and to act, and the purpose of philosophy is to direct the understanding and to regulate the conduct of man; anything that deviates from this aim is frivolous. Happiness can be acquired by the exercise of reason, the practice of virtue, and the moderate use of pleasure; which presupposes the health of body and soul. If the most important piece of knowledge is what we must avoid and do, then a young man cannot devote himself too early to the study of philosophy, and an old man cannot abandon it too late.

Oh my friends! Is there anything more ancient than truth? Did not truth exist before all the philosophers? The philosopher will therefore scorn all authorities and will proceed straight to the truth, brushing aside all the vain phantoms which appear on his way: the irony of Socrates and the sensual pleasures of Epicurus.[36]

---

[30]   Elea was in the south of Italy. A school of philosophers flourished there in the 5th century BC.

[31]   A school of philosophy founded by Epicurus in 311 BC. Epicurus was essentially concerned with humankind's quest for tranquility. He argued that the pleasures of the senses were important to virtue, which consisted of 'prudence in the pursuit of pleasure'. However, the *philosophes* usually avoided carefully any reference to his view that sexual love can be harmful. Happiness, for Epicurus, was to be derived from the moderation of desire. [eds]

[32]   The view that Epicurus was primarily an apologist of the 'lower pleasures' or of a 'pig philosophy' persisted into the nineteenth century. [eds]

[33]   Philosophical 'rivals' of the Epicureans. Stoicism was a school of philosophy founded by Zeno in the early part of the 3rd century BC. The central stoic belief was that virtue is the sole good and that health, happiness and possessions are of no account. People must free themselves from mundane desires. 'We can't be happy, but we can be good' epitomizes the stoic view. [eds]

[34]   The *philosophes* liked to identify with other renowned philosophers who were seen as victims of persecution, including Socrates. [eds]

[35]   The sections which follow are Diderot's reconstruction of the ideas of Epicurus. However, perhaps they reveal more about Diderot than they do about Epicurus. [eds]

[36]   Diderot here attacks those who have sought to distort the 'true' message of Epicurus and of other philosophers. [eds]

Why do people remain immersed in error? Because they take the terms of a statement for its proof. Create for yourself a set of principles, small in number, but rich in consequences. Do not neglect the study of nature, but apply yourself particularly to the science of morals. What would be the use of a profound knowledge of beings external to us, if we could, without this knowledge, dispel fear, prevent suffering, and satisfy our needs? The use of the dialectic[37] pushed to excess degenerates into the art of sowing thorns in all the sciences: I detest this art. True logic can be reduced to a few rules. In nature there are only things and ideas; and consequently, there are only two kinds of truths: some of existence, others of induction. The truths of existence belong to the senses; those of induction, to reason. Precipitance is the principal source of our errors. I shall therefore not tire of saying to you: *wait*. Without the appropriate use of the senses, there would not be any ideas or any preconceptions, that is, the anticipation of knowledge; and without preconceptions, neither opinion nor doubt would exist.[38] Far from being able to search for truth, we could not even create signs or symbols. Therefore multiply preconceptions by the diligent use of your senses; study the precise value of the signs that others have introduced and carefully determine the value of those which you introduce. If you make up your mind to speak, choose the most simple and ordinary expressions or live with the fear that you will not be understood and have to lose time interpreting yourself. When you listen to someone, try to be conscious of all the meanings conveyed by words. By the habitual use of these principles you will succeed in distinguishing that which is true, false, obscure, and ambiguous. But it is not enough that you know

how to put some truth into your arguments, for you must still know how to put some wisdom into your actions. In general when sensual pleasure does not entail any pain as a consequence, then do not hesitate to embrace it; if the pain is less than the pleasure, then you should still embrace it; embrace even the pain which promises a great pleasure. You will only calculate badly when you surrender yourself to a sensual pleasure that will cause you too much pain or will deprive you of greater pleasure.

About physiology in general. What goal shall we propose for ourselves in the study of physiology if not that of knowing the general causes of phenomena, so that after we are rid of all vain terrors, we might surrender ourselves without remorse to our reasonable desires; and after having enjoyed life, we might leave it without any regrets? Nothing is created out of nothing. The universe has always been and will always be. Only matter and the void exist.

[Diderot goes on here to give a full exposition of Epicurus' atomic theory regarding the physical nature of the universe and of man.[39]]

About theology. After having established the principle that there is nothing in nature but matter and the void, what shall we think of the gods?[40] Shall we abandon our philosophy and submit to popular opinions, or shall we say that the gods are corporeal beings? Since they are gods, they are happy; they enjoy themselves in a peaceful manner; nothing that happens on earth affects or troubles them; and it is sufficiently demonstrated by the phenomena of the physical and the moral world that they have had no part in the production of beings and that they do not take any in their conservation. It is nature itself that has placed the notion of their existence in our souls. What people are so barbaric that they

---

[37] The method of seeking knowledge by question and answer – a method used, but not invented, by Socrates. [eds]

[38] Compare, below, the discussion of scientific method in *Experiment*. [eds]

[39] Epicurus was a materialist but not a determinist. He believed that the movement of atoms is not invariably predictable by the laws of mechanics, but incorporates random and unpredictable elements. [eds]

[40] Epicurus believed that the gods exist but that they do not trouble themselves with the affairs of the human world. He was opposed to magic, astrology and divination. He generally expressed a hatred of religion, denied Providence and rejected immortality. Although he is here apparently persuaded by general consent that the gods exist, he thinks that many qualities and acts have been attributed to them in error. [eds]

do not have some kind of advance notion of the gods? Shall we be opposed to the general consent of mankind?[41] Shall we raise our voices against the voice of nature? Nature does not lie; the existence of the gods would be proven even by our prejudices. So many phenomena have been attributed to them only because the nature of these beings and the causes of phenomena were unknown; are not so many other errors an indication of the reliability of popular belief? If a man has been struck in his sleep by some sort of large simulacrum, and he were to retain the memory of it on waking, he might conclude that this image necessarily had its model wandering about nature; the voices that he could have heard did not permit him to doubt that this model had an intelligent nature; and the persistence of the apparition at different times and under the same form was conclusive evidence that it was immortal. But the being that is immortal is unalterable, and the being that is unalterable is perfectly happy, since it has no effect on anything and nothing affects it. The existence of the gods has therefore been and will therefore always be a sterile existence, and for the very reason that it cannot be altered; because it is necessary that the principle of activity, which is the source of all destruction and all reproduction, be eliminated in these beings. We have therefore nothing to hope nor to fear from them. Therefore what are prophecies? What are miracles? What are religions? If we owe some kind of worship to the gods, it would resemble the admiration that we naturally give to everything that presents an alluring image of perfection and happiness. We are inclined to believe that the gods have human shapes; this is what all peoples have assumed; and the human shape is the only one in which reason is used and virtue practised. If the gods were incorporeal beings, they would not have any senses, perceptions, pleasures, or pains. Their bodies in any case are not like ours; for they are composed of a similar but superior combination of atoms; the same organization, but the organs are infinitely more perfect; a special nature that is so fine and rare that nothing can affect, alter, augment, or diminish it, and action is not one of its attributes. We do not know the places where the gods frequent: this world is without doubt not worthy of them:

they might well have taken refuge in the empty spaces between adjoining worlds.

About morality. Happiness is the goal of life: it is the secret confession of the human heart and the clear purpose of actions, even those that seem to contradict it. The person who kills himself considers death a blessing. We cannot reform nature, but we can guide its general tendencies. A man can miscalculate and cause himself harm either by seeing happiness where it is not or by seeing happiness where it is but mistaking the means of obtaining it. What will be, therefore, the first step of our moral philosophy, if it is not an inquiry into what constitutes true happiness? Let this important subject be our present concern. Since we want to be happy from now on, let us not put off till tomorrow the study of what is happiness. The madman always intends to live well but never does so. To be supremely happy is granted only to immortal beings. A piece of folly that we must first of all not commit, is to forget that we are only men. Since we despair of never being as perfect as the gods whom we had proposed for models, let us be resolved not to be as happy. Since my eyes do not pierce through the immensity of space, shall I be disdainful about opening them to the objects that surround me? These objects will become an inexhaustible source of pleasure if I know how to enjoy or disregard them. Pain is always evil, pleasure always good; but there is no such thing as pure pleasure. Flowers grow at our feet and we must at least bend over to pick them. Nevertheless, O pleasure! it is for you alone that we do everything that we do; it is not you whom we avoid, but the pain that accompanies you only too often. You warm our cold reason; it is with your energy that strength of mind and willpower are born; it is you who move and transport us when we make a bed of roses for the young beauty who has charmed us and when defying the fury of tyrants we charge blindly and headlong into the fiery bulls that have been prepared for us. Pleasure takes all sorts of forms. It is therefore important to know the full price of all things presented to us by pleasure, so that we shall not be uncertain when the time is suitable for us to welcome or to reject them, to live or to die. After the health of the soul, there is nothing more precious than the health of the body. If the

---

[41] Is there any irony in this acquiescence in belief in the gods? [eds]

health of the body is particularly manifest in several limbs or organs, it is not general. If the soul is carried to excess in the practice of virtue, it is not entirely virtuous. The musician is not satisfied with tuning a few strings of his lyre; it would be desirable for the harmony of society to imitate him, and not allow our virtues and our passions to be either too slack or too strained and to make sounds that are either too flat or too sharp.[42]

If we have a good opinion of our fellow men, we shall take pleasure in performing our duties, because this is a sure method of being appreciated for our own work. We shall not scorn sensual pleasures, but we shall not deceive ourselves by comparing what is honourable with what is sensual. How can a person be happy if he has made a mistake in the choice of his career? How can one choose a career without knowing oneself? And how can people be content with their careers if the requirements of nature, the lusts of passion, and the flights of fancy are confused? We must keep a goal in mind if we do not want to leave everything to chance. It is not always impossible to take hold of the future. Everything must lead to the practice of virtue, the preservation of liberty and life, and the scorn of death. As long as we exist, death is nothing, and it is still nothing when we exist no more. We fear the gods only because we make them similar to men. Is not the impious individual the one who worships the gods of the common people? If true piety consists in bowing down before any piece of carved stone, then there would be nothing more widespread. But as it consists in judging soundly the nature of the gods, it is a rare virtue. What people call *natural law* is only the symbol of public usefulness. Public usefulness and common consent must be the two great rules of our actions. There is never any certainty that a crime will remain unknown: the one who commits it is therefore a madman who plays a game in which there is more to lose than to gain. Friendship is one of the greatest assets of life, and decency is one of the greatest social virtues. Be decent because you are not animals, and because you live in cities and not in the depths of the forest, etc.[43]

These are fundamental points of Epicurus' doctrines,[44] the only one of all the ancient philosophers who knew how to reconcile his moral code with what he understood to be man's true happiness and his precepts with the appetites and requirements of nature. He therefore had and will have at all times a great number of disciples. One can become a stoic, but one is born an *epicurean*...[45]

Source: *Épicurisme*, translated by S.Gendzier, volume v, 1755, pp.779–85.

14 PYRRHONIAN PHILOSOPHY by Diderot

PYRRHONIAN PHILOSOPHY or SCEPTICISM.[46] The Greeks were tired of so many disputes over what is true or false, good or bad, beautiful or ugly, when a new sect arose among them and won many proselytes in a short period of time. It was the Pyrrhonian school of philosophy or scepticism.

Pyrrho,[47] the disciple of Anaxarchus, of the Eleatic school, was the first to study and practice this pusillanimous and suspicious philosophy, which has been named after him, *Pyrrhonism*, and after its nature, *Scepticism*.

---

[42]   i.e. the ideal is moderation in all things. [eds]

[43]   Contrast, later, Rousseau's preference for country life (*Studies*, II). On this issue the *philosphes* were generally on the side of the city, civilization and progress. [eds]

[44]   We now return to the undisguised voice of Diderot. [eds]

[45]   i.e. stoicism embodies many principles which are inimical to human nature. [eds]

[46]   The *Encyclopédie* was censored by the publisher and printer Le Breton without Diderot's consent or knowledge. The article on 'Pyrrhonian philosophy' suffered some major slashing. For the full story of this betrayal, with the censored and fully re-established texts, see Douglas H. Gordon and Norman L. Torrey, *The Censoring of Diderot's Encyclopédie and the Re-established Text* (New York, 1947). The censored passages are given here in italics. [eds]

[47]   Pyrrho of Elis (*c.*365–*c.*270 BC), regarded as the founder of Scepticism as a school of philosophy. [eds]

[The Pyrrhonists argued that we can know nothing: they doubted everything. Diderot gives a history of Pyrrhonism in Greece and in later times, and then, for more recent times, discusses the French philosophers Montaigne, Bayle, Malebranche and Arnauld.]

But among the followers of *Pyrrhonism* we have forgotten Michel de Montaigne,[48] the author of those *Essays* that will be read as long as there are men who love truth, strength, and simplicity. The work of Montaigne is the touchstone of a good mind. Whoever dislikes to read him has some defect in feeling or judgement. There is almost no question that this author has not debated for or against and always in the same persuasive manner. The contradictions of his work are the faithful image of the contradictions in human understanding. He follows without any pose or affectation the train of his ideas, caring very little about where he begins, how he proceeds, or where he ends. The thing that he says, is what affects him at that moment. His thoughts are neither more coherent nor more disconnected when writing than when thinking or dreaming. Now, it is impossible for a man who thinks or dreams to be completely coherent. A mental impression should be able to stop without any apparent cause, and another impression could suddenly begin by itself. There is a necessary relationship between the two most disparate ideas; and this relationship is either in the senses or in words or in the memory, either inside or outside man. It is a rule to which even the insane are subject in their greatest derangement of reason. If we had the complete history of everything that takes place inside us, we would see that everything is related there, just as it is in the wisest and most sensible man.

As we go along, he [Montaigne] reveals, all aspects of himself, some good, some depraved, sometimes compassionate, sometimes vain, now incredulous, now superstitious. After having written effectively against the truth of miracles, he writes an apologia of auguries. But whatever he says, he is interesting and instructive. However among the ancients and the moderns *scepticism* did not have a more formidable defender than Bayle.[49]

Bayle was born in the year 1647. Nature gave him imagination, power, subtlety, memory, and education, everything that could help bring out his natural qualities. He learned Greek and Latin, devoting himself early and almost without respite to all kinds of readings and studies. Plutarch and Montaigne were his favourite authors. These were the seeds of *Pyrrhonism*, that were to develop subsequently within him in such a surprising way.

He began in 1684 his *République des Lettres*. Involved by this kind of work, he read all sorts of books, studied thoroughly the most disparate subjects, discussed questions of mathematics, philosophy, physics, theology, jurisprudence, history – what a field for a *Pyrrhonian*. The theosophist Malebranche[50] then appeared on the scene. Among a great number of opinions that were peculiar to him, he had advanced the notion that all sensual pleasures are good. Arnauld[51] believed he saw in this maxim the subversion of morality and attacked him. Bayle intervened in this quarrel, explained the terms, and exonerated Malebranche from Arnauld's accusations. *The latter was an obstinate and vain man, the head of a party, and an excessively bitter and quarrelsome person, who thought he was honour bound to engage Bayle in verbosity and obscurantism: he succeeded rather well. At that time the most outrageous vexations were being inflicted on the Protestants; France was made Catholic by ruining her; the eradication of heresy was advocated while the most sacred laws of humanity were violated and religion was dishonoured. This is what Bayle showed in his little pamphlet on the true character of an entirely Catholic France.* In a few other works he slipped in some principles likely to advance the cause of tolerance: he clearly explained himself on this

---

[48] Michel Eyquem de Montaigne (1533–92); his *Essays* were published between 1580 and 1588. [eds]

[49] Pierre Bayle (1647–1706), critic, philosopher and author of the *Dictionnaire Historique et Critique* (1697). [eds]

[50] Nicolas Malebranche (1638–1715), theologian and philosopher. [eds]

[51] Antoine Arnauld (1612–94), theologian, defender of Jansenism, and critic of Malebranche. [eds]

important subject in his philosophic commentary. This work, *the best that Bayle produced and the most useful*, was published in instalments. At first it was equally pleasing to all parties; then it dissatisfied the Catholics and continued to please the Protestants; later it became equally unsatisfactory to both sides and only retained the constant approval of the *philosophes. It is because they are the only truly tolerant men. We cannot recommend the reading of this work too highly: it is a masterpiece of reason and eloquence.*

The works which we have just briefly reviewed are not the only ones that this astonishing man wrote; and yet he only lived to the age of fifty-nine: he died in January 1706. *Do you want to know how you must judge him? Then consider that there has always existed, exists now, and always will exist but one kind of person who has spoken, speaks, and will speak ill of him; and conclude from this that it is not the truth but some particular interested motive that makes him speak. There are only one of three courses to choose in this world; write what one thinks, write the opposite of what one thinks, or be silent. The last is without contradiction the most secure and the least honest one. Bayle was writing against some proofs on the existence of God when he died. Some people have consequently felt pessimistic about his salvation. They have not considered that it is neither truth nor error which makes us innocent or guilty in the eyes of the sovereignly just and good Being, but the sincerity of our judgements.*

He will not reward us for having been intelligent, nor will he punish us for having been stupid. We behave as we will, but we reason as we can. We are free to do good and avoid evil, but we are not free to know the truth and escape from error. It is a misfortune, perhaps, to be mistaken, but it is not a crime. We are damned for our evil deeds and are not saved by our intellectual discoveries. I have a better opinion of the salvation of a man who preaches the lie that he believes in the depth of his heart than of the individual who announces the Gospel that he does not believe. The former can be a good man, while the latter is clearly an evil one. As for the dissension and agitation that certain opinions can stir up in the society of which one is a member, we cannot reach an unfavourable judgement of Bayle, who wrote in a country where freedom of the press was tolerated. Besides, if all truths are not suitable for publication, then this situation is certainly the consequence of bad legislation and the mistaken notion that political and religious matters should be intimately related. Wherever civil power supports

religion or seeks its support, the progress of reason must necessarily be retarded, and the resulting persecution becomes useless because minds can never be effectively coerced, and tolerance disappears or is limited: two almost equally disturbing suppositions. Tolerance must be general and from its generalization alone are born those two principal advantages: light and peace. A truth of whatever nature, if harmful for the moment, is necessarily useful in the future. A lie of whatever nature, useful perhaps for the moment, is necessarily harmful in the course of time. To think otherwise is to fail to understand the nature of either one or the other. Therefore, said the Persians and the sceptics with them, doubt is the first step along the path of knowledge and truth; he who discusses nothing is sure of nothing; he who doubts nothing discovers nothing; he who discovers nothing is blind and remains blind. Ignorance and falsehood are the causes of man's troubles; ignorance, which confuses everything, is opposed to everything, and leads to no conclusions; falsehood, which is never firmly enough established in all minds not to be suspected, exposed, and combatted: man finds peace only in the truth. Why have the questions of metaphysics always divided men? Because they are obscure and false. Why have the principles of natural morality always brought men together instead of stirring up dissension? Because they are clear, evident, and true. If I had the proof of some great truth, a proof that no man of good faith could reject, I would publish it immediately because of my conviction that there is no unmixed good in this world, that the truth is man's greatest good, and that he will sooner or later gather its sweetest fruits.

Bayle had few equals in the art of reasoning, perhaps no superior. No one knew how to discern more subtly the weakness of a system, no one knew how to point out more effectively its advantages; formidable when he proves, even more formidable when he objects, at the same time as he proves a point, he amuses, he portrays, he seduces. Although he accumulates doubt after doubt, he always proceeds methodically: he is a living polyp, breaking up into so many polyps that are all alive; he produces some more from the others. Whatever the thesis he has to prove, everything comes to his assistance: history, erudition, philosophy. If he has the truth on his side, no one can resist him; if he speaks in favour of falsehood, it assumes with his pen all the colours of truth: impartial or not, he always appears so; we never see the author, only the subject.

Whatever people say about the man of letters, the man himself is beyond reproach. He had an honest mind and a decent heart; he was obliging, sober, hard-working, without ambition, without pride, a friend of the truth, just even toward his enemies, tolerant, not very devout, not very credulous, absolutely undogmatic, cheerful, pleasant, consequently not very scrupulous in his narration, deceptive like all witty people who rarely hesitate to cut or add a slightly improper incident to a real situation when it thereby becomes more humorous or more interesting and often on the filthy side. I do not think that he attached any great value to continence, modesty, conjugal fidelity, and other virtues of this order; otherwise he would have been more reserved in his judgements. *To palliate his* Pyrrhonism, *whenever he assumed a sceptical manner, he always did it under pretext of restoring the rights of revelation, which he knew well how to sap when the occasion presented itself. He wrote alternatively an apologia of reason against authority and of authority against reason, very sure that men would not give up their appanage of reason and their liberty in favour of a yoke that galled them and that they asked nothing better than to shake off. He knew too much to believe everything or to doubt everything.* It has been said of his works *quamdiu vigebunt, lis erit,*[52] and we shall end our account of Bayle with this enigmatic reference to posterity.

It is clear from what has now been said that the first sceptics attacked reason only to mortify the pride of the dogmatic; that among modern sceptics some have sought to decry philosophy to give authority to revelation; others have done so to attack it more firmly, by undermining the security of the foundation on which it must rest, and that among ancient and modern sceptics there are some who have sincerely doubted, because in most questions they saw only reasons for uncertainty. For our part we conclude that, since everything in nature is connected, strictly speaking there is nothing of which man can have perfect, absolute, complete knowledge, not even of the most obvious axioms, because for that he would have to have knowledge of everything.

Since everything is connected, if man does not know everything, it necessarily follows that from one discussion to another he will come to something unknown; so starting from this unknown point there will still be grounds for accusing him of ignorance or obscurity, or uncertainity about the preceding point and of the one before that, and so on, to the most self-evident principle.

So there is a sort of restraint in the use of reason, which one has to accept, or resign oneself to drifting into uncertainty; a moment when its enlightenment, which had been increasing, begins to decrease and where all discussions must stop.

When, step by step, I have led a man to some self-evident proposition, I shall stop arguing. I shall not listen to anyone who denies the existence of bodies, the rules of logic, the evidence of the senses, the difference between true and false, good and evil, pleasure and pain, vice and virtue, decent and indecent, just and unjust, honest and dishonest, I shall turn my back on anyone who tries to lead me away from a simple question and plunge into dissertations on the nature of matter, of the understanding, of the substance of thought and other subjects, which have no defined limits.

A true whole man will not have two philosophies – one for his study and the other for society; he will not lay down principles in speculation which he will be forced to forget in practice.

What shall I say to someone who, although he sees, touches, hears and perceives, claims nevertheless that it is never just his sensations that he perceives; that he could have been organized, so that everything happens within him, without there being anything outside, and that perhaps he is the only being who exists? At once I shall be aware of the profound absurdity of this paradox and I shall take care not to waste my time in destroying in a man an opinion, which he does not hold, and to which I have nothing clearer to oppose than what he denies. To silence him I should have to get out of nature, take him out too, and argue from some point outside him and myself, which is impossible. This sophist at least lacks that conversational propriety, which consists of objecting only to things to which one adds a certain solidity oneself. Why should I waste my breath removing a doubt which you do not have? Is my time worth so little in your eyes? Do you spend so

---

[52] As long as they are esteemed, people will dispute them. [eds]

little on yours? Are there no more truths to investigate or clarify? Let us attend to something more important; or if we have only these current frivolities, let us go to sleep and digest.

Source: Pyrrhonienne ou sceptique, translated by S. Gendzier except final 6 paragraphs, translated by S. Clennell, volume xiii, 1765, pp.608–14.

Section 4   Science and Technology

15 CRAFT by Diderot

CRAFT. This name is given to any profession that requires the use of the hands, and is limited to a certain number of mechanical operations to produce the same piece of work, made over and over again. I do not know why people have a low opinion of what this word implies; for we depend on the *crafts* for all the necessary things of life. Anyone who has taken the trouble to visit casually the workshops will see in all places utility allied with the greatest evidence of intelligence: antiquity made gods of those who invented the *crafts*; the following centuries threw into the mud those who perfected the same work. I leave to those who have some principle of equity to judge if it is reason or prejudice that makes us look with such a disdainful eye on such indispensable men. The poet, the philosopher, the orator, the minister, the warrior, the hero would all be nude, and lack bread without this craftsman, the object of their cruel scorn.

Source: Métier, translated by S. Gendzier, volume x, 1765, pp.463–5.

16 EXPERIMENTAL by d'Alembert

EXPERIMENT (natural philosophy). We call *Experimental* philosophy that which uses *experiments* to discover the laws of Nature. *See* EXPERIENCE.

There are two parts to *experimental* physics which must not be confused, *experiment* properly so-called and *observation*. This latter, less refined and less subtle, is limited to the facts which are before our eyes, to accurately seeing and cataloguing all the different kinds of phenomena which the spectacle of Nature presents to us. The former, on the other hand, seeks to penetrate Nature more profoundly, to uncover that which she is hiding; to create, in some way, by

different combinations of substances, new phenomena so as to study these. In short, *experiment* is not limited to listening to Nature, but interrogates and plies it with questions.

The Ancients were content to read Nature, but they read very assiduously, and with better eyes than we imagine they did. They advanced several facts which were at first discarded by the moderns, but which further research has shown to be true. The method followed by the Ancients in cultivating observation rather than *experiment* was very philosophical and the most fitted of all to promote the greatest progress in physics of which it was capable in that first age of the human spirit. Before employing and exhausting our intelligence in looking for a fact in subtle combinations, we must be very sure that this fact is not close at hand and under our noses, as in geometry we must reserve our effort to find out that which has not been resolved by others. Nature is so varied and so rich, that a simple, reasonably complete, collection of facts would vastly advance our knowledge; and if it were possible to enlarge this collection to the point where nothing at all was lacking, this would perhaps be the sole task to which a physicist should restrict himself. It is at least the task with which he should begin and that is what the Ancients did. They treated Nature just as Hippocrates[53] treated the human body; another proof of the relationship and resemblance between their physics and their medicine. The wisest amongst them did make, so to speak, a table of what they saw, made it very well and stopped there. The only thing they knew about the magnet was its most obvious property of attracting iron; the marvels of electricity which surrounded them, and of which we find some traces in their works, did not strike them, because in order for these marvels to be realized they would have had to see their relationship to more obscure facts which *experiment* has been able to discover in these latter days. For one of the advantages, amongst many, of *experiment* is that of extending the field of observation. *Experiment* reveals one phenomenon to us and thereby opens our eyes to an infinity of others, which were, so to speak, just asking to be noticed. Observation, by the curiosity it inspires and the gaps which it leaves, leads to *experiment*; *experiment* leads back to

---

[53] Hippocrates of Kos (c.460–c.370 BC), Greek physician. [eds]

observation by way of that same curiosity, seeking ever more to fill and close the gaps. Thus *experiment* and observation can in one way be looked upon as the consequence and complement of each other.

The Ancients seem to have used *experiment* only for practical purposes and not in any way like us in order to satisfy a purely philosophical curiosity. They dissected or combined substances simply for useful or pleasing purposes without trying very hard to find out about their operation or structure. They did not even linger over the details in the descriptions they made of bodies, and if they need any justification for not having done so, there would in a sense be ample justification in the fact that the moderns have found little use in following a contrary method.

To get the true feel of ancient physics, we should perhaps look for it in Aristotle's[54] histories of animals rather than in his works on physics, which have fewer facts and more words, are more reasoned and less scholarly. For such is the intelligence and inanity of the human spirit, working both at the same time, that as long as materials are abundant and easy to collect, a man will be concerned scarcely to do more than amass and catalogue them. But the instant he is short of materials, he starts to talk about them; so that even when reduced to a small number of materials he still feels tempted to form a corpus of them and to outline a system of science out of them, or something a little less that has the look of such a system, but is really a small number of isolated and imperfect scraps of knowledge.

But while recognizing that such a spirit may have presided up to a certain point over Aristotle's works on physics, we must not lay to his charge the way in which they were abused by modern writers during the centuries of ignorance which lasted such a long time, nor the ineptitudes which his commentators would have us believe are the opinions of this great man.

I speak of these dark ages only to mention in passing some superior spirits who, abandoning this vague and obscure method of philosophizing, forsook words for things and sought real knowledge in their intelligence and in the study of Nature. The monk Bacon,[55] too little known and read today, must be included within the number of these first-rate spirits. From the depths of the most profound ignorance, he was able, by the force of his genius, to raise himself above his century and to leave it far behind him.

For the rest, the small number of great geniuses who, up to the actual Renaissance of Learning, studied nature in this way for herself, did not really devote themselves to what might be called *experimental* physics. Chemists rather than physicists, they seemed more interested in the decomposition of particular bodies and to the detail of the usages which they might make of these, rather than in the general study of Nature. Rich in an infinite variety of useful or curious, but separate, items of knowledge, they were unaware of the laws of movement, the laws of Hydrostatics, the weight of air, of which they saw the effects, and several other truths which are today the foundation and serve as the elements of modern physics.

The chancellor Bacon,[56] an Englishman like the monk (for this name and this people are successful in philosophy), was the first to embrace a very much wider perspective. He glimpsed the general principles which must serve as a foundation for the study of Nature, and proposed to gain a closer acquaintance by way of *experiment.* He foresaw a great number of discoveries which have since been made. Descartes,[57] who follows him closely, and who has been accused (perhaps rather unfairly) of having drawn his inspiration from the works of Bacon, opens up several routes into *experimental* physics, but he recommends it rather than practises it;

---

[54] Aristotle (384–324 BC), philosopher and scientist. [eds]

[55] Roger Bacon (*c.*1214–94), Franciscan friar and philosopher; among many other things he wrote a commentary on Aristotle's *Physics*. Not to be confused with Francis Bacon (see note 56 below). [eds]

[56] Francis Bacon (1561–1622), Chancellor of England and writer on scientific method. [eds]

[57] René Descartes (1596–1650), French mathematician and philosopher. [eds]

and it is this perhaps that has led him into several errors. For example he had the courage to express the first of the laws of motion, courage for which he should have the philosophers' recognition, since he has put those who have followed him on the track of accurate laws; but experience, or as we say below, reflections on the most common observations, should have taught him that the laws he had given were untenable. Descartes, and Bacon himself, in spite of all the obligations which philosophy owes them, would perhaps have served a yet more useful function, if they had been more practical rather than theoretical physicists. But the idle pleasure of meditation and even of conjecture ensnares the great spirits. They start much and finish little; they propose opinions, they set out what must be done to establish the justice and advantage of them, but they leave the task of getting the work done to others, who guided by a light not their own, do not go as far as their masters would have gone alone: thus some think or dream, while the others act or work. Consequently, the infancy of the sciences is long, or, to put it better, eternal.

But the spirit of *experimental* physics, which Bacon and Descartes had introduced, was imperceptibly spreading. The Academy del Cimento[58] at Florence, Boyle[59] and Mariotte[60] and after them several others, successfully accomplished a great number of *experiments*; academies were formed and pursued this type of philosophy with enthusiasm: the universities were slower, because they were already fully established when *experimental* physics was born, and for a long time yet followed their ancient methods. Little by little the physics of Aristotle, or rather that of his commentators, gave way to the physics of Descartes. If they had not yet reached the truth, they were at least on the way. They did several *experiments* and tried to account for them. It would have been better if they had been content to do them well and grasp their mutual similarity; but, we must not hope for so prompt a deliverance of

the spirit from all its prejudices. Newton[61] appeared and was the first to show what his predecessors had been able only to glimpse, namely the art of introducing geometry into physics and constructing an exact science by uniting *experiment* with calculation, to produce a science exact, profound, luminous and new. At least as great for his optical *experiments* as for his system of the world, he opened on all sides an immense and firm way ahead. England seized upon these views; the Royal Society looked upon them as its own from the moment of their birth. The academies of France were slower to put forward their claim and had more difficulty, for the same reason that the universities had for several years rejected the physics of Descartes: light at length prevailed; the generation opposed to these great men died out in the academies and universities, for which the academies these days seem to set the tone.

A new generation arose, for when the foundations of a revolution have been laid, it is almost always in the succeeding generation that the revolution is completed; rarely before then, because the obstacles will perish sooner than give way; rarely after then because, the barriers once crossed, the human spirit often advances quicker than the man himself wants until he meets a new obstacle which obliges him to rest for a long time.

Cast an eye over the University of Paris, and you will find convincing proof of what I am saying. The study of geometry and *experimental* physics is starting to become dominant there. Several young professors, very knowledgeable, full of spirit and courage (because both are needed for innovations, even innocent innovations) have dared to leave the beaten track and strike out on a new one; whilst in other schools, which we will spare the embarrassment of naming, Descartes's laws of movement and even peripatetic physics[62] still hold pride of place. The young masters of whom I am

---

[58]   A scientific academy.

[59]   Robert Boyle (1627–91), Irish chemist and physicist; published *Sceptical Chymist* (1661). [eds].

[60]   Edme Mariotte (1620–84), French physicist. [eds]

[61]   Isaac Newton (1642–1727), the greatest scientist of his age. Universally respected by the *philosophes* – and, indeed, by all eighteenth-century intellectuals. [eds]

[62]   i.e. Aristotelian physics. [eds]

speaking are training truly educated students, who at the end of their philosophical studies are instructed in the true principles of all the physico-mathematical sciences and who, far from having to forget (as they would have had to previously) what they had learned, are on the contrary, in a state to use their learning in order to become better acquainted with those parts of physics which please them most. The use that can be gained from this method is so great that one could wish that college philosophy courses should be increased by one year or that the metaphysics and logic parts of the first year course could be shortened, since the first year is usually devoted almost entirely to these subjects. I am far from wanting to abolish two sciences whose utility and indispensable necessity I recognize; but I believe that their length could be considerably shortened, if their content could be reduced to what is true and useful. They would gain from being comprised of fewer pages, and so would physics, which must follow them.

It is in these circumstances that the King has just established a chair of *experimental* physics in the University of Paris. The present state of physics amongst us, the interest which even those who know nothing about it are showing in it, the examples from abroad, where countries have long been enjoying the advantage of a like establishment, seems to us to demand that we put our minds to getting something similar. There never was a more favourable time for strengthening the interest in sound physics in such a useful and estimable body as the University of Paris, a time when physics has for some years past been spreading there with such success. The recognized merit of the academician who occupies this chair assures us of the success with which he will fill it. It is no part of my task to outline for him a plan which his capacity and experience have doubtless already long ago shown to him. I beg only that I be permitted a few general reflections on the real aim of *experiments*. These reflections will not perhaps be useless to the young students who are disposed to profit from this new foundation so advantageous to the progress of physics.

The first real object of *experimental* physics is the general properties of bodies, known to us, so to speak, in outline by observation, but whose effects only *experiment* can measure and determine; such as, for example, the phenomena of

gravity. No theory would have been able to reveal to us the law governing the vertical fall of heavy bodies, but once this law was known by *experiment*, everything appertaining to the movement of heavy bodies, whether rectilinear, curvilinear, inclined or vertical, can be gauged by a simple application of the theory. If *experiment* comes into it, this must be with only the same aim and in the same way as for the primitive laws of momentum.

In like manner, everyday observation teaches us that air weighs something, but only *experiment* can enlighten us as to the absolute quantity of that something. This *experiment* is the basis of aerometry, and reasoning completes the process. *See* AEROMETRY.

We know that fluids exert downward pressure and have resistance when they are at rest and exert forward force when they are in movement; but this vague knowledge could not be of very great use. In order to make it more precise, and consequently more real and more useful, we must have recourse to *experiment*.

This would be the place to make a few observations on the abuse of calculation and hypotheses in physics, if this had not already been done by geometricians themselves, who cannot be accused here of partiality. But when we get down to it, what is not abused by men? The geometricians' method has been used to enshroud metaphysics in mystery; geometrical figures have been put into treatises on the soul, and since the action of God has been reduced to theorems, need one be astonished if they have tried to do the same with the action of bodies? *See* DEGREE.

How much could I say here on the sciences which are called *physico-mathematical*, on physical astronomy amongst others, on acoustics, on optics and its different branches, on the way in which *experiment* and calculation must come together to make these sciences as perfect as possible; but in order not to make this article too long, I shall relegate these reflections and several others to the *entry* PHYSICS, which must not be separated from this one. For the present, I shall limit myself here to what is the true and unique province of *experimental* physics, to those phenomena which can be infinitely multiplied and the cause of which cannot be understood by reasoning, the links between which we cannot discern or at least the interconnections between which we see very dimly, very rarely and after having looked at them from many different angles; such are, for example, the phenomena of chemistry, electricity, the magnet and many, many others. These are the facts which a physicist must strive above all to know well. He cannot amass too many of them; the more he gathers, the closer he will be to seeing the connection between them. His object must be to reduce them to the order which is inherent in them, to explain the one by the other, as far as this is possible, and to make from them a chain, so to speak, with as few missing links as possible. There will always be enough of these; nature has arranged them in good order. He must always guard against wanting to give reasons for something which is not clear to him. He must mistrust that overwhelming desire to explain everything which Descartes introduced into physics, and which has made most of his followers content with vague principles and reasons, adequate to maintain either the pros or the cons. One cannot help laughing when one reads in certain works of physics the explanation for the variations in the barometer, for snow, for hail and for hundreds of other facts. These authors, with the [mistaken] principles and methods which they use, would have just as little trouble in explaining totally contradictory facts; they could demonstrate, for example, that when it rains, the barometer should rise, that snow should fall in summer and hail in winter. Explanations in a physics course should be, like reflections in history, short, wise, apposite, guided by the facts or enclosed within the facts themselves, by the way in which these are presented.

For the rest, when I banish from physics that mania for explanations, I am far from wanting to banish that spirit of conjecture, which, at one and the same time timid and enlightened, sometimes leads to discoveries, so long as it declares itself to be what it is until it has arrived at a definite discovery; or that spirit of analogy whose wise boldness pierces beyond what nature seems to want to show and anticipates facts before seeing them. These two talents, so precious and so rare sometimes mislead the man who does not use them carefully enough, but not the man who does.

I conclude with a short observation which does not relate directly to the subject of this article, but which I cannot forbid myself. When

imitating the foreign example by establishing a chair of *experimental* physics which we are lacking, why not follow the same example and establish three more very useful chairs, which we are entirely lacking – chairs of moral philosophy, public law and history, three subjects which do belong in a certain sense to *experimental* philosophy, when viewed in all its fullness? I certainly do not in any way wish to despise any branch of knowledge, but it does seem to me that instead of having at the Collège Royal two chairs for Arabic, which is no longer taught; two for Hebrew which is scarcely taught; two for Greek which is not taught much and should be taught more; two for oratory, for which nature is almost the sole teacher, that one chair for each of these subjects would be quite enough. It seems to me that the splendour and usefulness of this college would be enhanced by a chair of moral philosophy, the well developed principles of which would interest every nation; a chair of public law, of which even the elements are little known in France; and finally by a chair of history which should be occupied by a man who is both a man of letters and a *philosophe*, that is to say by a very rare kind of individual. This wish is not mine alone; it is that of a great number of good people; and although I have not much hope of anything coming of this proposal, there is no harm in making it.

Source: Expérimental, translated by J. Greenwood, volume vi, 1756, pp.298–301.

17 INOCULATION by Tronchin

INOCULATION (surgery, medicine, morality, politics), the noun synonymous with *insertion*, is the prevailing term to designate the operation by which one artifically communicates smallpox for the purpose of preventing the danger and the ravages of that illness when contracted naturally.

Even if all France were to be persuaded of the importance and usefulness of this practice, it could not be introduced in our country without the government's approval and assistance. And will the government ever resolve to encourage it without the most conclusive evidence in such matters?

It is therefore incumbent on the faculties of theology and medicine, the academies, the heads of the magistracy, and men of letters to banish the scruples fomented by ignorance and to make the people feel that its own interest, Christian charity, the good of the state, and the conservation of mankind are involved in the establishment of *inoculation*. When a question of public welfare arises, the duty of the thinking part of the nation is to enlighten those individuals susceptible of understanding and to drag along by the weight of authority that mob of people not affected by evidence of any kind.

Do we need more experiments? Are we not sufficiently aware of all the facts? Let the hospitals be directed to distinguish carefully in their annual registers the number of the sick and the dead in each kind of illness, a custom practised in England that will be recognized in time to have more and more usefulness. In one of these hospitals perform the experiment of inoculating one hundred subjects who will voluntarily submit to it. Have a hundred other patients of the same age treated for natural attacks of smallpox. Everything should take place with the assistance of the different masters in the art of curing, under the eyes and direction of an administrator whose enlightenment equals his devotion and good intentions. Then compare the register of deaths on both sides and give the results to the people. The means of clearing up and resolving doubts, if any remain, will not be lacking when with the power one will also have the will to do something constructive.

Inoculation, I repeat, will one day be prescribed in France, and people will be astonished that it was not adopted sooner.

Source: Inoculation, translated by S. Gendzier, volume viii, 1765, pp.755–71.

Section 5 Music

[For the Encyclopedists, music had one purpose only: to depict emotional states and scenes from nature. In the middle of the eighteenth century, French critics either had no concept of music as an autonomous language, or did not know how to criticize it as such. However, some of the more extreme views in the *Encyclopédie* were modified in the *Supplément*, published in 1776. In particular, later writers seemed concerned to limit the implications of 'imitation' for music.]

18 THE PRELIMINARY DISCOURSE TO THE ENCYCLOPEDIA by d'Alembert

Since the first process of thought consists in bringing together and uniting ideas of which we have direct experience, we have had to begin this *Discourse* by considering thought from that point of view, and reviewing the different sciences which result from it. But the concepts derived from the combination of direct observations are not the only ones of which our minds are capable. We must now turn to another sort of knowledge. It consists of the ideas which we form for ourselves, in creating in our imagination beings similar to those which are the object of our direct experience: this is what is called the imitation of Nature, a concept so well known and so commended by the ancients. Since the direct experiences which make the greatest impression on us are those which we most easily remember, these are also the ones which we strive to reawaken in ourselves by imitating their objects. Although agreeable objects make a stronger impression on us when they are really present rather than when they are represented, the charm they lose by being represented is to some extent compensated for by that which results from the pleasure of the imitation. With regard to the objects which, being present, excite only sad or agitated sentiments, their imitation is actually more agreeable than the objects themselves, because it places us at the exact distance where we can enjoy the pleasure of the emotion without experiencing the distress.

[D'Alembert discusses imitation in painting, sculpture and poetry.]

Finally Music, which speaks at the same time to the imagination and to the senses, holds the last place in the order of imitation, not because its imitation is less exact with regard to the objects which it attempts to represent, but because it seems, up to the present time, to be limited to a smaller number of images. We can attribute this less to the nature of the art than to a want of invention and resources in the majority of those who cultivate it. It will be worth giving some thought to this. Music, which was perhaps originally capable of representing nothing but noise, has gradually become a sort of discourse, or language, in which various feelings, or passions, can be expressed. But why restrict this expression to the passions alone? Why not extend it as far as possible, even to the extent of representing all sensations? Although the impressions which we receive from various organs differ from each other as much as the original objects differ, we can nevertheless compare them from a standpoint which is common to all of them, that is to say from the point of view of the pleasure or the distress they excite in our hearts. A frightening object or a terrifying noise each produces in us a comparable emotion, and we often refer to both objects by the same name or by synonymous terms. Consequently, I do not see why a musician who has to depict a frightening object should not do so successfully by seeking out a sound in nature which produces in us an emotion the most like that which is excited by the object. I advocate the same with regard to pleasurable feelings. To think otherwise would be to try to limit both art and pleasure. I admit that the kind of portrayal which we are speaking of here demands a subtle and profound study of the gradations which differentiate our feelings, so that it is not to be expected that those gradations will be discernible by the common man. Grasped by the man of genius, perceived by the man of taste, understood by the intelligent man, they are wasted on the masses. All music which does not depict is nothing but noise, and gives scarcely more pleasure than a sequence of pleasant-sounding words, deprived of sense or syntax. It is true that a musician who sought to depict everything might in some circumstances present us with sound pictures which were neither easily nor universally understood, but what we must conclude from this is that after having made an art out of writing music, we ought to make an art out of listening to it.

Source: Discours Préliminaire, translated by P. Howard, volume i, 1751, pp.i–xlv.

19 EXPRESSION by Louis de Cahusac

EXPRESSION (music). It is the tone which is the appropriate one for the feeling, the situation or the character of each part of the subject being treated. Poetry, Painting and Music are imitative arts. Since the first does not only consist in a structured arrangement of words, and the second is something quite different from a simple mixing of colours, similarly Music is far from being an abstract sequence of varied sounds. Each of these arts has and must have *expression*, because we cannot imitate without expressing, or rather *expression* is imitation itself.

There are two sorts of Music, instrumental and vocal, and *expression* is essential to both sorts,

however they are used. A concerto or a sonata must depict something or it is nothing but noise, harmonious if you will, but lifeless. The melody of a song or a cantata must express the words of the cantata or the song, or else the composer has not achieved his aim; and the melody, however beautiful, is only nonsense, and tiring for sensitive ears.

Source: Expression, translated by P. Howard, volume vi, 1756, pp.315–21.

20 SONATA by Jean-Jacques Rousseau

Now that instrumental writing has become the most important part of music, *sonatas* are very much in fashion, and all sorts of symphonies equally so; vocal music is scarcely more than an accessory.

Music is an imitative art; but this imitation is of a different kind from that of Poetry and Painting; and to experience it, it is necessary to be in the presence of the object which is being imitated, or at least in the presence of its image. This object is brought before us in words, and it is through the moving tones of the human voice, together with words, that the same object produces the appropriate feeling in the heart. Who has not felt how far instrumental music is distanced from this feeling and this power? To know the meaning of all this hotchpotch of *sonatas* with which we are overwhelmed, it would be necessary to do like the crass painter who had to write under his figures, 'this is a man', 'this is a tree', 'this is an ox'. I shall never forget the words of the famous M. de Fontenelle,[63] who, finding himself at a concert and exhausted by an endless symphony, called out loud in a fit of impatience, 'Sonata, what are you trying to tell me?'

Source: Sonate, translated by P. Howard, volume xv, 1765, p.348.

21 SYMPHONY by de Jaucourt, quoting Jean-Baptiste Dubos, 'Symphonie'

Music is not restricted to imitating in song, the language of man, and all the natural sounds which he emits instinctively. This art also aspires to imitate all the noises which move us most powerfully when we hear them in nature. To imi-

---

[63]   Bernard Bovier, sieur de Fontenelle (1657–1757), writer, critic and secretary from 1697 of the Académie des Sciences. [eds]

tate these sounds in which nothing is articulated, Music uses instruments only, and we usually call these imitations *symphonies*.

The truth of the imitation in a *symphony* consists in the resemblance of the *symphony* to the noise which it attempts to imitate. There is truth in a *symphony* which has been composed in imitation of a storm when the melody, harmony and rhythm of the *symphony* make us hear a noise like the howl of the winds and the roar of the waves as they crash together or which break against the rocks.

Source: Symphonie, translated by P. Howard, *Supplément*, volume xv, 1776, pp.740–1.

22 ART *by Jean François Marmontel*

Among the *liberal arts* some address the heart directly, like Eloquence and Poetry; other address more particularly the senses, like Music and Painting; some express themselves through the artificial and changeable signs of articulate sound; another uses natural and universal signs, the inflexion of the voice and the noise of a resonating body; yet others make use not of signs, but of the actual appearance of the objects which they express, its planes and contours, colours, light and shade; finally, another expresses nothing at all (I speak of Architecture), but its study is to observe what pleases the visual sense, whether in the relationship of dimensions or whether in the blending of forms, and its object is to unite ornament with utility.

Now among these *arts* some have nature for a model, and excellence consists in selecting and ordering not only as well as nature but better than her: this is how Poetry, Painting and Sculpture work; another expresses truth itself, and imitates nothing, but in the means that it employs it uses all the power of which those means are capable: thus Eloquence deploys all the resources of feeling and all the power of reason; another imitates either by resemblance or by analogy: thus Music for two instruments, one natural and the other artificial: in this way the human voice, and the instruments which aid the voice by accompanying it and, through the intermediary of the ear, to arouse new emotions in the heart.

If it is true, as a famous musician[64] has claimed, that the universal principle of harmony and melody are to be found in nature, it follows that nature should serve as the guide but not the model for Music. Doubtless all sounds and all harmonies exist in nature; but the *art* lies in combining them, and in composing a whole which pleases the ear and which arouses pleasant emotions in the heart. Now, let someone tell us what such a composition resembles. Is it from birdsong or from the intonations of the human voice that Music has taken its system of tonality and harmony?

This *art* is perhaps the most hidden secret which man has stolen from nature. The painter has only to open his eyes; will anyone say that the musician has only to listen to find models? It is true that Music often imitates nature; and embellished verisimilitude is one of its most fashionable pursuits, but to reduce it solely to imitation and to the expression of nature is to deny it the most astounding of its miracles, and the ear the most acute and the most cherished of its pleasures. Music, then, resembles on the one hand Poetry, which embellishes nature through imitation, and on the other hand Architecture, which seeks only to please the senses which it must address.

In studying the *arts*, one must grasp the idea that independent of the intellectual pleasures which mimicry and the much-advocated concept of imitation give us, each of the senses has its purely physical pleasures, like taste and smell; the ear above all has its own, and it seems that the more sensitive it is, the rarer are the pleasures in nature. For a thousand pleasing sensations that come to us through our sense of sight, there is perhaps one which comes through our sense of hearing: one might say that since this organ is specially intended to transmit to us word and thought, nature may therefore be thought to have favoured it enough. Everything in the universe seems to be made for the eye, and almost nothing for the ear. Thus of all the *arts*, that which has the most to gain from rivalling nature is the *art* of harmony and melody.

Source: Art, translated by P. Howard, *Supplément*, volume i, 1776, pp.585–97.

---

[64] The 'famous musician' is the French composer Jean Philippe Rameau (1683–1764). [eds]

23 VOCAL MUSIC by Jean François Marmontel

If instrumental music can please the ear without offering any distinct image or specific feeling to the mind, and if through the veil of an understated and indistinct expression it leaves each listener to imagine and feel what he will, according to the inclination and condition of his own heart, then that is sufficient. But we require of *vocal music* a more faithful imitation, either of the picture or of the feeling which the poem has provided for representation.

Source: *Chant*, translated by P. Howard, *Supplément*, volume ii, 1776, pp.320–3.

24 INSTRUMENTAL MUSIC Anonymous

The composer would do well always to keep in mind the idea of some person, some situation or some passion and to concentrate so completely on this idea that eventually he seems to hear speaking the very person who is in this situation. That will place him in a state to be moving, passionate or tender. He will find help in this respect in seeking among the great poets for passages of this sort, and in declaiming them, so as to approach composition in the state of heightened emotion to which this declamation will have brought him. He should only dispense with these precautions when he is firmly convinced that all composition which is not appropriate to express passion or which does not communicate intelligibly the language of feeling will be nothing but vain noise.

Source: *Instrumentale*, translated by P. Howard, *Supplément*, volume iii, 1777, pp.618–19.

Frederick the Great and Catherine the Great
Letters and Documents

Prepared for the Course Team by
Antony Lentin

Contents

Frederick the Great and Catherine the Great
Letters and Documents

Prussia under Frederick the Great (born 1712, ruled 1740–86) leaped to the fore in Europe and continued thereafter to exert a decisive influence. Consolidating the achievements of his father, Frederick-William I (1713–40), Frederick, ruling with extraordinary determination and clear-sightedness, welded a small, thinly-populated and under-resourced conglomeration of hereditary lands into a cohesive society and state, a serious contender for mastery in Germany and a recognized Great Power. This he demonstrated by his brilliant successes in the course of two great wars which he launched (1740–8 and 1756–63). Frederick was also an active participant in the thought and culture of the Enlightenment. Poet, flautist and composer, art-collector and designer of his own palace at Sans-Souci, he was above all a prolific man of letters, who styled himself 'the philosophe of Sans-Souci'; he corresponded widely, with, among others, Voltaire and d'Alembert. The Prussian philosopher, Kant, declared that 'our age is the age of Enlightenment, the century of Frederick' (Texts II, p.303). A recent scholar describes Frederick as 'probably the most effective populariser of the Enlightenment in Germany, if not Europe' (Blanning, 1989, p.275).

Catherine the Great (born 1729, ruled 1762–96), German-born, with no claim to the Russian throne, was brought to Russia to marry the heir to the throne. After his brief reign and overthrow, Catherine herself came to govern, as an intelligent and energetic absolute ruler, a vast state which came to the fore under Peter the Great (1696–1725) and continued thereafter to exert a major influence in Europe. Like Frederick, Catherine enjoyed dazzling successes in foreign policy, enhancing Russia's Great Power status in the course of two wars with Turkey (1768–74 and 1787–92) and three partitions of Poland.

Catherine too immersed herself in the works of the Enlightenment, particularly Voltaire and the Encyclopédie. She was, as she called herself, an inveterate 'scribbler', a translator, playwright and patron of the arts. At least until the French Revolution, she associated herself with 'Enlightenment' causes, and her legislative manifesto, the Nakaz (Instruction) of 1767, was banned in France as subversive. Catherine was hailed by the encyclopedists as one of their supporters. Her latest scholarly biographer describes her as 'truly a daughter of the Enlightenment' (Madariaga, 1989, p.302).

The following selection contains 103 letters and other documents, mainly in the form of extracts, 53 relating to Frederick, 50 to Catherine. Most are taken from Lentin (1985). Some documents have been further edited and abridged. For scholarly reference, each document is identified by reference to the original published source.

All the footnotes contained in these documents are the work of the editors. Accents added to Russian names indicate where the stress falls.

Frederick the Great, King of Prussia

Section 1 Frederick and monarchy

Document 1

Portrait of Frederick II

Contemporary published account, 1779

The King of Prussia is below the middle size, well made and remarkable active for his time of life. He has become hardy by exercise and a laborious life; for his constitution originally seems to have been none of the strongest. His look announces spirit and penetration. He has fine blue eyes; and in my opinion, his countenance, upon the whole, is agreeable. Some who have seen him are of a different opinion; all who judge him from his portraits only, must be so; for although I have seen a great many, which have a little resemblance of him, and some which have a great deal, yet none of them do him justice. His features acquire a wonderful degree of animation while he converses. He stoops considerably, and inclines his head almost constantly to one side. His tone of voice is the clearest and most agreeable in conversation I ever heard. He speaks a great deal; yet those who hear him regret he does not speak a great deal more. His observations are always lively, very often just; and few men possess the talent of repartee in greater perfection.

Figure 1 *J.H.C. Franke,* Frederick the Great, *1764, oil on canvas; photograph from Cambridge University Library.*

He hardly ever varies his dress, which consists of a blue coat, lined and faced with red, and a yellow waistcoat and breeches. He always wears boots with hussar tops, which fall in wrinkles about his ankles, and are oftener of a dark brown than a black colour. His hat would be thought extravagantly large in England, though it is of the size commonly used by the Prussian officers of cavalry. He generally wears one of the large side corners over his forehead and eyes, and the front cock on one side. He wears his hair queued behind, and dressed with a single buckle on each side. From their being very carelessly put up and unequally powdered, we may naturally conclude that the *friseur* has been greatly hurried in the execution of his office. He uses a very large gold snuffbox, the lid ornamented with diamonds, and takes an immoderate quantity of Spanish snuff, the marks of which very often appear on his waistcoat and breeches. These are also liable to be soiled by the paws of two or three Italian greyhounds, which he often caresses.[1]

A few days ago, I happened to take a very early walk, about a mile out of town,[2] and seeing some soldiers under arms in a field, at a small distance from the road, I went towards them. An officer on horseback, whom I took to be the major, for he gave the word of command, was uncommonly active, and often rode among the ranks, to reprimand or instruct the common men. When I came nearer, I was much surprised to find that this was the king himself. He had his sword drawn, and continued to exercise the corps for an hour after. He made them wheel, march, form the square, and fire by divisions and in platoons, observing all their motions with infinite attention; and, on account of some blunder, put two officers of the Prince of Prussia's regiment in arrest. In short, he seemed to exert himself with all the spirit of a young officer, eager to attract the notice of his general by uncommon alertness.

Source: J. Moore, *A View of society and manners in France, Switzerland and Germany,* volume II, Dublin, 1789, p.168.

---

[1] In 1991, Frederick was reburied next to his greyhounds at Sans-Souci, in accordance with his own wishes.

[2] Potsdam.

Document 2

Frederick II on himself and the state

Secret cabinet-order from Frederick II to Count von Finckenstein, Assistant Foreign Minister (in French), 10 January 1757
Should it be my fate to be taken prisoner,[3] I forbid anyone to entertain the slightest concern for my person, or to pay the least attention to anything I might write from my place of confinement. If such a misfortune should befall me, I shall sacrifice myself for the State, and everyone must then obey my brother.[4] I shall hold him and all my ministers and generals responsible on pain of death for seeing that neither a province nor a ransom is offered for my release, but that the war is continued and every advantage seized, just as if I had never existed.

Source: Oeuvres de Frédéric le Grand Vol XXV (1854), Berlin, p.320.

Document 3

Frederick II on hereditary monarchy

Letter from Frederick II to Voltaire (in French), 20 October 1774
We have two kings who are fit to be locked up and several weak monarchs, but no monsters. Weakness is an incorrigible fault; but we must blame nature, not the individual. I agree that harm is done through weakness; but in any country where the succession to the throne is established on a hereditary basis, a necessary consequence is that there must be some weak individuals in charge of nations, because no family whatever has supplied an uninterrupted succession of great men.[5] Believe me, not all human institutions will ever attain perfection. We must be content with second best, and not make violent protests against every incurable abuse.

Source: Voltaire's correspondence, edited by T. Besterman, volume LXXXIX, Geneva, 1963, p.12.

Document 4

Frederick II on 'the first servant of the state'

Confidential memorandum intended for the use of his heir (in French), 'Political Testament', 1752
In a State like this, the ruler must necessarily take charge of things personally, because if he is wise, he will pursue only the public interest, which is his own; whereas a minister always has his mind on things which further his own interests; and instead of promoting deserving candidates, appoints his own creatures and strives to consolidate his own position through the number of people whom he makes dependent on him. The monarch, on the other hand, will support the nobility, keep the clergy within its proper bounds, will not allow the princes of the blood to intrigue or plot, and will reward merit without those partisan views which ministers secretly entertain in everything they do.

But if it is vital that the ruler should personally direct the internal affairs of his State, how much more vital it is for him to conduct his foreign policy in person, to form the alliances which suit him, to make his own plans and take his own decisions in critical and awkward situations. Finances, domestic government, foreign policy and military affairs are so closely connected that it is impossible to deal with one of these branches in isolation from the others. When that happens, rulers do badly. In France four ministers rule the kingdom: the Ministers of Finance, Marine, War and Foreign Affairs. These four 'kings' never agree or concur; hence all the contradictions which we see in the French government: one man reverses out of jealousy the policy promoted by another abler man; no system, no planning; chance rules all, and everything in France is the result of court intrigues; the English know everything that is discussed at Versailles; there is no secrecy and consequently no proper foreign policy.

---

[3] During the Seven Years' War (1756–63). Frederick anticipated a Russian advance on Berlin, as Russians, Austrians and French made ready to close in on him.

[4] Prince August-Wilhelm of Prussia.

[5] Frederick had a low opinion of both his nominated heirs, August-Wilhelm, his brother (1722–58) and Frederick-William, his nephew (1744–97), later (1786–97) King Frederick-William II.

A well-run government must have a system as coherent as a system of philosophy: all the measures taken must be well reasoned; finances, foreign policy and military affairs must work to the same end, namely the consolidation of the State and the increase of its power. Now a system can only emanate from one mind; and this must be the monarch's. Idleness, luxury or stupidity prevent rulers from pursuing the noble task of bringing about their people's happiness. Such monarchs make themselves so contemptible that they become the laughing-stock of their contemporaries, and as far as history is concerned, their role is, at best, to mark a chronological period. They vegetate on the throne, unworthy to occupy it, intent on self-indulgence. Their negligence towards their peoples even becomes criminal. A monarch is not raised to this lofty rank or entrusted with supreme power in order to live in luxury, to grow fat on the people's substance and enjoy himself while everyone else suffers. The monarch is the first servant of the State. He is well paid in order that he may maintain the dignity of his rank; but he is required to contribute actively to the good of the State and to direct its principal affairs conscientiously, at the least. Certainly he needs assistance; to master all the details is too much for him; but he must listen to everyone's complaints and have justice promptly done to the potential victims of oppression. A woman came to petition a king of Epirus, who impatiently told her to leave him in peace: '*Why are you king, then,*' she retorted, '*if not to do me justice?*' A fine observation, which princes should bear constantly in mind.

Source: Die Politischen Testamente Friedrichs des Grossen, edited by G.B. Volz, Berlin, 1920, pp.37–9.

Document 5

Frederick on the king's role

Published essay (in French), 'Essay on the forms of government and the duties of sovereigns', 1777
The citizens only granted pre-eminence to one of their fellows in return for the services which they expected from him. These services consist in upholding the laws, ensuring that justice is scrupulously observed, opposing the corruption of manners as far as he can and defending the State against its enemies. The ruler must supervise agriculture, he must ensure abundant supplies for the community and promote industry and trade. He is like a sentry, permanently on guard against his neighbours and the activities of the enemies of the State. Just as all the springs of a watch operate to the same purpose, namely, to measure time, so too the springs of government should be set in such a way that all the different parts of the administration contribute equally to the greatest good of the State, that vital object that must never be lost sight of.

The ruler is linked by indissoluble bonds to the body of the State; consequently he feels the repercussion of all the ills that afflict his subjects, and likewise, society suffers the misfortunes which affect its ruler. There is only one good, namely, that of the State in general. If the ruler loses some provinces, he is no longer in the same position as before to assist his subjects. If misfortune has driven him into debt, it is the poor citizens who must pay; on the other hand, if the population is very small, if the people languish in poverty, the ruler lacks every resource. These are truths so incontrovertible that there is no need to stress them further. I repeat, then, the ruler represents the State; he and his peoples form a single body which can only be happy as long as they are both harmoniously united. The ruler is to the society he governs what the head is to the whole body: he must see, think and act for the whole community, in order to obtain for it all the benefits of which it is capable. If monarchical government is to be superior to republican, the monarch's decision is all-important; he must be active and upright, and must muster all his good qualities in order to fulfil his destined career.

This is my idea of his duties. He must acquire an accurate and detailed knowledge of his country's strengths and weaknesses, including monetary resources, population, finances, trade and the laws and character of the nation which he is to rule.

Since any individual who fails to act according to principle is inconsistent in his conduct, it is all the more important that the ruler, who is responsible for the people's welfare, should act according to a fixed system of politics, war, finances, trade and law.

These are the general duties that a ruler must carry out. In order not to fall short of them, he must constantly remind himself that he is a man, like the least of his subjects; if he is society's first judge, first general, first financier, first minister, it is not in order that he should merely symbolize their duties, but that he should carry them out. He is the first servant of the State, obliged to act with probity, wisdom, and complete disinterestedness, as if at any moment he were accountable to his citizens for his stewardship. So he is to blame, if he squanders the national revenue, which is the product of taxation, on luxury, ostentation and dissipation, when he should be promoting good moral conduct, which is the guardian of the laws, when he should be improving national education, and not undermining it by his bad example. This is the true idea that should be held of the duties of a monarch and is the only way to make monarchical government good and beneficial. If many rulers behave differently, we must attribute this to their lack of reflection on the institution of monarchy and the duties attaching to it. They have assumed a responsibility whose onerousness and importance they have underestimated; they have erred through lack of knowledge; for in our day ignorance causes more errors than wickedness.

This portrait of a monarch will perhaps be seen in the eyes of critics to resemble the ideal of the sage depicted by the Stoics, an ideal which has never existed in fact, and to which Marcus Aurelius[6] alone came closest. We hope that this humble essay may be able to produce some Marcus Aureliuses: that would be the finest reward we could hope for, and it would benefit humanity at the same time.

Source: Oeuvres de Frédéric le Grand, volume IX, Berlin, 1848, pp.198–210.

Document 6

Frederick II on monarchy and republicanism

Published essay (in French), 'Letters on love of Country', 1779

I remember you were of the opinion that one might expect to find true citizens in republics, but that you thought there were none in monarchies. Let me disabuse you of this error. Good monarchies, where the administration is wise and full of mildness, constitute in our day a form of government which is closer to oligarchy than to despotism, for it is the laws alone that rule. Let us go into some detail. Consider the number of people employed on the advisory committees, in the administration of justice and of finances, in diplomatic missions abroad, in commerce, in the armed forces, in the internal civilian administration; add to this those who have a voice in the provinces; all of them, let me inform you, share a part of the sovereign authority. So the ruler is not a despot ruling merely according to his own whim; he should be seen as the focal point where the *radii* of the circle converge. This form of government provides in its deliberations the secrecy which is lacking in republics; and the various branches of the administration, being interconnected, advance together like the four-horse chariots of the Romans, and operate in combination for the general welfare of the people. Moreover, you will always find less of the spirit of party faction in monarchies, if they have at their head a firm ruler, than in republics, which are often torn apart by citizens who intrigue and plot to overthrow one another. If there is in Europe an exception to what I have just been saying, it is perhaps the Ottoman Empire or some other government which, failing to recognize its true interest, has failed to bind closely enough the interests of the individuals with those of the monarch.

A well-ruled kingdom should be like a family, of which the monarch is the father, and the citizens his children; their good and bad fortune are shared between them, for the monarch cannot be happy when his people are wretched. When this union is well established, duty and gratitude produce good citizens: their identification with the State is absolute; they cannot dissociate themselves from it; they would have everything to lose and nothing to gain. You require examples? The government of Sparta was oligarchic and it produced a host of great patriots. Rome, after she lost her freedom, furnishes you with an Agrippa, a Thrasea Paetus, a Helvidius Priscus, a Corbulo, an Agricola,[7] emperors like Titus, Marcus Aurelius, Trajan and Julian; in a word, a large number of those mas-

---

[6]   Roman emperor AD 161–180, author of the stoic *Meditations* (among Frederick's favourite reading), and the prime example in antiquity of a paternalistic absolute ruler, dedicated to the service of the state.

[7]   Agrippa was Augustus's right-hand man; Thrasea Paetus, a Stoic, condemned to death for republican opposition under Nero; Helvidius Priscus, Paetus's son-in-law, exiled and later executed for opposition to Vespasian; Corbulo, successful general, recalled by Nero on suspicion of treason, committed suicide; Agricola, Governor of Britain, father-in-law of the historian Tacitus, who eulogized the above.

culine and virile men who put the interests and the advantage of the public good before their own.

Source: *Oeuvres de Frédéric le Grand*, volume IX, Berlin, 1848, pp.216–17.

Section 2 Frederick and war
Document 7

Frederick II on war

Published treatise (in French), The 'Anti-Machiavel, or Refutation of Machiavelli's "The Prince", [8] 1740
I ask: what can be the motive that makes a man seek to aggrandize himself? What can be his reason for plotting to base his power on the misery and destruction of others, and how can he believe that he will make a name for himself by merely making men unhappy? A monarch's fresh conquests do not make his existing possessions any richer; his peoples gain nothing from them, and he deceives himself if he imagines that they will make him any happier.

War is so rich in misfortunes, its outcome is so uncertain and its consequences are so disastrous for a country, that rulers can hardly reflect too long before embarking on it. I say nothing of the injustice and violence that they do to their neighbours, but confine myself to the miseries which fall directly upon their own subjects. I am convinced that if kings and rulers had a true picture of the people's sufferings, they would not be unmoved by them. But they lack the imagination to form an objective idea of the evils from which their status shields them. A ruler should be made to realize that his burning ambition sparks off all the fatal consequences to which war is prone: the taxes that cripple the people; the levies that deprive the country of all its young men; the epidemics that sweep through armies, where so many die in misery; the murderous sieges; the still crueller battles; the wounded, whom the loss of some limb deprives of the only means of subsistence, and the orphans, from whom the enemy fire has snatched those who braved the dangers and sold to the ruler their lives and their sustinence. So many men, useful to the State, cut off before their time! Never was there a tyrant who committed such cruelties in cold blood. Rulers who wage unjust wars are crueller than they. They sacrifice to their impetuous passion the happiness, health and the lives of an infinite number of men, whom it was their duty to protect and make happy, instead of so recklessly exposing them to everything that humanity has most to fear. It is therefore certain that the world's rulers cannot be too prudent and cautious in their actions, and cannot be too careful for the lives of their subjects, whom they should not regard as their slaves, but as their equals, and in a certain sense, as their masters.

Source: 'La réfutation du Prince de Machiavel', edited by C. Fleischauer, in *Studies on Voltaire and the Eighteenth Century*, volume V, Geneva, 1958, pp.180, 352–5.

Document 8

Frederick II on war

Letter from Frederick II to Electress Maria Antonia of Saxony (in French), 8 March 1766
Certainly, Madam, no society can exist without justice. Do unto others what you would have them do to you; this principle embodies the whole of virtue and Man's duties towards the society in which he lives. That is the basis of that Public [International] Law so well known in the German universities, but which is nearly always crushed by the law of the heavy guns. Thus, Madam, men's reason and their passion are constantly opposed to each other, and what the one sets up, the other knocks down. As for those, Madam, who are in charge of government, I think one should hear them before condemning them. I certainly do not regard these people as despots; if they are, it is only when they abuse their position. Their position places them in charge of society, and their basic duty is to further to the utmost of their ability the interests of that nation, that is to say, to maintain the security of its possessions, which is the first right of every citizen; next, to protect it from the designs of neighbours who seek to harm it, and lastly to defend it against enemy aggression. Now, Madam, put the mildest and most impartial man in charge of this task, and you will agree that in order to discharge his duties, he must act in a different way from that which his natural incli-

---

[8]   Machiavelli's *The Prince* (1519) advocated expediency over morality in statecraft. Frederick's *Anti-Machiavel*, corrected and polished by Voltaire, was published a few months before Frederick's first invasion of Silesia.

nation would dictate. He is like a tutor who, though generous as far as his own interests are concerned, is jealously concerned for those of his pupil. That, Madam, is my idea of the duty of monarchs, and so that is the basis upon which I act in my own small sphere.

Source: *Oeuvres de Frédéric le Grand*, volume XXIV, Berlin, 1854, p.109.

Document 9

Frederick II on war

Letter from Frederick II to Voltaire (in French), 30 July 1774
But I do not know where I stray. Is it for me to suggest ideas to that solitary *philosophe*, who from his study, furnishes the whole of Europe with ideas? I leave you to all those which your tireless imagination will suggest. It will doubtless tell you that it is as much use declaiming against snow and hail as against war; that these are inevitable evils; and that it is not worthy of a *philosophe* to take on lost causes. One asks a doctor to cure a fever, not to write a satire against it. If you have any cures, let us have them; if you have none, show sympathy for our misfortunes.

Source: *Voltaire's correspondence*, edited by T. Besterman, volume LXXXVIII, Geneva, 1963, pp.133–4.

Document 10

Frederick II on foreign policy

Confidential memorandum intended for the use of his heir (in French), 'Political Testament', 1752
An experienced politician should always adopt a flexible approach, adjusted to the circumstances in which he finds himself and the personalities with whom he has to deal. It is a great mistake in foreign policy always to be aggressive, to seek to decide every issue by force, or conversely, always to use gentle and subtle methods. A man who follows a uniform system is soon found out, and one must not be found out. If your method becomes well known, your enemies will correctly predict: *'If we do this, he will do so and so'*; while by changing and varying one's tactics, one baffles them, and they make wrong forecasts. But conduct as wise as this requires you to keep a permanent check on yourself, and far from following your personal inclinations, you must pursue meticulously the strategy which your real interests dictate. The main object is to hide your

intentions, and for that you must veil your character and only reveal a firmness moderated and tempered by justice. I have endeavoured to deal with my enemies on this basis. Each set of circumstances, each moment of time, each individual, requires a different approach. If it is time to break off negotiations, it is advisable to declare your intentions firmly and proudly; but it is no use for the storm to threaten, unless the lightning strikes simultaneously. If you have many enemies, you must divide them, isolate the most irreconcilable, attack him, negotiate with the rest, lull them to sleep, make separate peace, even if you have to lose by it; and then once the principal enemy is beaten, there is always time to return and fall on the others, under the pretext that they have failed to carry out their engagements.

Source: *Die Politischen Testamente Friedrichs des Grossen*, edited by G.B. Voltz, Berlin, 1920, pp.51, 54.

Document 11

Frederick II on Prussia and war

Confidential memorandum intended for the use of his heir (in French), 'Account of the government of Prussia', 1776
The geographical position of the State obliges us to maintain many troops: for our neighbours are Austria, Russia, France and Sweden. 220,000 men are kept on a war footing, including special batallions and auxiliary cavalry. Of this number, 180,000 men could be put in the field; but the moment it becomes necessary to raise three armies, it is obvious that we do not have many troops in comparison with our neighbours. I think that the discipline and tactics that have been introduced should remain on their present footing, provided that there is no change in the system of waging war; for then there is no alternative but to adapt to circumstances and change with them. But to equal or surpass the enemy, one must act in an orderly and disciplined fashion and encourage and reward the officers, so that noble emulation spurs them on to surpass the enemy. If the monarch does not personally participate in military affairs and if he fails to set the example, all is lost.

In foreign policy, we should look to the future as far as possible and ascertain future turns of events in Europe, whether to form alliances or to thwart the plans of our enemies. We should not believe that we can shape events;

but when they present themselves, we must seize them in order to exploit them. That is why finances must be in order, so that the government is ready to act the moment political considerations indicate that the time is ripe. War itself should be waged according to political principles, in order to inflict the bloodiest blow on the enemy. Small states are quickly crushed, unless they are active, vigorous and dynamic. These are a few of my reflections and ideas on the government of this country, which, until it acquires far greater strength and better frontiers, must be ruled by monarchs who are always alert, wary of their neighbours and ready to defend themselves from one day to the next against their enemies' designs.

Source: Oeuvres de Frédéric le Grand, volume IX, Berlin, 1848, pp.186, 190–1.

Document 12

Frederick on foreign policy

Confidential memorandum intended for the use of his heir[9] (in French), 'Account of the government of Prussia', 1776
As for the question of what acquisitions would suit this Prussian monarchy, the Saxon states would without doubt be the most appropriate: they would round it off and form a barrier for it by the mountains separating Saxony and Bohemia, which would have to be fortified. It is hard to predict how this acquisition could take place. The surest way would be to conquer Bohemia and Moravia, and exchange them for Saxony; or it could be done by other exchanges or with the Rhineland possessions, including Jülich or Berg; or by some other means. This acquisition is absolutely essential in order to give this State the solidity it lacks. For as soon as we are at war, the enemy can march straight on Berlin without meeting the least opposition in his path. I say nothing, however, of our rights of succession in Ansbach, Jülich and Berg, and Mecklenburg, because our claims there are well known, and we shall have to wait on events. As the State is not rich, we must above all avoid becoming involved in wars where there is nothing to gain; we exhaust ourselves to no purpose; and if a profitable occasion arose later, we would be unable to exploit it. All distant acquisitions are a burden upon the State. A village on the frontier is worth more than a principality sixty leagues away.

Source: Die Politischen Testamente Friedrichs des Grossen, edited by G.B. Voltz, Berlin, 1920, pp.241–2.

Document 13

Frederick II on eighteenth-century warfare

Letter from Frederick II to d'Alembert (in French), 18 October 1770
After all, standing armies do not depopulate the countryside or impair industry. In any country, there can only be a certain number of farmers in proportion to the amount of land available for cultivation, and a certain number of workers in proportion to the size of the market; the rest would become beggars or highwaymen. Moreover, these large armies cause money to circulate, and spread equally across the provinces the revenues that the people supply to the government. The costly upkeep of these armies shortens the length of the wars; instead of thirty years which they lasted over a century ago, rulers are obliged to end them far more quickly out of sheer insolvency. In our day, seven or eight annual campaigns at most exhaust the rulers' funds and make them amenable to peace negotiations.

It is also to be observed that these standing armies determine the conditions of war more definitely than was formerly the case. Today, at the first trumpet-blast, neither the farmer, the manufacturer, the lawyer, nor the scholar, are diverted from their work; they continue peacefully to pursue their normal occupations, leaving to the nation's defenders the task of avenging the nation. In former times, at the first alarm, troops were hastily levied, everyone became a soldier, the only thought was to repel the enemy; the fields lay fallow, the professions languished, and the soldiers, ill-paid, ill-kept, ill-disciplined, lived only by looting, and lived like bandits on the unhappy areas that were the scene of their depredations. All that has greatly changed; not that such disgraceful looting no longer exists in some armies; but the whole business of war bears no resemblance to the chaos that once prevailed.

Source: Oeuvres de Frédéric le Grand, volume XXIV, Berlin, 1848, pp.506–7.

---

[9]   This part of the memorandum was suppressed throughout the nineteenth century and published only in 1920.

Section 3 Frederick and society

Document 14

Frederick II on the nobility

Confidential memorandum intended for the use of his heir (in French), 'Political Testament', 1752
One object of the policy of the ruler of this State is to support its nobility; for whatever may befall, it may perhaps have a wealthier nobility, but never one more valiant or loyal. In order to guarantee them in their ownership of land, it is essential to prevent commoners from acquiring estates belonging to the nobility, and to per-suade commoners to invest their capital in trade; so that if some noble is obliged to sell his lands, the only purchasers are nobles. It is likewise essential to prevent the nobility from entering foreign service, in order to inspire them with *esprit de corps* and patriotism. This has been my constant endeavour, and throughout the first war[10] I took all possible steps to make the name of Prussians well known, to teach all the officers that, whatever province they might come from, they were all regarded as Prussians, and hence that all these provinces, though geographically separate, form a single unit. It is right that the nobility should choose to devote its services to its own country rather than to any other. For this reason, strict laws have been laid down against nobles who have gone to serve elsewhere without permission.

Source: Die Politischen Testamente Friedrichs des Grossen, edited by G.B. Volz, Berlin, 1920, pp.29–30.

Document 15

Frederick II on the officer class

Confidential memorandum intended for the use of his heir (in French), 'Account of the government of Prussia', 1776
If idle courtiers are preferred to military men, everyone will be seen to prefer idleness to the

soldier's laborious profession; and so, instead of our officers being noblemen, recourse will have to be had to commoners, which would be the first step towards military decadence and decline.[11]

Source:: Oeuvres de Frédéric le Grand, volume IX, Berlin, 1848, p.186.

Document 16

The Prussian officer class

Contemporary published account, c.1780
Another cause, which, in my opinion, greatly contributes to the excellence of the army, is the high birth of the officers. They are most of them of the first nobility of the country. They must all have been educated at the cadets' school[12] and have served as cadets. I have some very respect-able acquaintances among them. They are in every respect well-educated people, and upon the whole, very sensible men. The small pay of the subalterns obliges them to be economical, which is of great advantage to the service. They all have a martial appearance, and that alacrity in everything, which bespeaks men always ready to cut a knot with their own swords.

Source: J.C. Riesbeck, *Travels through Germany,* translated from French by Paul Henry Maty, volume III, London, 1787, p.22.

Document 17

Frederick II on the peasants

Published essay (in French), 'Essay on the forms of government and the duties of sovereigns', 1777
The monarch must frequently remind himself of the state of the poor: he should put himself in the place of a peasant or a manual worker and say to himself: 'If I had been born in the class of citizens whose hands constitute their capital, what would I wish the monarch to do?'

In most European states, there are prov-inces where the peasants are tied to the soil as

---

[10]   Frederick's first war over Silesia (1740–2), which sparked off the War of the Austrian Succession (1740–8)

[11]   Forced to grant temporary commissions to non-nobles by crippling casualties in the officer corps during the Seven Years' War, Frederick withdrew the commissions after the war. At the beginning of the nineteenth cen-tury, only 2 out of 422 staff-officers were not nobles.

[12]   The Noble Academy at Berlin. See Documents 43–4.

their masters' serfs. Of all conditions this is the most wretched and the most repugnant to humanity. Certainly, no man was born to be the slave of his fellow; we rightly detest such an abuse, and we imagine that all that would be required is the wish to abolish this barbarous custom. But this is not the case; serfdom is the result of ancient contracts made between land-owners and peasants. Agriculture is established on the basis of peasant services; if we sought to abolish in one blow this abominable mode of procedure, we would completely upset the agricultural system, and it would be necessary to indemnify the nobility for the loss of income which it would suffer.

Source: Oeuvres de Frédéric le Grand, volume IX, Berlin, 1848, pp.205–6.

Document 18

Frederick II on the peasants

Confidential memorandum intended for the use of his heir (in French), 'Political Testament', 1752
I have freed the peasants from some of the services which they performed in the past; instead of serving six days a week, as they used to, they have only three days of compulsory labour. This has stirred up the peasants of the nobility, who in many places have rebelled against their masters. The monarchy should hold a balance between peasant and noble, to prevent them from ruining each other. In Silesia, apart from Upper Silesia, the condition of the peasant is very good; in Upper Silesia he is a serf. Some day efforts will have to be made to emancipate him. I have set the example on my own estates[13] where I have started placing them on the same footing as those in Lower Silesia. However peasants should be prevented from buying lands belonging to nobles, and nobles from buying peasant land, because peasants cannot serve as officers in the army, and the nobles, by enclosing peasants holdings, would diminish the number of settlers and farmers.

Source: Die Politischen Testamente Friedrichs des Grossen, edited by G.B. Volz, Berlin 1920, pp.30–1.

Document 19

Peasant status in Prussia

Statute from Frederick's General Code, commissioned in 1780, published (in German), 1791
Whoever belongs to the peasant class cannot, without the permission of the State, follow a bourgeois profession or destine his children to this profession. Every peasant is obliged to cultivate his land, in accordance with the principles of rural economy, in such a way as to meet the needs of the community. The State can therefore compel him to do so, if necessary by force.

Source: Code général pour les états prussiens, volume II, Paris, 1794, pp.308–9.

Document 20

Frederick II on the abolition of serfdom in Pomerania

Cabinet order (in German), 23 May 1763
All forms of serfdom, whether in royal, noble or municipal villages, are henceforth absolutely and unequivocally abolished; and all who may seek to oppose this should be made to realize, if possible peacefully, but in the case of resistance, by force, that these settled ideas of His Majesty are directed to the needs of the whole province in its work.

Source: R. Stadelmann, Preussens Könige in ihrer Thätigkeit für die Landescultur, Part II, Friedrich der Grosse, Leipzig, 1882, p.340.

Document 21

Frederick II on population

Letter from Frederick II to Electress Maria Antonia of Saxony (in French), 9 April 1767
Your Royal Highness will perhaps be curious to know what we are doing here. Well, Madam, we are producing children; we are constantly giving birth and preparing for baptisms. This is very much the order of the day, for after that horrible massacre of the human race,[14] our most sacred duty is to make good the damage. If everyone

---

[13]   Crown lands comprised roughly one-quarter of Prussia's territory and yielded one-third of her revenue.

[14]   The Seven Years' War, in which Prussia lost roughly one-ninth of her population, including about one-fifth of the population of Pomerania, and one-quarter of that of the New Mark.

were of the same opinion, Europe would long remain peaceful.

Source: Oeuvres de Frédéric le Grand, volume XXIV, Berlin, 1854, p.133.

Document 22

Frederick II on agriculture

Letter from Frederick II to Voltaire (in French), 5 December 1775
There are no true riches except those which the earth produces. To improve your territory, to bring land under cultivation, to drain marshes, is to triumph over barbarism and to provide a livelihood for settlers of marriageable age, ready and willing to work at perpetuating the species and increasing the number of working citizens. Here we have imitated the agricultural methods of the English, which are very successful, and we have increased our cattle by a third. Their plough and seed-drill have not had the same success, the plough partly because our soil is too light, the seed-drill because it is too expensive for the common people and peasants. On the other hand, we have managed to grow rhubarb in our gardens. It retains all the qualities and is identical to the kind imported from the East. This year we have produced ten million pounds of silk and we have increased our beehives by one third.

Source: Voltaire's correspondence, edited by T. Besterman, volume XCII, Geneva, 1964, p.150.

Document 23

Frederick II on agriculture and industry

Letter from Frederick II to Voltaire (in French), 5 September 1777
I have returned from Silesia, and was very pleased with it. Agriculture there is making very marked progress; industry is prospering: we have exported five millions thalers' worth of linen, and one million two hundred thousands worth of cloth. A cobalt mine has been discovered in the mountains, which can supply the whole of Silesia.[15] We are producing a vitriol as good as

that made abroad. A most inventive man is developing an indigo identical to that of India; we can turn iron into steel in greater quantities and far more simply than by Réaumur's process. Since 1756 (when the war began) our population has increased by a hundred and eighty thousand. In short, it is as if all the scourges which ruined this poor province had never been; and I may tell you that I feel agreeably satisfied to see a province make such great progress.

Source: Voltaire's Correspondence, edited by Besterman, volume XCVII, Geneva, 1964, pp.73–4.

Section 4 Frederick, law and justice

Document 24

Frederick II on the rule of law

Confidential memorandum intended for the use of his heir (in French), 'Political Testament', 1768
It is not at all proper for the monarch to interfere in the process of the law; the laws alone should rule and the monarch's duty is confined to protecting them. Security of goods and property is the basis of society and all good government. This law holds good for the monarch as for the meanest of his subjects; he must see that it is observed, and punish with the utmost rigour any judges who may contravene it.

Source: Die Politischen Testamente Friedrichs des Grossen edited by G.B. Volz, Berlin, 1920, p.111.

Document 25

Frederick II on the administration of justice

Letter from Frederick II to Voltaire (in French), 13 August 1775
For myself, I confine myself in my own country to preventing the powerful from oppressing the poor, and to mitigating sentences which occasionally strike me as too severe.[16] This is one part of my work. When I tour the provinces, everyone comes to me; I investigate all complaints either personally or through others, and I make myself useful to persons of whose existence

---

[15] Cobalt was used as a pigment in the manufacture of ceramics.

[16] Sentences of death, hard labour or corporal punishment were referred to Frederick for personal review.

I was unaware before I received their petitions. This inspection makes the judges more attentive and prevents trials from being too harsh and rigorous.

Source: *Voltaire's correspondence*, edited by T. Besterman, volume XCI Geneva, 1964, pp.160–1.

Document 26

Frederick II on the administration of justice

Published essay (in French), 'Essay on the forms of government and the duties of sovereigns', 1777
The laws, if they are good, must be clearly expressed, so that they cannot be exploited by sharp practice, their spirit evaded and the fate of individuals decided arbitrarily and unsystematically. Procedure must be as short as possible, in order to prevent the ruin of the parties, who would otherwise spend in unnecessary costs what is due to them in justice and by good right. This branch of administration cannot be too closely supervised, so that every possible obstacle may be put in the way of the greed of judges and the boundless self-interest of lawyers. Everyone is to be kept to his duties by periodical visits to the provinces, where anyone who thinks himself wronged can venture to bring his complaints before the commission of enquiry; and those found guilty of sharp practice must be severely punished. It is perhaps superfluous to add that the punishment must never exceed the crime; that arbitrary force must never be applied in place of the law; and that it is better for a monarch to be too indulgent than too severe.

Source: *Oeuvres de Frédéric le Grand*, volume IX, Berlin, 1848, p.201.

Document 27

Prussian General Code

Frederick's General Code, commissioned in 1780, published (in German), 1791
The rights of man derive from his birth, his class and from actions or circumstances to which the laws have attributed a particular effect. The general rights of man are based on his natural liberty to pursue and to realize his own welfare without interfering with that of others. The particular rights and duties of members of the state derive from their individual relationships with each other and with the state. Whatever is not forbidden by natural laws or positive laws belongs in the category of things that are permitted.

The welfare of the State in general and its inhabitants in particular is the aim of civil society and the general object of the laws. The Head of State, whose duty is constantly to ensure the promotion of the public welfare, has the right to direct and determine the external actions of all the citizens in accordance with this aim. The laws and ordinances of the State can only restrict the freedom and rights of the citizens in so far as this is required by the object of society. Every member of the State is obliged to uphold the public welfare and security in accordance with his ability and his class. Individual rights and privileges of the members of the State must be subordinated to the rights and duties which tend to the increase of the public welfare, if there is a clear clash between them. For its part, the State is bound to indemnify anyone who is obliged to sacrifice his individual rights and privileges for the good of the State. Every inhabitant of the State has the right to demand its protection of his person and property.[17] On the other hand, no-one is authorized to take the law into his own hands. Disputes concerning rights, arising between the Head of State and his subjects, must be decided and resolved by the ordinary courts in accordance with the laws.

Source: *Code Général pour les états prussiens*, volume I, Paris, 1794, Introduction, pp.10–11.

Document 28

The rule of law in Prussia

Contemporary published account, c.1780
Far from endeavouring to undermine the rights of the nobility, the king takes all possible pains to maintain them in the full possession of them. He has assisted the Silesian nobility, who are the most powerful in his country, by lending them large sums of money, at one-and-a-half per cent.

---

[17]   The Code of Laws and General Code confirmed women's legal subjection to their husbands, who, however, were obliged to maintain them. Divorce was easier in Prussia than in Britain (see Document 38) and a divorced wife was entitled to a share of the matrimonial property.

The same thing has been done for the nobility of other provinces who have wanted his assistance. No community, city or religious order is in the least danger of having their privileges intruded upon, as long as they are not detrimental to the advantage of the whole. The rich monasteries in Silesia and the Western Prussia have not the least thing to apprehend. The Prussian government is generally considered in other countries as the most despotic that exists, though in fact nothing can be less so. The maxim which is the foundation of the British constitution: *Rex in regno suo superiores habet Deum et Legem [the king in his realm is under the authority of God and the law]*, is nowhere so well observed as it is here. People will not surely call a rigid observation of the laws which promote the good of the state – 'despotism'; and what instances are there of the king's ever having allowed himself anything that bespoke arbitrary sentiments? In no country are the rights of Reason, the rights of Nature, the customs and particular statutes which do not militate against the happiness of the whole, better observed and guarded than they are in the Prussian dominions. Nowhere does government direct all its steps so exactly according to the rules of right reason as it does here.

Source: J.C. Riesbeck, *Travels through Germany,* translated from French by Paul Henry Maty, volume II, London, 1787, pp.260–1.

Document 29

Frederick II on the case of the Miller Arnold[18]

Cabinet-order to all law courts (in German), 12 December 1779
This is an act of the most flagrant injustice, and directly contrary to the gracious will of his Majesty, who means to be a father to his country.

It is his Majesty's express will that throughout his dominions justice shall be impartially administered to every one of his subjects, whether they be noble or non-noble, whether they be rich or poor, without respect of persons. His Majesty is therefore determined severely to punish those judges who have decided in the case of the Miller Arnold, and to hold them out to all his courts as a dreadful instance of the consequence of neglected or perverted justice; and his Majesty would have them to know that the meanest peasant, nay even the beggar, is equally with his Majesty, entitled to the rights of humanity, and has an equal claim upon strict and impartial justice.

Source: Characteristic anecdotes and miscellaneous authentic papers of Frederick II, edited by B.H. Latrobe, London, 1788, p.285.

Document 30

Frederick II on the abolition of torture

Speech to the Academy of Sciences (in French), 'Dissertation on the reasons for laying down or repealing laws', 22 January 1750
Nothing is crueller than torture. The Romans tortured their slaves, whom they regarded as a kind of domestic chattel; but no citizen was ever put to the torture. In Germany,[19] criminals are tortured after conviction in order to make them confess their crimes with their own lips; in France, torture is used to discover evidence or to reveal accomplices. The English once had the ordeal by fire and water. Pardon me, I must protest against torture; I make so bold as to take humanity's side against a practice shameful to Christians and civilized peoples, and, I would add, as cruel as it is useless.

Quintilian,[20] wisest and most eloquent of orators, says in his discussion of torture, that it is

---

[18]   Christian Arnold, a miller from the New Mark, claimed that he had been wrongfully dispossessed of his mill through inability to pay the rent as a result of the unlawful diversion of water from the mill by a local official to feed his carp pond. When his appeal from the local manorial court was dismissed by the district court at Küstrin, Arnold petitioned Frederick, who investigated the facts and found in his favour. Frederick remitted the case, first to Küstrin, where the previous decision was confirmed, and then to the Supreme Court at Berlin, which upheld the judgement at Küstrin. Frederick on his own authority dismissed seven judges, gaoled them for nine months and ordered them to pay damages to Arnold. This judgement was reversed after Frederick's death.

[19]   i.e. outside Prussia.

[20]   Marcus Quintilianus (*c.*AD 35–*c.*100), Roman writer on rhetoric.

a question of temperament. A robust villain will deny his guilt; an innocent weakling will confess himself guilty. A man is accused; evidence exists, the judge is uncertain; he wishes to clarify himself, the poor wretch is put to the torture. If he is innocent, how barbarous to make him suffer martyrdom! If, overwhelmed by pain, he is forced to give evidence against himself, what dreadful inhumanity to put to agonizing pain and to condemn to death a virtuous citizen against whom there are nothing but suspicions! It would be better to pardon twenty guilty men than to sacrifice one innocent one. If laws are to be laid down for the good of the people, should we tolerate such laws, which authorize judges to commit these outrages and which revolt humanity? In Prussia torture was abolished eight years ago; we are sure of never confusing innocent and guilty, and justice is done no less than before.

Source: Oeuvres de Frédéric le Grand, volume IX, Berlin, 1848, pp.28–9.

Document 31

Frederick II on capital punishment

Letter from Frederick II to Condorcet[21] (in French), 24 October 1785
I turn to the subject of the laws, which Monsieur de Beccaria has so well explained[22] and on which you have written equally well. I am entirely of your opinion that the judges must not be in a hurry to pass sentence and that it is better to save a guilty man than to destroy an innocent one. However, I think experience has taught me

that one must not overlook any of the reins with which we lead men, namely, rewards and punishments; and that there are cases where the atrocity of the crime must be punished with rigour. Murderers and arsonists, for example, deserve the death penalty, because they have assumed a tyrannical power over men's lives and possessions. I agree that a life sentence is indeed a crueller punishment than death; but is it not as striking as the punishment which takes place before the eyes of the crowd, because such spectacles make more impression than occasional talk about the pains suffered by those who languish in gaol.

Source: Oeuvres de Frédéric le Grand, volume XXV, Berlin, 1854, pp.379–80.

Document 32

Frederick II commutes a death-sentence[23]

Cabinet-order from Frederick II to Baron von Zedlitz[24] (in French), 23 April 1776
I have great objections in my own mind to signing the sentence of death pronounced by the court against the incendiary Döpel. Both he and his accomplice Weiss are said to be still very young; and on that account it is my pleasure that neither of them be executed, but that they be confined in the house of correction, and care be taken that during their confinement they be better instructed in their duty to society, and made sensible of the dreadful nature of their crime. You are therefore directed to have the warrant altered accordingly.

Source: Characteristic anecdotes and miscellaneous authentic papers of Frederick II, edited by B.H. Latrobe, London, 1788, p.40.

---

[21]   Antoine Caritat de Condorcet (1743–94), *philosophe*, believed in inevitability of historical progress, adviser to the Prussian Academy of Sciences.

[22]   In *On Crimes and Punishments* (1764). See *Texts* I, pp.93.

[23]   Between 1775 and 1778 Frederick signed 46 death-warrants, an average of a dozen per year. Out of the 46 only two were for offences against property. The rest were for murder (mainly infanticide). Contrast the position in England (Study 3), and the absence of any right of automatic appeal there against sentence or conviction until 1907 *(sic)*.

[24]   Minister of Justice.

Document 33

Frederick II on unmarried mothers and infanticide

Letter from Frederick II to Voltaire (in French),
11 October 1777
No one can be arrested without my signature, or punished unless I have ratified the sentence. Most of these delinquents are girls who have killed their children;[25] there are few murders, and still fewer highway robberies. But as for those creatures who treat their offspring so cruelly, only those are executed whose act of murder we have been able to prove. I have done what I can to prevent these unfortunate women from doing away with their offspring. Masters are obliged to report their maidservants if they become pregnant; formerly these poor girls used to be forced to do public penance, in church; I relieved them of this. In every province there are homes in which they can have their confinement and have their children brought up. Notwithstanding all these facilities, I have still not succeeded in ridding their minds of the unnatural prejudice that makes them do away with their children. At this very moment I am contemplating the abolition of the stigma formerly attached to those who married unmarried mothers; I do not know whether I shall succeed. Perhaps I shall.

Source: Voltaire's correspondence, edited by T. Besterman, volume XCVII, Geneva, 1964, pp.122–3.

Document 34

Unmarried mothers in Prussia

Contemporary published account, 1773
The measures taken by his Prussian Majesty to promote the propagation of the species in his territories are not a little extraordinary. Pregnancy is rendered respectable, however it has been acquired: a big belly secures, by law, the licentious daughter from the reproaches of her parents, and a maidservant from the censures of her master and mistress, who are not suffered to turn her away or to ill-treat her or even to reprove her for what she has done. When a girl

is with child, she applies to a magistrate, who fixes the place where she is to lie in, and the inhabitants of the town or village pay the expenses of her delivery, if she or her family are not in circumstances to do it. The moment the child is born, it is put out to nurse at the expense of its parents, if they are capable of maintaining it; if they are not, the parish advances the money, and is reimbursed by the king.

Source: J.A.H. de Guibert, Observations on the military establishment and discipline of his Majesty the king of Prussia, translated from the French by J. Johnson, London, 1780, p.47.

Document 35

Military discipline in Prussia

Contemporary published account, 1779
The Prussian discipline on a general view is beautiful; in detail it is shocking. When the young rustic is brought to the regiment, he is at first treated with a degree of gentleness; he is instructed by words only how to walk, and to hold up his head, and to carry his firelock, and he is not punished, though he should not succeed in his earliest attempts: they allow his natural awkwardness and timidity to wear off by degrees. They seem cautious of confounding him at the beginning, or driving him to despair, and take care not to pour all the terrors of their discipline upon his astonished senses all at once. When he has been a little familiarized to his new state, he is taught the exercise of the firelock, first alone, and afterwards with two or three of his companions. This is not entrusted to a corporal or sergeant; it is the duty of a subaltern officer. In the park at Berlin, every morning, may be seen the lieutenants of the different regiments exercising with the greatest assiduity, sometimes a single man, at other times three or four together; and now, if the young recruit show neglect or remissness, his attention is roused by the officer's cane, which is applied with augmenting energy, till he has acquired the full command of his firelock. He is taught steadiness under arms, and the immobility of a statue; he is informed that all his members are to move

---

[25]   100 articles of Frederick's *General Code* (1791) were devoted to reforming the law on infanticide. The traditional penalty for infanticide, based on Roman law and revived by Frederick-William I, was for the guilty mother to be sewn in a sack and drowned. Frederick abolished this.

only at the word of command, and not at his own pleasure; that speaking, coughing, sneezing, are all unpardonable crimes; and when the poor lad is accomplished to their mind, they give him to understand that now it is perfectly known what he can do, and therefore the smallest deficiency will be punished with rigour. And although he should destine every moment of his time and all his attention to cleaning his arms, taking care of his clothes and practising the manual exercises, it is but barely possible for him to escape punishment. It is dreaded, that if they were occasionally moved from one garrison to another, the foreigners in the service, who are exceedingly prone to desertion, might then find opportunities which according to the present plan they cannot: for however desirous a Prussian soldier may be to desert, the thing is almost impossible. The moment a man is missing, a certain number of cannons are fired, which announce the desertion to the whole country. The peasants have a considerable reward for seizing a deserter, and are liable to severe penalties if they harbour or aid him in making his escape, and parties from the garrisons are sent after him in every direction.[26]

As to the common men, the leading idea of the Prussian discipline is to reduce them, in many respects, to the nature of machines; that they may have no volition of their own, but be solely actuated by that of their officers; that they may have such a superlative dread of those officers as annihilates all fear of the enemy; and that they may move forwards when ordered, without deeper reasoning or more concern than the flintlocks they carry along with them. The King imagines that discipline is the soul of an army; that men in the different nations of Europe are, in those qualities which are thought necessary for a soldier, nearly on a par; that in two armies of equal numbers, the degree of discipline will determine how far one is superior to the other. The great object therefore is to keep his own army at the highest possible degree of perfection

in this essential point. If that could be done by gentle means, undoubtedly he would prefer it. He is not naturally of a cruel disposition.

Source: J. Moore, *A view of society and manners in France, Switzerland and Germany,* volume II, Dublin, 1789, pp.101–13.

Section 5 Frederick and religion

Document 36

Frederick II on religion

Letter from Frederick II to Voltaire (in French), c.15 December 1766

You suppose that I think that the people needs the curb of religion in order to be controlled; I assure you these are not my sentiments. On the contrary, my experience places me entirely on the side of Bayle:[27] a society could not exist without laws, but it could certainly exist without religion, provided that there is a power, which, by punitive sanctions, can compel the masses to obey these laws. This is confirmed by the experiences of the savages discovered on the Marianne Islands,[28] who had not a metaphysical idea in their heads. It is proved still more by the government of China, where theism is the religion of all leading men in the state. However, as you see that in that vast kingdom the common people have abandoned themselves to the Buddhist superstition, I maintain that the same thing would happen elsewhere, and that a state purged of all superstition would not remain long in its purity but that new absurdities would take the place of the old ones, and within a short time, at that. The little dose of good sense spread across the surface of the globe is, I think, sufficient to found a world-wide society, rather like that of the Jesuits, but not a state. I see the present work of the *philosophes* as very useful, because men ought to be made to feel ashamed of fanaticism and intolerance, and because it is a service to humanity to fight these cruel and atrocious follies which turned our ancestors into ravening

---

[26]   In the Austro-Prussian war of the Bavarian Succession (1778–9) Frederick lost 3,500 men in battle and 16,000 by desertion.

[27]   On Bayle, see article 'Pyrrhonian Philosophy' in *Texts* I, pp.28–32.

[28]   The Maldive Islands.

beasts. To destroy fanaticism is to dry up the most deadly source of division and hatred in European memory, the bloody traces of which are found among all its peoples.

Source: *Voltaire's correspondence*, edited by T. Besterman, volume LXIII, Geneva, 1961, p 188.

Document 37

Frederick II on freedom of religion

Published essay (in French), 'Essay on the forms of government and the duties of sovereigns', 1777
There are few countries where the citizens share the same views on religion; often they differ completely, and some of them form different sects. The question therefore arises: must all citizens think alike, or can everyone be allowed to think as he wishes? Firstly, there are gloomy political thinkers who will tell you: 'Everyone must be of the same opinion, so that nothing may divide the citizens.' The theologian adds: 'Whoever does not share my beliefs is damned; so we must burn them in this world so that they may be better off in the next.' Our answer to that is that no society will ever share the same beliefs; that most Christian nations are anthropomorphite and that most Catholics are idolatrous; for I shall never be persuaded that a peasant can distinguish between *latria* and *hyperdulia*.[29] He genuinely worships the image that he invokes. So there are a variety of heretics in all the Christian sects. Moreover, each believes whatever seems plausible to it. One can force some poor wretch to pronounce a certain formula, from which he witholds his inner consent; so that the persecutor has gained nothing. But if we go back to the origin of society, it is perfectly clear that the monarch has no right to dictate the citizens' beliefs.

One would surely have to be mad to imagine that some men said to one of their fellows: 'We raise you above us, because we wish to be slaves, and we give you authority to dictate our thoughts as you wish.' On the contrary, they said: 'We need you to maintain the laws that we wish to obey, to rule us wisely and to protect us; for the rest, we ask you to respect our liberty.' Such is the sentence that has been pronounced, and there is no appeal against it. Moreover, this very tolerance is so beneficial to the societies where it is established, that it constitutes the happiness of the State. Whenever there is freedom of religion, everyone lives peacefully; while persecution has given rise to the bloodiest, longest and most destructive civil wars. The least of the evils brought by persecution is that it compels its victims to emigrate: France has had whole provinces where the population has declined and which still feel the effects of the revocation of the Edict of Nantes.[30]

Source: *Oeuvres de Frédéric le Grand*, volume IX, Berlin, 1848, pp.207–8.

Document 38

Frederick II on church and state

Confidential memorandum intended for the use of his heir (in French), 'Political Testament', 1752
Catholics, Lutherans, Protestants, Jews and numerous other Christian [*sic*] sects live peacefully in this State: if the monarch, inspired by misplaced zeal, thought fit to declare himself for one of these religions, we would immediately see factions form, disputes develop, persecutions gradually begin and finally the persecuted religion leave its own country and thousands of subjects enrich our neighbours by their numbers and industry.

It is politically quite immaterial whether a monarch has a religion or has no religion. All religions, when one examines them, are founded on a system of more or less absurd myths. It is impossible for a man of good sense who examines these matters not to see error; but these prejudices, these errors, this element of the miraculous, is made for man, and one must show the people enough respect not to scandalize it in its religious beliefs, whatever they may be.

I am in a certain sense the 'pope' of the Lutherans and head of the Protestant church.

---

[29]   The distinct categories of worship to, respectively, God and the Virgin Mary.

[30]   Louis XIV's revocation of the Edict of Nantes in 1685 ended the toleration extended to the Huguenots (Protestants) in France since 1598. Many Huguenot refugees settled in Prussia.

I appoint the clergy, and require of them only morality and mildness. I decide marriage-suits and am very indulgent in this respect, because basically marriage is only a civil contract which can be dissolved whenever both parties consent. Apart from brother and sister, mother and son, and father and daughter, I readily allow people to marry whom they please; for there is no harm in this sort of marriage.

The other Christian sects are all tolerated here; we silence the first man who seeks to ignite civil unrest and we treat the opinions of innovators with the ridicule they deserve. I am neutral between Rome and Geneva.[31] I try to maintain friendly relations with the Pope, in order to win over the Catholics and make them understand that the policy of rulers is the same, even though their nominal religion is different. However, I advise my successors not to trust the Catholic clergy without solid proofs of its loyalty.

Most of the Catholics are in Silesia. We allow them the free exercise of their religion; but to prevent the monasteries from stifling in celibacy the hopes of their families, it is forbidden to become a monk or nun before the age of majority. In other respects, I allow the clergy every liberty and the rights proper to them. The parish priests are quite reliable people; the monks are more inclined to support the House of Austria. For this reason, I make them pay thirty per cent of their revenues to the State, so that they may be of some use.[32] The Jesuits of Silesia, the most dangerous of all the monks of that communion, are extremely fanatical for the House of Austria. To set one group off against another, I have invited educated French Jesuits to come to raise educational standards among the Silesian nobility,[33] and thanks to the animosity which prevails between these French and German monks, I prevent them from conspiring together in favour of the house of Austria, which they might otherwise do.

Source: Die Politischen Testamente Friedrichs des Grossen edited by G.B. Volz, Berlin, 1920, pp.31–2.

Document 39

Frederick II on the case of de la Barre[34]

Letter from Frederick II to Voltaire (in French),
13 August 1766

I cannot find the execution at Abbeville as terrible as the unjust execution of Calas. Calas was innocent; he was the victim of fanaticism, and nothing in that terrible deed can excuse the judges. Far from it, they ignored the formal procedures and sentenced him to death without evidence, exhibits or witnesses.

The recent event at Abbeville is of a quite different nature. You will not dispute that every citizen must obey the laws of his country. Well, there are penalties laid down by the legislators for those who disturb the religion adopted by the nation. Discretion, decency, above all the respect that every citizen owes to the laws, oblige him not to insult the accepted religion and to avoid scandal and insolence. These are indeed bloody laws, which ought to be reformed by making the punishment proportionate to the crime; but as long as these rigorous laws remain the law of the land, the judges are bound to follow them.

I offer refuge to the *philosophes*, provided that they behave themselves, and that they are as peaceful as the fine title that they possess implies; for all the truths that they proclaim are not worth peace of mind, the only benefit that men can enjoy on this 'atom' that they inhabit. As for myself, being in favour of reason without enthusiasm, I should like men to be reasonable and, above all, peaceful. We know the crimes inspired by religious fanaticism. Let us beware of introducing such fanaticism into philosophy, whose character should be mildness and moderation. Philosophy should pity the tragic end of a young man who committed an act of folly; it should point out the excessive harshness of a law made in crude and ignorant times; but it should not encourage similar acts, or criticize judges who had no alternative than to decide as they did.

---

[31]   i.e. between Catholics and Protestants (particularly Calvinists).

[32]   The monasteries in Austria were exempt from taxation.

[33]   The Jesuits were renowned for their teaching skills (Voltaire was among their pupils).

[34]   See *Studies*, I, pp.33, 72, 109–110. De la Barre was executed at Abbeville.

Socrates did not worship the *deos majorum et minorum gentium*,[35] but he still attended public sacrifices. Gassendi[36] went to mass, and Newton attended sermons. Toleration in society should guarantee everyone the freedom to believe what he wishes; but this tolerance should not extend to condoning the effrontery and licence of young hooligans, who wantonly insult what the people revere. These are my sentiments, which accord with the guarantee of public freedom and security, the first object of any legislation.

Source: Voltaire's Correspondence, edited by T. Besterman, volume LXII 1961, Geneva, pp.113–15.

Document 40

Frederick II on freedom of religion

Cabinet-order (in German), 18 January 1781
His Majesty, from a thorough conviction that he thereby fulfils the duty of a good sovereign and father of his people, has laid down as an unalterable principle of his government, that every subject shall have liberty to believe whatever he can or will, and to serve God in whatever manner he likes, provided his principles of worship are not injurious to the peace of the state or subversive of morality. It is therefore his Majesty's will and pleasure that no constraint whatever in regard to the use or disuse of the new catechism and hymn-book, shall be laid upon any of the churches, but everyone is in this respect at liberty to think and to act as he pleases. As to the hymn-book, everyone is at liberty to sing: *Nun ruhen alle Wälder*,[37] or any other foolish, stupid nonsense he chooses. But the clergy must never forget toleration, as I shall never suffer them to persecute anyone.

Source: Characteristic anecdotes and miscellaneous authentic papers of Frederick II, edited by B.H. Latrobe, London, 1788, pp.49–51

Document 41

Frederick II on the Jesuits

Letter from Frederick II to Electress Maria Antonia of Saxony (in French), 1 February 1768
The Great Powers, to relieve their boredom, are making war on the poor Jesuits, who will soon be banished from half of Europe. What astonishes me in the conduct of these kings is that they follow the example of the Holy Office[38] and sequester the spoils of the outlawed party, doubtless to console themselves for losing the latter. For all that I am a heretic, I take great care not to follow their example, and I shall leave the Order in peace, as long as they do not seek to interfere in secular matters or to assassinate me or my relatives. Circuses keep lions and tigers for animal fights; why should Jesuits not be tolerated likewise? The most sociable of animals ought to have dealings with all other animals; and it is possible to live with Jesuits, Buddhist priests, Imams, and Rabbis, without biting them or being bitten by them. The greatest folly of our species is that we make use of demons in order to persecute one another and make life bitter for each other.

Source: Oeuvres de Frédéric le Grand, volume XXIV, Berlin, 1854, p.149.

Section 6 Frederick, education and enlightenment

Document 42

Frederick II on enlightenment and the masses

Letter from Frederick II to d'Alembert (in French), 8 January 1770
Take any monarchy: let us suppose that it has a population of ten million; of these ten million, let us first discount the farm-labourers, factory-

---

[35] The major and minor gods in the hierarchy of classical deities.

[36] Pierre Gassendi (1592–1655), French mathematician, philosopher and free-thinker.

[37] 'Now all the woodlands rest', a traditional Lutheran hymn, well known in its English version 'The duteous day now closeth'.

[38] The Inquisition.

workers, craftsmen and soldiers; that leaves about fifty thousand men and women; from these let us discount twenty-five thousand of the female sex. The rest will consist of the nobility and the upper middle class; of these, let us consider how many ignoramuses there will be, how many idiots, how many imbeciles and loose-livers; and the result of these calculations will be that, in a so-called civilized nation with a population of ten million, you will hardly find a thousand literate people, and even among these, what a difference in talents! Then suppose it were possible that these thousand philosophers all shared the same outlook, and were all equally free from prejudice, what effect would their teaching have on the people? If eight-tenths of the nation, busy gaining a livelihood, do not read at all, if another tenth is too frivolous, debauched or stupid to apply itself, the upshot is that the little good sense of which our species is capable can only reside in a tiny minority of the nation, beyond the reach of the remainder, and that consequently superstitious beliefs will always prevail among the majority. Imperfection, moral as well as physical, is the characteristic of the world we live in. It is a waste of energy to try and enlighten it, and sometimes the task is dangerous for those who undertake it. One should content oneself with being wise oneself, if one can be, and abandon the masses to error, while discouraging them from crimes which disturb the social order.

Source: *Oeuvres de Frédéric le Grand*, volume XXIV, Berlin, 1854, pp.471–2.

Document 43

Frederick II on the Noble Academy at Berlin

Published memorandum (in French), 'Instruction for the management of the Noble Academy at Berlin', 1765
The intention of the King and the purpose of this institution is to educate young gentlemen with a view to qualifying them, according to their vocation, for war or administration. The masters should therefore strive not merely to fill their minds with useful information but, more particularly, to make them intellectually capable of tackling any subject, and above all to cultivate their reason and form their judgement. They must consequently accustom their pupils to form clear and precise ideas and not to be satisfied with vague and confused ideas.

It is forbidden, on pain of imprisonment, for the masters to beat their pupils, who are persons of quality and should be inspired with nobility of soul; they should be punished in ways that arouse ambition, not that humiliate them.

Source: *Oeuvres de Frédéric le Grand*, volume IX, Berlin 1848, pp.77–83.

Document 44

The Noble Academy at Berlin

Contemporary published account, 1773
The Military Academy is agreeably situated on the banks of the Spree, opposite to the royal palace. In this school, which is under the wisest and best regulations, fifteen young gentlemen, selected from the corps of noble cadets, are maintained and educated at the king's expense. Their dress, which is a plain uniform, consists of a blue coat and breeches, with white buttons. To every three students an old, sensible and experienced officer is appointed as governor, to be constantly near his pupils and preside over their education. The three pupils sleep together in the same chamber, and have a lacquey in the livery of the house, for their attendant. The manner in which these young gentlemen are educated is admirably calculated to render them useful members of society and to inspire them with notions suited to their birth; for they are usually of the best families. They are instructed in all the living languages and in the different sciences, by excellent masters or professors, who are generally members of the Academy of Sciences. Each student has a monthly allowance of nine crowns for pocket money. Their governors are to take care that this money is not expended improperly. In winter they go in a body twice a week to the French comedy; in fine weather they make excursions to the country; one or two of their governors are always of these parties. These gentlemen likewise take it in turn to attend the students to the riding-house and in their other exercises.

Source: J.A.H. de Guibert, *Observations on the military establishment and discipline of his Majesty the King of Prussia*, translated from the French by J. Johnson, London, 1780, pp.43–4.

Document 45

Lessing[39] on freedom of expression at Berlin[40]

Letter from Lessing to Berlin publisher, Nicolai (in German), Hamburg, 25 August, 1769

Do not talk to me of your freedom of thought and expression at Berlin. It boils down to nothing more than freedom to peddle as many silly attacks as you like on religion. An honest man should be ashamed to make use of such freedom. Just let someone at Berlin try to write on other topics as freely as Sonnenfels[41] has at Vienna; let him try to tell the truth to the noble rabble at court as Sonnenfels has done; let him stand up at Berlin for the rights of the subject or against exploitation and despotism, as they do in France and Denmark, and you will soon find out which is the most slavish country in Europe to this day.

Source: E. Consentius, 'Friedrich der Grosse und die Zeitungs-Zensur', *Preussische Jahrbücher*, volume 115, Berlin, 1904, p.240.

Document 46

Freedom of expression at Berlin

Contemporary published account, 1779

Nothing surprised me more, when I first came to Berlin, than the freedom with which many people speak of the measures of government and the conduct of the King. I have heard political topics and others which I should have thought still more ticklish, discussed here with as little ceremony as at a London coffee-house. The same freedom appears in the booksellers' shops, where literary productions of all kinds are sold openly. The pamphlet lately published on the division of Poland, wherein the King is very roughly treated, is to be had without difficulty, as well as performances, which attack some of the most conspicuous characters with all the bitterness of satire. A

government, supported by an army of 180,000 men, may safely disregard the criticisms of a few speculative politicians, and the pen of the satirist.

Source: J. Moore, *A view of society and manners in France, Switzerland and Germany*, volume II, Dublin, 1789, p.130.

Document 47

Frederick II on German literature

Letter from Frederick II to Voltaire (in French), 24 July 1775

The Germans are aspiring to enjoy in their turn the benefits of the fine arts. They strive to equal Athens, Rome, Florence and Paris. For all my love of my native land, I cannot say that they have so far succeeded. They lack two things: language and taste. The language is too wordy; good society speaks French; and a few pedantic schoolmasters and professors cannot give German the politeness and easy turns-of-phrase that it can only acquire in high society. In addition, there is the variety of idioms; each province has its own, and so far no rules of preference have been laid down. As for taste, the Germans are particularly lacking in that. They have still not been able to imitate the authors of the age of Augustus; they produce a vicious mixture of Roman taste with English, French and Teutonic. They still lack that fine discernment which seizes on beauty where it finds it and can distinguish the mediocre from the perfect, the noble from the sublime, and can apply each of them in the right places. As long as there are plenty of 'r's' in their poetic vocabulary, they consider their verses harmonious; while as a rule they are only a meaningless jumble of puffed up verbiage. As far as history is concerned, they will not omit the slightest detail, however insignificant.

Their best works are on Public [International] Law. As for philosophy, since the genius of Leibniz and the great monad of Wolff,[42]

---

[39] Gotthold Ephraim Lessing (1729–81), playwright, author of *Nathan der Weise* ('Nathan the Wise'). Frederick attempted through his envoy at Hamburg to suppress the performance of Lessing's *Minna von Barnhelm* in 1767.

[40] On his accession, Frederick proclaimed freedom of the press; but he reimposed censorship a few months later at the start of the first Silesian War, laying down strict penalties for criticism of political conditions or army life.

[41] Joseph von Sonnenfels (1733–1817), Austrian exponent of Enlightenment.

[42] Johann Christian von Wolf (or Wolff) (1676–1754), popularizer of the philosophy of Leibniz, in which the basic element of being was called the 'monad'. Expelled from Prussia by Frederick-William I on suspicion of impiety, he was recalled by Frederick in 1740.

nobody tackles it any more. They imagine they are successful in drama, but so far nothing perfect has appeared.

Source: Voltaire's correspondence edited by T. Besterman, volume XCI Geneva, 1964, p.121

Document 48

Frederick II on German literature

Letter from Frederick II to Voltaire (in French), 8 September 1775
Taste will only spread in Germany after careful study of the classic writers, Greek as well as Roman and French. Two or three men of genius will improve the language and make it less barbarous, and will naturalize the foreign masterpieces in Germany. As for me, whose career is approaching its end, I shall not live to see those happy times. I would like to have contributed to their birth; but what could I do, a being preoccupied for two thirds of his career by continual wars, obliged to repair the evils caused by them, and born with talents too slight for such great tasks? Philosophy comes to us from Epicurus;[43] Gassendi, Newton and Locke[44] improved it; I do myself the honour of being their disciple, but no more.

Source: Voltaire's correspondence edited by T. Besterman, volume XCII, Geneva, 1964, pp.14–15.

Document 49

Winckelmann[45] on the Prussian Academy[46]

Letter from Winckelmann to his friend Stosch (in German), Rome, 17 December 1763
I thank you with all my heart for the kindly prospect you hold out for me in Berlin. I think, however, it will still be better for me to think of

Dresden. What a poor figure I should cut in Berlin, where no scholar can make a name for himself, especially by comparison with d'Alembert, whom the King has just invited there, and with other Frenchmen, who predominate in the Academy itself, and set the tone. My plan and a copy of the work on Italy will not suffice to prove to that great man that one of his born subjects has, as I hope, produced something worthwhile. Perhaps my *History of Art* could prove it, if it were not written in German.

Source: J.J. Winckelmann, *Briefe,* edited by H. Diepolder and W. Rehm, volume 2, Berlin, 1954, p.363.

Document 50

Music at Berlin

Contemporary published account, 1772
Upon the whole, my expectations from Berlin were not quite answered, as I did not find that the style of composition or manner of execution to which his Prussian Majesty has attached himself, fulfilled my ideas of perfection – I speak according to my own feelings; however it would be a presumption in me to oppose my single judgement to that of so enlightened a prince, if, luckily, mine were not the opinion of the greatest part of Europe. For, should it be allowed that his Prussian Majesty has fixed upon the Augustan age of music, it does not appear that he has placed his favour upon the best composers of that age. Vinci, Pergolesi, Handel and many others, who flourished in the best times of Graun[47] and Quantz,[48] I think superior to them in taste and genius. Of his Majesty's two favourites, the one is languid, and the other frequently common and insipid – and yet their names are religion at Berlin. Though a universal toleration prevails here as to different sects of Christians, yet in music, whoever dares to profess any other

---

[43]   See 'Epicurus as an Enlightenment hero' (*Studies*, I).

[44]   John Locke (1632–1704), English philosopher.

[45]   Johann Joachim Winckelmann (1717–68), writer on neo-classical aesthetics (see *Studies*, I).

[46]   See footnote 53

[47]   Karl Heinrich Graun (1701–59), German composer.

[48]   Johann Joachim Quantz (1697–1773), German flautist and composer, taught Frederick the flute.

tenets than those of Graun and Quantz, is sure to be persecuted.[49]

Source: C. Burney,[50] 'The present state of music in Germany' in P. Scholes *(ed.), Dr Burney's Musical Tours in Europe*, volume II, Oxford, 1959, p.207.

Document 51

Frederick II on inoculation

Letter from Frederick II to Electress Maria Antonia of Saxony[51] *(in French), 26 July 1763*

I learn with pleasure, Madam, that your family has been successfully inoculated against small-pox, and I offer you my sincere congratulations. The Paris *Parlement* has just pronounced judgement against this practice, so hard it is to destroy old, ignorant prejudices, and so much time is needed before men will do anything rational! However, the Duke of Orleans has had his children successfully inoculated; of a million people who have been inoculated at Berlin, no one has died; and after so many examples, it really is time to renounce such absurd rulings, which reflect so badly on the judges.

Source: Oeuvres de Frédéric le Grand, volume XXIV, Berlin, 1854, pp.41–2.

Document 52

Frederick II on Rousseau

Letter from Frederick II to George Keith, Earl Marischal (in French), 1 September 1762

Your letter, my dear Keith, about Rousseau of Geneva,[52] gave me great pleasure. I see that we think alike: we must assist that poor, wretched fellow, whose only sin is in holding odd opinions, which he thinks valid. I shall have a hundred crowns sent to you; please arrange to give him as many as his needs require. I think if one gives him things, he will accept them more readily than money. If we were not at war, if we were not ruined, I would have a hermitage with a garden built for him, where he could live as he believes our ancestors lived. I confess that my ideas are as far from his as the finite is from the infinite; he will never persuade me to browse on the grass and walk on all fours. It is true that all that asiatic luxury, that refined style of good living, voluptuousness and softness, is not essential for our preservation, and that we could live with more simplicity and frugality than we do. But why renounce the pleasures of life when we can enjoy them? The true philosophy, it seems to me, is that which contents itself with condemning the abuse, without forbidding the use; we should learn to do without everything, while renouncing nothing.

I must say that many of the modern philosophers displease me by the paradoxes they advance. They wish to proclaim new truths, and they come out with errors which are an insult to common sense. I stick to Locke, to my friend Lucretius, to my good old Emperor Marcus Aurelius; those men have told us all we can know, (apart from Epicurus' physics) and all that can make us moderate, virtuous and wise. After that, it is absurd to tell us that we are all equal, and that consequently we must live like savages, without laws, society or civilization, that the fine arts have harmed morals, and other similarly untenable paradoxes.

Source: Oeuvres de Frédéric le Grand, volume XX, Berlin, 1852, pp.288–90.

---

[49]   Frederick disliked the music of J.S. Bach (despite the latter's *Musical offering* to him). He employed C.P.E. Bach to accompany his performances on the flute.

[50]   Charles Burney (1726–1814), English musicologist.

[51]   Frederick persuaded the Electress to introduce inoculation in Saxony.

[52]   Persecuted by church and state in France, Rousseau was also spurned by the *philosophes* for his *Discourse on the Arts and Sciences, Discourse on Inequality* and *Social Contract*. In 1762, on the appearance of *Emile*, his controversial novel on education, a warrant was issued for his arrest. Rousseau fled to Geneva, but fell foul of the Swiss authorities. Frederick, while sharing the *philosophes'* antipathy to his ideas (cf. document 53), granted him asylum at Motiers, near Neuchâtel, a Prussian enclave in Switzerland, where he spent eighteen months (1762–3) under the protection of the Governor, George Keith, Earl Marischal of Scotland, a former Jacobite in Prussian service.

Document 53

Frederick II on the arts and the sciences

Published Speech to the Academy of Sciences[53] *(in French), 'Discourse on the usefulness of the arts and sciences in a state', 27 January 1772*

Some unenlightened or hypocritical persons have ventured to profess their hostility to the arts and sciences.[54] If they have been allowed to slander that which does most honour to humanity, we must be all the more entitled to defend it, for that is the duty of all who love society and who are grateful for what they owe to literature. Unfortunately, paradox often makes a greater impression on the public than truth; it is then that we must disabuse the public and refute the authors of such nonsense, not with insults but with sound reason. I am ashamed to state in this Academy that people have had the effrontery to ask whether the sciences are useful or harmful to society, a subject on which no one should entertain the slightest doubt. If we have any superiority over animals, it is certainly not in our bodily faculties, but in the greater understanding which nature has given us; and what distinguishes one man from another is genius and learning. Where lies the infinite difference between a civilized people and barbarians if not in the fact that the former are enlightened, while the others vegetate in brutish ignorance?

The nations which have enjoyed this superiority have been grateful to those who brought them this advantage. Hence the reputation justly enjoyed by those great thinkers of the world, those sages, who through their learned works, have enlightened their compatriots and their age.

Man in himself is little enough; he is born with faculties more or less ripe for development. But they require cultivation; his knowledge must increase if his ideas are to broaden; his memory must be filled if it is to supply the imagination with material on which to work, and his judgement must be refined if it is to discriminate between its own products. The greatest mind, without knowledge, is only a rough diamond that will acquire value only after it has been cut by the hands of a skilled jeweller. What minds have been thus lost to society, what great men of every kind stifled in the bud, whether through ignorance, or through the abject state in which they found themselves placed!

The true benefit of the State, its advantage and glory demand therefore that the people in it should be as well educated and enlightened as possible, in order to furnish it, in every field, with a number of trained subjects capable of acquitting themselves expertly in the different tasks entrusted to them. There are some false political thinkers, limited by their narrow ideas, who, without going deeply into the matter, have supposed that it is easier to rule an ignorant and stupid people than an enlightened nation. That is a really powerful argument, when experience proves that the more brutish the people are, the more they are capricious and obstinate, and that it is far more difficult to overcome its obstinacy than to explain realities to a people civilized enough to listen to reason! It would be a fine country where talents remained forever stifled and where there was only one man less narrow-minded than the rest! Such a State, inhabited by ignoramuses, would be like the lost paradise in Genesis, inhabited only by animals.

Although it is unnecessary to demonstrate to this illustrious audience and in this Academy that the arts and sciences bring both utility and fame to the peoples who possess them, it will perhaps not be without use to convince some less enlightened persons of the same thing, to arm them against the effects which some vile sophists might have on their minds. Let them compare a Canadian savage with any citizen of a civilized country of Europe, and all the advantage will be with the latter. How can one prefer

---

[53] In 1744 Frederick revived the Prussian Academy of Sciences and Letters (originally founded in 1701). The Academy's object was 'the cultivation of every interesting and useful aspect of the various branches of philosophy, mathematics, physics, natural history, political and literary history, as well as literary criticism'. Its first president was the French scientist Maupertuis, its proceedings were normally conducted in French, and its members, appointed by Frederick, were mostly French. After Maupertuis's death in 1759, Frederick took personal charge of the Academy, taking occasional advice from d'Alembert and later Condorcet. He never attended the Academy's sessions in person, however: his *Discourse on the Usefulness of the Arts and Sciences* (a riposte to Rousseau's *Discourse on the Arts and Sciences* (1750)) was delivered on his behalf.

[54] Rousseau in his *Discourse on the Arts and Sciences* (1750).

crude nature to nature perfected, lack of means of subsistence to a life of ease, rudeness to politeness, the security of possessions enjoyed under the protection of the laws to the law of the jungle and to anarchy, which destroys the fortunes and conditions of families?

Society, a community of men, could not do without either the arts or the sciences. Thanks to surveying and hydraulics, riparian regions are protected from flooding; without these arts, fertile lands would become unhealthy marshes, and would deprive numerous families of their livelihood. The higher lands could not do without surveyors to measure out and divide the fields. The physical sciences, firmly established by experiment, help to perfect agriculture and, in particular, horticulture. Botany, applied to the study of medicinal herbs, and chemistry, which can extract their essences, serve at least to fortify our hope during our illnesses, even if their property cannot cure us. Anatomy guides and directs the surgeon's hand in those painful but necessary operations that save our life at the expense of an amputated limb.

The mechanical sciences are useful in every field: if a load is to be raised or transported, they will move it. If we are to dig into the bowels of the earth to extract metals, the science of mechanics, with ingenious machines, pumps out the quarries and frees the miner from the superabundance of water which would cost him his life or his work. If we need mills to grind the most familiar and most basic form of food, the science of mechanics perfects them. It is the science of mechanics that helps craftsmen by improving the various kinds of craft at which they work. Every kind of machine lies within its province. And how many machines are needed in all the various fields! The craft of shipbuilding constitutes perhaps one of the greatest efforts of imagination; but how much knowledge the pilot must possess to steer his ship and brave wind and wave! He needs to have studied astronomy, to have good charts, an exact knowledge of geography and arithmetical skill, in order to ascertain the distance he has travelled and the point at which he is, and in this respect he will be helped in future by the chronometers which have just been perfected in England.[55] The arts and sciences go hand in hand: we owe them everything, they are the benefactors of mankind.

We agree that logic is beyond the riff-raff; this large section of the human race will always be the last to open its eyes to facts; but although in every country, it maintains a store of superstitions, it is also true to say that we have succeeded in disabusing it of its belief in witches, possession by devils, the philosopher's stone and other equally childish nonsense. We owe these advantages to the more meticulous study of nature which has been carried out. Physics has been combined with analysis and experiment; the brightest light has been brought to bear among these dark places which concealed so many truths from scholars of the past; and although we cannot attain to the knowledge of the first secret principles, which the Grand Geometrician[56] has reserved for himself alone, powerful geniuses have arisen who discovered the laws of gravity and motion. Chancellor Bacon, the precursor of the new philosophy, or rather, the man who guessed and predicted its progress, put Sir Isaac Newton on the track of his marvellous discoveries; Newton appeared after Descartes, who having discredited the errors of the past, replaced them with errors of his own. Since then, men have weighed the air, measured the skies, calculated the movement of the heavenly bodies with infinite accuracy, predicted eclipses, and discovered an unknown property of matter, the force of electricity, whose effects astound the imagination; and doubtless men will soon be able to predict the appearance of comets, as they do that of eclipses, (though we already owe to the learned Bayle[57] the dissipation of the fear which this phenomenon caused among the ignorant). Let us admit: while the weakness of our condition makes us humble, the works of these great men restore our courage and make us feel the dignity of our being.

Source: Oeuvres de Frédéric le Grand, volume IX, pp.171–7.

---

55   John Harrison's chronometers, tested by Captain Cook during his second voyage (see *Studies*, I).

56   i.e. God. The expression 'Grand Geometrician' was used by Freemasons.

57   In his *Miscellaneous Thoughts on the comet of 1680* (1682), 'wherein it is proved by several reasons drawn from philosophy and theology that comets are not presages of misfortune'.

Catherine the Great, Empress of Russia

Section 1 Catherine, enlightenment and the ruler

Document 1

Portrait of Catherine II

Contemporary account, published after Catherine's death

One could see that she had been handsome rather than pretty; her majestic brow was tempered by her eyes and pleasant smile; but everything was written in that brow. Without being a

Figure 2 *Catherine the Great. Van Vilk (Hachette). 1780s. (Bibliothèque Nationale, Paris)*

Lavater,[58] one could read it like a book: genius, justice, soundness, courage, depth, fair-mindedness, gentleness, calmness and firmness. The breadth of her brow suggested a good memory and imagination; one could see that it had room for everything. Her chin, rather pointed, was not altogether projecting, but it was far from receding, and had nobility about it. This being so, her face was not well built, but it was bound to give infinite pleasure, for frankness and gaiety were always on her lips. She should have had a good figure; but her fine bust had been acquired at the expense of her waist, which had been very slim; but people get very stout in Russia. Her hair was elaborately dressed; but if she had not bound it back so tightly, and had let it come down a little lower on her face, she would have looked much better.

One did not notice that she was short. She told me in confidence that she had been extremely lively, something which it was impossible to imagine. On entering the room, she invariably made three manly bows in the Russian fashion, one to the right, one to the left and one to the centre. Everything about her was measured and methodical. She had the art of listening, and had such habitual presence of mind that she seemed to be listening even when she was thinking of something else. She did not talk for the sake of talking, and inspired respect in those who talked to her. Her Imperial Majesty used to speak of the role that one must play in the world, but she knew that it was a role. Whatever else she might have been, and whatever class she might have had to play a role in, she would have carried it off with equal success, thanks to her profound judgement. But the role of Empress was that which best suited her countenance, her bearing, her greatness of mind and her genius as vast as her Empire.

Source: C.E. De Ligne,[59] *Mémoires*, volume II, Paris, 1827, pp.346–50.

---

[58]   Johann Kaspar Lavater (1741–1801), Swiss poet and physiognomist who held that character can be interpreted from the contours of the face.

[59]   Prince Charles de Ligne (1735–1814), Austrian visitor, received by Catherine in the 1780s.

Document 2

Catherine II on the conduct of a ruler

Notes by Catherine II found in a copy of Fénelon's Télémaque[60] *(in French), undated*
Be gentle, humane, accessible, sympathetic and liberal. Never let your greatness prevent you from condescending with kindness to the level of the lowly, or from putting yourself in their place; and never let this kindness undermine your authority or their respect. Let it be seen that you think and feel all that you should. Bear yourself so that good men will love you, wicked men fear you and all men respect you.

Keep in you those great qualities of soul which mark the man of honour, the great man and the hero. Beware of all artifice. Let contact with the world never alter your classical taste for honour and virtue. Never let petty ideas or evil designs find a way to your heart. Duplicity is unknown to great men: they despise its baseness.

I beg Providence to engrave those few words in my heart and in the hearts of those who will read them after me.

Source: Sochineniya Imperatritsy Yekateriny II, edited by A. Pypin, volume 12, St Petersburg, 1907, pp.645–6.

Document 3

Catherine II on the Encyclopedists

Letter from Catherine II to d'Alembert (in French), 13 November 1762
Monsieur d'Alembert, I have just read your reply, in which you refuse to make the move necessary in order to contribute to the education of my son.[61] Philosopher as you are, I appreciate that it costs you nothing to despise the so-called greatness and honours of this world; all that is little in your eyes and I am certainly of your opinion. But to be born or called to contribute to the happiness and even the education of a whole nation, and to refuse, seems to me to be refusing to do the good that is in your heart. Your philosophy is based on humanity; allow me to say that to decline to put it into action when you can, is to fall short of your capabilities. I know you too well as an honest man to attribute your refusal to vanity; I know that your reason is no more than the desire for repose in order to devote yourself to your writing and your friends; but what does that depend on? Bring all your friends with you; I promise all of you all the attractions and comforts which I can offer. Perhaps you will find more freedom and repose than in your own country. I confess that I have my son's education so much at heart and I need you so much that perhaps I urge you too strongly.

Source: D'Alembert, Oeuvres et correspondances inédites, publiées avec introduction, notes et appendice, Paris, 1887, pp. 204–6.

Document 4

Catherine II on the Encyclopédie

Letter from Catherine II to Falconet[62] *(in French), 28 March 1767*
Enough of the *Encyclopédie*! I cannot put that book aside! It is an inexhaustible source of excellent things, though there are some major inaccuracies here and there. But that is hardly surprising; for the authors have encountered every kind of opposition and unpleasantness: and they have certainly shown great courage and an invincible desire to serve and instruct those who persecuted them and yelled at them: *'No enlightenment! – we do not wish to learn anything!'*

Source: Correspondance de Falconet avec Catherine II 1767–1778, edited by L. Réau, Paris, 1921, p.14.

---

[60] François de Salignac de la Mothe-Fénelon (1651–1715), French theologian whose *Télémaque* (1699) was an allegorical tale about the ideal ruler.

[61] Grand Duke Paul (1754–1801), later (1796–1801) Emperor.

[62] Etienne - Maurice Falconet (1716–91), French sculptor, contributed article on sculpture to *Encyclopédie*. Commissioned by Catherine to produce the celebrated equestrian statue at St Petersburg of Peter the Great.

Document 5

Catherine II on Voltaire

Letter from Catherine II to Grimm[63] (in French), 1 October 1778

He was my master; it was he, or rather his works, that formed my way of thinking. I have told you more than once, I think: I am his pupil; when I was younger, I loved to please him; when I did something, it had to be worthy of telling him about it for it to please me, and then he was told of it straightway; he was so well used to this that he used to scold me if I left out any news and he learned it from elsewhere. My meticulousness on this point slackened in recent years because of pressure of events before and after the peace;[64] and because of the enormous work which I have taken on; I have got out of the habit of letter-writing and I feel less inclined and find less facility in writing. The famous writing-desk adorns my hermitage,[65] and also the two busts of Voltaire; I prefer the bust without the wig.

Source: Sbornik imperatorskogo russkogo istoricheskogo obshchestva, volume 23, St Petersburg, 1878, pp.102–4.

Document 6

Catherine II on Voltaire

Letter from Catherine II to Grimm (in French), 19 October 1778

Hardly had my letter of October 1st (which by the way I completed only today) been posted than I remembered all sorts of things that I had forgotten to ask you, in particular to order for me a hundred sets of the new edition of Voltaire's works. Give me a hundred complete sets of my master's work, so that I can have them distributed everywhere. I want them to serve as models; I want them to be studied, learned by heart; I want them to provide food for thought. They will produce true citizens, geniuses, heroes, and authors. They will encourage a thousand talents which will otherwise be lost in obscurity and ignorance.

Source: Sbornik imperatorskogo russkogo istoricheskogo obshchestva, volume 23, St Petersburg, 1878, pp.104–5.

Document 7

Catherine II on law-making

Letter from Catherine II to Grimm (in French), 29 November 1775

I am wearing out my pens, just like you do, scribbling so many pages: I really have done an enormous amount of scribbling since I have been here.[66] My latest *Regulations*[67] of 7th November contain 250 printed pages in quarto, and furthermore I swear that they are the best thing I have ever done: compared to this, I now regard the *Instruction for the laws*[68] as so much verbiage! Aha! There is something to make you sit up!

Source: Sbornik imperatorskogo russkogo istoricheskogo obshchestva, volume 23, St Petersburg, 1878, p.39.

Document 8

Catherine II on her achievements

Letter from Catherine II to Grimm (in French), 8 July 1781

On 28th June this year, Monsieur Bezborodko,[69] my 'factotum', came to bring me my statement

---

[63]   Friedrich Melchior, Baron von Grimm (1723–1807), Franco-German *philosophe* and critic. Contributed article on music in *Encyclopédie*. Acted as agent for Catherine in purchase of books and art collections in the West.

[64]   With Turkey (1774).

[65]   The Winter Palace at St Petersburg.

[66]   In Moscow.

[67]   The *Provincial Statute*.

[68]   See Document 21.

[69]   Catherine's secretary.

of accounts up to this year, to which he has to make an annual adjustment.

Here are the final results: Over the last nineteen years:– Provinces reorganized in accordance with the new system[70] ... ... 29. Towns founded and built in accordance with the new system ... ... 144. Conventions and treaties concluded ... ... 30. Victories won ... ... 78. Memorable edicts containing laws or foundations ... ... 88. Edicts for the relief of the people ... ... 123. Total: 492.

All this is in the normal business of running the state, and the list contains nothing special, as you see. Well, Sir, are you satisfied with us? Have we been idle?

Source: Sbornik imperatorskogo russkogo istoricheskogo obshchestva, volume 23, St Petersburg, 1878, p.216.

Section 2 Catherine and war

Document 9

Catherine II on war

Letter from Catherine II to Voltaire (in French), 3/14 August 1771

Talking of pride, I would like to make my full confession to you on this point. I have had some great successes during this war;[71] I have, quite naturally, rejoiced at them, saying: this war will win Russia a name for herself; people will see that this is a brave and indefatigable people, with men of eminent merit and all the qualities that make heroes: they will see that she lacks no resources, that those she has are by no means exhausted, and that she can defend herself and wage war with ease and vigour when she is unjustly attacked.

Full of these ideas, I have never given a thought to myself. At forty-two, I am hardly likely to improve in looks or intellect; in the nature of things, I must and will remain as I am. Why, then, should I be proud? If things go well, I say: so much the better. Should they go less well, I would do my best to restore them to the best of all possible conditions. That is my ambition, and I have no other. What I tell you is the truth. I shall go further: let me tell you that to spare

more bloodshed, I most sincerely long for peace: but this peace is still very far off, although the Turks, for other reasons, desire it ardently. But those folk do not know how to make peace. Equally I long for a peaceful settlement of Poland's insane quarrels.

Source: Voltaire and Catherine the Great. Selected Correspondence, edited by A. Lentin, Cambridge, 1974, p.115.

Document 10

Voltaire on Catherine's first war with Turkey

Letter from Voltaire to Catherine II (in French), 15th November 1768

On the one hand you are forcing the Poles to be tolerant and happy despite the papal nuncio: and on the other, you seem to be dealing with the Muslims in spite of Muhammad. If they make war on you, Madam, what Peter the Great once had in mind may well befall them, namely that Constantinople will become the capital of the Russian Empire. These barbarians deserve to be punished by a heroine, for the lack of respect they have hitherto had for ladies. Clearly, people who neglect all the fine arts and who lock up women, deserve to be exterminated.

Source: Voltaire and Catherine the Great. Selected Correspondence, edited by A. Lentin, Cambridge, 1974, pp.51–2.

Document 11

Diderot on Catherine's first war with Turkey

Memorandum from Diderot to Catherine II (in French), 1774

Thinking men are saddened by the length of the present war. They readily acknowledge that it is the sign of a great, proud and lofty spirit, such as your own, and, perhaps the mark of a very rational policy, to wish to end it by brute force, because such a triumph will make the Turks fear your military strength, and will make all the peoples of Europe respect your name, your nation, your genius and resolution. But the precious years of Your Majesty's life are slipping away, and it will be impossible for you to fulfil your great schemes for the happiness of your country. It is

---

[70] The *Provincial Statute.*

[71] Catherine's first war with Turkey (1768–74).

for Your Majesty, and Your Majesty alone, to weigh the pros and cons, which, in my eyes and in the eyes of the friends of peace, are enormous. But the *philosophe* and the monarch see things very differently.

Source: *Mémoires pour Catherine II*, edited by P. Vernière, Paris, 1963, pp.39–40.

Document 12

Radishchev[72] on war

Published book (in Russian) 'A Journey from St Petersburg to Moscow', 1790
You[73] will be to blame, if a mother mourns her son, or a wife her husband, slain on the battlefield; for the danger of falling captive can scarcely justify the murder, called war.[74]

Source: *Puteshestviye iz Peterburga v Moskvu*, edited by G. Ionin, Moscow, 1961, p.30.

Section 3 Catherine and religion

Document 13

Catherine II and religion

Secret Memoir (in Russian), published posthumously, c. 1787
A woman not born of the blood of our sovereigns, who deposed her husband by an armed insurrection, she received, in return for so virtuous a deed, the crown and sceptre of Russia, together with the title of 'Devout Sovereign', in the words of the prayer recited in church on behalf of our monarchs.

It cannot be said that she is unqualified to rule so great an Empire, if indeed a woman can support this yoke, and if human qualities alone are sufficient for this supreme office. She is endowed with considerable beauty, clever, affable, magnanimous and compassionate on principle. She loves glory, and is assiduous in her pursuit of it. She is prudent, enterprising, and quite well-read. However, her moral outlook is based on the modern philosophers, that is to say, it is not fixed on the firm rock of God's Law; and hence, being based on arbitrary worldly principles, it is liable to change with them.

I do not think I need to state whether she has faith in God's Law; for if she had, then God's Law itself might improve her heart and set her steps on the path of truth. But no: carried away by her indiscriminate reading of modern writers, she thinks nothing of the Christian religion, though she pretends to be quite devout. However much she conceals her thoughts, these are frequently revealed in her conversation, and her deeds prove it even more. Many books by Voltaire, undermining religion, have been translated by her order, such as *Candide, The Princess of Babylon*, and others; and Marmontel's *Bélisaire*, which makes no distinction between pagan and Christian virtue, was not merely translated by a society at her order, but she herself took part in translating it.[75] And her tolerance of, or rather permission for unlawful marriages, such as those of Princes Orlov and Golitsyn with their cousins, and of General Bauer with his step-daughter, proves this most of all. And so it may be said that even this indestructible bastion of conscience and virtue has been destroyed in her reign.

Source: Prince M.M. Shcherbatov,[76] *On the corruption of morals in Russia*, edited by A. Lentin, Cambridge, 1969, pp.235, 257.

---

[72]   See footnote 110.

[73]   Catherine.

[74]   In her notes on the book, Catherine commented: '"The murder, called war": what does he want: to be left defenceless, to fall captive to the Turks and Tartars, or to be conquered by the Swedes?'.

[75]   The Society for the Translation of Foreign Books was founded by Catherine in 1768, and published 112 titles by 1783 when its functions were taken over by the newly founded Russian Academy. *Candide* first appeared in a Russian translation in 1769 and was reprinted in 1779 and 1789. Marmontel's *Bélisaire* (1767), which was dedicated to Catherine, was translated by her and members of her entourage the same year. It was banned in France. Other translations included selections from the *Encyclopédie* and many of Rousseau's works.

[76]   Aristocrat, historian, moralist and courtier, Prince Mikhail Shcherbátov (1733–90) observed Catherine at close quarters. Resenting his failure to attain high office, he became probably her bitterest secret critic.

Document 14

Catherine II on religious toleration

Letter from Catherine II to Voltaire (in French),
28 November/9 December 1765
I would never have believed that the purchase of a library would bring me so many compliments: everyone is paying me them on my purchase of Monsieur Diderot's.[77] But confess, you, whom humanity should truly compliment for the help you have given to innocence and virtue in the persons of the Calas family[78] – it would have been cruel and unjust to separate a scholar from his books.

    Religious toleration is the rule with us: it is the law of the land, and persecution is forbidden. True, we have some fanatics, who, for lack of persecution, burn themselves to death:[79] but if those of other countries did as much there would be no great harm done; the world would only be the more peaceful for it, and Calas would not have been broken on the wheel.[80]

Source: Voltaire and Catherine the Great. Selected Correspondence,
edited by A. Lentin, Cambridge, 1974, p.40.

Document 15

Catherine II on religious toleration

Letter from Catherine II to Voltaire (in French),
c.22 December 1767
I think you would enjoy yourself at this assembly,[81] where orthodox sits next to heretic and muslim, and all three listen calmly to a heathen; and all four often put their heads together to make their opinions mutually acceptable. So well have they lost the habit of putting one another to the stake, that if anyone were ill-advised enough to suggest to a deputy that he should burn his neighbour to please the Supreme Being, I can say on behalf of all, that there is not one who would fail to reply: 'He is a man as I am; and according to the first paragraph of her Imperial Majesty's *Instruction*,[82] we must do one another all the good we can, and no evil.' I assure you, I am inventing nothing; if necessary, I could produce 640 signatures to vouch for me, with a bishop at the head of the list.

Source: Voltaire and Catherine the Great. Selected Correspondence,
edited by A. Lentin, Cambridge, 1974, p.49.

Document 16

Catherine II on freedom of religion

Imperial Manifesto (in French), December 1782
The protection which we are accustomed to give to foreigners who come into our Empire for the purposes of commerce and industry is generally known. Every person enjoys within our Realm the free exercise of the religion of his ancestors, finds complete security, the protection of the laws and of government, all the necessaries of life and the conveniences suitable to his rank.

Source: Edited from *An English Lady at the Court of Catherine the Great. The Journal of Baroness Elizabeth Dimsdale,*[83] 1781, edited by A.G. Cross, Cambridge, 1989, p.76.

Document 17

Catherine II on 'prejudices'

Notes, published posthumously (in French), 1762
Prejudices are an important and delicate matter. To forbid people to examine them privately and

---

[77] In 1765 Catherine purchased Diderot's library, but allowed him to keep it for life, together with a salary.

[78] For the Calas affair see *Studies*, I.

[79] The Schizmatics, or Old Believers, traditionally preferred self-martyrdom to enforced conversion to Orthodoxy. Catherine extended official toleration to them.

[80] This paragraph was reproduced by Voltaire in his *Lettres sur les panégyriques* (1767).

[81] The Legislative Commission.

[82] See document 21.

[83] Wife of Dr Thomas Dimsdale (document 39), whom Catherine made a baron of the Russian Empire.

to reject them where they find them false, is to forbid them to use reason. But when the people at large is concerned, to reject all prejudices or to tolerate them all are two excesses, each equally dangerous. The philosopher knows that there are national prejudices which must be respected, prejudices arising from upbringing, which must be tolerated, and religious prejudices, which must be upheld. (*Journal Encyclopédique*, 1 December 1761, p.8)

Source: *Sochineniya Imperatritsy Yekateriny II*, edited by A. Pypin, volume 12, St Petersburg, 1907, p.611.

Section 4 Catherine and her favourites

Document 18

Catherine II and her favourites

Secret Memoir (in Russian), published posthumously, c.1787
To add to the corruption of women's morals and of all decency, she has set other women the example of the possession of a long and frequent succession of lovers,[84] each equally honoured and enriched, thus advertising the cause of their ascendancy. Seeing a shrine erected to this vice in the heart of the Empress, women scarcely think it a vice in themselves to copy her; rather, I suppose, each thinks it a virtue in herself that she has not yet had so many lovers!

Although she is in her declining years, although grey hair now covers her head and time has marked her brow with the indelible signs of age, yet her licentiousness still does not diminish. She now realizes that her lovers cannot find in her the attractions of youth, and that neither rewards, nor power, nor gain can replace for them the effect which youthfulness can produce on a lover.

Source: Prince M.M. Shcherbatov, *On the corruption of morals in Russia*, edited by A. Lentin, Cambridge, 1969, p.245.

Document 19

Catherine II on her character and feelings

Memoirs, published posthumously (in French), c.1791
When I first came to Russia and for the first years of our marriage, however little this Prince [Grand Duke Peter[85]] had tried to make himself agreeable, I would have opened my heart to him. When I saw that of all around him I was the one to whom he paid least attention, precisely because I was his wife, it is no wonder that I failed to find the situation pleasant or to my taste, and that I was bored and perhaps depressed. This feeling of depression I kept under control far more than any other. My natural pride and my character made the idea of being unhappy unbearable to me. I used to tell myself: 'Happiness and unhappiness lie in the heart and soul of each individual. If you are unhappy, place yourself above misfortune, and act so that your happiness does not depend on any external event'.

Together with such an outlook of mind, I was endowed with great innate sensibility and a face that was at least interesting and which attracted from the first, without artifice or effort. My character was naturally so conciliatory that no one was ever in my company a quarter of an hour without readily falling into conversation with me, chatting to me as if we had known one another a long time. Naturally easy-going, I won the confidence of those who came into contact with me, because everyone felt that the most punctilious honesty and goodwill were the qualities which I sought most to emulate. If I may venture to use the expression, I make so bold as to claim that I was a bold and loyal knight, whose character was more male than female, though I was very far from being mannish. Together with the spirit and character of a man, I had the attractions of a most amiable woman. May I be forgiven my outspokenness in the truth of this avowal, which my pride dictates without hiding behind false modesty. Besides, this very account

---

[84] During the reign: G. Orlóv (1760–72), Vasíl'chikov (1772–4), Potémkin (1774–6), Zavadóvsky (1776–7), Zórich (1777–8), Rímsky-Kórsakov (1778–9), Lanskóy (1779–85), Yermólov (1785–6), Dmítriev-Mamónov (1786–9), Zúbov (1789–96).

[85] Ruled as Emperor Peter III (1761–2). Ousted, and murdered in the *coup* which brought Catherine to the throne.

should prove the truth of what I say about my outlook, feelings and character.

I said just now that people found me attractive, and hence I was half-way to temptation. In such a situation it is only human nature to go the whole way. To tempt and to be tempted are closely allied; and despite the finest maxims of morality that may be inculcated in one's head, the moment the feelings are involved, you are already far further along the way than you think; and I have yet to learn how to prevent their emergence. Maybe the remedy lies in flight; but there are occasions and situations where flight is impossible: how can you flee, avoid people, turn your back, in the middle of a court? Flight would itself cause gossip. Now if you do not take to flight, there is nothing so hard, in my opinion, as to escape from something which at heart you like. All arguments to the contrary will only be counsels of prudery, unrelated to the human heart. No one holds his heart in his hand, to squeeze or release it, fist clenched or open, at will.

Source: Mémoires de l'Impératrice Catherine II, edited by A. Herzen, London, 1859, pp.330–2.

Document 20

Catherine II on her 'favourites'

Letter from Catherine II to Potemkin (in Russian), c.1774
Well, Sir Hero, after this confession, may I hope for remission of my 'sins'? Please note that there are not fifteen of them, but only a third of that number.[86] The first occurred reluctantly, the fourth out of despair, which I did not think could in any way be accounted wantonness. As for the three others, if you consider the matter closely, God knows it was not done out of licentiousness, for which I have no liking. If, when I was young, it had been my lot to have a husband whom I could have loved, I would have remained faithful to him forever. The trouble is that my heart cannot bear to be without love even for a single hour.

Source: Sochineniya Imperatritsy Yekateriny II, edited by A. Pypin, volume 12, St Petersburg, 1907, p.698.

Section 5 Catherine, law and absolutism

Document 21

Catherine II, Nakaz or Instruction for the Commission for the Drawing-up of a New Code of Laws

Published document (in Russian), July 1767
1. The Christian religion teaches us to do good to one another, as far as possible. 2. Taking this religious precept as one which is, or ought to be, rooted in the hearts of the whole nation, we can only suppose that the desire of every honest citizen is, or will be, to see his country enjoy the highest level of prosperity, glory, happiness and stability. 3. And also to see each of his fellow-citizens under the protection of laws, which, without interfering with his well-being, protect him from any actions contrary to this precept. 4. But in order to bring about the speediest realization of this desire, which, we hope, is universal, we must examine the natural condition of this State. 5. For the laws most in accordance with nature are those whose particular character corresponds most closely to the character of the nation for which they have been laid down. 6. Russia is a European power.

Source: Nakaz Imperatritsy Yekateriny II, edited by N.D. Chechulin, St Petersburg, 1907, pp.1–2.

Document 22

Catherine II on the rule of law

Published document (in Russian), July 1767
33. The laws must protect as far as possible the security of each individual citizen. 34. The equality of all citizens consists in their all being subject to the same laws. 35. This equality requires effective regulations to prevent the rich from oppressing those less well off and from exploiting the ranks and offices entrusted to them purely in their capacity as civil servants. 36. Social or civil liberty does not consist in doing whatever one wishes. In a State, that is to say, in a society of men under laws, liberty can only mean being able to do what one ought to want to do and in not being forced to do what one ought

---

[86]   Saltykóv (1752–5) possibly fathered Grand Duke Paul; Poniatówski (1755–7), later King of Poland; Orlóv (1760–72), instrumental in engineering Catherine's accession; Vasíl'chikov (1772–4), replaced Orlóv, whose 'infidelities' distressed Catherine; Potémkin (1774–6), remained Catherine's closest friend and adviser even after his replacement as 'favourite'.

not to want to do. 37. We should form a clear and precise idea of liberty: liberty is the right to do whatever the laws permit. 38. If a citizen could do something forbidden by the laws, there could no longer be any liberty, because other citizens would have the same right. 39. Civil liberty is that peace of mind which results from the knowledge enjoyed by each citizen of his personal security. 40. For men to have this liberty, the law must be such that no citizen can fear another, but all fear the law alone. 41. As for the laws in general, nothing should be forbidden by the laws except what may be harmful, either to the individual or to society in general. 42. Any actions which contain no such element are outside the scope of the law, whose sole purpose is to produce the greatest security and benefit for those who live under it. 43. For the laws to be scrupulously observed, they should be so excellent and so well-provided with measures conducive to men's greatest good, that every individual would be firmly convinced that it was in his own interest to observe them scrupulously. 44. This is the height of perfection at which we should try to aim.

Source: Nakaz Imperatritsy Yekateriny II, edited by N.D. Chechulin, St Petersburg, 1907, pp.7–8.

Document 23

Catherine on absolutism

Published document (in Russian), July 1767
9. The ruler of Russia is absolute: for no power, other than that concentrated in his person, can operate with the effectiveness required by such a vast state. 10. A vast state presupposes absolute power in the person who rules it. Speed in decision-making has to compensate for slowness in implementation resulting from the remoteness of the localities concerned. 11. Any other form of government would be not merely harmful, but ultimately fatal to Russia. 12. Another consideration is the fact that it is better to obey the laws under one master than to depend on the will of many. 13. What is the object of absolute government? Not to deprive men of their natural freedom, but to guide their actions towards the greatest good. 14. Therefore the

government which can best accomplish this end, while placing the least restriction on natural freedom, is that which corresponds most closely to the aspirations which reasonable persons may be supposed to hold, and corresponds to the aim which men invariably aspire in the formation of civil society. 15. The aim and purpose of absolute government is the glory of the citizens, the state and the monarch. 16. And from this glory there results, in a nation ruled by a monarchy, a spirit of freedom, which can produce in these states as many great achievements and contribute as much to the happiness of the subjects, as freedom itself. 18. The essence of the government is formed by the intermediate and subordinate powers dependent on the sovereign power. 19. I said, 'the intermediate and subordinate powers, dependent on the sovereign power'; because certainly, it is the monarch who is the source of all political and civil power. 20. The fundamental laws of a state presuppose the existence of certain small channels, namely, the organs of government, through which the monarch's power is transmitted. 21. The laws allow these organs of government to make representations if a particular decree is contrary to the Code of Laws, or if it is harmful, obscure or impracticable; they lay down what decrees must be obeyed and the manner in which they are to be carried out. These laws undoubtedly make the constitution of any state firm and unshakeable. 22. There must be a Repository of the Laws. 23. This Repository can only reside in the organs of state which inform the people of the newly made laws and remind them of laws which they have forgotten. 24. As they receive the laws from the monarch, these state organs examine them carefully, and have the right to make representations if they find anything in them contrary to the Code of Laws etc., as mentioned earlier. 25. But if they do not find anything of this kind, they enter them in the record of existing laws and promulgate them to the people. 26. In Russia, the Senate is the Repository of the Laws. 27. The other state organs have the same duty and power to make representations to the Senate and to the monarch himself, in the manner described above.

Source: Nakaz Imperatritsy Yekateriny II, edited by N.D. Chechulin, St Petersburg, 1907, pp.3–4.

Document 24

A critic of the **Nakaz**: **Prince Shcherbatov**

Private observations on the Nakaz, *published posthumously (in Russian), c.1772*

9. Note. Whether a large state necessarily requires absolute power is a question yet to be decided.

10. Note. This thought is taken from Monsieur Montesquieu's book, *On the Spirit of the Laws,* Book VIII, Chapter 19.[87] I cannot agree with this opinion. True, if we suppose a conscientious monarch, one who despises pleasures for the good of his subjects, and all of whose decrees and orders are founded on perfect wisdom and justice, then of course such an absolutism could bring all the purported advantages. But such an absolutism would be preferable even to republican freedom. But such rulers are few, especially where not merit but birth alone has raised them to the throne; and therefore, when such a ruler governs, not according to the established laws but according to his own caprices, this is called despotism, which scarcely differs from loathsome tyranny.

13. Note. There can be no object other than this under any form of government; for, says Rousseau,[88] since great rulers were originally chosen by the people in order to guarantee their welfare, among the rights that they surrendered when drawing up the contract with these chosen rulers, the people could not have surrendered their natural freedom, this being something indispensable to their welfare. But here we must consider whether absolute power is in accordance with such an original contract. This seems doubtful to me, for can natural freedom be expected to be preserved where the legislative and executive power is united in the same person?

14. Note. From the preceding observation it is clear which form of government – republican or monarchical – achieves this end.

15. Note. In *On the Spirit of the Laws,* Book V, Chapter 9, Monsieur Montesquieu ascribes these principles to monarchical, not absolute government; but even so, it seems that glory has more effect on republicans than on those who live under monarchical government.

16. It is stated that a spirit of freedom can produce the same results as freedom itself. So this 'spirit of freedom' is not the same as freedom, and hence it is at most a mask of freedom.

18. Note. Montesquieu, Book II, chapter 4. But he adds: *'that is to say, where one man rules in accordance with fundamental laws'*. The omission of this phrase proves the desire for unlimited, despotic power.

19. Note. Montesquieu, *ibid.* But this author ascribes all this to monarchy, where the ruler is obliged to govern according to the fundamental laws of the state; and where, when he issues or confirms laws with the agreement of the organs of government, he is indeed the source of all political and civil power; but he himself is obliged to obey the law he has laid down. But this does not apply in countries where the ruler considers himself to be above the law. Here it is true that all power derives from him alone, but it is not always dispensed on the basis of that principle of justice for the sake of which peoples originally surrendered their freedom. And so it often leads to a breach of this original contract.

21. Note. The wisdom and magnanimity of Peter the Great are nowhere so evident as in his allowing the Senate to make representations against his decrees. And although this same rule has been extended by the present monarch, not only in the case of the Senate, but for all the Colleges, yet, since the time of Peter the Great, the Senate has never been known to make representations against the decrees of the sovereign. Why is this? Is it because rulers never make mistakes? That is impossible, for being human, they are subject to human weaknesses. Or is it because the senators either do not see the errors, or if they do see them, they dare not speak out?

23. Note. The words are those of Monsieur Montesquieu, *On the Spirit of the Laws,* Book II, Chapter 4. But that eminent writer is speaking of a form of government where one man governs according to fundamental laws, and not of one where his absolutism is unlimited, of which form of government that same writer in this chapter expresses himself as follows: 'In despotic states,

---

[87] 'A great empire presupposes a despotic authority in the person who rules'.

[88] In the *Social Contract* (1762).

where there are no fundamental laws, there is no repository of the laws'. And indeed, what laws can the government uphold in this case, when they are as inconstant as the thoughts and arbitrariness of the ruler? But neither in the *Nakaz* nor in the agenda of the Legislative Commission is there any mention of drawing up fundamental laws, which should surely have been the principle behind the whole enterprise. So even this *Nakaz* is conducive to a despotic form of government.

26. Note. The name 'Senate', by suggesting the idea of the Roman institution of the same name, makes us think it more significant than it is. For in fact, having no legislative power, and very limited executive power, it has little influence. For in all matters remotely doubtful, it reports to the monarch; and the monarch, without consulting the body of the Senate but simply after discussion with the Procurator-General,[89] gives her decisions, which are slavishly accepted by the Senate. Therefore since it has power neither to interpret the law nor to make representations against a decree of the sovereign, it is vain to call it the repository of the laws, since it only appears to be such, as is usually the case in all despotic governments, where the judges are not the guardians of the law, but instruments of the despot's will.

Source: Knyaz' M.M. Shcherbatov, Neizdannye sochineniya, edited by P.G. Lyubomirov, Moscow, 1935, pp.21–8.

Document 25

Diderot on the Nakaz

Diderot 'Observations on the Nakaz', published posthumously (in French), 1773
One should not ask *what is the object of an absolute government?*[90] It matters little what its object is; but *what is its effect?* Its effect is to make all liberty and property absolutely dependent on one man. If this master is a man of justice, enlightenment and firmness, everything will be directed, at least during his reign, towards the greatest good of all

men. But if it is rare to find even one of these qualities developed to a certain degree in a man, how much rarer is it to find all three well-developed and united together in him? If, then, the size of Russia demands a despot,[91] Russia is condemned to be ruled badly twenty times in return for one good reign. Whatever the country, therefore, the sovereign authority should be limited, and limited in a lasting manner. The difficult problem, then, is not to give laws, even good laws, to a people, but to protect these laws from any infringement by the monarch.

I see in Her Imperial Majesty's *Instruction* a plan for an excellent code of laws; but not a word on how to ensure the maintenance of the code. I see the name of despot renounced, but the essence retained, and despotism called monarchy.

Source: Diderot, Oeuvres politiques, edited by P. Vernière, Paris, 1963, pp.354–5, 457.

Document 26

Catherine II and the law

Secret memoir (in Russian), published posthumously, c.1787
Generally speaking, women are more prone to despotism than men; and as far as she is concerned, it can justly be averred that she is in this particular a woman among women. Nothing can irritate her more than when making some report to her, men quote the laws in opposition to her will. Immediately the retort flies from her lips: 'Can I not do this irrespective of the laws?' But she has found no one with the courage to answer that she can indeed, but only as a despot, and to the detriment of her glory. Many lawsuits attest to her arbitrariness; (1) the restoration to Már'ya Pávlovna Naryshkin by Talyzin of certain estates, which had been confirmed as his property by the title-deeds and by actual possession; (2) the case of the children of Prince Boris Vasíl'evich Golítsyn concerning the wrongful confiscation of the estates of their grandfather, Streshnev; although the injustice was recognised by the Senate, and a

---

[89]   The chief executive and supervisory minister.

[90]   See document 23, clause 13.

[91]   See document 23, clause 10.

report was submitted requesting permission for them to be restored to the rightful heirs, and although the postscript on the report 'So be it' seemed to indicate that their claim was being justly satisfied; yet later the explanation came from the Empress's study that the words 'So be it' meant 'Let them remain confiscated.'

Akim Ivánovich Apúkhtin reported to her through the College of War about the retirement of a certain major-general; he received the order that the man was to be retired without promotion. When he began to point out that the laws specifically laid it down that major-generals were to be promoted upon retirement, he received the answer that 'She was above the laws, and did not choose to grant him this reward.'

Source: Prince M.M. Shcherbatov, On the corruption of morals in Russia, edited by A. Lentin, Cambridge, 1969, pp.247–9.

Document 27

Catherine II on her rule

Letter from Catherine II to J.G. Zimmerman[92] (in French), January 1789
I have never hated or envied anyone. My wish and pleasure would have been to make men happy; but since everyone can only be so according to his character or understanding, my wishes have often encountered obstacles that were beyond my grasp. My ambition was certainly not a bad one; but perhaps it was too optimistic to believe men capable of becoming reasonable, just and happy. The human race in general is prone to injustice; this being so, it cannot be happy: that would be nonsense. If it listened to reason and justice, it would not need people like us. As for happiness, as I said before, everyone has his own idea of it.

I cherished philosophy, because at heart I have always been remarkably republican. I agree that this characteristic is perhaps rather extraordinary, given my unlimited political power; but at the same time no one in Russia will be able to say that I have abused that power.

Source: Sochineniya Imperatritsy Yekateriny II, edited by A. Pypin, volume 12, St Petersburg, 1907, pp.595–6.

Section 6 Catherine and serfdom

Document 28

Catherine II on serfdom

Published document (in Russian), July 1767
250. Civil society, like everything else, requires a certain order. There must be persons who govern and command, and others who obey. 251. This is the origin of every sort of subordination. It is lighter or heavier depending on the condition of those who obey. 252. Since Natural Law commands us to strive as much as we can for the welfare of all men, we are bound to relieve the position of those under our sway, as far as common sense permits. 253. Consequently we are bound to avoid reducing men to a state of slavery unless absolute necessity requries it, and if we do so, it is not for our own gain, but for the benefit of the State. 260. One should not suddenly and through a general law create a large number of free men. 261. The laws can favour giving personal property to slaves. 262. Let us conclude by repeating the principle that the form of government most in conformity with nature is that whose particular character corresponds most closely with the character of the nation for which it is established. 263. However, it is also necessary to remove the causes which have so often led to revolts of serfs against their masters; for unless we recognize these causes, it is impossible to prevent such occurrences by law, even though the tranquility of both parties depends on this.

Source: Nakaz Imperatritsy Yekateriny II, edited by N.D. Chechulin, St Petersburg, 1907, pp.74–6.

Document 29

Catherine II on the peasants

Memorandum from Catherine II to Diderot (in French), 1774
As for the common people, all they think of is the bread that nourishes them and the religion that consoles them. Their ideas will always be as primitive as their nature. The prosperity of the

---

[92] Johann Georg von Zimmerman (1728–95), Swiss moral philosopher, held out posthumous fame as a consolation for death.

state, progress, the next generation, are words which cannot affect them; they are connected with society only by their hardships, and of all that vast period of time which is called the future, they never conceive of anything except the next day. They are deprived by their poverty of a loftier interest.

Source: M. Tourneux, Diderot et Catherine II, Paris, 1899, pp.537–8.

Document 30

A critic of emancipation: Prince Shcherbatov

Essay, published posthumously (in Russian), 'Thoughts on the disadvantages of granting freedom to the peasants in Russia or of allowing them to own land', 1785
1766, the Free Economic Society was sent the following subject as the theme of an essay-competition: 'Whether it is more useful to society for the peasant to own his own land, or simply moveable chattels, and how far his rights to either form of property should be extended'. We can mark that year as the period when the immemorial bond between the peasants and their owners began to be severed. However moderate the language of the essay-title, and however much it was made clear that it was set simply as a question, it gave rise to rumour, to the spread of subversive ideas, and to insubordination.

At the Legislative Commission of 1767, 1768 and 1769, the incautious expression of views by the deputies spread this epidemic still further in the hearts of the commoners present there as deputies, who on their departure scattered these evil seeds to the remotest regions of Russia.

Even before the Commission was prorogued, indeed only a few months after the essay-competition, the year 1767 was remarkable in Russia for the murder of a large number of landowners by their peasants; while after the dismissal of the deputies, a still greater evil arose, when nearly all the peasants who had the slightest chance joined that enemy of the nation and the monarch, the Pretender Emel'yán Pugachóv, not only in several provinces, but in a considerable part of our vast country.[93] Loyalty to the sovereign was at an end, civilian blood was shed, towns and villages were devastated and a thousand noble families, true sons of the nation, whose ancestors shed their blood in order to extend and pacify the land, were cut off by a cruel and foul death, in those very regions which they had brought beneath Russia's sway. Their innocent blood, shed by the hands of miscreants who had formerly benefited from them, flowed in torrents; their corpses, mutilated, unburied, were consumed by wild beasts and birds of prey; their wives and daughters were outraged by the miscreants.

The short time that has elapsed since that catastrophe is still fresh in our memory. Perhaps later historians will not realise that this epidemic – the spirit of rebellion, false hope and insurrexion – affected not only those who showed their corruption by their open villainies, but also almost all the rest of the peasantry, who were only awaiting the opportunity to commit similar crimes. Even if they had the right to freedom and property, such a universal crime, as it were, ought to have disentitled them to it for some considerable time, and to have condemned them to serfdom even if they were not serfs, until the evil seeds were eradicated from their hearts.

Source: Chteniya v imperatorskom obshchestve istorii i drevnostey rossiiskikh, Book 3, part 5, Moscow, 1861, pp.98–115, 133.

Document 31

The condition of the serfs

Private journal, published posthumously, 1781
The peasants, that is to say the greater part of the subjects, are in an abject state of slavery, and are reckoned the property of the nobles and considerable people to whom they belong, as much as their horses or dogs. The wealth of a great man in Russia is not computed by the extent of land he possesses, or by the quantity of grain he can bring to market, but by the number of his slaves. Every slave pays about a rouble yearly to his owner. In general, every nobleman allots to the peasants that belong to him a certain portion of land to be cultivated by them, the produce of which, except what suffices for their own maintenance, is paid to the proprietor.

---

[93] Originally an uprising of Cossack and non-Russian peoples, the Pugachov rebellion (1773–4) later attracted serfs attached to industrial enterprises and, after Pugachov's capture of Kazan in July 1774, agricultural serfs.

Sometimes these slaves practise trades or engage in traffic, and all such persons pay a much greater sum to their owners than is done by labourers of the ground. In fact, a Russian peasant has no property which he can properly call his own. Another hardship which the Russian peasants are exposed to is being obliged to marry whatsoever person and at what time their superiors please; but this power is seldom insisted on.

Source: Edited from *An English Lady at the Court of Catherine the Great. The Journal of Baroness Elizabeth Dimsdale*, 1781, edited by A.G. Cross, Cambridge, 1989, pp.57–8.

Document 32

Enlightenment and the peasants

Contemporary published account, 1781
I must own, I was astonished at the barbarism in which the bulk of the people still continue. I am ready to allow that the principal nobles are perfectly civilized, and as refined in their entertainments, mode of living and social intercourse, as those of other European countries. But there is a wide difference between polishing a nation and polishing a few individuals. The merchants and peasants still universally retain their beards, their national dress, their original manners. The greatest part of the peasants, who form the bulk of the nation, are still almost as deficient in the arts as they were before Peter's time, although the sciences have flourished in the capital. But the civilization of a numerous and widely dispersed people cannot be the work of a moment, and can only be effected by a gradual and almost insensible progress.

Source: Archdeacon W. Coxe, *Travels into Poland, Russia, Sweden and Denmark*, volume II, Dublin, 1784, pp.318–19.

Section 7 Catherine and penal reform

Document 33

Catherine II on crime prevention

Published document (in Russian), July 1767
239. What methods are the most effective for the prevention of crime? 240. It is far better to prevent crimes than to punish them. 241. The prevention of crime is the object and aim of a good system of laws, which is none other than the art of leading men to the greatest good, or, if it is impossible to eradicate all evil, to leave them

with the minimum of evil. 243. Do you wish to prevent crime? Make the laws favour not so much the different classes of citizens, as each individual citizen. 244. Make people fear the laws and no one but the laws. 245. Do you wish to prevent crime? Spread enlightenment in society. 246. A good code of laws is one which simply prevents the dangerous whims of the individual from harming his fellows. 247. Crime can also be prevented by rewarding virtue. 248. Finally, the surest but most difficult method of improving men is by perfecting their education.

Source: Nakaz Imperatritsy Yekateriny II, edited by N.D. Chechulin, St Petersburg, 1907, pp.72–4.

Document 34

Catherine II on penal reform

Published document (in Russian), July 1767
63. All punishment that is not laid down out of necessity is tyrannical. Law does not derive solely from power. Matters which by their nature have no relation to good or evil, are outside the scope of the law. 67. Civil liberty triumphs when the criminal law deduces each penalty from the particular nature of each crime. Any arbitrariness in the imposition of the sentence ceases; the punishment should derive, not from the whim of the legislator but from the nature of the crime itself; and it is a question not of a man's suffering at the hands of man, but suffering the effects of his own action. 83. In this country, we shall strive not so much to punish crimes as to prevent them, and one should aim at instilling good conduct in the citizens through legislation rather than intimidating through punishment. 85. Observation teaches us that in countries where punishments are mild, the citizens are as much affected by them as they are elsewhere by harsh ones. 96. All punishments which can disfigure the human body ought to be abolished. 114. In states where moderation is observed, where the life, property and honour of even the humblest citizen is respected, no man's honour or property will be taken from him except after long and thorough investigation; no one is deprived of life except when the nation itself claims it; and the nation will claim no man's life without allowing him every possible means of defending it. 123. The use of torture is contrary to natural common sense; humanity itself cries out against it and demands its complete abolition. We see

today a nation renowned for its civil institutions,[94] which rejects it without any harmful consequences; hence it is not essential in its nature. 126. Those accused of serious offences should be able to choose their own judges, in conformity with the laws, or at least should be able to reject so many of them that the remainder would seem to be in court at the choice of the accused. 128. When a defendant is sentenced, it is not the judge who imposes the penalty upon him, but the law. 158. The laws should be written in simple language, and the complete code of laws should be published in a book readily available at a low price. 200. In order that punishment should not seem to be an act of violence committed upon a citizen by one or many adversaries, it should be public, as prompt as possible, necessary for the good of society, as moderate as possible in the circumstances, proportionate to the crime and fixed by the laws.

Source: Nakaz Imperatritsy Yekateriny II, edited by N.D. Chechulin, St Petersburg, 1907, pp. 14, 19, 23, 27–8, 30–1, 41–2, 57.

Document 35

Catherine II on torture

Published document (in Russian), July 1767
205. The aim of punishment is not to torment a creature endowed with feelings; its purpose is to prevent the criminal from harming society in future and to deter his fellow-citizens from committing similar crimes. For this, one should apply such punishment as, being proportioned to the crimes, will produce the most marked and durable effect on public opinion while at the same time being the least cruel to the offender. 206. Who is not filled with horror on seeing in history so many barbarous and useless examples of torture, invented and applied without the slightest compunction, by people calling themselves wise? Who does not shudder at the sight of those thousands of poor men who have suffered them and suffer them today, men often accused of crimes difficult or impossible to commit, crimes often fabricated out of ignorance and sometimes out of superstition? Who, I say, can see these men torn apart with great formalities by their fellow-men and brothers? The countries and

periods where punishments were cruellest, are those where the most atrocious crimes were committed. 208. If anywhere the laws were harsh, they have either been changed, or punishment for evil-doing has been waived because of the very severity of the laws. The extent of punishments should be relative to the actual condition and circumstances in which a nation finds itself. As men in society become enlightened, the sensibility of each individal citizen increases; and as sensibility develops in the citizens, the severity of punishments should be mitigated.

Source: Nakaz, Imperatritsy Yekateriny II, edited by N.D. Chechulin, St Petersburg, 1907, pp.59–61.

Document 36

A knouting at St Petersburg

Contemporary published account, 1781
One morning, as I was casually strolling through the streets of St Petersburg, near the marketplace, I observed a vast crowd of people flocking to one particular spot. Upon inquiring of my Russian servant the cause of this concourse, he informed me that the multitude was assembled in order to see a felon, who had been convicted of murder, receive the knout. Although I naturally shuddered at the very idea of being a spectator to the agonies of a fellow creature, yet my curiosity overcame my feelings. The executioner held in his hand the knout: this instrument is a thong, about the thickness of a crown-piece, and about three quarters of an inch broad, and rendered extremely hard by a peculiar kind of preparation; it is tied to a thick plaited whip, which is connected by means of an iron ring, with a small piece of leather that acts like a spring, and is fastened to a short wooden handle. The executioner, before every stroke, receded a few paces, and at the same time drew back the hand which held the knout; then, bounding forwards, he applied the flat end of the thong with considerable force to the naked back of the criminal in a perpendicular line, reaching six or seven inches from the collar towards the waist. He began by hitting the right shoulder, and continued his strokes parallel to each other quite to the left shoulder; nor ceased till he had inflicted

---

[94]   Britain.

333 lashes, the number prescribed by the sentence. At the conclusion of this terrible operation, the nostrils of the criminal were torn with pincers, his face marked with a hot iron, and he was reconducted to prison, in order to be transported to the mines of Nerchinsk, in Siberia.[95]

Source: Archdeacon W. Coxe,[96] *Travels into Poland, Russia, Sweden and Denmark,* volume II, Dublin, 1784, pp.295–7.

Document 37

Count Panin[97] on the Pugachov rebellion

Proclamation issued by Count P.I. Panin (in Russian), 25 August 1774
In all towns and villages where the inhabitants have seized and murdered their military governors, government officials of all kinds appointed by Her Majesty, their own landlords, priests or loyal subjects of any rank, or where they have aided and abetted by capturing them and handing them over to the traitors to be killed, both the murderers themselves and their traitorous accomplices shall, after Christian preparation, be put to death by the severing of the hands and feet followed by decapitation, and their bodies shall be placed on gibbets beside the main highways. All followers of such rebels shall without exception be severely knouted at the gallows. In all villages which rebelled against or disobeyed the lawful authorities, one man shall be placed on the gallows, one on the wheel and one hanged from the gibbet by the rib; and they shall not be taken down until further orders. If those responsible for the murder of the established authorities, their own landlords, priests and loyal subjects of any rank, cannot be discovered, then in the villages where the authorities, priests and loyal subjects of every rank were murdered or betrayed by the inhabitants, the latter shall be compelled to surrender those responsible by drawing lots, every third man to be hanged; and if this does not make them give them up, then every hundredth man chosen by lot shall indeed be hanged, and all remaining adults shall be knouted.

Source: Sochineniya Derzhavina, edited by Y. Grot, volume V, St Petersburg, 1869, pp.288–9.

Document 38

Catherine II on the Pugachov rebellion

Despatches from Catherine II to Count P.I. Panin (in Russian), 21 September 1774
Your sad Proclamation[98] is very much in accordance with the demands of the situation and it is written in a simple style readily comprehensible to the common people. It shows quite clearly the welcome you have in store for the Outlaw. And of course wherever the spirit of rebellion remains, the harsh measures are to be carried out, which you propose to employ where you are unable to put a final end by your Declaration to the venture of the fickle populace which has thrown off obedience to the authorities. And although my own feelings are very averse not only to the use of harsh punishments but even to severity, I acknowledge that in the present circumstances punishments are unfortunately necessary for the good of the Empire; I simply enjoin on you wherever possible to treat the miscreants at their execution in accordance with my habitual love of humanity and mercy,[99] and always remember that in this case I am like a mother shedding tears at the necessary punishment of her disobedient children.

Source: Sbornik imperatorskogo russkogo istoricheskogo obshchestva, volume VI, St Petersburg, 1871, pp.120–1.

---

[95] He died the next day of his injuries.

[96] William Coxe (1747–1828), English historian and traveller.

[97] Commander-in-chief entrusted with suppressing the Pugachov rebellion.

[98] i.e. Document 37.

[99] In accordance with this injunction, Pugachov was executed without the preliminary severing of hands and feet specified in Panin's proclamation.

Section 8 Catherine, education and enlightenment

Document 39

Catherine II on her inoculation

Letter from Catherine II to Voltaire (in French),
6/17 December 1768
Sir, I suppose you think me rather inconsistent: about a year ago I asked you to send me the complete works of my favourite author; last May I received the consignment I asked for, together with a bust of the most illustrious man of our age.

I have been equally satisfied with both: for the last six months they have comprised the finest adornment of my room and have been my daily reading-matter; but so far I have neither acknowledged receipt of them nor thanked you for them. My reasoning was as follows: a badly scrawled note, full of bad French, is a poor way of thanking such a man; I must pay him my compliments in a way which will please him. Different ideas came to mind; it would take too long to list them. In the end, I thought the best thing to do would be for me to set a personal example which might be of use to people. I remembered that, as luck would have it, I had not had small-pox. I sent to England for an expert in inoculation. The famous Dr Dimsdale agreed to come to Russia. This truly able man inoculated me on October 12th 1768. After the inoculation I was most surprised that the mountain had given birth to a mouse.[100] I have not had a moment's illness, and have been receiving people every day. I am going to have my only son inoculated immediately.

A French translation has just appeared of the Russian *Instruction* given to the deputies who are to draw up the project for our code of laws. There has not been time to print it. I hasten to send you the manuscript, to give you a clearer view of our basic principles. I do not think there is a single line which an honest man cannot approve.

I forgot to tell you that I supplemented the small amount or complete lack of medicine that is given during the inoculation with three or four excellent patent remedies, which I recommend every man of good sense not to neglect in similar circumstances: namely to have someone read to one *L'Ecossaise, Candide, L'Ingénu, L'homme aux quarante écus,* and *La Princesse de Babylone.* It is impossible to feel the least bit ill after that.

As for news from here, let me tell you, Sir, that everyone wants to be inoculated; a bishop is going to have it done, and more people have been inoculated here in one month than in eight at Vienna.

Source: Voltaire and Catherine the Great, Selected Correspondence, edited by A. Lentin, Cambridge, 1974, pp.52–4.

Document 40

Voltaire on inoculation

Letter from Voltaire to Catherine II (in French),
February 26, 1769
Oh, Madam, what a lesson your Majesty is giving to us petty Frenchmen, to our ridiculous Sorbonne and to the argumentative charlatans in our medical schools! You have been inoculated with less fuss than a nun taking an enema. The Crown Prince [Paul] has followed your example. We French can hardly be inoculated at all, except by decree of the *Parlement.* I do not know what has become of our nation.

Source: Voltaire and Catherine the Great. Selected Correspondence, edited by A. Lentin, Cambridge, 1974, p.56.

Document 41

The Cadet Corps at St Petersburg

Private journal, published posthumously, August 1781
General Betskoy, who has the Cadet Corps under his direction, invited us to his house, to see Prince Potemkin review a regiment of boys of about fourteen or fifteen years old. The review was in a field adjoining the house, and if people are to be brought up to kill one another, it is certainly a very fine Institution, established by the Empress. They are divided into certain companies, and are regularly trained to military exercises. There are sons of the people of the first rank, and a great number of the lower class. The

---

[100]   i.e. much ado about nothing. From Horace, *The Art of Poetry,* 1.139.

greatest care is taken of their education and likewise in regard to the military line. They are in number four hundred, and some of them are very fine young men. During six weeks in the summer, I was told, they form an encampment near the town, are reviewed and perform all the manoeuvres of war. Prizes are annually distributed amongst those who excel as well in their respective studies and employments and in their exercises. These prizes consist of books, gold and silver medals, ribbands and stars. Of those whose merit has entitled them to six prizes, three are annually selected for the purpose of travelling into foreign countries, with an allowance to each of one hundred and twenty pounds per annum.

The boys are all brought up in the hardest manner, and I believe in the winter not allowed to wear furs, and are habituated in all kinds of exercises, particularly to running and leaping. In one part of the field there was a part railed round which they call the Carosal. Near this Carosal stood a large leather horse. The highest part, I was informed, was at least six feet; and after the review was over, eight young men of about eighteen or nineteen, high in the Academy, leaped over it in every direction, sprung over its head, vaulted upon its back, turned themselves round upon it, poised themselves upon their hands with their head upon the saddle and their feet in the air; and then threw themselves from that posture upon the ground on their legs, with many similar feats which they performed with great ease and agility. This exercise I suppose may be of use in stretching their limbs, but afforded me no pleasure: for it appeared so dangerous that I expected every minute an accident would happen.

Source: Edited from *An English Lady at the Court of Catherine the Great. The Journal of Baroness Elizabeth Dimsdale*, 1781, edited by A.G. Cross, Cambridge, 1989, pp.44–5.

Document 42

Catherine II on the Smol'ny Institute[101] at St Petersburg

Letter from Catherine II to Voltaire (in French), 2/13 April 1772

Our young ladies perform both tragedy and comedy. Last year, they put on *Zaire*[102] and for the New Year they performed *Semira*, a Russian tragedy, indeed the best tragedy, of Monsieur Sumarokov, of whom you have heard.[103] Oh, Sir, you will oblige me immensely, if for the sake of these dear children you will undertake the task which you call a pleasure and which would be so difficult for anyone else.[104] You will thereby give me a most feeling token of that friendship of which I am so distinguished an object. Moreover, these young ladies are charming, as all who see them agree. Some of them are already fourteen and fifteen years of age. I am sure they would win your approval if you saw them. I have been tempted more than once to send you some letters which I have received from them and which were certainly not devised by their teachers: they are too childish for that: for the moment, every line brims with innocence, charm and high spirits. I do not know whether this 'battalion of girls' as you call them, will turn out to be amazons, but we are very far from wishing to turn them into nuns, or wear them out by constant caterwauling in church, as the practice is at St-Cyr.[105] On the contrary, we educate them with a view to making them the delight of their future families; we want them to be neither prudes nor coquettes, but agreeable young ladies, capable of raising their own children and running their own homes.

Source: Voltaire and Catherine the Great. Selected Correspondence, edited by A. Lentin, Cambridge, 1974, pp.134–5.

---

[101] The Smol'ny Institute at St Petersburg, Russia's first school for girls. Founded by Catherine in 1769 as a boarding-school for young ladies of the nobility, the Smol'ny Institute was avowedly 'progressive', inspired by ideas drawn from Locke and Fénelon. It aimed to produce a 'new mother'.

[102] Tragedy by Voltaire (1732).

[103] A.P. Sumarokov (1717–77), Russian neo-classical tragedian.

[104] To expurgate, at Catherine's request, French classics for performance by pupils at the Smol'ny Institute.

[105] Institution founded in Paris in 1685 by Mme de Maintenón to provide a Christian education for young women of the nobility.

Document 43

The Smol'ny Institute at St Petersburg

Private journal, published posthumously, August 1781
The Seminary for the Education of the Female
Nobility, usually called *Le Couvent des Demoiselles
Nobles,* is situated at the extremity of the suburbs
of St Alexander Nevsky. This building was constructed by the Empress Elizabeth, and intended
for a nunnery, but was wisely converted to its
present use by the present Empress, who
ordered upon her coming to the Crown that the
nuns who were in it might do as they liked, leave
it immediately or continue in it as long as they
lived, but no more should be permitted to go in,
and her Majesty has endowed it with a salary of
some thousand pounds a year. General Betskoy,
the Director of all those useful Societies, invited
the Baron, Mr Howard[106] and myself to see it,
and to show us a particular mark of respect, met
us there.

The number of children of rank are about
three hundred. The whole number is seven hundred. They are taken in from two years old to
four, and go out after being there fifteen years.
There are five classes. The first wear white silk,
and long green aprons and bibs, the second
light brown, the third and the others were in
plain colours, and the lowest in chocolate. The
dress of the bourgeoises is coarser than that of
the young ladies.

The classes are kept by themselves according to their rank and age, and separately
instructed in history and geography. They
obtain, besides a grammatical knowledge of their
native tongue, the French, German and Italian
languages, and receive lessons in dancing, music
and drawing, according to the bent of their
geniuses. Great attention is paid to all the
classes: if any of them appear to have a taste
for the polite arts, it is cultivated, and they have
the best masters appointed to instruct them, as
the Empress often expresses a wish that some of
the inferior rank may come out qualified to

undertake a governess's place and prevent so
many French teachers being encouraged in Russia. In the room[107] of these finer accomplishments, the lower class of the bourgeoises are
employed in the management of household
affairs, they prepare and wash their own linen,
are taught to make bread and are trained to the
art of cookery.

Mr Howard looked into every part of the
Convent, and asked many questions. We went
into the kitchen and into the bakehouse to taste
the bread which was just drawn out of the oven:
in short, no place was omitted; and from the
conversation Mr Howard and I had together, I
thought he approved of things in general very
much, and remarked what cheerful countenances there appeared in all the children; but he,
I think, very justly, disapproved of their hair
being powdered, and looked close to their
heads, and turning to me, said: 'I would not suffer any children in my school to powder. Don't
you think it is wrong, for it is only a covering for
dirt in children.' We were shown the garden,
and at the further end of it into a room which is
the dairy. A table was spread with cheese and
cream, brown bread, and the finest butter I had
tasted since I left England.

After we had regaled ourselves, we
returned to Madame La Font's[108] parlour, and
she showed us the theatre, an elegant circular
room, neatly painted. Madame La Font and the
young ladies very politely invited us to come and
see them act a play, but our time was too much
taken up, we could not accept the invitation. We
went into another room, which was hung with
the designs, paintings, charts, genealogical table,
and other trophies of the young ladies. Prizes
are annually distributed among those who distinguish themselves. They consist chiefly of ribbands, which are worn in bows at their side.

We returned home, and I believe I may say
all of us exceedingly pleased with our morning's
entertainment. This noble Establishment
afforded me much pleasure, and the sight of the
great order and regularity, and good manage-

---

[106]   John Howard (1726–90), the prison reformer. See *Studies*, I.

[107]   i.e. instead of.

[108]   The headmistress.

ment everything was conducted with, and the happy countenances of all the children impressed such an agreeable idea on my memory, that I think I shall never forget it.

Source: Edited from *An English Lady at the Court of Catherine the Great. The Journal of Baroness Elizabeth Dimsdale*, 1781, edited by A.G. Cross, Cambridge, 1989, pp.47–9.

Document 44

Catherine II on national education

Letter from Catherine II to Grimm (in French), 27 February 1775

But listen a moment, you *philosophes* who form no sect. You would be charming, adorable people if you would have the kindness to draw up a plan of studies for young people, from the ABC to university level inclusive. You will tell me it is indiscreet of me to ask you this; but I am told that there must be three types of schools; and since I have never followed any formal course of studies or been to Paris, and have neither learning nor intelligence, the result is that I have no idea what the curriculum should or even could be, or where to find all this out, if not from you. I really do need to have some idea of how a university is run, and how to organize a system of secondary and primary schools. While waiting to see whether or not you will listen to my prayer, I know what I am going to do: I shall flip through the *Encyclopédie*, I shall certainly find in it everything I should and should not do.[109]

Source: *Sbornik imperatorskogo russkogo istoricheskogo obshchestva*, volume 23, St Petersburg, 1878, p.19.

Section 9 Catherine, literature and revolution

Document 45

Radíshchev on censorship and serfdom

Published book (in Russian), 'A Journey from St Petersburg to Moscow',[110] 1790

(a) The government, having recognized the usefulness of printing, has allowed everyone the right to make use of it; but having also recognized that control of thought will nullify its good intention in granting freedom of the press, it has entrusted censorship, or the supervision of printed books, to the Board of Public Morals. Now the Board's duty in this respect may simply be to forbid the sale of harmful books. But even this form of censorship is unnecessary. One stupid official of the Board of Public Morals can do the greatest harm to enlightenment and put back the advance of reason for years. He will prohibit some useful invention, some new thought, and thus deprive everyone of something great.

Let everyone publish whatever enters his head. If anyone finds himself libelled, let him seek his remedy at law. I am serious. Words are not always deeds, thoughts are not crimes. These are the rules laid down in the *Instruction for a New Code of Law.*[111]

(b) Free men, who have committed no crime, are put in chains and sold like cattle. Oh, laws! Your wisdom often lies only in your

---

[109] In the event, Catherine's *Statute on National Education* (1786), providing for primary and secondary education and theoretically open to all classes, was modelled on the Austrian system introduced by Joseph II. Catherine founded no new universities (Moscow University was founded by the Empress Elisabeth in 1755).

[110] Alexander Radishchev (1749–1802) was educated at Catherine's court and studied at Leipzig under her patronage (document 41). He availed himself of the public right, granted by Catherine in 1783, to set up a printing press (hitherto a state monopoly) subject to registration and the submission of publications to the police. In 1790 he published his polemical *Journey from St. Petersburg to Moscow* (available in an English translation by L. Wiener, Harvard University Press, 1958), which the St Petersburg police chief apparently approved without reading.

[111] In the discussion of 'treason', where Catherine criticizes censorship.

style! Is this not an open mockery of you? And, still worse, a mockery of the sacred name of freedom. Oh, if these slaves, weighed down with their heavy bonds, were to go mad in their despair, and, with the iron that fetters their freedom, should smash our heads, the heads of their inhuman masters, and should stain their fields crimson with our blood! What would the state lose thereby? Great men would soon arise from them to take the place of the slain, but men with another outlook and without the right to oppress.

Source: Puteshestviye iz Peterburga v Moskvu, edited by G. Ionin, Moscow, 1961, pp.104–5, 141.

Document 46

Catherine II on Radishchev's Journey from St Petersburg to Moscow

Catherine's notes, forwarded to the Secret Chancellery (in Russian), June/July 1790
This book was published in 1790. The name of the publisher does not appear, nor is there any indication of permission to publish at the beginning; however, at the end, it says: '*By permission of the Board of Public Morals*'. This is probably a lie, or the result of an oversight. The aim of this book is clear on every page: the author, filled and infected with the French madness, seeks in every conceivable way to lessen respect for authority and the authorities and to make the people discontented with their masters and superiors. He is certainly a Martinist,[112] or something similar, is quite knowledgeable and well-read. He is of a gloomy disposition, sees everything in dark black colours and hence has a jaundiced outlook. He has considerable imagination and is quite outspoken in his writing.

The author is an absolute deist and not an adherent of the Eastern Orthodox creed. The author sets out his purpose, namely to demonstrate the inadequacy and faults of the existing form of government. According to his philosophy (the current French one), all classes are to be equal in the name of Man and his supposed rights. A principle is advanced which is destructive of the laws, indeed the very principle which has turned France upside down.[113] He purports to lament the deplorable condition of the peasant class, although it is indisputable that there is no better lot in the whole world than that enjoyed by our peasants under a good master. Throughout the book it is obvious that the author has little respect for the Christian religion and has arbitrarily substituted for it certain ideas not in conformity with Christianity and the civil law. Spleen and impatience have been everywhere vented against everything that is established, and have produced a particular line of thought, borrowed, however, from various semi-philosophers of the age, such as Rousseau and Raynal[114] and similar hypochondriacs.

The author refers to the peasants and their lack of freedom and the troops who are also not free because of the discipline and organization, and he inclines towards stirring up peasants against landowners and men against officers; the author does not like the words 'peace' and 'quiet'. Kings are harshly attacked: one passage ends with these words: '*How power should be combined with freedom for their mutual benefit*'. It may be assumed that he is aspiring to follow the current immoral example of France; this is more likely in as much as the author everywhere seeks the opportunity to attack the ruler and authority. An ode, quite manifestly seditious, in which kings are threatened with execution. The example of Cromwell is presented in a praiseworthy light. These pages are of criminal intent, absolutely seditious. He places his hopes in a peasant rebellion. There is included a eulogy of Mirabeau,[115] who is fit to be hanged many times over.

Source: Addendum to D.A. Babkin, *Protsess A.N. Radishcheva,* Moscow-Leningrad, 1952, pp.157–8, 160.

---

[112]   Freemason, follower of the mystic Saint Martin. Radishchev was not in fact a mason.

[113]   Radishchev upheld the rights and equality of man, the social contract, and the peasants' right to self-defence against their masters.

[114]   Radishchev admitted that he was influenced by Raynal's anti-colonial *Philosophical and political history of the two Indies* (1781).

[115]   Honoré Gabriel Riqueti, Comte de Mirabeau (1749–91), French writer, orator and revolutionary.

Document 47

Radishchev's 'confession'

*Questions drafted by Catherine II and put to Radish-
chev under interrogation in the Secret Chancellery, and
report of his answers (in Russian), July 1790*

Question 5: What was your intention in writing
this book?

Answer: My main aim in writing the book
was to win fame as an author and to enhance his
[*sic*] public reputation. However, now that it has
been pointed out to him, he sees for himself that
it is full of base, audacious and licentious
expressions, which he profoundly regrets. He
did not, however, take France as his model,
though he himself admits the similarity of circumstances, for he wrote the book before the
French Revolution.

Question 6: Were you not a member of the
Martinist circle?

Answer: Not only has he never been a Martinist, but he denounces their views, as appears
in the book itself on pages 93 and 315.

Question 9: Is he not a deist? for the
thoughts expressed on pages 114, 115 and 116
are not in accordance with the Eastern Orthodox creed.

Answer: To this he replied that he had
always been a Christian, and remained true to
the dogmas in which he was born. As for what he
wrote on those pages, he wrote it entirely out of
intellectual speculation and the desire to show
that he is more a philosopher than a Christian.

Question 10: On pages 119, 120, 121, 122,
123, why do you denounce the existing form of
government and describe its faults?

Answer: To this he replied. I never intended
to denounce the existing form of government. I
considered the *Provincial Statute* a wise piece of
legislation, such as is not found elsewhere. On
those pages I wrote of the abuses that can occur,
of which, I confess, it was not my business to
judge and which, moreover, he cannot identify,
since he wrote out of his head in reliance on
popular rumour about various alleged abuses.

Question 14: Why did he denounce the condition of the peasant class, although he knows
that there is no better lot anywhere than that
enjoyed by the Russian peasants under a good
master?

Answer: My denunciation was only aimed at
one event described there. Moreover I am myself
convinced that under a good master our
peasants are better off than anywhere. I wrote
that part out of my head, thinking that among
the landowners there are some monsters, as it
were, who, abandoning the laws of honour and
decency, sometimes commit such appalling acts,
and by writing about them, I thought to deter
such wicked men from this kind of disgraceful
actions.

Question 23: Why do you wish to abolish
censorship?

Answer: I confess my error. I thought that
one could do without censorship, but now I see
from my own experience that it is beneficial,
particularly so when it exists as it does under our
present Lawgiver, when indeed it can save many
erroneous thinkers like myself from the ruin to
which I have truly brought myself as a result of
my weak reasoning.

Question 24: Between pages 306 and 340,
among the thoughts on censorship appear the
following words: '*He was a czar. In whose head, say,
can there be more inconsistencies, than in the head of a
czar?*' What do you think of these words?

Answer: I confess that they are very audacious; but nowhere there did I intend any
allusion to the sacred person of Her Imperial
Majesty. I was only referring to those rulers
notorious in history for their wicked actions. As
for the Autocrat who astounds the world with
her sage and humane rule, I can only say, by
contrast, that if I offended her, it was the result
of temporary madness on my part. I wrote those
bold words without any reason, since I have
always revered the sacred person of Her Imperial
Majesty in my heart.[116]

Source: Arkhiv Knyazya Vorontsova, Book 5, Moscow, 1872,
pp.431–2, 433, 434, 438–9, 440–1.

---

[116] Catherine ordered Radishchev to be tried and sentenced (*sic*) by the St Petersburg criminal court.
Sentence of death was imposed and confirmed by the Senate and the Imperial Council. In September,
Catherine commuted the sentence to ten years' exile in Siberia. The Russian ambassador in London
commented: 'What a sentence, and what a commutation for a mere indiscretion! What will they do, then, for
crime and for real revolt?' Catherine allowed Radishchev to travel at a leisurely pace, accompanied by his
family. He was allowed to return after Catherine's death, but took his own life in 1802.

Document 48

Catherine II on the French Revolution

Letter from Catherine II to Grimm (in French),
14 April 1792

The Jacobins[117] everywhere proclaim that they are going to kill me, and that for this purpose they have despatched three or four men, of whose whereabouts I hear from all quarters. I think if they really had such a design, they would not spread the news around so as to reach me. At Warsaw, Mazzei[118] has made a bet that by 3rd May I shall no longer be in this world. I consider myself conscience-bound to write to you on that date, so that you may know that I am still alive.

As soon as I can, I shall give those scoundrels a drubbing, and show them what is what.[119] So, at the end of the Eighteenth Century, it is apparently praiseworthy to assassinate people! And then they tell me that it was Voltaire who preached all this! See how they dare to slander people. I think that Voltaire would rather stay where he was buried than find himself in the company of Mirabeau at St Geneviève's.[120] But when will someone put an end to all these crimes? It is strange in all this that all the courts are following the lead of the King and Queen of France, who, in all their actions, have only shown inaction.[121]

Source: Sbornik imperatorskogo russkogo istoricheskogo obshchestva, volume 23, St Petersburg, 1878, p.565.

Document 49

Catherine II on freemasonry in Russia

Questions drafted by Catherine II and put to Novikóv[122] under interrogation in the Secret Chancellery, and her comments on his replies (in Russian), Summer 1792

Question 3

Since you knew that the establishment and profession of any new religious or dissenting sect is harmful to the state and prohibited by the government, you must now reveal your reason and motive for devoting yourself to this subversive activity, and when you first began it, under what circumstances, and also who first involved you in this sect?

Comments

He says: 'I never thought that freemasonry was objectionable to the government'. So he says. This in itself proves that he gave no thought to obedience, still less to complying with the positive laws of state under which all secret meetings are strictly forbidden. But of course he was unaware of this; yes, and did not want to make himself aware either. As to his allegation that they met openly, this is a lie, proved by the fact that in the rules of their meetings, written in his hand, he refers to the meetings as secret.

---

[117]   Extreme revolutionary party then in the ascendancy in France.

[118]   Italian revolutionary.

[119]   Catherine refers to the second (1793) partition of Poland.

[120]   The Panthéon in Paris, where Voltaire's body was reinterred after the Revolution.

[121]   The following year Louis XVI and Marie-Antoinette were guillotined.

[122]   Novikóv, a prominent editor and publicist of philanthropic views, was a Mason and Rosicrucian. In 1792, Catherine, who had hitherto tolerated Masonic activities, had Novikóv incarcerated without trial in the fortress of Schlüsselburg and charged with (a) holding secret meetings, (b) swearing obedience to the Duke of Brunswick, (c) correspondence in cipher with the Prussian Minister, Wöllner, (d) unauthorized publication of masonic books, (e) trying to enlist the Grand Duke Paul into masonry. Like Radishchev, he was sentenced to death. Catherine commuted this to 15 years' imprisonment. Novikóv was released after her death, a broken man,

Regarding the fact that he and others named in his writings, such as Prince Trubetskóy and others (as is clear from his papers), corresponded with the Princes of Brunswick[123] and Cassel, the Prussian Minister, Wöllner, and others, without government permission, and asked to be admitted under their protection and direction, and thereby placed themselves under absolute obedience to them – such conduct on their part, as subjects of an autocrat, can certainly not be considered well-intentioned; rather it may be inferred that they acted in violation of their duties to monarch and state.

Question 12

It is known, from two orders of prohibition made against you at the wish of her Imperial Majesty and from papers taken from you, that you had the audacity to print and sell books such as inspire aversion to the Church and the Christian faith, and also to obedience to the authorities.

Question 13

Who wrote, translated and censored these books, and were the university authorities aware of this?

Question 15

In the answers that you gave in Moscow, you said that you published these forbidden books only for distribution among the Masons: but in fact it has emerged that you put them on sale, and furthermore called these books 'moral' and written to rebut freethinkers. These expressions of yours reveal your cunning and your dissimulation of your evil intentions. Common sense alone proves this: for if they had been moral books, the government would not have forbidden you to print them; and if you yourself had really thought them moral, there would have been no need to restrict their circulation to the Masons. So should you not reveal the real truth about this?

Comments

Not only Novikov, but the entire membership is guilty of translating, printing, concealing the books from inspection and selling them after inspection. For they saw that the books were harmful to the state and had already been banned by the government; even so they printed them secretly and sold them. Does this not clearly prove their criminal intent against the government?

Question 25

Here in Russia it is absolutely forbidden by law to maintain any secret correspondence in code. You, however, concealed your meetings from the government, and invented a code in letters and secret signs. You are to explain why you instituted such a correspondence.

Question 31

Is it consistent with your oath of allegiance to the state, to swear an oath in your meeting that you will have no secret from the principal of the lodge?

Comments

The force of the oath sworn by them must be construed as in the question: for in Russia no oath of any kind may be taken without permission of the government.

Source: Sbornik imperatorskogo russkogo istoricheskogo obshchestva, volume 2, St Petersburg, 1868, pp.112, 115, 123, 125, 127.

Document 50

Catherine II on enlightenment and revolution

Letter from Catherine II to Grimm (in French), 22 February 1794
Do you remember that the late King of Prussia[124] claimed to have been told by Helvétius[125] that the

---

[123] Grand Master of the Rosicrucians.

[124] Frederick the Great.

[125] Claude Adrien Helvétius (1715–71), anticlerical *philosophe*. His *On Man, his intellectual faculties and his education* (1772) was dedicated to Catherine.

aim of the *philosophes* was to overturn all thrones, and that the *Encylopédie* was written with no other end in view than to destroy all kings and all religions? Do you also remember that you never wished to be included among the *philosophes*? Well, you were right. The sole aim of the whole movement, as experience is proving, is to destroy. But whatever they may say and do, the world will never do without some authority.

Source: Sbornik imperatorskogo russkogo istoricheskogo obshchestva, volume 23, St Petersburg, 1878, p.539.

References

Blanning, T.C.W. (1989) 'Frederick the Great and Enlightened Absolutism', in H.M. Scott (ed.), *Enlightened Absolutism. Reform and Reformers in Later Eighteenth-Century Europe*, Macmillan, London.

Lentin, A. (ed.) (1985) *Enlightened Absolutism (1760–1790), A Documentary Sourcebook*, Avero Eighteenth-Century Publications, Newcastle-upon-Tyne.

Madariaga, I. de (1989) 'Catherine the Great', in H.M. Scott (ed.), *Enlightened Absolutism. Reform and Reformers in Later Eighteenth-Century Europe*, Macmillan, London.

Cesare Beccaria
Extracts from On Crimes and Punishments

Prepared for the Course Team by
Clive Emsley

Contents

Cesare Beccaria
Extracts from On Crimes and Punishments

Cesare Beccaria (1738–94) was born into the nobility of northern Italy, educated by Jesuits in Parma, and graduated with a degree in Law from the University of Pavia in 1758. He spent most of his adult life occupying public offices in the administration of his native Milan. Typical of many of the intelligentsia of eighteenth-century Italy, much of his thought was directed to practical, and especially economic, ends. He is credited with being among the first to propose the introduction of a metric system, and his Elementi di economia pubblica, *published ten years after his death, explored and developed many of the ideas of political economy. However he is best remembered for his pamphlet* Dei Delitti e delle Pene *('On Crimes and Punishments') from which the following extracts are taken.*

The pamphlet, first published anonymously in Tuscany in 1764, was an instant success allegedly running through six editions in eighteen months. Translations into other European languages rapidly followed; a translation into French, by the philosophe the Abbé Morellet, appeared in 1766; an English edition was published the following year. The English translator commented that 'perhaps no book, on any subject, was ever received with more avidity, more generally read, or more universally applauded'.

As will be clear from the extracts, the book is redolent with the Enlightenment tenets of rationality and humanitarianism. In some respects Beccaria exaggerated the evils of the criminal justice system of his day; already, when he wrote, reformers were beginning to question many of the existing procedures and the different legal and penal systems in Europe were being moderated by some of those who worked within them. Beccaria's pamphlet provided an eloquent and powerful focus for the reformers; indeed much of its success probably stemmed from the fact that it gave voice to the thoughts and the hopes of others. (All footnotes with [Paolucci] or [Beccaria] after them are derived from the edition given in the source at the end of this text).

Introduction

If we glance at the pages of history, we will find that laws, which surely are, or ought to be, compacts of free men, have been, for the most part, a mere tool of the passions of some, or have arisen from an accidental and temporary need. Never have they been dictated by a dispassionate student of human nature who might, by bringing the actions of multitude of men into focus, consider them from this single point of view: the *greatest happiness shared by the greatest number.*[1] Happy are those few nations that have not waited for the slow succession of coincidence and human vicissitude to force some little turn for the better after the limit of evil has been reached, but have facilitated the intermediate progress by means of good laws. And humanity owes a debt of gratitude to that philosopher who, from the obscurity of his isolated study, had the courage to scatter among the multitude the first seeds, so long unfruitful, of useful truths.[2]

The true relations between sovereigns and their subjects, and between nations, have been discovered. Commerce has been reanimated by the common knowledge of philosophical truths diffused by the art of printing, and there has sprung up among nations a tacit rivalry of industriousness that is most humane and truly worthy of rational beings. Such good things we owe to the productive enlightenment of this age. But very few persons have studied and fought against the cruelty of punishments and irregularities of criminal procedures, a part of legislation that is as fundamental as it is widely neglected in almost all of Europe. Very few persons have undertaken

---

[1] 'La massima felicità divisa nel maggior numero'. Many approximations of this celebrated formula are no doubt to be found in the extensive literature of eudemonistic [eudemonia: a moral philosophy which regards actions as good if they tend to produce happiness] and hedonistic ethics which originated with the ancient Greeks, but there is no question that Jeremy Bentham, who made the formula famous, first encountered it here. [Paolucci]

[2] Perhaps Jean-Jacques Rousseau. [Paolucci]

to demolish the accumulated errors of centuries by rising to general principles, curbing, at least, with the sole force that acknowledged truths possess, the unbounded course of ill-directed power which has continually produced [...] the most cold-blooded barbarity. And yet the groans of the weak, sacrificed to cruel ignorance and to opulent indolence; the barbarous torments, multiplied with lavish and useless severity, for crimes either not proved or wholly imaginary; the filth and horrors of a prison, intensified by that cruellest tormentor of the miserable, uncertainty – all these ought to have roused that breed of magistrates who direct the opinions of men.

The immortal Montesquieu[3] has cursorily touched upon this subject. Truth, which is one and indivisible, has obliged me to follow the illustrious steps of that great man, but the thoughtful men for whom I write will easily distinguish my traces from his. I shall deem myself happy if I can obtain, as he did, the secret thanks of the unknown and peace-loving disciples of reason, and if I can inspire that tender thrill with which persons of sensibility respond to one who upholds the interests of humanity.

Adherence to a strictly logical sequence would now lead us to examine and distinguish the various kinds of crimes and modes of punishment; but these are by their nature so variable, because of the diverse circumstances of time and place, that the result would be a catalogue of enormous and boring detail. By indicating only the most general principles and the most dangerous and commonest errors, I will have done enough to disabuse both those who, from a mistaken love of liberty, would be ready to introduce anarchy, and those who would like to see all men subjected to a monastic discipline.

But what are to be the proper punishments for such crimes? Is the death-penalty really *useful* and *necessary* for the security and good order of society? Are torture and torments *just,* and do they attain the *end* for which laws are instituted? What is the best way to prevent crimes? Are the same punishments equally effective for all times? What influence have they on customary behaviour? These problems deserve to

be analysed with that geometric precision which the mist of sophisms, seductive eloquence, and timorous doubt cannot withstand. If I could boast only of having been the first to present to Italy, with a little more clarity, what other nations have boldly written and are beginning to practise, I would account myself fortunate. But if, by defending the rights of man and of unconquerable truth, I should help to save from the spasm and agonies of death some wretched victim of tyranny or of no less fatal ignorance, the thanks and tears of one innocent mortal in his transports of joy would console me for the contempt of all mankind.

The origin of punishments, and the right to punish

Laws are the conditions under which independent and isolated men united to form a society. Weary of living in a continual state of war, and of enjoying a liberty rendered useless by the uncertainty of preserving it, they sacrificed a part so that they might enjoy the rest of it in peace and safety. The sum of all these portions of liberty sacrificed by each of his own good constitutes the sovereignty of a nation, and their legitimate depository and administrator is the sovereign. But merely to have established this deposit was not enough; it had to be defended against private usurpations by individuals each of whom always tries not only to withdraw his own share but also to usurp for himself that of others. Some tangible motives had to be introduced, therefore, to prevent the despotic spirit, which is in every man, from plunging the laws of society into its original chaos. These tangible motives are the punishments established against infractors of the laws. I say 'tangible motives' because experience has shown that the multitude adopt no fixed principles of conduct and will not be released from the sway of that universal principle of dissolution which is seen to operate both in the physical and the moral universe, except for motives that directly strike the senses. These motives, by dint of repeated representation to the mind, counterbalance the powerful

---

[3]   Beccaria was greatly excited and influenced by Montesquieu's *Persian Letters* (1721) and *The Spirit of the Laws* (1748). [Paolucci]

impressions of the private passions that oppose the common good. Not eloquence, not declamations, not even the most sublime truths have sufficed, for any considerable length of time, to curb passions excited by vivid impressions of present objects.

It was, thus, necessity that forced men to give up part of their personal liberty, and it is certain, therefore, that each is willing to place in the public fund only the least possible portion, no more than suffices to induce others to defend it.[4] The aggregate of these least possible portions constitutes the right to punish; all that exceeds this is abuse and not justice; it is fact but by no means right.[5]

Punishments that exceed what is necessary for protection of the deposit of public security are by their very nature unjust, and punishments are increasingly more just as the safety which the sovereign secures for his subjects is the more sacred and inviolable, and the liberty greater.

Mildness of punishments

It is evident that the purpose of punishment is neither to torment and afflict a sensitive being, nor to undo a crime already committed. Can there, in a body politic which, far from acting on passion, is the tranquil moderator of private passions – can there be a place for this useless cruelty, for this instrument of wrath and fanaticism, or of weak tyrants? Can the shrieks of a wretch recall from time, which never reverses its course, deeds already accomplished? The purpose can only be to prevent the criminal from

inflicting new injuries on its citizens and to deter others from similar acts. Always keeping due proportions, such punishments and such method of inflicting them ought to be chosen, therefore, which will make the strongest and most lasting impression on the minds of men, and inflict the least torment on the body of the criminal.

Who, in reading history, can keep from cringing with horror before the spectacle of barbarous and useless torments, cold-bloodedly devised and carried through by men who called themselves wise? What man of any sensibility can keep from shuddering when he sees thousands of poor wretches driven by a misery either intended or tolerated by the laws (which have always favoured the few and outraged the many) to a desperate return to the original state of nature – when he sees them accused of impossible crimes, fabricated by timid ignorance, or found guilty of nothing other than being true to their own principles, and sees them lacerated with meditated formality and slow torture by men gifted with the same senses, and consequently with the same passions? Happy spectacle for a fanatical multitude!

For a punishment to attain its end, the evil which it inflicts has only to exceed the advantage derivable from the crime; in this excess of evil one should include the certainty of punishment and the loss of the good which the crime might have produced.[6] All beyond this is superfluous and for that reason tyrannical. Men are regulated in their conduct by the repeated impression of evils they know, and not according

---

[4] Cf. Rousseau, *Social Contract*, II, 4: 'It is granted that all which an individual alienates by the social compact is only that part of his power, his property, and his liberty, the use of which is important to the community; but we must also grant that the sovereign is the only judge of what is important to the community'. [Paolucci]

[5] Note that the word 'right' is not opposed to the word 'might'; the first is rather a modification of the second – that modification, to be precise, which is most advantageous to the greater number. And by 'justice' I mean nothing more than the bond required to maintain the unity of particular interests which would otherwise dissolve into the original state of insociability. [Beccaria]
Care must be taken not to attach to this word 'justice' the idea of some real thing, as of a physical force or of an existent being; it is simply a human way of conceiving things, a way that has an enormous influence on everyone's happiness. Much less have I in mind that other kind of justice which emanates from God, and which relates directly to the punishments and rewards of the life to come. [Paolucci]

[6] Considering the law of the 'state of nature', Locke writes (*Second Treatise*, II, 12): 'Each transgression may be punished to that degree and with so much severity as will suffice to make it an ill bargain to the offender, give him cause to repent, and terrify others from doing the like' (Library of Liberal Arts edn., No. 31 [New York, 1952], p. 9). [Paolucci]

to those of which they are ignorant. Given, for example, two nations, in one of which, in the scale of punishments proportioned to the scale of crimes, the maximum punishment is perpetual slavery, and in the other the wheel; I say that the first shall have as much fear of its maximum punishment as the second; whatever reason might be adduced for introducing to the first the maximum punishment of the other could similarly be adduced to justify intensification of punishments in the latter, passing imperceptibly from the wheel to slower and more ingenious torments, and at length to the ultimate refinements of a science only too well known to tyrants.

In proportion as torments become more cruel, the spirits of men, which are like fluids that always rise to the level of surrounding objects, become callous, and the ever lively force of the passions brings it to pass that after a hundred years of cruel torments the wheel inspires no greater fear than imprisonment once did. The severity of punishment of itself emboldens men to commit the very wrongs it is supposed to prevent; they are driven to commit additional crimes to avoid the punishment for a single one. The countries and times most notorious for severity of penalties have always been those in which the bloodiest and most inhumane of deeds were committed, for the same spirit of ferocity that guided the hand of the legislators also ruled that of the parricide and assassin. On the throne it dictated iron laws for vicious-spirited slaves to obey, while in private, hiddenly, it instigated the slaughter of tyrants only to make room for new ones.

Two other baneful consequences derive from the cruelty of punishments, interfering with the avowed purpose of preventing crimes. The first is that it is not easy to establish a proper proportion between crime and punishment because, however much an industrious cruelty may have multiplied the variety of its forms, they cannot exceed in force the limits of endurance determined by human organization and sensibility. When once those limits are reached, it is impossible to devise, for still more injurious and atrocious crimes, any additional punishment that

could conceivably serve to prevent them. The other consequence is that impunity itself results from the atrocity of penalties. Men are bound within limits, no less in evil than in good; a spectacle too atrocious for humanity can only be a passing rage, never a permanent system such as the laws must be, for if [the laws] are really cruel, they must either be changed or fatal impunity will follow from the laws themselves.

I conclude with this reflection that the scale of punishments should be relative to the state of the nation itself. Very strong and sensible impressions are demanded for the callous spirits of a people that has just emerged from the savage state. A lightning bolt is necessary to stop a ferocious lion that turns upon the shot of a rifle. But to the extent that spirits are softened in the social state, sensibility increases and, as it increases, the force of punishment must diminish if the relation between object and sensory impression is to be kept constant.[7]

The death penalty

This useless prodigality of torments, which has never made men better, has prompted me to examine whether death is really useful and just in a well-organized government.

What manner of right can men attribute to themselves to slaughter their fellow beings? Certainly not that from which sovereignty and the laws derive. These are nothing but the sum of the least portions of the private liberty of each person; they represent the general will, which is the aggregate of particular wills. Was there ever a man who can have wished to leave to other men the choice of killing him? Is it conceivable that the least sacrifice of each person's liberty should include sacrifice of the greatest of all goods, life? And if that were the case, how could such a principle be reconciled with the other, that man is not entitled to take his own life? He must be, if he can surrender that right to others or to society as a whole.

The punishment of death, therefore, is not a right, for I have demonstrated that it cannot be such; but it is the war of a nation against a citizen whose destruction it judges to be necessary

---

[7] Cf. Montesquieu, *Spirit*, VI, 12: 'Experience shows that in countries remarkable for the lenity of their laws the spirit of the inhabitants is as much affected by slight penalties as in other countries by severer punishments'. [Paolucci]

or useful. If, then, I can show that death is neither useful nor necessary I shall have gained the cause of humanity.

There are only two possible motives for believing that the death of a citizen is necessary. The first: when it is evident that even if deprived of liberty he still has connections and power such as endanger the security of the nation – when, that is, his existence can produce a dangerous revolution in the established form of government. The death of a citizen thus becomes necessary when a nation is recovering or losing its liberty or, in time of anarchy, when disorders themselves take the place of laws. But while the laws reign tranquilly, in a form of government enjoying the consent of the entire nation, well defended externally and internally by force, and by opinion, which is perhaps even more efficacious than force, where executive power is lodged with the true sovereign alone, where riches purchase pleasures and not authority, I see no necessity for destroying a citizen, except if his death were the only real way of restraining others from committing crimes; this is the second motive for believing that the death penalty may be just and necessary.

It is not the intensity of punishment that has the greatest effect on the human spirit, but its duration, for our sensibility is more easily and more permanently affected by slight but repeated impressions than by a powerful but momentary action. The sway of habit is universal over every sentient being; as man speaks and walks and satisfies his needs by its aid, so the ideas of morality come to be stamped upon the mind only by long and repeated impressions. It is not the terrible yet momentary spectacle of the death of a wretch, but the long and painful example of a man deprived of liberty, who, having become a beast of burden, recompenses with his labours the society he has offended, which is the strongest curb against crimes. That efficacious idea – efficacious, because very often repeated to ourselves – 'I myself shall be reduced to so long and miserable a condition if I commit a similar misdeed' is far more potent than the idea of death, which men envision always at an obscure distance.

The death penalty becomes for the majority a spectacle and for some others an object of compassion mixed with disdain; these two sentiments rather than the salutary fear which the laws pretend to inspire occupy the spirits of the spectators. But in moderate and prolonged punishments the dominant sentiment is the latter, because it is the only one. The limit which the legislator ought to fix on the rigour of punishments would seem to be determined by the sentiment of compassion itself, when it begins to prevail over every other in the hearts of those who are the witnesses of punishment, inflicted for their sake rather than for the criminal's.

For a punishment to be just it should consist of only such gradations of intensity as suffice to deter men from committing crimes. Now, the person does not exist who, reflecting upon it, could choose for himself total and perpetual loss of personal liberty, no matter how advantageous a crime might seem to be. Thus the intensity of the punishment of a life sentence of servitude, in place of the death penalty, has in it what suffices to deter any determined spirit. It has, let me add, even more. Many men are able to look calmly and with firmness upon death – some from fanaticism, some from vanity, which almost always accompanies man even beyond the tomb, some from a final and desperate attempt either to live no longer or to escape their misery. But neither fanaticism nor vanity can subsist among fetters or chains, under the rod, under the yoke, in a cage of iron, where the desperate wretch does not end his woes but merely begins them. Our spirit resists violence and extreme but momentary pains more easily than it does time and incessant weariness, for it can, so to speak, collect itself for a moment to repel the first, but the vigour of its elasticity does not suffice to resist the long and repeated action of the second.

With the death penalty, every example given to the nation presupposes a new crime; with the penalty of a lifetime of servitude a single crime supplies frequent and lasting examples. And if it be important that men frequently observe the power of the laws, penal execution ought not to be separated by long intervals; they, therefore, presuppose frequency of the crimes. Thus, if this punishment is to be really useful, it somehow must not make the impression on men that it should; that is, it must be useful and not useful at the same time. To anyone raising the argument that perpetual servitude is as painful as death and therefore equally cruel, I will reply that, adding up all the moments of unhappiness of servitude, it may well be even more cruel; but these are drawn out over an entire lifetime, while the pain of death exerts its whole force in a moment. And precisely this is the advantage of penal servitude, that it inspires terror in the spectator more than in the sufferer, for the former considers the entire sum of unhappy moments, while the latter is distracted from the thought of future misery by that of the present moment. All evils are magnified in the imagination, and the sufferer finds compensations and consolations unknown and incredible to spectators who substitute their own sensibility for the callous spirit of a miserable wretch.

This, more or less, is the line of reasoning of a thief or an assassin – men who find no motive weighty enough to keep them from violating the laws, except the gallows or the wheel.[8] I know that cultivation of the sentiments of one's own spirit is an art that is learned through education; but although a thief may not be able to give a clear account of his motives, that does not make them any the less operative: 'What are these laws that I am supposed to respect, that place such a great distance between me and the rich man? He refuses me the penny I ask of him and, as an excuse, tells me to sweat at work that he knows nothing about. Who made these laws? Rich and powerful men who have never deigned to visit the squalid huts of the poor, who have never had to share a crust of moldy bread amid the innocent cries of hungry children and the tears of a wife. Let us break these bonds, fatal to the majority and only useful to a few indolent tyrants; let us attack the injustice at its source. I will return to my natural state of independence; I shall at least for a little time live free and happy with the fruits of my courage and industry. The day will perhaps come for my sorrow and repentance, but it will be brief, and for a single day of suffering I shall have many years of liberty and of pleasures. As king over a few, I will correct the mistakes of fortune and will see these tyrants grow pale and tremble in the presence of one whom with an insulting flourish of pride they used to dismiss to a lower level

than their horses and dogs.' Then religion presents itself to the mind of the abusive wretch and, promising him an easy repentance and an almost certain eternity of happiness, does much to diminish for him the horror of that ultimate tragedy.

But he who foresees a great number of years, or even a whole lifetime to be spent in servitude and pain, in sight of his fellow citizens with whom he lives in freedom and friendship, slave of the laws which once afforded him protection, makes a useful comparison of all this with the uncertainty of the result of his crimes, and the brevity of the time in which he would enjoy their fruits. The perpetual example of those whom he actually sees the victims of their own carelessness makes a much stronger impression upon him than the spectacle of a punishment that hardens more than it corrects him.

The death penalty cannot be useful, because of the example of barbarity it gives men. If the passions or the necessities of war have taught the shedding of human blood, the laws, moderators of the conduct of men, should not extend the beastly example, which becomes more pernicious since the inflicting of legal death is attended with much study and formality. It seems to me absurd that the laws, which are an expression of the public will, which detest and punish homicide, should themselves commit it, and that to deter citizens from murder, they order a public one. Which are the true and most useful laws? Those pacts and those conditions which all would observe and propose, while the voice of private interest, which one cannot help hearing, is either silent or in accord with that of the public. What are the sentiments of each and every man about the death penalty? Let us read them in the acts of indignation and contempt with which everyone regards the hangman, who is, after all, merely the innocent executor of the public will, a good citizen contributing to the public good, an instrument as necessary to the internal security of a people as valorous soldiers are to the external. What then is the origin of this contradiction? And why, in spite of reason, is

---

[8]   Breaking on the wheel was a form of execution used in continental Europe for particularly severe offences. The guilty man was stretched over a wooden cross and had his limbs broken by the executioner with an iron bar. The body was then exhibited on a wheel. [eds]

this sentiment indelible in men? Because men, in the most secret recess of their spirits, in the part that more than any other still conserves the original form of their first nature, have always believed that one's own life can be in the power of no one, except necessity alone which, with its sceptre of iron, rules the universe.

What must men think when they see learned magistrates and high ministers of justice, who, with calm indifference, cause a criminal to be dragged, by slow proceedings, to death; and while some wretch quakes in the last throes of anguish, awaiting the fatal blow, the judge who, with insensitive coldness, and perhaps even with secret satisfaction in his personal authority, passes by to enjoy the conveniences and the pleasures of life? 'Ah!' they will say, 'these laws are but the pretexts of force; the studied and cruel formalities of justice are nothing but a conventional language for immolating us with great security, like victims destined for sacrifice to the insatiable idol of despotism. Assassination, which is represented to us as a terrible misdeed, we see employed without any repugnance and without excitement. Let us take advantage of the example given us. Violent death seemed to be a terrible spectacle in their descriptions, but we see that it is the affair of a moment. How much less terrible must it be for one who, not expecting it, is spared almost all there is in it of pain!'

Such are the dangerous and fallacious arguments employed, if not with clarity, at least confusedly, by men disposed to crimes, in whom, as we have seen, the abuse of religion is more potent than religion itself.

If one were to cite against me the example of all the ages and of almost all the nations that have applied the death penalty to certain crimes, my reply would be that the example reduced itself to nothing in the face of truth, against which there is no prescription; the history of men leaves us with the impression of a vast sea of errors, among which, at great intervals, some rare and hardly intelligible truths appear to float on the surface. Human sacrifices were once common to almost all nations, yet who will dare to defend them? That only a few societies, and for a short time only, have abstained from applying

the death penalty, stands in my favour rather than against me, for that conforms with the usual lot of great truths; which are about as long-lasting as a lightning flash in comparison with the long dark night that envelops mankind. The happy time has not yet arrived in which truth shall be the portion of the greatest number, as error has heretofore been. And from this universal law those truths only have been exempted which Infinite Wisdom has chosen to distinguish from others by revealing them.

The voice of a philosopher is too weak to contend against the tumults and the cries of so many who are guided by blind custom, but the few wise men who are scattered over the face of the earth shall in their heart of hearts echo what I say; and if the truth, among the infinite obstacles that keep it from a monarch, in spite of himself, should ever reach as far as his throne, let him know that it comes there with the secret approval of all men; let him know that in his worthy presence the bloody fame of conquerors will be silences, and that posterity, which is just, assigns him first place among the peaceful trophies of the Tituses, of the Antonines, and of the Trajans.[9]

How fortunate humanity would be if laws were for the first time being decreed for it, now that we see on the thrones of Europe monarchs who are beneficent, who encourage peaceful virtues, the sciences, the arts, who are fathers to their peoples, crowned citizens, the increase of whose authority constitutes the happiness of subjects, because it removes that intermediate despotism, the more cruel because less secure, which represses popular expressions of esteem which are ever sincere and ever of good omen when they can reach the throne! If these monarchs, I say, suffer the old laws to subsist, it is because of the infinite difficulties involved in stripping from errors the venerated rust of many centuries. This surely is a reason for enlightened citizens to desire, with greater ardour, the continual increase of their authority.

Banishment and confiscations

Anyone who disturbs the public peace, who does not obey the laws, that is, the conditions under

---

[9] Titus Flavius Sabinus Vespasianus (AD 407–81), Marcus Ulpius Trajanus (AD 52–117), and Antoninus Pius (AD 86–161) were all Roman emperors who were noted for their beneficence and concern for the welfare of their subjects [Beccaria]

which men agree to support and defend one another, must be excluded from society – he must be banished from it.

It seems that banishment should be imposed on those who, being accused of an atrocious crime, have against them a great probability, but no certainty of guilt; but for this it is necessary to have a statute as little arbitrary and as precise as possible, which condemns to banishment whoever has forced upon the nation the fatal alternative either of fearing or of unjustly punishing him, leaving him, however, the sacred right to prove his innocence. The motives should, therefore, be stronger against a citizen than against a foreigner, against a person accused for the first time than against one who has often been accused.

But should a person banished and excluded forever from the society of which he was a member be deprived of his possessions? Such a question may be viewed in various aspects. The loss of possessions is a punishment greater than that of banishment; in some cases, therefore, according to the crimes, all or a part of one's possessions should be forfeited, and in others, none. Forfeiture of all should follow when the banishment prescribed by the law is such that it nullifies all ties between society and a delinquent citizen; in that case, the citizen dies and the man remains. With respect to the body politic, [civil death] should produce the same effect as natural death. It would seem, then, that the possessions of which the criminal is deprived should pass to his legitimate heirs rather than to the ruler, since death and such banishment are the same with regard to the body politic. But it is not on the grounds of this subtlety that I dare to disapprove of the confiscation of goods. If some have maintained that confiscations have served to restrain vengeful acts and abuses of personal power, they fail to consider that, although punishments produce some good, they are not always therefore just, for to be so they must be necessary; even a useful injustice cannot be tolerated by the legislator who means to close all doors against that watchful tyranny which entices with temporary advantages and with the apparent happiness of a few illustrious persons, disdainful of the ruin to come and the tears of multitudes in obscurity. Confiscations put a price on the heads of the weak, cause the innocent to suffer the punishment of the guilty, and force the innocent themselves into the desperate necessity of committing crimes. What spectacle can be sadder than that of a family dragged into infamy and misery by the crimes of its head which the submission ordained by the laws would hinder the family from preventing, even if it had the means to do so.

Infamy

Infamy is a mark of public disapprobation that deprives the criminal of public esteem, of the confidence of his country, and of that almost fraternal intimacy which society inspires. It cannot be determined by law. The infamy which the law inflicts, therefore, must be the same as that which arises from the relations of things, the same that is dictated by universal morality, or by the particular morality of particular systems, which are legislators of vulgar opinions and of that particular nation. If one [set of opinions] differs from the other, either the law suffers a loss of public respect or the ideas of morality and probity vanish in spite of declamations that can never withstand the weight of example. Whoever declares actions to be infamous that are in themselves indifferent diminishes the infamy of actions that are really such.

Corporal and painful punishments should not be applied to crimes founded on pride, which derive glory and nourishment out of pain itself; far more suitable are ridicule and infamy – punishments that check the pride of fanatics with the pride of the onlookers, and from the tenacity of which even truth itself can hardly work its way loose, with slow and obstinate efforts. Thus by opposing forces against forces, and opinions against opinions, the wise legislator breaks down the admiration and surprise of the populace occasioned by a false principle, the correctly deduced consequences of which tend to conceal from popular minds the original absurdity.

The punishments of infamy should neither be too frequent nor fall upon a great number of persons at one time – not the first, because the true and too often repeated effects of matters of opinion weaken the force of opinion itself, and not the second, because the infamy of many resolves itself into the infamy of none.

This is the way to avoid confounding the relations and the invariable nature of things, which, not being limited by time and operating incessantly, confounds and overturns all limited regulations that stray from its course. It is not only the arts of taste and pleasure that have as their universal principle the faithful imitation of nature, but politics itself, at least that which is true and lasting, is subject to this universal maxim, for it is nothing other than the art of properly directing and co-ordinating the immutable sentiments of men.

Promptness of punishment

The more promptly and the more closely punishment follows upon the commission of a crime, the more just and useful will it be. I say more just, because the criminal is thereby spared the useless and cruel torments of uncertainty, which increase with the vigour of imagination and with the sense of personal weakness; more just, because privation of liberty, being itself a punishment, should not precede the sentence except when necessity requires. Imprisonment of a citizen, then, is simply custody of his person until he be judged guilty; and this custody, being essentially penal, should be of the least possible duration and of the least possible severity. The time limit should be determined both by the anticipated length of the trial and by seniority among those who are entitled to be tried first. The strictness of confinement should be no more than is necessary to prevent him from taking flight or from concealing the proofs of his crimes. The trial itself should be completed in the briefest possible time. What crueller contrast than the indolence of a judge and the anguish of a man under accusation – the comforts and pleasures of an insensitive magistrate on one side, and on the other the tears, the squalor of a prisoner? In general, the weight of punishment and the consequence of a crime should be that which is most efficacious for others, and which inflicts the least possible hardship upon the person who suffers it; one cannot call legitimate any society which does not maintain, as an infallible principle, that men have wished to subject themselves only to the least possible evils.

I have said that the promptness of punishment is more useful because when the length of time that passes between the punishment and the misdeed is less, so much the stronger and more lasting in the human mind is the association of these two ideas, *crime and punishment*, they then come insensibly to be considered, one as the cause, the other as the necessary inevitable effect. It has been demonstrated that the association of ideas is the cement that forms the entire fabric of the human intellect; without this cement pleasure and pain would be isolated sentiments and of no effect. The more men depart from general ideas and universal principles, that is, the more vulgar they are, the more apt are they to act merely on immediate and familiar associations, ignoring the more remote and complex ones that serve only men strongly impassioned for the object of their desires; the light of attention illuminates only a single object, leaving the others dark. They are of service also to more elevated minds, for they have acquired the habit of rapidly surveying many objects at once, and are able with facility to contrast many partial sentiments one with another, so that the result, which is action, is less dangerous and uncertain.

Of utmost importance is it, therefore, that the crime and the punishment be intimately linked together, if it be desirable that, in crude, vulgar minds, the seductive picture of a particularly advantageous crime should immediately call up the associated idea of punishment. Long delay always produces the effect of further separating these two ideas; thus, though punishment of a crime may make an impression, it will be less as a punishment than as a spectacle, and will be felt only after the horror of the particular crime, which should serve to reinforce the feeling of punishment, has been much weakened in the hearts of the spectators.

Another principle serves admirably to draw even closer the important connection between a misdeed and its punishment, namely, that the latter be as much in conformity as possible with the nature of the crime. This analogy facilitates admirably the contrast that ought to exist between the inducement to crime and the counterforce of punishment, so that the latter may deter and lead the mind toward a goal the very opposite of that toward which the seductive idea of breaking the laws seeks to direct it.

Those guilty of lesser crimes are usually punished either in the obscurity of a prison or by transportation, to serve as an example, with a distant and therefore almost useless servitude, to nations which they have not offended. Since men are not induced on the spur of the moment to commit the gravest crimes, public punishment of a great misdeed will be regarded by the majority as something very remote and of improbable occurrence; but public punishment of lesser crimes, which are closer to men's hearts, will make an impression which, while deterring them from these, deters them even further from the graver crimes. A proportioning of punishments to one another and to crimes should comprehend not only their force but also the manner of inflicting them.

The certainty of punishment. Mercy

One of the greatest curbs on crimes is not the cruelty of punishments, but their infallibility, and, consequently, the vigilance of magistrates, and that severity of an inexorable judge which, to be a useful virtue, must be accompanied by a mild legislation. The certainty of a punishment, even if it be moderate, will always make a stronger impression than the fear of another which is more terrible but combined with the hope of impunity; even the least evils, when they are certain, always terrify men's minds, and hope, that heavenly gift which is often our sole recompense for everything, tends to keep the thought of greater evils remote from us, especially when its strength is increased by the idea of impunity which avarice and weakness only too often afford.

Sometimes a man is freed from punishment for a lesser crime when the offended party chooses to forgive – an act in accord with beneficence and humanity, but contrary to the public good – as if a private citizen, by an act of remission, could eliminate the need for an example, in the same way that he can waive compensation for the injury. The right to inflict punishment is a right not of an individual, but of all citizens, or of their sovereign. An individual can renounce his own portion of right, but cannot annul that of others.

As punishments become more mild, clemency and pardon become less necessary. Happy the nation in which they might some day be considered pernicious! Clemency, therefore, that virtue which has sometimes been deemed a sufficient substitute in a sovereign for all the duties of the throne, should be excluded from perfect legislation, where the punishments are mild and the method of judgement regular and expeditious. This truth will seem harsh to anyone living in the midst of the disorders of a criminal system, where pardons and mercy are necessary to compensate for the absurdity of the laws and the severity of the sentences. This, which is indeed the noblest prerogative of the throne, the most desirable attribute of sovereignty, is also, however, the tacit disapprobation of the beneficent dispensers of public happiness for a code which, with all its imperfections, has in its favour the prejudice of centuries, the voluminous and imposing dowry of innumerable commentators, the weighty apparatus of endless formalities, and the adherence of the most insinuating and least formidable of the semi-learned. But one ought to consider that clemency is a virtue of the legislators and not of the executors of the laws, that it ought to shine in the code itself rather than in the particular judgements. To make men see that crimes can be pardoned or that punishment is not their necessary consequence foments a flattering hope of impunity and creates a belief that, because they might be remitted, sentences which are not remitted are rather acts of oppressive violence than emanations of justice. What is to be said, then, when the ruler grants pardons, that is, public security to a particular individual, and, with a personal act of unenlightened beneficence, constitutes a public decree of impunity? Let the laws, therefore, be inexorable, and inexorable their executors in particular cases, but let the legislator be tender, indulgent, and humane. Let him, a wise architect, raise his building upon the foundation of self-love and let the general interest be the result of the interests of each; he shall not then be constrained, by partial laws and tumultuous remedies, to separate at every moment the public good from that of individuals, and to build the image of public well-being upon fear and distrust. Wise and compassionate philosopher, let him permit men, his brothers, to enjoy in peace that small portion of happiness which the grand system established by the First Cause, by that *which is*, allows them to enjoy in this corner of the universe.

How to prevent crimes

It is better to prevent crimes than to punish them. This is the ultimate end of every good legislation, which, to use the general terms for assessing the good and evils of life, is the art of leading men to the greatest possible happiness or to the least possible unhappiness.

But heretofore, the means employed have been false and contrary to the end proposed. It is impossible to reduce the turbulent activity of mankind to a geometric order, without any irregularity and confusion. As the constant and very simple laws of nature do not impede the planets from disturbing one another in their movements, so in the infinite and very contrary attractions of pleasure and pain, disturbances and disorder cannot be impeded by human laws. And yet this is the chimera of narrow-minded men when they have power in their grasp. To prohibit a multitude of indifferent acts is not to prevent crimes that might arise from them, but is rather to create new ones; it is to define by whim the ideas of virtue and vice which are preached to us as eternal and immutable. To what should we be reduced if everything were forbidden us that might induce us to crime! It would be necessary to deprive man of the use of his senses. For one motive that drives men to commit a real crime there are a thousand that drive them to commit those indifferent acts which are called crimes by bad laws; and if the probability of crimes is proportionate to the number of motives, to enlarge the sphere of crimes is to increase the probability of their being committed. The majority of the laws are nothing but privileges, that is, a tribute paid by all to the convenience of some few.

Do you want to prevent crimes? See to it that the laws are clear and simple and that the entire force of a nation is united in their defence, and that no part of it is employed to destroy them. See to it that the laws favour not so much classes of men as men themselves. See to it that men fear the laws and fear nothing else. For fear of the laws is salutary, but fatal and fertile for crimes is one man's fear of another. Enslaved men are more voluptuous, more depraved, more cruel than free men. These study the sciences, give thought to the interests of their country, contemplate grand objects and imitate them, while enslaved men, content with the present moment, seek in the excitement of debauchery a distraction from the emptiness of the condition in which they find themselves. Accustomed to an uncertainty of outcome in all things, the outcome of their crimes remains for

them problematical, to the advantage of the passions that determine them. If uncertainty regarding the laws befalls a nation which is indolent because of climate, its indolence and stupidity are confirmed and increased; if it befalls a voluptuous but energetic nation, the result is a wasteful diffusion of energy into an infinite number of little cabals and intrigues that sow distrust in every heart, make treachery and dissimulation the foundation of prudence; if it befalls a brave and powerful nation, the uncertainty is removed finally, but only after having caused many oscillations from liberty to slavery and from slavery back to liberty.

Do you want to prevent crimes? See to it that enlightenment accompanies liberty. Knowledge breeds evils in inverse ratio to its diffusion, and benefits in direct ratio. A daring impostor, who is never a common man, is received with adorations by an ignorant people, and with hisses by an enlightened one. Knowledge, by facilitating comparisons and by multiplying points of view, brings on a mutual modification of conflicting feelings, especially when it appears that others hold the same views and face the same difficulties. In the face of enlightenment widely diffused throughout the nation, the calumnies of ignorance are silenced and authority trembles if it be not armed with reason. The vigorous force of the laws, meanwhile, remains immovable, for no enlightened person can fail to approve of the clear and useful public compacts of mutual security when he compares the inconsiderable portion of useless liberty he himself has sacrificed with the sum total of liberties sacrificed by other men, which, except for the laws, might have been turned against him. Any person of sensibility, glancing over a code of well-made laws and observing that he has lost only a baneful liberty to injure others, will feel constrained to bless the throne and its occupant.

Another way of preventing crimes is to direct the interest of the magistracy as a whole to observance rather than corruption of the laws. The greater the number of magistrates, the less dangerous is the abuse of legal power; venality is more difficult among men who observe one another, and their interest in increasing their personal authority diminishes as the portion that would fall to each is less, especially in comparison with the danger involved in the undertaking. If the sovereign, with his apparatus and pomp, with the severity of his edicts, with the permission he grants for unjust as well as just claims to be advanced by anyone who thinks himself oppressed, accustoms his subjects to fear magistrates more than the laws, [the magistrates] will profit more from this fear than personal and public security will gain from it.

Another way of preventing crimes is to reward virtue. Upon this subject I notice a general silence in the laws of all the nations of our day. If the prizes offered by the academies to discoverers of useful truths have increased our knowledge and have multiplied good books, why should not prizes distributed by the beneficent hand of the sovereign serve in a similar way to multiply virtuous actions? The coin of honour is always inexhaustible and fruitful in the hands of the wise distributor.

Finally, the surest but most difficult way to prevent crimes is by perfecting education – a subject much too vast and exceeding the limits I have prescribed for myself, a subject, I venture also to say, too intimately involved with the nature of government for it ever to be, even in the far-off happy ages of society, anything more than a bare field, only here and there cultivated by a few sages. A great man, who enlightens the world that persecutes him,[10] has indicated plainly and in detail what principal maxims of education are truly useful to men: they are, that it should consist less in a barren multiplicity of things than in a selection and precise definition of them; in substituting originals for the copies of the moral as well as physical phenomena which chance or wilful activity may present to the fresh minds of youths; in leading them toward virtue by the easy way of feeling, and in directing them away from evil by the infallible one of necessity and inconvenience, instead of by the uncertain means of command which obtains only simulated and momentary obedience.

Conclusion

From what has thus far been demonstrated, one may deduce a general theorem of considerable utility, though hardly conformable with custom, the usual legislator of nations; it is this: *In order for punishment not to be, in every instance, an act of violence of one or of many against a private citizen, it must be essentially public, prompt, necessary, the least possible in the given circumstances, proportionate to the crimes, dictated by the laws.*[11]

Source: Cesare Beccaria, *On Crimes and Punishments*, translated and with an introduction by Henry Paolucci, Bobbs-Merrill, Indianapolis, New York, 1963.

---

[10]   Reference is to Rousseau's *Emile.* [Paolucci]

[11]   See Article VII of the 'Declaration of the Rights of Man and of the Citizen,' passed by the revolutionary National Assembly of France, on August 26, 1789: 'The law ought to impose no other penalties but such as are absolutely and evidently necessary; and no one ought to be punished, but in virtue of a law promulgated before the offence, and legally applied'. [Paolucci]

John Howard
Extracts from An Enquiry into the Present State of Prisons

Prepared for the Course Team by
Colin Cunningham

Contents

John Howard
Extracts from An Enquiry into the Present State of Prisons

John Howard (1726–90) was the son of a well-to-do carpet trader in the City of London. Like his father he was a member of the dissenting church; and his reputation is that of a humanitarian philanthropist. Instead of a career in trade Howard purchased a small estate at Cardington in Bedfordshire, and lived as a country gentleman of modest means. He ran his estate as an improving landlord, building cottages and generally fostering improved agriculture. This and his election to the Royal Society (1756) and to the Society for the Encouragement of Arts, Manufactures and Commerce (1758) reveals interests that are fairly typical of an intellectual in the age of Enlightenment. In the 1750s he travelled to Portugal, and was himself imprisoned after capture by a French privateer. His experience of the horrors of gaol may

have stimulated a concern to alleviate suffering; but his active interest in prison reform did not begin for another seventeen years. In 1773 he was elected High Sheriff of Bedfordshire and, most unusually for the time, took seriously his duty to inspect the county gaol. What he found horrified him and launched him on a campaign for prison reform that took him into virtually every prison in England and Wales and most in Europe. In 1777, just ten years after Beccaria's On Crimes and Punishments appeared in England, he published his Enquiry, which was one the most significant early texts of prison reform; and his name is firmly linked to that movement in the Howard League for Prison Reform which is still active today.

Section I

General view of distress in prisons

There are prisons, into which whoever looks will, at first sight of the people confined there, be convinced, that there is some great error in the management of them: the sallow meagre countenances declare, without words, that they are very miserable: many who went in healthy, are in a few months changed to emaciated dejected objects. Some are seen pining under diseases, '*sick and in prison*'; expiring on the floors, in loathsome cells, of pestilential fevers, and the confluent small-pox: victims, I must not say to the cruelty, but I will say to the inattention, of sheriffs, and gentlemen in the commission of the peace.

The cause of this distress is, that many prisons are scantily supplied, and some almost totally unprovided with the necessaries of life.

There are several Bridewells[1] (to begin with them) in which prisoners have no allowance of

FOOD at all. In some, the keeper farms[2] what little is allowed them: and where he engages to supply each prisoner with one or two penny-worth of bread a day, I have known this shrunk to half, sometimes less than half the quantity, cut or broken from his own loaf.

It will perhaps be asked, does not their work maintain them? for every one knows that those offenders are committed to *hard labour*. The answer to that question, though true, will hardly be believed. There are very few Bridewells in which any work is done, or can be done. The prisoners have neither tools, nor materials of any kind; but spend their time in sloth, profaneness and debauchery, to a degree which, in some of those houses that I have seen, is extremely shocking.

The same complaint, *want of food*, is to be found in many COUNTY-GAOLS.[3] In about half

---

[1] Bridewells: otherwise known as houses of correction, these prisons were for minor offenders; dishonest apprentices, prostitutes and vagrants etc., who were sent for corrective discipline and set to work. The name comes from the first such prison established in a derelict royal palace at St Bride's Well in London. [eds]

[2] 'farms': since gaolers were not paid they made their living by selling food, drink and favours to the inmates. It was a regular practice also to sell off, or charge for, a portion of the basic allowance of food supplied by the authorities. [eds]

[3] County gaols: in addition to Bridewells there were small lockups known as town gaols and the major prisons, county gaols, associated with the assize circuits. These held debtors and felons both awaiting trial, awaiting sentence or execution or serving sentences of imprisonment. [eds]

these, debtors have no bread; although it is granted to the highwayman, the house-breaker, and the murderer; and medical assistance, which is provided for the latter, is withheld from the former. In many of these Gaols, debtors who would work are not permitted to have any tools, lest they should furnish felons with them for escape or other mischief. I have often seen those prisoners eating their water-soup (bread boiled in mere water) and heard them say, 'We are locked up and almost starved to death'.

As to the relief provided for Debtors by the benevolent act, 32d of George II[4] (commonly called the lords act, because it originated in their house). I did not find in all England and Wales (except the counties of Middlesex and Surrey) TWELVE DEBTORS who had obtained from their creditors the four-pence a day, to which they had a right by that act: the means of procuring it were out of their reach. In one of my journeys I found near six hundred prisoners, whose debts were under twenty pounds each: some of them did not owe above three or four pounds: and the expense of suing for the aliment is in many places equal to those smaller debts; for which some of these prisoners had been confined several months.

MANY prisons have NO WATER. This defect is frequent in Bridewells, and Town-Gaols. In the felons courts of some County-Gaols there is no water: in some places where there is water, prisoners are always locked up within doors, and have no more than the keeper or his servants to think fit to bring them: in one place they are limited to three pints a day each – a scanty provision for drink and cleanliness!

And as to AIR, which is no less necessary than either of the two preceding articles, and given us by Providence quite *gratis*, without any care or labour of our own; yet, as if the bounteous goodness of Heaven excited our envy, methods are contrived to rob prisoners of this *genuine cordial of life*, as Dr Hales[5] very properly

calls it: I mean by preventing that circulation and change of the salutiferous fluid, without which animals cannot live and thrive. It is well known that air which has performed its office in the lungs, is feculent and noxious.

Air which has been breathed, is made poisonous to a more intense degree by the effluvia from the sick; and what else in prisons is offensive. My reader will judge of its malignity, when I assure him, that my cloaths were in my first journeys so offensive, that in a post-chaise I could not bear the windows drawn up: and was therefore often obliged to travel on horseback. The leaves of my memorandum-book were often so tainted, that I could not use it till after spreading it an hour or two before the fire: and even my antidote, a vial of vinegar, has after using it in a few prisons, become intolerably disagreeable. I did not wonder that in those journies many gaolers made excuses; and did not go with me into the felons wards.

In many Gaols, and in most Bridewells, there is no allowance of STRAW for prisoners to sleep on; and if by any means they get a little, it is not changed for months together, so that it is almost worn to dust. Some lie upon rags, others upon the bare floors. When I have complained of this to the keepers, their justification has been, 'The county allows no straw; the prisoners have none but at my cost'.[6]

The evils mentioned hitherto affect the *health* and *life* of prisoners: I have now to complain of what is pernicious to their MORALS; and that is, the confining [of] all sorts of prisoners together: debtors and felons; men and women; the young beginner and the old offender: and with all these, in some counties, such as are guilty of misdemeanours only; who should have been committed to Bridewell, to be corrected by diligence and labour; but for want of food, and the means of procuring it in those prisons, are in pity sent to such County-Gaols as afford these offenders prison-allowance.

---

[4]   The 'benevolent' act 1769 required that debtors should be maintained in prison by their creditors. [eds]

[5]   Stephen Hales (1677–1761), physiologist, inventor, Fellow of the Royal Society was an Anglican priest and a friend of the antiquarian William Stukeley. Best known for his work on health and agriculture he invented a system of ventilation for use in gaols.

[6]   'at my cost': although there was usually a basic allowance of food, other items were not regularly supplied. It was assumed that the gaoler would provide these out of the profits of the rest of his enterprise. [eds]

Few prisons separate men and women in the day-time. In some counties the Gaol is also the Bridewell: in others those prisons are contiguous, and the yard common. There the petty offender is committed for instruction to the most profligate. In some Gaols you see (and who can see it without pain?) boys of twelve or fourteen eagerly listening to the stories told by practised and experienced criminals, of their adventures, successes, stratagems, and escapes.

I must here add, that in some few Gaols are confined idiots and lunatics. These serve for sport to idle visitants at assizes, and other times of general resort. The insane, where they are not kept separate, disturb and terrify other prisoners. No care is taken of them, although it is probable that by medicines, and proper regimen, some of them might be restored to their senses and to usefulness in life.

I am ready to think, that none who give credit to what is contained in the foregoing pages, will wonder at the havock made by GAOL-FEVER.[7]

Sir John Pringle[8] observes, that 'jails have often been the cause of malignant fevers'; and he informs us, that in the late rebellion in Scotland, above 200 men of one regiment were infected with the jail-fever, by some deserters brought from prisons in England.

Dr Lind,[9] Physician to the Royal Hospital at Haslar, near Portsmouth, shewed me in one of the wards a number of sailors ill of the gaol-fever; brought on board their ship by a man who had been discharged from a prison in London. The ship was laid up on the occasion. That gentleman, in his *Essay on the Health of Seamen*, asserts, that 'The source of infection to our armies and fleets are undoubtedly the jails; we can often trace the importers of it directly from them. It often proves fatal in impressing men on

the hasty equipment of a fleet. The first English fleet sent last war to America, lost by it above 2000 men.' In another place he assures us, that 'the seeds of infection were carried from the guard-ships into our squadrons – and the mortality, thence occasioned, was greater than by all other diseases or means of death put together.'

It were easy to multiply instances of this mischief, but those which have been mentioned are, I presume, sufficient to shew, even if no mercy were to due prisoners, that the Gaol-Distemper is a national concern of no small importance.

How directly contrary this [is] to the intention of our laws with regard to these offenders; which certainly is to correct and reform them! Instead of which, their confinement doth notoriously promote and increase the very vices it was designed to suppress. Multitudes of young creatures, committed for some trifling offence, are totally ruined there.

Section II

Bad customs in prison

A cruel custom obtains in most of our Gaols, which is that of the prisoners demanding of a new comer GARNISH, FOOTING OR (as it is called in London Gaols) CHUMMAGE.[10] 'Pay or strip', are the fatal words. I say *fatal*, for they are so to some, who having no money, are obliged to give up part of their scanty apparel; and if they have no bedding or straw to sleep on, contract diseases, which I have known to prove mortal.

GAMING in various forms is very frequent: cards, dice, skittles, Mississippi and Porto-bello tables, billiards, fives, tennis, etc. In the country the three first are most common; and especially cards. There is scarce a County-Gaol but is

---

[7]   Gaol-fever: this was typhus. In the eighteenth century it was believed to be transmitted by aerial contagion. In fact it is spread by lice. [eds]

[8]   Sir John Pringle (1707–82): Dr John Pringle published *Observations on the Nature and Care of Hospital and Jayl Fevers* in 1750. In it he showed that gaol fever, hospital fever and army fever were one and the same.

[9]   Dr James Lind (1716–94): see Part C, Lind. Lind was surgeon-general in charge of the huge naval hospital at Haslar near Portsmouth built between 1746 and 1762. Previously the navy had relied on outside contractors to treat sick and wounded, often in hulks. [eds]

[10]   Garnish, footing, chummage: this unofficial payment was regularly requested of newcomers to a gaol. The payment was often in the form of buying drinks and was usually paid to the most senior prisoner in the ward. [eds]

furnished with them: and one can seldom go in without seeing prisoners at play. In London, all the sorts that I have named are in use. I am not an enemy to diverting exercise: yet the riot, brawling, and profaneness, that are the usual consequents of their play; the circumstances of debtors gaming away the property of their creditors, which I know they have done in some prisons to a considerable amount; accomplishing themselves in the frauds of gamblers, who, if they be not themselves prisoners, are sure to haunt where gaming is practised; hindering their fellow-prisoners who do not play from walking in the yards while they do, of which inconvenience I have heard them complain: these seem to me cogent reasons for prohibiting all kinds of gaming within the walls of a prison.

LOADING prisoners with HEAVY IRONS, which make their walking, and even lying down to sleep, difficult and painful, is another custom which I cannot but condemn. In some County-Gaols the *women* do not escape this severity: but in London they do: and therefore it is not necessary in the country. The practice must be mere tyranny; unless it proceed from avarice; which I rather suspect; because county-gaolers do sometimes grant dispensations, and indulge their prisoners, men as well as women, with what they call 'the choice of irons', if they will pay for it.

The Marquis Beccaria, in his *Essay on Crimes and Punishments*, page 75, observes that 'Imprisonment being only the means of securing the person of the accused, until he be tried – ought … to be attended with as little severity as possible'. The distress occasioned by chains is increased by varying the towns where Quarter Sessions and Assizes are held: so that prisoners have to walk in irons ten or fifteen miles to their trial: and sometimes to towns that have no prison: where numbers of both sexes are shut up together for many days and nights in one room.

Section IV

An account of foreign prisons

France
In or near Paris are the *Conciergerie, Grand* and *Petit Chatelet, Fort L'Evéque*, the *Bicêtre*, and some others.

My first question at each prison commonly was, 'Whether the Gaoler or Keeper resided in the House?' and the answer was always in the affirmative.

Most Prisons in the city have three or four gates; from 4 to $4\frac{1}{2}$ feet high; separated from each other by a little area or court. Within the inner gate is, in some prisons, a *Turnstile*. The number and lowness of the gates (at each of which you must stoop) and the turnstiles, effectually prevent the prisoners rushing out.

In most of the prisons there are five or six *Turnkeys*; viz two or three at the gates: one walking in the yard, to prevent conferring and plotting (a circumstance to which French Gaolers are very attentive): one at the women's ward: and every day one of them is abroad, or otherwise at leisure. This liberty they have in rotation. They are strictly prohibited, under severe penalties, from receiving anything of the prisoners, directly or indirectly, on any pretence whatever. The Gaoler is obliged to board them; and to pay each of them at least one hundred livres a year. It must be paid quarterly, in presence of the Deputy of the Attorney-General.

I was surprised at seeing that none of the prisoners were in *Irons*. No Gaoler (I was informed) may put them on a prisoner, without an express order from the Judge. And yet in some of the Prisons, there were more criminals than in any of our London Gaols. When I was first there, the number had been recently increased by an insurrection on account of the scarcity of corn. My Reader will perhaps presently see reason to conclude, that the manner in which Prisons are conducted makes the confinement more tolerable, and chains less needful. Indeed it was evident, from the very appearance of the prisoners in most of the Gaols, that humane attention was paid to them.

Most of the courts are paved; and they are washed three or four times a day. One would hardly believe how this freshens the air in the upper rooms. I felt this very sensibly once and again when I was in the chambers: and an Englishman, who had the misfortune to be a prisoner, made the same remark. But I seldom or ever found in any French Prison that offensive smell which I had often perceived in English Gaols. I sometimes thought these courts were the cleanest places in Paris. One circumstance that contributes to it, besides the number of Turnkeys, is, that most of them are near the river.

Prisoners, especially criminals, attend Mass every day, and the Gaoler or a Turnkey with them: but such of them as are Protestants are excused. No person is admitted into any Prison during the time of Divine Service.

As condemned criminals generally throw off all reserve, and by relating their various adventures and success prove pernicious tutors to young and less practised offenders; care is taken to prevent this mischief, by sending those who are sentenced to the Gallies, to a separate Prison at the *Port de St. Bernard*:[11] where they are kept till there is a proper number of them to be carried off. Some continue there many months; but their term commences two days after sentence.

The chambers are opened at seven in the morning from November 1st to Easter; at six from Easter to November: and shut in the evening at six from November 1st to Easter; at seven from Easter to November. But debtors have an hour more at night. This they commonly spend in the court; as they do not choose to be there in the day-time, among felons. Common-side prisoners are obliged to come out of their night-rooms at the fore-mentioned morning-hours. Experience having shewn, that idleness and lying in bed, are productive of the *Scurvy* and other distempers. Women are kept quite separate from men. Where there is but one court-yard, as in the *Conciergerie*, they have the use of it from twelve till two; and the men are shut up. I happened to be in that prison at those hours. The court is fifty-five yards by thirty-eight; and has a fine piazza[12] on three sides; on one side the piazza is double. This was the largest prison in the city before the fire in January 1776.

Those who sleep on straw, pay the Gaoler no fee at entrance, or discharge; but they pay one sou or halfpenny a day; and have clean straw once a month: those in the dungeons, once a fortnight. These are seldom let out; never in the yard.

The Chamber-Rents are all regulated. Those who sleep on beds pay ten sous entrance, and the same when discharged. If they lie alone, they pay five sous a day, if two in a bed, three sous each. The Gaoler finds them clean sheets in summer once in three weeks; in winter once a month. Those who board with him, and have a bed, not a room to themselves, pay a sum not exceeding three livres a day ($2s\ 7d\frac{1}{2}$): but nothing at entrance or discharge. Such boarders as have a chamber to themselves and firing, pay twenty sous a week more: if no fire-place fifteen sous.

Both these sorts have clean sheets in summer once a fortnight; in winter, in three weeks. The Gaoler's servants attend them. There are also half-boarders; and some who have an entire chamber, but no board.

All the Regulations are read in the Chapel to Prisoners, the first Sunday of every month, by the Chaplain; and they hang up in the Prison for common inspection. If any Prisoner tears, or otherwise damages them, he suffers corporal punishment: if a Register or Gaoler does so, he is fined twenty livres: if a Turnkey, he is discharged.

Gaolers and Turnkeys are obliged to visit once a day at least, all the dungeons. I was sorry to find the humanity which is so conspicuous in the 'forementioned, and other excellent rules, so deficient as to continue the use of those subterraneous abodes; which are totally dark, and beyond imagination horrid and dreadful. Poor creatures are confined in them night and day for weeks, for months together. They visit these, I say, daily: and if they find any prisoners sick, they must acquaint the Physician and Surgeon; who visit them; and if needful, order them to more wholesome rooms till they recover.

Flanders

At GHENT in the Prison at the superb *Maison de Ville* each criminal has from the city about fourpence halfpenny English, a day: and provision being there about one-third cheaper than in *London*, some of them save a little out of that allowance after paying for the weekly washing of their linen.

Here is a Prison belonging to the rich Monastery of *Benedictines* in the *Abbey of St Peter*. There are now thirty-five of the fraternity: who have many Lordships, and part of the City in their jurisdiction. The Prison joins to the Abbot's Court-House. Three dreary dungeons down nineteen steps: a little window in each: no prisoners. I went down; but my noting the dimensions of the windows &c. so enraged the Keeper, that he would not indulge my curiosity any farther.

There is at *Ghent* a new Prison building by the States of *Austrian Flanders*. It is a House of

---

[11]   The Prison at the Port de St Bernard was a holding institution where the condemned were kept before being marched in chains across France to the various Bagnes or to the galleys. [eds]

[12]   piazza: a covered colonnade. This was what Howard urged as providing both for circulation of air and covered exercise space for prisoners. [eds]

Correction for all those Provinces (as that at *Vilforde for Austrian Brabant*) and is called LA MAISON DE FORCE. It is situated near a *Canal.* The plan is an *Octagon*: only four sides finished: in one of them were in 1775 one hundred and fifty-nine men criminals: this year one hundred and ninety-one. Another of the sides is for women, of whom there were fifty-nine. In the middle of this court is a bason of running water, for washing all the Linen of the House.

On each of the four floors there is a corridor, or arcade, six feet nine inches wide, quite open to the air of the yard, which, however, is not attended with any inconvenience, even in winter. In the recess of every corridor, except the lowest, is a range of bed-rooms, six feet nine inches by four feet ten, and eight feet eight inches high: the doorway two feet. These are uniformly furnished with a bedstead, six feet and a half by two and a half, a straw bed, a mattress, a pillow, a pair of sheets, two blankets in winter and one in summer. Each room has a little bench, and a shutter to the lattice window (in the door), which, when opened and turned down, serves for a table. In the wall is a little cupboard, two feet by one, and ten inches deep. All the rooms are vaulted to prevent fire from running from story to story. No person is on any pretence admitted into the bed-room of another. They have a clean shirt once a week, and clean sheets once a month. The women have not separate rooms. Some of theirs are ten feet and a half by nine and a half.

In order to [secure] the admission of a prisoner, previous notice must be given by the City or Province that sends him. When he comes, he is shaved, and washed: a Surgeon examines him; and if healthy, he is cloathed with the uniform of the House, which is marked with the number of his room; to it he is conducted by one of the most orderly of the prisoners; who is appointed to that service, and who also acquaints him with the Rules of the House. Commitment from one year to twenty or more.

A bell is rung in the morning to summon the prisoners into the dining-room; in the summer at five; in winter the hour varies with the length of the days. Half an hour after the bell rings, their names are called over; and they go to Prayers in a Chapel. They are then allowed half an hour to breakfast. At noon they have two hours, for dinner; making their beds (which in fair weather they bring out to air); and for recreation. I was present during the whole time the men criminals were at dinner, and much admired the regularity, decency, and order, with which the whole was conducted. Every thing was done at a word given by a Director; no noise or confusion appeared; and this company of near one hundred and ninety stout criminals was governed with as much apparent ease as the most sober and well-disposed assembly in civil society. At night they have an hour for supper &c. The bell gives notice of all these successive hours: it is rung at a window over the gate-way by a *Centinel*, who there overlooks the whole yard; and, should there be any disturbance, is to give the alarm to a company who keep guard.

On the ground-floors of the building are work-rooms. Those for the men are too small for the looms &c. The women's work-room is one hundred and seventeen feet long, twenty-six wide, and nine to the springing of the arch. In this many were spinning and combing wool; mending linen, &c. Others were washing in places proper for that purpose.

An exact account is kept of every circumstance relating to each man's work, in a Book that has fourteen columns. The

1st	Column contains the Names of Prisoners.
2	The Sort of Stuff on which each Man is employed; as *Shalloon, Cloth, Dimity* &c.
3	The Number that is marked on the Piece.
4	The Day it was begun.
5	The Day it was finished.
6	Measure of the whole Piece.
7	Number of Working-Days, the Prisoner was upon it.
8	The Task due per Day.
9	Surplus Work upon the Piece beyond Task.
10	Price of the Piece per Ell.
11	Observations, or Occasional Circumstances: such as *Sick, Lame, difficult Work, first Piece* &c.
12	Payment to Prisoners for Surplus Work.
13	Deficiency of Task.
14	Punishment for the Default.

This last column is written by the Magistrates themselves.

Source: John Howard F.R.S. , *An Enquiry into the Present State of the Prisons in England and Wales with Preliminary observations and an account of some Foreign Prisons,* Warrington, 1777.

James Boswell
Extracts from Journal of a Tour to the Hebrides

Prepared for the Course team by
Angus Calder

Contents

James Boswell
Extracts from Journal of a Tour to the Hebrides

James Boswell (1740–95) was the son of Alexander Boswell, an Ayrshire landowner of ancient family, who became Lord Auchinleck as one of the judges in the Court of Session, Scotland's supreme court in criminal causes. Boswell loved and feared his father. After an erratic youth, including a brief conversion to Roman Catholicism and much debauchery in London, he contrived to meet the great English writer Samuel Johnson in 1763. They became devoted friends. Boswell then embarked on a version of the Grand Tour which included legal studies in Holland, a visit to Berlin where he tried but failed to interview Frederick the Great, a detour to Switzerland where he met Rousseau (whose mistress, it seems, he later managed to sleep with), a visit to Voltaire in France, a sojourn in Italy – and then a bold journey to find General Paoli, leader of local nationalist resistance to the French, in the mountains of Corsica. His Account of Corsica (1768) made him famous as 'Corsica Boswell'. Meanwhile, he settled down as an advocate (barrister) in Edinburgh, maintaining his friendship with Johnson on lengthy visits to London.

He recorded in a detailed journal the trip which he made with Johnson to the Hebrides in 1773. They left Edinburgh on 18 August and returned there on 9 November. Autumnal winds and rain made much of their travel arduous and even, when at sea, dangerous. The good Doctor, as readers soon learned when his Journey to the Western Islands was published in 1775, bore all stoically. Boswell's more excitable account, adapted from his journals, did not reach the public until 1785, the year after his friend's death. It came out as a 'trailer' for Boswell's monumental Life of Johnson, published in 1791.

The first extract here is as printed in 1785. Boswell worked up his account of Johnson's arrival in Edinburgh from notes. His very detailed diary, kept from 18 August to 26 October, was found in a croquet box in a cupboard in Malahide Castle near Dublin in 1930. The second extract is from that. Comparison shows that Boswell, editing his extempore impressions with the devoted help of his friend, the great Shakespearian scholar, Edmond Malone, polished but did not distort them.

Both extracts will be found in the Pottle edition cited in the source: pp.6–12 and pp.202–13. We have made some internal cuts.

Introduction

Luckily Mr Justice (now Sir Robert) Chambers[1], who was about to sail for the East Indies, was going to take leave of his relations at Newcastle, and he conducted Dr Johnson to that town. Mr Scott of University College, Oxford (now Dr Scott of the Commons), accompanied him from thence to Edinburgh. With such propitious convoys did he proceed to my native city. But lest metaphor should make it be supposed he actually went by sea, I choose to mention that he travelled in post-chaises, of which the rapid motion was one of his most favourite amusements.

Dr Samuel Johnson's character – religious, moral, political, and literary – nay, his figure and manner, are, I believe, more generally known than those of almost any man, yet it may not be superfluous here to attempt a sketch of him. Let my readers then remember that he was a sincere and zealous Christian, of high-Church-of-England and monarchical principles, which he would not tamely suffer to be questioned; steady and inflexible in maintaining the obligations of piety and virtue, both from a regard to the order of society and from a veneration for the Great Source of all order; correct, nay stern, in his taste; hard to please and easily offended, impetuous and irritable in his temper, but of a most humane and benevolent heart; having a mind stored with a vast and various collection of learning and knowledge, which he communicated with peculiar perspicuity and force, in rich and choice expression. He united a most logical head with a most fertile imagination, which gave him an extraordinary advantage in arguing, for he could reason close or wide as he saw best for the moment. He could, when he chose it, be the greatest sophist that ever wielded a weapon in the schools of decla-

---

[1] Robert Chambers (1737–1803): lawyer and later a judge in India. While Vinerian Professor of Laws at Oxford, Chambers received much help from Johnson in the preparation of his lectures. [eds]

mation, but he indulged this only in conversation, for he owned that he sometimes talked for victory; he was too conscientious to make error permanent and pernicious by deliberately writing it. He was conscious of his superiority. He loved praise when it was brought to him, but was too proud to seek for it. He was somewhat susceptible of flattery. His mind was so full of imagery that he might have been perpetually a poet. It has been often remarked that in his poetical pieces (which is to be regretted are so few, because so excellent) his style is easier than in his prose. There is deception in this: it is not easier but better suited to the dignity of verse; as one may dance with grace whose motions in ordinary walking – in the common step – are awkward. He had a constitutional melancholy the clouds of which darkened the brightness of his fancy and gave a gloomy cast to his whole course of thinking; yet, though grave and awful in his deportment when he thought it necessary or proper, he frequently indulged himself in pleasantry and sportive sallies. He was prone to superstition but not to credulity. Though his imagination might incline him to a belief of the marvellous and the mysterious, his vigorous reason examined the evidence with jealousy. He had a loud voice and a slow deliberate utterance which no doubt gave some additional weight to the sterling metal of his conversation. Lord Pembroke said once to me at Wilton, with a happy pleasantry and some truth, that 'Dr Johnson's sayings would not appear so extraordinary were it not for his *bow-wow way*', but I admit the truth of this only on some occasions. The *Messiah* played upon the Cante.'bury organ is more sublime than when played upon an inferior instrument, but very slight music will seem grand when conveyed to the ear through that majestic medium. *While therefore Doctor Johnson's sayings are read, let his manner be taken along with them.* Let it, however, be observed that the sayings themselves are generally great; that, though he might be an ordinary composer at times, he was for the most part a Handel. – His person was large, robust, I may say approaching to the gigantic, and grown unwieldly from corpulency. His countenance was naturally of the cast of an ancient statue, but somewhat disfigured by the scars of that *evil* which it was formerly imagined the *royal touch* could cure. He was now in his sixty-fourth year, and was becoming a little dull of hearing. His sight had always been somewhat weak, yet so much does mind govern and even supply the deficiency of organs that his perceptions were uncommonly quick and accurate. His head and sometimes also his body shook with a kind of motion like the effect of a palsy; he appeared to be frequently disturbed by cramps or convulsive contractions, of the nature of that distemper called St Vitus's dance.[2] He wore a full suit of plain brown clothes with twisted-hair buttons of the same colour, a large bushy greyish wig, a plain shirt, black worsted stockings, and silver buckles. Upon this tour, when journeying, he wore boots and a very wide brown cloth great-coat with pockets which might have almost held the two volumes of his folio dictionary, and he carried in his hand a large English oak stick. Let me not be censured for mentioning such minute particulars. Everything relative to so great a man is worth observing. I remember Dr Adam Smith, in his rhetorical lectures at Glasgow, told us he was glad to know that Milton wore latchets in his shoes instead of buckles. When I mention the oak stick, it is but letting Hercules have his club; and by and by my readers will find this stick will bud and produce a good joke.

This imperfect sketch of 'the *combination* and the *form*' of that Wonderful Man whom I venerated and loved while in this world, and after whom I gaze with humble hope now that it has pleased ALMIGHTY GOD to call him to a better world, will serve to introduce to the fancy of my readers the capital object of the following Journal, in the course of which I trust they will attain to a considerable degree of acquaintance with him.

His prejudice against Scotland was announced almost as soon as he began to appear in the world of letters. In his *London, a Poem*, are the following nervous lines:

---

[2] Such they appeared to me; but since the first edition, Sir Joshua Reynolds has observed to me that Dr Johnson's extraordinary gestures were only habits, in which he indulged himself at certain times. When in company where he was not free, or when engaged earnestly in conversation, he never gave way to such habits, which proves that they were not involuntary. I still however think that these gestures were involuntary; for surely had not that been the case, he would have restrained them in the public streets. [Boswell]

For who would leave, unbribed, Hibernia's
land?
Or change the rocks of Scotland for the
Strand?
There none are swept by sudden fate away,
But all, whom hunger spares, with age
decay.[3]

The truth is, like the ancient Greeks and
Romans, he allowed himself to look upon all
nations but his own as barbarians: not only
Hibernia and Scotland, but Spain, Italy, and
France are attacked in the same poem. If he was
particularly prejudiced against the Scots, it was
because they were more in his way; because he
thought their success in England rather
exceeded the due proportion of their real merit;
and because he could not but see in them that
nationality which I believe no liberal-minded
Scotsman will deny. He was indeed, if I may be
allowed the phrase, at bottom much of a *John
Bull*, much of a *true-born Englishman*. There was a
stratum of common clay under the rock of marble. – He was voraciously fond of good eating,
and he had a great deal of that quality called
humour, which gives an oiliness and a gloss to
every other quailty.

I am, I flatter myself, completely a citizen
of the world. In my travels through Holland,
Germany, Switzerland, Italy, Corsica, France, I
never felt myself from home; and I sincerely love
'every kindred and tongue and people and
nation.' I subscribe to what my late truly learned
and philosophical friend Mr Crosbie[4] said: that
the English are better animals than the Scots;
they are nearer the sun, their blood is richer and
more mellow; but when I humour any of them in
an outrageous contempt of Scotland, I fairly own
I treat them as children. And thus I have, at
some moments, found myself obliged to treat
even Dr Johnson.

To Scotland, however, he ventured; and he
returned from it in great good humour, with his
prejudices much lessened, and with very grateful
feelings of hospitality with which he was treated,
as is evident from that admirable work, his *Journey to the Western Islands of Scotland*,[5] which, to my

utter astonishment, has been misapprehended,
even to rancour, by many of my countrymen.

Saturday, 14 August, 1773

On Saturday the fourteenth of August, 1773, late
in the evening, I received a note from him that
he was arrived at Boyd's Inn, at the head of the
Canongate. I went to him directly. He embraced
me cordially, and I exulted in the thought that I
now had him actually in Caledonia. Mr Scott's
amiable manners and attachment to our
Socrates at once united me to him. He told me
that before I came in the Doctor had unluckily
had a bad specimen of Scottish cleanliness. He
then drank no fermented liquor. He asked to
have his lemonade made sweeter, upon which
the waiter with his greasy fingers lifted a lump of
sugar and put it into it. The Doctor in indignation threw it out of the window. Scott said he
was afraid he would have knocked the waiter
down. Mr Johnson told me that such another
trick was played him at the house of a lady in
Paris. He was to do me the honour to lodge
under my roof. I regretted sincerely that I had
not also a room for Mr Scott. Mr Johnson and I
walked arm-in-arm up the High Street to my
house in James's Court; it was a dusky night; I
could not prevent his being assailed by the evening effluvia of Edinburgh. I heard a late baronet
of some distinction in the political world in the
beginning of the present reign observe that
'walking the streets of Edinburgh at night was
pretty perilous and a good deal odoriferous'.
The peril is much abated by the care which the
magistrates have taken to enforce the city laws
against throwing foul water from the windows;
but, from the structure of the houses in the old
town, which consist of many storeys in each of
which a different family lives, and there being no
covered sewers, the odour still continues. A
zealous Scotsman would have wished Mr Johnson to be without one of his five senses upon this
occasion. As we marched slowly along, he grum-
bled in my ear, 'I smell you in the dark!'. But he
acknowledged that the breadth of the street and

---

[3] Boswell is over-sensitive. The lines mean the opposite of what he thinks they say. London is under attack, not
Scotland. [eds]

[4] Andrew Crosbie (d. 1785): advocate at the Scottish bar and famed for his conversational prowess. [eds]

[5] Published in 1775, ten years before Boswell's account. [eds]

the loftiness of the buildings on each side made a noble appearance.

My wife had tea ready for him, which it is well known he delighted to drink at all hours, particularly when sitting up late, and of which his able defence against Mr Jonas Hanway[6] should have obtained him a magnificent reward from the East Indian Company. He showed much complacency upon finding that the mistress of the house was so attentive to his singular habit; and as no man could be more polite when he chose to be so, his address to her was most courteous and engaging, and his conversation soon charmed her into a forgetfulness of his external appearance.

Wednesday, 22 September, 1773

The sheriff had excellent peats, and the evening went on admirably. Mr Johnson said the Lords Orrery, till this, have been writers. The first wrote several plays. The second was Bentley's antagonist; the third[7] wrote the Life of Swift, and several other pieces. His son Hamilton, Earl of Orrery, wrote several papers in the *Adventurer* and *World*. He said he knew well Swift's Lord Orrery. He was a feeble-minded man. He was much hurt by the counter-Life written by Delany. Mr Johnson comforted him by saying they were both right. He had seen most of the good side of Swift, my Lord of the bad. MacLeod asked if it was not wrong in Orrery to expose the defects of a man with whom he lived in intimacy. MR JOHNSON. 'Why no, sir, after the man is dead, and it is done historically.' He said if Lord Orrery had been rich, he would have been a very liberal patron. That his conversation was like his writing, neat and elegant, but without strength. That he grasped at more than his abilities could reach. Tried to pass for a better talker, and a better writer, and a better thinker than he was.

I mentioned my lord's affectation of ending all his letters about Swift in different ways, and never 'I am, etc.,' (an observation which I have heard Sheridan make); and that a foreign lady said to me that this was peculiar to, or at least most frequent among, the English. I took up a volume of Dryden, containing *The Conquest of Granada, Amboyna, The Assignation*, etc., and all of the dedications had such conclusions. Mr Johnson said it was more elegant than 'I am'.

Orrery's attack on his son in his will led us to talk of the dispositions a man should have when dying. I said I did not see why a man should alter his behaviour to those whom he thought ill of when well, merely because he was dying. Mr Johnson said, 'I should not scruple to speak against a party when dying; but not against an individual.' He said it was told of Sixtus Quintus[8] that on his death-bed, in the intervals of his last pangs, he signed death-warrants. Mr Macqueen said he should not do so. He would have more tenderness to heart. Said Mr Johnson, 'I believe I should not either; but Mr Macqueen and I are cowards. It would not be from tenderness of heart, for the heart is as tender when a man is in health as when sick, though his resolution may be stronger. Sixtus Quintus was a sovereign as well as a priest, and if the criminals deserved death, he was doing his duty to the last. You would not think a judge died ill who should be carried off by an apoplectic fit while pronouncing sentence of death. Consider a class of men whose business it is to distribute death – soldiers, who die scattering bullets. Nobody thinks they die ill on that account.'

Talking of biography, he said he did not know any literary man's life in England well-written. It should tell us his studies, his manner of life, the means by which he attained to excellence, his opinion of his own works, and such particulars.

---

[6] Jonas Hanway (1712–86): English philanthropist and traveller; his 'Essay on Tea' (1757) which attacked the 'pernicious' custom of tea-drinking was criticized by both Johnson and Goldsmith. [eds]

[7] Roger Boyle, first earl of Orrery (1621–79) wrote eight heroic plays. Charles Boyle, fourth earl (1676–1731) was editor of the *Letters of Phalaris* which were shown to be spurious by Richard Bentley (1662–1742), Master of Trinity College, Cambridge, and renowned classical scholar. John Boyle, fifth earl of Orrery (1707–62) wrote *Remarks on Swift* (1751). [eds]

[8] Sixtus V (Felice Pevetti; 1521–90) became Pope in 1585. [eds]

His notion as to the poems given by Macpherson as the works of Ossian, was confirmed here.[9] Mr Macqueen always evaded the point, saying that Mr Macpherson's pieces fell far short of what he knew in Erse,[10] and were said to be Ossian's. Said Mr Johnson, 'I hope they do. I am not disputing that you may have poetry of great merit, but that Macpherson's is not a translation from ancient poetry. You do not believe it. I say before you, you do not believe it, though you are very willing that the world should believe it.' Mr Macqueen could not answer to this. Said Mr Johnson, 'I look upon Macpherson's *Fingal* to be as gross an imposition as ever the world was troubled with. Had it been really an ancient work, a true specimen how men thought at that time, it would have been a curiosity of the first rate. As a modern production, it is nothing.'

Mr Johnson said he could never get the meaning of an Erse song. They told him the chorus was generally unmeaning. 'I take it,' said he, 'they are like a song which I remember. It was composed in Queen Elizabeth's time on the Earl of Essex, and the burthen was

Radaratwo, radarati, radaratadara tandore.'

'But,' said Mr Macqueen, 'there would be words to it which had meaning.' Said Mr Johnson, 'I recollect one stanza:

O then bespoke the prentices all,
Living in London both proper and tall,
Fore Essex's sake they would fight all.
Radaratwo, radarati, etc.[11]

When Mr Macqueen began again upon the beauty of Ossian's poetry, Mr Johnson cried, 'Ay, radaratwo, radarati.' Mr Rorie MacLeod, son to the sheriff, said he believed Macpherson's book to be a forgery; for that the Erse songs of Ossian which he had heard had no resemblance

to Macpherson's English. Mr Macqueen is the most obstinate man I ever found. He has not firmness of mind sufficient to break. He is like a supple willow. No sooner is he pressed down than he rises again, just where he was. He always harped on this: 'Macpherson's translations are far inferior to Ossian's originals.' 'Yes,' said I, 'because they are not the same. They are inferior as a shilling is to a guinea, because they are not the same.' It was really disagreeable to see how Macqueen shuffled about the matter.

Thursday, 23 September, 1773

I took Ossian down to the parlour in the morning and tried a test proposed by Mr Rorie. Mr Macqueen had said he had some of him in the original. I made him read what he had, which was a passage on page 50, quarto edition, and Rorie looked on with me on the English, and said it was pretty like. But when Mr Macqueen read a description of Cuchullin's' sword, with a verse translation by Sir James Foulis, Rorie said that was much liker than Macpherson's. Mr Macqueen repeated in Erse a description of one of the horses in Cuchullin's car. Rorie said Macpherson's English was nothing like it.

When Mr Johnson came down, I told him that Mr Macqueen had repeated a passage pretty like; and that he himself had required Macpherson's Ossian to be no liker than Pope's Homer. 'Well,' said he, 'this is just what I always said. He has found names, and stories, and phrases – nay passages in old songs – and with them has compounded his own compositions, and so made what he gives to the world as the translation of an ancient poem.' 'But,' said I, 'it was wrong in him to pretend that there was a poem in six books.' JOHNSON. 'Yes, sir. At a time too when the Highlanders knew nothing of *books* and

---

[9] James Macpherson (1736–96) published *Fragments of Ancient Poetry* ... (1760); this he followed with *Fingal* (1762) and *Temora* (1763), both purporting to be translations from the work of an ancient Gaelic poet 'Ossian'. Samuel Johnson, and others, challenged the poems' authenticity. (Macpherson was never able to produce authentic manuscripts of the poems.) It is now agreed that the Ossianic poems were a mixture of liberally edited traditional Gaelic poems and passages of Macpherson's own invention. [eds]

[10] Gaelic (Scots or Irish dialects). The Reverend Donald Macqueen was a learned Skye minister. [eds]

[11] This droll quotation, I have since found, was from a song in honour of the Earl of Essex, called *Queen Elizabeth's Champion*, which is preserved in a collection of Old Ballads, in three volumes, published in London in different years between 1720 and 1730. [Boswell]

nothing of *six* – or perhaps were got the length of counting six. We have been told, by Condamine,[12] of a nation that could count no more than four. I'd tell Monboddo[13] that. It would help him. There's as much charity in helping a man downhill as in helping him uphill.' BOSWELL. 'I don't think there's as much charity'. JOHNSON. 'Yes sir, if his *tendency* be downwards. Till he's at the bottom, he flounders. Get him to it. and he's quiet. Swift tells that Stella had a trick, which she learnt from Addison, to encourage a very absurd man in absurdity, rather than strive to pull him out of it.'

Mr Macqueen evaded our questions about Ossian in so strange a manner that I said if Macpherson was capitally tried for forgery, two such witnesses would hang him; because the truth that comes from an unwilling witness makes the strongest impression, gives the fullest conviction. Mr Johnson said, 'I should like to see Mr Macqueen examined in one of our courts of justice about Ossian.' Said I, 'Were he to evade as he had done now, in one of our courts, he would be committed.' JOHNSON. 'I hope he would. Sir, he has told Blair[14] a little more than he believes, which is published; and he sticks to it. Sir, he is so much at the head of things here that he has never been accustomed to be closely examined; and so he goes on quite smoothly.' BOSWELL. 'He has never had anybody to work him.' JOHNSON. 'No, sir. And a man is seldom disposed to work himself; though he ought to work himself, to be sure.' Mr Macqueen stood patiently by while all this passed.[15]

Last night Mr Johnson gave us an account of the whole process of tanning, and of the nature of milk and the various operations upon it, as making whey, etc. His variety of knowledge is quite amazing, and it gives one much satisfaction to find such a genius bestowing his attention on the useful arts. Ullinish[16] was much struck with his knowledge; 'and,' said he, 'he is a great orator, sir. It is music to hear this man speak.' A strange thought struck me: to try if he knew anything of an art (or invention, or whatever it should be called), which is no doubt very useful in life, but which certainly lies far out of the way of a philosopher and poet – I mean the trade of a butcher. I began with observing that Banks[17] tells us the art was not known in Otaheite [Tahiti]; for instead of bleeding their dogs to death, they strangle them. This he told me himself; and I supposed that their hogs would certainly be slaughtered in the same way. Mr Johnson said, 'This would be owing to their not having knives, though they have sharp stones with which they can cut a carcass in pieces tolerably.' By degrees, he showed that he knew something even of butchery. He said an ox was knocked down and a calf stunned, but a sheep had its throat cut without anything done to stupefy it. That the butchers had no view to the ease of the animals, but only to make them quiet, which they did not mind with sheep. He said Hales was of opinion that every animal should be blooded without having any blow given to it, because it bleeds better. I said it would be cruel. Mr Johnson said, 'No, sir. There is not much pain if the jugular vein be properly cut.' He said the kennels of Southwark run with blood two or three days in the week. That he was afraid there were slaughter-houses in more streets in London than one thinks – speaking with a kind of horror of butchering. And yet he

---

[12]   Charles Marie de Lacondamine (1701–74), French geographer, explorer of the Amazon and supporter of inoculation. [eds]

[13]   James Burnett, Lord Monboddo (1714–99), Scottish judge, anthropologist and *philosophe* whose views Johnson derided. [eds]

[14]   Hugh Blair (1718–1800), Scottish preacher, who encouraged and defended Macpherson. [eds]

[15]   I think it but justice to say, that I believe Dr Johnson meant to ascribe Mr Macqueen's conduct to inaccuracy and enthusiasm, and did not mean any severe imputation against him. [Boswell]

[16]   Alexander MacLeod of Ullinish, Sherrif Depute and their host. [eds]

[17]   Sir Joseph Banks (1744–1820), the naturalist, who had recently sailed with Cook on his first voyage to 'Otaheite' (Tahiti). [eds]

said that any of us would kill a cow rather than not have beef. I said we *could* not. 'Yes,' said he, 'any one may. The business of a butcher is a trade indeed; that is to say, there is an apprenticeship served to it. But it may be learnt in a month.'

We set out this morning in Ullinish's boat. As we sailed along, Mr Johnson got into one of his fits of railing at the Scots. He owned that we were a very learned nation for about 100 years, from about 1550 to about 1650. But that we lost our learning during the Civil War and had never recovered it. He said we afforded the only instance of a people among whom the arts of civil life did not advance in proportion with learning; that we had hardly any trade, any money, or any elegance before the Union. That it was strange how with all the advantages that other nations have, we had not any of those arts which are the fruit of industry, till we came in contact with a civilized nation. 'We have taught you,' he said; 'and we'll do the same in time to all barbarous nations – to the Cherokees – and at last to the orang-outangs' – laughing as if Monboddo[18] had been present. I said we had wine before the Union. 'No sir,' said he; 'you had some weak stuff, the refuse of France, which would not make you drunk.' BOSWELL. 'I assure you, sir, there was a great deal of drunkenness.' JOHNSON. 'No, sir; there were people who died of dropsies which they contracted in trying to get drunk.'

I must here glean some of his conversation at Ullinish, which I have omitted. He said for five years of his life he made him a bowl of punch every night. He repeated his remark that a man in a ship was worse than a man in a jail. 'The man in a jail,' said he, 'has more room, better food, and commonly better company, and is in safety.' 'Ay, but,' said Mr Macqueen, 'the man in the ship has the pleasing hope of getting to shore.' JOHNSON. 'Sir, I am not talking of a man's getting to shore, but of a man while he is in a ship; and then, I say, he is worse than a man

while he is in a jail. A man in a jail *may* have the pleasing hope of getting out. A man confined for a certain time *has* it.' MacLeod[19] mentioned his schemes for carrying on fisheries, with spirit, and how he would wish to understand well the construction of boats. I said he might go to a dockyard and work, as Peter the Great did. 'Nay,' said Mr Johnson, 'he need not work. Peter the Great had not the sense to see that the mere mechanical work may be done by anybody, and that there is the same art in constructing a vessel whether the boards are well or ill wrought. Sir Christopher Wren might as well have served his time to a bricklayer, and first indeed to a brickmaker.'

There is a beautiful little island in the Loch of Dunvegan, called Isay. MacLeod said he would give it to Mr Johnson, on condition of his residing on it three months in the year, nay, one month. Mr Johnson was highly pleased with the fancy. I have seen him please himself with little things, even with mere ideas, as this was. He talked a great deal of this island – how he would build a house, how he would fortify it, how he would have cannon, how he would plant, how he would sally out and *take* the Isle of Muck; and then he laughed with a glee that was astonishing, and could hardly leave off. I have seen him do so at a small matter that struck him, and was a sport to no one else. Langton told me that one night at the Club[20] he did so while the company were all grave around him; only Garrick in his smart manner addressed him, 'Mighty pleasant, sir; mighty pleasant, sir.' Poor Langton's Will was a sport of this kind; but there I own Mr Johnson carried me along with him, as he made it really most ludicrous; and perhaps the contrast of Chambers's gravity, who had helped Langton to make the Will, gave additional keenness to our risibility. MacLeod humoured Mr Johnson finely as to his island; told him that as it was the practice in this country to name every man by his lands, he begged leave to drink him in the

---

[18]   Monboddo argued that orang-outangs were primitive childlike versions of human beings: 'the infantine state of our species'. Since Darwin this view sounds less absurd than it did to Johnson and most of his contemporaries. [eds]

[19]   Norman MacLeod of Dunvegan, chief of the clan. [eds]

[20]   The famous 'Literary Club' around Johnson, of which Boswell was a member, along with Bennet Langton. [eds]

manner: '*Island Isay,* your health!' Ullinish, Talisker, and Mr Macqueen all joined in their different manners, while Mr Johnson bowed to each in excellent good humour.

We had a fine sail this day. There cannot be a finer harbour than the basin which we saw sheltered from every wind. MacLeod showed us an arm of the sea which runs up with very deep water for a mile, upon which he intends to build a town. We sailed up another arm. The shore was varied with hills and rocks and cornfields, and natural wood or bushes. We landed near to the house of Fernilea. He himself was waiting on the shore, with a horse for Mr Johnson. The rest of us walked up. We found at Fernilea a very comfortable house. His wife is daughter to Bernera.[21] When I took off my *scalck,* with hearty readiness he said, 'Fare fa' you!'[22] His parlour was paved with flagstones, not in squares, but just in the shapes which they naturally had in the quarry. I liked this better. It had more variety. I preferred it by the same rule that Mr Johnson prefers the

variety of the English conclusions of letters to the common style, 'I am, etc.' We had here an excellent dinner, in particular a remarkable leg of boiled mutton with turnips and carrots. MacLeod has really shown us a chief and his clan. We saw some of them with him at Dunvegan. We now saw him with some of them. On both sides there was the most agreeable kindness. I expressed to MacLeod the joy which I had in seeing this. Said he, 'Government has deprived us of our ancient power, but it cannot deprive us of our domestic satisfactions. I would rather drink a bottle of punch in one of their houses' (meaning his people) 'than a bottle of claret in my own.' Here he said at once what every chieftain should think. All that he can get by raising his rents is more luxury in his own house. Is it not far better to share the profits of his estate to a certain degree with his kinsmen, and so have both social intercourse and patriarchal influence? Fernilea seemed to be a worthy, sensible, kind man.

Source: Boswell's Journal of a Tour to the Hebrides with Samuel Johnson LL.D. 1773, edited by Frederick A. Pottle and Charles H. Bennett, Heinemann, 1963.

---

[21]   To Donald Macleod of Bernera. Her husband was Alexander MacLeod of Fernilea. [eds]

[22]   i.e., 'Fair fall you.' [eds]

Franz Joseph Haydn
The Creation

Prepared for the Course Team by
Patricia Howard

Contents

Franz Joseph Haydn
The Creation

In the late Spring of 1791, during his first visit to England, Haydn attended a week-long festival of Handel's music in Westminster Abbey. Among the works performed were the oratorios Messiah *and* Israel in Egypt, *the anthem 'Zadok the Priest'. Haydn was so struck by the brilliance of the performances and the enthusiasm of the audiences that he later described the effect on him as sending him back to begin his studies from scratch: 'it was as if he had known nothing up to that time; he pondered every* [1] *note and learned from those excellent scores the nature of true musical grandeur.' The result of Haydn's ponderings appears in* The Creation, *first performed in Vienna in April 1798. Everything about the work proclaims Haydn's debt to Handel, from the text, originally prepared for Handel, and based on such richly English sources as Milton's poem* Paradise Lost *and the Authorized Version of the Bible, to the lyrical arias and majestic choruses, so reminiscent of* Messiah.

Part One

Sources

The first day

1   INTRODUCTION: Representation of Chaos

2   RECITATIVE with CHORUS

Raphael   In the beginning God created the heaven and the earth; and the earth was without form, and void; and darkness was upon the face of the deep.

Genesis 1:1–4

Chorus   And the Spirit of God moved upon the face of the waters. And God said, Let there be light: and there was light.

Uriel   And God saw the light, that it was good: and God divided the light from the darkness.

3   ARIA with CHORUS

        Now vanish before the holy beams
        The gloomy shades of ancient night
        The first of days appears.
        Now chaos ends, and order fair prevails.
        Affrighted fly hell's spirits black in throngs:
        Down they sink in the deep abyss
        To endless night.

Paradise Lost, Bk. VI, 864–6

Chorus   Despairing cursing rage attends their rapid fall
        A new-created world springs up at God's command.

P.L., VI, 867–77

---

[1]   The quotation comes from a biography of Haydn based on interviews with the composer, Giuseppe Carpani, *Le Haydine*, Milan, 1812, p.162.

The second day

4   RECITATIVE

Raphael   And God made the firmament, and divided the waters   *G. 1:7*
which were under the firmament from the waters which were
above the firmament: and it was so.

> Now furious storms tempestuous rage,
> Like chaff, by the winds impelled are the clouds,
> By sudden fire the sky is inflamed,
> And awful thunders are rolling on high.

Now from the floods in steam ascend reviving showers of rain,   *P.L., VII, 210–15*
The dreary wasteful hail, the light and flaky snow.

5   CHORUS with SOLO

Gabriel   The marv'llous work behold amaz'd
The glorious hierarchy of heaven;
And to th' ethereal vaults resound
The praise of God, and of the second day.

Chorus   And to th' ethereal vaults resound
The praise of God, and of the second day.

The third day

6   RECITATIVE   *G. 1:9–10*

Raphael   And God said, Let the waters under the heavens be
gathered together to one place, and let the dry land appear: and
it was so. And God called the dry land earth, and the gathering of
waters called He seas: and God saw that it was good.

7   AIR

> Rolling in foaming billows,   *P.L., VII, 285–7*
> Uplifted, roars the boisterous sea.
> Mountains and rocks now emerge,
> Their tops among the clouds ascend.
> Through th' open plains, outstretching wide,   *P.L., VII, 298–302*
> In serpent error rivers flow.
> Softly purling, glides on
> Through silent vales the limpid brook.

8   RECITATIVE

Gabriel   And God said, Let the earth bring forth grass, the herb   *G. 1:11*
yielding seed, and the fruit-tree yielding fruit after his kind, whose
seed is in itself, upon the earth: and it was so.

9   ARIA

> With verdure clad the fields appear,   *P.L., VII, 315–26*
> Delightful to the ravish'd sense;
> By flowers sweet and gay
> Enhanced is the charming sight.
> Here fragrant herbs their odours shed;
> Here shoots the healing plant.
> With copious fruit the expanded boughs are hung;
> In leafy arches twine the shady groves;
> O'er lofty hills majestic forests wave.

10 RECITATIVE

Uriel   And the heavenly host proclaimed the third day, praising
God, and saying,

11 CHORUS

Awake the harp, the lyre awake,   *P.L., VII, 256–9*
And let your joyful song resound.
Rejoice in the Lord, the mighty God;
For He both heaven and earth
Has clothed in stately dress.

The fourth day

12 RECITATIVE

Uriel   And God said, Let there be lights in the firmament of   *G.1:14–16*
heaven, to divide the day from the night, and to give light upon
the earth; and let them be for signs, and for seasons, and for days,
and for years. He made the stars also.

13 RECITATIVE

In splendour bright is rising now the sun,
And darts his rays; a joyful happy spouse,   *Psalm 19:5*
A giant proud and glad
To run his measur'd course
With softer beams, and milder light,
Steps on the silver moon through silent night.
The space immense of th' azure sky
A countless host of radiant orbs adorns.
And the sons of God announced the fourth day,
In song divine, proclaiming thus His power:

14 CHORUS

The heavens are telling the glory of God,   *Ps. 19:1–4*
The wonder of His work displays the firmament.

Trio   To day that is coming speaks it the day,
The night that is gone to following night.

Chorus   The heavens are telling the glory of God,
The wonder of His work displays the firmament.

Trio   In all the lands resounds the word,
Never unperceived, ever understood.

Chorus   The heavens are telling the glory of God,
The wonder of His work displays the firmament.

Part Two

The fifth day

[   ] **15** RECITATIVE

Gabriel And God said, Let the waters bring forth abundantly   G. 1:20
the moving creature that hath life, and fowl that may fly above
the earth in the open firmament of heaven.

[   ] **16** ARIA

On mighty pens uplifted soars   *P.L., VII, 421–35*
The eagle aloft, and cleaves the air,
In swiftest flight, to the blazing sun.
His welcome bids to morn the merry lark,
And cooing calls the tender dove his mate.
[   ]   From ev'ry bush and grove resound
The nightingale's delightful notes;
No grief affected yet her breast,
Nor to a mournful tale were tun'd
Her soft enchanting lays.

[   ] **17** RECITATIVE

Raphael And God created great whales, and every living   G. 1:21
creature that moveth; and God blessed them, saying

Be fruitful all, and multiply.   *P.L., VII, 396–403*
Ye winged tribes, be multiplied,
And sing on every tree; multiply,
Ye finny tribes, and fill each wat'ry deep;
Be fruitful, grow, and multiply,
And in your God and Lord rejoice.

[   ] **18** RECITATIVE

And the angels struck their immortal harps, and the wonders of
the fifth day sung.

[   ] **19** TRIO

Gabriel Most beautiful appear, with verdure young adorn'd,
The gently sloping hills; their narrow sinuous veins
Distil, in crystal drops, the fountain fresh and bright.

Uriel In lofty circles play, and hover in the air,   *P.L., VII, 433–4*
The cheerful host of birds; and as they flying whirl
Their glittering plumes are dy'd as rainbows by the sun.

Raphael See flashing through the deep in thronging swarms   *P.L., VII, 400–1*
The fish a thousand ways around.
Upheaved from the deep, th' immense Leviathan   *P.L., VII, 412–16*
Sports on the foaming wave.

Trio How many are Thy works, O God!   *P.L., VII, 602–604*
Who may their number tell?

[   ] **20** CHORUS and TRIO

The Lord is great, and great His might,
His glory lasts for ever and for evermore.

The sixth day

21 RECITATIVE

Raphael And God said, Let the earth bring forth the living   *G. 1:24*
creature after his kind, cattle, and creeping thing, and beast of
the earth, after his kind.

22 RECITATIVE

Straight opening her fertile womb,   *P.L., VII, 453–81*
The earth obey'd the word,
And teem'd creatures numberless,
In perfect forms, and fully grown.

Cheerful, roaring, stands the tawny lion. With sudden leap
The flexible tiger appears. The nimble stag
Bears up his branching head. With flying mane,
And fiery look, impatient neighs the noble steed.
The cattle, in herds, already seek their food
On fields and meadows green.
And o'er the ground, as plants, are spread
The fleecy, meek, and bleating flocks.
Unnumber'd as the sands, in swarms arose
The hosts of insects. In long dimension
Creeps, with sinuous trace, the worm.

23 ARIA

Now heaven in fullest glory shone   *P.L., VII, 499–516*
Earth smil'd in all her rich attire;
The room of air with fowl is filled;
The water swell'd by shoals of fish;
By heavy beasts the ground is trod:
But all the work was not complete;
There wanted yet that wondrous being,
That, grateful, should God's power admire,
With heart and voice His goodness praise.

24 RECITATIVE

Uriel And God created Man in His own image, in the image of   *G. 1:27*
God created He him. Male and female created He them.
He breathed into his nostrils the breath of life, and Man became   *G. 2:7*
a living soul.

25 ARIA

In native worth and honour clad,   *P.L., IV, 288–301*
With beauty, courage, strength, adorn'd,
Erect, with front serene, he stands
A man, the lord and king of nature all.
His large and arched brow sublime
Of wisdom deep declares the seat!
And in his eyes with brightness shines
The soul, the breath and image of his God.
With fondness leans upon his breast
The partner for him form'd,
A woman, fair and graceful spouse.
Her softly-smiling virgin looks,
Of flow'ry spring the mirror,
Bespeak him love, and joy, and bliss.

26 RECITATIVE

Raphael And God saw everything that He had made, and behold,   *G. 1:31*
it was very good. And the heavenly choir, in song divine, thus
closed the sixth day.

27 CHORUS

Achieved is the glorious work;
The Lord beholds it, and is pleas'd
In lofty strains let us rejoice,
Our song let be the praise of God.

27a TRIO

Gabriel and
Uriel   On Thee each living soul awaits;   *Ps. 104:27–30*
From Thee, O Lord, all seek their food;
Thou openest Thy hand,
And fillest all with good.

Raphael   But when Thy face, O Lord, is hid,
With sudden terror they are struck;
Thou tak'st their breath away,
They vanish into dust.

Gabriel, Uriel
and Raphael   Thou sendest forth Thy breath again,
And life with vigour fresh returns;
Revived earth unfolds new strength
And new delights.

27b CHORUS

Achieved is the glorious work;
Our song let be the praise of God.
Glory to His Name for ever.
He sole on high exalted reigns.
                                    Hallelujah!

Part Three

28 INTRODUCTION (Morning)
RECITATIVE

Uriel   In rosy mantle appears, by music sweet awak'd,
The morning young and fair.
From heaven's angelic choir
Pure harmony descends on ravish'd earth.
Behold the blissful pair,   *P.L., IV, 689*
Where hand in hand they go: their glowing looks
Express the thanks that swell their grateful hearts.
A louder praise of God their lips
Shall utter soon; then let our voices ring,
United with their song.

29 DUET AND CHORUS

Adam and Eve By Thee with bliss, O bounteous Lord,   *P.L., V, 153–208*
               Both heaven and earth are stor'd.
               This world so great, so wonderful.
               Thy mighty hand has fram'd.

Chorus   For ever blessed be His power,
               His Name be ever magnified.

Adam   Of stars the fairest, pledge of day,
               That crown'st the smiling morn;
               And thou, bright sun, that cheer'st the world,
               Thou eye and soul of all;

Chorus   Proclaim in your extended course
               Th' almighty power and praise of God.

Eve   And thou that rul'st the silent night
               And all ye starry hosts,
               Ev'rywhere spreads wide His praise
               In choral songs about.

Adam   Ye mighty elements, by His power
               Your ceaseless changes make;
               Ye dusky mists, and dewy streams,
               That rise and fall thro' th' air;

Chorus   Resound the praise of God our Lord.
               Great His name, and great His might.

Eve   Ye purling fountains, tune His praise;
               And wave your tops, ye pines.
               Ye plants, exhale, ye flowers, breathe
               To Him your balmy scent.

Adam   Ye that on mountains stately tread,
               And ye that lowly creep;
               Ye birds that sing at heaven's gate,
               And ye that swim the stream;

Eve and Adam Ye creatures all, extol the Lord;

Chorus   Ye creatures all, extol the Lord;
               Him celebrate, Him magnify.

Eve and Adam Ye valleys, hills, and shady woods,
               Made vocal by our song,
               From morn till eve you shall repeat
               Our grateful hymns of praise.

Chorus   Hail! bounteous Lord! Almighty, hail!
               Thy word call'd forth this wondrous frame.
               The heavens and earth Thy power adore;
               We praise Thee now and evermore.

☐   30 RECITATIVE

Adam   Our duty we have now perform'd,
             In offering up to God our thanks.
             Now follow me, dear partner of my life,
             Thy guide I'll be; and every step
             Pours new delights into our breasts,
             Shows wonders everywhere.
             Then mayst thou feel and know the high degree
             Of bliss the Lord allotted us,
             And with devoted heart His bounties celebrate.
             Come, follow me, thy guide I'll be.

☐   *Eve*   O thou for whom I am, my help, my shield,   *P.L., IV, 440–1; 635–8*
             My all, thy will is law to me;
             So God our Lord ordains; and from obedience
             Grows my pride and happiness.

☐   31 DUET

Adam   Graceful consort, at thy side
             Softly fly the golden hours;
             Ev'ry moment brings new rapture,
             Ev'ry care is lull'd to rest.

Eve   Spouse adored, at thy side
             Purest joys o'erflow the heart;
             Life and all I have is thine;
             My reward thy love shall be.

☐   *Both*   The dew-dropping morn, O how she quickens all!   *P.L., IV, 641–56*
             The coolness of even, O how she all restores!
             How grateful is of fruits the savour sweet!
             How pleasing is of fragrant bloom the smell!
             But without thee, what is to me
             The morning dew, the breath of even,
             The sav'ry fruit, the fragrant bloom?
                 With thee is every joy enhanced,
                 With thee delight is ever new,
                 With thee is life incessant bliss,
                 Thine, thine it all shall be.

☐   32 RECITATIVE

Uriel   O happy pair! and happy still might be   *P.L., IV, 774–5*
             If not misled by false conceit.
             Ye strive at more than granted is;
             And more desire to know, than know ye should.

☐   33 CHORUS

             Sing the Lord, ye voices all,
             Magnify His name thro' all creation,
             Celebrate His power and glory,
             Let His name resound on high.
             Praise the Lord. Utter thanks.
             Jehovah's praise for ever shall endure.
                                         Amen.

THE CREATION.

PART I.

No. 1. INTRODUCTION.—REPRESENTATION OF CHAOS.

No. 2.

RECITATIVE (Bass).—"IN THE BEGINNING."

RAPHAEL.

And God made the fir - ma - ment, and di - vi - ded the wa-ters which were un-der the fir- ma -

- ment   from the wa - ters   which were   a- bove the fir - ma - ment: and   it   was   so.

Allegro assai.

Allegro assai.

Now   fu - rious storms tem- pes - tu- ous rage,

RECITATIVE (BASS).—"AND GOD SAID, LET THE WATERS."

RAPHAEL.

And God said, Let the wa-ters un-der the heav-ens be gath-er-ed to-geth-er to

one . . place, and let the dry land ap-pear : and it was so. And God call-ed the dry land

earth, and the gathering of waters call-ed he seas, and God saw that it was good.

No. 7.   **AIR (BASS).—"ROLLING IN FOAMING BILLOWS."**

Allegro assai.

si - lent vales . the lim - pid brook,

pp

p

115

through si - lent vales the lim - pid brook.

pp

No. 8. RECITATIVE (SOPRANO).—"AND GOD SAID, LET THE EARTH."

GABRIEL.

And God said, Let the earth bring forth grass, the herb yield-ing

mf

4

seed, and the fruit- tree yield-ing fruit af - ter his kind, whose seed is in it -

7

- self, up - on the earth: and it was so.

f

AIR (SOPRANO).—"WITH VERDURE CLAD."

GABRIEL.

No. 10.   Recitative (Tenor).—"AND THE HEAVENLY HOST."

No. 11.   Chorus.—"AWAKE THE HARP."

No. 12.   RECITATIVE (TENOR).—"AND GOD SAID, LET THERE BE LIGHTS."

END OF PART I.

Part B
Reactions to Classical Antiquity

Contents

David Hume
Of the Standard of Taste

Prepared for the Course Team by
Robert Wilkinson

Contents

David Hume
Of the Standard of Taste

This essay is addressed to the class of well-educated men of letters of the day. Hume could take it for granted that they could read Greek and Latin, and would have read most of the classics that were available at the time in the original. He could also assume their acquaintance with literary classics in other European languages, and consequently in this piece Hume feels free to take examples from Italian, Spanish and French literature from the fourteenth century to his own day.

The piece is written in a belletristic rather than a scholarly manner, without learned apparatus or precise citation. Hume was quite able to adopt a scholarly approach if he so chose, as is shown, for example, by his long and learned essay Of the Populousness of Ancient Nations (1751). The relaxed mode of writing, by Humean standards, in the present essay allows him to address his readers in an informal way, and to flatter them by assuming them to be well-read.

Of the Standard of Taste

The great variety of Taste, as well as of opinion, which prevails in the world, is too obvious not to have fallen under every one's observation. Men of the most confined knowledge are able to remark a difference of taste in the narrow circle of their acquaintance, even where the persons have been educated under the same government, and have early imbibed the same prejudices. But those who can enlarge their view to contemplate distant nations and remote ages, are still more surprised at the great inconsistence and contrariety. We are apt to call *barbarous* whatever departs widely from our own taste and apprehension; but soon find the epithet of reproach retorted on us. And the highest arrogance and self-conceit is at last startled, on observing an equal assurance on all sides, and scruples, amidst such a contest of sentiment, to pronounce positively in its own favour.

As this variety of taste is obvious to the most careless inquirer, so will it be found, on examination, to be still greater in reality than in appearance. The sentiments of men often differ with regard to beauty and deformity of all kinds, even while their general discourse is the same. There are certain terms in every language which import blame, and others praise; and all men who use the same tongue must agree in their application of them. Every voice is united in applauding elegance, propriety, simplicity, spirit in writing; and in blaming fustian, affectation, coldness, and a false brilliancy. But when critics come to particulars, this seeming unanimity vanishes; and it is found, that they had affixed a very different meaning to their expressions. In all matters of opinion and science,[1] the case is opposite; the difference among men is there oftener found to lie in generals than in particulars, and to be less in reality than in appearance. An explanation of the terms commonly ends the controversy: and the disputants are surprised to find that they had been quarrelling, while at bottom they agreed in their judgement.

Those who found morality on sentiment, more than on reason,[2] are inclined to comprehend ethics under the former observation, and to maintain, that, in all questions which regard conduct and manners, the difference among men is really greater than at first sight it appears. It is indeed obvious, that writers of all nations and all ages concur in applauding justice, humanity, magnanimity, prudence, veracity; and in blaming the opposite qualities. Even poets and other authors, whose compositions are chiefly

---

[1]   See note 12 below. [eds]

[2]   An issue considered at length in Hume's *Enquiry Concerning the Principle of Morals* (1751). [eds]

calculated to please the imagination, are yet found, from Homer down to Fenelon,[3] to inculcate the same moral precepts, and to bestow their applause and blame on the same virtues and vices. This great unanimity is usually ascribed to the influence of plain reason, which, in all these cases, maintains similar sentiments in all men, and prevents those controversies to which the abstract sciences are so much exposed. So far as the unanimity is real, this account may be admitted as satisfactory. But we must also allow, that some part of the seeming harmony in morals may be accounted for from the very nature of language. The word *virtue*, with its equivalent in every tongue, implies praise, as that of *vice* does blame; and no one, without the most obvious and grossest impropriety, could affix reproach to a term, which in general acceptation is understood in a good sense: or bestow applause, where the idiom requires disapprobation. Homer's general precepts, where he delivers any such, will never be controverted; but it is obvious, that, when he draws particular pictures of manners, and represents heroism in Achilles, and prudence in Ulysses, he intermixes a much greater degree of ferocity in the former, and of cunning and fraud in the latter, than Fenelon would admit of. The sage Ulysses, in the Greek poet, seems to delight in lies and fictions, and often employs them without any necessity or even advantage. But his more scrupulous son, in the French epic writer, exposes himself to the most imminent perils, rather than depart from the most exact line of truth and veracity.

The admirers and followers of the Alcoran insist on the excellent moral precepts interspersed throughout that wild and absurd performance. But it is to be supposed, that the Arabic words, which correspond to the English, equity, justice, temperance, meekness, charity, were such as, from the constant use of that tongue, must always be taken in a good sense: and it would have argued the greatest ignorance, not of morals, but of language, to have mentioned them with any epithets, besides those of applause and approbation. But would we know, whether the pretended prophet had really attained a just sentiment of morals, let us attend to his narration, and we shall soon find, that he bestows praise on such instances of treachery, inhumanity, cruelty, revenge, bigotry, as are utterly incompatible with civilized society. No steady rule of right seems there to be attended to; and every action is blamed or praised, so far only as it is beneficial or hurtful to the true believers.

The merit of delivering true general precepts in ethics is indeed very small. Whoever recommends any moral virtues, really does no more than is implied in the terms themselves. That people who invented the word *charity*, and used it in a good sense, inculcated more clearly, and much more efficaciously, the precept, *Be charitable*, than any pretended legislator or prophet, who should insert such a *maxim* in his writings. Of all expressions, those which, together with their other meaning, imply a degree either of blame or approbation, are the least liable to be perverted or mistaken.

It is natural for us to seek a *Standard of Taste*; a rule by which the various sentiments of men may be reconciled; at least a decision afforded confirming one sentiment, and condemning another.

There is a species of philosophy, which cuts off all hopes of success in such an attempt, and represents the impossibility of ever attaining any standard of taste. The difference, it is said, is very wide between judgement and sentiment. All sentiment is right; because sentiment has a reference to nothing beyond itself, and is always real, wherever a man is conscious of it. But all determinations of the understanding are not right; because they have a reference to something beyond themselves, to wit, real matter of fact; and are not always conformable to that standard. Among a thousand different opinions which different men may entertain of the same subject,

---

[3] Francois de Salignac de la Mothe-Fénelon (1651–1715), Archbishop of Cambrai, and a writer of considerable quality. Hume has in mind here his best-known work *Télémaque* (1699), a prose narrative of the imaginary adventures of Telemachus, in Greek legend the son of Ulysses. The work was written for the instruction of the young man to whom Fénelon was tutor, namely the Duc de Bourgogne, son of the Dauphin, and this partly explains the way in which the character of the hero is portrayed (which is as Hume describes it in the text). In Homer's *Odyssey*, Telemachus is portrayed as valiant and pious (as he is by Fénelon), but somewhat diffident and without his father's energy or decisiveness. cf. *Odyssey*, Bks. I–IV. [eds]

there is one, and but one, that is just and true: and the only difficulty is to fix and ascertain it. On the contrary, a thousand different sentiments, excited by the same object, are all right; because no sentiment represents what is really in the object. It only marks a certain conformity or relation between the object and the organs or faculties of the mind; and if that conformity did not really exist, the sentiment could never possibly have being. Beauty is no quality in things themselves: it exists merely in the mind which contemplates them; and each mind perceives a different beauty. One person may even perceive deformity, where another is sensible of beauty; and every individual ought to acquiesce in his own sentiment, without pretending to regulate those of others. To seek the real beauty, or real deformity, is as fruitless an inquiry, as to pretend to ascertain the real sweet or real bitter. According to the disposition of the organs, the same object may be both sweet and bitter; and the proverb has justly determined it to be fruitless to dispute concerning tastes. It is very natural, and even quite necessary, to extend this axiom to mental, as well as bodily taste; and thus common sense, which is so often at variance with philosophy, especially with the sceptical kind, is found, in one instance at least, to agree in pronouncing the same decision.

But though this axiom, by passing into a proverb, seems to have attained the sanction of common sense; there is certainly a species of common sense, which opposes it, at least serves to modify and restrain it. Whoever would assert an equality of genius and elegance between Ogilby[4] and Milton, or Bunyan and Addison, would be thought to defend no less an extravagance, than if he had maintained a mole-hill to be as high as Teneriffe, or a pond as extensive as the ocean. Though there may be found persons, who give the preference to the former authors; no one pays attention to such a taste; and we pronounce, without scruple, the sentiment of these pretended critics to be absurd and ridiculous. The principle of the natural equality of tastes is then totally forgot, and while we admit it on some occasions, where the objects seem near an equality, it appears an extravagant paradox, or rather a palpable absurdity, where objects so disproportioned are compared together.

It is evident that none of the rules of composition are fixed by reasonings a priori,[5] or can be esteemed abstract conclusions of the understanding, from comparing those habitudes and relations of ideas, which are eternal and immutable. Their foundation is the same with that of all the practical sciences, experience; nor are they any thing but general observations, concerning what has been universally found to please in all countries and in all ages. Many of the beauties of poetry, and even of eloquence, are founded on falsehood and fiction, on hyperboles, metaphors, and an abuse or perversion of terms from their natural meaning. To check the sallies of the imagination, and to reduce every expression to geometrical truth and exactness, would be the most contrary to the laws of criticism; because it would produce a work, which, by universal experience, has been found the most insipid and disagreeable. But though poetry can never submit to exact truth, it must be confined by rules of art, discovered to the author either by genius or observation. If some negligent or irregular writers have pleased, they have not pleased by their transgressions of rule or order, but in spite of these transgressions: they have possessed other beauties, which were conformable to just criticism; and the force of these beauties has been able to overpower censure, and give the mind a satisfaction superior to the

---

[4] John Ogilby (1600–76), an older contemporary of Milton (1608–74), published verse translations of Homer, Aesop and Virgil, and now a more or less forgotten minor figure in the history of English literature. Interestingly, posterity has not sustained Hume's dismissal of John Bunyan (1628–88), who is regarded as a writer at least as important as Addison, if not more so. [eds]

[5] a priori (lit. 'from what is prior'). A statement is known to be true a priori if its truth can be established without an appeal to experience. I can know a priori that a bachelor is unmarried, since in order to know it I need only know the meaning of the words 'bachelor' and 'unmarried': I do not need to investigate the circumstances of any bachelors to test its truth. By contrast, in order to justify my claim to know that 'John Doe is a bachelor', I need to check a fact about John Doe, i.e. whether he is married or not. I need to appeal to experience to test this second claim, which is known a posteriori (lit. from what is posterior). [eds]

disgust[6] arising from the blemishes. Ariosto[7] pleases; but not by his monstrous and improbable fictions, by his bizarre mixture of the serious and comic styles, by the want of coherence in his stories, or by the continual interruptions of his narration. He charms by the force and clearness of his expression, by the readiness and variety of his inventions, and by his natural pictures of the passions, especially those of the gay[8] and amorous kind: and, however his faults may diminish our satisfaction, they are not able entirely to destroy it. Did our pleasure really arise from those parts of his poem, which we denominate faults, this would be no objection to criticism in general: it would only be an objection to those particular rules of criticism, which would establish such circumstances to be faults, and would represent them as universally blamable. If they are found to please, they cannot be faults, let the pleasure which they produce be ever so unexpected and unaccountable.

But though all the general rules of art are founded only on experience, and on the observation of the common sentiments of human nature, we must not imagine, that, on every occasion, the feelings of men will be conformable to these rules. Those finer emotions of the mind are of a very tender and delicate nature, and require the concurrence of many favourable circumstances to make them play with facility and exactness, according to their general and established principles. The least exterior hindrance to such small springs, or the least internal disorder, disturbs their motion, and confounds the operations of the whole machine. When we would make an experiment of this nature, and would try the force of any beauty or deformity, we must choose with care a proper time and place, and bring the fancy to a suitable situation and disposition. A perfect serenity of mind, a recollection of thought, a due attention to the object; if any of these circumstances be wanting, our experiment will be fallacious, and we shall be unable to judge of the catholic and universal beauty. The relation, which nature has placed between the form and the sentiment, will at least be more obscure; and it will require greater accuracy to trace and discern it. We shall be able to ascertain its influence, not so much from the operation of each particular beauty, as from the durable admiration which attends those works that have survived all the caprices of mode and fashion, all the mistakes of ignorance and envy.

The same Homer who pleased at Athens and Rome two thousand years ago, is still admired at Paris and at London. All the changes of climate, government, religion, and language, have not been able to obscure his glory. Authority or prejudice may give a temporary vogue to a bad poet or orator; but his reputation will never be durable or general. When his compositions are examined by posterity or by foreigners, the enchantment is dissipated, and his faults appear in their true colours. On the contrary, a real genius, the longer his works endure, and the more wide they are spread, the more sincere is the admiration which he meets with. Envy and jealousy have too much place in a narrow circle; and even familiar acquaintance with his person may diminish the applause due to his performances: but when these obstructions are removed, the beauties, which are naturally fitted to excite agreeable sentiments, immediately display their energy; and while the world endures, they maintain their authority over the minds of men.

It appears, then, that amidst all the variety and caprice of taste, there are certain general principles of approbation or blame, whose influence a careful eye may trace in all operations of

---

[6] i.e. displeasure. [eds]

[7] Ludovico Ariosto (1474–1533), wrote *Orlando Furioso* (published in its complete form in 1532), a major classic poem of Italian literature. The subject of the poem was neatly summed up by Byron as 'ladye-love and war, romance and knightly worth' (*Childe Harold's Pilgrimage* (1812–13) Canto IV, xi, 1.9). One would not expect either the subject-matter or the style to appeal to those whom classical models were the norm. However, Hume is not alone in judging that the poem has features which more than compensate for this. Gibbon calls him 'the incomparable Ariosto' and Voltaire commented: '*Je vous avoue que cet Arioste est mon homme*' ('I tell you that this Ariosto is my sort of man'). [eds]

[8] Not just light-hearted or merry, but associated with what we call the social life. [eds]

the mind. Some particular forms or qualities, from the original structure of the internal fabric are calculated to please, and others to displease; and if they fail of their effect in any particular instance, it is from some apparent defect or imperfection in the organ. A man in a fever would not insist on his palate as able to decide concerning flavours; nor would one affected with the jaundice pretend to give a verdict with regard to colours. In each creature there is a sound and a defective state; and the former alone can be supposed to afford us a true standard of taste and sentiment. If, in the sound state of the organ, there be an entire or a considerable uniformity of sentiment among men, we may thence derive an idea of the perfect beauty; in like manner as the appearance of objects in daylight, to the eye of a man in health, is denominated their true and real colour, even while colour is allowed to be merely a plantasm of the senses.

Many and frequent are the defects in the internal organs, which prevent or weaken the influence of those general principles, on which depends our sentiment of beauty or deformity. Though some objects, by the structure of the mind, be naturally calculated to give pleasure, it is not to be expected that in every individual the pleasure will be equally felt. Particular incidents and situations occur, which either throw a false light on the objects, or hinder the true from conveying to the imagination the proper sentiment and perception.

One obvious cause why many feel not the proper sentiment of beauty, is the want of that *delicacy* of imagination which is requisite to convey a sensibility of those finer emotions. This delicacy every one pretends to: every one talks of it; and would reduce every kind of taste or sentiment to its standard. But as our intention in this Essay is to mingle some light of the understanding with the feelings of sentiment, it will be proper to give a more accurate definition of delicacy than has hitherto been attempted. And not to draw our philosophy from too profound a source, we shall have recourse to a noted story in Don Quixote.[9]

It is with good reason, says Sancho to the squire with the great nose, that I pretend to have a judgement in wine: this is a quality hereditary in our family. Two of my kinsmen were once called to give their opinion of a hogshead, which was supposed to be excellent, being old and of a good vintage. One of them tastes it, considers it; and, after mature reflection, pronounces the wine to be good, were it not for a small taste of leather which he perceived in it. The other, after using the same precautions, gives also his verdict in favour of the wine; but with the reserve of a taste of iron, which he could easily distinguish. You cannot imagine how much they were both ridiculed for their judgement. But who laughed in the end? On emptying the hogshead, there was found at the bottom an old key with a leathern thong tied to it.

The great resemblance between mental and bodily taste will easily teach us to apply this story. Though it be certain that beauty and deformity, more than sweet and bitter, are not qualities in objects, but belong entirely to the sentiment, internal or external, it must be allowed, that there are certain qualities in objects which are fitted by nature to produce those particular feelings. Now, as these qualities may be found in a small degree, or may be mixed and confounded with each other, it often happens that the taste is not affected with such minute qualities, or is not able to distinguish all the particular flavours, amidst the disorder in which they are presented. Where the organs are so fine as to allow nothing to escape them, and at the same time so exact as to perceive every ingredient in the composition, this we call delicacy of taste, whether we employ these terms in the literal or metaphorical sense. Here then the general rules of beauty are of use, being drawn from established models, and from the observation of what pleases or displeases, when presented singly and in a high degree; and if the same qualities, in a continued composition, and in a smaller degree, affect not the organs with a sensible delight or uneasiness, we exclude the person from all pretensions to this delicacy. To produce these general rules or avowed patterns of composition, is like finding the key with the leathern thong, which justified the verdict of Sancho's kinsmen, and confounded those pretended judges who had condemned them.

[9]   *Don Quixote de la Mancha* (Part I, 1605; Part II, 1615) by Miguel de Cervantes Saavedra (1547–1616). The incident cited occurs in Part II, ch.13. [eds]

Though the hogshead had never been emptied, the taste of the one was still equally delicate, and that of the other equally dull and languid; but it would have been more difficult to have proved the superiority of the former, to the conviction of every bystander. In like manner, though the beauties of writing had never been methodized, or reduced to general principles; though no excellent models had ever been acknowledged, the different degrees of taste would still have subsisted, and the judgement of one man been preferable to that of another; but it would not have been so easy to silence the bad critic, who might always insist upon his particular sentiment, and refuse to submit to his antagonist. But when we show him an avowed principle of art; when we illustrate this principle by examples, whose operation, from his own particular taste, he acknowledges to be conformable to the principle; when we prove that the same principle may be applied to the present case, where he did not perceive or feel its influence: he must conclude, upon the whole, that the fault lies in himself, and that he wants the delicacy which is requisite to make him sensible of every beauty and every blemish in any composition or discourse.

It is acknowledged to be the perfection of every sense or faculty, to perceive with exactness its most minute objects, and allow nothing to escape its notice and observation. The smaller the objects are which become sensible to the eye, the finer is that organ, and the more elaborate its make and composition. A good palate is not tried by strong flavours, but by a mixture of small ingredients, where we are still sensible of each part, notwithstanding its minuteness and its confusion with the rest. In like manner, a quick and acute perception of beauty and deformity must be the perfection of our mental taste; nor can a man be satisfied with himself while he suspects that any excellence or blemish in a discourse has passed him unobserved. In this case, the perfection of the man, and the perfection of the sense of feeling, are found to be united. A very delicate palate, on many occasions, may be a great inconvenience both to a man himself and to his friends. But a delicate taste of wit or beauty must always be a desirable quality,

because it is the source of all the finest and most innocent enjoyments of which human nature is susceptible. In this decision the sentiments of all mankind are agreed. Wherever you can ascertain a delicacy of taste, it is sure to meet with approbation; and the best way of ascertaining it is, to appeal to those models and principles which have been established by the uniform consent and experience of nations and ages.

But though there be naturally a wide difference, in point of delicacy, between one person and another, nothing tends further to increase and improve this talent, than *practice* in a particular art, and the frequent survey or contemplation of a particular species of beauty. When objects of any kind are first presented to the eye or imagination, the sentiment which attends them is obscure and confused; and the mind is, in a great measure, incapable of pronouncing concerning their merits or defects. The taste cannot perceive the several excellences of the performance, much less distinguish the particular character of each excellency, and ascertain its quality and degree. If it pronounce the whole in general to be beautiful or deformed, it is the utmost that can be expected; and even this judgement, a person so unpractised will be apt to deliver with great hesitation and reserve. But allow him to acquire experience in those objects, his feeling becomes more exact and nice:[10] he not only perceives the beauties and defects of each part, but marks the distinguishing species of each quality, and assigns it suitable praise or blame. A clear and distinct sentiment attends him through the whole survey of the objects; and he discerns that very degree and kind of approbation or displeasure which each part is naturally fitted to produce. The mist dissipates which seemed formerly to hang over the object; the organ acquires greater perfection in its operations, and can pronounce, without danger of mistake, concerning the merits of every performance. In a word, the same address and dexterity which practice gives to the execution of any work, is also acquired by the same means in the judging of it.

So advantageous is practice to the discernment of beauty, that, before we can give judgement on any work of importance, it will even be

---

[10]   i.e. discriminating, capable of registering nuances. [eds]

requisite that that very individual performance be more than once perused by us, and be surveyed in different lights with attention and deliberation. There is a flutter or hurry of thought which attends the first perusal of any piece, and which confounds the genuine sentiment of beauty. The relation of the parts is not discerned: the true characters of style are little distinguished. The several perfections and defects seem wrapped up in a species of confusion, and present themselves indistinctly to the imagination. Not to mention, that there is a species of beauty, which, as it is florid and superficial, pleases at first; but being found incompatible with a just expression either of reason or passion, soon palls upon the taste, and is then rejected with disdain, at least rated at a much lower value.

It is impossible to continue in the practice of contemplating any order of beauty, without being frequently obliged to form *comparisons* between the several species and degrees of excellence, and estimating their proportion to each other. A man who has had no opportunity of comparing the different kinds of beauty, is indeed totally unqualified to pronounce an opinion with regard to any object presented to him. By comparison alone we fix the epithets of praise or blame, and learn how to assign the due degree of each. The coarsest daubing contains a certain lustre of colours and exactness of imitation, which are so far beauties, and would affect the mind of a peasant or Indian with the highest admiration. The most vulgar ballads are not entirely destitute of harmony or nature; and none but a person familiarized to superior beauties would pronounce their members harsh, or narration uninteresting. A great inferiority of beauty gives pain to a person conversant in the highest excellence of the kind, and is for that reason pronounced a deformity; as the most finished object with which we are acquainted is naturally supposed to have reached the pinnacle of perfection, and to be entitled to the highest applause. One accustomed to see, and examine, and weigh the several performances, admired in different ages and nations, can alone rate the merits of a work exhibited to his view, and assign its proper rank among the productions of his genius.

But to enable a critic the more fully to execute this undertaking, he must preserve his mind free from all *prejudice*, and allow nothing to enter into his consideration, but the very object which is submitted to his examination. We may observe, that every work of art, in order to produce its due effect on the mind, must be surveyed in a certain point of view, and cannot be fully relished by persons whose situation, real or imaginary, is not conformable to that which is required by the performance. An orator addresses himself to a particular audience, and must have a regard to their particular genius, interests, opinions, passions, and prejudices; otherwise he hopes in vain to govern their resolutions, and inflame their affections. Should they even have entertained some prepossessions against him, however unreasonable, he must not overlook this disadvantage: but, before he enters upon the subject, must endeavour to conciliate their affection, and acquire their good graces. A critic of a different age or nation, who should peruse this discourse, must have all these circumstances in his eye, and must place himself in the same situation as the audience, in order to form a true judgement of the oration. In like manner, when any work is addressed to the public, though I should have a friendship or enmity with the author, I must depart from this situation, and, considering myself as a man in general, forget, if possible, my individual being, and my peculiar circumstances. A person influenced by prejudice complies not with this condition, but obstinately maintains his natural position, without placing himself in that point of view which the performance supposes. If the work be addressed to persons of a different age or nation, he makes no allowance for their peculiar views and prejudices; but, full of the manners of his own age and country, rashly condemns what seemed admirable in the eyes of those for whom alone the discourse was calculated. If the work be executed for the public, he never sufficiently enlarges his comprehension, or forgets his interest as a friend or enemy, as a rival or commentator. By this means his sentiments are perverted; nor have the same beauties and blemishes the same influence upon him, as if he had imposed a proper violence on his imagination, and had forgotten himself for a moment. So far his taste evidently departs from the true standard, and of consequence loses all credit and authority.

It is well known, that, in all questions submitted to the understanding, prejudice is destructive of sound judgement, and perverts all operations of the intellectual faculties: it is no less contrary to good taste; nor has it less influence to corrupt our sentiment of beauty. It belongs to *good sense* to check its influence in both cases; and in this respect, as well as in many others, reason, if not an essential part of taste, is at least requisite to the operations of this latter faculty. In all the nobler productions of genius, there is a mutual relation and correspondence of parts; nor can either the beauties or blemishes be perceived by him whose thought is not capacious enough to comprehend all those parts, and compare them with each other, in order to perceive the consistence and uniformity of the whole. Every work of art has also a certain end or purpose for which it is calculated; and is to be deemed more or less perfect, as it is more or less fitted to attain this end. The object of eloquence is to persuade, of history to instruct, of poetry to please, by means of the passions and the imagination. These ends we must carry constantly in our view when we peruse any performance; and we must be able to judge how far the means employed are adapted to their respective purposes. Besides, every kind of composition, even the most poetical, is nothing but a chain of propositions and reasonings; not always, indeed, the justest and most exact, but still plausible and specious,[11] however disguised by the colouring of the imagination. The persons introduced in tragedy and epic poetry must be represented as reasoning, and thinking, and concluding, and acting, suitably to their character and circumstances; and without judgement, as well as taste and invention, a poet can never hope to succeed in so delicate an undertaking. Not to mention, that the same excellence of faculties which contributes to the improvement of reason, the same clearness of conception, the same exactness of distinction, the same vivacity of apprehension, are essential to the operations of true taste, and are its infallible concomitants. It seldom or never happens, that a man of sense, who has experience in any art, cannot judge of its beauty; and it is no less rare to meet with a man who has a just taste without a sound understanding.

Thus, though the principles of taste be universal, and nearly, if not entirely, the same in all men; yet few are qualified to give judgement on any work of art, or establish their own sentiment as the standard of beauty. The organs of internal sensation are seldom so perfect as to allow the general principles their full play, and produce a feeling correspondent to those principles. They either labour under some defect, or are vitiated by some disorder; and by that means excite a sentiment, which may be pronounced erroneous. When the critic has no delicacy, he judges without any distinction, and is only affected by the grosser and more palpable qualities of the object: the finer touches pass unnoticed and disregarded. Where he is not aided by practice, his verdict is attended with confusion and hesitation. Where no comparison has been employed, the most frivolous beauties, such as rather merit the name of defects, are the object of his admiration. Where he lies under the influence of prejudice, all his natural sentiments are perverted. Where good sense is wanting, he is not qualified to discern the beauties of design and reasoning, which are the highest and most excellent. Under some or other of these imperfections, the generality of men labour, and hence a true judge in the finer arts is observed, even during the most polished ages, to be so rare a character: strong sense, united to delicate sentiment, improved by practice, perfected by comparison, and cleared of all prejudice, can alone entitle critics to this valuable character; and the joint verdict of such, wherever they are to be found, is the true standard of taste and beauty.

But where are such critics to be found? By what marks are they to be known? How distinguish them from pretenders? These questions are embarrassing; and seem to throw us back into the same uncertainty from which, during the course of this Essay, we have endeavoured to extricate ourselves.

But if we consider the matter aright, these are questions of fact, not of sentiment. Whether any particular person be endowed with good sense and a delicate imagination, free from prejudice, may often be the subject of dispute, and be liable to great discussion and inquiry: but that such a character is valuable and estimable, will be agreed in by all mankind. Where these doubts occur, men can do no more than in other

---

[11] 'Specious' also means 'plausible': Hume uses two words for the sake of euphony and rhythm, and to reinforce his point. [eds]

disputable questions which are submitted to the understanding: they must produce the best arguments that their invention suggests to them; they must acknowledge a true and decisive standard to exist somewhere, to wit, real existence and matter of fact; and they must have indulgence to such as differ from them in their appeals to this standard. It is sufficient for our present purpose, if we have proved, that the taste of all individuals is not upon an equal footing, and that some men in general, however difficult to be particularly pitched upon, will be acknowledged by universal sentiment to have a preference above others.

But, in reality, the difficulty of finding, even in particulars, the standard of taste, is not so great as it is represented. Though in speculation we may readily avow a certain criterion in science,[12] and deny it in sentiment, the matter is found in practice to be much more hard to ascertain in the former case than in the latter. Theories of abstract philosophy, systems of profound theology, have prevailed during one age: in a successive period these have been universally exploded: their absurdity has been detected: other theories and systems have supplied their place, which again gave place to their successors: and nothing has been experienced more liable to the revolutions of chance and fashion than these pretended decisions of science. The case is not the same with the beauties of eloquence and poetry. Just expressions of passion and nature are sure, after a little time, to gain public applause, which they maintain for ever. Aristotle, and Plato, and Epicurus, and Descartes,[13] may successively yield to each other: but Terence and Virgil maintain an universal, undisputed empire over the minds of men. The abstract philosophy of Cicero has lost its credit: the vehemence of his oratory is still the object of our admiration.

Though men of delicate taste be rare, they are easily to be distinguished in society by the soundness of their understanding, and the superiority of their faculties above the rest of mankind. The ascendant, which they acquire, gives a prevalence to that lively approbation with which they receive any productions of genius, and renders it generally predominant. Many men, when left to themselves, have but a faint and dubious perception of beauty, who yet are capable of relishing any fine stroke which is pointed out to them. Every convert to the admiration of the real poet or orator, is the cause of some new conversion. And though prejudices may prevail for a time, they never unite in celebrating any rival to the true genius, but yield at last to the force of nature and just sentiment. Thus, though a civilized nation may easily be mistaken in the choice of their admired philosopher, they never have found long to err, in their affection for a favourite epic or tragic author.

But notwithstanding all our endeavours to fix a standard of taste, and reconcile the discordant apprehensions of men, there still remain two sources of variation, which are not sufficient indeed to confound all the boundaries of beauty and deformity, but will often serve to produce a difference in the degrees of our approbation or blame. The one is the different humours of particular men; the other, the particular manners and opinions of our age and country. The general principles of taste are uniform in human nature: where men vary in their judgements, some defect or perversion in the faculties may commonly be remarked; proceeding either from prejudice, from want of practice, or want of delicacy: and there is just reason for approving one taste, and condemning another. But where there is such a diversity in the internal frame or external situation as is entirely blameless on both sides, and leaves no room to give one the preference above the other; in that case a certain degree of diversity in judgement is unavoidable, and we seek in vain

---

12   As Hume makes clear, this is not science in the modern sense, but any body of systematic knowledge, including theology. [eds]

13   The first four members of this list are philosophers: Plato (427–348 BC), Aristotle (384–322 BC), Epicurus (341–270 BC), and, from a much later period, René Descartes (1596–1650). For Terence, see note 19 below. Virgil (Publius Virgilius Maro, 70–19 BC) was a great Roman poet, whose major work was the epic poem, *The Aeneid*. Marcus Tullius Cicero (106–43 BC) wrote some philosophical works, but posterity has endorsed Hume's view that his enduring significance is as one of the greatest orators. Hume assumes that his audience (i.e. educated men) is familiar with all these figures. [eds]

for a standard, by which we can reconcile the contrary sentiments.

A young man, whose passions are warm, will be more sensibly touched with amorous and tender images, than a man more advanced in years, who takes pleasure in wise, philosophical reflections, concerning the conduct of life, and moderation of the passions. At twenty, Ovid may be the favourite author, Horace at forty, and perhaps Tacitus at fifty.[14] Vainly would we, in such cases, endeavour to enter into the sentiments of others, and divest ourselves of those propensities which are natural to us. We choose our favourite author as we do our friend, from a conformity of humour and disposition. Mirth or passion, sentiment or reflection; whichever of these most predominates in our temper, it gives us a peculiar sympathy with the writer who resembles us.

One person is more pleased with the sublime,[15] another with the tender, a third with raillery. One has a strong sensibility[16] to blemishes, and is extremely studious of correctness; another has a more lively feeling of beauties, and pardons twenty absurdities and defects for one elevated or pathetic[17] stroke. The ear of this man is entirely turned towards conciseness and energy; that man is delighted with a copious, rich, and harmonious expression. Simplicity is affected[18] by one; ornament by another. Comedy, tragedy, satire, odes, have each its partisans, who prefer that particular species of writing to all others. It is plainly an error in a critic, to confine his approbation to one species or style of writing, and condemn all the rest. But it is almost impossible not to feel a predilection for that which suits our particular turn and disposition. Such performances are innocent and unavoidable, and can never reasonably be the object of dispute, because there is no standard by which they can be decided.

For a like reason, we are more pleased, in the course of our reading, with pictures and characters that resemble objects which are found in our own age and country, than with those which describe a different set of customs. It is not without some effort that we reconcile ourselves to the simplicity of ancient manners, and behold princesses carrying water from the spring, and kings and heroes dressing their own victuals. We may allow in general, that the representation of such manners is no fault in the author, nor deformity in the piece; but we are not so sensibly touched with them. For this reason, comedy is not easily transferred from one age or nation to another. A Frenchman or Englishman is not pleased with the *Andria* of Terence, or *Clitia* of Machiavel; where the fine lady, upon whom all the play turns, never once appears to the spectators, but is always kept behind the scenes, suitably to the reserved humour of the ancient Greeks and modern Italians.[19] A man of learning and reflection can make allowance for these peculiarities of man

---

[14]   Publius Ovidius Naso (43 BC–AD 18), is a major Roman poet, some of whose works are of an erotic nature, e.g. *Ars Amatoria* (*The Art of Love*), which is perhaps why Hume thinks that they would appeal to twenty-year-olds (men, that is). For Horace, see note 20 below. Publius (or Gaius) Cornelius Tacitus (*c.* AD 55–117) was a great historian. Again, Hume assumes that his audience is familiar with all these writers.

[15]   Sublime: an aesthetic experience based on terror, awe or fear. [eds]

[16]   i.e. deeply sensitive to. [eds]

[17]   i.e. moving. [eds]

[18]   i.e. liked. [eds]

[19]   *Andria* (*The Woman of Andros*), one of the six surviving plays by Publius Terentius Afer (Terence, *c.* 195–159 BC), a great Roman writer of comedy. In this play, the character Glycerium, the woman of Andros herself, does not appear on stage. *Clitia* (*Clizia* is the Italian title) is a play by Niccoló di Bernardo dei Machiavelli (1469–1527), now best remembered for his work of political theory *Il Principe* (*The Prince*, 1513). By coincidence, Machiavelli had published a free translation of the *Andria; Clizia* is a blend of contemporary situation and a plot by Terence's predecessor, Plautus (Titus Maccius Plautus, 254–184 BC), the other major Roman writer of comedy whose works have survived. Again, the leading character in *Clizia* does not appear. [eds]

ners; but a common audience can never divest themselves so far of their usual ideas and sentiments, as to relish pictures which nowise resemble them.

But here there occurs a reflection, which may, perhaps, be useful in examining the celebrated controversy concerning ancient and modern learning; where we often find the one side excusing any seeming absurdity in the ancients from the manners of the age, and the other refusing to admit this excuse, or at least admitting it only as an apology for the author, not for the performance. In my opinion, the proper boundaries in this subject have seldom been fixed between the contending parties. Where any innocent peculiarities of manners are represented, such as those above mentioned, they ought certainly to be admitted; and a man who is shocked with them, gives an evident proof of false delicacy and refinement. The poet's *monument more durable than brass*,[20] must fall to the ground like common brick or clay, were men to make no allowance for the continual revolutions of manners and customs, and would admit of nothing but what was suitable to the prevailing fashion. Must we throw aside the pictures of our ancestors, because of their ruffs and farthingales? But where the ideas of morality and decency alter from one age to another, and where vicious manners are described, without being marked with the proper characters[21] of blame and disapprobation, this must be allowed to disfigure the poem, and to be a real deformity. I cannot, nor is it proper I should, enter into such sentiments; and however I may excuse the poet, on account of the manners of his age, I can never relish the composition. The want of humanity and of decency, so conspicuous in the characters drawn by several of the ancient poets, even sometimes by Homer and the Greek tragedians,[22] diminishes considerably the merit of their noble performances, and gives modern authors an advantage over them. We are not interested in the fortunes and sentiments of such rough heroes; we are displeased to find the limits of vice and virtue so much confounded; and whatever indulgence we may give to the writer on account of his prejudices, we cannot prevail on ourselves to enter into his sentiments, or bear an affection to characters which we plainly discover to be blamable.

The case is not the same with moral principles as with speculative opinions of any kind. These are in continual flux and revolution. The son embraces a different system from the father. Nay, there scarcely is any man, who can boast of great constancy and uniformity in this particular. Whatever speculative errors may be found in the polite writings of any age or country, they detract but little from the value of those compositions. There needs but a certain turn of thought or imagination to make us enter into all the opinions which then prevailed, and relish the sentiments or conclusions derived from them. But a very violent effort is requisite to change our judgement of manners, and excite sentiments of approbation or blame, love or hatred, different from those to which the mind, from long custom, has been familiarized. And where a man is confident of the rectitude of that moral standard

---

[20]   *monument more durable than brass*: part of a line from Horace (Quintus Horatius Flaccus, 65–8 BC, Roman poet and satirist), *Carminae* (*Odes*) Book III, xxx, l.1:

   Exegi monumentum aere perennius.
(I have completed a monument more durable than brass)
   This is a well-known line of an oft quoted poet, hence Hume feels no need here to attribute the quotation. The poem is a classic statement of the theme *ars longa, vita brevis* (art is long, life is short), i.e. works of art immortalize their creators far more effectively than any other form of memorial. Shakespeare's Sonnet 55 is one of many later poems on exactly this theme:

   Not marble nor the gilded monuments
   Of princes shall outlive this powerful rhyme. (ll. 1–2) [eds]

[21]   i.e. characteristics. [eds]

[22]   The 'Greek tragedians' he has in mind are Aeschylus (525–456 BC), Sophocles (496–406 BC) and Euripides (*c.* 480–406 BC). [eds]

by which he judges, he is justly jealous[23] of it, and will not pervert the sentiments of his heart for a moment, in complaisance[24] to any writer whatsoever.

Of all speculative errors, those which regard religion are the most excusable in compositions of genius; nor is it ever permitted to judge of the civility or wisdom of any people, or even of single persons, by the grossness or refinement of their theological principles. The same good sense that directs men in the ordinary occurrences of life, is not hearkened to in religious matters, which are supposed to be placed altogether above the cognizance of human reason. On this account, all the absurdities of the Pagan system of theology must be overlooked by every critic, who would pretend to form a just notion of ancient poetry; and our posterity, in their turn, must have the same indulgence to their forefathers. No religious principles can ever be imputed as a fault to any poet, while they remain merely principles, and take not such strong possession of his heart as to lay him under the imputation of *bigotry or superstition*. Where that happens, they confound the sentiments of morality, and alter the natural boundaries of vice and virtue. They are therefore eternal blemishes, according to the principle above mentioned; nor are the prejudices and false opinions of the age sufficient to justify them.

It is essential to the Roman Catholic religion to inspire a violent hatred of every other worship, and to represent all Pagans, Mahometans, and heretics, as the objects of divine wrath and vengeance. Such sentiments, though they are in reality very blamable, are considered as virtues by the zealots of that communion, and are represented in their tragedies and epic poems as a kind of divine heroism. This bigotry has disfigured two very fine tragedies of the French theatre, POLIEUCTE[25] and ATHALIA; where an intemperate zeal for particular modes of worship is set off with all the pomp imaginable, and forms the predominant character of the heroes. 'What is this,' says the sublime Joad to Josabet, finding her in discourse with Mathan the priest of Baal, 'Does the daughter of David speak to this traitor? Are you not afraid lest the earth should open, and pour forth flames to devour you both? Or lest these holy walls should fall and crush you together? What is his purpose? Why comes that enemy of God hither to poison the air, which we breathe, with his horrid presence?' Such sentiments are received with great applause on the theatre of Paris; but at London the spectators would be full as much pleased to hear Achilles tell Agamemnon, that he was a dog in his forehead, and a deer in his heart; or Jupiter threaten Juno with a sound drubbing, if she will not be quiet.

---

[23]   i.e. protective. [eds]

[24]   i.e. deference. [eds]

[25]   *Polieucte* (French title *Polyeucte*, 1642), a tragedy by Pierre Corneille (1606–84) and *Athalia* (French title *Athalie*, 1691), by Jean Racine (1639–99). In many ways one would not expect *Polyeucte* to appeal to Hume, since the main character, Polyeucte himself, is what Hume would have termed a religious 'enthusiast', i.e. a zealot. Polyeucte, a recent convert to Christianity, commits a very public act of iconoclasm in a pagan temple and chooses not to try to avoid the death sentence for this crime, which is duly carried out. Other Enlightenment figures who, like Hume, valued toleration in religious matters found the character of Polyeucte unsympathetic. Voltaire remarks: 'I thought I could discern amongst the audience, at performances, a secret joy that Polyeucte was going to carry out that action [i.e. iconoclasm], because they hoped he would be punished and that Severus [a pagan] would marry his wife' (Dedicatory Epistle to his own play *Zaïre*, 1732): Lessing commented wryly: 'Polyeucte wants to become a martyr, he hopes for death and torture, regarding them as the first step toward an infinitely happy existence; I admire the pious enthusiasm, but I would be afraid of annoying his soul in the bosom of eternal beatitude, were I to feel any compassion for him' (Letter to his friend Moses Mendelssohn, 18th December, 1756).

Racine's masterpiece *Athalie* is his version of a Biblical story (second book of Kings, XI and XII) and embodies an orthodox Catholic view of the working of divine providence in history. Hume here translates a speech by the high priest Joad, who has come upon his wife Josabet in conversation with Mathan, a priest of Baal (II, v, ll.1–8). D'Alembert did not much care for the character of Joad either, describing him as an 'insolent, seditious and fanatical priest' (Letter to Voltaire, 11th December, 1769). [eds]

Religious principles are also a blemish in any polite composition, when they rise up to superstition, and intrude themselves into every sentiment, however remote from any connection with religion. It is no excuse for the poet, that the customs of his country had burdened life with so many religious ceremonies and observ- ances, that no part of it was exempt from that yoke. It must for ever be ridiculous in Petrarch to compare his mistress, Laura, to Jesus Christ.[26] Nor is it less ridiculous in that agreeable liber- tine, Boccace,[27] very seriously to give thanks to God Almighty and the ladies, for their assistance in defending him against his enemies.

Source: David Hume, *Essays: Moral, Political and Literary*, Oxford University Press, 1963.

---

[26] Petrarch is Francesco Petrarca (1304–74), a major Italian poet. Hume has in mind here Petrarch's series of love poems, inspired by a woman he calls Laura. The poems are collectively referred to as the *Rime in Vita e Morte di Madonna Laura* (*Poems concerning the Life and Death of Lady Laura*), also known more briefly as the *Canzoniere* (*Book of Songs*). I think Hume is here referring to a daring comparison Petrarch makes between the face of Laura (his Heaven, which he hopes to see) and the face of Christ imprinted on a shroud, the object of a pilgrimage by a pious old man:

> *e viene a Roma, seguendo 'l desio,*
> *per mirar la sembianza di colui*
> *ch'ancor lassù nel ciel vedere spera.*
> *Cosi, lasso! talor vo cercand'io,*
> *Donna, quanto è possibile, in altrui*
> *la disiata vostra forma vera.*

(and [the old man] comes to Rome, pursuing his desire to see the likeness [on the sacred relic] of Him whom he hopes to see again in heaven. Thus alas do I sometimes seek, my lady, so far as it is possible, your desired, true form in others [other ladies].) From the sonnet beginning '*Movesi il vecchierel canuto e bianco*', no 16 in the standard numbering of Petrarch's poems. [eds]

[27] Giovanni Boccaccio (1313?–75), a significant figure in Italian literature. His best known work is the *Decameron* (1348–58), a collection of one hundred stories told by a group of ten young people to one another over a period of ten days (hence the title). Some of the stories are risqué: hence Hume's epithet 'agreeable libertine'. (Even in the 1960s, some English translations of the *Decameron* left the most explicit passages in Italian, on the curious principle, one supposes, that those who can read saucy material in Italian are less likely to be depraved and corrupted by it than those who can read it only in English – a late version of Gibbon's notion that certain items are best left in the decent obscurity of a learned language.) The conjunction of 'God Almighty and the ladies', two subjects which greatly exercised Boccaccio, is common in the *Decameron*; see, for example, the Proem to the *Decameron*, especially the closing lines. Alternatively, Hume may be thinking of these words from the Epilogue to the *Decameron*: 'Most noble damsels, for whose solace I addressed me to this long and toilsome task, meseems that, aided by the divine grace, the bestowal whereof I impute to the efficacy of your pious prayers, and in no wise to merits of mine, I have now brought this work to the full and perfect consummation which in the outset thereof I promised you. Wherefore, it but remains for me to render, first to God, and then to you, my thanks, and so to give a rest to my pen and weary hand' (trans. J.M. Rigg, Everyman's Library reprint). [eds]

Joshua Reynolds
Extracts from Discourses on Art

Prepared for the Course Team by
Gill Perry

Contents

Joshua Reynolds
Extracts from Discourses on Art

Sir Joshua Reynolds (1723–92) was first president of the Royal Academy of Arts, founded under royal charter in 1768. During his presidency Reynolds produced his Discourses, a series of fifteen lectures delivered to students and academicians between 1769 and 1790. These were delivered at the Royal Academy's annual prize-giving ceremonies. The Discourses form an important document in the history of European art theory. The Royal Academy was formed to teach and disseminate the principles of an academic art practice, to give the discipline of painting and sculpture the status of a 'liberal' art. Thus Reynolds wrote in Discourse III of his wish to give 'to painting its true dignity, which entitles it to the name of a Liberal art, and ranks it as a sister of poetry'. 'Liberal' here denotes an activity of a free man, a gentleman, and thereby distinguishes art from mere craftsmanship or mechanical trades.

Although the Discourses, delivered over a period of twenty years, reveal some shifts in opinion, they are consistent in advocating the acquisition of knowledge in order to produce great art. The importance of study from antique (Greek and Roman) and Italian Renaissance (in particular Michaelangelo and Raphael) sources is a recurring theme. However, the Discourses were primarily intended as lectures, as guidelines for an art practice as well as theoretical treatises. Reynolds's tendency in later lectures to qualify and revise some of the theoretical ambitions of the earlier Discourses reveals both the influence of contemporary developments in philosophy and aesthetics, and his experiences and interests as a practising artist. It has often been pointed out that the Royal Academy's ambitions to establish a school of High Art, for which the hierarchy of genre and history painting was all-important, were rarely fulfilled by the work of the majority of Academicians. During the eighteenth century portraits were the most popular form of art commissioned by British patrons, and form the major part of Reynolds's output.

The following edited extracts from Discourses III and VII have been selected because they contain several themes that were central in Reynolds's work: his concept of the Grand Style, the extent to which the artist should copy from nature and learn from the Ancients, and his ideas on 'genius' and 'taste'. In places the punctuation reflects the breathing pauses of public oral delivery.

Discourse III[1]

GENTLEMEN,

THE first endeavours of a young Painter, as I have remarked in a former discourse, must be employed in the attainment of mechanical dexterity, and confined to the mere imitation of the object before him. Those who have advanced beyond the rudiments, may, perhaps, find advantage in reflecting on the advice which I have likewise given them, when I recommended the diligent study of the works of our great predecessors; but I at the same time endeavoured to guard them against an implicit submission to the authority of any one master however excellent; or by a strict imitation of his manner, precluding themselves from the abundance and variety of Nature. I will now add that Nature herself is not to be too closely copied. There are excellencies in the art of painting beyond what is commonly called the imitation of nature: and these excellencies I wish to point out. The students who, having passed through the initiatory exercises, are more advanced in the art, and who, sure of their hand, have leisure to exert their understanding, must now be told, that a mere copier of nature can never produce any thing great; can never raise and enlarge the conceptions or warm the heart of the spectator.

[1] 14 December, 1770.

THE wish of the genuine painter must be more extensive: instead of endeavouring to amuse mankind with the minute neatness of his imitations, he must endeavour to improve them by the grandeur of his ideas; instead of seeking praise, by deceiving the superficial sense of the spectator, he must strive for fame, by captivating the imagination.

THE principle now laid down, that the perfection of this art does not consist in mere imitation, is far from being new or singular. It is, indeed, supported by the general opinion of the enlightened part of mankind. The poets, orators, and rhetoricians of antiquity, are continually enforcing this position; that all the arts receive their perfection from an ideal beauty, superior to what is to be found in individual nature. They are ever referring to the practice of the painters and sculptors of their times, particularly Phidias,[2] (the favourite artist of antiquity,) to illustrate their assertions. As if they could not sufficiently express their admiration of his genius by what they knew, they have recourse to poetical enthusiasm.[3] They call it inspiration; a gift from heaven. The artist is supposed to have ascended the celestial regions, to furnish his mind with this perfect ideal of beauty. 'He,' says Proclus,[4] 'who takes for his model such forms as nature produces, and confines himself to an exact imitation of them, will never attain to what is perfectly beautiful. For the works of nature are full of disproportion, and fall very short of the true standard of beauty. So that Phidias, when he formed his Jupiter, did not copy any object ever presented to his sight; but contemplated only that image which he had conceived in his mind from Homer's description.' And thus Cicero,[5] speaking of the same Phidias: 'Neither did this artist,' says he 'when he carved the image of Jupiter or Minerva, set before him any one human figure, as a pattern, which he was to copy; but having a more perfect idea of beauty fixed in his mind, this he steadily contemplated, and to the imitation of this all his skill and labour were directed'.

THE Moderns are not less convinced than the Ancients of this superior power existing in the art; nor less sensible of its effects. Every language has adopted terms expressive of this excellence. The *gusto grande* of the Italians, the *beau ideal* of the French, and the *great style, genius* and *taste* among the English, are but different appellations of the same thing. It is this intellectual dignity, they say, that ennobles the painter's art; that lays the line between him and the mere mechanic; and produces those great effects in an instant, which eloquence and poetry, by slow and repeated efforts, are scarcely able to attain.

SUCH is the warmth with which both the Ancients and Moderns speak of this divine principle of the art; but, as I have formerly observed, enthusiastic admiration seldom promotes knowledge. Though a student by such praise may have his attention roused, and a desire excited, of running in this great career; yet it is possible that what has been said to excite, may only serve to deter him. He examines his own mind, and perceives there nothing of that divine inspiration, with which, he is told, so many others have been favoured. He never travelled to heaven to gather new ideas; and he finds himself possessed of no other qualifications than what mere common observation and a plain understanding can confer. Thus he becomes gloomy at the splendour of figurative declamation,[6] and thinks it hopeless, to pursue an object which he supposes out of the reach of human industry.

---

[2] Phidias (born *c.* 500 BC), Greek sculptor who was patronized by Pericles, and whose work was known to an 18th century audience largely through Roman copies. [eds]

[3] Literally, 'God within'; the word could mean possession in both a good and bad sense. [eds]

[4] Reynolds is quoting here from an antique source, the *Timaeus* of Plato, cited by Junius in his *de Pictura Veterum* (lit., The Painting of the Ancients). [eds]

[5] Marcus Tullius Cicero (106–43 BC): a Roman orator and statesman who followed the common practice of publishing his speeches. He also produced writings on rhetoric, religion and moral and political philosophy. [eds]

[6] i.e. metaphorical speech. [eds]

BUT on this, as upon many other occasions, we ought to distinguish how much is to be given to enthusiasm, and how much to reason. We ought to allow for, and we ought to commend, that strength of vivid expression which is necessary to convey, in its full force, the highest sense of the most complete effect of art; taking care at the same time, not to lose in terms of vague admiration, that solidity and truth of principle, upon which alone we can reason, and may be enabled to practise.

IT is not easy to define in what this great style consists; nor to describe, by words, the proper means of acquiring it, if the mind of the student should be at all capable of such an acquisition. Could we teach taste or genius by rules, they would be no longer taste and genius. But though there neither are, nor can be, any precise invariable rules for the exercise, or the acquisition, of these great qualities, yet we may truly say that they always operate in proportion to our attention in observing the works of nature, to our skill in selecting, and to our care in digesting, methodizing, and comparing our observations. There are many beauties in our art, that seem, at first, to lie without[7] the reach of precept, and yet may easily be reduced to practical principles. Experience is all in all; but it is not every one who profits by experience; and most people err, not so much from want of capacity to find their object, as from not knowing what object to pursue. This great ideal perfection and beauty are not to be sought in the heavens, but upon the earth. They are about us, and upon every side of us. But the power of discovering what is deformed in nature, or in other words, what is particular and uncommon, can be acquired only by experience; and the whole beauty and grandeur of the art consists, in my opinion, in being able to get above all singular forms, local customs, particularities, and details of every kind.

ALL the objects which are exhibited to our view by nature, upon close examination will be found to have their blemishes and defects. The most beautiful forms have something about them like weakness, minuteness, or imperfection. But it is not every eye that perceives these blemishes. It must be an eye long used to the contemplation and comparison of these forms; and which, by a long habit of observing what any set of objects of the same kind have in common, has acquired the power of discerning what each wants in particular. This long laborious comparison should be the first study of the painter, who aims at the greatest style. By this means, he acquires a just idea of beautiful forms; he corrects nature by herself, her imperfect state by her more perfect. His eye being enabled to distinguish the accidental deficiencies, excrescences, and deformities of things, from their general figures, he makes out an abstract idea of their forms more perfect than any one original; and what may seem a paradox, he learns to design naturally by drawing his figures unlike to any one object. This idea of the perfect state of nature, which the Artist calls the Ideal Beauty, is the great leading principle, by which works of genius are conducted. By this Phidias acquired his fame. He wrought[8] upon a sober principle, what has so much exited the enthusiasm of the world; and by this method you, who have courage to tread the same path, may acquire equal reputation.

THIS is the idea which has acquired, and which seems to have a right to the epithet of *divine*, as it may be said to preside, like a supreme judge, over all the productions of nature; appearing to be possessed of the will and intention of the Creator, as far as they regard the external form of living beings. When a man once possesses this idea in its perfection, there is no danger, but that he will be sufficiently warmed by it himself, and be able to warm and ravish every one else.

THUS it is from a reiterated experience, and a close comparison of the objects in nature, that an artist becomes possessed of the idea of that central form, if I may so express it, from which every deviation is deformity. But the investigation of this form, I grant, is painful, and I know but of one method of shortening the road; this is, by a careful study of the works of the ancient sculptors; who, being indefatigable in the school of nature, have left models of that perfect form behind them, which an artist would prefer as supremely beautiful, who had spent his whole life in that single contemplation. But if

---

[7] i.e. beyond. [eds]

[8] i.e. acted or worked. [eds]

industry carried them thus far, may not you also hope for the same reward from the same labour? We have the same school opened to us, that was opened to them; for nature denies her instructions to none, who desire to become her pupils.

TO the principle I have laid down, that the idea of beauty in each species of beings is an invariable one, it may be objected, that in every particular species there are various central forms, which are separate and distinct from each other, and yet are undeniably beautiful; that in the human figure, for instance, the beauty of Hercules is one, of the Gladiator another, of the Apollo another; which makes so many different ideas of beauty.[9]

IT is true, indeed, that these figures are each perfect in their kind, though of different characters and proportions; but still none of them is the representation of an individual, but of a class. And as there is one general form, which, as I have said, belongs to the human kind at large, so in each of these classes there is one common idea and central form, which is the abstract of the various individual forms belonging to that class. Thus, though the forms of childhood and age differ exceedingly, there is a common form in childhood, and a common form in age, which is the more perfect, as it is more remote from all peculiarities. But I must add further, that though the most perfect forms of each of the general divisions of the human figure are ideal, and superior to any individual form of that class; yet the highest perfection of the human figure is not to be found in any one of them. It is not in the Hercules, nor in the Gladiator, nor in the Apollo; but in that form which is taken from them all, and which partakes equally of the activity of the Gladiator, of the delicacy of the Apollo, and of the muscular strength of the Hercules. For perfect beauty in any species must combine all of the characters which are beautiful in that species. It cannot consist in any one to the exclusion of the rest: no one, therefore, must be predominant, that no one may be deficient.

THE knowledge of these different characters, and the power of separating and distinguishing them, is undoubtedly necessary to the painter, who is to vary his compositions with figures of various forms and proportions, though he is never to lose sight of the general idea of perfection in each kind.

THERE is, likewise, a kind of symmetry, or proportion, which may properly be said to belong to deformity. A figure lean or corpulent, tall or short, though deviating from beauty, may still have a certain union of the various parts, which may contribute to make them on the whole not unpleasing.

WHEN the Artist has by diligent attention acquired a clear and distinct idea of beauty and symmetry; when he has reduced the variety of nature to the abstract idea; his next task will be to become acquainted with the genuine habits of nature, as distinguished from those of fashion. For in the same manner, and on the same principles, as he has acquired the knowledge of the real forms of nature, distinct from accidental deformity, he must endeavour to separate simple chaste nature, from those adventitious, those affected and forced airs or actions, with which she is loaded by modern education.

PERHAPS I cannot better explain what I mean, than by reminding you of what was taught us by the Professor of Anatomy,[10] in respect to the natural position of movement of the feet. He observed that the fashion of turning them outwards was contrary to the intent of nature, as might be seen from the structure of the bones, and from the weakness that proceeded from that manner of standing. To this we may add the erect position of the head, the projection of the chest, the walking with straight knees, and many such actions, which we know to be merely the result of fashion, and what nature never warranted, as we are sure that we have been taught them when children.

HOWEVER the mechanic and ornamental arts may sacrifice to fashion, she must be entirely excluded from the Art of Painting; the painter

---

[9]   Reynolds is referring here to some famous Greek sculptures. The 'Apollo' is probably the 'Apollo Belvedere' in the Vatican (Pl. 9). [eds]

[10]   The Professor of Anatomy in 1770 was Dr William Hunter. [eds]

must never mistake this capricious changeling for the genuine offspring of nature; he must divest himself of all prejudices in favour of his age or country; he must disregard all local and temporary ornaments, and look only on those general habits which are every where and always the same. He addresses his works to the people of every country and every age; he calls upon posterity to be his spectators, and says with Zeuxis, *in oeternitatem pingo.*[11]

THE neglect of separating modern fashions from the habits of nature, leads to that ridiculous style which has been practised by some painters, who have given to Grecian Heroes the airs and graces practised in the court of Lewis the Fourteenth; an absurdity almost as great as it would have been to have dressed them after the fashion of that court.

TO avoid this error, however, and to retain the true simplicity of nature, is a task more difficult than at first sight it may appear. The prejudices in favour of the fashions and customs that we have been used to, and which are justly called a second nature, make it too often difficult to distinguish that which is natural, from that which is the result of education; they frequently even give a predilection in favour of the artificial mode; and almost every one is apt to be guided by those local prejudices, who has not chastised[12] his mind, and regulated the instability of his affections by the eternal invariable idea of nature.

HERE then, as before, we must have recourse to the Ancients as instructors. It is from a careful study of their works that you will be enabled to attain to the real simplicity of nature; they will suggest many observations, which would probably escape you, if your study were confined to nature alone. And, indeed, I cannot help suspecting, that in this instance the ancients had an easier task than the moderns. They had, probably, little or nothing to unlearn, as their manners were nearly approaching to this desirable simplicity; while the modern artist, before he can see the truth of things, is obliged to remove a veil, with which the fashion of the times has thought proper to cover her.

HAVING gone thus far in our investigation of the great style in painting, if we now should suppose that the artist has formed the true idea of beauty, which enables him to give his works a correct and perfect design; if we should suppose also, that he has acquired a knowledge of unadulterated habits of nature, which gives him simplicity; the rest of his task is, perhaps, less than is generally imagined. Beauty and simplicity have so great a share in the composition of a great style, that he who has acquired them has little else to learn. It must not, indeed, be forgotten, that there is a nobleness of conception, which goes beyond any thing in the mere exhibition even of perfect form; there is an art of animating and dignifying the figures with intellectual grandeur, of impressing the appearance of philosophic wisdom, or heroic virtue. This can only be acquired by him that enlarges the sphere of his understanding by a variety of knowledge, and warms his imagination with the best productions of ancient and modern poetry.

IF deceiving the eye were the only business of the art, there is no doubt, indeed, but the minute painter would be more apt to succeed: but it is not the eye, it is the mind, which the painter of genius desires to address; nor will he waste a moment upon those smaller objects, which only serve to catch the sense,[13] to divide the attention, and to counteract his great design of speaking to the heart.

THIS is the ambition which I wish to excite in your minds; and the object I have had in my view, throughout this discourse, is that one great idea, which gives to painting its true dignity, which entitles it to the name of a Liberal Art, and ranks it as a sister of poetry.

As for the various departments of painting, which do not presume to make such high pretensions, they are many. None of them are without their merit, though none enter into competition with this universal presiding idea of the art. The painters who have applied themselves more particularly to low and vulgar characters, and who express with precision the various shades of passion, as they are exhibited by vulgar minds, (such as we see in the works of

---

[11]   I paint for all time. [eds]

[12]   i.e. corrected, reformed. [eds]

[13]   i.e. distract. [eds]

Hogarth,) deserve great praise; but as their genius has been employed on low and confined subjects, the praise which we give must be as limited as its object. The merry-making, or quarrelling, of the Boors of Teniers; the same sort of productions of Brouwer, or Ostade,[14] are excellent in their kind; and the excellence and its praise will be in proportion, as, in those limited subjects, and peculiar[15] forms, they introduce more or less of the expression of those passions, as they appear in general and more enlarged nature. This principle may be applied to the Battle-pieces of Bourgognone, the French Gallantries of Watteau, and even beyond the exhibitions of animal life, to the Landscapes of Claude Lorraine, and the Sea-Views of Vandervelde. All these painters have, in general, the same right, in different degrees, to the name of a painter, which a satirist, an epigrammatist, a sonneteer, a writer of pastorals, or descriptive poetry, has to that of a poet.

IN the same rank, and perhaps of not so great merit, is the cold painter of portraits. But his correct and just imitation of his object has its merit. Even the painter of still life, whose highest ambition is to give a minute representation of every part of those low objects which he sets before him, deserves praise in proportion to his attainment; because no part of this excellent art, so much the ornament of polished life, is destitute of value and use. These, however, are by no means the views to which the mind of the student ought to be *primarily* directed. Having begun by aiming at better things, if from particular inclination, or from the taste of the time he lives in, or from necessity, or from failure in the highest attempts, he is obliged to descend lower, he will bring into the lower sphere of art a grandeur of composition and character, that will raise and ennoble his works far above their natural rank.

DISCOURSE VII[16]

GENTLEMEN,

IT has been my uniform endeavour, since I first addressed you from this place, to impress you strongly with one ruling idea. I wished you to be persuaded, that success in your art depends almost entirely on your own industry; but the industry which I principally recommended, is not the industry of the *hands*, but of the *mind*.

As our art is not a divine *gift*, so neither is it a mechanical *trade*. Its foundations are laid in solid science: and practice, though essential to perfection, can never attain that to which it aims, unless it works under the direction of principle.

SOME writers upon art carry this point too far, and suppose that such a body of universal and profound learning is requisite, that the very enumeration of its kinds is enough to frighten a beginner. Vitruvius, after going through the many accomplishments of nature, and the many acquirements of learning, necessary to an architect, proceeds with great gravity to assert, that he ought to be well skilled in the civil law; that he may not be cheated in the title of the ground he builds on.[17] But without such exaggeration, we may go so far as to assert, that a painter stands in need of more knowledge than is to be picked off his palate, or collected by looking on his model, whether it be in life or in picture. He can never be a great artist, who is grossly illiterate.

EVERY man whose business is description, ought to be tolerably conversant with the poets, in some language or other; that he may imbibe a poetical spirit, and enlarge his stock of ideas. He ought to acquire an habit of comparing and digesting his notions. He ought not to be wholly unacquainted with that part of philosophy which gives an insight into human nature, and relates to the manners, characters, passions,

---

[14]   Teniers, Brouwer and Ostade were seventeenth century Dutch painters, famous for their genre subjects; hence Reynolds's reference to 'low and confined subjects'. [eds]

[15]   i.e. specialized. [eds]

[16]   10 December, 1776. [eds]

[17]   Marcus Vitruvius Pollio (1st century AD), Roman architect and military engineer. Reynolds refers here to his *De architectura* (Architecture). [eds]

and affections. He ought to know *something* concerning the mind, as well as *a great deal* concerning the body of man. For this purpose, it is not necessary that he should go into such a compass of reading, as must, by distracting his attention, disqualify him for the practical part of his profession, and make him sink the performer in the critic. Reading, if it can be made of favourite recreation of his leisure hours, will improve and enlarge his mind, without retarding his actual industry. What such partial and desultory reading cannot afford, may be supplied by the conversation of learned and ingenious men, which is the best of all substitutes for those who have not the means or opportunities of deep study.

OF these studies, and this conversation, the desired and legitimate offspring is a power of distinguishing right from wrong; which power applied to works of art, is denominated *Taste*. Let me then, without further introduction, enter upon an examination, whether taste be so far beyond our reach, as to be unattainable by care; or be so very vague and capricious, that no care ought to be employed about it.

IT has been the fate of arts to be enveloped in mysterious and incomprehensive language, as if it was thought necessary that even the terms should correspond to the idea entertained of the instability and uncertainty of the rules which they expressed.

TO speak of genius and taste, as in any way connected with reason or common sense, would be, in the opinion of some towering talkers, to speak like a man who possessed neither; who had never felt that enthusiasm, or, to use their own inflated language, was never warmed by the Promethean fire, which animates the canvas and vivifies the marble.

IF, in order to be intelligible, I appear to degrade art by bringing her down from her visionary situation in the clouds, it is only to give her a more solid mansion upon the earth. It is necessary that at some time or other we should see things as they really are, and not impose on ourselves by that false magnitude with which objects appear when viewed indistinctly as through a mist.

WE will allow a poet to express his meaning, when his meaning is not well known to himself, with a certain degree of obscurity, as it is one source of the sublime. But when, in plain prose, we gravely talk of courting the muse in shady bowers; waiting the call and inspiration of Genius, finding out where he inhabits, and where he is to be invoked with the greatest success; of attending to times and seasons when the imagination shoots with the greatest vigour, whether at the summer solstice or the vernal equinox; sagaciously observing how much the wild freedom and liberty is cramped by attention to established rules; and how this same imagination begins to grow dim in advanced age, smothered and deadened by too much judgement; when we talk such language, or entertain such sentiments as these, we generally rest contented with mere words, or at best entertain notions not only groundless, but pernicious.

GENIUS and taste, in their common acceptation, appear to be very nearly related; the difference lies only in this, that genius has superadded to it a habit or power of execution: or we may say, that taste when this power is added, changes it name, and is called genius. They both, in the popular opinion, pretend to an entire exemption from the restraint of rules. It is supposed that their powers are intuitive; that under the name of genius great works are produced, and under the name of taste an exact judgement is given, without our knowing why, and without our being under the least obligation to reason, precept, or experience.

ONE can scarce state these opinions without exposing their absurdity; yet they are constantly in the mouths of men, and particularly of artists. They who have thought seriously on this subject, do not carry the point so far; yet I am persuaded, that even among those few who may be called thinkers, the prevalent opinion allows less than it ought to the powers of reason; and considers the principles of taste, which give all their authority to the rules of art, as more fluctuating, and as having less solid foundations, than we shall find, upon examination, they really have.

WE apply the term *Taste* to that act of the mind by which we like or dislike, whatever be the subject. Our judgement upon an airy nothing, a fancy which has no foundation, is called by the same name which we give to our determination concerning those truths which refer to the most general and most unalterable principles of human nature; to the works which are only to be produced by the greatest efforts of the human understanding. However inconvenient this may be, we are obliged to take words as we find them; all we can do is to distinguish the *things* to which they are applied.

WE may let pass those things which are at once subjects of taste and sense, and which having as much certainty as the senses themselves, give no occasion to enquiry or dispute. The natural appetite or taste of the human mind is for *Truth*; whether that truth results from the real agreement or equality of original ideas among themselves; from the agreement of the representation of any object with the thing represented; or from the correspondence of the several parts of any arrangement with each other. It is the very same taste which relishes a demonstration in geometry, that is pleased with the resemblance of a picture to an original, and touched with the harmony of music.

ALL these have unalterable and fixed foundations in nature, and are therefore equally investigated by reason, and known by study; some with more, some with less clearness, but all exactly in the same way. A picture that is unlike, is false. Disproportionate ordonnance[18] of parts is not right; because it cannot be true, until it ceases to be a contradiction to assert, that the parts have no relation to the whole. Colouring is true when it is naturally adapted to the eye, from brightness, from softness, from harmony, from resemblance; because these agree with their object, *nature*, and therefore are true; as true as mathematical demonstration; but known to be true only to those who study these things.

BUT beside *real*, there is also *apparent* truth, or opinion, or prejudice. With regard to real truth, when it is known, the taste which conforms to it, is, and must be, uniform. With regard to the second sort of truth which may be called truth upon sufferance, or truth by courtesy, it is not fixed, but variable. However, whilst these opinions and prejudices, on which it is founded, continue, they operate as truth; and the art whose office it is to please the mind, as well as instruct it, must direct itself according to *opinion*, or it will not attain its end.

IN proportion as these prejudices are known to be generally diffused or long received,

the taste which conforms to them approaches nearer to certainty, and to a sort of resemblance to real science, even where opinions are found to be no better than prejudices. And since they deserve, on account of their duration and extent, to be considered as really true, they become capable of no small degree of stability and determination[19] by their permanent and uniform nature.

AS these prejudices become more narrow, more local, more transitory, this secondary taste becomes more and more fantastical; recedes from real science; is less to be approved by reason, and less followed in practice; though in no case perhaps to be wholly neglected, where it does not stand, as it sometimes does, in direct defiance of the most respectable opinions received amongst mankind.

MY notion of nature comprehends not only the forms which nature produces, but also the nature and internal fabric and organization, as I may call it, of the human mind and imagination. The terms beauty, or nature, which are general ideas, are but different modes of expressing the same thing, whether we apply these terms to statues, poetry, or picture. Deformity is not nature, but an accidental[20] deviation from her accustomed practice. This general idea therefore ought to be called Nature, and nothing else, correctly speaking, has a right to that name. But we are so far from speaking, in common conversation, with any such accuracy, that, on the contrary, when we criticize Rembrandt and other Dutch painters, who introduced into their historical pictures exact representations of individual objects with all their imperfections, we say, – though it is not in a good taste, yet it is nature.

THIS misapplication of terms must be very often perplexing to the young student. Is not art, he may say, an imitation of nature? Must he not therefore who imitates here with the greatest fidelity, be the best artist? By this mode of reasoning Rembrandt has a higher place than Raffaelle. But a very little reflection will serve to show us that these particularities cannot be nature: for how can that be the nature of man, in which no two individuals are the same?

---

[18]   i.e. arrangement. [eds]

[19]   i.e. decisiveness. [eds]

[20]   i.e. chance and non-essential. [eds]

IT plainly appears, that as a work is conducted under the influence of general ideas, or partial, it is principally to be considered as the effect of a good or a bad taste.

As beauty therefore does not consist in taking what lies immediately before you, so neither, in our pursuit of taste, are those opinions which we first received and adopted, the best choice, or the most natural to the mind and imagination. In the infancy of our knowledge we seize with greediness the good that is within our reach; it is by after-consideration, and in consequence of discipline, that we refuse the present for a greater good at a distance. The nobility or elevation of all arts, like the excellency of virtue itself, consists in adopting this enlarged and comprehensive idea; and all criticism built upon the more confined view of what is natural, may properly be called *shallow* criticism, rather than false: its defect is, that the truth is not sufficiently extensive.

HE who thinks nature, in the narrow sense of the word, is alone to be followed, will produce but a scanty entertainment for the imagination: every thing is to be done with which it is natural for the mind to be pleased, whether it proceeds from simplicity or variety, uniformity or irregularity; whether the scenes are familiar or exotic; rude and wild, or enriched and cultivated; for it is natural for the mind to be pleased with all these in their turn. In short, whatever pleases has in it what is analogous to the mind, and is therefore, in the highest and best sense of the word, natural.

IT is the sense of nature or truth which ought more particularly to be cultivated by the professors of art; and it may be observed, that many wise and learned men, who have accustomed their minds to admit nothing for truth but what can be proved by mathematical demonstration, have seldom any relish for those arts which address themselves to the fancy, the rectitude and truth of which is known by another kind of proof: and we may add, that the acquisition of this knowledge requires as much circumspection and sagacity, as is necessary to attain those truths which are more capable of demonstration. Reason must ultimately determine our choice on every occasion; but this reason may still be exerted ineffectually by applying to taste principles which, though right as far as they go, yet do not reach the object. No man, for instance, can deny, that it seems at first view very reasonable, that a statue which is to carry down to posterity the resemblance of an individual should be dressed in the fashion of the times, in the dress which he himself wore: this would certainly be true, if the dress were part of the man; but after a time, the dress is only an amusement for an antiquarian; and if it obstructs the general design of the piece, it is to be disregarded by the artist. Common sense must here give way to a higher sense. In the naked form, and in the disposition of the drapery, the difference between one artist and another is principally seen. But if he is compelled to exhibit the modern dress, the naked form is entirely hid, and the drapery is already disposed by the skill of the tailor. Were a Phidias to obey such absurd commands, he would please no more than an ordinary sculptor; since, in the inferior parts of every art, the learned and the ignorant are nearly upon a level.

THESE were probably among the reasons that induced the sculptor of that wonderful figure of Laocoon[21] to exhibit him naked, notwithstanding he was surprised in the act of sacrificing to Apollo, and consequently ought to have been shown in his sacerdotal habits, if those greater reasons had not preponderated. Art is not yet in so high estimation with us, as to obtain so great a sacrifice as the ancients made, especially the Grecians; who suffered themselves to be represented naked, whether they were generals, lawgivers, or kings.

I SHALL now say something on that part of taste, which, as I have hinted to you before, does not belong so much to the external form of things, but is addressed to the mind, and depends on its original frame, or, to use the expression, the organization of the soul; I mean the imagination and the passions. The principles of these are as invariable as the former, and are to be known and reasoned upon in the same manner, by an appeal to common sense deciding upon the common feelings of mankind. This

---

[21] 'Laocoon' is a sculpture from the 2nd century BC (See Study), the work of three sculptors, Agesander, Polydorus and Athenodorus (fl.c.150 BC). The work became influential as a sculptural representation of pathos, and the 'classicism' of the work was discussed and criticized in the writings of the German archaeologist and historian, Johann Winkelmann (1717–68), and by Gotthold Lessing (1729–81), man of letters. [eds]

sense, and these feelings, appear to me of equal authority, and equally conclusive. Now this appeal implies a general uniformity and agreement in the minds of men. It would be else an idle and vain endeavour to establish rules of art; it would be pursuing a phantom to attempt to move affections with which we were entirely unacquainted. We have no reason to suspect there is a greater difference between our minds than between our forms; of which, though there are no two alike, yet there is a general similitude that goes through the whole race of mankind; and those who have cultivated their taste can distinguish what is beautiful or deformed, or, in other words, what agrees with or deviates from the general idea of nature, in one case, as well as in the other.

THE internal fabric of our minds, as well as the external form of our bodies, being nearly uniform; it seems then to follow of course, that as the imagination is incapable of producing any thing originally of itself, and can only vary and combine those ideas with which it is furnished by means of the senses, there will be necessarily an agreement in the imaginations as in the senses of men. There being this agreement, it follows, that in all cases, in our lightest amusements, as well as in our most serious actions and engagements of life, we must regulate our affections of every kind by that of others. The well-disciplined mind acknowledges this authority, and submits its own opinion to the public voice. It is from knowing what are the general feelings and passions of mankind, that we acquire a true idea of what imagination is; though it appears as if we had nothing to do but to consult our own particular sensations, and these were sufficient to ensure us from all error and mistake.

EVERY art, like our own, has in its composition fluctuating as well as fixed principles. It is an attentive enquiry into their difference that will enable us to determine how far we are influenced by custom and habit, and what is fixed in the nature of things.

To distinguish how much has solid foundation, we may have recourse to the same proof by which some hold that wit ought to be tried; whether it preserves itself when translated. That wit is false, which can subsist only in one language; and that picture which pleases only one age or one nation, owes its reception to some local or accidental association of ideas.

WE may apply this to every custom and habit of life. Thus the general principles of urbanity, politeness, or civility, have been ever the same in all nations; but the manner, whether by bowing the body, kneeling, prostration, pulling off the upper part of our dress, or taking away the lower, is a matter of custom.

THUS in regard to ornaments, it would be unjust to conclude that because they were at first arbitrarily contrived, they are therefore undeserving of our attention; on the contrary, he who neglects the cultivation of those ornaments, acts contrary to nature and reason. As life would be imperfect without its highest ornaments, the Arts, so these arts themselves would be imperfect without *their* ornaments. Though we by no means ought to rank these with positive and substantial beauties, yet it must be allowed that a knowledge of both is essentially requisite towards forming a complete, whole, and perfect taste. It is in reality from the ornaments that arts receive their peculiar[22] character and complexion;[23] we may add, that in them we find the characteristical mark of a national taste; as by throwing up a feather in the air, we know which way the wind blows, better than by a more heavy matter.

THE striking distinction between the works of the Roman, Bolognian, and Venetian schools, consists more in that general effect which is produced by colours, than in the more profound excellencies of the art; at least it is from thence that each is distinguished and known at first sight. Thus it is the ornaments, rather than the proportions of architecture, which at the first glance distinguish the different orders from each

---

[22]   i.e. individual. [eds]

[23]   i.e. temperament, nature. [eds]

other; the Doric is known by its triglyphs, the Ionic by its volutes, and the Corinthian by its acanthus.[24]

IT appears to be the same right turn of mind which enables a man to acquire the *truth*, or the just idea of what is right, in the ornaments, as in the more stable principles of art. It has still the same centre of perfection, though it is the centre of a smaller circle.

TO illustrate this by the fashion of dress, in which there is allowed to be a good or bad taste. The component parts of dress are continually changing from great to little, from short to long; but the general form still remains: it is still the same general dress which is comparatively fixed, though on a very slender foundation; but it is on this which fashion must rest. He who invents with the most success, or dresses in the best taste, would probably, from the same sagacity employed to greater purposes, have discovered equal skill, or have formed the same correct taste, in the highest labours of art.

IT is in dress as in things of greater consequence. Fashions originate from those only who have the high and powerful advantages of rank, birth, and fortune. Many of the ornaments of art, those for which no reason can be given, are transmitted to us, are adopted, and acquire their consequence from the company in which we have been used to see then. As Greece and Rome are the foundations from whence have flowed all kinds of excellence, to that veneration which they have a right to claim for the pleasure and knowledge which they have afforded us, we voluntarily add our approbation of every ornament and every custom that belonged to them, even to the fashion of their dress. For it may be observed that, not satisfied with them in their own place, we make no difficulty of dressing statues of modern heroes or senators in the fashion of the Roman armour or peaceful robe; we go so far as hardly to bear a statue in any other drapery.

THE figures of the great men of those nations have come down to us in sculpture. In sculpture remain almost all the excellent specimens of ancient art. We have so far associated personal dignity to the persons thus represented, and the truth of art to their manner of representation, that it is not in our power any longer to separate them. This is not so in painting; because having no excellent ancient portraits, that connection was never formed. Indeed we could no more venture to paint a general officer in a Roman military habit, than we could make a statue in the present uniform. But since we have no ancient portraits, – to show how ready we are to adopt those kind of prejudices, we make the best authority among the moderns serve the same purpose. The great variety of excellent portraits with which Vandyck has enriched this nation, we are not content to admire for their real excellence, but extend our approbation even to the dress which happened to be the fashion of that age.[25] We all very well remember how common it was a few years ago for portraits to be drawn in this fantastick dress; and this custom is not yet entirely laid aside. By this means it must be acknowledged very ordinary pictures acquired something of the air and effect of the works of Vandyck, and appeared therefore at first sight to be better pictures than they really were; they appeared so, however, to those only who had the means of making this association; and when made, it was irresistible. But this association is nature, and refers to that secondary truth that comes from conformity to general prejudice and opinion; it is therefore not merely fantastical. Besides the prejudice which we have in favour of ancient dresses, there may be likewise other reasons for the effect which they produce; among which we may justly rank the simplicity of them, consisting of little more than one single piece of drapery, without those whimsical capricious forms by which all other dresses are embarrassed.

THUS, though it is from the prejudice we have in favour of the ancients, who have taught us architecture, that we have adopted likewise

---

[24] triglyphs: block or tablet with three vertical grooves.
volutes: spiral curves.
acanthus: leaves of the acanthus plant. [eds]

[25] Sir Anthony Van Dyck (1599–1641), a Dutch portrait painter who worked in England where he was patronized by the Court of Charles I. He became known for the 'Van Dyck habit', the elaborate ceremonial dress depicted in many of his portrait commissions. [eds]

their ornaments; and though we are satisfied that neither nature nor reason are the foundation of those beauties which we imagine we see in that art, yet if any one, persuaded of this truth, should therefore invent new orders of equal beauty, which we will suppose to be possible, they would not please; nor ought he to complain, since the old has that great advantage of having custom and prejudice on its side. In this case we leave what has every prejudice in its favour, to take that which will have no advantage over what we have left, but novelty; which soon destroys itself, and at any rate is but a weak antagonist against custom.

ANCIENT ornaments, having the right of possession, ought not to be removed, unless to make room for that which not only has higher pretensions, but such pretensions as will balance the evil and confusion which innovation always brings with it.

To this we may add, that even the durability of the materials will often contribute to give a superiority to one object over another. Ornaments in buildings, with which taste is principally concerned, are composed of materials which last longer than those of which dress is composed;

the former therefore make higher pretensions to our favour and prejudice.

SOME attention is surely due to what we can no more get rid of than we can go out of ourselves. We are creatures of prejudice; we neither can nor ought to eradicate it; we must only regulate it by reason; which kind of regulation is indeed little more than obliging the lesser, the local and temporary prejudices, to give way to those which are more durable and lasting.

HE therefore who in his practice of portrait-painting wishes to dignify his subject, which we will suppose to be a lady, will not paint her in the modern dress, the familiarity of which alone is sufficient to destroy all dignity. He takes care that his work shall correspond to those ideas and that imagination which he knows will regulate the judgement of others; and therefore dresses his figure something with the general air of the antique for the sake of dignity, and preserves something of the modern for the sake of likeness. By this conduct his works correspond with those prejudices which we have in favour of what we continually see; and the relish of the antique simplicity corresponds with what we may call the more learned and scientific prejudice.

Source: Sir Joshua Reynolds, *Discourses on Art*, edited by Robert R. Wark, Yale University Press, 1975.

Robert Adam
Extracts from The Works in Architecture of Robert and James Adam, Esquires

Prepared for the Course Team by
Colin Cunningham

Contents

Robert Adam
Extracts from The Works in Architecture of Robert and James Adam, Esquires

Robert Adam (1728–92) was the second surviving son of William Adam, a leading Scottish architect, entrepreneur, building contractor and a gentleman of moderate means. William gave Robert a liberal education, first at Edinburgh High School, and then, from 1743, at Edinburgh University, where he met several of the leading thinkers of his generation, such as David Hume and Adam Smith. Robert joined his father's office in 1746, taking on the business in partnership with his elder brother John on his father's death in 1748. He gained a thorough grounding in all the common business of building, not least from the firm's involvement as contractors for Fort George in the Highlands. However by 1754 he had amassed savings of about £5,000, which he used on a lengthy grand tour through France to Italy.

Between 1754 and 1758 he studied the buildings of Italy, particularly the ruins of ancient Rome. He employed the French draughtsman Charles-Louis Clérissau to help record the ancient monuments. He also made friends with the mercurial Italian artist Giambattista Piranesi, collected casts of antique works and made hundreds of detailed drawings. Adam considered making a new, corrected, edition of Desgodetz's Les Edifices Antiques de Rome (1682), the best guide to the ruins available at that time. Instead he travelled to Spalatro (modern Split in former Yugoslavia) to survey the remains, which he published as the Ruins of the Palace of the Emperor Diocletian at Spalatro in 1764.

In 1758, Robert returned to London and set up as an architect and interior decorator. He soon acquired important patrons, built Harewood House (1759), Croome Court and Kedleston (1760), and remodelled Bowood (1761), Syon House (1762) and Osterley Park (1763).

By 1773 the partnership of Robert and and his younger brother James had suffered a long and expensive lawsuit over the patent of a type of Roman cement, or stucco, and been almost ruined in their attempts to construct a prestigious block of housing, the Adelphi, on the Strand shore of the Thames (demolished in the 1930s). Partly to re-establish the firm's position Adam planned a lavish publication. This book, The Works in Architecture of Robert and James Adam, appeared in three volumes, the first in 1773, the second in 1779 and the third at the time of his younger brother's death in 1822.

The first two volumes were arranged in five separate 'numbers' of eight plates each. Originally these were produced separately, and their formats vary slightly. In Volume I there is a preface to each 'number' (of which the first is much the longest) and quite extensive descriptions of some of the plates. Volume II has only a single brief preface; and Volume III has only a printer's advertisement, and the twenty-four plates are not divided into 'numbers'. Our excerpts preserve the eccentric spelling, capitalization and punctuation of the original.

The footnotes in this section are complex. Mostly they are the work of Adam himself with interpolative notes by the volume's editors – these are placed within square brackets at the appropriate point and signed 'eds'.

Volume I

I PREFACE to The SEAT of the DUKE of NORTHUMBERLAND, at SION

SOME apology may, perhaps, be requisite, for giving to the world a book of architecture, after so many works of this kind have been published in Italy, France and England during the tow last centuries.

The novelty and variety of the following designs, will, we flatter ourselves, not only excuse, but justify our conduct, in communicating them to the world. —— We have not trod in the path of others, nor derived aid from their labours. In the works which we have had the honour to execute, we have not only met with the approbation of our employers, but even with the imitation of other artists, to such a degree, as in some measure to have brought about, in this country; a kind of revolution in the whole system of this useful and elegant art. These circumstances induced us to hope, that to collect and engrave our works would afford both entertainment and instruction.

To enter upon an enquiry into the state of this art in Great Britain, till the late changes it has undergone, is no part of our present design. We leave that subject to the observation of the skilful; who we doubt not, will easily perceive, within these few years, a remarkable improvement in the form, convenience, arrangement, and relief of apartments; a greater movement[1] and variety, in

---

[1] *Movement* is meant to express, the rise and fall, the advance and recess, with other diversity of form, in the different parts of a building, so as to add greatly to the picturesque of the composition. For the rising and falling, advancing and receding, with the convexity and concavity, and other forms of the great parts, have the same effect in architecture, that hill and dale, fore-ground and distance, swelling and sinking have in landscape : That is, they serve to produce an agreeable and diversified contour, that groups and contrasts like a picture, and creates a variety of light and shade, which gives great spirit, beauty and effect to the composition.

It is not always that such variety can be introduced into the design of any building but where it can be obtained without encroaching upon its useful purposes, it adds much to its merit, as an object of beauty and grandeur.

The effect of the height and convexity of the dome of St. Peter's, contrasted with the lower square front, and the concavity of its court, is a striking instance of this sort of composition. [St Peter's dome designed by Michelangelo, 1558–60, completed by Giacomo della Porta, 1588–90 (see Pl. 32). [Façade by Carlo Maderna, c.1607–15; colonnades by Bernini, 1656ff. – eds.] The college and church *des quatre nations* at Paris [possibly the Val de Grace, designed by François Mansart, 1645–50, completed 1667. – eds], is though small, another of the same kind; and with us, we really do not recollect any example of so much movement and contrast, as in the south front of Kedleston house in Derbyshire, one of the seats of the Right Honourable Lord Scarsdale, of which building we shall have occasion to speak more at large hereafter. [Adam never did include plates of Kedleston in *The Works.* – eds] [Adam]

[Adam concludes with a note on the English baroque architect, Vanburgh.]

[2] *The massive entablature.* It is well known to every one who has made architecture, in any degree, the object of his attention, that the entablature constitutes a principal part or each order, and is itself formed of three great divisions, the architrave, freeze and cornice. [See note 18 below on the orders, Pl. 31, and architecture cassette. – eds]

It is not here meant to find fault with the whole, or its component parts, but so far only as it has been abused by the misapplication, ignorance, and want of invention in many modern artists.

Nothing can be more noble and striking, when properly applied, than a fine order of columns, with their bases, capitals, and entablatures ; nothing more sterile and disgustful, than to see for ever the dull repetition of Dorick, Ionick, and Corinthian entablatures, in their usual proportions, reigning round every apartment, where no order can come or ought to come; and yet it is astonishing to think that this has been almost invariably the case in the apartments of every house in Europe, that has any pretensions to magnificence, from the days of Bramante down to our time. [Donato Bramante (1444–1514), high renaissance architect; most famous work the tempietto (little temple) of S. Pietro, Montorio, Rome (1502). – eds] In smaller rooms, where height is wanting, the architrave has sometimes been omitted, and sometimes both architrave and freeze, but their places were ponderously supplied by a cornice of most ample dimensions fit for the temple of Jupiter Tonans, from which it was imitated perhaps, or more probably, copied. [Temple of Jupiter Tonans (Jupiter the Thunderer) now identified as the Temple of Vespasian in the Forum at Rome; illustrated in Desgodetz's *Les Edifices Antiques de Rome* (1682). – eds]

To describe here in what manner this tiresome repetition may be avoided, would be to anticipate the purpose of the present work, which, among other things, is intended to point out a new stile of composition for those parts of interior decoration. [Adam]

the outside composition, and in the decoration of the inside, an almost total change.

The massive entablature,[2] the ponderous compartment ceiling,[3] the tabernacle frame,

---

[3]   *Compartment ceiling:* a name given to all ceilings that are divided into various pannels, surrounded with mouldings, a mode to which we do not here mean to object, there being many beautiful compositions of this kind, both ancient and modern; but the epithet of *ponderous* is applied to distinguish those that were in use in this country, during the last century, from those of the present times; the stile of the former being of the most enormous weight and depth.

These absurd compositions took their rise in Italy, under the first of their modern masters, who were no doubt led into that idea from the observations of the soffits [underside of architectural element such as a cornice or arch. – eds] used by the ancients in the porticos of their temples and other public works. These the ancients, with their usual skill and judgement, kept of a bold and massive style, suiting them to the strength, magnitude, and height of the building, and making an allowance for their being on the exterior part, and adjoining to other great objects; all which served to diminish and lighten the effect of their compartments. – But on the inside of their edifices the ancients were extremely careful to proportion both the size and depth of their compartments and pannels, to the distance from the eye and the objects with which they were to be compared; and, with regard to the decoration of their private and bathing apartments, they were all delicacy, gaiety, grace, and beauty. If the reader is desirous to examine more minutely into these truths, let him consult the Rotunda [now known as the Pantheon. See Pl. 27. – eds], the Temple of Peace [now known as the Basilica of Maxentius. – eds], the ruins of Adrian's villa [the grandiose country palace of the emperor Hadrian at Tivoli. – eds], the Palace of the Emperors [the series of imperial palaces which cover the Palatine Hill in Rome. See Pl. 28.– eds], and other Cryptæ [covered or subterranean passages. – eds] at Rome, with the inimitable remains on the Baian shore. [In the eighteenth century most Roman remains were still partly underground and unexcavated (see also footnote 5 below). Excavation had only just begun at Herculaneum and Pompeii, on the Baian shore, when Adam visited Italy. – eds] – We shall only add, that from this mistake of the first modern Italian artists, all Europe has been misled, and has been servilely groaning under this load for these three centuries past.

Michael Angelo, Raphael, Pyrro Ligerio, Dominichino, Giorgio Vasari, and Algardi, with great taste and knowledge, threw off these prejudices, and boldly aimed at restoring the antique. [All painters, sculptors and architects of high and late renaissance in Italy. Domenichino the only one not to have worked as an architect, but involved with decoration of Farnese Palace, Rome, an important source for Adam's style of painted decoration. – eds]

But at this time the rage of painting became so prevalent in Italy, that instead of following these great examples, they covered every ceiling with large fresco compositions, which, tho' extremely fine and well painted, were very much misplaced, and must necessarily, from the attitude in which they are beheld, tire the patience of every spectator. Great compositions should be placed so as to be viewed with ease. Grotesque ornaments and figures, in any situation, are perceived with the glance of an eye, and require little examination.

The heavy compartment ceilings were afterwards adopted in France; and Le Potre adorned them with all the trappings of his luxuriant imagination. Inigo Jones introduced them into England, with as much weight, but less fancy and embellishment. [Antoine Le Pautre (1621–81), known for his designs for fantastic palaces and for design of the Hôtel de Beauvais (1652). Inigo Jones (1573–1652) imported the classical style into England. Much influenced by Italian architect Andrea Palladio (1508–80). Best known for the Queen's House, Greenwich (1616–18; see Pl. 33) and the Banqueting House, Whitehall (1619–22). – eds]

Vanburgh, Campbell, and Gibbs, followed too implicitly the authority of this great name. [Sir John Vanburgh (1664–1726), outstanding architect of the English baroque (see Pl. 34). Colen Campbell (1676–1729) and James Gibbs (1682–1754), leading architects of the generation before Adam. Both closely associated with English neo-Palladian style, though Gibbs's work shows more of the baroque. – eds] Kent's genius for the picturesque, and the vast reputation he deservedly acquired, made him in some measure withstand this prevalent abuse; he has much merit in being the first who began to lighten his compartments, and to introduce grotesque paintings with his ornaments in stucco. His works, however, are evidently those of a beginner. [William Kent (1685–1748), architect, painter and designer of furniture, interior decoration and landscape gardens. Designed the well-known interior decoration of Chiswick House, London (*c.*1726–9). – eds] Mr. Stuart [James 'Athenian' Stuart (1713–88); another Scot, and a rival of Adam, who superseded him as interior decorator at Kedleston. With Nicholas Revett, Stuart published the *Antiquities of Athens* (1762), the first archaeologically accurate survey of Greek, rather than Roman, monuments (second vol. 1789). The book had considerable influence on late eighteenth century taste. – eds], with his usual elegance and taste has contributed greatly towards introducing the true style of antique decoration; and it seems to have been reserved for the present times to see compartment ceilings, and those of every kind, carried to a degree of perfection in Great Britain, that far surpasses any of the former attempts of other modern nations. [Adam]

almost the only species of ornament[4] formerly known, in this country, are now universally exploded, and in their place, we have adopted a beautiful variety of light mouldings, gracefully formed, delicately enriched and arranged with propriety and skill. We have introduced a great diversity of ceilings, freezes, and decorated pilasters, and have added grace and beauty to the whole, by a mixture of grotesque[5] stucco, and painted ornaments, together with the flowing rainceau,[6] with its fanciful figures and winding foliage.

---

[4]   *Tabernacle Frame:* a collective term, made use of by English artists to express the whole dressing of a door, window, nich, or chimney, when the dressing consists of columns or pilasters with an entablature and pediment over them. This term seems not to have been borrowed from the Latin, Italian, or French, the usual sources from whence our technical phrases flow. We are therefore of opinion, that it has taken its rise in this country from the general custom of decorating all the altar-pieces of our churches in this style.

In Roman catholic countries, that part of the altar where the cup containing the Host is placed, is called tabernacle; and by an easy transition, from a part to the whole, we have given the alter-piece the name of tabernacle.

This piece of decoration, which is extremely noble and beautiful, when well composed, is only condemned from its misapplication and frequent repetition in inside finishing, where it is by much too heavy and bold to admit of the gay and the elegant, unless in very great apartments. [Adam]

[5]   By *grotesque* is meant that beautiful light stile of ornament used by the ancient Roamns, in the decoration of their palaces, baths and villas. It is also to be seen in some of their amphitheatres, temples and tombs; the greatest part of which being vaulted and covered with ruins, have been dug up and cleared by the modern Italians, who for these reasons, give them the name of *grotte*, which is perhaps a corruption of the Latin *Criptæ*, a word borrowed from the Greeks, as the Romans did most of their terms in architecture; and hence the modern word *grotesque*, and the English word *grotto*, signifying a cave.

In the times of Raphael Michael Angelo, Julio Romano, Polidoro , Giov. d'Udine, Vasari , Zuchero and Algardi, there is no doubt but there was much greater remains of the grotte, than what are now to be seen, and in imitation of them were decorated the loggias of the Vatican, the villas Madama, Pamfili Caprarola, the old palace at Florence; and indeed whatever else is elegant or admirable in the finishings of modern Italy. [Raphael was responsible for decoration of the Vatican *loggie* and designed the Villa Madama, Rome, which had grotesques by Romano and da Udine derived from sources such as the Golden House of Nero. Vasari painted an extensive series in the Palazzo Vecchio (The Signoria), Florence. Zucchero contributed to decoration of the Palazzo Farnese, Caprarola. The Palazzo Pamphili has a gallery designed by Borromini, painted by Pietro da Cortona. – eds] The French, who till of late never adopted the ornaments of the ancients, and jealous as all mankind are of the reputation of their national taste, have branded those ornaments with the vague and fantastical appellation of arabesque, a stile which, though entirely distinct from the grotesque, has, notwithstanding, been most absurdly and universally confounded with it by the ignorant.

This classical stile of ornament, by far the most perfect that has ever appeared for inside decorations, and which has stood the test of many ages, like other works of genius, requires not only fancy and imagination in the composition, but taste and judgement in the application; and when these are happily combined, this gay and elegant mode is capable of inimitable beauties.

Vitruvius with great reason condemns an over licentiousness in compositions of this kind, and blames the painters of his time for introducing monstrous extravagancies. [Marcus Vitruvius Pollio, a Roman engineer, famous for his book *De Architectura*, the only surviving architectural treatise from the ancient world. – eds] We mean not to vindicate any thing that deserves suchs appellations but surely in light and gay compositions, designed merely to amuse, it is not altogether necessary to exclude the whimsical and the bisarre. [Adam]

[6]   *Rainceau*, apparently derived from *rain*, an old French word, signifying the branch of a tree. This French term is also used by the artists of this country, to express the winding and twisting of the stalk or stem of the acanthus plant; which flowing round in many graceful turnings, spreads its foliage with great beauty and variety, and is often intermixed, with human figures, animals and birds, imaginary or real; also with flowers and fruits.

This gay and fanciful diversity of agreeable objects, well composed, and delicately executed in stucco of painting, attains a wonderfull power of pleasing.

We hope this minute explanation of these terms will be excused. It is intended to supply in some measure a general deficiency which we have found upon this subject, in all the encyclopedias and technical dictionaries. [Adam]

Whether our works have not contributed to diffuse these improvements in architecture, through this country, we shall leave to the impartial public. – We, by no means, presume to find fault, with the compositions, or to decry the labours of other authors; many of whom have much merit and deserve great praise. Our ambition is to share with others, not to appropriate to ourselves the applause of the public; and, if we have any claim to approbation, we found it on this alone : That we flatter ourselves, we have been able to seize, with some degree of success, the beautiful spirit of antiquity, and to translate it, with novelty and variety, through all our numerous works.

We intended to have prefixed to our designs a dissertation concerning the rise and progress of architecture in Great Britain; and to have pointed out the various stages of its improvements from the time, that our ancestors, relinquishingn the gothick style, began to aim at an imitation of the Grecian manner, until it attained that degree of perfection at which it has now arrived. We have made many observations, and collctted various materials to enable us to illustrate this curious and entertaining subject; but to digest and arrange these would require more time than we can command amidst the multiplied occupations of an active profession. We, therefore, reserve the subject for some period of greater leisure.

The rules and orders of architecture, are so generally known, and may be found in so many books,[7] that it would be tedious, and even absurd, to treat of them in this work. We beg leave, however, to observe that among architects destitute of genius and incapable of venturing into the great line of their art, the attention paid to those rules and proportions is frequently minute and frivolous. The great masters of antiquity were not so rigidly scrupulous, they varied the proportions as the general spirit of their composition required, clearly perceiving, that however necessary these rules may be to form the taste and correct the licentiousness of the scholar, they often cramp the genius and circumscribe the ideas of the master.

We have given a short explanation of the plates, accompanied with such observations as we imagined might be both useful and entertaining.

We have thought it proper to colour with the tints, used in the execution, a few copies of each number, not only that posterity might be enabled to judge with more accuracy concerning the taste of the present age, and that foreign connoisseurs might have it in their power to indulge their curiosity with respect to our national style of ornament; but that the public in general might have an opportunity of cultivating the beautiful art of decoration, hitherto so little understood in most of the countries of Europe.

We hope it will be thought no more than justice to ourselves, thus to ascertain the originality of our designs. and enable the world to discover, where they have been imitated with judgment, and where they have been servilely copied or misapplied. — An artist who feels in himself an inability of presenting to the public any thing from his own store of invention, has no title to be offended if an author is solicitous to vindicate himself to posterity from any imputation of plagiarism.

As this work will not only exhibit designs in architecture, but also in every kind of ornamental furniture, we imagine it may be particularly useful to those whose professions require taste and elegance in that way.

PLANS of SION HOUSE, FROM THE DESIGNS of ROBERT ADAM

IN the year 1762, the Duke of Northumberland came to the resolution of fitting up the apartments of Sion House, in a magnificent manner. He communicated his intentions to me, and having expressed his desire, that the whole might be executed intirely in the antique style, he was pleased, in terms very flattering, to signify his confidence in my abilities to follow out his idea.

Upon this plan, the alterations and inside decorations of Sion House were begun, and as the idea was to me a favourite one, the subject great, the expence unlimited, and the Duke himself a person of extensive knowledge and correct taste in architecture, I endeavoured to render it a noble and elegant habitation, not unworthy of a proprietor, who possessed not only wealth to execute a great design, but skill to judge of its merit.

---

[7] Adam cites a number of these later in the prefaces. Many were in his own collection. [eds]

Some inequality in the levels on the old floors, some limitations from the situation of the old walls, and some want of additional heights to the enlarged apartments, were the chief difficulties with which I had to struggle. These difficulties I flatter myself are in great measure surmounted, so as not only to procure much convenience in the arrangement of the apartments, but likewise an elegant form and graceful proportion in the principal rooms.

The inequality of levels has been managed in such a manner as to increase the scenery and add to the movement, so that an apparent defect has been converted into a real beauty.

[The descriptions of individual plates are printed in the folder of the engravings.]

[Adam gives a lengthy explanation of the plan (Plate I .i.5, i.e. Engraving 5 in the folder), the first part of which is printed on the engraving. The description is continued here.]

Variety and gracefulness of form, so particularly courted by the ancients, have not been objects of much attention to modern artists. Bramante, Raphael, and Michael Angelo, those great restorers of the arts, almost entirely neglected this pleasing source of beauty. Pyrro Ligorio in his Papa Giulio and lodge in the Vatican garden,[8] and some few masters of the Roman school, excited by the example of the ancients, and by an admiration of those remains of their works, which were always before their eyes, made some feeble efforts to revive this elegant mode, which since their time has been but little cultivated by Paladio, Jones,[9] or any of the celebrated masters of this art; and it is only of late, that it has been again introduced into Great Britain with some rays of its ancient splendor.

A proper arrangement and relief of apartments are branches of architecture in which the French have excelled all other nations: these have united magnificence with utility in the hotels[10] of the nobility, and have rendered them objects of universal imitation.

To understand thoroughly the art of living, it is necessary, perhaps, to have passed some time amongst the French, and to have studied the customs of that social and conversible people. In one particular, however, our manners prevent us from imitating them. Their eating rooms seldom or never constitute a piece in their great apartments, but lie out of the suite, and in fitting them up, little attention is paid to beauty of decoration. The reason of this is obvious; the French meet there only at meals, when they trust to the display of the table for show and magnificence, not to the decoration of the apartment; and as soon as the entertainment is over, they immediately retire to the rooms of company. It is not so with us. Accustomed by habit, or induced by the nature of our climate, we indulge more largely in the enjoyment of the bottle. Every person of rank here is either a membre of the legislation,[11] or is entitled by his condition to take part in the political arrangements of his country, and to enter with ardour into those discussions to which they give rise; these circumstances lead men to live more with one another, and more detached from the society of the ladies. The eating rooms are considered as the apartments of conversation, in which we are to pass a great part of our time. This renders it desireable to have them fitted up with elegance and splendor, but in a style different from that of other apartments. Instead of being hung with damask, tapestry, &c. they are always finished with stucco, and adorned with statues and paintings, that they may not retain the smell of the victuals.

But leaving a digression, which perhaps may appear not uninstructive, as it points out the necessity of varying the style of architecture so as to accommodate it to the manners and habits of different nations, we shall now return to a more regular inspection of the plan before us.

The hall, both in our houses and in those of France, is a spacious apartment, intended as

---

[8]   The lodge is the Casino di Pio IV (1558). [eds]

[9]   See note on Inigo Jones and Palladio in footnote 3 above. [eds]

[10]   i.e. town houses. [eds]

[11]   i.e. parliament, social status, rank. [eds]

the room of access where servants in livery attend. It is here a room of great dimension, is finished with stucco, as halls always are, and is formed with a recess at each end, one square and the other circular, which have a noble effect and increase the variety.

The anti-rooms on each side are for the attendance of servants out of livery, and also for that of tradesmen, &c. these are relieved[12] by the back stairs in the towers. That on the side of the great apartment is square, and is decorated with columns of verd antique marble, as represented in the plan and sections, which standing insulated, serve to form the room and heighten the scenery. The anti-room, on the side of the private apartment. is formed into an oval, a figure seldom or never used by the ancients, but has been sometimes introduced by the moderns with success, and was here in some respect necessary from the oblong shape of the room.

Next to the anti-rooms are the public and private eating-rooms, the publick one is a room of great extent, finished with stucco, and adorned with niches and statues of marble; it is formed into a great circular recess at each end, decorated with screens of columns. The private one also has its recesses and stucco finishing, and is relieved by a back-stair for the use of the servants.

Next to the great eating-room, lies a splendid with-drawing room, for the ladies, or salle de compagnie, as it is called by the French; this is varied from the other rooms, by the forms of its ceiling, which is coved and painted in compartments. It gives access into a gallery of great length, tho' rather too narrow and too low to be in the just proportion we could have wished. It is, however, finished in a style to afford great variety and amusement; and is, for this reason, an admirable room for the reception of company before dinner, or for the ladies to retire to after it : For the with-drawing room lying between this and the eating room, prevents the noise of the men from being troublesome; and for this rea-son we would always recommend the intervention of a room, in great apartments, to prevent such inconvenience.

The little closets or cabinets, the one circular for china, and the other square for miniatures, at each end of the gallery, serve only for an additional amusement. The gallery itself, as well as the private apartments, is relieved by the circular back stairs, and gives access to the ranges of apartments on both sides.

The great circular saloon, is a noble room, entering from the hall, and leading into the gallery and great stairs, relieves all the other apartments: this serves also for a room of great rendezvous, and for public entertainments, with illuminations, dancing, and music. The form is new and singular; it is a circle within a circle, the smaller opening into a larger, by eight peircings, adorned with columns, and terminated with niches and statues, so that the scenery, like the decorations of a theatre, apparently increases the extent, and leaves room for the imagination to play.

The private apartments are now the only part of the plan remaining undescribed; on the one hand is the Duchess's bed-chamber, an anti-room for the attendance of her maids, her toilet or dressing-room, her powdering-room, water-closet, and outer anti-room, with back stairs leading to intersols[13] for the maids bed-room and wardrobes, &c. On the other hand is a dressing-room for the Duke, a powdering-room, writing-room, water-closet and stairs to intersols for His Grace's valet-de-chambre, and wardrobe, &c. In these, little form is necessary, and none is here attempted, except what may serve in some measure to diversity the scene.

We should not have dared to enter so minutely into the description of this plan, if we did not imagine that this is one of those branches of our art, which has not hitherto been treated of with any accuracy, or studied with any care; though of all others the most essential, both to the splendor and convenience of life.

---

[12] i.e. have a way out or in. [eds]

[13] Intersol: floor half way between major stories. With the exaggerated height of major apartments, it was frequently possible, in houses such as Syon, to accommodate servants' rooms in this way. [eds]

II PREFACE to The VILLA of EARL MANSFIELD, at KENWOOD

VARIOUS avocations[14] have retarded the publishing of our second number longer than we intended. During this interval, we have listened with respect to the opinion of the public concerning the first number; and we have had the most flattering approbation from men of taste, both at home and abroad.

Encouraged by this, we now resume our task, with greater confidence, by publishing the plans, elevations, and sections of Kenwood; a beautiful villa belonging to Lord Mansfield, the friend of every elegant art and useful science.[15]

We have reserved the remaining designs of Sion for some future number; as we were persuaded that by giving specimens of some of our other works, we should add greater variety to our undertaking, without diminishing its utility. – As in this work we aim, not only at affording entertainment to the connoisseur, but wish also to convey some instruction to the artist; we shall, from time to time, make such observations as naturally arise from the subjects before us. – Should we differ in any of these observations from the opinion of either antient or modern authors, we do not mean to engage in any controversy, being only desirous of submitting our ideas to the consideration of the public. At the same time we may affirm, that whatever we venture either to publish, or to recommend, is the result of much experience, and of a careful search into the purest sources of antiquity. – Architecture has not, like some other arts, an immediate standard in nature, to which the artist can always refer, and which would enable the skilful instantly to decide with respect to the degree of excellence attained in any work. In architecture, it must be formed and improved by

a correct taste, and diligent study of the beauties exhibited by great masters in their productions; and it is only by profound meditation upon these, that one becomes capable of distinguishing between what is graceful and what is inelegant; between that which possesses, and that which is destitute of harmony.

We have observed in our first number, that many of the disputes among modern architects are extremely frivolous. There is nothing with respect to which they have differed more, than the rules for the diminution of columns. This, however, is a subject of greater importance than those which frequently engage their attention. The column is not only one of the noblest and most graceful pieces of decoration, but in all round bodies, especially such as stand insulated,[16] there is a delicacy of proportion to be observed, that those of another form, and in other situations, do not require.

[Adam explains his method of calculating the taper of columns.]

The proportion of columns has also been a subject of much enquiry. But as this greatly depends on the situation of these columns, whether they make parts of outside, or inside decoration, whether they stand insulated, or engaged,[17] whether raised much above the eye, or level with it; these are circumstances which very much affect such proportions, and consequently leave an uncertainty, which can only be properly ascertained by the correct taste of the skilful and experienced artist.

Having mentioned the diminution and proportion of columns, we are naturally led to make some observations with regard to their capitals; an object of great distinction and delicacy in the detail of architecture. – In the first place, we acknowledge only three orders;[18] the Doric, the Ionic, and the Corinthian: for as to

---

[14]   i.e. distractions. [eds]

[15]   Kenwood House, Hampstead, Middlesex (now an art gallery). Adam remodelled the house (1767–9), and added a library, one of his finest rooms. [eds]

[16]   i.e. isolated, freestanding. [eds]

[17]   i.e. linked to the wall surface, attached. [eds]

[18]   Order: the name given to the column in classical architecture, with base, shaft, capital and entablature (see Pl. 31). Vitruvius specified Doric, Ionic and Corinthian. Renaissance architects, among them Palladio, recognized in addition Composite (a mix of Corinthian and Ionic) and Tuscan (a plainer version of Doric). There were various elaborate rules for the ratio of the height of the column to its base diameter, and the proportional relationship of all its parts. [eds]

the Tuscan, it is, in fact, no more than a bad and imperfect Doric; and the Composite, or Roman order, in our opinion, is a very disagreeable and awkward mixture of the Corinthian and Ionic, without either grace or beauty. We do not however mean to condemn the composing of capitals; a liberty which has often been taken by the antients with great success; and in a former part of this work, we have exhibited an attempt of our own in this way; and shall, during the course of it have other oportunities of the same kind.

The Doric capital, when properly adorned, is capable of great elegance : But where rich decoration is required, in order to give it all it's grace, the neck, or space between the astragal and the annulets,[19] should be made of much greater height than the common proportion prescribed by Paladio and many other moderns: and that neck should be enriched in the various ways which we shall have occasion to represent in the course of our work.

The Corinthian capital itself does not, in our opinion, admit of more dignity and magnificence, than a rich Ionic with it's volutes square in the front. – Angular volutes, as in the Temples of Concord and Manly Fortune at Rome, and in the Temple of Erectheus at Athens,[20] have always appeared to us less solid, less grave, and less graceful; and, in our opinion, they have been injudiciously adopted by Michael Angelo, Scamozzi,[21] and many other modern architects. Their reason for this was, in order to avoid the irregularity of appearance in this capital when viewed in profile which differs so very much from it's aspect in front. But notwithstanding this difference, the profile itself, as well as the front, are susceptible of such beauties, that we are inclinable to hazard some defects, rather than to sacrifice the elegant result of the whole composition.

The great size of the volute of the Grecian Ionic has always appeared to us by much too heavy, and those used by the Romans seem rather to border on the other extreme. We have therefore generally taken a mean between them, which we think has a happy effect; making them in width about one half of the superior[22] diameter of the column, and observing that the center of the eye of the volute is nearly perpendicular to the extremity of the said diameter.

We have also adopted the Grecian manner of forming the volute with a double fillet, which, by producing more light and shade, gives great relief, and far exceeds in grace and beauty that used by the Romans. In imitation of the Greeks, we likewise bend the channel, or hollow band, from whence the volutes spring, in the middle of the capital; which band, in case of rich decoration, should be filled with a winding foliage; or some such ornament, from the center of the capital to the eye of the volute. But the members of chief importance towards completing this capital, are the astragal and neck, which neck, as in the Doric, should be filled sometimes with various enrichments, more or less ornamented, and sometimes, perhaps should be left altogether plain, according to the stile of the building where it is employed. In a future number, we shall have occasion to give an example of it, executed at Sion-House, with all the embellishment of which it is capable.

The foliage and stems of the Corinthian capital make it not only magnificent, but also extremely gay and graceful. It has besides some advantages over the Ionic in point of form; all it's sides are regular, and the concavity of it's abacus contrasts in a beautiful manner with convexity of the vase. The form of the vase is sometimes executed in a most defective manner, by

---

[19] Astragal is a small moulding, of semi-circular section, placed around the top or bottom of columns. An annulet is a small fillet or head band encircling a column (see Pl. 31). In eighteenth century architecture the annulets were more often than not omitted. Adam is here stressing the archaeological soundness of his scholarship. [eds]

[20] The Temple of Fortuna Virilis at Rome and the Erechtheion at Athens both have angle volutes (spiral curves) on their corner columns only in the traditional Greek manner. Adam seems to be confusing the Temple of Concord with the Temple of Saturn in Rome, which has angle volutes on all its columns. See Pls 29 and 30. [eds]

[21] Vincenzo Scamozzi (1552 1616) was the most important of Palladio's immediate followers. The difficulty of differing front and side views of the Ionic capital is shown in Engraving 13. [eds]

[22] i.e. upper. [eds]

swelling it towards the middle, and bending it inwards at the bottom. in a cimarecta shape;[23] which is both unpleasant, and rests ill upon the shaft of the column. – This error has probably been introduced from a defect in the drawing of the plates of Desgodetz,[24] whom, notwithstanding his great parade of precision and accuracy we have often found guilty of considerable oversight and mistakes, not only in his mensuration, but also in the delineation of many of the antient monuments. This capital, as well as the preceeding, we think may be formed into various compositions, of great beauty and elegance, as we shall endeavour to shew by some examples hereafter.

We shall not at present enter into any particular detail with respect to the entablatures or the bases of the different orders, but refer to the specimens of each now published, and to what we are about to publish. We must however beg leave to observe, that we can see no reason for assigning to each order it's precise entablature fixed down unalterably both in figure and dimension. Different circumstances of situation and propriety ought to vary the form, and also the proportion, of all entablatures. A latitude in this respect, under the hand of an ingenious and able artist is often productive of great novelty, variety and beauty.

[Adam discusses the difference between Greek and Roman mouldings, then gives descriptions of the eight plates of Kenwood.]

III PREFACE to the SEAT of the EARL OF BUTE, at LUTON PARK

WE proceed to lay before the public another number of our Works. It contains a part of the designs of LUTON HOUSE. one of the seats of the EARL OF BUTE.[25] We are happy in having this opportunity of expressing to the world that gratitude which we never ceased to feel, for the protection, favour, and friendship with which we have always been honoured by his Lordship.

After having made various designs for Luton House in different styles, the Earl of Bute fixed upon the following, and directed it to be carried into execution. In consequence of his Lordship's orders, the work was begun in 1767; and whatever reputation the Architect may acquire at present by this plan, that which most flatters his vanity, and will do him the greatest honour with posterity, is the approbation of the noble proprietor, so justly esteemed for his great taste and discerning judgment in the celebrated works of the ancients, and in every branch of the fine arts.

The situation of the house is particularly fortunate. It stands on the easy declivity of a hill or bank; at the bottom of which, along the vale, runs the river Lee, a clear and beautiful stream, spreading into an artificial lake, upwards of a mile and half in length, and in some places of great breadth, as it covers a space of near fifty acres.

The bank on which the House is built, as well as the rising grounds on the opposite side of the lake, are beautifully diversified by gentle risings and fallings: and the whole park is adorned with lofty forest trees of different kinds, happily disposed, so as to create variety in the views, and produce a striking effect in the landscape.

The House itself, which is built of a bright coloured stone, of a bluish cast, and admirably wrought, adds greatly to the magnificence and splendour of a scene universally admired.

[Adam then gives brief descriptions of the eight plates of Luton Hoo.]

IV PREFACE to PUBLIC BUILDINGS

PUBLIC Buildings are the most splendid monuments of a great and opulent people. The purposes for which they are intended, admit of magnificence in the design, and require solidity in the construction.

Such buildings, must, of course, contain great and spacious apartments for the meeting of numerous assemblies; and, consequently, they

---

[23] A moulding concave in its upper part and convex below. See Pl. 7. [eds]

[24] Antoine Desgodetz, *Les Edifices Antiques de Rome*, 1682. This had been through many editions, and was the standard source in Adam's time. He had even considered making a new edition with his own plates. [eds]

[25] Lord Elgin, third Earl of Bute (1713–92), was the lover of George III's mother, and had considerable influence on the King at the beginning of his reign. [eds]

are susceptible of more grandeur, as well in their external decoration, as in their internal distribution.

[Adam expands on the difference in scope between public and private architecture, drawing a parallel between the grandeur of Italian renaissance painting and the detail of Flemish art.]

Horace[26] complains, that, in his time, the Romans were become extremely expensive in the private houses and gardens; which circumstance rendered them less capable of expending large sums upon, and of attending to, the decoration and magnificence of their public buildings. Our ancestors, says he, were exceedingly economical with regard to themselves and their private houses, but profuse and magnificent in whatever concerned the public edifices, particularly those which related to the service of the Gods.[27]

The bigoted zeal and superstitious pomp of the Roman-Catholic religion have produced a like profusion and magnificence in the public works of modern Italy; and to that cause, however incompatible it may seem to be with the general science and liberal ideas, Italy owes it's vast progress and present splendor in the arts of elegance.

---

[26]   Quintus Horatius Flaccus (65–8 BC), a Roman poet whose lyrical descriptions of rural retreat and leisure were widely popular in the enlightenment period. [eds]

[27]   Jam pauca aratro jugera regiæ
        Moles relinquent: undique latius
        Extenta visentur Lucrino
        Stagna Lacu.
['Now the royal piles leave few acres for the plough; artificial basins may everywhere be seen of greater surface area than the Lucrine Lake.' Horace is referring to the private villas on the shore of Campania around Herculaneum. – eds]
And afterwards:
        Privatus illis census erat brevis,
        Commune magnum: nulla decempedis
        Metata privatis opacam
        Porticus excipiebat Arcton:
        Nec fortuitum spernere cespitem
        Leges sinebant, oppida publico
        Sumptu jubentes, & deorum
        Templa novo decorare saxo.
        LIB. II. CARMEN 15.
['For them, private property was of little significance, but public property was very important indeed. For private individuals no colonnade measured out with rods looked out on the gloomy north, nor did the laws allow them to despise any turf hut thrown up by accident, ordering them to decorate the towns at public expense and the temples of the gods with new stonework' (Horace, *Odes* II. 15). – eds]
We cannot help thinking that there is somewhat very singular in this observation of Horace. At the time in which the poet wrote, there were certainly greater public works erected and restored at Rome, than ever had been in any former period.
Suetonius, in the Life of Augustus, says, "Principes viros hortatus est, ut pro facultate quisque monumentis vel novis, vel refectis, et excultis urbem adornaret. Multa itaque opera a multis extructa sunt."
['He (Augustus) urged the leading citizens that each according to his ability should adorn the city either with new or with restored and improved monuments. And so many works were erected by many people' (Suetonius, *Life of Augustus*). – eds]
We shall here mention some of the principal buildings erected in the reign of Augustus, and, for a more particular account of them, refer our readers to the "Campus Martius" of Piranezi, where they will find quoted every ancient authority on this subject. [Adam had become friends with Giambattista Piranesi, Italian architect, while in Rome. Piranesi dedicated his book to 'Robertus Adam, Architectus', and also engraved a number of plates in the *Works* for Adam. – eds]
[Adam lists twenty-six Roman buildings, including the Pantheon, dating them from the foundation of Rome.]
We shall only farther observe, that, from this formidable list, we think, we have clearly proved, that notwithstanding the above quoted lines of Horace, it was not possible the grandeur and decoration of public works could be neglected at a time when the ingenious Vitruvius lived, and the splendid Augustus reigned. [Adam]

Great-Britain, since the first acquired power and opulence, has never had the same motive for calling forth abilities and talents or the fine arts : neither has the form of our government, nor the decent simplicity of our religion, ever demanded any such exertion; nor is it probable that they ever will while we continue a free and flourishing people. Though, therefore, we have, within a short period of years, made considerable progress in almost every art; and demonstrated, by many convincing proofs, that this country, when roused, is capable of admirable efforts of native genius; yet we must not expect that the fine arts will ever meet with their most ample reward, or attain their utmost degree of perfection, deprived as they are of that emulation which is excited by public works, and by the honourable applause of a refined and discerning Public.

[Adam then gives brief description of his eight plates of public buildings. These are: the Admiralty Screen, Whitehall (1760), Chelsea Hospital Council Chamber (1776), the Royal Society of Arts, London (1772), two plates, The Register House, Edinburgh (1774), three plates, and various pieces of furniture.]

V PREFACE to DESIGNS for the KING and QUEEN, and the PRINCESS DOWAGER of WALES, &c

WHOEVER attempts to trace the progress of nations in science or in taste, will meet with singular appearances, of which it is not easy to give account. In Italy, national genius awakened at once, and exerted itself with vigour, in every direction. The sixteenth century is the splendid age of that country; and during the course of it, flourished the great poets, historians, painters, sculptors, architects, and musicians, whom the Italians still consider as the models of perfect composition, and follow as their masters and guides. In England, the first efforts of national genius, though more circumscribed, were not less vigorous. This country can boast of possessing a great dramatic poet, long before any

nation on the north side of the Alps had produced an author worthy of that name. The exertions of England in the culture of science have been still greater, and more meritorious. Bacon early pointed out the path by which genuine philosophy should advance to the discovery of truth. By adhering to it, Newton penetrated into the secrets of nature, and explained its laws. Locke traced and developed the operations of the human mind.

But whilst England led the way in those important investigations, she could not boast of the same pre-eminence in the fine arts. In painting, sculpture, architecture, and music, her progress was extremely slow; and in all of them she has been far excelled by other nations of modern Europe.

If however, we were to distinguish any one of these arts as more cultivated and more successful in England, we should not hesitate to say it was Architecture. Inigo Jones, who had long studied in Italy, rescued this art in a considerable degree from the Gothicism of former times, and began to introduce into his country a love of that elegance and refinement which characterise the productions of Greece and Rome.

Instructed and encouraged by his example, Sir Christopher Wren[28] became more chaste; and having the felicity to be employed in executing the most magnificent work of English architecture, he was enabled to display greater extent of genius.

Vanburgh[29] understood better than either the art of living among the great. A commodious arrangement of apartments was therefore his peculiar[30] merit. But his lively imagination scorned the restraint of any rule in composition; and his passion for what was fancifully magnificent, prevented him from discerning what was truly simple, elegant, and sublime.

Campbell, Gibbs, and Kent, have each their peculiar share of merit.

But whilst England was thus adorned with a succession of considerable masters in architecture, the various departments of painting, as well

---

[28]   Sir Christopher Wren (1632–1723), architect of St. Paul's Cathedral, London, is the last major British architect to be introduced in Adam's prefaces. See note 3. [eds]

[29]   See note on Vanburgh in footnote 3 above. [eds]

[30]   i.e. special. [eds]

as of the kindred arts connected with it, have been almost wholly engrossed[31] by foreigners. It is by the pencils of strangers that the lineaments of the heroes, statesmen, and beauties, of former times are known to their descendants.

The progress of all these arts in Great Britain may be considered as the peculiar distinction of the present reign. Inferior to our ancestors in science, we surpass them in taste. The study of what is elegant and beautiful, sensibility, discernment, and a correctness of eye, are become more general; and arts formerly little known begin to be naturalized amongst us. Cherished by the patronage of a people, opulent, discerning, and capable of estimating merit, the genius of native artists has been called forth into new and laudable exertions. Many of the inferior branches dependant on painting, architecture, and sculpture, have been carried, within that short period, to a degree of perfection which has far exceeded the efforts of artists in any other part of modern Europe.

Without detracting from the talents and merit of other artists, we are encouraged, by the public approbation, to flatter ourselves, that our works have somewhat contributed to difuse juster ideas and a better taste in architecture. It was with a view of rendering them more generally useful, that we first engaged in this publication.

This Number, which is the last of the First Volume, contains some of our designs for the King, the Queen, and her Royal Highness the late Princess Dowager of Wales. Tho these we have subjoined the design of a magnificent harpsichord, executed here for the Empress of Russia.

[Adam then gives brief descriptions of his eight plates. These are: a design for a screen and gateway for Carlton House, London (three plates), two designs for chimney-pieces, an Illumination and Transparency in honour of the King's birthday 1762, partly executed, a Sedan-Chair for the Queen, a design for a painted ceiling in the Queen's House, and a design for a harpsichord for Catherine the Great. See Pls 39, 41 and 45–6.]

Source: Robert Adam, *The Works in Architecture of Robert and James Adam, Esquires,* Volume I, London, 1778.

Volume II

[Volume II, published in 1779, contains a single preface, with plates arranged in groups of eight as in Volume I. The plates are:

I. Derby House, Grosvenor Square, London (1773).

II. 20 St. James's Square, London, for Sir Watkin Williams Wynn (1771).

III. Lansdowne House, Berkeley Square, London (1762-8) designed for the 3rd Earl of Bute and completed for John Shelburne lst Marquis Lansdowne.

IV. Seat of the Duke of Northumberland at Syon, listed below.

V. Designs for Public and private buildings:

    i. Mistley Church, Essex (1776), three plates.

    ii. Design for a British Coffee House.

    iii. Porter's lodge for Ashburnham House, Dover Street, London (1773).

    iv. Theatre Royal, Drury Lane, London (1775), two plates.

    v. Design for a garden seat for the Duke of Montagu at Richmond.

See Pls 40, 44 and 47.]

Source: Robert Adam, *The Works in Architecture of Robert and James Adam, Esquires,* Volume II, London, 1779.

Volume III

[Volume III, published in 1822 after the death of James Adam, contains only twenty-five plates, eight of which complete the series of designs for Syon. It also includes three plates of a 'Pavilion erected for the Fète Champètre in the garden of the Earl of Derby at the Oaks in Surrey, the 9th of June, 1774.' See Pls 42 and 43. The plates are not labelled in the same way as those in Volumes I and II, lacking the numbers of Volume, section and plate.]

Source: Robert Adam, *The Works in Architecture of Robert and James Adam, Esquires,* Volume III, London, 1822.

---

[31] i.e. taken over. [eds]

Edward Gibbon
Extracts from The History of the Decline and Fall of the Roman Empire

Prepared for the Course Team by Richard Allen, Lorna Hardwick, Anne Laurence and Antony Lentin

Contents

In the second century of the Christian Era, the empire of Rome comprehended the fairest part of the earth, and the most civilized portion of
mankind. The frontiers of that extensive monarchy were guarded by
ancient renown and disciplined valor. The gentle, but powerful, influence of laws and manners had gradually cemented the union of the provinces. Their peaceful inhabitants enjoyed and abused the advantages of

Edward Gibbon
Extracts from The History of the Decline and Fall of the Roman Empire

In his History of the Decline and Fall of the Roman Empire *Edward Gibbon (1737–94) surveys the evolution of Europe from the second century AD ('the age of the Antonines') to the fall of Constantinople in 1453 and the dawn of the Renaissance. The present selection, which represents only a small part of the whole work, comprises Chapter IX, most of Chapter XX, and two shorter extracts, one from the beginning of Chapter I, the other from the end of Chapter XXXVIII. There are also brief extracts on Roman architecture from Chapters XIII and XIV. Chapters I, IX, XII, XIV appeared in Volume One, first published in 1776. Chapter XXVIII is from Volume Three, first published in 1781.*

'I have described' wrote Gibbon, 'the triumph of barbarism and religion'. In Chapter IX, The State of Germany till the Invasion of the Barbarians, passing a critical eye over the habits of the wild Germanic tribes, he juxtaposes his basic predilection for 'the classical' with the significant recognition that so-called 'barbarian' societies contained the seeds of life from which modern Europe evolved. In Chapter XX, he examines The Motives, Progress, and Effects of the Conversion of Constantine to Christianity as a philosophical historian, applying his well-known irony to the pious conclusions of ecclesiastical historians. In the final brief section from Chapter XXXVIII, General Observations on the Fall of the Roman Empire in the West,

he looks back complacently from the cultural heights of the late eighteenth century, blithely unaware of the revolutionary upheavals about to break forth, and provides a comforting assurance of almost limitless progress within the existing framework of European society. Gibbon's preoccupation with 'barbarism and religion' reveal much about the concerns of Enlightenment Europe. According to Professor Dawson, 'it is impossible to find any European writer, not even Voltaire himself, whose work reflects more perfectly the spirit of what is called "the Enlightenment", in all its strengths and all its limitations' (Introduction to the Everyman edition, 1956).

Although Gibbon was astonishingly accurate, errors in reference and interpretation do occur in his footnotes and these have spawned, in the many editions since his death, a second set of notes from various editors. The text we have printed here is taken from the edition edited by J.B. Bury in 1909, and his remarks within Gibbon's footnotes appear unsigned within square brackets. The original footnote numbers are given in brackets after the footnote number. We have also included translations (denoted by square brackets and signed 'eds') of the main Latin and French quotations in the footnotes, except where they are already paraphrased in Gibbon's text; and where Gibbon's interpretations are either positively misleading, or need glossing for a present-day readership, we have included an editorial note to clarify matters.

Chapter I

The Extent and Military Force of the Empire in the Age of the Antonines

In the second century of the Christian Era, the empire of Rome comprehended the fairest part of the earth, and the most civilized portion of mankind. The frontiers of that extensive monarchy were guarded by ancient renown and disciplined valour. The gentle, but powerful, influence of laws and manners had gradually cemented the union of the provinces. Their peaceful inhabitants enjoyed and abused the advantages of

Introduction

wealth and luxury. The image of a free constitution was preserved with decent reverence. The Roman senate appeared to possess the sovereign authority, and devolved on the emperors all the executive powers of government. During a happy period of more than fourscore years, the public administration was conducted by the virtue and abilities of Nerva, Trajan, Hadrian, and the two Antonines. It is the design of this and of the two succeeding chapters, to describe the prosperous condition of their empire; and afterwards, from the death of Marcus Antoninus, to deduce the most important circumstances of its decline and fall: a revolution which will ever be remembered, and is still felt by the nations of the earth.

AD 96–180

The principal conquests of the Romans were achieved under the republic; and the emperors, for the most part, were satisfied with preserving those dominions which had been acquired by the policy of the senate, the active emulation of the consuls, and the martial enthusiasm of the people. The seven first centuries were filled with a rapid succession of triumphs; but it was reserved for Augustus to relinquish the ambitious design of subduing the whole earth, and to introduce a spirit of moderation into the public councils. Inclined to peace by his temper and situation, it was easy for him to discover that Rome, in her present exalted situation, had much less to hope than to fear from the chance of arms; and that, in the prosecution of remote wars, the undertaking became every day more difficult, the event[1] more doubtful, and the possession more precarious and less beneficial. The experience of Augustus added weight to these salutary reflections, and effectually convinced him that, by the prudent vigour of his counsels, it would be easy to secure every concession which the safety or the dignity of Rome might require from the most formidable barbarians. Instead of exposing his person and his legions to the arrows of the Parthians, he obtained, by an honourable treaty, the restitution of the standards and prisoners which had been taken in the defeat of Crassus.[2]

Moderation of Augustus

His generals, in the early part of his reign, attempted the reduction of Ethiopia and Arabia Felix. They marched near a thousand miles to the south of the tropic; but the heat of the climate soon repelled the invaders and protected the unwarlike natives of those sequestered regions.[3] The northern countries of Europe scarcely deserved the expense and labour of conquest. The forests and morasses of Germany were filled with a hardy race of barbarians, who despised life when it was separated from freedom; and though, on the first attack, they seemed to yield to the weight of the Roman power, they soon, by a signal act of despair,

---

[1]   i.e. outcome. [eds]

[2]   (1) Dion Cassius (l. Liv. p.736) with the annotations of Reimar, who has collected all that Roman vanity has left upon the subject. The marble of Ancyra, on which Augustus recorded his own exploits, asserts that *he compelled* the Parthians to restore the ensigns of Crassus. [Gibbon]

[3]   (2) Strabo (l. xvi. p.780) Pliny the elder (Hist. Natur. l. vi. 32,35) and Dion Cassius (l.liii. p.723, and l. liv p.734 have left us very curious details concerning these wars. The Romans made themselves masters of Mariaba, or Merab, a city of Arabia Felix, well known to the Orientals (see Abulfeda and the Nubian geography, p.52). They were arrived within three days' journey of the Spice country, the rich object of their invasion. [Gibbon]

regained their independence, and reminded Augustus of the vicissitude of fortune.[4] On the death of that emperor his testament was publicly read in the senate. He bequeathed, as a valuable legacy to his successors, the advice of confining the empire within those limits which nature seemed to have placed as its permanent bulwarks and boundaries: on the west the Atlantic ocean; the Rhine and Danube on the north; the Euphrates on the east; and towards the south the sandy deserts of Arabia and Africa.[5]

Happily for the repose of mankind, the moderate system recommended by the wisdom of Augustus was adopted by the fears and vices of his immediate successors. Engaged in the pursuit of pleasure or in the exercise of tyranny, the first Caesars seldom showed themselves to the armies, or to the provinces; nor were they disposed to suffer, that those triumphs which *their* indolence neglected should be usurped by the conduct and valour of their lieutenants. The military fame of a subject was considered as an insolent invasion of Imperial prerogative; and it became the duty, as well as interest, of every Roman general, to guard the frontiers entrusted to his care, without aspiring to conquests which might have proved no less fatal to himself than to the vanquished barbarians.[6]

Imitated by his successors

The only accession which the Roman empire received during the first century of the Christian era, was the province of Britain. In this single instance the successors of Caesar and Augustus were persuaded to follow the example of the former, rather than the precept of the latter. The proximity of its situation to the coast of Gaul seemed to invite their arms; the pleasing, though doubtful, intelligence of a pearl fishery attracted their avarice;[7] and as Britain was viewed in the light of a distinct and insulated world, the conquest scarcely formed any exception to the general system of continental measures. After a war of about forty years, undertaken by the most stupid,[8] maintained by the most dissolute, and

Conquest of Britain was the first exception to it

---

[4] (3) By the slaughter of Varus and his three legions. See the first book of the Annals of Tacitus, Sueton. in August. c. 23, and Velleius Paterculus, l. ii c.117, &c. Augustus did not receive the melancholy news with all the temper and firmness that might have been expected from his character. [Gibbon]

[5] (4) Tacit. Annal. l. ii. Dion Cassius, l. lvi. p.832, and the speech of Augustus himself, in Julian's Caesars. It receives great light from the learned notes of his French translator, M. Spanheim. [Gibbon]

[6] (5) Germanicus, Suetonius Paulinus, and Agricola were checked and recalled in the course of their victories. Corbulo was put to death. Military merit, as it is admirably expressed by Tacitus, was, in the strictest sense of the word, *imperatoria virtus*. [i.e. manly excellence and courage which the Emperor alone might display. – eds] [Gibbon]

[7] (6) Caesar himself conceals that ignoble motive; but it is mentioned by Suetonius, c.47. The British pearls proved, however, of little value, on account of their dark and livid colour. Tacitus observes, with reason (in Agricola, c.12), that it was an inherent defect 'Ego facilius crediderim naturam margaritis deesse quam nobis avaritiam.' [I should more easily have believed that it was the quality of the pearls which fell short rather than our own cupidity. – eds] [Gibbon]

[8] (7) Claudius, Nero, and Domitian. A hope is expressed by Pomponius Mela l. iii. c. 6 (he wrote under Claudius), that, by the success of the Roman arms, the island and its savage inhabitants would soon be better known. It is amusing enough to peruse such passages in the midst of London. [Gibbon]

terminated by the most timid of all the emperors, the far greater part of the island submitted to the Roman yoke.[9] The various tribes of Britons possessed valour without conduct, and the love of freedom without the spirit of union. They took up arms with savage fierceness, they laid them down, or turned them against each other, with wild inconstancy; and while they fought singly, they were successively subdued. Neither the fortitude of Caractacus, nor the despair of Boadicea, nor the fanaticism of the Druids, could avert the slavery of their country, or resist the steady progress of the Imperial generals, who maintained the national glory, when the throne was disgraced by the weakest or the most vicious of mankind. At the very time when Domitian, confined to his palace, felt the terrors which he inspired, his legions, under the command of the virtuous Agricola, defeated the collected force of the Caledonians at the foot of the Grampian hills; and his fleets, venturing to explore an unknown and dangerous navigation, displayed the Roman arms round every part of the island. The conquest of Britain was considered as already achieved; and it was the design of Agricola to complete and ensure his success by the easy reduction of Ireland, for which, in his opinion, one legion and a few auxiliaries were sufficient.[10] The western isle might be improved into a valuable possession, and the Britons would wear their chains with the less reluctance, if the prospect and example of freedom was on every side removed from before their eyes.

But the superior merit of Agricola soon occasioned his removal from the government of Britain; and for ever disappointed this rational, though extensive, scheme of conquest. Before his departure the prudent general had provided for security as well as for dominion. He had observed that the island is almost divided into two unequal parts by the opposite gulfs or, as they are now called, the Friths of Scotland. Across the narrow interval of about forty miles he had drawn a line of military stations, which was afterwards fortified, in the reign of Antoninus Pius, by a turf rampart, erected on foundations of stone.[11] This wall of Antoninus, at a small distance beyond the modern cities of Edinburgh and Glasgow, was fixed as the limit of the Roman province. The native Caledonians preserved, in the northern extremity of the island, their wild independence, for which they were not less indebted to their poverty than to their valour. Their incursions were frequently repelled and chastised; but their country was never subdued.[12] The masters of the fairest and most wealthy climates of the globe turned with contempt from gloomy hills

---

[9]   (8) See the admirable abridgment, given by Tacitus, in the Life of Agricola, and copiously, though perhaps not completely, illustrated by our own antiquarians, Camden and Horsley. [Gibbon]

[10]   (9) The Irish writers, jealous of their national honour, are extremely provoked on this occasion, both with Tacitus and with Agricola. [Gibbon]

[11]   (10) See Horsley's Britannia Romana, l. ic. 10. [Gibbon]

[12]   (11) The poet Buchanan celebrates, with elegance and spirit (see his Sylvæ, v.), the unviolated independence of his native country. But, if the single testimony of Richard of Cirencester was sufficient to create a Roman province of Vespasiana to the north of the wall, that independence would be reduced within very narrow limits. [Gibbon]

assailed by the winter tempest, from lakes concealed in a blue mist, and from cold and lonely heaths, over which the deer of the forest were chased by a troop of naked barbarians.[13]

Chapter IX

The State of Germany till the Invasion of the Barbarians, in the Time of the Emperor Decius

The government and religion of Persia have deserved some notice from their connection with the decline and fall of the Roman empire. We shall occasionally mention the Scythian or Sarmatian tribes, which, with their arms and horses, their flocks and herds, their wives and families, wandered over the immense plains which spread themselves from the Caspian Sea to the Vistula, from the confines of Persia to those of Germany. But the warlike Germans, who first resisted, then invaded, and at length overturned, the Western monarchy of Rome, will occupy a much more important place in this history, and possess a stronger, and, if we may use the expression a more domestic,[14] claim to our attention and regard. The most civilized nations of modern Europe issued from the woods of Germany, and in the rude institutions of those barbarians we may still distinguish the original principles of our present laws and manners. In their primitive state of simplicity and independence, the Germans were surveyed by the discerning eye, and delineated by the masterly pencil, of Tacitus, the first of historians who applied the science of philosophy to the study of facts. The expressive conciseness of his descriptions has deserved to exercise the diligence of innumerable antiquarians, and to excite the genius and penetration of the philosophic historians of our own times. The subject, however various and important, has already been so frequently, so ably, and so successfully discussed, that it is now grown familiar to the reader, and difficult to the writer. We shall therefore content ourselves with observing, and indeed with repeating, some of the most important circumstances of climate, of manners, and of institutions, which rendered the wild barbarians of Germany such formidable enemies to the Roman power.

Ancient Germany, excluding from its independent limits the province westward of the Rhine, which had submitted to the Roman yoke, extended itself over a third part of Europe. Almost the whole of modern Germany, Denmark, Norway, Sweden, Finland, Livonia,[15] Prussia, and the

Extent of Germany

---

[13] (12) See Appian (in Proem.) and the uniform imagery of Ossian's poems, which, according to every hypothesis, were composed by a native Caledonian. [Gibbon]
Ossian, a legendary Gaelic warrior and bard, supposed to have lived in the third century. In 1763 James Macpherson published *Temora*, an epic in eight books, which he claimed was a translation of an original poem by Ossian. The fabrication was accepted by many, but challenged by Dr Johnson, and others. See Oxford *Johnson*, edited by Green, p.789. [eds]

[14] The Angles, Saxons, Jutes, Franks, Visi-Goths and Lombards, who first established English, French, Spanish and Italian powers were of course Germanic tribes. [eds]

[15] Roughly present-day Lithuania. [eds]

greater part of Poland, were peopled by the various tribes of one great nation, whose complexion, manners, and language denoted a common origin, and preserved a striking resemblance. On the west, ancient Germany was divided by the Rhine from the Gallic, and on the south by the Danube from the Illyrian,[16] provinces of the empire. A ridge of hills, rising from the Danube, and called the Carpathian Mountains, covered Germany on the side of Dacia or Hungary. The eastern frontier was faintly marked by the mutual fears of the Germans and the Sarmatians, and was often confounded by the mixture of warring and confederating tribes of the two nations. In the remote darkness of the north the ancients imperfectly descried a frozen ocean that lay beyond the Baltic Sea and beyond the peninsula, or islands,[17] of Scandinavia.

Some ingenious writers[18] have suspected that Europe was much colder formerly than it is at present; and the most ancient descriptions of the climate of Germany tend exceedingly to confirm their theory. The general complaints of intense frost and eternal winter are perhaps little to be regarded, since we have no method of reducing to the accurate standard of the thermometer the feelings or the expressions of an orator born in the happier regions of Greece or Asia. But I shall select two remarkable circumstances of a less equivocal nature. 1. The great rivers which covered the Roman provinces, the Rhine and the Danube, were frequently frozen over, and capable of supporting the most enormous weights. The barbarians, who often chose that severe season for their inroads, transported, without apprehension or danger, their numerous armies, their cavalry, and their heavy waggons, over a vast and solid bridge of ice.[19] Modern ages have not presented an instance of a like phenomenon. 2. The reindeer, that useful animal, from whom the savage of the North derives the best comforts of his dreary life, is of a constitution that supports, and even requires, the most intense cold. He is found on the rock of Spitzberg, within ten degrees of the pole; he seems to delight in the snows of Lapland and Siberia; but at present he cannot subsist, much less multiply, in any country to the south of the Baltic.[20]

Climate

---

[16] Roughly parts of Austria, Hungary, Slovenia, Croatia, Serbia, Bosnia, Montenegro and Albania. [eds]

[17] (1) The modern philosophers of Sweden seem agreed that the waters of the Baltic gradually sink in a regular proportion, which they have ventured to estimate at half an inch every year. Twenty centuries ago, the flat country of Scandinavia must have been covered by the sea; while the high lands rose above the waters, as so many islands of various forms and dimensions. Such indeed is the notion given us by Mela, Pliny, and Tacitus, of the vast countries round the Baltic. See in the Bibliothèque Raisonnée, tom. xl. and xlv., a large abstract of Dalin's History of Sweden, composed in the Swedish language. [Gibbon]

[18] (2) In particular, Mr. Hume, and the Abbé du Bos, and M. Pelloutier, Hist. des Celtes, tom. i. [Gibbon]

[19] (3) Diodorus Siculus, l. v. p.340, edit. Wessel. Herodian l. vi. p.221. Jornandes, c. 55. On the banks of the Danube, the wine, when brought to table, was frequently frozen into great lumps, *frusta vini*. Ovid Epist. ex Ponto, l. iv. 7, 7–10. Virgil Georgic. l. iii. 355. The fact is confirmed by a soldier and a philosopher, who had experienced the intense cold of Thrace. See Xenophon, Anabasis, l. vii, p.560, edit. Hutchinson. [Gibbon]

[20] (4) Buffon, Histoire Naturelle, tom. xii. p.79, 116. [Gibbon]

In the time of Caesar, the reindeer, as well as the elk and the wild bull, was a native of the Hercynian forest, which then overshadowed a great part of Germany and Poland.[21] The modern improvements sufficiently explain the causes of the diminution of the cold. These immense woods have been gradually cleared, which intercepted from the earth the rays of the sun.[22] The morasses have been drained, and, in proportion as the soil has been cultivated, the air has become more temperate. Canada, at this day, is an exact picture of ancient Germany. Although situated in the same parallel with the finest provinces of France and England, that country experiences the most rigorous cold. The reindeer are very numerous, the ground is covered with deep and lasting snow, and the great river of St Lawrence is regularly frozen, in a season when the waters of the Seine and the Thames are usually free from ice.[23]

It is difficult to ascertain, and easy to exaggerate, the influence of the climate of ancient Germany over the minds and bodies of the natives. Many writers have supposed, and most have allowed, though, as it should seem, without any adequate proof, that the rigorous cold of the North was favourable to long life and generative vigour, that the women were more fruitful, and the human species more prolific, than in warmer or more temperate climates.[24] We may assert, with greater confidence, that the keen air of Germany formed the large and masculine limbs of the natives, who were, in general, of a more lofty stature than the people of the South,[25] gave them a kind of strength better adapted to violent exertions than to patient labour, and inspired them with constitutional bravery, which is the result of nerves and spirits. The severity of a winter campaign, that chilled the courage of the Roman troops, was scarcely felt by these hardy children of the North,[26] who, in their turn, were unable to resist the summer heats, and dissolved away in languor and sickness under the beams of an Italian sun.[27]

Its effects on the natives

---

[21] (5) Caesar de Bell. Gallic. vi. 23, &c. The most inquisitive of the Germans were ignorant of its utmost limits, although some of them had travelled in it more than sixty days' journey. [Gibbon]

[22] (6) Cluverius (Germania Antiqua, l. iii. c. 47) investigates the small and scattered remains of the Hercynian Wood. [Gibbon]

[23] (7) Charlevoix, Histoire du Canada. [Gibbon]

[24] (8) Olaus Rudbeck asserts that the Swedish women often bear ten or twelve children, and not uncommonly twenty or thirty; but the authority of Rudbeck is much to be suspected. [Gibbon]

[25] (9) In hos artus, in hæc corpora, quæ miramur, excrescunt. [They develop those limbs and that physique which we so much admire. – eds] Tacit. Germania, c.20. Cluver. l. i. c. 14. [Gibbon]

[26] (10) Plutarch. in Mario. The Cimbri, by way of amusement, often slid down mountains of snow on their broad shields. [Gibbon]

[27] (11) The Romans made war in all climates, and by their excellent discipline were in a great measure preserved in health and vigour. It may be remarked that man is the only animal which can live and multiply in every country from the equator to the poles. The hog seems to approach the nearest to our species in that privilege. [Gibbon]

There is not anywhere upon the globe a large tract of country which   *Origin of the Germans*
we have discovered destitute of inhabitants or whose first population can
be fixed with any degree of historical certainty. And yet, as the most
philosophic minds can seldom refrain from investigating the infancy of
great nations, our curiosity consumes itself in toilsome and disappointed
efforts. When Tacitus considered the purity of the German blood, and
the forbidding aspect of the country, he was disposed to pronounce those
barbarians *Indigenæ*, or natives of the soil. We may allow with safety, and
perhaps with truth, that ancient Germany was not originally peopled by
any foreign colonies already formed into a political society;[28] but that the
name and nation received their existence from the gradual union of
some wandering savages of the Hercynian woods. To assert those savages
to have been the spontaneous production of the earth which they
inhabited would be a rash inference, condemned by religion, and unwar-
ranted by reason.

Such rational doubt is but ill suited with the genius of popular van-   *Fables and conjectures*
ity. Among the nations who have adopted the Mosaic history of the world,
the ark of Noah has been of the same use, as was formerly to the Greeks
and Romans the siege of Troy. On a narrow basis of acknowledged truth,
an immense but rude superstructure of fable has been erected; and the
wild Irishman,[29] as well as the wild Tartar,[30] could point out the individual
son of Japhet from whose loins his ancestors were lineally descended. The
last century abounded with antiquarians of profound learning and easy
faith,[31] who, by the dim light of legends and traditions, of conjectures and
etymologies, conducted the great-grandchildren of Noah from the Tower
of Babel to the extremities of the globe. Of these judicious critics, one of
the most entertaining was Olaus Rudbeck, professor in the university of
Upsal.[32] Whatever is celebrated either in history or fable, this zealous
patriot ascribes to his country. From Sweden (which formed so
considerable a part of ancient Germany) the Greeks themselves derived
their alphabetical characters, their astronomy, and their religion. Of that
delightful region (for such it appeared to the eyes of a native) the Atlantis

---

[28] (12) Tacit. German. c. 3. The emigration of the Gauls followed the course of
the Danube, and discharged itself on Greece and Asia. Tacitus could discover only
one inconsiderable tribe that retained any traces of a Gallic origin. [Gibbon]

[29] (13) According to Dr. Keating (History of Ireland, p.13,14), the giant
Partholanus, who was the son of Seara, the son of Esra, the son of Sru, the son of
Framant, the son of Fathaclan, the son of Magog, the son of Japhet, the son of
Noah, landed on the coast of Munster, the 14th day of May in the year of the
world one thousand nine hundred and seventy-eight. Though he succeeded in his
great enterprise, the loose behaviour of his wife rendered his domestic life very
unhappy, and provoked him to such a degree, that he killed – her favourite
greyhound. This, as the learned historian very properly observes, was the *first*
instance of female falsehood and infidelity ever known in Ireland. [Gibbon]

[30] (14) Genealogical History of the Tartars by Abulghazi Bahadur Khan.
[Gibbon]

[31] i.e. credulity. [eds]

[32] (15) His work, entitled Atlantica, is uncommonly scarce. Bayle has given two
most curious extracts from it. République des Lettres, Janvier et Février, 1685.
[Gibbon]

of Plato, the country of the Hyperboreans, the gardens of the Hesperides, the Fortunate Islands, and even the Elysian Fields, were all but faint and imperfect transcripts. A clime so profusely favoured by Nature could not long remain desert after the flood. The learned Rudbeck allows the family of Noah a few years to multiply from eight to about twenty thousand persons. He then disperses them into small colonies to replenish the earth, and to propagate the human species. The German or Swedish detachment (which marched, if I am not mistaken, under the command of Askenaz the son of Gomer, the son of Japhet) distinguished itself by a more than common diligence in the prosecution of this great work. The northern hive cast its swarms over the greatest part of Europe, Africa, and Asia; and (to use the author's metaphor) the blood circulated back from the extremities to the heart.

But all this well-laboured system of German antiquities is annihilated by a single fact, too well attested to admit of any doubt, and of too decisive a nature to leave room for any reply. The Germans, in the age of Tacitus, were unacquainted with the use of letters;[33] and the use of letters is the principal circumstance that distinguishes a civilized people from a herd of savages, incapable of knowledge or reflection. Without that artificial help the human memory soon dissipates or corrupts the ideas entrusted to her charge; and the nobler faculties of the mind, no longer supplied with models or with materials, gradually forget their powers: the judgement becomes feeble and lethargic, the imagination languid or irregular. Fully to apprehend this important truth, let us attempt, in an improved society, to calculate the immense distance between the man of learning and the *illiterate* peasant. The former, by reading and reflection, multiplies his own experience, and lives in distant ages and remote countries; whilst the latter, rooted to a single spot, and confined to a few years of existence, surpasses but very little his fellow labourer the ox in the exercise of his mental faculties. The same and even a greater difference will be found between nations than between individuals; and we may safely pronounce that without some species of writing no people has ever preserved the faithful annals of their history, ever made any considerable progress in the abstract sciences, or ever possessed, in any tolerable degree of perfection, the useful and agreeable arts of life.

The Germans ignorant of letters

Of these arts the ancient Germans were wretchedly destitute. They passed their lives in a state of ignorance and poverty, which it has pleased some declaimers to dignify with the appellation of virtuous simplicity. Modern Germany is said to contain about two thousand three hundred

of arts and agriculture

---

[33] (16) Tacit. Germ. ii. 19. Literarum secreta viri pariter ac foeminæ ignorant. [Both the men and women are equally ignorant of the mysteries of the alphabet. – eds] We may rest contented with this decisive authority, without entering into the obscure disputes concerning the antiquity of the Runic characters. The learned Celsius, a Swede, a scholar and a philosopher, was of opinion, that they were nothing more than the Roman letters, with the curves changed into straight lines for the ease of engraving. See Pelloutier, Histoire des Celtes, l. ii. c. 11. Dictionnaire Diplomatique, tom. i. p.223. We may add, that the oldest Runic inscriptions are supposed to be of the third century, and the most ancient writer who mentions the Runic characters is Venantius Fortunatus (Carm. vii. 18), who lived towards the end of the sixth century. Barbara Fraxineis pingatur RUNA tabellis. [Strange Runic inscriptions drawn on on ashwood tablets. – eds] [Gibbon]

walled towns.[34] In a much wider extent of country the geographer Ptolemy could discover no more than ninety places which he decorates with the name of cities;[35] though, according to our ideas, they would but ill deserve that splendid title. We can only suppose them to have been rude fortifications, constructed in the centre of the woods, and designed to secure the women, children, and cattle, whilst the warriors of the tribe marched out to repel a sudden invasion.[36] But Tacitus asserts, as a well-known fact, that the Germans, in his time, had *no* cities;[37] and that they affected to despise the works of Roman industry as places of confinement rather than of security.[38] Their edifices were not even contiguous, or formed into regular villas;[39] each barbarian fixed his independent dwelling on the spot to which a plain, a wood, or a stream of fresh water had induced him to give the preference. Neither stone, nor brick, nor tiles were employed in these slight habitations.[40] They were indeed no more than low huts of a circular figure, built of rough timber, thatched with straw, and pierced at the top to leave a free passage for the smoke. In the most inclement winter, the hardy German was satisfied with a scanty garment made of the skin of some animal. The nations who dwelt towards the North clothed themselves in furs; and the women manufactured for their own use a coarse kind of linen.[41] The game of various sorts with which the forests of Germany were plentifully stocked supplied its inhabitants with food and exercise.[42] Their monstrous herds of cattle, less remarkable indeed for their beauty than for their utility,[43] formed the principal object of their wealth. A small quantity of corn was the only produce exacted from the earth: the use of orchards or artificial

---

[34]   (17) Recherches Philosophiques sur les Américains, tom. iii. p.228. The author of that very curious work is, if I am not misinformed, a German by birth. [Gibbon]

[35]   (18) The Alexandrian Geographer is often criticized by the accurate Cluverius. [Gibbon]

[36]   (19) See Caesar, and the learned Mr. Whitaker in his history of Manchester, vol. i. [Gibbon]

[37]   (20) Tacit. Germ. 16. [Gibbon]

[38]   (21) When the Germans commanded the Ubii of Cologne to cast off the Roman yoke, and with their new freedom to resume their ancient manners, they insisted on the immediate demolition of the walls of the colony. 'Postulamus a vobis, muros coloniæ, munimenta servitii, detrahatis; etiam fera animalia, si clausa teneas, virtutis obliviscuntur.' [We ask you to demolish the walls of the colonia which keeps you in servitude; for even wild animals forget their courage if they are kept in captivity. – eds] Tacit. Hist. iv. 64. [Gibbon]

[39]   (22) The straggling villages of Silesia are several miles in length. See Cluver l. i. c. 13. [Gibbon]

[40]   (23) One hundred and forty years after Tacitus a few more regular structures were erected near the Rhine and Danube. Herodian, l. vii. p.234. [Gibbon]

[41]   (24) Tacit. Germ. 17. [Gibbon]

[42]   (25) Tacit. Germ. 5. [Gibbon]

[43]   (26) Caesar de Bell. Gall. vi. 21. [Gibbon]

meadows was unknown to the Germans; nor can we expect any improvements in agriculture from a people whose property every year experienced a general change by a new division of the arable lands, and who, in that strange operation, avoided disputes by suffering a great part of their territory to lie waste and without tillage.[44]

Gold, silver, and iron were extremely scarce in Germany. Its barbarous inhabitants wanted both skill and patience to investigate those rich veins of silver, which have so liberally rewarded the attention of the princes of Brunswick and Saxony. Sweden, which now supplies Europe with iron, was equally ignorant of its own riches; and the appearance of the arms of the Germans furnished a sufficient proof how little iron they were able to bestow on what they must have deemed the noblest use of that metal. The various transactions of peace and war had introduced some Roman coins (chiefly silver) among the borderers of the Rhine and Danube; but the more distant tribes were absolutely unacquainted with the use of money, carried on their confined traffic by the exchange of commodities, and prized their rude earthen vessels as of equal value with the silver vases, the presents of Rome to their princes and ambassadors.[45] To a mind capable of reflection such leading facts convey more instruction than a tedious detail of subordinate circumstances. The value of money has been settled by general consent to express our wants and our property, as letters were invented to express our ideas; and both these institutions, by giving more active energy to the powers and passions of human nature, have contributed to multiply the objects they were designed to represent. The use of gold and silver is in a great measure factitious;[46] but it would be impossible to enumerate the important and various services which agriculture, and all the arts, have received from iron, when tempered and fashioned by the operation of fire and the dexterous hand of man. Money, in a word, is the most universal incitement, iron the most powerful instrument, of human industry; and it is very difficult to conceive by what means a people, neither actuated by the one nor seconded by the other, could emerge from the grossest barbarism.[47]

and of the use of metals

If we contemplate a savage nation in any part of the globe, a supine indolence and a carelessness of futurity will be found to constitute their general character. In a civilized state every faculty of man is expanded and exercised; and the great chain of mutual dependence connects and embraces the several members of society. The most numerous portion of it is employed in constant and useful labour. The select few, placed by fortune above that necessity, can, however, fill up their time by the pursuits of interest or glory, by the improvement of their estate or of their understanding, by the duties, the pleasures, and even the follies, of social life. The Germans were not possessed of these varied resources. The care of the house and family, the management of the land and cattle, were

Their indolence

---

[44] (27) Tacit. Germ. 26. Caesar, vi. 22. [Gibbon]

[45] (28) Tacit. Germ. 5. [Gibbon]

[46] i.e. artificial and conventional. [eds]

[47] (29) It is said that the Mexicans and Peruvians, without the use of either money or iron, had made a very great progress in the arts. Those arts, and the monuments they produced, have been strangely magnified. See Recherches sur les Américains, tom. ii. p.153, &c. [Gibbon]

delegated to the old and the infirm, to women and slaves. The lazy warrior, destitute of every art that might employ his leisure hours, consumed
his days and nights in the animal gratifications of sleep and food. And
yet, by a wonderful diversity of nature (according to the remark of a
writer who had pierced into its darkest recesses), the same barbarians are
by turns the most indolent and the most restless of mankind. They
delight in sloth, they detest tranquillity.[48] The languid soul, oppressed
with its own weight, anxiously required some new and powerful sensation;
and war and danger were the only amusements adequate to its fierce
temper. The sound that summoned the German to arms was grateful[49] to
his ear. It roused him from his uncomfortable lethargy, gave him an
active pursuit, and, by strong exercise of the body, and violent emotions
of the mind, restored him to a more lively sense of his existence. In the
dull intervals of peace these barbarians were immoderately addicted to
deep gaming and excessive drinking; both of which, by different means,
the one by inflaming their passions, the other by extinguishing their reason, alike relieved them from the pain of thinking. They gloried in passing whole days and nights at table; and the blood of friends and relations
often stained their numerous and drunken assemblies.[50] Their debts of
honour (for in that light they have transmitted to us those of play) they
discharged with the most romantic fidelity. The desperate gamester, who
had staked his person and liberty on a last throw of the dice, patiently
submitted to the decision of fortune, and suffered himself to be bound,
chastised, and sold into remote slavery, by his weaker but more lucky
antagonist.[51]

    Strong beer, a liquor extracted with very little art from wheat or
barley, and *corrupted* (as it is strongly expressed by Tacitus) into a certain
semblance of wine, was sufficient for the gross purposes of German
debauchery. But those who had tasted the rich wines of Italy, and afterwards of Gaul, sighed for that more delicious species of intoxication.
They attempted not, however (as has since been executed with so much
success), to naturalize the vine on the banks of the Rhine and Danube;
nor did they endeavour to procure by industry the materials of an advantageous commerce. To solicit by labour what might be ravished by arms
was esteemed unworthy of the German spirit.[52] The intemperate thirst of
strong liquors often urged the barbarians to invade the provinces on
which art or nature had bestowed those much envied presents. The
Tuscan who betrayed his country to the Celtic nations attracted them into
Italy by the prospect of the rich fruits and delicious wines, the productions of a happier climate.[53] And in the same manner the German

Their taste for strong liquors

---

[48] (30) Tacit. Germ. 15. [Gibbon]

[49] i.e. pleasing. [eds]

[50] (31) Tacit. Germ. 22, 23. [Gibbon]

[51] (32) Tacit. Germ. 24. The Germans might borrow the *arts* of play from the
Romans, but the *passion* is wonderfully inherent in the human species. [Gibbon]

[52] (33) Tacit. Germ. 14. [Gibbon]

[53] (34) Plutarch. in Camillo. T. Liv. v. 33. [Gibbon]

auxiliaries, invited into France during the civil wars of the sixteenth century, were allured by the promise of plenteous quarters in the provinces of Champagne and Burgundy.[54] Drunkenness, the most illiberal but not the most dangerous of *our* vices, was sometimes capable, in a less civilized state of mankind, of occasioning a battle, a war, or a revolution.

The climate of ancient Germany has been mollified,[55] and the soil *State of population* fertilized, by the labour of ten centuries from the time of Charlemagne.[56] The same extent of ground, which at present maintains, in ease and plenty, a million of husbandmen and artificers, was unable to supply an hundred thousand lazy warriors with the simple necessaries of life.[57] The Germans abandoned their immense forests to the exercise of hunting, employed in pasturage the most considerable part of their lands, bestowed on the small remainder a rude and careless cultivation, and then accused the scantiness and sterility of a country that refused to maintain the multitude of its inhabitants. When the return of famine severely admonished them of the importance of the arts, the national distress was sometimes alleviated by the emigration of a third, perhaps, or a fourth part of their youth.[58] The possession and the enjoyment of property are the pledges which bind a civilized people to an improved country. But the Germans, who carried with them what they most valued, their arms, their cattle, and their women, cheerfully abandoned the vast silence of their woods for the unbounded hopes of plunder and conquest. The innumerable swarms, that issued, or seemed to issue, from the great storehouse of nations, were multiplied by the fears of the vanquished and by the credulity of succeeding ages. And from facts thus exaggerated, an opinion was gradually established, and has been supported by writers of distinguished reputation, that, in the age of Caesar and Tacitus, the inhabitants of the North were far more numerous than they are in our days.[59] A more serious inquiry into the causes of population seems to have convinced modern philosophers of the falsehood, and indeed the impossibility, of the supposition. To the names of Mariana and of Machiavel[60] we can oppose the equal names of Robertson and Hume.[61]

---

[54] (35) Dubos, Hist. de la Monarchie Françoise, tom. i. p.193. [Gibbon]

[55] i.e. rendered less harsh. [eds]

[56] AD 742–814, King of the Franks and emperor of the West (800). [eds]

[57] (36) The Helvetian nation, which issued from the country called Switzerland, contained, of every age and sex, 368,000 persons (Caesar de Bell. Gall. i. 29). At present, the number of people in the Pays de Vaud (a small district on the banks of the Leman Lake, much more distinguished for politeness than for industry) amounts to 112,591. See an excellent Tract of M. Muret, in the Mémoires de la Société de Berne. [Gibbon]

[58] (37) Paul Diaconus, c. 1, 2, 3. Machiavel, Davila, and the rest of Paul's followers, represent these emigrations too much as regular and concerted measures. [Gibbon]

[59] (38) Sir William Temple and Montesquieu have indulged, on this subject, the usual liveliness of their fancy. [Gibbon]

[60] (39) Machiavel, Hist. di Firenze, l. i. Mariana, Hist. Hispan. l. v. c. l. [Gibbon]

[61] (40) Robertson's Cha. V. Hume's Politic. Ess. [Gibbon]

A warlike nation like the Germans, without either cities, letters, arts,   *German freedom*
or money found some compensation for this savage state in the enjoy-
ment of liberty. Their poverty secured their freedom, since our desires
and our possessions are the strongest fetters of despotism. 'Among the
Suiones (says Tacitus) riches are held in honour. They are *therefore* subject
to an absolute monarch, who instead of entrusting his people with the
free use of arms, as is practised in the rest of Germany, commits them to
the safe custody, not of a citizen, or even of a freedman, but of a slave.
The neighbours of the Suiones, the Sitones, are sunk even below servitude; they obey a woman.'[62] In the mention of these exceptions, the great
historian sufficiently acknowledges the general theory of government. We
are only at a loss to conceive by what means riches and despotism could
penetrate into a remote corner of the North, and extinguish the generous flame that blazed with such fierceness on the frontier of the Roman
provinces, or how the ancestors of those Danes and Norwegians, so distinguished in later ages by their unconquered spirit, could thus tamely
resign the great character of German liberty.[63] Some tribes, however, on
the coast of the Baltic, acknowledged the authority of kings, though without relinquishing the rights of men;[64] but in the far greater part of Germany the form of government was a democracy, tempered, indeed, and
controlled, not so much by general and positive laws as by the occasional
ascendant of birth or valour, of eloquence or superstition.[65]

Civil governments, in their first institutions, are voluntary   *Assemblies of the people*
associations for mutual defence. To obtain the desired end it is absolutely
necessary that each individual should conceive himself obliged to submit
his private opinion and actions to the judgement of the greater number
of his associates. The German tribes were contented with this rude but
liberal outline of political society. As soon as a youth, born of free
parents, had attained the age of manhood, he was introduced into the
general council of his countrymen, solemnly invested with a shield and
spear, and adopted as an equal and worthy member of the military
commonwealth. The assembly of the warriors of the tribe was convened
at stated seasons, or on sudden emergencies. The trial of public offences,
the election of magistrates, and the great business of peace and war, were

---

[62]   (41) Tacit. Germ. 44, 45. Freinshemius (who dedicated his supplement to Livy,
to Christina of Sweden) thinks proper to be very angry with the Roman who
expressed so very little reverence for Northern queens. [Gibbon]

[63]   (42) May we not suspect that superstition was the parent of despotism? The
descendants of Odin (whose race was not extinct till the year 1060) are said to
have reigned in Sweden above a thousand years. The temple of Upsal was the
ancient seat of religion and empire. In the year 1153 I find a singular law prohibiting the use and possession of arms to any, except the king's guards. Is it not
probable that it was coloured by the pretence of reviving an old institution? See
Dalin's History of Sweden in the Bibliothèque Raisonnée, tom. xi. and xiv. [Gib-
bon]

   Gibbon refers to the eleventh century conversion to Christianity of the
Swedish royal house. [eds]

[64]   (43) Tacit. Germ. c. 43. [Gibbon]

[65]   (44) Id. c. 11, 12, 13, &c. [Gibbon]

determined by its independent voice. Sometimes, indeed, these important questions were previously considered and prepared in a more select council of the principal chieftains.[66] The magistrates might deliberate and persuade, the people only could resolve and execute; and the resolutions of the Germans were for the most part hasty and violent. Barbarians accustomed to place their freedom in gratifying the present passion, and their courage in overlooking all future consequences, turned away with indignant contempt from the remonstrances of justice and policy, and it was the practice to signify by a hollow murmur their dislike of such timid councils. But, whenever a more popular orator proposed to vindicate the meanest citizen from either foreign or domestic injury, whenever he called upon his fellow countrymen to assert the national honour, or to pursue some enterprise full of danger and glory, a loud clashing of shields and spears expressed the eager applause of the assembly. For the Germans always met in arms, and it was constantly to be dreaded lest an irregular multitude, inflamed with faction and strong liquors, should use those arms to enforce, as well as to declare, their furious resolves. We may recollect how often the diets of Poland have been polluted with blood, and the more numerous party has been compelled to yield to the more violent and seditious.[67]

A general of the tribe was elected on occasions of danger; and, if the danger was pressing and extensive, several tribes concurred in the choice of the same general. The bravest warrior was named to lead his countrymen into the field, by his example rather than by his commands. But this power, however limited, was still invidious.[68] It expired with the war, and in time of peace, the German tribes acknowledged not any supreme chief.[69] *Princes* were, however, appointed, in the general assembly, to administer justice, or rather to compose differences,[70] in their respective districts. In the choice of these magistrates as much regard was shown to birth as to merit.[71] To each was assigned, by the public, a guard, and a council of an hundred persons, and the first of the princes appears to have enjoyed a pre-eminence of rank and honour which sometimes tempted the Romans to compliment him with the regal title.[72]

Authority of the princes and magistrates

---

[66] (45) Grotius changes an expression of Tacitus, pertractantur into prætractantur. The correction is equally just and ingenious. [Gibbon]

pertractantur, be thoroughly discussed; *prætractantur,* be discussed beforehand. [eds]

[67] (46) Even in *our* ancient parliament, the barons often carried a question not so much by the number of votes as by that of their armed followers. [Gibbon]

[68] i.e. barely tolerated. [eds]

[69] (47) Caesar de Bell. Gall. vi. 23. [Gibbon]

[70] (48) Minuunt controversias [they make disputes smaller. – eds] is a very happy expression of Caesar's. [Gibbon]

[71] (49) Reges ex nobilitate, duces ex virtute sumant. [They choose their kings for their noble birth, their military leaders for their courage. – eds] Tacit. Germ. 7. [Gibbon]

[72] (50) Cluver, Germ. Ant. l. i. c. 38. [Gibbon]

The comparative view of the powers of the magistrates, in two remarkable instances, is alone sufficient to represent the whole system of German manners. The disposal of the landed property within their district was absolutely vested in their hands, and they distributed it every year according to a new division.[73] At the same time they were not authorized to punish with death, to imprison, or even to strike a private citizen.[74] A people thus jealous of their persons, and careless of their possessions, must have been totally destitute of industry and the arts, but animated with a high sense of honour and independence.

more absolute over the property than over the persons of the Germans

The Germans respected only those duties which they imposed on themselves. The most obscure soldier resisted with disdain the authority of the magistrates. 'The noblest youths blushed not to be numbered among the faithful companions of some renowned chief, to whom they devoted their arms and service. A noble emulation prevailed, among the companions to obtain the first place in the esteem of their chief; amongst the chiefs, to acquire the greatest number of valiant companions. To be ever surrounded by a band of select youths was the pride and strength of the chiefs, their ornament in peace, their defence in war. The glory of such distinguished heroes diffused itself beyond the narrow limits of their own tribe. Presents and embassies solicited their friendship, and the fame of their arms often ensured victory to the party which they espoused. In the hour of danger it was shameful for the chief to be surpassed in valour by his companions; shameful for the companions not to equal the valour of their chief. To survive his fall in battle was indelible infamy. To protect his person, and to adorn his glory with the trophies of their own exploits, were the most sacred of their duties. The chiefs combated for victory, the companions for the chief. The noblest warriors, whenever their native country was sunk in the laziness of peace, maintained their numerous bands in some distant scene of action, to exercise their restless spirit, and to acquire renown by voluntary dangers. Gifts worthy of soldiers, the warlike steed, the bloody and ever victorious lance, were the rewards which the companions claimed from the liberality of their chief. The rude plenty of his hospitable board was the only pay that *he* could bestow, or they would accept. War, rapine, and the free will offerings of his friends, supplied the materials of this munificence.'[75] This institution, however it might accidentally weaken the several republics,[76] invigorated the general character of the Germans, and even ripened amongst them all the virtues of which barbarians are susceptible – the faith and valour, the hospitality and the courtesy, so conspicuous long afterwards in the ages of chivalry. The honourable gifts, bestowed by the chief on his brave companions have been supposed, by an ingenious writer, to contain the first rudiments of the fiefs,[77] distributed after the conquest of the Roman provinces, by the barbarian lords among their vassals, with a similar duty

Voluntary engagements

---

[73]   (51) Caesar, vi. 22. Tacit. Germ. 26. [Gibbon]

[74]   (52) Tacit. Germ. 7. [Gibbon]

[75]   (53) Tacit. Germ. 13, 14. [Gibbon]

[76]   i.e. states or communities. [eds]

[77]   Under feudal law, an estate held on condition of homage and service to a superior lord. [eds]

of homage and military service.[78] These conditions are, however, very repugnant to the maxims of the ancient Germans, who delighted in mutual presents; but without either imposing or accepting the weight of obligations.[79]

'In the days of chivalry, or more properly of romance, all the men were brave, and all the women were chaste;' and, notwithstanding the latter of these virtues is acquired and preserved with much more difficulty than the former, it is ascribed, almost without exception, to the wives of the ancient Germans. Polygamy was not in use, except among the princes, and among them only for the sake of multiplying their alliances. Divorces were prohibited by manners rather than by laws. Adulteries were punished as rare and inexpiable crimes; nor was seduction justified by example and fashion.[80] We may easily discover that Tacitus indulges an honest pleasure in the contrast of barbarian virtue with the dissolute conduct of the Roman ladies: yet there are some striking circumstances that give an air of truth, or at least of probability, to the conjugal faith and chastity of the Germans.

German chastity

Although the progress of civilization has undoubtedly contributed to assuage the fiercer passions of human nature, it seems to have been less favourable to the virtue of chastity, whose most dangerous enemy is the softness of the mind. The refinements of life corrupt while they polish the intercourse of the sexes. The gross appetite of love becomes most dangerous, when it is elevated, or rather, indeed, disguised, by sentimental passion. The elegance of dress, of motion, and of manners, gives a lustre to beauty, and inflames the senses through the imagination. Luxurious entertainments, midnight dances, and licentious spectacles present at once temptation and opportunity to female frailty.[81] From such dangers the unpolished wives of the barbarians were secured by poverty, solitude, and the painful cares of a domestic life. The German huts, open on every side to the eye of indiscretion or jealousy, were a better safeguard of conjugal fidelity than the walls, the bolts, and the eunuchs of a Persian harem. To this reason another may be added of a more honourable nature. The Germans treated their women with esteem and confidence, consulted them on every occasion of importance, and fondly believed that in their breasts resided a sanctity and wisdom more than human. Some of these interpreters of fate, such as Velleda, in the

Its probable causes

---

[78] (54) Esprit des Loix, l. xxx. c. 3. The brilliant imagination of Montesquieu is corrected, however, by the dry cold reason of the Abbé de Mably. Observations sur l'Histoire de France, tom. i. p.356. [Gibbon]

[79] (55) Gaudent muneribus, sed nec data imputant, nec acceptis obligantur. [They enjoy presents but expect no return, nor do they feel obligation in receiving. – eds] Tacit. Germ. c. 21. [Gibbon]

[80] (56) The adulteress was whipped through the village. Neither wealth nor beauty could inspire compassion, or procure her a second husband. Tacit. Germ. C. 18, 19. [Gibbon]

[81] (57) Ovid employs two hundred lines in the research of places the most favourable to love. Above all he considers the theatre as the best adapted to collect the beauties of Rome, and to melt them into tenderness and sensuality. [Gibbon]

Batavian war, governed, in the name of the deity, the fiercest nations of Germany.[82] The rest of the sex, without being adored as goddesses, were respected as the free and equal companions of soldiers; associated even by the marriage ceremony to a life of toil, of danger, and of glory.[83] In their great invasions, the camps of the barbarians were filled with a multitude of women, who remained firm and undaunted amidst the sound of arms, the various forms of destruction, and the honourable wounds of their sons and husbands.[84] Fainting armies of Germans have more than once been driven back upon the enemy by the generous[85] despair of the women, who dreaded death much less than servitude. If the day was irrecoverably lost, they well knew how to deliver themselves and their children with their own hands, from an insulting victor.[86] Heroines of such a cast may claim our admiration; but they were most assuredly neither lovely nor very susceptible of love. Whilst they affected to emulate the stern virtues of *man,* they must have resigned that attractive softness in which principally consist the charm and weakness of *woman.* Conscious pride taught the German females to suppress every tender emotion that stood in competition with honour, and the first honour of the sex has ever been that of chastity. The sentiments and conduct of these high-spirited matrons may, at once, be considered as a cause, as an effect, and as a proof, of the general character of the nation. Female courage, however it may be raised by fanaticism, or confirmed by habit, can only be a faint and imperfect imitation of the manly valour that distinguishes the age or country in which it may be found.

The religious system of the Germans (if the wild opinions of savages *Religion* can deserve that name) was dictated by their wants, their fears, and their ignorance.[87] They adored the great visible objects and agents of Nature, the Sun and the Moon, the Fire and the Earth; together with those imaginary deities who were supposed to preside over the most important occupations of human life. They were persuaded that, by some ridiculous arts of divination, they could discover the will of the superior beings, and that human sacrifices were the most precious and acceptable offerings to their altars. Some applause has been hastily bestowed on the sublime notion entertained by that people of the Deity whom they neither confined within the walls of a temple nor represented by any human figure; but when we recollect that the Germans were unskilled in architecture,

---

[82]   (58) Tacit. Hist. iv. 61, 65. [Gibbon]

[83]   (59) The marriage present was a yoke of oxen, horses, and arms. See Germ. c. 18. Tacitus is somewhat too florid on the subject. [Gibbon]

[84]   (60) The change of *exigere* into *exugere* is a most excellent correction. [Gibbon] *exigere*, to examine the wounds; *exugere*, to suck out, or dry off. [eds]

[85]   i.e. invigorating. [eds]

[86]   (61) Tacit. Germ. c. 7. Plutarch. in Mario. Before the wives of the Teutones destroyed themselves and their children, they had offered to surrender, on condition that they should be received as the slaves of the vestal virgins. [Gibbon]

[87]   (62) Tacitus has employed a few lines, and Cluverius one hundred and twenty-four pages, on this obscure subject. The former discovers in Germany the gods of Greece and Rome. The latter is positive that, under the emblems of the sun, the moon, and the fire, his pious ancestors worshipped the Trinity in unity. [Gibbon]

and totally unacquainted with the art of sculpture, we shall readily assign the true reason of a scruple, which arose not so much from a superiority of reason as from a want of ingenuity. The only temples in Germany were dark and ancient groves, consecrated by the reverence of succeeding generations. Their secret gloom, the imagined residence of an invisible power, by presenting no distinct object of fear or worship, impressed the mind with a still deeper sense of religious horror;[88] and the priests, rude and illiterate as they were, had been taught by experience the use of every artifice that could preserve and fortify impressions so well suited to their own interest.

The same ignorance which renders barbarians incapable of conceiving or embracing the useful restraints of laws exposes them naked and unarmed to the blind terrors of superstition. The German priests, improving this favourable temper of their countrymen, had assumed a jurisdiction even in temporal concerns which the magistrate could not venture to exercise; and the haughty warrior patiently submitted to the lash of correction, when it was inflicted, not by any human power, but by the immediate order of the god of war.[89] The defects of civil policy were sometimes supplied by the interposition of ecclesiastical authority. The latter was constantly exerted to maintain silence and decency in the popular assemblies; and was sometimes extended to a more enlarged concern for the national welfare. A solemn procession was occasionally celebrated in the present countries of Mecklenburgh and Pomerania. The unknown symbol of the *Earth*, covered with a thick veil, was placed on a carriage drawn by cows; and in this manner the goddess, whose common residence was in the isle of Rugen, visited several adjacent tribes of her worshippers. During her progress, the sound of war was hushed, quarrels were suspended, arms laid aside, and the restless Germans had an opportunity of tasting the blessings of peace and harmony.[90] The *truce of God*, so often and so ineffectually proclaimed by the clergy of the eleventh century, was an obvious imitation of this ancient custom.[91]

Its effects in peace

But the influence of religion was far more powerful to inflame than to moderate the fierce passions of the Germans. Interest and fanaticism often prompted its ministers to sanctify the most daring and the most unjust enterprises, by the approbation of Heaven, and full assurances of success. The consecrated standards, long revered in the groves of superstition were placed in the front of the battle;[92] and the hostile army was devoted[93] with dire execrations to the gods of war and of thunder.[94] In the

in war

---

[88] (63) The sacred wood, described with such sublime horror by Lucan, was in the neighbourhood of Marseilles; but there were many of the same kind in Germany. [Gibbon]

[89] (64) Tacit. Germania, c. 7. [Gibbon]

[90] (65) Tacit. Germania, c.40. [Gibbon]

[91] (66) See Dr. Robertson's History of Charles V. vol. i. note 10. [Gibbon]

[92] (67) Tacit. Germ. c. 7. These standards were only the heads of wild beasts. [Gibbon]

[93] i.e. dedicated. [eds]

[94] (68) See an instance of this custom, Tacit. Annal. xiii. 57. [Gibbon]

faith of soldiers (and such were the Germans) cowardice is the most unpardonable of sins. A brave man was the worthy favourite of their martial deities; the wretch who had lost his shield was alike banished from the religious and the civil assemblies of his countrymen. Some tribes of the north seem to have embraced the doctrine of transmigration,[95] others imagined a gross paradise of immortal drunkenness.[96] All agreed that a life spent in arms, and a glorious death in battle, were the best preparations for a happy futurity, either in this or in another world.

The immortality so vainly promised by the priests was, in some degree, conferred by the bards. That singular order of men has most deservedly attracted the notice of all who have attempted to investigate the antiquities of the Celts, the Scandinavians, and the Germans. Their genius and character, as well as the reverence paid to that important office, have been sufficiently illustrated. But we cannot so easily express, or even conceive, the enthusiasm of arms and glory which they kindled in the breast of their audience. Among a polished people, a taste for poetry is rather an amusement of the fancy than a passion of the soul. And yet, when in calm retirement we peruse the combats described by Homer or Tasso,[97] we are insensibly seduced by the fiction, and feel a momentary glow of martial ardour. But how faint, how cold is the sensation which a peaceful mind can receive from solitary study! It was in the hour of battle, or in the feast of victory, that the bards celebrated the glory of heroes of ancient days, the ancestors of those warlike chieftains who listened with transport to their artless but animated strains. The view of arms and of danger heightened the effect of the military song; and the passions which it tended to excite, the desire of fame and the contempt of death, were the habitual sentiments of a German mind.[98]

The bards

Such was the situation and such were the manners of the ancient Germans. Their climate, their want of learning, of arts, and of laws, their notions of honour, of gallantry, and of religion, their sense of freedom, impatience of peace, and thirst of enterprise, all contributed to form a people of military heroes. And yet we find that, during more than two hundred and fifty years that elapsed from the defeat of Varus to the reign of Decius, these formidable barbarians made few considerable attempts,

Causes which checked the progress of the Germans

---

[95]   (69) Caesar, Diodorus, and Lucan seem to ascribe this doctrine to the Gauls, but M. Pelloutier (Histoire des Celtes, l. iii. c. 18) labours to reduce their expressions to a more orthodox sense. [Gibbon]
Transmigration: i.e. of souls after death. [eds]

[96]   (70) Concerning this gross but alluring doctrine of the Edda, see Fable xx in the curious version of that book, published by M. Mallet, in his Introduction to the History of Denmark. [Gibbon]

[97]   Homer and Tasso: ancient Greek, and sixteenth century Italian epic poets respectively. [eds]

[98]   (71) See Tacit. Germ. c. 3. Diodor. Sicul. l. v. Strabo, l. iv. p.197. The classical reader may remember the rank of Demodocus in the Phæacian court, and the ardour infused by Tyrtæus into the fainting Spartans. Yet there is little probability that the Greeks and the Germans were the same people. Much learned trifling might be spared, if our antiquarians would condescend to reflect that similar manners will naturally be produced by similar situations. [Gibbon]

and not any material impression, on the luxurious and enslaved provinces of the empire. Their progress was checked by their want of arms and discipline, and their fury was diverted by the intestine division of ancient Germany.

Want of arms

I. It has been observed, with ingenuity, and not without truth, that the command of iron soon gives a nation the command of gold. But the rude tribes of Germany, alike destitute of both those valuable metals, were reduced slowly to acquire, by their unassisted strength, the possession of the one as well as the other. The face of a German army displayed their poverty of iron. Swords and the longer kind of lances they could seldom use. Their *frameæ*[99] (as they called them in their own language) were long spears headed with a sharp but narrow iron point, and which, as occasion required, they either darted from a distance, or pushed in close onset. With this spear and with a shield their cavalry was contented. A multitude of darts, scattered[100] with incredible force, were an additional resource of the infantry. Their military dress, when they wore any, was nothing more than a loose mantle. A variety of colours was the only ornament of their wooden or their osier shields. Few of the chiefs were distinguished by cuirasses,[101] scarce any by helmets. Though the horses of Germany were neither beautiful, swift, nor practised in the skilful evolutions of the Roman manage, several of the nations obtained renown by their cavalry; but, in general, the principal strength of the Germans consisted in their infantry[102] which was drawn up in several deep columns, according to the distinction of tribes and families. Impatient of fatigue or delay, these half-armed warriors rushed to battle with dissonant shouts and disordered ranks; and sometimes, by the effort of native valour, prevailed over the constrained and more artificial[103] bravery of the Roman mercenaries. But as the barbarians poured forth their whole souls on the first onset, they knew not how to rally or to retire. A repulse was a sure defeat; and a defeat was most commonly total destruction. When we recollect the complete armour of the Roman soldiers, their discipline, exercises, evolutions, fortified camps, and military engines, it appears a just matter of surprise how the naked and unassisted valour of the barbarians could dare to encounter in the field the strength of the legions and the various troops of the auxiliaries, which seconded their operations. The contest was too unequal, till the introduction of luxury had enervated the vigour, and a spirit of disobedience and sedition had relaxed the discipline, of the Roman armies. The introduction of barbarian auxiliaries into those armies was a measure attended with very obvious dangers, as it might gradually instruct the Germans in the arts of war and

and of discipline

---

[99]   *Franca* in Old English meant 'javelin'. [eds]

[100]   (72) Missilia spargunt [they scatter missiles. – eds], Tacit. Germ. c. 6. Either that historian used a vague expression, or he meant that they were thrown at random. [Gibbon]

[101]   Breast plate and back plate. [eds]

[102]   (73) It was the principal distinction from the Sarmatians, who generally fought on horseback. [Gibbon]

[103]   i.e. acquired through training in military skills. [eds]

of policy. Although they were admitted in small numbers and with the strictest precaution, the example of Civilis was proper to convince the Romans that the danger was not imaginary, and that their precautions were not always sufficient.[104] During the civil wars that followed the death of Nero, that artful and intrepid Batavian, whom his enemies condescended to compare with Hannibal and Sertorius,[105] formed a great design of freedom and ambition. Eight Batavian cohorts, renowned in the wars of Britain and Italy, repaired to his standard. He introduced an army of Germans into Gaul, prevailed on the powerful cities of Treves and Langres to embrace his cause, defeated the legions, destroyed their fortified camps, and employed against the Romans the military knowledge which he had acquired in their service. When at length, after an obstinate struggle, he yielded to the power of the empire, Civilis secured himself and his country by an honourable treaty. The Batavians[106] still continued to occupy the islands of the Rhine,[107] the allies, not the servants, of the Roman monarchy.

II. The strength of ancient Germany appears formidable when we consider the effects that might have been produced by its united effort. The wide extent of country might very possibly contain a million of warriors, as all who were of an age to bear arms were of a temper to use them. But this fierce multitude, incapable of concerting or executing any plan of national greatness, was agitated by various and often hostile intentions. Germany was divided into more than forty independent states; and even in each state the unions of the several tribes was extremely loose and precarious. The barbarians were easily provoked; they knew not how to forgive an injury, much less an insult; their resentments were bloody and implacable. The casual disputes that so frequently happened in their tumultuous parties of hunting or drinking were sufficient to inflame the minds of whole nations; the private feud of any considerable chieftains diffused itself among their followers and allies. To chastise the insolent, or to plunder the defenceless, were alike causes of war. The most formidable states of Germany affected to encompass their territories with a wide frontier of solitude and devastation. The awful distance preserved by their neighbours attested the terror of their arms, and in some measure defended them from the danger of unexpected incursions.[108]

Civil dissensions of Germany

---

[104] (74) The relation of this enterprise occupies a great part of the fourth and fifth books of the History of Tacitus, and is more remarkable for its eloquence than perspicuity. Sir Henry Saville has observed several inaccuracies. [Gibbon]

[105] (75) Tacit. Hist. iv. 13. Like them, he had lost an eye. [Gibbon]
Quintus Sertorius (*c.*123–72 BC), Roman statesman and commander in Spain. [eds]

[106] Batavia was roughly present-day Holland. [eds]

[107] (76) It was contained between the two branches of the old Rhine, as they subsisted before the face of the country was changed by art and nature. See Cluver. German. Antiq. l. iii. c. 30, 37. [Gibbon]

[108] (77) Caesar de Bell. Gall. l. vi. 23. [Gibbon]

'The Bructeri (it is Tacitus who now speaks) were totally exterminated by the neighbouring tribes,[109] provoked by their insolence, allured by the hopes of spoil, and perhaps inspired by the tutelar[110] deities of the empire. Above sixty thousand barbarians were destroyed, not by the Roman arms, but in our sight, and for our entertainment. May the nations, enemies of Rome, ever preserve this enmity to each other! We have now attained the utmost verge of prosperity,[111] and have nothing left to demand of fortune except the discord of the barbarians.·[112] These sentiments, less worthy of the humanity than of the patriotism of Tacitus, express the invariable maxims of the policy of his countrymen. They deemed it a much safer expedient to divide than to combat the barbarians, from whose defeat they could derive neither honour nor advantage. The money and negotiations of Rome insinuated themselves into the heart of Germany, and every art of seduction was used with dignity to conciliate those nations whom their proximity to the Rhine or Danube might render the most useful friends as well as the most troublesome enemies. Chiefs of renown and power were flattered by the most trifling presents, which they received either as marks of distinction or as the instruments of luxury. In civil dissensions, the weaker faction endeavoured to strengthen its interest by entering into secret connections with the governors of the frontier provinces. Every quarrel among the Germans was fomented by the intrigues of Rome; and every plan of union and public good was defeated by the stronger bias of private jealousy and interest.[113]

Fomented by the policy of Rome

The general conspiracy which terrified the Romans under the reign of Marcus Antoninus[114] comprehended almost all the nations of Germany, and even Sarmatia, from the mouth of the Rhine to that of the Danube.[115] It is impossible for us to determine whether this hasty confederation was formed by necessity, by reason, or by passion; but we may rest assured, that the barbarians were neither allured by the indolence or provoked by the ambition of the Roman monarch. This dangerous invasion required

Transient union against Marcus Antoninus

---

[109] (78) They are mentioned however in the ivth and vth centuries by Nazarius, Ammianus, Claudian, &c., as a tribe of Franks. See Cluver. Germ. Antiq. l. iii. c. 13. [Gibbon]

[110] i.e. protecting. [eds]

[111] (79) *Urgentibus* is the common reading, but good sense; Lipsius, and some MSS declare for *Vergentibus*. [Gibbon]

If the word is read as *urgentibus*, the translation is 'whilst the destinies of the empire drive it on'; *vergentibus* gives 'whilst the destinies of the empire stand on the utmost edge of prosperity'. [eds]

[112] (80) Tacit. Germania, c. 33. The pious Abbé de la Blèterie is very angry with Tacitus, talks of the devil who was a murderer from the beginning, &c., &c. [Gibbon]

[113] (81) Many traces of this policy may be discovered in Tacitus and Dion; and many more may be inferred from the principles of human nature. [Gibbon]

[114] Marcus Aurelius Antoninus (AD 121–180), Roman Emperor AD 161–180. [eds]

[115] (82) Hist. August. p.31. Ammian. Marcellin. l. xxxi. c. 5. Aurel. Victor. The Emperor Marcus was reduced to sell the rich furniture of the palace, and to enlist slaves and robbers. [Gibbon]

all the firmness and vigilance of Marcus. He fixed generals of ability in the several stations of attack, and assumed in person the conduct of the most important province on the Upper Danube. After a long and doubtful conflict, the spirit of the barbarians was subdued. The Quadi and the Marcomanni,[116] who had taken the lead in the war, were the most severely punished in its catastrophe. They were commanded to retire five miles[117] from their own banks of the Danube, and to deliver up the flower of the youth, who were immediately sent into Britain, a remote island, where they might be secure as hostages and useful as soldiers.[118] On the frequent rebellions of the Quadi and Marcomanni, the irritated emperor resolved to reduce their country into the form of a province. His designs were disappointed by death. This formidable league, however, the only one that appears in the two first centuries of the Imperial history, was entirely dissipated without leaving any traces behind in Germany.

In the course of this introductory chapter, we have confined ourselves to the general outlines of the manners of Germany, without attempting to describe or to distinguish the various tribes which filled that great country in the time of Caesar, of Tacitus, or of Ptolemy. As the ancient or as new tribes successively present themselves in the series of this history, we shall concisely mention their origin, the situation, and their particular character. Modern nations are fixed and permanent societies, connected among themselves by laws and government, bound to their native soil by arts and agriculture. The German tribes were voluntary and fluctuating associations of soldiers, almost of savages. The same territory often changed its inhabitants in the tide of conquest and emigration. The same communities, uniting in a plan of defence or invasion, bestowed a new title on their new confederacy. The dissolution of an ancient confederacy restored to the independent tribes their peculiar[119] but long forgotten appellation. A victorious state often communicated its own name to a vanquished people. Sometimes crowds of volunteers flocked from all parts to the standard of a favourite leader; his camp became their country, and some circumstance of the enterprise soon gave a common denomination to the mixed multitude. The distinctions of the ferocious invaders were perpetually varied by themselves, and confounded by the astonished subjects of the Roman empire.[120]

Distinction of the German tribes

---

[116]   (83) The Marcomanni, a colony, who, from the banks of the Rhine, occupied Bohemia and Moravia, had once erected a great and formidable monarchy under their king Maroboduus. See Strabo, l. vii. Vell. Pat. ii. 105. Tacit. Annal. ii. 63. [Gibbon]

[117]   (84) Mr. Wotton (History of Rome, p.166) increases the prohibition to ten times the distance. His reasoning is specious but not conclusive. Five miles were sufficient for a fortified barrier. [Gibbon]

[118]   (85) Dion, l. lxxi. and lxxii. [Gibbon]

[119]   i.e. individual. [eds]

[120]   (86) See an excellent dissertation on the origin and migrations of nations, in the Mémoires de l'Académie des Inscriptions, tom. xviii. p.48–71. It is seldom that the antiquarian and the philosopher are so happily blended. [Gibbon]

Wars and the administration of public affairs are the principal sub- *Numbers*
jects of history; but the number of persons interested in these busy scenes
is very different, according to the different condition of mankind. In
great monarchies millions of obedient subjects pursue their useful occupations in peace and obscurity. The attention of the writer, as well as of
the reader, is solely confined to a court, a capital, a regular army, and the
districts which happen to be the occasional scene of military operations.
But a state of freedom and barbarism, the season of civil commotions, or
the situation of petty republics,[121] raises almost every member of the community into action and consequently into notice. The irregular divisions
and the restless motions of the people of Germany dazzle our imagination, and seem to multiply their numbers. The profuse enumeration of
kings and warriors, of armies and nations, inclines us to forget that the
same objects are continually repeated under a variety of appellations, and
that the most splendid appellations have been frequently lavished on the
most inconsiderable objects.

Chapter XIII

The Reign of Diocletian

Before we dismiss the consideration of the life and character of *Description of Salona, and*
Diocletian, we may, for a moment, direct our view to the place of his *the adjacent country*
retirement. Salona, a principal city of his native province of Dalmatia, was
near two hundred Roman miles (according to the measurement of the
public highways) from Aquileia and the confines of Italy, and about two
hundred and seventy from Sirmium, the usual residence of the emperors
whenever they visited the Illyrian frontier.[122] A miserable village still
preserves the name of Salona, but so late as the sixteenth century, the
remains of a theatre, and a confused prospect of broken arches and
marble columns, continued to attest its ancient splendour.[123] About six or
seven miles from the city, Diocletian constructed a magnificent palace,
and we may infer from the greatness of the work, how long he had
meditated his design of abdicating the empire. The choice of a spot
which united all that could contribute either to health or to luxury did
not require the partiality of a native. 'The soil was dry and fertile, the air
is pure and wholesome, and, though extremely hot during the summer
months, this country seldom feels those sultry and noxious winds to which
the coast of Istria and some parts of Italy are exposed. The views from the
palace are no less beautiful than the soil and climate were inviting.

---

[121] (87) Should we suspect that Athens contained only 21,000 citizens, and
Sparta no more than 39,000? See Hume and Wallace on the number of mankind
in ancient and modern times. [Gibbon]

[122] (122) See the Itiner. p.269, 272, edit. Wessel. [Gibbon]

[123] (123) The Abate Fortis, in his Viaggio in Dalmazia, p.43 (printed at Venice in
the year 1774, in two small volumes in quarto), quotes a Ms. account of the
antiquities of Salona, composed by Giambattista Giustiniani about the middle of
the xvith century. [See Mr. Jackson's work on Dalmatia, and Mr. Freeman's essay
in Historical Essays, 2nd series.] [Gibbon]

Towards the west lies the fertile shore that stretches along the Hadriatic, in which a number of small islands are scattered in such a manner as to give this part of the sea the appearance of a great lake. On the north side lies the bay, which led to the ancient city of Salona, and the country beyond it, appearing in sight, forms a proper contrast to that more extensive prospect of water, which the Hadriatic presents both to the south and to the east. Towards the north, the view is terminated by high and irregular mountains, situated at a proper distance, and, in many places, covered with villages, woods and vineyards.[124]

Though Constantine, from a very obvious prejudice, affects to mention the palace of Diocletian with contempt,[125] yet one of their successors, who could only see it in a neglected and mutilated state, celebrates its magnificence in terms of the highest admiration.[126] It covered an extent of ground consisting of between nine and ten English acres. The form was quadrangular, flanked with sixteen towers. Two of the sides were near six hundred, and the other two near seven hundred, feet in length. The whole was constructed of a beautiful freestone, extracted from the neighbouring quarries of Trau or Tragutium,[127] and very little inferior to marble itself. Four streets, intersecting each other at right angles, divided the several parts of this great edifice, and the approach to the principal apartment was from a very stately entrance, which is still denominated the Golden Gate. The approach was terminated by a *peristylium*[128] of granite columns, on one side of which we discover the square temple of Æsculapius, on the other the octagon temple of Jupiter. The latter of those deities Diocletian revered as the patron of his fortunes, the former as the protector of his health. By comparing the present remains with the precepts of Vitruvius, the several parts of the building, the baths, bedchamber, the *atrium*, the *basilica*,[129] and the Cyzicene, Corinthian, and Egyptian halls have been described with some degree of precision, or at least of probability. Their forms were various, their proportions just, but

Of Diocletian's palace

---

[124] (124) Adam's Antiquities of Diocletian's Palace at Spalatro, p.6. We may add a circumstance or two from the Abate Fortis; the little stream of the Hyader, mentioned by Lucan, produces most exquisite trout, which a sagacious writer, perhaps a monk, supposes to have been one of the principal reasons that determined Diocletian in the choice of his retirement. Fortis, p.45. The same author (p.38) observes that a taste for agriculture is reviving at Spalatro; and that an experimental farm has lately been established near the city, by a society of gentlemen. [Gibbon]

[125] (125) Constantin. Orat. ad Coetum Sanct. c. 25. In this sermon, the emperor or the bishop who composed it for him affects to relate the miserable end of all the persecutors of the church. [Gibbon]

[126] (126) Constantin. Porphyr. de Statu Imper. p.86 [iii. p.125, ed. Bonn]. [Gibbon]

[127] (127) Tragurium is the name; now Trogir. [eds]

[128] i.e. a colonnaded or square cloister. [eds]

[129] *atrium*: an open court or hall; *basilica*: an oblong building with double colonnades and a semi-circular apse at one end, used as a place of public assembly. [eds]

they were all attended with two imperfections, very repugnant to our modern notions of taste and conveniency. These stately rooms had neither windows nor chimneys. They were lighted from the top (for the building seems to have consisted of no more than one storey), and they received their heat by the help of pipes that were conveyed along the walls. The range of principal apartments was protected towards the south west by a portico five hundred and seventeen feet long, which must have formed a very noble and delightful walk, when the beauties of painting and sculpture were added to those of the prospect.

Had this magnificent edifice remained in a solitary country, it would have been exposed to the ravages of time; but it might, perhaps, have escaped the rapacious industry of man. The village of Aspalathus,[130] and, long afterwards, the provincial town of Spalatro, have grown out of its ruins. The Golden Gate now opens into the market place. St John the Baptist has usurped the honours of Æsculapius; and the temple of Jupiter under the protection of the Virgin, is converted into the cathedral church. For this account of Diocletian's palace we are principally indebted to an ingenious artist of our own time and country, whom a very liberal curiosity carried into the heart of Dalmatia.[131] But there is room to suspect that the elegance of his designs and engraving has somewhat flattered the objects which it was their purpose to represent. We are informed by a more recent and very judicious traveller that the awful ruins of Spalatro are not less expressive of the decline of the arts than of the greatness of the Roman empire in the time of Diocletian.[132] If such was indeed the state of architecture, we must naturally believe that painting and sculpture had experienced a still more sensible decay. The practice of architecture is directed by a few general and even mechanical rules. But sculpture, and, above all, painting, propose to themselves the imitation not only of the forms of nature, but of the characters and passions of the human soul. In those sublime arts, the dexterity of the hand is of little avail, unless it is animated by fancy and guided by the most correct taste and observation.

Decline of the Arts

---

[130] (128) D'Auville, Géographie Ancienne, tom. i. p.162. [Gibbon]

[131] (129) Messieurs Adam and Clérisseau, attended by two draughtsmen, visited Spalatro in the month of July, 1757. The magnificent work which their journey produced was published in London seven years afterwards. [Gibbon]

[132] (130) I shall quote the words of the Abate Fortis. 'E'bastevolmente nota agli amatori dell' Architettura, e dell' Antichità, l'opera del Signor ADAMS, che a donato molto a que' superbi vestigi coll'abituale eleganza del suo toccalapis e del bulino. In generale la rozzezza del scalpello, e'l cattivo gusto del secolo vi gareggiano colla magnificenza del fabricato.' [The works of Mr. Adams (*sic*) are well known to lovers of architecture and antiquity; he has given a great deal to those superb remains with the usual elegance of his pencil and engraver's chisel. In general, the roughness of the sculptor's chisel and the poor taste of the age spoil the magnificence of the design. – eds] See Viaggio in Dalmazia, p.40. [Gibbon]

Chapter XIV

Troubles after the Abdication of Diocletian and Reunion of the Empire under the Authority of Constantine

In the use of victory, Constantine neither deserved the praise of clemency, nor incurred the censure of immoderate rigour.[133] He inflicted the same treatment to which a defeat would have exposed his own person and family, put to death the two sons of the tyrant, and carefully extirpated his whole race. The most distinguished adherents of Maxentius must have expected to share his fate, as they had shared his prosperity and his crimes: but, when the Roman people loudly demanded a greater number of victims, the conqueror resisted, with firmness and humanity, those servile clamours which were dictated by flattery as well as by resentment. Informers were punished and discouraged; the innocent who had suffered under the late tyranny were recalled from exile, and restored to their estates. A general act of oblivion quieted the minds and settled the property of the people, both in Italy and in Africa.[134] The first time that Constantine honoured the senate with his presence, he recapitulated his own services and exploits in a modest oration, assured that illustrious order of his sincere regard, and promised to re-establish its ancient dignity and privileges. The grateful senate repaid these unmeaning professions by the empty titles of honour, which it was yet in their power to bestow; and, without presuming to ratify the authority of Constantine, they passed a decree to assign him the first rank among the three *Augusti* who governed the Roman world.[135] Games and festivals were instituted to preserve the fame of his victory, and several edifices, raised at the expense of Maxentius, were dedicated to the honour of his successful rival. The triumphal arch of Constantine still remains a melancholy proof of the decline of the arts, and a singular testimony of the meanest vanity. As it was not possible to find in the capital of the empire a sculptor who was capable of adorning that public monument, the arch of Trajan, without any respect either for his memory or for the rules of propriety, was stripped of its most elegant figures. The difference of times and persons, of actions and characters, was totally disregarded. The Parthian captives appear prostrate at the feet of a prince who never carried his arms beyond the Euphrates; and curious antiquarians can still discover the head of Trajan on the trophies of Constantine. The new ornaments which

His reception

---

[133]   (82) Zosimus, the enemy of Constantine, allows (l. ii. p.88 [17]) that only a few of the friends of Maxentius were put to death, but we may remark the expressive passage of Nazarius (Panegyr. Vet. x. 6.): Omnibus qui labefactare statum ejus poterant cum stirpe deletis. [All who could undermine his position were killed, together with their families. – eds] The other orator (Panegyr. Vet. ix. 20, 21) contents himself with observing that Constantine, when he entered Rome, did not imitate the cruel massacres of Cinna, of Marius, or of Sylla. [Gibbon]

[134]   (83) See the two Panegyrics, and the laws of this and the ensuing year, in the Theodosian Code. [Gibbon]

[135]   (84) Panegyr. Vet. ix. 20. Lactantius de M. P. c. 44. Maximin, who was confessedly the oldest Caesar, claimed, with some show of reason, the first rank among the Augusti. [Gibbon]

it was necessary to introduce between the vacancies of ancient sculpture are executed in the rudest and most unskilful manner.[136]

Chapter XX

The Motives, Progress, and Effects of the Conversion of Constantine – Legal Establishment and Constitution of the Christian or Catholic Church

The public establishment of Christianity may be considered as one of those important and domestic revolutions which excite the most lively curiosity and afford the most valuable instruction. The victories and the civil policy of Constantine no longer influence the state of Europe; but a considerable portion of the globe still retains the impression which it received from the conversion of that monarch; and the ecclesiastical institutions of his reign are still connected, by an indissoluble chain, with the opinions, the passions, and the interests of the present generation.

In the consideration of a subject which may be examined with impartiality, but cannot be viewed with indifference, a difficulty immediately arises of a very unexpected nature: that of ascertaining the real and precise date of the conversion of Constantine. The eloquent Lactantius, in the midst of his court, seems impatient[137] to proclaim to the world the glorious example of the sovereign of Gaul;[138] who, in the first moments of his reign, acknowledged and adored the majesty of the true and only

Date of the conversion of Constantine

AD 306

---

[136] (85) Adhuc cuncta opera quæ magnifice construxerat, urbis fanum, atque basilicam, Flavii meritis patres sacravere. Aurelius Victor. [All works which he had previously built as a holy shrine and basilica of the city, the Flavian fathers dedicated in their own praise. – eds] With regard to the theft of Trajan's trophies, consult Flaminius Vacca, apud Montfaucon, Diarium Italicum, p.250, and l'Antiquité Expliquée of the latter, tom. iv. p.171. [Cp. Petersen, Römische Mittheilungen, 1889, 314 *sqq*. The question has been investigated anew by H. Stuart Jones, who has shown that the sculptures belong to different periods, and has made it probable that the emperor represented in the sacrificial scenes is Claudius Gothicus, whom Constantine claimed as his grandfather (see above, chap. xiii.). A statement of the results of Mr. Jones's studies will be found in Appendix 24. Lanciani (Pagan and Christian Rome, p.20; Ruins and Excavations, p.193) referred the sculptures to the Arch of Titus. For the famous inscriptions on the Arch of Constantine, see also Appendix 24.] [Gibbon]

[137] (1) The date of the Divine Institutions of Lactantius has been accurately discussed, difficulties have been started, solutions proposed, and an expedient imagined of two *original* editions: the former published during the persecution of Diocletian, the latter under that of Licinius. See Dufresnoy, Prefat. p.v. Tillemont, Mém. Ecclésiast. tom. vi. p.465–470. Lardner's Credibility, part ii. vol. vii. p.78–86. For my own part, I am *almost* convinced that Lactantius dedicated his Institutions to the sovereign of Gaul, at a time when Galerius, Maximin, and even Licinius, persecuted the Christians; that is, between the years 306 and 311. [The work was probably begun about 304, and finished perhaps by 308, certainly before 311.] [Gibbon]

[138] i.e. Constantine [eds]

God.[139] The learned Eusebius has ascribed the faith of Constantine to the miraculous sign which was displayed in the heavens whilst he meditated and prepared the Italian expedition.[140] The historian Zosimus maliciously asserts that the emperor had imbrued his hands in the blood of his eldest son, before he publicly renounced the gods of Rome and of his ancestors.[141] The perplexity produced by these discordant authorities is derived from the behaviour of Constantine himself. According to the strictness of ecclesiastical language, the first of the *Christian* emperors was unworthy of that name, till the moment of his death; since it was only during his last illness that he received, as a catechumen,[142] the imposition of hands,[143] and was afterwards admitted, by the initiatory rites of baptism, into the number of the faithful.[144] The Christianity of Constantine must be allowed in a much more vague and qualified sense; and the nicest accuracy is required in tracing the slow and almost imperceptible gradations by which the monarch declared himself the protector, and at length the proselyte, of the church. It was an arduous task to eradicate the habits and prejudices of his education, to acknowledge the divine power of Christ, and to understand that the truth of *his* revelation was incompatible with the worship of the gods. The obstacles which he had probably experienced in his own mind instructed him to proceed with caution in the momentous change of a national religion; and he insensibly discovered[145] his new opinions, as far as he could enforce them with safety and with effect. During the whole course of his reign, the stream of

AD 312

AD 326

AD 337

---

[139]   (2) Lactant. Divin. Institut. i. l. vii. 27. The first and most important of these passages is indeed wanting in twenty-eight manuscripts; but it is found in nineteen. If we weigh the comparative value of those manuscripts, one of 900 years old, in the king of France's library, may be alleged in its favour; but the passage is omitted in the correct manuscript of Bologna, which the P. de Montfaucon ascribes to the sixth or seventh century (Diarium Italic. p.409). The taste of most of the editors (except Isæus, see Lactant. edit. Dufresnoy, tom. i. p.596) has felt the genuine style of Lactantius. [On these and other minor interpolations, see Brandt's papers in the Sitzungsberichte of the Vienna Academy, 118 and 119 (1889).] [Gibbon]

[140]   (3) Euseb. in Vit. Constant. l. i. c. 27–32. [Gibbon]

[141]   (4) Zosimus, l. ii. p.104 [c. 29]. [Gibbon]

[142]   A new convert under instruction before baptism. [eds]

[143]   (5) That rite was *always* used in making a catechumen (see Bingham's Antiquities, l. x. c. l, p.419; Dom. Chardou, Hist. des Sacremens, tom. i. p.62), and Constantine received it for the *first* time (Euseb. in Vit. Constant. l. iv. c. 61) immediately before his baptism and death. From the connexion of these two facts, Valesius (ad loc. Euseb.) has drawn the conclusion, which is reluctantly admitted by Tillemont (Hist. des Empereurs, tom. iv. p.628), and opposed with feeble arguments by Mosheim (p.968). [Gibbon]

[144]   (6) Euseb. in Vit. Constant. l. iv. c. 61, 62, 63. The legend of Constantine's baptism at Rome, thirteen years before his death, was invented in the eighth century, as a proper motive for his *donation*. Such has been the gradual progress of knowledge that a story of which Cardinal Baronius (Annal. Ecclesiast. AD 324, No. 43–49) declared himself the unblushing advocate is now feebly supported, even within the verge of the Vatican. See the Antiquitates Christianæ, tom. ii. p.232; a work published with six approbations at Rome, in the year 1751, by Father Mamachi, a learned Dominican. [Gibbon]

[145]   i.e. revealed. [eds]

Christianity flowed with a gentle, though accelerated, motion; but its general direction was sometimes checked, and sometimes diverted, by the accidental circumstances of the times, and by the prudence, or possibly by the caprice, of the monarch. His ministers were permitted to signify the intentions of their master in the various language which was best adapted to their respective principles;[146] and he artfully balanced the hopes and fears of his subjects by publishing in the same year two edicts: *AD 321* the first of which enjoined the solemn observance of Sunday,[147] and the second directed the regular consultation of the Aruspices.[148] While this important revolution yet remained in suspense, the Christians and the Pagans watched the conduct of their sovereign with the same anxiety, but with very opposite sentiments. The former were prompted by every motive of zeal, as well as vanity, to exaggerate the marks of his favour, and the evidences of his faith. The latter, till their just apprehensions were changed into despair and resentment, attempted to conceal from the world, and from themselves, that the gods of Rome could no longer reckon the emperor in the number of their votaries. The same passions and prejudices have engaged the partial writers of the times to connect the public profession of Christianity with the most glorious or the most ignominious era of the reign of Constantine.

Whatever symptoms of Christian piety might transpire in the dis- *His Pagan superstition* courses or actions of Constantine, he persevered till he was near forty years of age in the practice of the established religion;[149] and the same conduct, which in the court of Nicomedia might be imputed to his fear, could be ascribed only to the inclination or policy of the sovereign of Gaul. His liberality restored and enriched the temples of the gods: the medals which issued from his Imperial mint are impressed with the fig- ures and attributes of Jupiter and Apollo, of Mars and Hercules; and his filial piety increased the council of Olympus by the solemn apotheosis of his father Constantius.[150] But the devotion of Constantine was more

---

[146] (7) The quæstor, or secretary, who composed the law of the Theodosian Code, makes his master say with indifference, 'hominibus supradictæ religionis' [men of the aforesaid religion. – eds] (l. xvi. tit. ii. leg. 1). The minister of ecclesi- astical affairs was allowed a more devout and respectful style, (τῆς ἐνθέσμου καὶ ἁγιωτάτης καθολικῆς θρησκείας), the legal, most holy, and catholic worship. See Euseb. Hist. Eccl. l. x. c. 6. [Gibbon]

[147] (8) Cod. Theodos. l. ii. tit. viii. leg. l. Cod. Justinian. l. iii. tit. xii. leg. iii. Con- stantine styles the Lord's day *dies solis* [the day of the sun. – eds], a name which could not offend the ears of his Pagan subjects. [Gibbon]

[148] (9) Cod. Theod. l. xvi. tit. x. leg. 1. Godefroy, in the character of a commen- tator, endeavours (tom. vi. p.257) to excuse Constantine; but the more zealous Baronius (Annal. Eccl. AD 321, No. 18) censures his profane conduct with truth and asperity. [Gibbon]

Aruspices: pagan priests who foretold events by examining the entrails of birds. [eds]

[149] (10) Theodoret (l. i. c. 18) seems to insinuate that Helena gave her son a Christian education; but we may be assured, from the superior authority of Euse- bius (in Vit. Constant. l. iii. c. 47), that she herself was indebted to Constantine for the knowledge of Christianity. [Gibbon]

[150] (11) See the medals of Constantine in Ducange and Banduri. As few cities had retained the privilege of coining, almost all the medals of that age issued from the mint under the sanction of the Imperial authority. [Gibbon]

peculiarly directed to the genius of the Sun, the Apollo of Greek and Roman mythology; and he was pleased to be represented with the symbols of the God of Light and Poetry. The unerring shafts of that deity, the brightness of his eyes, his laurel wreath, immortal beauty, and elegant accomplishments, seem to point him out as the patron of a young hero. The altars of Apollo were crowned with the votive offerings of Constantine; and the credulous multitude were taught to believe that the emperor was permitted to behold with mortal eyes the visible majesty of their tutelar deity, and that, either waking or in a vision, he was blessed with the auspicious omens of a long and victorious reign. The Sun was universally celebrated as the invincible guide and protector of Constantine; and the Pagans might reasonably expect that the insulted god would pursue with unrelenting vengeance the impiety of his ungrateful favourite.[151]

As long as Constantine exercised a limited sovereignty over the provinces of Gaul, his Christian subjects were protected by the authority, and perhaps by the laws, of a prince who wisely left to the gods the care of vindicating their own honour. If we may credit the assertion of Constantine himself, he had been an indignant spectator of the savage cruelties which were inflicted, by the hands of Roman soldiers, on those citizens whose religion was their only crime.[152] In the East and in the West, he had seen the different effects of severity and indulgence; and, as the former was rendered still more odious by the example of Galerius, his implacable enemy, the latter was recommended to his imitation by the authority and advice of a dying father. The son[153] of Constantius immediately suspended or repealed the edicts of persecution, and granted the free exercise of their religious ceremonies to all those who had already professed themselves members of the church. They were soon encouraged to depend on the favour as well as on the justice of their sovereign, who had imbibed a secret and sincere reverence for the name of Christ and for the God of the Christians.[154]

He protects the Christians of Gaul. AD 306–312

About five months after the conquest of Italy, the emperor made a solemn and authentic declaration of his sentiments, by the celebrated edict of Milan, which restored peace to the Catholic Church. In the personal interview of the two western princes, Constantine, by the ascendant of genius and power, obtained the ready concurrence of his colleague

AD 313. March. Edict of Milan.

[151] (12) The panegyric of Eumenius (vii. inter Panegyr. Vet.), which was pronounced a few months before the Italian war, abounds with the most unexceptionable evidence of the Pagan superstition of Constantine, and of his particular veneration for Apollo, or the Sun; to which Julian alludes (orat. vii. p.228, ἀπολείπων σε). See Commentaire de Spanheim sur les Césars, p.317. [Gibbon]

[152] (13) Constantin. Orat. ad sanctos, c. 25. But it might easily be shown that the Greek translator has improved the sense of the Latin original; and the aged emperor might recollect the persecution of Diocletian with a more lively abhorrence than he had actually felt in the days of his youth and Paganism. [Gibbon]

[153] i.e. Constantine. [eds]

[154] (14) See Euseb. Hist. Eccles. l. viii. 13, 1, ix. 9, and in Vit. Const. l. i. c. 16, 17. Lactant. Divin. Institut. i. l. Cæcilius de Mort. Persecut. c. 25. [Gibbon]

Licinius; the union of their names and authority disarmed the fury of Maximin; and, after the death of the tyrant of the East, the edict of Milan was received as a general and fundamental law of the Roman world.[155] The wisdom of the emperors provided for the restitution of all the civil and religious rights of which the Christians had been so unjustly deprived. It was enacted that the places of worship, and public lands, which had been confiscated, should be restored to the church, without dispute, without delay, and without expense; and this severe injunction was accompanied with a gracious promise that, if any of the purchasers had paid a fair and adequate price, they should be indemnified from the Imperial treasury. The salutary regulations which guard the future tranquillity of the faithful are framed on the principles of enlarged and equal toleration; and such an equality must have been interpreted by a recent sect as an advantageous and honourable distinction. The two emperors proclaim to the world that they have granted a free and absolute power to the Christians, and to all others, of following the religion which each individual thinks proper to prefer, to which he has addicted his mind, and which he may deem the best adapted to his own use. They carefully explain every ambiguous word, remove every exception and exact from the governors of the provinces a strict obedience to the true and simple meaning of an edict which was designed to establish and secure, without any limitation, the claims of religious liberty. They condescend to assign two weighty reasons which have induced them to allow this universal toleration: the human intention of consulting the peace and happiness of their people; and the pious hope that, by such a conduct, they shall appease and propitiate *the Deity*, whose seat is in heaven. They gratefully acknowledge the many signal proofs which they have received of the divine favour; and they trust that the same Providence will for ever continue to protect the prosperity of the prince and people. From these vague and indefinite expressions of piety, three suppositions may be deduced, of a different, but not of an incompatible, nature. The mind of Constantine might fluctuate between the Pagan and the Christian religions. According to the loose and complying notions of Polytheism, he might acknowledge the God of the Christians as *one* of the *many* deities who composed the hierarchy of heaven. Or perhaps he might embrace the philosophic and pleasing idea that, notwithstanding the variety of names, of rites, and of opinions, all the sects and all the nations of mankind are united in the worship of the common Father and Creator of the universe.[156]

---

[155] (15) Cæcilius (de Mort. Persecut. c. 48) has preserved the Latin original; and Eusebius (Hist. Eccles. l. x. c. 5) has given a Greek translation of this perpetual edict, which refers to some provisional regulations. [O. Seeck holds that there was no such thing as the Edict of Milan, Zeitschrift für Kirchengeschichte, 12, p.181; cp. Geschichte des Untergangs der antiken Welt, i. p.457.] [Gibbon]

[156] (16) A panegyric of Constantine, pronounced seven or eight months after the edict of Milan (see Gothofred. Chronolog. Legum. p.7, and Tillemont, Hist. des Empereurs, tom. iv. p.246), uses the following remarkable expression: 'Summe rerum sator, cujus tot nomina sunt, quot linguas gentium esse voluisti, quem enim te ipse dici velis, scire non possumus'. [Oh supreme father of the world, whose names are as many as you have determined there to be human languages, for we cannot know by which name you yourself want to be called. – eds] Panegyr. Vet. ix. 26. In explaining Constantine's progress in the faith, Mosheim (p.971, &c.) is ingenious, subtle, prolix. [Gibbon]

more frequently influenced by views
…iderations of abstract and speculative
…avour of Constantine may naturally be
…entertained for the moral character of
…sion that the propagation of the gospel
…private and public virtue. Whatever lati-
…ay assume in his own conduct, whatever
…or his own passions, it is undoubtedly his
…s should respect the natural and civil obli-
ga… …operation of the wisest laws is imperfect and
precar… …inspire virtue, they cannot always restrain vice.
Their power… …ent to prohibit all that they condemn, nor can
they always punis… …actions which they prohibit. The legislators of
antiquity had summoned to their aid the powers of education and of
opinion. But every principle which had once maintained the vigour and
purity of Rome and Sparta was long since extinguished in a declining and
despotic empire. Philosophy still exercised her temperate sway over the
human mind, but the cause of virtue derived very feeble support from
the influence of the Pagan superstition. Under these discouraging circumstances, a prudent magistrate might observe with pleasure the progress of a religion, which diffused among the people a pure, benevolent,
and universal system of ethics, adapted to every duty and every condition
of life; recommended as the will and reason of the Supreme Deity, and
enforced by the sanction of eternal rewards or punishments. The experience of Greek and Roman history could not inform the world how far the
system of national manners might be reformed and improved by the precepts of a divine revelation; and Constantine might listen with some confidence to the flattering, and indeed reasonable, assurances of Lactantius.
The eloquent apologist seemed firmly to expect, and almost ventured to
promise, *that* the establishment of Christianity would restore the innocence and felicity of the primitive age; *that* the worship of the true God
would extinguish war and dissension among those who mutually considered themselves as the children of a common parent; *that* every
impure desire, every angry or selfish passion, would be restrained by the
knowledge of the gospel; and *that* the magistrates might sheathe the
sword of justice among a people who would be universally actuated by the
sentiments of truth and piety, of equity and moderation, of harmony and
universal love.[157]

The passive and unresisting obedience which bows under the yoke
of authority, or even of oppression, must have appeared, in the eyes of an
absolute monarch, the most conspicuous and useful of the evangelic
virtues.[158] The primitive Christians derived the institution of civil
government, not from the consent of the people, but from the decrees of

---

[157] (17) See the elegant description of Lactantius (Divin. Institut. v. 8), who is
much more perspicuous and positive than it becomes a discreet prophet.
[Gibbon]

[158] (18) The political system of the Christians is explained by Grotius, de Jure
Belli et Pacis [the Law of War and Peace. – eds], l. i. c. 3, 4. Grotius was a
republican and an exile, but the mildness of his temper inclined him to support
the established powers. [Gibbon]

heaven. The reigning emperor, though he had usurped the sceptre by treason and murder, immediately assumed the sacred character of vicegerent of the Deity. To the Deity alone he was accountable for the abuse of his power; and his subjects were indissolubly bound, by their oath of fidelity, to a tyrant who had violated every law of nature and society. The humble Christians were sent into the world as sheep among wolves; and, since they were not permitted to employ force, even in the defence of their religion, they should be still more criminal if they were tempted to shed the blood of their fellow creatures in disputing the vain privileges, or the sordid possessions, of this transitory life. Faithful to the doctrine of the apostle[159] who in the reign of Nero had preached the duty of unconditional submission, the Christians of the three first centuries preserved their conscience pure and innocent of the guilt of secret conspiracy or open rebellion. While they experienced the rigour of persecution, they were never provoked either to meet their tyrants in the field or indignantly to withdraw themselves into some remote and sequestered corner of the globe.[160] The Protestants of France, of Germany, and of Britain, who asserted with such intrepid courage their civil and religious freedom, have been insulted by the invidious comparison between the conduct of the primitive and of the reformed Christians.[161] Perhaps, instead of censure, some applause may be due to the superior sense and spirit of our ancestors, who had convinced themselves that religion cannot abolish the unalienable rights of human nature.[162] Perhaps the patience of the primitive church may be ascribed to its weakness, as well as to its virtue. A sect of unwarlike plebeians, without leaders, without arms, without fortifications, must have encountered inevitable destruction in a rash and fruitless resistance to the master of the Roman legions. But the Christians, when they deprecated the wrath of Diocletian, or solicited the favour of Constantine, could allege, with truth and confidence, that they held the principle of passive obedience, and that, in the space of three centuries, their conduct had always been conformable to their principles. They

---

[159] i.e. Paul. See Romans 13. [eds]

[160] (19) Tertullian. Apolog. c. 32, 34, 35, 36. Tamen nunquam Albiniani, nec Nigriani vel Cassiani inveniri potuerunt Christiani. [However, neither the Albiniani nor the Nigriani nor the Cassiani were able to show themselves as Christians. – eds] Ad Scapulam, c. 2. If this assertion be strictly true, it excludes the Christians of that age from all civil and military employments, which would have compelled them to take an active part in the service of their respective governors. See Moyle's Works, vol. ii. p.349. [Gibbon]

[161] (20) See the artful Bossuet (Hist. des Variations des Eglises Protestantes, tom. iii. p.210–258), and the malicious Bayle (tom. ii. p.620). I *name* Bayle, for he was certainly the author of the Avis Aux Refugiés [Counsel for Refugees. – eds]; consult the Dictionnaire Critique de Chauffepié, tom. i. part ii. p.145. [Gibbon]

[162] (21) Buchanan is the earliest, or at least the most celebrated, of the reformers, who has justified the theory of resistance. See his Dialogue de Jure Regni apud Scotos [The Law of the Throne amongst Scots. – eds]. tom. ii. p.28, 30, edit. fol. Ruddiman. [Gibbon]
The 'unalienable rights of human nature' are those of self-defence. [eds]

might add that the throne of the emperors would be established on a fixed and permanent basis, if all their subjects, embracing the Christian doctrine, should learn to suffer and to obey.

In the general order of Providence, princes and tyrants are considered as the ministers of Heaven, appointed to rule or to chastise the nations of the earth. But sacred history affords many illustrious examples of the more immediate interposition of the Deity in the government of his chosen people. The sceptre and the sword were committed to the hands of Moses, of Joshua, of Gideon, of David, of the Maccabees; the virtues of those heroes were the motive or the effect of the divine favour, the success of their arms was destined to achieve the deliverance or the triumph of the church. If the judges of Israel were occasional and temporary magistrates, the kings of Judah derived from the royal unction of their great ancestor an hereditary and indefeasible right, which could not be forfeited by their own vices, nor recalled by the caprice of their subjects. The same extraordinary providence, which was no longer confined to the Jewish people, might elect Constantine and his family as the protectors of the Christian world; and the devout Lactantius announces, in a prophetic tone, the future glories of his long and universal reign.[163] Galerius and Maximin, Maxentius and Licinius, were the rivals who shared with the favourite of Heaven the provinces of the empire. The tragic deaths of Galerius and Maximin soon gratified the resentment, and fulfilled the sanguine expectations, of the Christians. The success of Constantine against Maxentius and Licinius removed the two formidable competitors who still opposed the triumph of the second David, and his cause might seem to claim the peculiar[164] interposition of Providence. The character of the Roman tyrant disgraced the purple and human nature: and, though the Christians might enjoy his precarious favour, they were exposed, with the rest of his subjects, to the effects of his wanton and capricious cruelty. The conduct of Licinius soon betrayed the reluctance with which he had consented to the wise and humane regulations of the edict of Milan. The convocation of provincial synods[165] was prohibited in his dominions; his Christian officers were ignominiously dismissed; and, if he avoided the guilt, or rather danger, of a general persecution, his partial oppressions were rendered still more odious by the violation of a solemn and voluntary engagement.[166] While the East, according to the lively expression of Eusebius, was involved in the shades of infernal darkness, the auspicious rays of celestial light warmed and illuminated the provinces of the West. The piety of Constantine was

Divine right of Constantine

---

[163]   (22) Lactant. Divin. Institut. i. l. Eusebius, in the course of his history, his life, and his oration, repeatedly inculcates the divine right of Constantine to the empire. [Gibbon]

[164]   i.e. special. [eds]

[165]   i.e. Church councils. [eds]

[166]   (23) Our imperfect knowledge of the persecution of Licinius is derived from Eusebius (Hist. Eccles. l. x. c. 8; Vit. Constantin. l. i. c. 49–56, l. ii. c. l, 2). Aurelius Victor mentions his cruelty in general terms. [Cp. Görres, die Licinianische Christenverfolgung [i.e. Licinius' *Persecution of Christians.* – eds]. He has shown that the persecution was not attended with much bloodshed. Some bishops were executed. P. 32 *sqq*] [Gibbon]

admitted as an unexceptionable proof of the justice of his arms; and his use of victory confirmed the opinion of the Christians, that their hero was inspired and conducted by the Lord of Hosts. The conquest of Italy produced a general edict of toleration; and, as soon as the defeat of Licinius had invested Constantine with the sole dominion of the Roman world, he immediately, by circular letters, exhorted all his subjects to imitate, without delay, the example of their sovereign, and to embrace the divine truth of Christianity.[167]

AD 324

The assurance that the elevation of Constantine was intimately connected with the designs of Providence instilled into the minds of the Christians two opinions, which, by very different means, assisted the accomplishment of the prophecy. Their warm and active loyalty exhausted in his favour every resource of human industry; and they confidently expected that their strenuous efforts would be seconded by some divine and miraculous aid. The enemies of Constantine have imputed to interested motives the alliance which he insensibly contracted with the Catholic church, and which apparently contributed[168] to the success of his ambition. In the beginning of the fourth century, the Christians still bore a very inadequate proportion to the inhabitants of the empire; but among a degenerate people, who viewed the change of masters with the indifference of slaves, the spirit and union of a religious party might assist the popular leader to whose service, from a principle of conscience, they had devoted their lives and fortunes.[169] The example of his father had instructed Constantine to esteem and to reward the merit of the Christians; and in the distribution of public offices, he had the advantage of strengthening his government, by the choice of ministers or generals in whose fidelity he could repose a just and unreserved confidence. By the influence of these dignified missionaries, the proselytes of the new faith must have multiplied in the court and army; the Barbarians of Germany, who filled the ranks of the legions, were of a careless temper, which acquiesced without resistance in the religion of their commander; and, when they passed the Alps, it may fairly be presumed that a great number of the soldiers had already consecrated their swords to the service of Christ and of Constantine.[170] The habits of mankind, and the interest of religion, gradually abated the horror of war and bloodshed, which had so

Loyalty and zeal of the Christian party

---

[167]   (24) Euseb. in. Vit. Constant. l. ii. c. 24–42, 48–60. [Gibbon]

[168]   (24a) [This seems a necessary correction of 'contributes,' which appears in the quarto ed.]

[169]   (25) In the beginning of the last century, the Papists of England were only a *thirtieth,* and the Protestants of France only a *fifteenth,* part of the respective nations, to whom their spirit and power were a constant object of apprehension. See the relations which Bentivoglio (who was then nuncio at Brussels, and afterwards cardinal) transmitted to the court of Rome (Relazione, tom. ii. p.211, 241). Bentivoglio was curious, well-informed, but somewhat partial. [Gibbon]

[170]   (26) This careless temper of the Germans appears almost uniformly in the history of the conversion of each of the tribes. The legions of Constantine were recruited with Germans (Zosimus, l. ii. p.86 [c. 15]); and the court even of his father had been filled with Christians. See the first book of the Life of Constantine, by Eusebius. [Gibbon]

long prevailed among the Christians; and, in the councils which were assembled under the gracious protection of Constantine, the authority of the bishops was seasonably employed to ratify the obligation of the military oath, and to inflict the penalty of excommunication on those soldiers who threw away their arms during the peace of the church.[171] While Constantine, in his own dominions, increased the number and zeal of his faithful adherents, he could depend on the support of a powerful faction in those provinces which were still possessed or usurped by his rivals. A secret disaffection was diffused among the Christian subjects of Maxentius and Licinius; and the resentment which the latter did not attempt to conceal served only to engage them still more deeply in the interest of his competitor. The regular correspondence which connected the bishops of the most distant provinces enabled them freely to communicate their wishes and their designs, and to transmit without danger any useful intelligence, or any pious contributions, which might promote the service of Constantine, who publicly declared that he had taken up arms for the deliverance of the church.[172]

Expectation and belief of a miracle

The enthusiasm which inspired the troops, and perhaps the emperor himself, had sharpened their swords, while it satisfied their conscience. They marched to battle with the full assurance that the same God, who had formerly opened a passage to the Israelites through the waters of Jordan, and had thrown down the walls of Jericho at the sound of the trumpets of Joshua, would display his visible majesty and power in the victory of Constantine. The evidence of ecclesiastical history is prepared to affirm that their expectations were justified by the conspicuous miracle to which the conversion of the first Christian emperor has been almost unanimously ascribed. The real or imaginary cause of so important an event deserves and demands the attention of posterity; and I shall endeavour to form a just estimate of the famous vision of Constantine, by a distinct consideration of the *standard,* the *dream,* and the *celestial sign;* by separating the historical, the natural, and the marvellous parts of this extraordinary story which, in the composition of a specious argument, have been artfully confounded in one splendid and brittle mass.

The 'Labarum,' or standard of the cross

I. An instrument of the tortures which were inflicted only on slaves and strangers became an object of horror in the eyes of a Roman citizen; and the ideas of guilt, of pain, and of ignominy were closely united with

---

[171]   (27) De his qui arma projiciunt in *pace,* placuit eos abstinere a communione. [Those who threw down their arms in time of peace were banned from communion. – eds] Concil. Arelat. Canon iii. The best critics apply these words to the *peace of the church.* [Gibbon]

[172]   (28) Eusebius always considers the second civil war against Licinius as a sort of religious crusade. At the invitation of the tyrant, some Christian officers had resumed their *zones;* or, in other words, had returned to the military service. Their conduct was afterwards censured by the 12th canon of the Council of Nice; if this particular application may be received, instead of the loose and general sense of the Greek interpreters, Balsamon, Zonaras, and Alexis Aristenus. See Beveridge, Pandect. Eccles. Græc. tom. i. p.72, tom. ii. p.78, Annotation. [Gibbon]

the idea of the cross.[173] The piety rather than the humanity of Constantine soon abolished in his dominions the punishment which the Saviour of mankind had condescended to suffer;[174] but the emperor had already learned to despise the prejudices of his education, and of his people, before he could erect in the midst of Rome his own statue, bearing a cross in its right hand, with an inscription which referred the victory of his arms, and the deliverance of Rome, to the virtue of that salutary sign, the true symbol of force and courage.[175] The same symbol sanctified the arms of the soldiers of Constantine; the cross glittered on their helmets, was engraved on their shields, was interwoven into their banners; and the consecrated emblems which adorned the person of the emperor himself were distinguished only by richer materials and more exquisite workmanship.[176] But the principal standard which displayed the triumph of the

---

[173] (29) Nomen ipsum *crucis* absit non modo a corpore civium Romanorum, sed etiam a cogitatione, oculis, auribus. [For the very name of the cross be far not only from the body of Roman citizens but also from their thoughts, eyes and ears. – eds] Cicero pro Rabirio, c. 5. The Christian writers, Justin, Minucius Felix, Tertullian, Jerom, and Maximus of Turin, have investigated with tolerable success the figure or likeness of a cross in almost every object of nature or art; in the intersection of the meridian and equator, the human face, a bird flying, a man swimming, a mast and yard, a plough, a *standard*, &c. &c. &c. See Lipsius de Cruce, l. i. c. 9. [Gibbon]

[174] (30) See Aurelius Victor, who considers this law as one of the examples of Constantine's piety. An edict so honourable to Christianity deserved a place in the Theodosian Code, instead of the indirect mention of it, which seems to result from the comparison of the vth and xviiith titles of the ixth book. [Gibbon]

[175] (31) Eusebius, in Vit. Constantin. l. i. c. 40. The statue, or at least the cross and inscription, may be ascribed with more probability to the second, or even the third, visit of Constantine to Rome. Immediately after the defeat of Maxentius, the minds of the senate and people were scarcely ripe for this public monument. [Gibbon]

[176] (32) Agnoscas regina libens mea signa necesse est;
   In quibus effigies *crucis* aut gemmata refulget
   Aut longis solido ex auro præfertur in hastis.
   Hoc signo invictus, transmissis Alpibus Ultor
   Servitium solvit miserabile Constantinus.
   *   *   *   *   *   *   *   *
   Christus *purpureum* gemmanti textus in auro
   Signabat *Labarum*, clypeorum insignia Christus
   Scripserat; ardebat summis *crux* addita cristis.
      Prudentius, in Symmachum, l. ii. 464, 486. [Gibbon]
[Oh Queen, you must with pleasure acknowledge my standards; the image of the cross is either gleaming on these with jewels or made from solid gold borne before on the long pikes/spears. By this standard triumphant, Constantine crossed the Alps victorious and banished wretched slavery. Decked in jewel encrusted gold, Christ adorned the purple Labarum, Christ had inscribed the emblems of the shields; the cross blazed forth, attached to the highest crests.] [eds]

cross was styled the *Labarum*,[177] an obscure though celebrated name, which has been vainly derived from almost all the languages of the world. It is described[178] as a long pike intersected by a transversal beam. The silken veil which hung down from the beam was curiously enwrought with the images of the reigning monarch and his children. The summit of the pike supported a crown of gold which inclosed the mysterious monogram, at once expressive of the figure of the cross and the initial letters of the name of Christ.[179] The safety of the labarum was entrusted to fifty guards, of approved valour and fidelity; their station was marked by honours and emoluments; and some fortunate accidents soon introduced an opinion that, as long as the guards of the labarum were engaged in the execution of their office, they were secure and invulnerable amidst the darts of the enemy. In the second civil war Licinius felt and dreaded the power of this consecrated banner, the sight of which, in the distress of battle, animated the soldiers of Constantine with an invincible enthusiasm, and scattered terror and dismay through the ranks of the adverse legions.[180] The Christian emperors, who respected the example of Constantine, displayed in all their military expeditions the standard of the cross; but, when the degenerate successors of Theodosius had ceased to appear in person at the head of their armies, the labarum was deposited as a venerable but useless relic in the palace of Constantinople.[181] Its honours are still preserved on the medals of the Flavian family. Their grateful devotion has placed the monogram of Christ in the midst of the ensigns of Rome. The solemn epithets of, safety of the republic, glory of the army, restoration of public happiness, are equally applied to the

---

[177] (33) The derivation and meaning of the word *Labarum* or *Laborum*, which is employed by Gregory Nazianzen, Ambrose, Prudentius, &c. still remain totally unknown; in spite of the efforts of the critics, who have ineffectually tortured the Latin, Greek, Spanish, Celtic, Teutonic, Illyric, Armenian, &c. in search of an etymology. See Ducange, in Gloss. Med. et infim. Latinitat. sub voce *Labarum*, and Godefroy, ad God. Theodos. tom. ii. p.143. [Gibbon]

[178] (34) Euseb. in Vit. Constant. l. i. c. 30, 31. Baronius (Annal. Eccles. AD 312, No. 26) has engraved a representation of the Labarum. [Gibbon]

[179] (35) Transversâ X literâ, summo capite circumflexo, Christum in scutis notat. [He notes Christ on the shields [in the form of] an oblique letter X [+] with the top bent round [P]. – eds] Cæcilius de M. P. c. 44. Cuper (add. M. P. in edit. Lactant. tom. ii. p.500) and Baronius (AD 312, No. 25) have engraved from ancient monuments several specimens (as thus P or P) of these monograms, which became extremely fashionable in the Christian world. [Gibbon]

[180] (36) Euseb. in Vit. Constantin. l. ii. c. 7, 8, 9. He introduces the Labarum before the Italian expedition; but his narrative seems to indicate that it was never shown at the head of an army, till Constantine, above ten years afterwards, declared himself the enemy of Licinius and the deliverer of the church. [Gibbon]

[181] (37) See Cod. Theod. l. vi. tit. xxv. Sozomen, l. i. c. 2. Theophan. Chronogr. p.11. Theophanes lived towards the end of the eighth century, almost five hundred years after Constantine. The modern Greeks were not inclined to display in the field the standard of the empire and of Christianity; and, though they depended on every superstitious hope of *defence,* the promise of *victory* would have appeared too bold a fiction. [Gibbon]

religious and military trophies; and there is still extant a medal of the emperor Constantius, where the standard of the labarum is accompanied with these memorable words, BY THIS SIGN THOU SHALT CONQUER.[182]

II. In all occasions of danger or distress, it was the practice of the primitive Christians to fortify their minds and bodies by the sign of the cross, which they used, in all their ecclesiastical rites, in all the daily occurrences of life, as an infallible preservative against every species of spiritual or temporal evil.[183] The authority of the church might alone have had sufficient weight to justify the devotion of Constantine, who, in the same prudent and gradual progress, acknowledged the truth, and assumed the symbol, of Christianity. But the testimony of a contemporary writer, who in a former treatise has avenged the cause of religion, bestows on the piety of the emperor a more awful and sublime character. He affirms, with the most perfect confidence, that, in the night which preceded the last battle against Maxentius, Constantine was admonished in a dream to inscribe the shields of his soldiers with the *celestial sign of God*, the sacred monogram of the name of Christ; that he executed the commands of heaven; and that his valour and obedience were rewarded by the decisive victory of the Milvian Bridge. Some considerations might perhaps incline a sceptical mind to suspect the judgement or the veracity of the rhetorician, whose pen, either from zeal or interest, was devoted to the cause of the prevailing faction.[184] He appears to have published his deaths of the persecutors at Nicomedia about three years after the Roman victory; but the interval of a thousand miles, and a thousand days, will allow an ample latitude for the invention of declaimers, the credulity of party, and the tacit approbation of the emperor himself; who might listen without indignation to a marvellous tale, which exalted his fame and promoted his designs. In favour of Licinius, who still dissembled his animosity to the Christians, the same author has provided a similar vision, of a form of prayer, which was communicated by an angel, and repeated by the whole army before they engaged the legions of the tyrant Maximin.

The dream of Constantine

---

[182]   (38) The Abbé du Voisin, p.103, &c. alleges several of these medals, and quotes a particular dissertation of a Jesuit, the Père de Grainville, on this subject. [Gibbon]

[183]   (39) Tertullian. de Corona, c. 3. Athanasius, tom. i. p.101. The learned Jesuit Petavius (Dogmata Theolog. l. xv. c. 9, 10) has collected many similar passages on the virtues of the cross, which in the last age embarrassed our Protestant disputants. [Gibbon]

[184]   (40) Cæcilius, de M.P. c. 44. It is certain that this historical declamation was composed and published while Licinius, sovereign of the East, still preserved the friendship of Constantine and of the Christians. Every reader of taste must perceive that the style is of a very different and inferior character to that of Lactantius; and such indeed is the judgement of Le Clerc and Lardner (Bibliothèque Ancienne et Moderne, tom. ii. p.438. Credibility of the Gospel, &c. part ii. vol. vii. p.94). Three arguments from the title of the book, and from the names of Donatus and Cæcilius, are produced by the advocates for Lactantius (see the P. Lestocq, tom. ii. p.46–60). Each of these proofs is singly weak and defective; but their concurrence has great weight. I have often fluctuated, and shall *tamely* follow the Colbert Ms. in calling the author (whoever he was) Cæcilius. [Gibbon]

The frequent repetition of miracles serves to provoke, where it does not subdue, the reason of mankind;[185] but, if the dream of Constantine is separately considered, it may be naturally explained either by the policy or the enthusiasm of the emperor. Whilst his anxiety for the approaching day, which must decide the fate of the empire, was suspended by a short and interrupted slumber, the venerable form of Christ, and the well known symbol of his religion, might forcibly offer themselves to the active fancy of a prince who reverenced the name, and had perhaps secretly implored the power, of the God of the Christians. As readily might a consummate statesman indulge himself in the use of one of those military stratagems, one of those pious frauds, which Philip[186] and Sertorius had employed with such art and effect.[187] The preternatural origin of dreams was universally admitted by the nations of antiquity, and a considerable part of the Gallic army was already prepared to place their confidence in the salutary sign of the Christian religion. The secret vision of Constantine could be disproved only by the event;[188] and the intrepid hero who had passed the Alps and the Apennine might view with careless despair the consequences of a defeat under the walls of Rome. The senate and people, exulting in their own deliverance from an odious tyrant, acknowledged that the victory of Constantine surpassed the powers of man, without daring to insinuate that it had been obtained by the protection of the *Gods*. The triumphal arch which was erected about three years after the event proclaims, in ambiguous language, that, by the greatness of his own mind and by an *instinct* or impulse of the Divinity, he had saved and avenged the Roman republic.[189] The pagan orator, who had seized an earlier opportunity of celebrating the virtues of the conqueror, supposes that he alone enjoyed a secret and intimate commerce with the Supreme Being, who delegated the care of mortals to his subordinate deities; and

---

[185]   (41) Cæcilius, de M.P. c. 46. There seems to be some reason in the observation of M. de Voltaire (Oeuvres, t. xiv. p.307), who ascribes to the success of Constantine the superior fame of his Labarum above the angel of Licinius. Yet even this angel is favourably entertained by Pagi, Tillemont, Fleury, &c. who are fond of increasing their stock of miracles. [Gibbon]

[186]   Philip II of Macedon (382–336 BC), father of Alexander the Great. [eds]

[187]   (42) Besides these well-known examples, Tollius (Preface to Boileau's translation of Longinus) has discovered a vision of Antigonus, who assured his troops that he had seen a pentagon (the symbol of safety) with these words, "In this conquer". But Tollius has most inexcusably omitted to produce his authority; and his own character, literary as well as moral, is not free from reproach (see Chauffepié, Dictionnaire Critique, t. iv. p.460). Without insisting on the silence of Diodorus, Plutarch, Justin, &c. it may be observed that Polyænus, who in a separate chapter (l. iv. c. 6) has collected nineteen military stratagems of Antigonus, is totally ignorant of this remarkable vision. [Gibbon]

[188]   i.e. outcome. [eds]

[189]   (43) Instinctu Divinitatis, mentis magnitudine. [At the instigation of the Divinity, through the greatness of his mind. – eds] [Seeck thinks this an allusion to the dream.] The inscription on the triumphal arch of Constantine, which has been copied by Baronius, Grutor, &c., may still be perused by every curious traveller. [See vol. i., Appendix 24.] [Gibbon]

thus assigns a very plausible reason why the subjects of Constantine should not presume to embrace the new religion of their sovereign.[190]

III. The philosopher, who with calm suspicion examines the dreams and omens, the miracles and prodigies, of profane or even of ecclesiastical history, will probably conclude that, if the eyes of the spectators have sometimes been deceived by fraud, the understanding of the readers has much more frequently been insulted by fiction. Every event, or appearance, or accident, which seems to deviate from the ordinary course of nature, has been rashly ascribed to the immediate action of the Deity; and the astonished fancy of the multitude has sometimes given shape and colour, language and motion, to the fleeting but uncommon meteors of the air.[191] Nazarius and Eusebius are the two most celebrated orators who, in studied panegyrics, have laboured to exalt the glory of Constantine. Nine years after the Roman victory, Nazarius[192] describes an army of divine warriors, who seemed to fall from the sky: he marks their beauty, their spirit, their gigantic forms, the stream of light which beamed from their celestial armour, their patience in suffering themselves to be heard, as well as seen, by mortals; and their declaration that they were sent, that they flew, to the assistance of the great Constantine. For the truth of this prodigy, the Pagan orator appeals to the whole Gallic nation, in whose presence he was then speaking; and seems to hope that the ancient apparitions[193] would now obtain credit from this recent and public event. The Christian fable of Eusebius, which in the space of twenty-six years might arise from the original dream, is cast in a much more correct and elegant mould. In one of the marches of Constantine, he is reported to have seen with his own eyes the luminous trophy of the cross, placed above the meridian sun, and inscribed with the following words: BY THIS CONQUER. This amazing object in the sky astonished the whole army, as well as the emperor himself, who was yet undetermined in the choice of a religion; but his astonishment was converted into faith by the vision of the ensuing night. Christ appeared before his eyes; and, displaying the same celestial sign of the cross, he directed Constantine to frame a similar standard, and to march, with an

Appearance of a cross in the sky

AD 321

AD 338

---

[190]   (44) Habes profecto aliquid cum illâ mente Divinâ secretum; quæ delegatâ nostrâ Diis Minoribus curâ uni se tibi dignatur ostendere. [You have assuredly some secret commerce with that celestial Spirit, which deigns to show itself to you alone, our care being delegated to the lesser Gods. – eds] Panegyr. Vet. ix. 2. [Gibbon]

[191]   (45) M. Freret (Mémoires de l'Académie des Inscriptions, t. iv. p.411–437) explains, by physical causes, many of the prodigies of antiquity; and Fabricius, who is abused by both parties, vainly tries to introduce the celestial cross of Constantine among the solar halos. Bibliothec. Græc. tom. vi. p.8–29. [Gibbon]

[192]   (46) Nazarius inter Panegyr. Vet. x. 14, 15. It is unnecessary to name the moderns, whose undistinguishing and ravenous appetite has swallowed even the Pagan bait of Nazarius. [Gibbon]

[193]   (47) The apparitions of Castor and Pollux, particularly to announce the Macedonian victory, are attested by historians and public monuments. See Cicero de Naturâ Deorum [*The Nature of the Gods.* – eds], ii, 2, iii. 5, 6. Florus, ii. 12. Valerius Maximus, l. i. c. 8, No. 1. Yet the most recent of these miracles is omitted, and indirectly denied, by Livy (xlv. 1). [Gibbon]

assurance of victory, against Maxentius and all his enemies.[194] The learned bishop of Caesarea appears to be sensible that the recent discovery of this marvellous anecdote would excite some surprise and distrust among the most pious of his readers. Yet instead of ascertaining the precise circumstances of time and place, which always serve to detect falsehood or establish truth;[195] instead of collecting and recording the evidence of so many living witnesses, who must have been spectators of this stupendous miracle;[196] Eusebius contents himself with alleging a very singular testimony: that of the deceased Constantine, who, many years after the event, in the freedom of conversation, had related to him this extraordinary incident of his own life, and had attested the truth of it by a solemn oath. The prudence and gratitude of the learned prelate forbade him to suspect the veracity of his victorious master; but he plainly intimates that, in a fact of such a nature, he should have refused his assent to any meaner authority. This motive of credibility could not survive the power of the Flavian family; and the celestial sign, which the Infidels might afterwards deride,[197] was disregarded by the Christians of the age which immediately followed the conversion of Constantine.[198] But the Catholic Church, both of the East and of the West, has adopted a prodigy, which favours, or seems to favour, the popular worship of the cross. The vision of Constantine maintained an honourable place in the legend of superstition, till the bold and sagacious spirit of criticism

---

[194]   (48) Eusebius, l. i. c. 28, 29, 30. The silence of the same Eusebius, in his Ecclesiastical History, is deeply felt by those advocates for the miracle who are not absolutely callous. [Gibbon]

[195]   (49) The narrative of Constantine seems to indicate that he saw the cross in the sky before he passed the Alps against Maxentius. The scene has been fixed by provincial vanity at Treves, Besançon, &c. See Tillemont, Hist. des Empereurs, tom. iv. p.573. [Professor Flinders Petrie plausibly suggests that what Constantine saw was the phenomenon of mock suns (not uncommon in northern, but rare in southern, latitudes). The real sun, with three mock suns, might have appeared to his eyes as a cross.] [Gibbon]

[196]   (50) The pious Tillemont (Mém. Ecclés, tom. vii. p.1317) rejects with a sigh the useful Acts of Artemius, a veteran and a martyr, who attests as an eye witness the vision of Constantine. [Gibbon]

[197]   (51) Gelasius Cyzic, in Act. Concil. Nicen. l. i. c. 4. [Gibbon]

[198]   (52) The advocates for the vision are unable to produce a single testimony from the Fathers of the fourth and fifth centuries, who, in their voluminous writings, repeatedly celebrate the triumph of the church and of Constantine. As these venerable men had not any dislike to a miracle, we may suspect (and the suspicion is confirmed by the ignorance of Jerom) that they were all unacquainted with the life of Constantine by Eusebius. This tract was recovered by the diligence of those who translated or continued his Ecclesiastical History, and who have represented in various colours the vision of the cross. [Gibbon]

presumed to depreciate the triumph, and to arraign the truth of the first Christian emperor.[199]

    The protestant and philosophic readers of the present age will incline to believe that, in the account of his own conversion, Constantine attested a wilful falsehood by a solemn and deliberate perjury. They may not hesitate to pronounce that, in the choice of a religion, his mind was determined only by a sense of interest; and that (according to the expression of a profane poet)[200] he used the altars of the church as a convenient footstool to the throne of the empire. A conclusion so harsh and so absolute is not, however, warranted by our knowledge of human nature, of Constantine, or of Christianity. In an age of religious fervour, the most artful statesmen are observed to feel some part of the enthusiasm which they inspire; and the most orthodox saints assume the dangerous privilege of defending the cause of truth by the arms of deceit and falsehood. Personal interest is often the standard of our belief, as well as of our practice; and the same motives of temporal advantage which might influence the public conduct and professions of Constantine would insensibly dispose his mind to embrace a religion so propitious to his fame and fortunes. His vanity was gratified by the flattering assurance that *he* had

The conversion of Constantine might be sincere

---

[199] (53) Godefroy was the first who, in the year 1643 (Not. ad Philostorgium, l. i. c. 6, p.16), expressed any doubt of a miracle which had been supported with equal zeal by Cardinal Baronius and the Centuriators of Magdeburg. Since that time, many of the Protestant critics have inclined towards doubt and disbelief. The objections are urged, with great force, by M. Chauffepié (Dictionnaire Critique, tom. iv. p.6–11), and, in the year 1774, a doctor of Sorbonne, the Abbé du Voisin, published an Apology, which deserves the praise of learning and moderation. [Gibbon]

[200] (54) Lors Constantin dit ces propres paroles:

    J'ai renversé le culte des idoles;
    Sur les débris de leurs temples fumans
    Au Dieu du Ciel j'ai prodigué l'encens.
    Mais tous mes soins pour sa grandeur suprême
    N'eurent jamais d'autre objet que moi-même;
    Les saints autels n'étoient à mes regards
    Qu'un marchepié du trône des Césars.
    L'ambition, la fureur, les délices
    Etoient mes Dieux, avoient mes sacrifices.
    L'or des Chrétiens, leurs intrigues, leur sang
    Ont cimenté ma fortune et mon rang.

The poem which contains these lines may be read with pleasure, but cannot be named with decency. [Gibbon]

    [When Constantine said these very words:
    I have put down the worship of idols;
    On the ruins of their smoking temples;
    I have offered incense to the God of Heaven;
    But all my care for his supreme grandeur;
    Had no object but myself;
    The sacred altars had my attention only;
    As a footstool to the throne of the Caesars;
    Ambition, passion, delight were my gods and had my sacrifices;
    The gold of Christians, their schemes, their blood;
    Have secured my fortune and my rank.] [eds]

been chosen by Heaven to reign over the earth; success had justified his divine title to the throne, and that title was founded on the truth of the Christian revelation. As real virtue is sometimes excited by undeserved applause, the specious piety of Constantine, if at first it was only specious, might gradually, by the influence of praise, of habit, and of example, be matured into serious faith and fervent devotion. The bishops and teachers of the new sect, whose dress and manners had not qualified them for the residence of a court, were admitted to the Imperial table; they accompanied the monarch in his expeditions; and the ascendant which one of them, an Egyptian or a Spaniard,[201] acquired over his mind was imputed by the Pagans to the effect of magic.[202] Lactantius, who has adorned the precepts of the gospel with the eloquence of Cicero,[203] and Eusebius, who has consecrated the learning and philosophy of the Greeks to the service of religion,[204] were both received into the friendship and familiarity of their sovereign: and those able masters of controversy could patiently watch the soft and yielding moments of persuasion, and dexterously apply the arguments which were the best adapted to his character and understanding. Whatever advantages might be derived from the acquisition of an Imperial proselyte, he was distinguished by the splendour of his purple, rather than by the superiority of wisdom or virtue, from the many thousands of his subjects who had embraced the doctrines of Christianity. Nor can it be deemed incredible that the mind of an unlettered soldier should have yielded to the weight of evidence, which, in a more enlightened age, has satisfied or subdued the reason of a Grotius, a Pascal, or a Locke. In the midst of the incessant labours of his great office, this soldier employed, or affected to employ, the hours of the night in the diligent study of the Scriptures and the composition of theological discourses; which he afterwards pronounced in the presence of a numerous and applauding audience. In a very long discourse, which is still extant, the royal preacher expatiates on the various proofs of religion; but he dwells with peculiar complacency on the Sibylline verses,[205] and the

The fourth eclogue of Virgil

---

[201] (55) This favourite was probably the great Osius, bishop of Cordova, who preferred the pastoral care of the whole church to the government of a particular diocese. His character is magnificently, though concisely, expressed by Athanasius (tom. i. p.703). See Tillemont, Mém. Ecclés. tom. vii. p.524–561. Osius was accused, perhaps unjustly, of retiring from court with a very ample fortune. [Gibbon]

[202] (56) See Eusebius (in Vit. Constant. passim), and Zosimus, l. ii. p.104 [c. 29]. [Gibbon]

[203] (57) The Christianity of Lactantius was of a moral rather than of a mysterious cast. 'Erat pæne rudis (says the orthodox Bull) disciplinæ Christianæ, et in rhetoricâ melius quam in theologiâ versatus.' [He was almost unskilled in Christian doctrine, and was better versed in rhetoric than in theology. – eds] Defensio Fidei Nicenæ [Defence of the Nicene Faith. – eds], sect. ii. c.14. [Gibbon]

[204] (58) Fabricius, with the usual diligence, has collected a list of between three and four hundred authors quoted in the Evangelical Preparation of Eusebius. See Bibliothec. Græc. l. v. c. 4, tom. vi. p.37–56. [Gibbon]

[205] (59) See Constantine. Orat. ad Sanctos [Address to the Saints. – eds], c. 19,20. He chiefly depends on a mysterious acrostic, composed in the sixth age after the Deluge by the Erythræan Sybil, and translated by Cicero into Latin. The initial letters of the thirty-four Greek verses form this prophetic sentence: JESUS CHRIST, SON OF GOD, SAVIOUR OF THE WORLD. [Gibbon]

fourth eclogue of Virgil.[206] Forty years before the birth of Christ, the Mantuan bard, as if inspired by the celestial muse of Isaiah, had celebrated with all the pomp of oriental metaphor, the return of the Virgin, the fall of the serpent, the approaching birth of a God-like child, the offspring of the great Jupiter, who should expiate the guilt of human kind, and govern the peaceful universe with the virtues of his father; the rise and appearance of an heavenly race, a primitive nation throughout the world; and the gradual restoration of the innocence and felicity of the golden age. The poet was perhaps unconscious of the secret sense and object of these sublime predictions, which have been so unworthily applied to the infant son of a consul or a triumvir;[207] but, if a more splendid, and indeed specious, interpretation of the fourth eclogue contributed to the conversion of the first Christian emperor, Virgil may deserve to be ranked among the most successful missionaries of the gospel.[208]

The awful mysteries of the Christian faith and worship were concealed from the eyes of strangers, and even of catechumens,[209] with an affected secrecy, which served to excite their wonder and curiosity.[210] But the severe rules of discipline which the prudence of the bishops had instituted were relaxed by the same prudence in favour of an Imperial proselyte, whom it was so important to allure, by every gentle condescension, into the pale of the church; and Constantine was permitted, at least by a tacit dispensation, to enjoy *most* of the privileges, before he had contracted *any* of the obligations, of a Christian. Instead of retiring from the congregation when the voice of the deacon dismissed the profane multitude, he prayed with the faithful, disputed with the bishops, preached on the most sublime and intricate subjects of theology, celebrated with sacred rites the vigil of Easter, and publicly declared himself, not only a partaker, but in some measure a priest and hierophant[211] of the Christian

Devotion and privileges of Constantine

---

[206]   (60) In his paraphrase of Virgil, the emperor has frequently assisted and improved the literal sense of the Latin text. See Blondel des Sybilles, l. i. c. 14, 15, 16. [Gibbon]

[207]   (61) The different claims of an elder and younger son of Pollio, of Julia, of Drusus, of Marcellus, are found to be incompatible with chronology, history, and the good sense of Virgil. [Gibbon]

[208]   (62) See Lowth, de Sacra Poesi Hebræorum Prælect [Sacred Poetry of Select Hebrew Authors. – eds]. xxi. p.289–293. In the examination of the fourth eclogue, the respectable bishop of London has displayed learning, taste, ingenuity, and a temperate enthusiasm, which exalts his fancy without degrading his judgement. [Gibbon]

[209]   Those converts undergoing instruction before baptism. [eds]

[210]   (63) The distinction between the public and the secret parts of divine service, the *missa catechumenorum,* and the *missa fidelium,* and the mysterious veil which piety or policy had cast over the latter, are very judiciously explained by Thiers, Exposition du Saint Sacrement, l. i. c. 8–12, p.59–91; but as, on this subject, the Papists may reasonably be suspected, a Protestant reader will depend with more confidence on the learned Bingham, Antiquities, l. x. c. 5. [Gibbon]

[211]   An official expounder of sacred rites and ceremonies. [eds]

mysteries.[212] The pride of Constantine might assume, and his services had deserved, some extraordinary distinction: an ill-timed rigour might have blasted the unripened fruits of his conversion; and, if the doors of the church had been strictly closed against a prince who had deserted the altars of the gods, the master of the empire would have been left destitute of any form of religious worship. In his last visit to Rome, he piously disclaimed and insulted the superstition of his ancestors by refusing to lead the military procession of the equestrian order and to offer the public vows to the Jupiter of the Capitoline Hill.[213] Many years before his baptism and death, Constantine had proclaimed to the world that neither his person nor his image should ever more be seen within the walls of an idolatrous temple; while he distributed through the provinces a variety of medals and pictures, which represented the emperor in an humble and suppliant posture of Christian devotion.[214]

The pride of Constantine, who refused the privileges of a catechumen, cannot easily be explained or excused; but the delay of his baptism may be justified by the maxims and the practice of ecclesiastical antiquity. The sacrament of baptism[215] was regularly administered by the bishop himself, with his assistant clergy, in the cathedral church of the diocese, during the fifty days between the solemn festivals of Easter and Pentecost; and this holy term admitted a numerous band of infants and adult persons into the bosom of the church. The discretion of parents often suspended the baptism of their children till they could understand the obligations which they contracted; the severity of ancient bishops exacted from the new converts a noviciate of two or three years; and the catechumens themselves, from different motives of a temporal or a spiritual nature, were seldom impatient to assume the character of perfect and initiated Christians. The sacrament of baptism was supposed to contain a full and absolute expiation of sin; and the soul was instantly restored to its original purity, and entitled to the promise of eternal salvation. Among the proselytes of Christianity, there were many who judged it imprudent to precipitate a salutary rite, which could not be repeated; to throw away an inestimable privilege, which could never be recovered. By the delay of their baptism, they could venture freely to indulge their passions in the enjoyments of this world, while they still retained in their own hands the

Delay of his baptism till the approach of death

---

[212]   (64) See Eusebius in Vit. const. l. iv. c. 15–32, and the whole tenor of Constantine's Sermon. The faith and devotion of the emperor has furnished Baronius with a specious argument in favour of his early baptism. [Gibbon]

[213]   (65) Zosimus, l. ii. p.105 [29, ad fin.]. [Gibbon]

[214]   (66) Eusebius in Vit. Constant. l. iv. c. 15, 16. [Gibbon]

[215]   (67) The theory and practice of antiquity with regard to the sacrament of baptism have been copiously explained by Dom. Chardon, Hist. des Sacremens, tom. i. p.3–405; Dom. Martenne, de Ritibus Ecclesiæ Antiquis [Rites of the Ancient Church. – eds], tom. i.; and by Bingham, in the tenth and eleventh books of his Christian Antiquities. One circumstance may be observed, in which the modern churches have materially departed from the ancient custom. The sacrament of baptism (even when it was administered to infants) was immediately followed by confirmation and the holy communion. [Gibbon]

means of a sure and easy absolution.[216] The sublime theory of the gospel had made a much fainter impression on the heart than on the understanding of Constantine himself. He pursued the great object of his ambition through the dark and bloody paths of war and policy; and, after the victory, he abandoned himself, without moderation, to the abuse of his fortune. Instead of asserting his just superiority above the imperfect heroism and profane philosophy of Trajan and the Antonines, the mature age of Constantine forfeited the reputation which he had acquired in his youth. As he gradually advanced in the knowledge of truth, he proportionably declined in the practice of virtue; and the same year of his reign in which he convened the council of Nice was polluted by the execution, or rather murder, of his eldest son. The date is alone sufficient to refute the ignorant and malicious suggestions of Zosimus,[217] who affirms that, after the death of Crispus, the remorse of his father accepted from the ministers of Christianity the expiation which he had vainly solicited from the Pagan Pontiffs. At the time of the death of Crispus, the emperor could no longer hesitate in the choice of a religion; he could no longer be ignorant that the church was possessed of an infallible remedy, though he chose to defer the application of it, till the approach of death had removed the temptation and danger of a relapse. The bishops, whom he summoned in his last illness to the palace of Nicomedia, were edified by the fervour with which he requested and received the sacrament of baptism, by the solemn protestation that the remainder of his life should be worthy of a disciple of Christ, and by his humble refusal to wear the imperial purple after he had been clothed in the white garment of a neophyte.[218] The example and reputation of Constantine seemed to countenance the delay of baptism.[219] Future tyrants were encouraged to believe that the innocent blood which they might shed in a long reign would instantly be washed away in the waters of regeneration: and the abuse of religion dangerously undermined the foundations of moral virtue.

---

[216]   (68) The fathers, who censured this criminal delay, could not deny the certain and victorious efficacy even of a deathbed baptism. The ingenious rhetoric of Chrysostom could find only three arguments against these prudent Christians. 1. That we should love and pursue virtue for her own sake, and not merely for the reward. 2. That we may be surprised by death without an opportunity of baptism. 3. That, although we shall be placed in heaven, we shall only twinkle like little stars, when compared to the suns of righteousness who have run their appointed course with labour, with success, and with glory. Chrysostom in Epist. ad Hebræos [Letter to the Hebrews. – eds], Homil. xiii. apud Chardon, Hist. des Sacremens tom. i. p.49. I believe that this delay of baptism, though attended with the most pernicious consequences, was never condemned by any general or provincial council, or by any public act or declaration of the church. The zeal of the bishops was easily kindled on much slighter occasions. [Gibbon]

[217]   (69) Zosimus, l. ii. p.104 [c.29]. For this disingenuous falsehood he has deserved and experienced the harshest treatment from all the ecclesiastical writers, except Cardinal Baronius (AD 324, No. 15–28), who had occasion to employ the Infidel on a particular service against the Arian Eusebius. [Gibbon]

[218]   A new convert in the primitive Christian church. [eds]

[219]   (70) Eusebius, l. iv. c. 61, 62, 63. The bishop of Caesarea supposes the salvation of Constantine with the most perfect confidence. [Gibbon]

The gratitude of the church has exalted the virtues and excused the failings of a generous patron, who seated Christianity on the throne of the Roman world; and the Greeks, who celebrate the festival of the Imperial saint, seldom mention the name of Constantine without adding the title of *equal to the Apostles*.[220] Such a comparison, if it allude to the character of those divine missionaries, must be imputed to the extravagance of impious flattery. But, if the parallel is confined to the extent and number of their evangelic victories, the success of Constantine might perhaps equal that of the Apostles themselves. By the edicts of toleration he removed the temporal disadvantages which had hitherto retarded the progress of Christianity; and its active and numerous ministers received a free permission, a liberal encouragement, to recommend the salutary truths of revelation by every argument which could affect the reason or piety of mankind. The exact balance of the two religions continued but a moment; and the piercing eye of ambition and avarice soon discovered that the profession of Christianity might contribute to the interest of the present, as well as of a future, life.[221] The hopes of wealth and honours, the example of an emperor, his exhortations, his irresistible smiles, diffused conviction among the venal and obsequious crowds which usually fill the apartments of a palace. The cities which signalized a forward zeal by the voluntary destruction of their temples were distinguished by municipal privileges, and rewarded with popular donatives; and the new capital of the East gloried in the singular advantage that Constantinople was never profaned by the worship of idols.[222] As the lower ranks of society are governed by imitation, the conversion of those who possessed any eminence of birth, of power, or of riches, was soon followed by dependent multitudes.[223] The salvation of the common people was purchased at an easy rate, if it be true that, in one year, twelve thousand men were baptized at Rome, besides a proportionable number of women and children; and that a white garment, with twenty pieces of gold, had been

---

[220]   (71) See Tillemont, Hist. des Empereurs, tom. iv. p.429. The Greeks, the Russians, and, in the darker ages, the Latins themselves have been desirous of placing Constantine in the catalogue of saints. [Gibbon]

[221]   (72) See the third and fourth books of his life. He was accustomed to say that, whether Christ was preached in pretence or in truth, he should still rejoice (l. iii. c. 58). [Gibbon]

[222]   (73) M. de Tillemont (Hist. des Empereurs, tom. iv. p.374, 616) has defended, with strength and spirit, the virgin purity of Constantinople against some malevolent insinuations of the Pagan Zosimus. [Gibbon]

[223]   (74) The author of the Histoire Politique et Philosophique des deux Indes [*Political and Philosophical History of the two Indies*. – eds] (tom. i. p.9) condemns a law of Constantine, which gave freedom to all the slaves who should embrace Christianity. The emperor did indeed publish a law which restrained the Jews from circumcising, perhaps from keeping, any Christian slaves (see Euseb. in Vit. Constant. l. iv. c. 27 and Cod. Theod. l. xvi. tit. ix. with Godefroy's Commentary, tom. vi. p.247). But this imperfect exception related only to the Jews; and the great body of slaves, who were the property of Christian or Pagan masters, could not improve their temporal condition by changing their religion. I am ignorant by what guides the Abbé Raynal was deceived; as the total absence of quotations is the unpardonable blemish of his entertaining history. [Gibbon]

promised by the emperor to every convert.[224] The powerful influence of Constantine was not circumscribed by the narrow limits of his life, or of his dominions. The education which he bestowed on his sons and nephews secured to the empire a race of princes whose faith was still more lively and sincere, as they imbibed, in their earliest infancy, the spirit, or at least the doctrine, of Christianity. War and commerce had spread the knowledge of the gospel beyond the confines of the Roman provinces; and the Barbarians, who had disdained an humble and proscribed sect, soon learned to esteem a religion which had been so lately embraced by the greatest monarch and the most civilized nation of the globe.[225] The Goths and Germans who enlisted under the standard of Rome revered the cross which glittered at the head of the legions, and their fierce countrymen received at the same time the lessons of faith and of humanity. The kings of Iberia and Armenia worshipped the God of their protector; and their subjects, who have invariably preserved the name of Christians, soon formed a sacred and perpetual connection with their Roman brethren. The Christians of Persia were suspected, in time of war, of preferring their religion to their country; but, as long as peace subsisted between the two empires, the persecuting spirit of the Magi[226] was effectually restrained by the interposition of Constantine.[227] The rays of the gospel illuminated the coast of India. The colonies of Jews, who had penetrated into Arabia and Ethiopia,[228] opposed the progress of Christianity; but the labour of the missionaries was in some measure facilitated by a previous knowledge of the Mosaic revelation; and Abyssinia still reveres the memory of Frumentius, who, in the time of Constantine, devoted his life to the conversion of those sequestered regions.

[c. AD 330 and following years]

---

[224] (75) See Acta Sti Silvestri [Life of Saint Silvester. – eds], and Hist. Eccles. Nicephor. Callist. l. vii. c.34, ap. Baronium, Annal. Eccles. AD 324, No. 67. 74. Such evidence is contemptible enough; but these circumstances are in themselves so probable that the learned Dr. Howell (History of the World, vol. iii. p.14) has not scrupled to adopt them. [Gibbon]

[225] (76) The conversion of the Barbarians under the reign of Constantine is celebrated by the ecclesiastical historians (see Sozomen, l. ii. c. 6, and Theodoret, l. i. c. 23, 24). But Rufinus, the Latin translator of Eusebius, deserves to be considered as an original authority. His information was curiously collected from one of the companions of the Apostle of Ethiopia, and from Bacurius, an Iberian prince, who was count of the domestics. Father Mamachi has given an ample compilation on the progress of Christianity, in the first and second volumes of his great but imperfect work. [Rufinus, at first a friend, afterwards an opponent of Jerome, also translated some works of Origen.] [Gibbon]

[226] A Persian priestly caste, three of whom are said to have visited the infant Christ in Bethlehem. [eds]

[227] (77) See in Eusebius (in Vit. Constant. l. ib. c. 9) the pressing and pathetic epistle of Constantine in favour of his Christian brethren of Persia. [J. Labourt, Le Christianisme dans l'empire Perse sous la dynastie Sassanide, 1904. [Christianity in the Persian Empire under the Sassanid Dynasty. – eds]] [Gibbon]

[228] (78) See Basnage, Hist, des Juifs, tom. vii. p.182, tom. viii. p.333, tom. ix. p.810. The curious diligence of this writer pursues the Jewish exiles to the extremities of the globe. [Gibbon]

Under the reign of his son Constantius, Theophilus,[229] who was himself of Indian extraction, was invested with the double character of ambassador and bishop. He embarked on the Red Sea with two hundred horses of the purest breed of Cappadocia, which were sent by the emperor to the prince of the Sabæans,[230] or Homerites. Theophilus was entrusted with many other useful or curious presents, which might raise the admiration and conciliate the friendship of the Barbarians; and he successfully employed several years in a pastoral visit to the churches of the torrid zone.[231]

The irresistible power of the Roman emperors was displayed in the important and dangerous change of the national religion. The terrors of a military force silenced the faint and unsupported murmurs of the Pagans, and there was reason to expect that the cheerful submission of the Christian clergy, as well as people, would be the result of conscience and gratitude. It was long since established, as a fundamental maxim of the Roman constitution, that every rank of citizens were alike subject to the laws, and that the care of religion was the right as well as duty of the civil magistrate. Constantine and his successors could not easily persuade themselves that they had forfeited, by their conversion, any branch of the Imperial prerogatives, or that they were incapable of giving laws to a religion which they had protected and embraced. The emperors still continued to exercise a supreme jurisdiction over the ecclesiastical order; and the sixteenth book of the Theodosian code represents, under a variety of titles, the authority which they assumed in the government of the Catholic church.

Change of the national religion

AD 312–438

But the distinction of the spiritual and temporal powers,[232] which had never been imposed on the free spirit of Greece and Rome, was introduced and confirmed by the legal establishment of Christianity. The office of supreme pontiff, which, from the time of Numa[233] to that of Augustus, had always been exercised by one of the most eminent of the senators, was at length united to the Imperial dignity. The first magistrate of the state, as often as he was prompted by superstition or policy,

Distinction of the spiritual and temporal powers

---

[229] (79) Theophilus had been given in his infancy as a hostage by his country-men of the isle of Diva, and was educated by the Romans in learning and piety. The Maldives, of which Male, or *Diva*, may be the capital, are a cluster of 1900 or 2000 minute islands in the Indian ocean. The ancients were imperfectly acquainted with the Maldives; but they are described in the two Mahometan travellers of the ninth century, published by Renaudot, Geograph. Nubiensis, p.30, 31. D'Herbelot, Bibliothèque Orientale, p.704. Hist. Générale des Voyages, tom. viii. [Gibbon]

[230] Present day Yemen. [eds]

[231] (80) Philostorgius, l. iii. c. 4, 5, 6, with Godefroy's learned observations. The historical narrative is soon lost in an inquiry concerning the seat of paradise, strange monsters, &c. [Gibbon]

[232] (81) See the epistle of Osius, ap. Athanasium, vol. i. p.840. The public remonstrance which Osius was forced to address to the son contained the same principles of ecclesiastical and civil government which he had secretly instilled into the mind of the father. [Gibbon]

[233] One of the legendary early Roman kings. [eds]

performed with his own hands the sacerdotal functions;[234] nor was there any order of priests, either at Rome or in the provinces, who claimed a more sacred character among men, or a more intimate communication with the Gods. But in the Christian church, which entrusts the service of the altar to a perpetual succession of consecrated ministers, the monarch, whose spiritual rank is less honourable than that of the meanest deacon, was seated below the rails of the sanctuary, and confounded with the rest of the faithful multitude.[235] The emperor might be saluted as the father of his people, but he owed a filial duty and reverence to the fathers of the church; and the same marks of respect which Constantine had paid to the persons of saints and confessors were soon exacted by the pride of the episcopal order.[236] A secret conflict between the civil and ecclesiastical jurisdictions embarrassed the operations of the Roman government; and a pious emperor was alarmed by the guilt and danger of touching with a profane hand the ark of the covenant. The separation of men into the two orders of the clergy and of the laity was, indeed, familiar to many nations of antiquity; and the priests of India, of Persia, of Assyria, of Judea, of Ethiopia, of Egypt, and of Gaul, derived from a celestial origin the temporal power and possessions which they had acquired. These venerable institutions had gradually assimilated themselves to the manners and government of their respective countries;[237] but the opposition or contempt of the civil power served to cement the discipline of the primitive church. The Christians had been obliged to elect their own magistrates, to raise and distribute a peculiar[238] revenue, and to regulate the internal policy of their republic[239] by a code of laws, which were ratified by the consent of the people and the practice of three hundred years.

---

[234]   (82) M. de la Bastie (Mémoires de l'Académie des Inscriptions, tom. xv. p.38–61) has evidently proved that Augustus and his successors exercised in person all the sacred functions of pontifex maximus, or high-priest of the Roman empire. [Gibbon]

[235]   (83) Something of a contrary practice had insensibly prevailed in the church of Constantinople; but the rigid Ambrose commanded Theodosius to retire below the rails, and taught him to know the difference between a king and a priest. See Theodoret, l. v. c. 18. [Gibbon]

[236]   (84) At the table of the emperor Maximus, Martin, bishop of Tours, received the cup from an attendant, and gave it to the presbyter, his companion, before he allowed the emperor to drink; the empress waited on Martin at table. Sulpicius Severus, in Vit Sti Martin, c. 23, and Dialogue ii. 7. Yet it may be doubted, whether these extraordinary compliments were paid to the bishop or the saint. The honours usually granted to the former character may be seen in Bingham's Antiquities, l. ii. c. 9, and Vales, ad Theodoret. l. iv. c. 6. See the haughty ceremonial which Leontius, bishop of Tripoli, imposed on the empress. Tillemont, Hist. des Empereurs, tom. iv. p.754. Patres Apostol. tom. ii. p.179. [Gibbon]

[237]   (85) Plutarch, in his treatise of Isis and Osiris, informs us that the kings of Egypt, who were not already priests, were initiated, after their election, into the sacerdotal order. [Gibbon]

[238]   i.e. special to themselves. [eds]

[239]   i.e. community. [eds]

When Constantine embraced the faith of the Christians, he seemed to contract a perpetual alliance with a distinct and independent society; and the privileges granted or confirmed by that emperor, or by his successors, were accepted, not as the precarious favours of the court, but as the just and unalienable rights of the ecclesiastical order.

The Catholic Church was administered by the spiritual and legal jurisdiction of eighteen hundred bishops;[240] of whom one thousand were seated in the Greek, and eight hundred in the Latin, provinces of the empire. The extent and boundaries of their respective dioceses had been variously and accidentally decided by the zeal and success of the first missionaries, by the wishes of the people, and by the propagation of the gospel. Episcopal churches were closely planted along the banks of the Nile, on the sea-coast of Africa, in the proconsular Asia,[241] and through the southern provinces of Italy. The bishops of Gaul and Spain, of Thrace and Pontus, reigned over an ample territory, and delegated their rural suffragans[242] to execute the subordinate duties of the pastoral office.[243] A Christian diocese might be spread over a province or reduced to a village; but all the bishops possessed an equal and indelible character: they all derived the same powers and privileges from the apostles, from the people, and from the laws. While the *civil* and *military* professions were separated by the policy of Constantine, a new and perpetual order of *ecclesiastical* ministers, always respectable, sometimes dangerous, was established in the church and state. The important review of their station and attributes may be distributed under the following heads: I. Popular election. II. Ordination of the clergy. III. Property. IV. Civil jurisdiction. V. Spiritual censures. VI. Exercise of public oratory. VII. Privilege of legislative assemblies.

I. The freedom of elections subsisted long after the legal establishment of Christianity;[244] and the subjects of Rome enjoyed in the church the privilege which they had lost in the republic, of choosing the

State of the bishops under the Christian emperors

I. Election of bishops

---

[240]   (86) The numbers are not ascertained by any ancient writer, or original catalogue; for the partial lists of the eastern churches are comparatively modern. The patient diligence of Charles a S^to Paolo, of Luke Holstenius, and of Bingham, has laboriously investigated all the episcopal sees of the Catholic Church, which was almost commensurate with the Roman empire. The ninth book of the Christian Antiquities is a very accurate map of ecclesiastical geography. [Gibbon]

[241]   Part of present-day Turkey. [eds]

[242]   i.e. assistant bishops. [eds]

[243]   (87) On the subject of the rural bishops, or *Chorepiscopi*, who voted in synods, and conferred the minor orders, see Thomassin, Discipline de l'Eglise, tom. i. p.447, &c. and Chardon, Hist. des Sacremens, tom. v. p.395, &c. They do not appear till the fourth century; and this equivocal character, which had excited the jealousy of the prelates, was abolished before the end of the tenth both in the East and the West. [F. Gillmann, Das Institut der Chorbischöfe im Orient, 1903.] [Gibbon]

[244]   (88) Thomassin (Discipline del'Eglise, tom. ii. l. ii. c. i–8, p.673–721) has copiously treated of the election of bishops during the five first centuries, both in the East and in the West; but he shows a very partial bias in favour of the episcopal aristocracy. Bingham (l. iv. c. 2) is moderate; and Chardon (Hist. des Sacremens, tom. v. p.108–128) is very clear and concise. [Gibbon]

magistrates whom they were bound to obey. As soon as a bishop had closed his eyes, the metropolitan issued a commission to one of his suffragans to administer the vacant see, and prepare, within a limited time, the future election. The right of voting was vested in the inferior clergy, who were best qualified to judge of the merit of the candidates; in the senators or nobles of the city, all those who were distinguished by their rank or property; and finally in the whole body of the people, who, on the appointed day, flocked in multitudes from the most remote parts of the diocese,[245] and sometimes silenced, by their tumultuous acclamations, the voice of reason and the laws of discipline. These acclamations might accidentally fix on the head of the most deserving competitor; of some ancient presbyter, some holy monk, or some layman, conspicuous for his zeal and piety. But the episcopal chair was solicited, especially in the great and opulent cities of the empire, as a temporal rather than as a spiritual dignity. The interested views, the selfish and angry passions, the arts of perfidy and dissimulation, the secret corruption, the open and even bloody violence, which had formerly disgraced the freedom of election in the commonwealths of Greece and Rome, too often influenced the choice of the successors of the apostles. While one of the candidates boasted the honours of his family, a second allured his judges by the delicacies of a plentiful table, and a third, more guilty than his rivals, offered to share the plunder of the church among the accomplices of his sacrilegious hopes.[246] The civil as well as ecclesiastical laws attempted to exclude the populace from this solemn and important transaction. The canons of ancient discipline, by requiring several episcopal qualifications of age, station, &c., restrained in some measure the indiscriminate caprice of the electors. The authority of the provincial bishops, who were assembled in the vacant church to consecrate the choice of the people, was interposed to moderate their passions and to correct their mistakes. The bishops could refuse to ordain an unworthy candidate, and the rage of contending factions sometimes accepted their impartial mediation. The submission, or the resistance, of the clergy and people, on various occasions, afforded different precedents, which were insensibly converted into positive laws and provincial customs;[247] but it was everywhere admitted, as a fundamental maxim of religious policy, that no bishop could be imposed on an orthodox church without the consent of its members. The emperors, as the guardians of the public peace, and as the first citizens of

---

[245] (89) Incredibilis multitudo, non solum ex eo oppido (*Tours*), sed etiam ex vicinis urbibus ad suffragia ferenda convenerat, &c. [An amazing crowd, not only from the town but also from the neighbouring cities gathered to cast their votes. – eds] Sulpicius Severus, in Vit. Martin. c. 7. The council of Laodicea (canon xiii.) prohibits mobs and tumults; and Justinian confines the right of election to the nobility. Novell. cxxiii. 1. [Gibbon]

[246] (90) The epistles of Sidonius Apollinaris (iv. 25, vii. 5. 9) exhibit some of the scandals of the Gallican church; and Gaul was less polished and less corrupt than the East. [Gibbon]

[247] (91) A compromise was sometimes introduced by law or by consent: either the bishops or the people chose one of the three candidates who had been named by the other party. [Gibbon]

Rome and Constantinople, might effectually declare their wishes in the choice of a primate; but those absolute monarchs respected the freedom of ecclesiastical elections; and, while they distributed and resumed the honours of the state and army, they allowed eighteen hundred perpetual magistrates to receive their important offices from the free suffrages of the people.[248] It was agreeable to the dictates of justice, that these magistrates should not desert an honourable station from which they could not be removed; but the wisdom of councils endeavoured, without much success, to enforce the residence, and to prevent the translation, of bishops. The discipline of the West was indeed less relaxed than that of the East; but the same passions which made those regulations necessary rendered them ineffectual. The reproaches which angry prelates have so vehemently urged against each other serve only to expose their common guilt and their mutual indiscretion.

II. The bishops alone possessed the faculty of *spiritual* generation; and this extraordinary privilege might compensate, in some degree, for the painful celibacy[249] which was imposed as a virtue, as a duty, and at length as a positive obligation. The religions of antiquity, which established a separate order of priests, dedicated a holy race, a tribe or family, to the perpetual service of the Gods.[250] Such institutions were founded for possession rather than conquest. The children of the priests enjoyed, with proud and indolent security, their sacred inheritance; and the fiery spirit of enthusiasm[251] was abated by the cares, the pleasures, and the endearments of domestic life. But the Christian sanctuary was open to every ambitious candidate who aspired to its heavenly promises or temporal possessions. The office of priests, like that of soldiers or magistrates, was strenuously exercised by those men whose temper and abilities had prompted them to embrace the ecclesiastical profession or who had been selected by a discerning bishop as the best qualified to promote the glory

II. Ordination of the clergy

---

[248] (92) All the examples quoted by Thomassin (Discipline de l'Eglise, tom. ii. l. ii. c. 6, p.704–714) appear to be extraordinary acts of power, and even of oppression. The confirmation of the bishop of Alexandria is mentioned by Philostorgius as a more regular proceeding (Hist. Eccles. l. ii. II). [Gibbon]

[249] (93) The celibacy of the clergy during the first five or six centuries is a subject of discipline, and indeed of controversy, which has been very diligently examined. See in particular Thomassin, Discipline de l'Eglise, tom. l. ii. c. lx. lxi. p.886–902, and Bingham's Antiquities, l. iv. c. 5. By each of these learned but partial critics, one half of the truth is produced, and the other is concealed. [Gibbon]

[250] (94) Diodorus Siculus attests and approves the hereditary succession of the priesthood among the Egyptians, the Chaldeans, and the Indians (l. i. p.84 [c. 73], l. ii. p.142, 153 [29, 40 and 41 ad fin.], edit. Wesseling). The magi are described by Ammianus as a very numerous family: 'per sæcula multa ad præsens unâ eâdemque prosapiâ multitudo creata, Deorum cultibus dedicata' (xxiii. 6). [Through many centuries to the present, a multitude appointed as priests from one and same family and dedicated to the rites of the Gods. – eds] Ausonius celebrates the *Stirps Druidarum* [Race of Druids. – eds] (De Professorib. Burdigal. iv.); but we may infer from the remark of Caesar (vi. 13), that, in the Celtic hierarchy, some room was left for choice and emulation. [Gibbon]

[251] i.e. excessive religious zeal. [eds]

and interest of the church. The bishops[252] (till the abuse was restrained by the prudence of the laws) might constrain the reluctant, and protect the distressed; and the imposition of hands for ever bestowed some of the most valuable privileges of civil society. The whole body of the Catholic clergy, more numerous perhaps than the legions, was exempted by the emperors from all service, private or public, all municipal offices, and all personal taxes and contributions which pressed on their fellow citizens with intolerable weight; and the duties of their holy profession were accepted as a full discharge of their obligations to the republic.[253] Each bishop acquired an absolute and indefeasible right to the perpetual obedience of the clerk whom he ordained: the clergy of each episcopal church, with its dependent parishes, formed a regular and permanent society; and the cathedrals of Constantinople[254] and Carthage[255] maintained their peculiar establishment of five hundred ecclesiastical ministers. The ranks[256] and numbers were insensibly multiplied by the superstition of the times, which introduced into the church the splendid ceremonies of a Jewish or Pagan temple; and a long train of priests, deacons, sub-deacons, acolytes, exorcists, readers, singers, and door-keepers, contributed, in their respective stations, to swell the pomp and harmony of religious worship. The clerical name and privilege were extended to many pious fraternities, who devoutly supported the ecclesiastical throne.[257] Six hundred *parabolani,* or adventurers, visited the sick at Alex-

---

[252] (95) The subject of the vocation, ordination, obedience, &c. of the clergy is laboriously discussed by Thomassin (Discipline de l'Eglise, tom. ii. p.l–83) and Bingham (in the fourth book of his Antiquities, more especially the fourth, sixth, and seventh chapters). When the brother of St Jerom was ordained in Cyprus, the deacons forcibly stopped his mouth, lest he should make a solemn protestation which might invalidate the holy rites. [Gibbon]

[253] (96) The charter of immunities which the clergy obtained from the Christian emperors is contained in the sixteenth book of the Theodosian code; and is illustrated with tolerable candour by the learned Godefroy, whose mind was balanced by the opposite prejudices of a civilian and a protestant. [Gibbon]
republic: i.e. state. [eds]

[254] (97) Justinian. Novell. ciii. Sixty presbyters or priests, one hundred deacons, forty deaconesses, ninety sub-deacons, one hundred and ten readers, twenty-five chanters, and one hundred door-keepers; in all, five hundred and twenty-five. This moderate number was fixed by the emperor, to relieve the distress of the church, which had been involved in debt and usury by the expense of a much higher establishment. [Gibbon]

[255] (98) Universus clerus ecclesiæ Carthaginiensis ... fere *quinginti* vel amplius; inter quos quamplurimi erant lectores infantuli. [The entire clerisy of the Church of Carthage ... almost five hundred or more, amongst whom a very large number were child officials. – eds] Victor Vitensis de Persecut. Vandal. v. 9. p.78, edit. Ruinart. This remnant of a more prosperous state subsisted under the oppression of the Vandals. [Gibbon]

[256] (99) The number of *seven* orders has been fixed in the Latin church, exclusive of the episcopal character. But the four inferior ranks, the minor orders, are now reduced to empty and useless titles. [Gibbon]

[257] (100) See Cod. Theodos. l. xvi. tit. 2, leg. 42, 43. Godefroy's Commentary, and the Ecclesiastical History of Alexandria, show the danger of these pious institutions, which often disturbed the peace of that turbulent capital. [Gibbon]

andria; eleven hundred *copiatæ*, or gravediggers, buried the dead at Constantinople; and the swarms of monks, who arose from the Nile, overspread and darkened the face of the Christian world.

[In the remaining 2,700 words of Chapter XX, Gibbon continues his discussion of the organization, powers and influence of the Church.]

Chapter XXXVIII

General observations on the Fall of the Roman Empire in the West

As the happiness of a *future* life is the great object of religion, we may hear, without surprise or scandal, that the introduction, or at least the abuse, of Christianity had some influence on the decline and fall of the Roman empire. The clergy successfully preached the doctrines of patience and pusillanimity; the active virtues of society were discouraged; and the last remains of the military spirit were buried in the cloister; a large portion of public and private wealth was consecrated to the specious demands of charity and devotion; and the soldiers' pay was lavished on the useless multitudes of both sexes, who could only plead the merits of abstinence and chastity. Faith, zeal, curiosity, and the more earthly passions of malice and ambition kindled the flame of theological discord; the church, and even the state, were distracted by religious factions, whose conflicts were sometimes bloody, and always implacable; the attention of the emperors was diverted from camps to synods; the Roman world was oppressed by a new species of tyranny; and the persecuted sects became the secret enemies of their country. Yet party-spirit, however pernicious or absurd, is a principle of union as well as of dissension. The bishops, from eighteen hundred pulpits, inculcated the duty of passive obedience to a lawful and orthodox sovereign; their frequent assemblies, and perpetual correspondence, maintained the communion of distant churches: and the benevolent temper of the gospel was strengthened, though confined, by the spiritual alliance of the Catholics. The sacred indolence of the monks was devoutly embraced by a servile and effeminate age; but, if superstition had not afforded a decent retreat, the same vices would have tempted the unworthy Romans to desert, from baser motives, the standard of the republic. Religious precepts are easily obeyed, which indulge and sanctify the natural inclinations of their votaries; but the pure and genuine influence of Christianity may be traced in its beneficial, though imperfect, effects on the Barbarian proselytes of the North. If the decline of the Roman empire was hastened by the conversion of Constantine, his victorious religion broke the violence of the fall, and mollified the ferocious temper of the conquerors.[258]

This awful revolution may be usefully applied to the instruction of the present age. It is the duty of a patriot to prefer and promote the exclusive interest and glory of his native country; but a philosopher may be permitted to enlarge his views, and to consider Europe as one great republic, whose various inhabitants have attained almost the same level of politeness and cultivation. The balance of power will continue to fluctuate, and the prosperity of our own or the neighbouring kingdoms may be alternately exalted or depressed; but these partial events cannot

---

[258]   i.e. the Germanic tribes. [eds]

essentially injure our general state of happiness, the system of arts, and laws, and manners, which so advantageously distinguish, above the rest of mankind, the Europeans and their colonies. The savage nations of the globe are the common enemies of civilized society; and we may inquire with anxious curiosity, whether Europe is still threatened with a repetition of those calamities which formerly oppressed the arms and institutions of Rome. Perhaps the same reflections will illustrate the fall of that mighty empire, and explain the probable causes of our actual security.

I. The Romans were ignorant of the extent of their danger, and the number of their enemies. Beyond the Rhine and Danube, the northern countries of Europe and Asia were filled with innumerable tribes of hunters and shepherds, poor, voracious, and turbulent; bold in arms, and impatient to ravish the fruits of industry. The Barbarian world was agitated by the rapid impulse of war; and the peace of Gaul or Italy was shaken by the distant revolutions of China. The Huns, who fled before a victorious enemy, directed their march towards the West; and the torrent was swelled by the gradual accession of captives and allies. The flying tribes who yielded to the Huns assumed in *their* turn the spirit of conquest; the endless column of Barbarians pressed on the Roman empire with accumulated weight; and, if the foremost were destroyed, the vacant space was instantly replenished by new assailants. Such formidable emigrations can no longer issue from the North; and the long repose, which has been imputed to the decrease of population, is the happy consequence of the progress of arts and agriculture. Instead of some rude villages, thinly scattered among its woods and morasses, Germany now produces a list of two thousand three hundred walled towns; the Christian kingdoms of Denmark, Sweden, and Poland, have been successively established; and the Hanse merchants, with the Teutonic knights, have extended their colonies along the coast of the Baltic, as far as the Gulf of Finland. From the Gulf of Finland to the Eastern Ocean, Russia now assumes the form of a powerful and civilized empire. The plough, the loom, and the forge, are introduced on the banks of the Volga, the Oby, and the Lena; and the fiercest of the Tartar hordes have been taught to tremble and obey. The reign of independent Barbarism is now contracted to a narrow span; and the remnant of Calmucks or Uzbecks, whose forces may be almost numbered, cannot seriously excite the apprehensions of the great republic of Europe.[259] Yet this apparent security should not tempt us to forget that new enemies, and unknown dangers, may *possibly* arise from some obscure people, scarcely visible in the map of the world. The Arabs or Saracens, who spread their conquests from India to Spain, had languished in poverty and contempt, till Mahomet breathed into those savage bodies the soul of enthusiasm.

---

[259] (6) The French and English editors of the Genealogical History of the Tartars have subjoined a curious, though imperfect, description of their present state. We might question the independence of the Calmucks, or Eluths, since they have been recently vanquished by the Chinese, who, in the year 1759, subdued the lesser Bucharia, and advanced into the country of Badakshan, near the sources of the Oxus (Mémoires sur les Chinois, tom. i. p.325–400). But these conquests are precarious, nor will I venture to ensure the safety of the Chinese empire. [Gibbon]

II. The empire of Rome was firmly established by the singular and perfect coalition of its members. The subject nations, resigning the hope, and even the wish, of independence, embraced the character of Roman citizens; and the provinces of the West were reluctantly torn by the Barbarians from the bosom of their mother country.[260] But this union was purchased by the loss of national freedom and military spirit; and the servile provinces, destitute of life and motion, expected their safety from the mercenary troops and governors, who were directed by the orders of a distant court. The happiness of a hundred millions depended on the personal merit of one or two men, perhaps children, whose minds were corrupted by education, luxury, and despotic power. The deepest wounds were inflicted on the empire during the minorities of the sons and grandsons of Theodosius; and, after those incapable princes seemed to attain the age of manhood, they abandoned the church to the bishops, the state to the eunuchs, and the provinces to the Barbarians. Europe is now divided into twelve powerful, though unequal, kingdoms, three respectable commonwealths, and a variety of smaller, though independent, states; the chances of royal and ministerial talents are multiplied, at least with the number of its rulers; and a Julian, or Semiramis, may reign in the North, while Arcadius and Honorius again slumber on the thrones of the South. The abuses of tyranny are restrained by the mutual influence of fear and shame; republics have acquired order and stability; monarchies have imbibed the principles of freedom, or, at least, of moderation; and some sense of honour and justice is introduced into the most defective constitutions by the general manners of the times. In peace, the progress of knowledge and industry is accelerated by the emulation of so many active rivals: in war, the European forces are exercised by temperate and undecisive contests. If a savage conqueror should issue from the deserts of Tartary, he must repeatedly vanquish the robust peasants of Russia, the numerous armies of Germany, the gallant nobles of France, and the intrepid freemen of Britain; who, perhaps, might confederate for their common defence. Should the victorious Barbarian carry slavery and desolation as far as the Atlantic Ocean, ten thousand vessels would transport beyond their pursuit the remains of civilized society; and Europe would revive and flourish in the American world which is already filled with her colonies and institutions.[261]

III. Cold, poverty, and a life of danger and fatigue, fortify the strength and courage of Barbarians. In every age they have oppressed the polite and peaceful nations of China, India, and Persia, who neglected, and still neglect, to counterbalance these natural powers by the resources of military art. The war-like states of antiquity, Greece, Macedonia, and Rome, educated a race of soldiers; exercised their bodies, disciplined their courage, multiplied their forces by regular evolutions, and

---

[260]   (7) The prudent reader will determine how far this general proposition is weakened by the revolt of the Isaurians, the independence of Britain and Armorica, the Moorish tribes, or the Bagaudæ of Gaul and Spain (vol. i. p.280, vol. iii. p.352, 402, 480). [Gibbon]

[261]   (8) America now contains about six millions of European blood and descent: and their numbers, at least in the North, are continually increasing. Whatever may be the changes of their political situation, they must preserve the manners of Europe; and we may reflect with some pleasure that the English language will probably be diffused over an immense and populous continent. [Gibbon]

converted the iron which they possessed into strong and serviceable weapons. But this superiority insensibly declined with their laws and manners; and the feeble policy of Constantine and his successors armed and instructed, for the ruin of the empire, the rude valour of the Barbarian mercenaries. The military art has been changed by the invention of gunpowder; which enables man to command the two most powerful agents of nature, air and fire. Mathematics, chemistry, mechanics, architecture, have been applied to the service of war; and the adverse parties oppose to each other the most elaborate modes of attack and of defence. Historians may indignantly observe that the preparations of a siege would found and maintain a flourishing colony;[262] yet we cannot be displeased that the subversion of a city should be a work of cost and difficulty, or that an industrious people should be protected by those arts, which survive and supply the decay of military virtue. Cannon and fortifications now form an impregnable barrier against the Tartar horse; and Europe is secure from any future eruption of Barbarians; since, before they can conquer, they must cease to be barbarous. Their gradual advances in the science of war would always be accompanied, as we may learn from the example of Russia, with a proportionable improvement in the arts of peace and civil policy; and they themselves must deserve a place among the polished nations whom they subdue.

Should these speculations be found doubtful or fallacious, there still remains a more humble source of comfort and hope. The discoveries of ancient and modern navigators, and the domestic history, or tradition, of the most enlightened nations, represent the *human savage*, naked both in mind and body, and destitute of laws, of arts, of ideas, and almost of language.[263] From this abject condition, perhaps the primitive and

---

[262] (9) On avoit fait venir (for the siege of Turin) 140 pièces de canon; et il est a remarquer que chaque gros canon monté revient à environ 2000 écus; il y avoit 110,000 boulets; 106,000 cartouches d'une façon, et 300,000 d'une autre; 21,000 bombes; 27,700 grenades, 15,000 sacs à terre, 30,000 instruments pour le pionnage; 1,200,000 livres de poudre. Ajoutez à ces munitions, le plomb, le fer, et le fer blanc, les cordages, tout ce qui sert aux mineurs, le souphre, le salpêtre, les outils de toute espèce. Il est certain que les frais de tous ces preparatifs de destruction suffiroient pour fonder et pour faire fleurir la plus nombreuse colonie. [140 cannon had been brought up and, it is worth noting, each large mounted cannon costs around 2,000 crowns. There were 110,000 bullets, 106,000 cartridges of one type and 300,000 of another, 21,000 bombs, 27,700 grenades, 15,000 sacks of earth, 30,000 digging tools and 1,200,000 pounds of powder. To these munitions must be added lead, iron, tin, ropes, everything for the use of miners: sulphur, saltpetre and tools of every kind. There can be no doubt that expense of all these preparations for destruction would be sufficient to found and maintain the largest colony in a flourishing condition. – eds] Voltaire, Siècle de Louis XIV. c. xx. in his Works. tom. xi. p.391. [Gibbon]

[263] (10) It would be an easy though tedious task to produce the authorities of poets, philosophers, and historians. I shall therefore content myself with appealing to the decisive and authentic testimony of Diodorus Siculus (tom. i. l. i. p.11, 12, l. iii. p.184, &c., edit. Wesseling). The Ichthyophagi [i.e. fish-eaters. – eds], who in his time wandered along the shores of the Red Sea, can only be compared to the natives of New Holland [i.e. present-day north Australia. – eds] (Dampier's Voyages, vol. i. p.464–469). Fancy or perhaps reason may still suppose an extreme and absolute state of nature far below the level of these savages, who had acquired some arts and instruments. [Gibbon]

universal state of man, he has gradually arisen to command the animals,
to fertilize the earth, to traverse the ocean, and to measure the heavens.
His progress in the improvement and exercise of his mental and
corporeal faculties[264] has been irregular and various, infinitely slow in the
beginning, and increasing by degrees with redoubled velocity; ages of
laborious ascent have been followed by a moment of rapid downfall; and
the several climates of the globe have felt the vicissitudes of light and
darkness. Yet the experience of four thousand years[265] should enlarge our
hopes, and diminish our apprehensions; we cannot determine to what
height the human species may aspire in their advance towards perfection;
but it may safely be presumed that no people, unless the face of nature is
changed, will relapse into their original barbarism. The improvements of
society may be viewed under a threefold aspect. 1. The poet or
philosopher illustrates his age and country by the efforts of a *single* mind;
but these superior powers of reason or fancy are rare and spontaneous
productions, and the genius of Homer, or Cicero, or Newton, would
excite less admiration, if they could be created by the will of a prince or
the lessons of a preceptor. 2. The benefits of law and policy, of trade and
manufactures, of arts and sciences, are more solid and permanent; and
many individuals may be qualified, by education and discipline, to
promote, in their respective stations, the interest of the community. But
this general order is the effect of skill and labour; and the complex
machinery may be decayed by time or injured by violence. 3. Fortunately
for mankind, the more useful, or, at least, more necessary arts can be
performed without superior talents, or national subordination; without
the powers of *one* or the union of *many*. Each village, each family, each
individual, must always possess both ability and inclination to perpetuate
the use of fire[266] and of metals; the propagation and service of domestic
animals; the methods of hunting and fishing; the rudiments of
navigation; the imperfect cultivation of corn or other nutritive grain; and
the simple practice of the mechanic trades. Private genius and public
industry may be extirpated; but these hardy plants survive the tempest,
and strike an everlasting root into the most favourable soil. The splendid
days of Augustus and Trajan were eclipsed by a cloud of ignorance; and
the Barbarians subverted the laws and palaces of Rome. But the scythe,
the invention or emblem of Saturn,[267] still continued annually to mow the

---

[264]   (11) See the learned and rational work of the President Goguet, de l'Origine
des Loix, des Arts, et des Sciences. He traces from facts or conjectures (tom. i.
p.147–337, edit. 12mo) the first and most difficult steps of human invention.
[Gibbon]

[265]   Bibles of Gibbon's time and subsequently, record that the world was created
four thousand years BC. [eds]

[266]   (12) It is certain, however strange, that many nations have been ignorant of
the use of fire. Even the ingenious natives of Otaheite [Tahiti. – eds], who are
destitute of metals, have not invented any earthen vessels capable of sustaining
the action of fire and of communicating the heat to the liquids which they
contain. [Gibbon]

[267]   (13) Plutarch. Quæst. Rom. in tom. ii. p.275. Macrob. Saturnal. l. i. c. 8,
p.152, edit. London. The arrival of Saturn (or his religious worship) in a ship may
indicate that the savage coast of Latium [i.e. Italian coast near Rome. – eds] was
first discovered and civilized by the Phoenicians. [Gibbon]

harvests of Italy: and the human feasts of the Læstrygons[268] have never been renewed on the coast of Campania.

Since the first discovery of the arts, war, commerce, and religious zeal have diffused, among the savages of the Old and New World, those inestimable gifts: they have been successively propagated; they can never be lost. We may therefore acquiesce in the pleasing conclusion that every age of the world has increased, and still increases, the real wealth, the happiness, the knowledge, and perhaps the virtue, of the human race.[269]

Source: Edward Gibbon, *The History of the Decline and Fall of the Roman Empire,* reprinted from edition edited by J.B. Bury, Methuen and Co., London, 1909.

---

[268] (14) In the ninth and tenth books of the Odyssey, Homer has embellished the tales of fearful and credulous sailors, who transformed the cannibals of Italy and Sicily into monstrous giants. [Gibbon]

[269] (15) The merit of discovery has too often been stained with avarice, cruelty, and fanaticism; and the intercourse of nations has produced the communication of disease and prejudice. A singular exception is due to the virtue of our own times and country. The five great voyages successively undertaken by the command of his present Majesty were inspired by the pure and generous love of science and of mankind. The same prince, adapting his benefaction to the different stages of society, has founded a school of painting in his capital, and has introduced into the island of the South Sea the vegetables and animals most useful to human life. [Gibbon]

Part C
'The Best of all Possible Worlds'

Contents

Voltaire
Candide or Optimism

The complete translation of Donald Frame

Contents

Introduction

Characteristic of all Voltaire's life were the acclaim and harassment that marked its close. At the age of eighty-three he returned to his native Paris for a triumph such as few authors have ever enjoyed. Delegations from the Académie Française and the Comédie Française, personages as diverse as Mme du Barry and Mme Necker, Diderot and Franklin, Gluck and the English ambassador, came to pay him their respects. Crowds cheered him in the streets. At the sixth performance of his tragedy *Irène*, he in his box and later his bust on the stage were crowned with wreaths amid wild acclaim. Yet he had come to Paris with no clear authorization after twenty-four years of exile. When he died there ten weeks later (May 30, 1778) the religious authorities denied him burial, and his body was removed secretly at night to be interred in the abbey of Scellières in Champagne.

The oppressive power of Voltaire's opponents must be kept in mind if his tales are to appear in their true perspective. Great satire creates the illusion that its targets are more comic than sinister. Imprisonments, exiles, a beating had whetted Voltaire's will to fight; the longer he lived the more constantly he used his wit to forge weapons of war. His tales, all written after he was fifty, are the weapons that have worn best. Their lustre must not blind us, however, to the fact that when Voltaire died his long battle for liberty and justice was not won.

The acclaim, like the harassment, came to Voltaire early as well as late. François-Marie Arouet, who adopted the nobiliary pen-name 'de Voltaire' at twenty-three, was born in 1694 of an intelligent, ambitious bourgeois family and given a strong classical education at the distinguished Collège Louis-le-Grand, where his Jesuit masters enjoyed his precocity and rated him as 'a talented boy, but a notable scamp'. He resisted his father's pressure to follow him into the law, and devoted himself early to literature. In the hedonistic society of the Regency after the death of Louis XIV (1715) he won renown – also imprisonment and brief exile – for his wit. In his twenty-fourth year he scored his first success as a tragedian with *Oedipe* (1718). Though even his best tragedies, such as *Zaïre* (1732), *Mahomet*

(1742), and *Mérope* (1734), are little more than documents today, for much of his life Voltaire's greatest fame was as the leading successor to Corneille and Racine in classical French verse tragedy, which he spiced with themes from Shakespeare and the East, colourful and violent visual effects, and thinly veiled social and religious criticism.

Five years later he made another successful début in the epic with *La Henriade*, today quite dated but enormously popular in its time, and still probably the best Fench epic in the classical mode. His subject was a lifelong hero, Henry IV, fighter for religious peace and tolerance in France and author (1598) of the Edict of Nantes.

In 1725 a sneer at Voltaire by the Chevalier de Rohan led to a sharp reply, and this to a beating by lackeys directed by Rohan under the indifferent eyes of other aristocrats whom Voltaire had thought his friends. He challenged Rohan,who accepted; but on the morning set for the duel Voltaire was arrested and put in the Bastille, which he was allowed to leave two weeks later for an exile of over two years (1726–9) in England.

His exposure to English freedoms in his early thirties, following the harsh awakening to his lack of status in the eyes of French nobles, turned his mind to social inequalities as never before. He studied English hard and learned it rather well, made friends, with Swift, Pope, Congreve, Bolingbroke, and others, and hailed English freedom of worship, thought, and speech, as well as the Quakers, Shakespeare, Bacon, Locke, Newton, and the parliamentary system, in his *Philosophical Letters,* or *Letters Concerning the English Nation*, whose long-delayed publication in 1734 brought about the burning of the book and a warrant for the author's arrest. The openness and power of his ironic attack on French abuses and inequities give this date great importance.

Meanwhile Voltaire had triumphed in another field with his *History of Charles XII* (1731). Less important than two later works, *The Century of Louis XIV* (1751) and the *Essay on the Manners and the Spirit of Nations* (1756), which brought all civilization and all civilizations into the purview of history, his account of the Swedish warrior-king showed what harm such a man can do even to his own country, and demonstrated Voltaire's mastery at shaping masses of material into a clear and enjoyable story.

The persecution brought on by the *Philosophical Letters* found Voltaire prepared. Financially secure since his early thirties after studious and successful investment, he had a safe asylum in the independent duchy of Lorraine at the Château of Cirey with his beloved mistress Emilie, Marquise du Châtelet. Here he settled down for eleven years (1733–44) with Emilie and her accommodating husband, writing indefatigably, delving deeply, though as an amateur, into the science of his time, especially that of Newton. An even greater lover of science than Voltaire, Mme du Châtelet also loved the philosophical optimism of Leibniz and Wolff, which Voltaire treated gently until her death but ridiculed ten years later in *Candide*.

In his early fifties (1744–50) Voltaire was mainly occupied at court, with some success: appointment as historiographer-royal and as gentleman of the King's chamber, election to the Académie Française. His uneasiness and his disgust with this life, however, appear already in his first philosophical tale, *Zadig* (1747). The death of Mme du Châtelet in 1749 left him sad and unsettled. For ten years Frederick the Great of Prussia, culturally an ardent Francophile, had been urging Voltaire to come to his 'German Versailles' in Potsdam, near Berlin. Hoping to find a philosopher-king, Voltaire at last accepted.

His stay in Berlin (1750–3) started like a honeymoon and ended in a violent though not permanent break. Frederick was no comfortable master for a spirited subordinate, nor Voltaire a comfortable courtier for an authoritarian monarch. Both were better at using than at supporting irony. French courtiers aroused Voltaire's jealousy and fomented bad feeling. Voltaire's shady speculation with a Jew named Hirschel led to a squalid lawsuit that angered Frederick. The last straw came when Maupertuis,[1] president of the Academy of Berlin, by sheer force of authority had the mathematician and philosopher Koenig condemned as a forger

and dismissed from the Academy in disgrace. Voltaire, convinced that Koenig was in the right, protested; Frederick sided with his President. When Maupertuis published some inept *Letters*, Voltaire ridiculed him scathingly in his *Diatribe of Doctor Akakia*. Frederick had this burned and Voltaire arrested, and subjected him on his departure later to another humiliating arrest and detainment – not without reason – in Frankfurt.

Back in France, Voltaire was soon in trouble over a pirated edition of the *Essay on the Manners*, and permission to return to Paris was not granted. Needing a safe retreat with Cirey gone, he chose Lake Geneva, renting a house between Lausanne and the lake and buying another just outside Geneva which he named Les Délices. To Voltaire, now sixty, this was a happy home, which could comfortably accommodate his niece – and mistress – Mme Denis, a considerable household, and many visitors. Here, at his own private theatre, he could indulge a favourite passion by directing his own plays and acting in them with his guests. Since stage performances were banned in Calvinist Geneva, he was presently required to move his to Lausanne. In return he encouraged his friend d'Alembert to criticize the ban in his article on Geneva in the *Encyclopédie*, which led Jean-Jacques Rousseau to answer the article and Voltaire with his eloquent *Letter to D'Alembert* (1758). Voltaire and Rousseau, friendly at first, were now at odds for good. When other matters in d'Alembert's article worsened Voltaire's relations with the Genevans, he started looking for a home outside Genevan territory. In 1758 he bought the large property of Ferney on French soil but still on Lake Geneva and only four miles from the town.

The Patriarch of Ferney, as he came to be called, now added to his many other activities those of a country gentleman. He took a strong paternal interest in his village, planting trees, raising wheat and cows, developing pasture land, a stone quarry, a tile works, a tannery, factories of silk stockings, lace, and Swiss watches, obtaining lighter and more equitable taxes for the whole region, establishing a school and a hospital, even

---

[1] Pierre Louis Moreau de Maupertuis (1698–1759), French mathematician and supporter of Newtonian physics. [eds]

building a church. He took many unfortunates into his home: victims of injustice like the Calas and Sirven families; others who provided him a chance for matchmaking, such as a grand-niece of Corneille, for whose dowry he published a critical edition of that playwright's works; and later a particular favourite, Mlle Varicourt, destined for a convent for economy's sake and in despair until Voltaire took her in, nicknamed her 'Belle et Bonne', and eventually married her to the Marquis de Villette. Visitors of great distinction flocked to Ferney as to a capital of letters. Meanwhile Voltaire worked as tirelessly as ever, usually in bed, on his enormous and fascinating correspondence, on some plays, but mainly on keen, satiric, short pieces of all sorts including his witty *Philosophical Dictionary* and most of his tales. The great philosophic struggle was on in earnest, with Voltaire the main leader of the fight to *écraser l'infâme* ('crush infamy'): the infamy of intolerance and authoritarian suppression of freedom in thought and word. Publication of that great secular monument the *Encyclopédie* was completed, after much opposition and repeated suspensions, in 1765. Voltaire contributed considerably to it by writing and soliciting articles, by encouragement and spirited defence.

Nor was the old warrior content to seek justice simply in the abstract. Again and again he fought tirelessly for the victims of judicial injustice and religious intolerance: Jean Calas, Protestant of Toulouse, condemned and executed for the murder of his son, unanimously rehabilitated (1765); Sirven, another Protestant of Toulouse, condemned for killing his daughter (1764), fleeing arrest with his wife and two remaining daughters, exonerated (1771); Lally, a former commander in India, executed in 1766, rehabilitated in 1778; the Perra family, Martin, Montbailli; La Barre, whose torture and death were a bitter blow; La Barre's friend d'Etallonde, whom Voltaire greatly helped. This unsparing dedication to the victims of persecution led to the final transfiguration of Voltaire's public image: in Paris on his final visit, as in Geneva two years before, enthusiastic crowds hailed him as the defender of Calas.

Voltaire was always a man of action. Highly volatile, sensitive, ambitious, emotional, irascible and generous, vindictive and compassionate, he found his greatest satisfaction and release in work. But work, to satisfy him, must act on others. He once complained that Rousseau wrote for the sake of writing, while he himself wrote in the interest of action. Hence his lack of fondness for meditation or speculation. When Martin, in the conclusion of *Candide*, recommends work without reasoning as the only way of making life endurable, he is not challenging the priority of reason like Rousseau; he is condemning the *libido ratiocinandi* of Pangloss, displayed perhaps most clearly in Chapter 5. There Candide, lying injured in the ruins of Lisbon, begged Pangloss for oil and wine, and was treated to a theory of the origin of the earthquake.

'"Nothing is more probable," said Candide, "but for the love of God, a little oil and wine."

"What do you mean, probable?" replied the philosopher. "I maintain that the matter is proved." Candide lost consciousness ...' What Voltaire, like Martin, condemns is impractical reasoning and theorizing not leading to action.

Thus Voltaire is not a philosopher in any usual sense. Convinced like Descartes that clarity and distinctness are the prime criteria of truth; convinced that man, an insect living a few seconds on an atom of mud, cannot understand the grand designs of his infinite Creator, that systems claiming to explain the unfathomable are imposture and vanity, he is equally convinced that there is much worth knowing and worth doing. Science, which had given men some certain knowledge of the measurable, he found useful; but since science was impeded by repressive dogmatism, even here action for freedom was as necessary as research. The most vital study, for Voltaire, was that of the means and the obstacles to human betterment; the most vital action was to remove those obstacles. In the France of his time the chief obstacles seemed to be social injustice and religious intolerance; these were the infamy that he strove to crush.

His main weapon was wit, wit prompted but not controlled by emotion. Passion, as the angel points out in *Zadig* (Chapter 20), is necessary but dangerous, the wind that moves our vessel but may sink it. Voltaire put his faith in reason as the test of truth. Abuses must be exposed to the light of reason clearly, satirically, in the nakedness of their absurdity; the reader must see that the emperor has no clothes.

This being the main purpose of Voltaire's tales, they must not seek fully to reproduce the rich texture of human nature, motive, or situation; we must neither believe in his characters, nor be involved with them, too completely; the ideas must be dominant and clear. There is no harm, in *Candide*, in bringing the Baron and Pangloss back to life; they have useful roles to play later, and their apparent deaths are further proof that human misfortune is universal. Despite Voltaire's debt to Swift, the two are very different. Voltaire never makes the same pretence of truth about his tales that Swift, with his utterly veracious narrator and his precise physical measurements does about *Gulliver's Travels*; he does not seek the richness of ambiguity and texture that Swift derives in part from this deadpan humour of his; his points must be unmistakable and full of impact. Uncertainties in Voltaire – the relative importance of Jesrad's assertions and of Zadig's 'But ...', the precise scope of Candide's 'cultivate our garden' – are of another order than in Swift: the rarity of happiness for the good, the futility of idle reasoning are crystal clear.

The ideas, of course, are not everything. Voltaire's best tales sweep along on lively plots, often Oriental, often both exploiting and parodying contemporary romances of sentiment and adventure, often using travel to give the protagonist experience of the world. This experience he must gain, and his gain is ours. Along the way we are treated to ever-varied pyrotechnics as an anecdote here, a comment there, sheds the light of ridicule on Voltaire's favourite abuses. Always the movement is rapid, the style lean and sparkling. Always the story, however entertaining, is ancillary to the ideas.

In some tales the ideas are simple. *Memnon* (1749) teaches us the folly of aspiring to perfect wisdom; *Bababec* (1750), that good deeds are better than useless asceticism; *Scarmentado* (1756),

that intolerance is universal; *The World as It Is* (1748) and *Plato's Dream* (1756), that we and our globe might be worse; *Berthier* (1759), that most Jesuits are proud, some boring; *Story of a Good Brahman* (1761), that man does not want happiness at the price of imbecility; *Jeannot and Colin* (1765), that vanity is profitless; *An Indian Adventure* (1766), that all creatures are cruel to one another; *The One-Eyed Porter* (1774), that happiness is in the eye of the beholder; *Memory's Adventure* (1775), that man would be lost without memory and the senses.

In others the themes are complex. *Count Chesterfield's Ears* (1775) ranges from the inanity of the concept *soul* through the beauty of Tahitian love festivals to picturesque theories of human motivation. *Ingenuous* (1767) hits at the folly of sectarians, the cruelty of oppressors, and the evils of arbitrary power, while presenting the noble savage as a good-natured brute needing education to become truly a man. *Micromegas* (1752) is a lesson in relativity, the presumption of puny man, and the dignity that scientific knowledge gives him. The two greatest tales, *Candide* and *Zadig*, focus on the problem of evil, which most of the others touch upon. In *Zadig* (1747), probably because of Mme du Châtelet, Voltaire gives the hermit a stong argument for a beneficent Providence whose ways are beyond us, and the story ends happily. However Zadig still argues as the hermit-angel flies off, and the story suggests that goodness, wisdom, and valour rarely lead to happiness. *Candide* (1759), written at white heat after Emilie's death, disillusionment with Frederick, and the Lisbon earthquake, demonstrates that our life is either suffering or boredom, philosophical optimism is the acme of folly, the concept of Providence is wishful thinking, and our sole salvation lies in fruitful work cultivating our garden.

Candide
or Optimism

Translated from the German of Dr Ralph[2] With the Additions Found in the Doctor's Pocket When He Died at Minden in the Year of Our Lord 1759
[1759]

1
How Candide was brought up in a fine castle, and how he was expelled therefrom

In Westphalia, in the castle of My Lord the Baron of Thunder-ten-tronckh, there was a young man whom nature had endowed with the gentlest of characters. His face bespoke his soul. His judgement was rather sound and his mind of the simplest; this is the reason, I think, why he was named Candide. The old servants of the house suspected that he ·was the son of My Lord the Baron's sister and of a good and honourable gentleman of the neighbourhood whom that lady never would marry because he could prove only seventy-one quarterings[3] and the rest of his genealogical tree had been lost by the injuries of time.

My Lord the Baron was one of the most powerful lords in Westphalia, for his castle had a door and windows. His great hall was even adorned with a piece of tapestry. All the dogs of his stable yards formed a pack of hounds when necessary; his grooms were his huntsmen; the village vicar was his Grand Almoner. They all called him My Lord, and they laughed at the stories he told.

My lady the Baroness, who weighed about three hundred and fifty pounds, attracted very great consideration by that fact, and did the honours of the house with a dignity that made her even more respectable. Her daughter Cunégonde, aged seventeen, was rosy-complexioned, fresh, plump, appetizing. The Baron's son appeared in all respects worthy of his father. The tutor Pangloss[4] was the oracle of the house, and little Candide listened to his lessons with all the candour of his age and character.

Pangloss taught metaphysico-theologo-cosmolo-nigology.[5] He proved admirably that there is no effect without a cause and that, in this best of all possible worlds,[6] My Lord the Baron's castle was the finest of castles, and My Lady the best of all possible Baronesses.

'It is demonstrated,' he said, 'that things cannot be otherwise, for, everything being made for an end, everything is necessarily for the best end. Note that noses were made to wear spectacles, and so we have spectacles. Legs were visibly instituted to be breeched, and we have breeches. Stones were formed to be cut and to make into castles; so My Lord has a very handsome castle; the greatest baron in the province should be the best housed; and, pigs being made to be eaten, we eat pork all year round: consequently, those who have asserted that all is well have said a foolish thing; they should have said that all is for the best.'

---

[2] For some weeks after its publication Voltaire denied authorship of *Candide*, as he often did with works potentially dangerous to himself. [Frame]

[3] Divisions on a coat of arms indicating degrees of nobility. Sixty-four was considered the maximum. [Frame]

[4] From the Greek: 'all tongue.' [Frame]

[5] The '-nigo-' suggests the French *nigaud*, 'booby.' [Frame]

[6] The systematic optimism ridiculed throughout *Candide* is a caricature of that of Leibniz (1646–1716), popularized by Alexander Pope in his *Essay on Man* (1733–4), and systematized by Christian Wolff (1679–1754). [Frame]

Candide listed attentively and believed innocently; for he thought Mademoiselle Cunégonde extremely beautiful, though he never made bold to tell her so. He concluded that after the happiness of being born Baron of Thunder-ten-tronckh, the second degree of happiness was to be Mademoiselle Cunégonde; the third, to see her every day; and the fourth, to listen to Doctor Pangloss, the greatest philosopher in the province and consequently in the whole world.

One day Cunégonde, walking near the castle in the little wood they called The Park, saw in the bushes Doctor Pangloss giving a lesson in experimental physics to her mother's chambermaid, a very pretty and very docile little brunette. Since Mademoiselle Cunégonde had much inclination for the sciences, she observed breathlessly the repeated experiments of which she was a witness; she clearly saw the Doctor's sufficient reason, the effects and the causes, and returned home all agitated, all pensive, all filled with the desire to be learned, thinking that she might well be the sufficient reason of young Candide, who might equally well be hers.

She met Candide on the way back to the castle, and blushed; Candide blushed too; she said good morning to him in a faltering voice; and Candide spoke to her without knowing what he was saying. The next day, after dinner, as everyone was leaving the table, Cunégonde and Candide found themselves behind a screen; Cunégonde dropped her handkerchief, Candide picked it up, she innocently took his hand, the young man innocently kissed the young lady's hand with a very special vivacity, sensibility, and grace; their lips met, their eyes glowed, their knees trembled, their hands wandered. My Lord the Baron of Thunder-ten-tronckh passed near the screen and, seeing this cause and this effect, expelled Candide from the castle with great kicks in the behind; Cunégonde swooned; she was slapped in the face by My Lady the Baroness as soon as she had come to herself; and all was in consternation in the finest and most agreeable of all possible castles.

2

What became of Candide among the Bulgarians[7]

Candide, expelled from the earthly paradise, walked for a long time without knowing where, weeping, raising his eyes to heaven, turning them often toward the finest of castles, which enclosed the most beautiful of future Baronesses; he lay down to sleep without supper in the midst of the fields between two furrows; the snow was falling in fat flakes. The next day Candide, frozen, dragged himself toward the neighbouring town, which was named Valdberghoff-trarbk-dikdorff, with no money, dying of hunger and fatigue. He stopped sadly at the door of an inn. Two men dressed in blue noticed him.

'Comrade,' said one, 'there's a very well-built young man, and he's of the right height.'

They advanced toward Candide and very civilly invited him to dinner.

'Gentlemen,' said Candide with charming modesty, 'you do me great honour, but I haven't the money to pay my bill.'

'Ah, sir,' said one of the men in blue, 'persons of your figure and merit never pay for anything; aren't you five feet five?'

'Yes, gentlemen, that is my height,' he said with a bow.

'Ah, sir, sit down to table; not only will we pay your expenses, but we will never allow a man like you to lack money; men are made only to help one another.'

'You are right,' said Candide. 'That is what Monsieur Pangloss always told me, and I clearly see that all is for the best.'

They urge him to accept a few crowns, he takes them and wants to make out a promissory note; they want none, they all sit down to table.

'Don't you love tenderly …?'

'Oh yes,' he replied, 'I love Mademoiselle Cunégonde tenderly.'

'No,' said one of the gentlemen, 'we are asking you whether you do not tenderly love the King of the Bulgarians.'

---

[7]   Voltaire chose this name to represent the Prussians of Frederick the Great because he had reason to think that Frederick was a pederast and because the French *bougre*, like the English 'bugger', comes from *Bulgare* (Bulgarian). Note the treatment of the Baron's son in Chapter 4 and his adventures narrated to Chapters 15 and 28. [Frame]

'Not at all,' he said, 'for I have never seen him.'

'What! He is the most charming of Kings, and you must drink his health.'

'Oh! most gladly, gentlemen'; and he drinks.

'That is sufficient,' they say to him, 'you are now the prop, the support, the defender, the hero of the Bulgarians; your fortune is made, and your glory is assured.'

They immediately put irons on his legs and they take him to the regiment. They make him turn right, turn left, raise the ramrod, return the ramrod, take aim, fire, march on the double, and they give him thirty strokes with a stick; the next day he drills a little less badly and he gets only twenty strokes; the day after they give him only ten, and he is regarded as a prodigy by his comrades.

Candide, completely stupefied, could not yet understand too well how he was a hero. He took it into his head one fine spring day to go for a stroll, walking straight ahead, believing that it was a privilege of the race of humans, as of the race of animals, to use their legs as they please.[8] He had not gone two leagues when up came four other heroes, six feet tall; they overtake him, they bind him, they put him in a dungeon. He was asked, juridically, which he liked better, to be beaten thirty-six times by the whole regiment, or to receive twelve lead bullets at once in his brain. In vain he told them that the will is free and that he wanted neither of these; he had to make a choice. By virtue of the gift of God that is called *liberty*, he decided to run the gauntlet thirty-six times; he did it twice. The regiment was made up of two thousand men. That gave him four thousand strokes of the ramrod, which laid open his muscles and nerves from the nape of his neck to his rump. As they were about to proceed to the third run, Candide, at the end of his rope, asked

them as a favour to be kind enough to smash in his head; he obtained this favour. They bandage his eyes; they make him kneel; at that moment the King of the Bulgarians passes, inquires about the victim's crime; and since this King was a man of great genius, he understood, from all he learned about Candide, that this was a young metaphysician very ignorant of the ways of this world, and he granted him his pardon with a clemency that will be praised in all newspapers and in all ages. A worthy surgeon cured Candide in three weeks with the emollients prescribed by Dioscorides.[9] He already had a little bit of skin, and could walk, when the King of the Bulgarians gave battle to the King of the Abarians.[10]

3
How Candide escaped from among the Bulgarians, and what became of him

Nothing could be so beautiful, so smart, so brilliant, so well drilled as the two armies. Trumpets, fifes, oboes, drums, cannons formed a harmony such as was never heard even in hell.

First the cannons felled about six thousand men on each side; then the musketry removed from the best of worlds some nine or ten thousand scoundrels who infected its surface. The bayonet also was the sufficient reason for the death of some thousands of men. The whole might well amount to about thirty thousand souls. Candide, trembling like a philosopher, hid himself as best he could during this heroic butchery.

Finally, while both kings were having *Te Deums*[11] sung, each in his own camp, he decided to go reason elsewhere about effects and causes. He passed over heaps of dead and dying and first reached a neighbouring village; it was in ashes; it was an Abarian village which the Bulgarians had

---

[8]   This whole chapter satirizes the drillmastership of Frederick the Great. The desertion is suggested by Voltaire's memory of a Frenchman named Courtilz, whose release from prison into a hospital Voltaire had procured from Frederick. [Frame]

[9]   Dioscorides: Greek physician of the first century AD. [eds]

[10]   This name, which designates a Scythian tribe, represents the French who were involved in the Seven Years' War (1756–63) opposite the Prussians. [Frame]

[11]   A Latin hymn of praise to God, often sung to celebrate a victory in battle. [eds]

burned in accordance with the rules of inter-national law. Here old men riddled with wounds watched their wives die, with their throats cut, holding their children to their bleeding breasts; there, girls, disembowelled after satisfying the natural needs of a few heroes, were gasping their last sighs; others, half-burned, screamed to be given the *coup de grâce*. Brains were spattered over the ground beside severed arms and legs.

Candide fled full speed to another village; it belonged to some Bulgarians, and the Abarian heroes had treated it in the same way. Candide, still treading on quivering limbs or through ruins, arrived at last outside the theatre of war, carrying a few small provisions in his knapsack, and never forgetting Mademoiselle Cunégonde. His provisions ran out when he was in Holland; but having heard that everyone in that country was rich, and that they were Christians, he had no doubt that he would be treated as well as he had been in the castle of My Lord the Baron before he had been expelled from it on account of the lovely eyes of Mademoiselle Cunégonde.

He asked alms of several grave personages, who all replied that if he continued that practice he would be shut up in a house of correction to teach him how to live.

He then addressed a man who had just talked about charity for one solid hour unaided in a large assembly. This orator, looking askance at him, said to him: 'What brings you here? Are you here for the good cause?'

'There is no effect without a cause,' replied Candide modestly, 'everything is linked by necessity and arranged for the best. It was necessary for me to be expelled from the pres-ence of Mademoiselle Cunégonde and to run the gauntlet, and now to beg my bread until I can earn it; all this could not happen differently.'

'My friend,' said the orator to him, 'do you believe that the Pope is antichrist?'

'I had never heard that before,' replied Candide; 'but whether he is or not, I have no bread.'

'You do not deserve to eat any,' said the other. 'Hence, scoundrel; hence, wretch; never

come near me again in your life.'

The orator's wife, who had put her head out the window, seeing a man who doubted that the Pope was antichrist, poured out on his head a full ... O Heavens! to what excess is religious zeal carried in ladies!

A man who had not been baptized, a good Anabaptist[12] named Jacques, saw the cruel and ignominious treatment accorded to one of his bretheren, a two-footed creature with a soul;[13] he took him home, cleaned him up, gave him some bread and some beer, made him a present of two florins, and even volunteered to teach him to work in his factories of Persian cloth that is made in Holland. Candide, wanting to fall pros-trate at his feet, cried:

'Doctor Pangloss was certainly right to tell me that all is for the best in this world, for I am infinitely more touched by your extreme gener-osity than by the harshness of that gentleman in the black coat and of my lady his wife.'

The next day on a walk he met a beggar all covered with sores, his eyes dull as death, the end of his nose eaten away, his mouth awry, his teeth black, talking out of his throat, tormented with a violent cough, and spitting out a tooth at each spasm.

4

How Candide met his old philosophy teacher, Doctor Pangloss, and what happened

Candide, moved even more by compassion than by horror, gave this frightful beggar the two flo-rins he had received from his honest Anabaptist Jacques. The Phantom gazed fixedly at him, shed tears, and threw his arms around his neck. Candide recoiled in terror.

'Alas!' said the wretch to the other wretch, 'don't you recognize your dear Pangloss any more?'

'What do I hear? You, my dear master! You in this horrible state! Why, what misfortune has happened to you? Why are you no longer in the

---

[12]   A Protestant sect founded in Germany (1521) which believed in adult (as opposed to infant) baptism and the creation of a community in which everything was shared equally. [eds]

[13]   The phrase goes back to Plato's so-called *Definitions*. [Frame]

finest of castles? What has become of Mademoiselle Cunégonde, the pearl of young ladies, the masterpiece of nature?'

'I am exhausted,' said Pangloss.

Immediately Candide took him into the Anabaptist's stable, where he made him eat a little bread; and when Pangloss had recovered: 'Well,' he said, 'Cunégonde?'

'She is dead,' the other replied.

Candide swooned at these words; his friend restored him to his senses with a little bad vinegar that happened to be in the stable. Candide opened his eyes.

'Cunégonde is dead! Ah, best of worlds, where are you? But what illness did she die of? Could it have been for having seen me expelled with great kicks from the fine castle of My Lord, her father?'

'No,' said Pangloss, 'she was disembowelled by Bulgarian soldiers after being raped as much as anyone can be; they smashed in the head of My Lord the Baron, who tried to defend her; My Lady the Baroness was cut to pieces; the poor pupil was treated precisely like his sister; and as for the castle, not a stone is left standing upon another, not a barn, not a sheep, not a duck, not a tree; but we have been well avenged, for the Abarians did as much in a neighbouring barony that belonged to a Bulgarian lord.'

At this account Candide swooned again; but having come back to his senses and said all that was appropriate, he inquired about the cause and effect, the sufficient reason, which had put Pangloss in such a piteous state.

'Alas!' said Pangloss, 'it is love; love, the consoler of the human race, the preserver of the universe, the soul of all emotional beings, tender love.'

'Alas!' said Candide, 'I have known this love, this sovereign of hearts, this soul of our soul; all it has ever brought me was one kiss and twenty kicks in the arse. How could this beautiful cause produce in you so abominable an effect?'

Pangloss answered in these terms:

'O my dear Candide! You knew Paquette that pretty attendant upon our august Baroness; I tasted in her arms the delights of paradise, which produced these torments of hell by which you see me devoured; she was infected and she may have died of it. Paquette had received this present from a very learned Franciscan, who had gone back to the source; for he had got it from an old countess, who had received it from a cavalry captain, who owed it to a marquise, who had it from a page, who had received it from a Jesuit, who as a novice had got it in a direct line from one of the companions of Christopher Columbus. For my part I shall give it to no one, for I am dying.'

'O Pangloss!' exclaimed Candide, 'that is a strange genealogy! Wasn't the devil the root of it?'

'Not at all,' replied the great man. 'It was an indispensable thing in the best of worlds, a necessary ingredient; for if Columbus had not caught, in an island in America, this disease which poisons the source of generation, which often even prevents generation, and which is obviously opposed to the great purpose of nature, we would not have either chocolate or cochineal. It should also be noted that to this day this malady is peculiar to us in our continent, like religious controversy. The Turks, the Indians, the Persians, the Chinese, the Siamese, the Japanese are not yet acquainted with it; but there is sufficient reason for their making its acquaintance, in their turn, within a few centuries. Meanwhile it has made marvellous progress among us, and especially in those great armies composed of decent, well-brought-up mercenaries, which decide the destiny of states; one may confidently assert that when thirty thousand men fight a pitched battle against an equal number of troops, there are about twenty thousand on each side with the pox.'

'That is admirable,' said Candide, 'but we must get you cured.'

'How can I be?' said Pangloss. 'I haven't a sou, my friend; and in the whole area of this globe you cannot be bled or given an enema without paying, or without someone paying for you.'

This last speech made up Candide's mind; he went and threw himself at the feet of his charitable Anabaptist Jacques and painted him such a touching picture of the state to which his friend was reduced that the good man had no hesitation in taking in Doctor Pangloss; he had him cured at his own expense. In the cure Pangloss lost only one eye and one ear.[14] He

---

[14] The control of syphilis with mercury was one of the very few relatively successful treatments available to eighteenth-century medicine; the results of mercury poisoning, however, could be as bad as the original disease. [eds]

wrote a good hand and knew arithmetic perfectly. The Anabaptist Jacques made him his book-keeper.

Two months later, having to go to Lisbon on business, he took his two philosophers on his ship with him. Pangloss explained to him how everything was for the very best. Jacques was not of this opinion.

'Surely,' he said, 'men must have corrupted nature a little, for they were not born wolves, and they have become wolves: God gave them neither twenty-four-pounder cannon nor bayonets, and they have made bayonets and cannon to destroy one another. I could put bankrupticies into account, and the justice which seizes the goods of the bankrupt to defraud their creditors of them.'

'All that was indispensable,' replied the one-eyed Doctor, 'and private misfortunes make up the general good; so that the more private misfortunes there are, the more all is well.'

While he was reasoning, the air darkened, the winds blew from the four corners of the world, and the ship was assaulted by the most horrible tempest in sight of the port of Lisbon.

5
Tempest, shipwreck, earthquake, and what happened to Doctor Pangloss, Candide, and the Anabaptist Jacques

Half the passengers, weakened, nearly dying of those inconceivable tortures that the rolling of a ship imparts to the nerves and all the humours of a body tossed in opposite directions, had not even the strength to worry about the danger. The other half were uttering screams and prayers; the sails were torn, the masts shattered, the vessel split open. Those who could worked, no one co-operated, no one commanded. The Anabaptist was helping a little with the work; he was on the main deck; a frenzied sailor struck him a hard blow and stretched him on the planks, but got such a jolt from the blow he gave him that he fell out of the ship headfirst. He was caught on a piece of broken mast and remained dangling from it. The good Jacques runs to his aid,

helps him to climb back up, and by this effort is flung headfirst into the sea in full view of the sailor, who lets him perish without even deigning to look at him. Candide approaches, sees his benefactor come up again for a moment and then be swallowed up forever. He wants to throw himself into the sea after him; the philosopher Pangloss stops him, proving to him that the Lisbon roads had been formed expressly for this Anabaptist to be drowned in. While he was proving this *a priori*, the ship splits open and everyone perishes with the exception of Pangloss, Candide, and that brute of a sailor who had drowned the virtuous Anabaptist; the scoundrel swam successfully ashore and Pangloss and Candide were carried there on a plank.

When they had recovered themselves a little, they walked toward Lisbon; they had a little money left, with which they hoped to be saved from hunger after escaping from the tempest.

Hardly have they set foot in the city, weeping over the death of their benefactor, when they feel the earth tremble under their feet; the sea rises boiling in the port and shatters the vessels that are at anchor.[15] Whirlwinds of flame and ashes cover the streets and public squares, the houses crumble, the roofs are tumbled down upon the foundations, and the foundations disintegrate; thirty thousand inhabitants of every age and of either sex are crushed beneath the ruins. Said the sailor, whistling and swearing: 'There'll be something to pick up here.' Said Pangloss: 'What can be the sufficient reason for this phenomenon?' 'It is the end of the world,' exclaimed Candide.

The sailor runs headlong into the midst of the debris, braves death to find money, finds some, seizes it, gets drunk, and when he has slept it off buys the favours of the first girl of good will he meets upon the ruins of demolished houses and in the midst of the dying and the dead. Pangloss meanwhile was tugging at his sleeve: 'My friend,' he said, 'this is not good, you are departing from universal reason, you are choosing your time badly.'

''Sblood and zounds!' the other replied. 'I am a sailor, and born at Batavia; I have stamped on the crucifix four times on four trips to

---

[15]   The Lisbon earthquake and fire (November 1, 1755), which killed over 30,000 people and reduced the city to ruins, led Voltaire to make strong attacks on philosophical optimism, especially in his *Poem on the Lisbon Disaster* (written in 1755) and in *Candide*. [Frame]

Japan;[16] you certainly picked the right man, you and your universal reason!'

Candide had been wounded by some splinters of stone; he was stretched out in the street and covered with debris. He said to Pangloss: 'Alas! get me a little wine and oil, I am dying.'

'This earthquake is not a new thing,' replied Pangloss. 'The town of Lima suffered the same shocks in America last year; same causes, same effects; there is certainly a vein of sulphur underground from Lima to Lisbon.'

'Nothing is more probable,' said Candide, 'but for the love of God, a little oil and wine.'

'What do you mean, probable?' replied the philosopher. 'I maintain that the matter is proved.' Candide lost consciousness, and Pangloss brought him a little water from a neighbouring fountain.

The next day, having found a few victuals as they slipped through the ruins, they restored their strength a bit. Then they worked like the rest to relieve the inhabitants who had escaped death. A few citizens whom they had helped gave them as good a dinner as could be provided in such a disaster. True, the meal was sad, the guests watered their bread with their tears; but Pangloss consoled them by assuring them that things could not be otherwise.

'For,' he said, 'all this is for the very best. For if there is a volcano in Lisbon, it could not be anywhere else. For it is impossible that things should not be where they are. For all is well.'

A little dark man, a familiar of the Inquisition, who was beside him, spoke up politely and said: 'Apparently the gentleman does not believe in original sin; *for*, if all is for the best, then there has been neither fall nor punishment.'

'I very humbly beg Your Excellency's pardon,' replied Pangloss still more politely, 'for the fall of man and the curse necessarily entered into the best of possible worlds.'

'Then the gentleman does not believe in free will?' said the familiar.

'Your Excellency will excuse me,' said Pangloss; 'free will can coexist with absolute necessity, for it was necessary that we should be free; for after all, predetermined will ...'

Pangloss was in the middle of his sentence when the familiar gave a nod to his armed attendant, who was pouring him out some port, or Oporto, wine.

6

How they held a fine auto-da-fé to prevent earthquakes, and how Candide was flogged

After the earthquake, which had destroyed three-quarters of Lisbon, the country's wise men had found no more efficacious means of preventing total ruin than to give the people a fine auto-da-fé;[17] it was decided by the University of Coimbra that the spectacle of a few persons burned by a slow fire in great ceremony is an infallible secret for keeping the earth from quaking.

They had consequently seized a Biscayan convicted of having married his godchild's godmother, and two Portuguese who when eating a chicken had taken out the bacon;[18] after dinner they came and bound Doctor Pangloss and his disciple Candide, the one for having spoken, and the other for having listened with an air of approbation; both were taken separately into extremely cool apartments in which one was never bothered by the sun;[19] a week later they were each clad in a sanbenito,[20] and their heads were adorned with paper mitres; Candide's mitre

---

[16]   To discourage trade with the Christians, the Japanese required European merchants to stamp on the cross as a sign of rejection of Christianity. [Frame]

[17]   From the Portuguese, 'act of the faith': the ceremony attendant to a judgement by the Inquisition: hence the burning of heretics as a result of such a judgement. [Frame]

[18]   Thus showing that they were Jews still secretly faithful to Judaism. [Frame]

[19]   Prison cells. [Frame]

[20]   A yellow robe worn by heretics condemned to the stake by the Inquisition. [Frame]

and sanbenito were painted with flames upside down and with devils that had neither tails nor claws; but Pangloss's devils wore claws and tails, and his flames were right side up.

Thus dressed, they marched in procession and heard a very pathetic sermon followed by some beautiful music in a droning plain-song. Candide was flogged in time to the singing, the Biscayan and the two men who wouldn't eat the bacon were burned, and Pangloss was hanged although this is not the custom. On the same day the earth quaked again with a fearful crash.

Candide, terrified, dumbfounded, bewildered, bleeding and quivering all over, said to himself:

'If this is the best of all possible worlds, then what are the others? I could let it pass if I had only been flogged, that happened also with the Bulgarians; but, O my dear Pangloss, greatest of philosophers, was it necessary that I see you hanged without knowing why! O my dear Anabaptist, best of men, was it necessary that you be drowned in the port! O Mademoiselle Cunégonde, pearl of young ladies, was it necessary that your belly be slit open!'

He was going back barely supporting himself, preached at, flogged, absolved and blessed, when an old woman accosted him and said: 'My son, take courage, follow me.'

7
How an old woman took care of Candide, and how he recovered that which he loved

Candide did not take courage, but he followed the old woman into a hovel; she gave him a jar of ointment to rub on and left him food and drink; she showed him a fairly clean little bed; beside the bed there was a suit of clothes.

'Eat, drink, sleep,' she said, 'and may Our Lady of Atocha, My Lord Saint Anthony of Padua, and My Lord Saint James of Compostela take care of you. I shall come back tomorrow.'

Candide, still astounded at all he had seen, at all he had suffered, and even more at the old woman's charity, tried to kiss her hand.

'It is not my hand you should kiss,' said the old woman. 'I shall come back tomorrow. Rub yourself with ointment, eat, and sleep.'

Candide for all his misfortunes ate and slept. The next day the old woman brings him some breakfast, examines his back, rubs it herself with another ointment; later she brings him dinner; she returns toward evening and brings supper. The day after, she again performed the same ceremonies.

'Who are you?' Candide kept asking her. 'Who has inspired you with such kindness? How can I possibly thank you?'

The good woman never made any answer; she returned toward evening and brought no supper. 'Come with me,' she said, 'and don't say a word.'

She takes him by the arm and walks with him into the country for about a quarter of a mile; they arrive at an isolated house surrounded with gardens and canals. The old woman knocks on a little door. It is opened; she takes Candide by a hidden staircase into a gilded boudoir, leaves him on a brocaded sofa, closes the door, and goes away. Candide thought he was dreaming and considered his whole life as a sinister dream and the present moment as a sweet dream.

The old woman soon reappeared; she was supporting with difficulty a trembling woman of majestic stature, gleaming with precious stones and covered with a veil. 'Remove that veil,' said the old woman to Candide. The young man approaches, he lifts the veil with a timid hand. What a moment! What a surprise! He thinks he sees Mademoiselle Cunégonde, he did indeed see her, it was she herself. His strength fails him, he cannot utter a word, he falls at her feet. Cunégonde falls on the sofa. The old woman plies them copiously with aromatic spirits; they regain their senses, they speak to each other; at first it is only disconnected words, questions and answers at cross purposes, sighs, tears, cries. The old woman recommends that they makes less noise, and leaves them by themselves.

'What! Is it you?' said Candide. 'You are alive! I find you again here in Portugal! Then you were not raped? Your belly was not slit open, as the philosopher Pangloss had assured me?'

'Oh yes,' said the fair Cunégonde, 'but people do not always die of those two accidents.'

'But were your father and mother killed?'

''Tis only too true,' said Cunégonde, weeping.

'And your brother?'

'My brother was killed too.'

'And why are you in Portugal, and how did you learn I was here, and by what strange adventure did you have me brought to this house?'

'I will tell you all that,' replied the lady; 'but first you must tell me everything that has happened to you since the innocent kiss that you gave me and the kicks that you received.'

Candide obeyed her with profound respect; and though he was dumfounded, though his voice was weak and trembling, though his spine still hurt a little, he told her in the most naive manner all that he had undergone since the moment of their separation. Cunégonde kept raising her eyes to heaven; she shed tears at the death of the good Anabaptist and of Pangloss; after which she spoke in these terms to Candide, who did not miss a word and devoured her with his eyes.

8
Cunégonde's story

'I was in bed and fast asleep when it pleased Heaven to send the Bulgarians to our fine castle of Thunder-ten-tronkch; they slaughtered my father and brother and cut my mother into pieces. A big Bulgarian six feet tall, seeing that I had lost consciousness at the sight of this, set about raping me; this brought me to, I regained my senses, I screamed, I struggled, I bit, I scratched, I tried to tear that big Bulgarian's eyes out, not knowing that all that was happening in my father's castle was a matter of custom; the brute stabbed me with a knife in the left side and I still bear the mark.' 'Alas! I certainly hope I shall see it,' said the naive Candide. 'You shall see it,' said Cunégonde, 'but let me go on.' 'Go on,' said Candide. She took up the thread of her story thus:

'A Bulgarian captain came in, he saw me all bleeding, and the soldier did not disturb himself. The captain grew angry at the lack of respect this brute showed him, and killed him upon my body. Then he had my wounds dressed and took me to his quarters as a prisoner of war. I laundered the few shirts he had, I did his cooking; he found me very pretty, I must admit; and I shall not deny that he was very well built and had soft white skin; for the rest little wit, little philosophy; it was easy to see that he had not been brought up by Doctor Pangloss. After three months, having lost all his money as well as his taste for me, he sold me to a Jew named Don Issachar, who traded in Holland and Portugal and had a passionate love of women. This Jew grew much attached to my

person but could not triumph over it; I resisted him better than I did the Bulgarian soldier. A person of honour may have been raped once, but her virtue gains strength from it. The Jew, to tame me, brought me to this country house that you see. I had thought until then that there was nothing on earth so splendid as the castle of Thunder-ten-tronckh. I was undeceived.

'The Grand Inquisitor noticed me one day at Mass; he eyed me a great deal, and sent word to me that he had secret affairs to speak to me about. I was taken to his palace, I informed him of my birth; he pointed out to me how much it was beneath my rank to belong to an Israelite. On his behalf it was proposed to Don Issachar to yield me to His Lordship. Don Issachar, who is the court banker and a man of influence, would do no such thing. The Inquisitor threatened him with an auto-da-fé. Finally my Jew, intimidated, made a bargain by which the house and I would belong to them both in common, the Jew would have Monday, Wednesday, and the Sabbath day for him, and the Inquisitor would have the other days of the week. This agreement has lasted for six months. It has not been without quarrels, for it has often been undecided whether the night between Saturday and Sunday belongs to the old law or the new. For my part, thus far I have resisted them both, and I think that is the reason why I have still been loved.

'Finally, to turn aside the scourge of earthquakes and to intimidate Don Issachar, My Lord the Inquisitor was pleased to celebrate an auto-da-fé. He did me the honour of inviting me. I had a very good seat; they served the ladies with refreshments between the Mass and the execution. Truly I was seized with horror on seeing them burn those two Jews and that worthy Biscayan who had married the godmother of his godchild; but what was my surprise, my fright, my distress, when I saw, in a sanbenito and under a mitre, a face resembling that of Pangloss! I rubbed my eyes, I looked attentively, I saw him hanged; I fell into a faint; hardly was I regaining my senses when I saw you stripped stark naked; that was the height of horror, consternation, grief, despair. I will tell you truthfully that your skin is even whiter and more perfectly rosy than that of my Bulgarian captain. This sight redoubled all the feelings that crushed me, that devoured me. I cried out, I tried to say "stop barbarians!" but my voice failed me, and my cries would have been useless. When you had been well flogged, I said: "How can it be that the charming Candide and the wise Pangloss are in Lisbon one to receive a hundred lashes and the other to be hanged by order of My Lord the Inquisitor whose dearly beloved I am?" Then Pangloss deceived me most cruelly when he told me that all is for the very best.'

'Agitated, bewildered, now beside myself and now ready to die of faintness, I had my mind filled with the massacre of my father, mother, and brother, the insolence of my horrid Bulgarian soldier, the stab he gave me, my slavery, my work as a cook, my Bulgarian captain, my horrid Don Issachar, my abominable Inquisitor, the hanging of Doctor Pangloss, that long *miserere* in droning plain-song during which they were whipping you, and above all the kiss I gave you behind a screen the day I saw you for the last time. I praised God, who was bringing you back to me through so many trials. I charged my old woman to take care of you and to bring you here as soon as she could. She has carried out my commission very well; I have enjoyed the inexpressible pleasure of seeing you again, hearing you, speaking to you. You must be ravenously hungry; my appetite is good; let's begin with supper.'

So they both sit down to table and after supper resume their places on that handsome sofa that has been already mentioned; they were there when Señor Don Issachar, one of the masters of the house, arrived. It was the Sabbath day. He was coming to enjoy his rights and expound his tender love.

9
What happened to Cunégonde, Candide, the Grand Inquisitor, and a Jew

This Issachar was the most choleric Hebrew ever seen in Israel since the Babylonian captivity.

'What!' he said. 'Bitch of a Galilean, My Lord the Inquisitor isn't enough? This scoundrel must share with me too?'

So saying, he draws a long dagger which he always carried and, not thinking that his adversary was armed, throws himself upon Candide; but our good Westphalian had received a fine sword from the old woman together with the

suit. He draws his sword, although he had a very gentle character, and stretches out the Israelite stone dead on the floor at the feet of the fair Cunégonde.

'Holy Virgin!' she cried, 'what is to become of us? A man killed in my house! If the law comes, we are lost.'

'If Pangloss had not been hanged,' said Candide, 'he would give us good advice in this extremity, for he was a great philosopher. Failing him, let us consult the old woman.'

She was very prudent, and was beginning to state her advice, when another little door opened. It was one hour after midnight, it was the beginning of Sunday. That day belonged to My Lord the Inquisitor. He came in and saw the flogged Candide sword in hand, a dead man stretched on the floor, Cunégonde terrified, and the old woman giving advice.

Here is what went on in that moment in Candide's soul, and how he reasoned: 'If this holy man calls for help, he will have me burned without fail; he may do as much to Cunégonde; he has had me pitilessly whipped; he is my rival; I have started killing, there is no hesitating.'

This reasoning was clear-cut and swift, and without giving the Inquisitor the time to recover from his surprise, he pierces him through and through and tosses him beside the Jew.

'Now here's another one,' said Cunégonde; 'there is no more chance of pardon; we are excommunicated, our last hour is come. How could you, who were born so mild, manage to kill one Jew and one Inquisitor in two minutes?'

'My fair lady,' replied Candide, 'when a man is in love, jealous, and whipped by the Inquisition, he is out of his mind.'

The old woman then spoke up and said: 'There are three Andalusian horses in the stable with their saddles and bridles: let the brave Candide prepare them; My Lady has moidores[21] and diamonds; let us mount quickly, although I can ride on only one buttock, and let us go to Cádiz; the weather could not be finer, and it is a great pleasure to travel in the cool of the night.'

Immediately Candide saddles the three horses. Cunégonde, the old woman, and he do thirty miles at one stretch. While they were riding away, the Holy Hermandad[22] arrives in the

---

[21]   A gold coin of Portugal and Brazil. [Frame]

[22]   The Holy Brotherhood, an association formed in Spain with a police force to track down criminals. [Frame]

house; they bury His Lordship in a beautiful church and they toss Don Issachar on the dump.

Candide, Cunégonde, and the old woman were already in the little town of Avacena in the midst of the mountains of the Sierra Morena; and they were talking as follows in an inn.

10
In what distress Candide, Cunégonde, and the old woman arrive at Cádiz; and about their embarkation

'Now who can have stolen my pistoles[23] and my diamonds?' said Cunégonde, weeping. 'What shall we live on? What shall we do? Where shall we find Inquisitors and Jews to give me others?'

'Alas!' said the old woman. 'I strongly suspect a reverend Franciscan father who slept in the same inn with us yesterday at Badajoz; God keep me from forming a rash judgement, but he came into our room twice and he left long before us.'

'Alas!' said Candide, 'the good Pangloss had often proved to me that the goods of the earth are common to all men, that each has an equal right to them. That Franciscan, according to these principles, should certainly have left us enough to complete our trip. Have you nothing at all left then, my fair Cunégonde?'

'Not a maravedi,'[24] said she. 'What should we do?' said Candide. 'Let's sell one of the horses,' said the old woman. 'I'll ride on the crupper behind my lady, although I can ride on only one buttock, and we will get to Cádiz.'

In the same hostelry there was a Benedictine prior; he bought the horse at a bargain. Candide, Cunégonde, and the old woman passed through Lucena, Chillas, Lebrixa, and at last reached Cádiz. There a fleet was being equipped and troops assembled to bring to terms the reverend Jesuit Fathers in Paraguay, who were accused of causing one of their tribes, near the town of San Sacramento, to revolt against the kings of Spain and Portugal.[25] Candide, having served with the Bulgarians, performed the Bulgarian drill before the general of the little army with so much grace, celerity, skill, pride, and agility, that they gave him an infantry company to command. Here he is a captain; he embarks with Mademoiselle Cunégonde, the old woman, two valets, and the two Andalusian horses that had belonged to His Lordship the Grand Inquisitor of Portugal.

During the whole crossing they reasoned a great deal about the philosophy of poor Pangloss.

'We are going to another universe,' said Candide; 'no doubt it is in that one that all is well. For it must be admitted that one might groan a little over what happens in the physical and the moral domain in ours.'

'I love you will all my heart,' said Cunégonde, 'but my soul is still frightened by what I have seen, what I have undergone.'

'All will be well,' replied Candide; 'the sea of this new world is already better than the seas of our Europe; it is calmer, the winds are more constant. It is certainly the new world that is the best of possible universes.'

'God grant it,' said Cunégonde; 'but I have been so horribly unhappy in mine that my heart is almost closed to hope.'

'You complain,' the old woman said to them. 'Alas! You have not undergone misfortunes such as mine.'

Cunégonde almost burst out laughing, and thought this good woman very comical to claim to be more unfortunate than herself.

'Alas!' she said to her, 'my dear woman, unless you have been raped by two Bulgarians, been stabbed twice in the belly, had two of your castles demolished and two mothers and two fathers slaughtered before your eyes, and seen two of your beloveds flogged in an auto-da-fé, I don't see that you can outdo me; plus the fact that I was born a Baroness with seventy-two quarterings, and now I have been a cook.'

'My Lady,' replied the old woman, 'you do not know my birth, and if I showed you my bottom you would not speak as you do and you would suspend your judgement.'

---

[23] A Spanish gold coin. [Frame]

[24] A small Spanish copper coin. [Frame]

[25] This revolt occurred in 1756. [Frame]

This speech aroused extreme curiosity in the minds of Cunégonde and Candide. The old woman spoke to them in these terms.

11
The old woman's story

'My eyes were not always bloodshot and red-rimmed; my nose did not always touch my chin, and I was not always a servant. I am the daughter of Pope Urban X and the Princess of Palestrina.[26] Until the age of fourteen I was brought up in a palace to which all the castles of your German barons would not have served as stables, and one of my dresses was worth more than all the magnificence of Westphalia. I grew in beauty, graces, and talents, in the midst of pleasures, respect, and hopes. Already I inspired love, my bosom was forming; and what a bosom! White, firm, sculptured like that of the Venus de' Medici. And what eyes! What eyelids! What black eyebrows! What flames shone in my two irises and dimmed the glistening of the stars, as the neighbourhood poets used to tell me. The women who dressed and undressed me fell into ecstasies when they looked at me in front and behind, and all the men would have liked to be in their place.

'I was betrothed to a sovereign prince of Massa-Carrara. What a prince! As handsome as I, formed of sweetness and charms, agleam with wit and afire with love. I loved him as one loves for the first time, with idolatrous frenzy. The nuptials were prepared. The pomp, the magnificence were unheard of; there were continual festivities, tournaments, comic operas, and all Italy composed for me sonnets not one of which was passable.

'The moment of my happiness was at hand when an old marquise who had been my prince's mistress invited him to have some chocolate at her house. He died in less than two hours in frightful convulsions. But that is only a trifle. My mother, in despair, yet much less afflicted than I, decided to tear herself away for a time from such a fateful place. She had a very beautiful estate near Gaeta.[27] We embarked on a local galley, gilded like the altar of St Peter's in Rome. Suddenly a pirate from Salé[28] swoops down on us and boards us. Our soldiers defended themselves like soldiers of the Pope; they all fell on their knees, throwing away their arms, and begging the pirates for absolution *in articulo mortis.*[29]

'Immediately they stripped them naked as monkeys, and my mother too, our ladies of honour too, and me too. The diligence with which those gentlemen undress people is a wonderful thing. But what surprised me more was that they put their fingers in a place in all of us where we women ordinarily admit only the nozzle of a syringe. This ceremony seemed quite strange to me; that is how one judges of everything when one has never been out of one's country. I soon learned that this was to see whether we had not hidden some diamonds there; it is a custom established from time immemorial among the civilized nations that roam the seas. I learned that My Lords the religious Knights of Malta never fail to do this when they capture Turkish men and women; it is a rule of international law that has never been broken.

'I shall not tell you how hard it is for a young princess to be taken to Morocco as a slave with her mother. You can imagine well enough all that we had to suffer in the pirate ship. My mother was still very beautiful; our ladies of honour, our mere chambermaids had more charms than can be found in all Africa. As for me, I was ravishing, I was beauty and grace itself, and I was a virgin. I was not so for long: that flower that had been reserved for the handsome Prince of Massa-Carrara was ravished from me by the pirate captain. He was an abominable Negro

---

[26] Author's posthumous note: 'Observe the author's extreme discretion. There has been up to now no Pope named Urban X. The author fears to assign a bastard daughter to a known Pope. What circumspection! What delicacy of conscience!' [Frame]

[27] An Italian port north-west of Naples. [Frame]

[28] A Moroccan port on the Atlantic near Rabat, once a headquarters for pirates. [Frame]

[29] At the point of death. [Frame]

who yet thought he was doing me much honour. Indeed My Lady the Princess of Palestrina and I had to be very strong to endure all we underwent until we arrived in Morocco. But let's get on; these are things so common that they are not worth speaking of.

'Morocco was swimming in blood when we arrived. Fifty sons of the Emperor Muley Ismael each had a faction; which produced in effect fifty civil wars, of blacks against blacks, blacks against tans, tans against tans, mulattos against mulattos. It was a continual carnage over the whole extent of the empire.

'Hardly had we landed when some blacks, of a faction hostile to that of my pirate, came up to take his booty from him. After the diamonds and the gold, we were the most precious thing he had. I was witness to a combat such as you never see in your European climates. The blood of the northern peoples is not ardent enough. They are not mad about women to the point that is common in Africa. It seems as though your Europeans have milk in their veins; it is vitriol, it is fire that flows in those of the inhabitants of Mount Atlas and the neighbouring countries. They fought with the fury of the lions, tigers, and snakes of the country to see who should have use. One Moor seized my mother by the right arm, my captain's lieutenant held her back by the left arm; a Moorish soldier took her by one leg, one of the pirates held her by the other. In a moment nearly all our girls found themselves pulled in this way by four soldiers. My captain kept me hidden behind him. He had his scimitar in hand, and was killing everything that opposed his rage. Finally I saw all our Italian women and my mother torn, cut, massacred, by the monsters who were fighting over them. My fellow captives, those who had captured them, soldiers, sailors, blacks, tans, whites, mulattos, and finally my captain – all were killed, and I remained dying on a heap of dead. Similar scenes were taking place, as everyone knows, over an area of more than three hundred square leagues, without anyone failing to say the five prayers a day ordained by Mohammed.

'I extricated myself with great difficulty from the press of so many heaped-up bleeding corpses, and I dragged myself beneath a big orange tree at the edge of a nearby stream; there I fell down from fright, weariness, horror, despair, and hunger. Soon afterward my exhausted senses gave themselves up to a sleep that was more like a swoon than a rest. I was in this state of weakness and insensibility, between life and death, when I felt something pressing on me and moving on my body. I opened my eyes and saw a white man of good appearance who was sighing and muttering between his teeth: *"O che sciagura d'essere senza coglioni!"*[30]

12

Continuation of the old woman's misfortunes

'Astounded and delighted to hear the language of my homeland, and no less surprised at the words this man was uttering, I replied that there were worse misfortunes than the one he was complaining of. I informed him in a few words of the horrors I had suffered, and I fell back into a faint. He took me into a neighbouring house, had me put to bed and given food, served me, consoled me, flattered me, told me he had never seen anything as beautiful as I and that he never so much regretted what no one could restore to him.

'"I was born in Naples," he told me; "there they caponize two or three thousand boys every year; some die of it, others acquire a voice more beautiful than a woman's, others go and govern states. This operation was performed on me with great success, and I was a musician in the chapel of My Lady the Princess of Palestrina."

'"Of my mother!" I cried out.

'"Of your mother!" he exclaimed, weeping. "What! Can you be that young princess that I brought up until the age of six, and who already then promised to be as beautiful as you are?"

'"I am indeed; my mother is four hundred yards from here, cut into quarters under a heap of dead."

'I told him everything that had happened to me; he too told me his adventures, and informed me that he had been sent by a Christian power to the King of Morocco to conclude a treaty with that monarch by which he would be furnished with gunpowder, cannon, and ships to help him to exterminate the commerce of the

---

[30] 'Oh, what an affliction to be without testicles!' [Frame]

other Christians. "My mission is performed," this honest eunuch said; "I am going to embark at Ceuta and I will take you back to Italy. *Ma che sciagura d'essere senza coglioni!*"

'I thanked him with tears of emotion, and instead of taking me to Italy he conducted me to Algiers and sold me to the Dey of that province. Hardly was I sold when the plague which has spread all over Africa, Asia, and Europe broke out furiously in Algiers. You have seen earthquakes; but, My Lady, have you ever had the plague?'

'Never,' replied the Baroness.

'If you had had it,' the old woman went on, 'you would admit that it is far worse than an earthquake. It is very common in Africa; I was struck with it. Imagine what a situation for the daughter of a Pope, aged fifteen, who in three months' time had undergone poverty and slavery, had been raped almost every day, had seen her mother cut into quarters, had endured hunger and war, and was now dying of the plague in Algiers. However, I did not die of it; but my eunuch and the Dey and almost all the seraglio of Algiers perished.

'When the first ravages of this frightful plague were over, the Dey's slaves were sold. A merchant bought me and took me to Tunis. He sold me to another merchant, who resold me at Tripoli; from Tripoli I was resold to Alexandria, from Alexandria resold to Smyrna, from Smyrna to Constantinople. I finally belonged to an Aga of the Janizaries, [31] who was soon ordered to go and defend Azov against the Russians who were besieging it.

'The Aga, who was a very gallant man, took his whole seraglio with him and lodged us in a little fort on the Maeotian Marsh, [32] guarded by two black eunuchs and twenty soldiers. They killed a prodigious number of Russians, but these repaid us with interest. Azov was put to fire and sword, and there was no pardon for sex nor for age; nothing remained but our little fort; the enemy tried to take us by famine. The twenty Janizaries had sworn never to surrender. The extremities of hunger to which they were reduced forced them to eat our two eunuchs, for fear of violating their oath. A few days later they resolved to eat the women.

'We had with us a very pious and very compassionate imam, [33] who preached them a fine sermon by which he persuaded them not to kill us completely. "Just cut off one buttock from each of these ladies," he said, "you will make very good cheer; if you have come back, you will have as much again in a few days; heaven will be pleased with you for so charitable an action, and you will be rescued."

'He had great eloquence; he persuaded them. They performed this horrible operation on us. The imam applied to us the same balm that they put on children who have just been circumcised. We were all at the point of death.

'Scarcely had the Janizaries eaten the meal we had furnished them when the Russians arrived in flat-bottomed boats; not one Janizary escaped. The Russians paid no attention to the state we were in. There are French surgeons everywhere; one of them, who was very skilful, took care of us; he cured us; and I shall remember all my life that when my wounds were fully closed, he made propositions to me. For the rest, he told us all to console ourselves; he assured us that the same sort of thing had happened in many sieges and that it was a law of war.

'As soon as my companions could walk, they were sent to Moscow. I fell to the lot of a Boyar, [34] who made me his gardener and gave me twenty lashes a day. But when this lord was broken on the wheel two years later with some thirty other Boyars for some petty fuss at court, I profited by this adventure; I fled; I crossed the whole of Russia; I was long a servant in an inn at Riga, then at Rostock, at Wismar, at Leipzig, Cassel, Utrecht, Leyden, the Hague, Rotterdam; I have grown old in misery and opprobrium, having only half a backside, always remembering that I was the daughter of a Pope; a hundred

---

[31]   A high officer of the guards of the Turkish Sultan. [Frame]

[32]   Ancient name for the Sea of Azov. [Frame]

[33]   A Mohammedan priest. [Frame]

[34]   Russian nobleman. [Frame]

times I wanted to kill myself, but I still loved life. This ridiculous foible is perhaps one of our most disastrous inclinations. For is there anything more stupid than to want to bear continually a burden that we always want to throw to the ground? To regard our being with horror, and to cling to our being? In fine, to caress the serpent that devours us until it has eaten up our heart?

'I have seen, in the countries that fate has driven me through and in the inns where I have served, a prodigious number of persons who loathed their existence; but I have seen only twelve who voluntarily put an end to their misery: three Negroes, four Englishmen, four Genevans, and a German professor named Robeck.[35] I ended up by being a servant to the Jew Don Issachar; he put me in your service, my fair young lady; I have attached myself to your destiny, and I have been more occupied with your adventures than with mine. I would never even have spoken to you of my misfortunes if you had not piqued me a little and if it were not customary on shipboard to tell stories to conquer boredom. In short, My Lady, I have experience, I know the world; have some fun, get each passenger to tell you his story; and if there is a single one who has not often cursed his life, who has not often said to himself that he was the unhappiest of men, throw me into the sea headfirst.'

13
How Candide was obliged to part from the fair Cunégonde and the old woman

The fair Cunégonde, having heard the old woman's story, showed her all the courtesy due to a person of her rank and merit. She accepted the proposition and got all the passengers one after the other to tell her their adventures; Candide and she admitted that the old woman was right.

'It is a great pity,' said Candide, 'that the wise Pangloss was hanged contrary to custom in an auto-da-fé; he would tell us wonderful things about the physical evil and the moral evil that cover earth and sea, and I would feel strong

enough to dare to offer him, respectfully, a few objections.'

As each one was telling his story the vessel moved on. They landed in Buenos Aires. Cunégonde, Captain Candide, and the old woman called on the governor, Don Fernando d'Ibaraa y Figueora y Mascarenes y Lampourdos y Souza. This lord had the pride befitting a man who bore so many names. He spoke to men with the noblest disdain, bearing his nose so high, raising his voice so pitilessly, assuming so imposing a tone, affecting so lofty a bearing, that all who addressed him were tempted to give him a beating. He loved women with a frenzy. Cunégonde seemed to him the most beautiful thing he had ever seen. The first thing he did was ask if she were not the Captain's wife. The air with which he asked his question alarmed Candide: he did not dare say she was his wife because in fact she was not; he did not dare say she was his sister, because she was not that either; and although this diplomatic lie was once very fashionable among the ancients [36] and might be useful to the moderns, his soul was too pure to be disloyal to the truth. 'Mademoiselle Cunégonde,' he said, 'is to do me the honour of marrying me, and we beseech Your Excellency to deign to perform our wedding ceremony.'

Don Fernando d'Ibaraa y Figueora y Mascarenes y Lampourdos y Souza, twirling his moustache, smiled bitterly and ordered Captain Candide to go pass his company in review. Candide obeyed; the governor remained with Mademoiselle Cunégonde. He declared his passion to her, protested that the next day he would marry her publicly in church, or otherwise, as it might please her charms. Cunégonde asked him for a quarter of an hour to collect herself, to consult the old woman, and to make up her mind.

The old woman said to Cunégonde:
'My Lady, you have seventy-two quarterings and not a penny; it depends on you alone to be the wife of the greatest lord in South America, who has a very handsome moustache; is it for you to pride yourself on an invincible fidelity? You have been raped by the Bulgarians; a Jew

---

[35] Author of theses on the folly of loving life, who drowned himself in 1739 at the age of sixty-seven. [Frame]

[36] A reference to Abraham and Sarah (Genesis 12:12–13 and again 20:2–3) and to Isaac and Rebekah (Genesis 26:7–9). [Frame]

and an Inquisitor have enjoyed your good graces. Misfortunes confer rights. I admit that if I were in your place, I would have no scruple over marrying My Lord the Governor and making the fortune of Captain Candide.'

While the old woman was speaking with all the prudence that age and experience give, a little vessel was seen to enter the port; it brought an alcaide and some alguazils,[37] and here is what had happened.

The old woman had guessed correctly that it was a long-sleeved Franciscan who stole Cunégonde's money and jewels in the town of Badajoz when she was fleeing in haste with Candide. This monk tried to sell some of the precious stones to a jeweller. The merchant recognized them as belonging to the Grand Inquisitor. The Franciscan, before being hanged, admitted that he had stolen them; he indicated the persons and the route they were taking. The flight of Cunégonde and Candide was already known. They were followed to Cádiz; with no loss of time a ship was sent in pursuit of them. The ship was already in the port of Buenos Aires. The rumour spread that an alcaide was about to land and that they were pursuing the murderers of His Lordship the Grand Inquisitor. The prudent old woman saw in an instant all that was to be done.

'You cannot flee,' she said to Cunégonde, 'and you have nothing to fear; it was not you that killed His Lordship; besides, the governor, who loves you, will not allow you to be maltreated; stay.'

She immediately ran to Candide. 'Flee,' she said, 'or you're going to be burned within an hour.' There was not a moment to lose; but how could he part with Cunégonde, and where was he to take refuge?

14
How Candide and Cacambo were received by the Jesuits in Paraguay

Candide had brought from Cádiz a valet of a type often found on the coasts of Spain and in the colonies. He was one-quarter Spanish, born of a half-breed in Tucuman;[38] he had been a choirboy, sacristan, sailor, monk, merchant's representative, soldier, lackey. His name was Cacambo, and he loved his master very much, because his master was a very good man. He saddled the two Andalusian horses as fast as possible.

'Come, master, let us take the old woman's advice, leave, and run for it without looking behind us.'

Candide shed tears. 'Oh my dear Cunégonde! Must I abandon you just when My Lord the Governor is going to perform our marriage! Cunégonde, brought here from so far, what will become of you?'

'She will get along as best she can,' said Cacambo; 'women are never at a loss; God looks after them; let's run for it.'

'Where are you taking me? Where are we going? What shall we do with Cunégonde?' said Candide.

'By St James of Compostela,' said Cacambo, 'you were going to make war on the Jesuits; let's make war for them; I know the roads well enough, I will take you to their kingdom, they will be delighted to have a captain who can drill Bulgarian style, you will make a prodigious fortune; when you don't get your due in one world you find it in another. It is a very great pleasure to see and do new things.'

'Then you have already been in Paraguay?' said Candide.

'Oh yes indeed,' said Cacambo, 'I was a servant in the College of the Assumption, and I know the government of *Los Padres*[39] as well as I know the streets of Cádiz. It is an admirable thing, this government. The kingdom is already more than three hundred leagues in diameter; it is divided into thirty provinces; *Los Padres* have everything and the people nothing; it is the masterpiece of reason and justice. For my part, I know nothing so divine as *Los Padres*, who here make war on the King of Spain and the King of Portugal, and who in Europe confess those Kings; who here kill Spaniards, and in Madrid send them to heaven; this enchants me; let's get on; you are going to be the happiest of men.

---

[37] A municipal officer and some police officers. [Frame]

[38] A province in northern Argentina. [Frame]

[39] 'The Fathers,' i.e., the Jesuits. [Frame]

What pleasure *Los Padres* will have when they learn that a captain is coming to them who knows the Bulgarian drill!'

As soon as they had reached the first barrier, Cacambo told the outpost that a captain asked to speak to My Lord the Commandant. They went to notify the main guard. A Paraguayan officer ran to the feet of the Commandant to impart the news to him. First Candide and Cacambo were disarmed; their two Andalusian horses were seized. The two strangers were brought in between two ranks of soldiers; the Commandant was at the end, three-cornered hat on head, gown tucked up, sword at side, and a half-pike in hand. He made a sign; and immediately twenty-four soldiers surround the two newcomers. A sergeant tells them they must wait, that the Commandant cannot speak to them, that the Reverend Provincial Father does not permit any Spaniard to open his mouth except in his presence or to remain more than three hours in the country.

'And where is the Reverend Provincial Father?' said Cacambo.

'He is at the parade after having said Mass,' replied the sergeant, 'and you will not be able to kiss his spurs until three hours from now.'

'But,' said Cacambo, 'the captain, who is dying of hunger as I am, is not a Spaniard, he is a German; mightn't we have breakfast while waiting for His Reverence?'

The sergeant immediately went and reported this statement to the Commandant.

'Praise God!' said this lord. 'Since he is a German I can speak to him; let him be brought to my arbour.'

Candide was taken immediately into a leafy bower adorned with a very pretty colonnade in green and gold marble and with trellises which enclosed parrots, two kinds of humming-birds, guinea fowl, and all the rarest of birds. An excellent breakfast stood prepared in vessels of gold; and while the Paraguayans ate corn out of wooden bowls in the open fields in the blaze of the sun, the Reverend Father Commandant entered the arbour.

He was a very handsome young man, full-faced, rather white-skinned, high-coloured, with arched eyebrows, keen eyes, red ears, vermilion lips, his manner proud, but with a pride that was neither that of a Spaniard nor that of a Jesuit. Candide and Cacambo were given back their arms, which had been taken from them, as well as their two Andalusian horses; Cacambo fed them oats near the arbour and kept his eye constantly on them for fear of a surprise.

Candide first kissed the hem of the Commandant's robe, then they sat down to table.

'So you are a German?' the Jesuit said to him in that language.

'Yes, Reverend Father,' said Candide.

Each one, as he pronounced these words, looked at the other with extreme surprise and an emotion which they could not master.

'And what part of Germany are you from?' said the Jesuit.

'From the filthy province of Westphalia,' said Candide; 'I was born in the castle of Thunder-ten-tronckh.'

'Heavens! Is it possible!' cried the Commandant. 'What a miracle!' cried Candide.

'Can it be you?' said the Commandant.

'That is not possible,' said Candide. They both fall over backwards, they embrace, they shed torrents of tears.

'What! Can that be you, Reverend Father? You, the brother of the fair Cunégonde! You, who were killed by the Bulgarians! You, the son of My Lord the Baron! You a Jesuit in Paraguay! I must admit that this world is a strange thing. O Pangloss! Pangloss! How happy you would be if you had not been hanged!'

The Commandant sent away the Negro slaves and the Paraguayans who were serving drink in rock-crystal goblets. He thanked God and St Ignatius a thousand times; he clasped Candide in his arms; their faces were bathed in tears.

'You would be even more astounded, more touched, more beside yourself,' said Candide, 'if I told you that Mademoiselle Cunégonde your sister, whom you thought disembowelled, is in full health.'

'Where?'

'In your neighbourhood, with My Lord the Governor of Buenos Aires; and I was coming to make war on you.'

Each word they uttered in this long conversation piled prodigy upon prodigy. Their whole souls flew from their tongues, listened in their ears, sparkled in their eyes. Since they were Germans, they stayed long at table, waiting for the Reverend Father Provincial; and the Commandment spoke thus to his dear Candide.

15

How Candide killed the brother of his dear Cunégonde

'All my life I shall have present in my memory the horrible day when I saw my father and mother killed and my sister raped. When the Bulgarians were withdrawn, that adorable sister was not found, and my mother my father, and I, two serving girls and three little boys who had all been slaughtered were put into a cart to be taken and buried in a Jesuit chapel two leagues from the castle of my forefathers. A Jesuit threw holy water on us; it was horribly salt; a few drops got into my eyes; the father noticed a tiny movement in my eyelid; he put his hand on my heart and felt it beating; I was rescued, and after three weeks it was as if nothing had happened. You know, my dear Candide, that I was very pretty, I became even more so; so the Reverend Father Kroust,[40] superior of the house, conceived the most tender friendship for me; he gave me the dress of a novice; some time later I was sent to Rome. The Father General needed some young German Jesuit recruits. The sovereigns of Paraguay receive as few Spanish Jesuits as they can; they prefer foreigners, since they feel more their masters. I was judged fit by the Reverend Father General to go and labour in this vineyard. We set out, a Pole, a Tyrolese, and I. On arriving, I was honoured with a subdeaconate and a lieutenancy; today I am a colonel and priest. We shall give the King of Spain's troops a vigorous reception; I warrant you they will be excommunicated and beaten. Providence sends you here to second us. But is it really true that my dear sister Cunégonde is in the neighbourhood with the Governor of Buenos Aires?'

Candide assured him on his oath that nothing could be truer. Their tears began to flow again.

The Baron seemed unable to tire of embracing Candide; he kept calling him his brother, his saviour.

'Ah!' he said, 'my dear Candide, perhaps we can enter the city together as conquerors and regain my sister Cunégonde.'

'That is all I wish for,' said Candide; 'for I was counting on marrying her, and I still hope to.'

'You, insolent wretch!' replied the Baron, 'You would have the impudence to marry my sister who has seventy-two quarterings! I am amazed at your effrontery in daring to speak to me of so rash a plan!'

Candide, petrified at such a speech, replied: 'Reverend Father, all the quarterings in the world have nothing to do with it; I have saved your sister from the arms of a Jew and an Inquisitor; she has obligations enough toward me, she wants to marry me; Doctor Pangloss always told me that men are equal, and certainly I shall marry her.'

'We'll see about that, you scoundrel!' said the Jesuit Baron of Thunder-ten-tronckh, and at the same time he struck him a great blow to the face with the flat of his sword. That same instant Candide drew his own and thrust it up to the hilt in the Jesuit Baron's belly; but as he drew it out all smoking he began to weep: 'Alas! Good Lord!' he said. 'I have killed my former master, my friend, my brother-in-law; I am the kindest man in the world, and here I am killing three men already, and two of the three are priests.'

Cacambo, who was standing watch at the door to the arbour, ran up.

'There is nothing left for us but to sell our lives dear,' said his master to him. 'No doubt they will be coming into the arbour, we must die arms in hand.'

Cacambo, who had seen the likes of this before, did not lose his head; he took the Jesuit robe worn by the Baron, put it over Candide's body, gave him the dead man's square bonnet, and got him to mount his horse. All this was done in the twinkling of an eye. 'Let's gallop, master. Everyone will take you for a Jesuit on his way to give order, and we will have passed the frontiers before they can come after us.'

---

[40]   Father Antoine Kroust, Jesuit, rector at Colmar from 1753 to 1763, hostile to Voltaire and the *philosophes*. [Frame]

He was already in flight as he uttered these words, and shouted in Spanish: 'Make way, make way for the Reverend Father Colonel.'

16
What happened to the two travellers with two girls, two monkeys, and the savages called Oreillons[41]

Candide and his valet were beyond the barriers, and as yet no one in the camp knew of the death of the German Jesuit. The vigilant Cacambo had taken care to fill his bag with bread, chocolate, ham, fruit, and a few bottles of wine. On their Andalusian horses they plunged into an unknown land where they found no road. Finally there appeared before them a beautiful meadow interlaced with streams. Our two travellers give food to their mounts. Cacambo proposes to his master that they eat, and sets the example.

'How,' said Candide, 'can you expect me to eat ham, when I have killed the son of My Lord the Baron and find myself condemned never to see the fair Cunégonde again in my life? What will it profit me to prolong my wretched days, since I must drag them out far from her in remorse and despair? And what will the *Journal de Trévoux*[42] say?'

As he spoke thus, he did not fail to eat. The sun was setting. The two wanderers heard a few little cries that seemed to be uttered by women. They did not know whether these were cries of pain or of joy; but they jumped to their feet hastily with the anxiety and alarm that everything inspires in an unknown country. These sounds came from two girls, stark naked, who were running lightly along the edge of the meadow, while two monkeys followed them and bit their buttocks. Candide was moved with pity; he had learned to shoot among the Bulgarians, and he could have knocked a nut off a bush without touching the leaves. He takes his double-barrelled Spanish gun, fires, and kills the two monkeys.

'God be praised, my dear Cacambo, I have delivered these two poor creatures from great peril; if I committed a sin in killing an Inquisitor and a Jesuit, I have certainly made up for it by saving the lives of these two girls. Perhaps they are two young ladies of quality, and this adventure may earn us great advantages in this country.'

He was going to continue, but his tongue was silenced when he saw these two girls tenderly embrace the two monkeys, burst into tears over their bodies, and fill the air with the most grievous cries.

'I was not expecting such goodness of soul,' he said at last to Cacambo, who answered him: 'You've done a fine piece of work there, my master; you have killed the two lovers of these young ladies.'

'Their lovers! Can this be possible? You are making fun of me, Cacambo; how can I believe you?'

'My dear master,' replied Cacambo, 'you are always astonished at everything; why do you find it so strange that in some countries there are monkeys who obtain the good graces of the ladies? They are one-quarter men as I am one-quarter Spaniard.'

'Alas!' replied Candide, 'I remember hearing Doctor Pangloss say that in other times similar accidents had happened and that these mixtures had produced Aegipans, fauns, and satyrs; that many great personages of antiquity had seen them; but I took that for fables.'

'You ought to be convinced now,' said Cacambo, 'that it is the truth, and you see how people behave who have not received a certain education; all I fear is that these ladies may get us into bad trouble.'

These solid reflections led Candide to leave the meadow and plunge into a wood. There he ate supper with Cacambo, and they both, after cursing the Inquisitor of Portugal, the Governor of Buenos Aires, and the Baron, fell asleep on some moss. When they woke up they found that they could not move; the reason was that during the night the Oreillons, the inhabitants of the country, to whom the two ladies had denounced them, had bound them with ropes of bark. They were surrounded by about fifty stark-naked

---

[41]   From the Spanish *Orejones*, suggesting 'pierced ears' or 'big ears'. The French name likewise suggests *oreilles* 'ears'. [Frame]

[42]   The Jesuit journal, founded in 1701 and edited for many years by Guillaume-François Berthier. [Frame]

Oreillons armed with arrows and stone clubs and hatchets; some were boiling up a great cauldron, others were preparing spits; and all were shouting: 'It's a Jesuit, it's a Jesuit; we shall be avenged and we shall have a good meal; let's eat Jesuit, let's eat Jesuit.'

'I told you so, my dear master,' exclaimed Cacambo sadly; 'I said that those two girls would do us a bad turn.'

Candide, perceiving the cauldron and the spits, exclaimed: 'We are certainly going to be roasted or boiled. Ah! what would Doctor Pangloss say if he saw what the pure state of nature is like? All is well; so be it; but I confess it is very cruel to have lost Mademoiselle Cunégonde and to be put on a spit by the Oreillons.'

Cacambo never lost his head. 'Do not despair about anything,' he said to the disconsolate Candide; 'I understand a bit of the lingo of these people, I'm going to speak to them.'

'Do not fail,' said Candide, 'to point out to them what frightful inhumanity it is to cook men and how unchristian it is.'

'Gentlemen,' said Cacambo, 'so you are counting on eating a Jesuit today; that is a very good thing to do; nothing is more just than to treat one's enemies thus. In fact natural law teaches us to kill our neighbour, and this is how people behave all over the world. If we do not exercise our right to eat him, that is because we have other ingredients for a good meal; but you do not have the same resources as we do; certainly it is better to eat one's enemies than to abandon the fruits of victory to the crows and the ravens. But, gentlemen, you would not want to eat your friends. You think you are going to put a Jesuit on the spit, and it is your defender, it is the enemy of your enemies that you are about to roast. For my part I was born in your country; the gentleman you see here is my master; and far from being a Jesuit, he has just killed a Jesuit, he is wearing his spoils, that is the reason for your mistake. To verify what I am telling you, take his robe, carry it to the first barrier of the kingdom of *Los Padres*, find out whether my master has not killed a Jesuit officer. It won't take you long; you can still eat us if you find I have lied to you. But if I have told you the truth, you know the principles of international law, its customs and rules, too well not to spare us.'

The Oreillons found this speech very reasonable; they deputized two notables to go with all diligence and find out the truth; the two deputies acquitted themselves of their commission like intelligent men and soon returned bearing good news. The Oreillons untied their two prisoners, paid them all sorts of courtesies, offered them girls, gave them refreshments, and conducted them all the way to the confines of their states, shouting joyfully: 'He's not a Jesuit, he's not a Jesuit!'

Candide could not tire of wondering at the reason for his deliverance. 'What a race!' he said. 'What men! What customs! If I had not had the good fortune of giving a great sword-thrust through the body of Mademoiselle Cunégonde's brother, I would have been eaten without mercy. But after all, the pure state of nature is good, since these people, instead of eating me, offered me a thousand courtesies as soon as they learned that I was not a Jesuit.'

17
Arrival of Candide and his valet in the country of Eldorado,[43] and what they saw there

When they were at the frontiers of the Oreillons, Cacambo said to Candide: 'You see, this hemisphere is no better than the other; take my word for it, let's go back to Europe by the shortest route.'

'How can we go back there?' said Candide. 'And where could we go? If I go to my own country, the Bulgarians and Abarians are slaughtering everyone; if I go back to Portugal I am burned; if we stay in this country we run the risk at any moment of being put on the spit. But how can one bring oneself to leave the part of the world where Mademoiselle Cunégonde lives?'

'Let's turn toward Cayenne,' said Cacambo; 'there we will find Frenchmen; they go all over the world; they may help us; perhaps God will have pity on us.'

It was not easy to go to Cayenne. They knew about what direction they had to go; but mountains, rivers, precipices, brigands, savages,

---

[43]   'The Golden (Country)', which a lieutenant of Pizarro claimed to have discovered. [Frame]

were terrible obstacles on all sides. Their horses died of fatigue; their provisions were used up. For the whole month they lived on wild fruits, and at last found themselves by a little river bordered with coconut trees, which supported their lives and hopes.

Cacambo, who always gave as good advice as the old woman, said to Candide: 'We are at the end of our rope, we have walked far enough; I see an empty canoe on the bank, let us fill it with coconuts, cast ourselves into this little bark, and drift with the current; a river always leads to some inhabited spot. If we do not find pleasant things, at least we shall find new things.'

'Let's go,' said Candide, 'let us recommend ourselves to Providence.'

They drifted a few leagues between banks now flowery, now barren, now smooth, now rugged. The river kept getting wider; finally it disappeared under an arch of frightful rocks that rose to the heavens. The two travellers had the hardihood to abandon themselves to the waters underneath this arch. The river, at this point narrowed, carried them along with horrible rapidity and noise. After twenty-four hours they saw daylight again, but their canoe smashed on the reefs. They had to drag themselves from rock to rock for a whole league; finally they discovered an immense horizon bordered by inaccessible mountains. The country was cultivated for pleasure as well as for need; everywhere the useful was attractive. The roads were covered, or rather adorned, with carriages brilliant in form and material, bearing men and women of singular beauty, and drawn rapidly by big red sheep which in swiftness surpassed the finest horses of Andalusia, Tetuan, and Meknes.[44]

'All the same,' said Candide, 'here is a country that is better than Westphalia.' With Cacambo he set foot on land near the first village he came upon. A few village children covered with badly torn gold brocade were playing quoits at the entrance to the village. Our two men from the other world watched them with enjoyment. Their quoits were rather wide round pieces, yellow, red, and green, which shone with singular brilliance. The travellers took a notion

to pick up a few of them; they were gold, emerald, and rubies, the least of which would have been the greatest ornament of the Mogul's throne.

'No doubt,' said Cacambo, 'these children are the sons of the King of the country playing quoits.'

The village schoolmaster appeared at the moment, to call them back to school. 'That,' said Candide, 'is the tutor of the royal family.'

The little beggars immediately left their game, leaving on the ground their quoits and everything they had been playing with. Candide picks them up, runs to the tutor, and humbly presents them to him, giving him to understand by signs that Their Royal Highnesses had forgotten their gold and their precious stones. The village schoolmaster, smiling, threw them on the ground, looked at Candide's face for a moment with much surprise, and continued on his way.

The travellers did not fail to pick up the gold, the rubies, and the emeralds. 'Where are we?' exclaimed Candide. 'Kings' children must be well brought up in this country, since they teach them to despise gold and jewels.' Cacambo was as surprised as Candide. Finally they approached the first house in the village. It was built like a European palace. A crowd of people was bustling at the door, and even more inside the house. You could hear very pleasant music and smell a delicious odour of cooking. Cacambo approached the door and head them speaking Peruvian; it was his mother tongue; for everyone knows that Cacambo was born in Tucuman[45] in a village where only that language was known. 'I will serve as your interpreter,' he said to Candide; 'let's go in, this is an inn.'

Instantly two boys and two girls of the hostelry, dressed in cloth of gold, their hair bound up with ribbons, invited them to sit at the host's table. They served four soups each garnished with two parrots, a boiled condor that weighed two hundred pounds, two roast monkeys of excellent flavour; three hundred colibri humming-birds on one platter and six hundred other humming-birds on another; exquisite stews, delicious pastries; all this on

---

[44] Tetuan and Meknes: towns in Morocco. [Frame]

[45] A province in northern Argentina. [Frame]

platters of a sort of rock crystal. The boys and girls of the inn poured several liquors made of sugar cane.

The guests were for the most part merchants and coachmen, all of the greatest politeness, who asked Cacambo many questions with the most circumspect discretion and who answered his in a wholly satisfactory manner.

When the meal was over, Cacambo, like Candide, thought to pay his bill full well by throwing on the host's table two of those big gold pieces that he had picked up; the host and hostess burst out laughing and held their sides for quite a while. Finally they recovered themselves.

'Gentlemen,' said the host, 'we can easily see that you are foreigners; we are not accustomed to see any. Pardon us if we began to laugh when you offered us in payment the pebbles of our highroads. No doubt you have none of this country's money, but it is not necessary to have any in order to dine here. All the hostelries established for the convenience of commerce are paid for by the government. You had a bad meal here because this is a poor village; but everywhere else you will be received as you deserve to be.'

Cacambo explained to Candide all the host's remarks, and Candide listened to them with the same amazement and the same bewilderment with which his friend Cacambo reported them. 'What kind of country is this, then,' they said to each other, 'unknown to the rest of the world, and where all nature is of a sort so different from ours? Probably this is the country where all is well; for there absolutely must be one of that sort. And no matter what Doctor Pangloss said about it, I often noticed that all was pretty bad in Westphalia.'

18
What they saw in the Land of Eldorado

Cacambo manifested all his curiosity to his host; the host said to him: 'I am very ignorant, and I get along all right that way; but we have here an old man who has retired from the court, who is the most learned man in the kingdom and the most communicative.' Immediately he took Cacambo to the old man. Candide was now playing only second fiddle and going along with his valet. They entered a house that was very simple, for the door was only of silver and the panelling in the apartments only of gold, but wrought with so much taste that the richest panelling did not eclipse it. True, the antechamber was encrusted only with rubies and emeralds, but the order in which everything was arranged fully made up for this extreme simplicity.

The old man received the two foreigners on a sofa stuffed with humming-bird feathers, and had them served liqueurs in diamond vases; after which he satisfied their curiosity in these terms:

'I am a hundred and seventy-two years old, and I learned from my late father, equerry to the King, of the astounding revolutions in Peru that he had witnessed. The kingdom we are in is the ancient homeland of the Incas, who left it very imprudently to go and subjugate part of the world, and who were finally destroyed by the Spaniards.

'The princes of their family who remained in their native country were wiser; they ordained, with the consent of the nation, that no inhabitant should ever leave our little kingdom; and that is what has preserved our innocence and happiness for us. The Spaniards gained some confused knowledge of this country; they called it El Dorado; and an Englishman named Lord Raleigh even came near it about a hundred years ago; but since we are surrounded by inaccessible rocks and precipices, we have up to now always been sheltered from the rapacity of the nations of Europe, who have an inconceivable rage for the pebbles and mud of our land, and who would kill us all to the last man to get some.'

The conversation was long; it bore on the form of government, customs, women, public spectacles, arts. Finally Candide, who always had a taste for metaphysics, had Cacambo ask whether there was a religion in the country.

The old man blushed a little. 'What,' he said, 'can you doubt it? Do you take us for ingrates?' Cacambo humbly asked what was the religion of Eldorado. The old man blushed again.

'Can there be two religions?' he said. 'We have, I think, the religion of everyone; we worship God from morning till evening.'

'Do you worship only one single God?' said Cacambo, who was still serving as interpreter for Candide's doubts.

'It appears,' said the old man, 'that there are not two, or three or four. I must admit that the people of your world ask very singular questions.'

Candide could not tire of having this good old man questioned; he wanted to know how they prayed to God in Eldorado.

'We do not pray to him,' said the good and respectable sage; 'we have nothing to ask him for; he has given us all we need, we thank him without ceasing.'

Candide had a curiosity to see some priests; he asked where they were. The good old man smiled.

'My friends,' he said, 'we are all priests; the King and all the heads of families solemnly sing hymns of thanksgiving every morning, and five or six thousand musicians accompany them.'

'What! you have no monks to teach, to dispute, to govern, to intrigue, and to have people burned who are not of their opinion?'

'We would have to be crazy,' said the old man; 'we are all of the same opinion, and we do not understand what you mean with your monks.'

At all these remarks Candide remained in ecstasy and said to himself:

'This is very different from Westphalia and the castle of My Lord the Baron; if our friend Pangloss had seen Eldorado, he would no longer have said that the castle of Thunder-ten-tronckh was the best thing on earth; travel is certainly necessary.'

After this long conversation, the good old man had a carriage harnessed with six sheep and gave the two travellers twelve of his servants to take them to court. 'Excuse me,' he said to them, 'if my age deprives me of the honour of accompanying you. The King will receive you in a way that will not leave you discontented, and you will doubtless pardon the customs of the country if there are some that displease you.'

Candide and Cacambo climbed into the carriage, the six sheep flew, and in less than four hours they arrived at the King's palace, situated at one end of the capital. The portal was two hundred and twenty feet high and a hundred wide; it is impossible to describe what material it was. It is easy to see what prodigious superiority it must have had over those pebbles and sand that we call gold and precious stones.

Twenty beautiful girls of the watch received Candide and Cacambo as they got out of the carriage, took them to the baths, dressed them in robes woven from humming-bird down; after which the men and women grand officers of the crown took them to His Majesty's apartment between two files of a thousand musicians each, according to the ordinary custom. When they approached the throne room, Cacambo asked one grand officer how they should go about saluting His Majesty: whether you crawled on your knees or on your belly, whether you put your hands on your head or on your backside, whether you licked the dust of the room, in short what the ceremony was.

'The custom,' said the grand officer, 'is to embrace the King and kiss him on both cheeks.'

Candide and Cacambo threw their arms around the neck of His Majesty, who received them with all the grace imaginable and politely asked them to supper.

While waiting, they were shown the town, the public buildings rising to the clouds, the market places adorned with a thousand columns, the fountains of pure water, those of rose water, and those of cane-sugar liqueurs, which flowed continually in great squares paved with a kind of precious stone which gave off a perfume like that of cloves and cinnamon.

Candide asked to see the law courts; they told him that there were none and that people never went to law. He inquired whether there were prisons, and they told him no. What surprised him even more and pleased him most was the Palace of Sciences, in which he saw a great gallery two thousand paces long all full of instruments for mathematics and physics.

After spending all afternoon touring about the thousandth part of the city, they were taken back to the King's palace; Candide sat down to the table with His Majesty, his valet Cacambo, and several ladies. Never was better cheer made, and never had a man more wit at supper than His Majesty. Cacambo explained the King's witty remarks to Candide, and even when translated they still appeared witty. Of all that astounded Candide this was not what astounded him least.

They stayed a month in this hospitable place. Candide never stopped saying to Cacambo:

'It is true, my friend, once again, that the castle where I was born is not worth the country where we are now; but after all, Mademoiselle Cunégonde is not here, and no doubt you have some mistress in Europe. If we stay here, we shall only be like the others, whereas if we return to our own world with just twelve sheep laden with the pebbles of Eldorado, we shall be richer than all the Kings put together, we shall have no more Inquisitors to fear, and we shall easily be able to recover Mademoiselle Cunégonde.'

Cacambo liked this idea; people are so fond of running about, showing off before the folks at home, and parading what they have seen on their travels, that the two happy men resolved to be so no longer and to ask His Majesty for leave to go.

'You are doing a foolish thing,' the King said to them. 'I know that my country is not much; but when a person is reasonably well off somewhere he should stay there. I certainly have no right to detain foreigners; that is a tyranny that does not exist either in our customs or in our laws; all men are free; leave when you will, but the way out is very difficult. It is impossible to go back up the rapid river on which by a miracle you came here and which runs under acres of rock. The mountains that surround my ·whole kingdom are ten thousand feet high and as perpendicular as walls; they are each more than ten leagues wide, you can descend them only by way of precipices. However, since you absolutely want to leave, I am going to give orders to the directors of machinery to make a machine that can transport you comfortably. When you have been taken to the other side of the mountains, no one will be able to accompany you farther; for my subjects have made a vow never to go beyond the mountain walls, and they are too wise to break their vow. Ask of me anything else you like.'

'We ask of Your Majesty,' said Cacambo, 'only a few sheep loaded with victuals, pebbles, and some of the country's mud.'

The King laughed. 'I do not understand,' he said, 'the taste your people of Europe have for our yellow mud; but take as much as you want, and much good may it do you.'

He immediately gave orders to his engineers to make a machine to hoist these two extraordinary men out of the kingdom. Three thousand good physicists worked on it; it was ready in two weeks and cost no more than twenty million pounds sterling in the money of the country. They put Candide and Cacambo on the machine; there were two big red sheep saddled and bridled to serve them as mounts when they had crossed the mountains; twenty pack sheep laden with victuals, thirty bearing presents of the most curious products of the country, and fifty laden with gold, precious stones, and diamonds. The King embraced the two wanderers tenderly.

A fine spectacle was their departure and the ingenious manner in which they and their sheep were hoisted to the top of the mountains. The physicists took leave of them after setting them down safely, and Candide was left with no other desire and object than to go and present his sheep to Mademoiselle Cunégonde.

'We have enough,' he said, 'to pay the Governor of Buenos Aires, if Mademoiselle Cunégonde can be ransomed. Let us head for Cayenne and take ship, and then we shall see what kingdom we can buy.'

19

What happened to them in Surinam, and how Candide made the acquaintance of Martin

Our two travellers' first day was rather pleasant. They were encouraged by the idea of finding themselves possessors of more treasures than Asia, Europe, and Africa could assemble. Candide in transport wrote Cunégonde's name on the trees. On the second day two of their sheep got stuck in the marshes and went down with their loads; two other sheep died of fatigue a few day later; seven or eight then died of hunger in a desert; a few days later some others fell from precipices. Finally, after a hundred days of travel, they had only two sheep left.

Candide said to Cacambo: 'My friend, you see how perishable are the riches of this world; there is nothing solid but virtue and the happiness of seeing Mademoiselle Cunégonde again.'

'I admit it,' said Cacambo, 'but we still have two sheep left with more treasures than the King of Spain will ever have, and I see in the distance a town that I suspect is Surinam which belongs to the Dutch. We are at the end of our troubles and the beginning of our happiness.'

As they approached the town they met a Negro stretched on the ground, with only half his clothes left, that is to say a pair of blue cloth shorts; the poor man had his left leg and his right hand missing. 'Oh good, Lord!' said Candide to him in Dutch. 'What are you doing there, my friend, in that horrible state I see you in?'

'I am waiting for my master Monsieur Vanderdendur, the famous merchant,' the Negro replied.

'Was it Monsieur Vanderdendur,' said Candide, 'who treated you this way?'

'Yes, sir,' said the Negro, 'it is the custom. They give us a pair of cloth shorts twice a year for all our clothing. When we work in the sugar mills and we catch our finger in the millstone, they cut off our hand; when we try to run away, they cut off a leg; both things have happened to me. It is at this price that you eat sugar in Europe. However, when my mother sold me for ten patacóns[46] on the Guinea coast, she said to me: "My dear child, bless our fetishes, worship them always, they will make you live happily; you have the honour to be a slave to our lords the whites, and thereby you are making the fortune of your father and mother." Alas! I don't know if I made their fortune, but they didn't make mine. Dogs, monkeys, parrots are a thousand times less miserable than we are. The Dutch fetishes who converted me tell me every Sunday that we are all, whites and blacks, children of Adam. I am no genealogist, but if those preachers are telling the truth we are all second cousins. Now you must admit that no one could treat his relatives in a more horrible way.'

'O Pangloss!' exclaimed Candide 'you had not guessed this abomination; this does it, at last I shall have to renounce your optimism.'

'What is optimism?' said Cacambo.

'Alas,' said Candide, 'it is the mania of maintaining that all is well when we are miserable!' And he shed tears as he looked at his Negro, and he entered Surinam weeping.

The first thing they inquired about was whether there was not some ship in the port that could be sent to Buenos Aires. The man they addressed proved to be a Spanish ship's captain, who offered to make an honest bargin with them. He arranged to meet them at an inn.

Candide and the faithful Cacambo went and waited for him there with their two sheep.

Candide, whose heart was on his lips, told the Spaniard all his adventures and admitted to him that he wanted to carry off Mademoiselle Cunégonde.

'I shall take good care not to take you to Buenos Aires,' said the captain. 'I would be hanged and you too. The fair Cunégonde is His Lordship's favourite mistress.'

This was a bolt from the blue for Candide; he wept for a long time; finally he drew Cacambo aside.

'My dear friend,' he said to him, 'here is what you must do. We each have in our pockets five or six millions' worth of diamonds; you are cleverer than I; go to get Mademoiselle Cunégonde in Buenos Aires. If the Governor makes any difficulties, give him a million; if he still doesn't give in, give him two; you haven't killed an Inquisitor, they won't suspect you. I will fit out another ship; I will go to Venice and wait for you; it is a free country where there is nothing to fear either from Bulgarians, or Abarians, or Jews, or Inquisitors.'

Cacambo applauded his wise resolution. He was in despair at parting from a good master who had become his intimate friend; but the pleasure of being useful to him overcame the grief of leaving him. They embraced, shedding tears. Candide recommended to him not to forget the good old woman. Cacambo left that very day. He was a very good man, this Cacambo.

Candide stayed on some time in Surinam and waited for another captain to be willing to take him to Italy, him and the two sheep he had left. He took servants and bought everything he needed for a long voyage. At last Monsieur Vanderdendur, master of a big ship, came to see him.

'How much do you want,' he asked this man, 'to take me straight to Venice me, my men, my baggage, and the two sheep you see here?' The captain agreed to ten thousand piasters.[47] Candide did not hesitate.

'Oho!' said the prudent Vanderdendur to himself, 'this foreigner gives ten thousand

---

[46]   Patacón (or pataca): a Portuguese and Brazilian silver coin. [Frame]

[47]   A coin, usually silver, or Turkey and Egypt; also used to signify the Spanish peso. [Frame]

piaters right away! He must be very rich.' Then returning a moment later, he signified that he could not sail for less than twenty thousand. 'Very well, you shall have them,' said Candide.

'Whew!' said the merchant softly to himself, 'this man gives twenty thousand piasters as easily as ten thousand.' He came back again and said that he could not take him to Venice for less than thirty thousand piasters. 'Then you shall have thirty thousand,' said Candide.

'Oho!' said the Dutch merchant to himself again, 'thirty thousand piasters means nothing to this man; no doubt the two sheep are carrying immense treasures; let's not insist any further; let's get the thirty thousand piasters paid first, and then we shall see.'

Candide sold two little diamonds the smaller of which was worth more than all the money the captian was asking. He paid him in advance. The two sheep were put aboard. Candide was following in a little boat to join the ship in the roads; the captain seizes his chance, sets sail, weighs anchor; the wind favours him. Candide, bewildered and stupefied, soon loses sight of him. 'Alas!' he cried 'that's a trick worthy of the Old World.' He returns to shore sunk in grief, for after all he had lost enough to make the fortune of twenty monarchs.

He goes to see the Dutch judge; and since he was somewhat upset, he knocks roughly on the door; he enters, expounds his adventure, and exclaims a little louder than was fitting. The judge began by making him pay ten thousand piasters for the noise he had made. Then he listened to him patiently, promised to look in to his affair as soon as the merchant had returned, and charged him another ten thousand piastres for the costs of the hearing.

This procedure completed Candide's despair; true, he had endured misfortunes a thousand times more painful; but the cold–bloodedness of the judge, and of the captain by whom he had been robbed, inflamed his bile and plunged him into a black melancholy. The wickedness of men appeared to his mind in all its ugliness; he fed only on sad ideas.

Finally when a French ship was on the point of leaving for Bordeaux, since he had no more sheep laden with diamonds to put on board, he hired a cabin at a proper price and let it be known in the town that he would pay the passage and food and two thousand piastres to a decent man who would like to make the voyage with him, on condition that this man should be the most disgusted with his lot, and the most unfortunate in the province.

A throng of aspirants presented themselves that a fleet could not have held. Candide, wanting to choose among the most promising, picked out about twenty persons who seemed to him sociable enough and who all claimed to deserve the preference. He assembled them in his inn and gave them supper on condition that each would take an oath to tell his story faithfully; promising to choose the one who should seem to him the most to be pitied and the most discontented with his lot for the best reasons, and to give the others rewards.

The session lasted until four in the morning. Candide, as he listened to all their adventures, remembered what the old woman had said to him on the way to Buenos Aires, and the wager she had made that there was no one on the ship to whom very great misfortunes had not happened. At each adventure that was told him he thought of Pangloss.

'That Pangloss,' said he, 'would be much embarrassed to try to prove his system. I wish he were here. Certainly if all is well it is in Eldorado and not in the rest of the world.'

Finally he made up his mind in favour of a poor scholar who had worked ten years for the booksellers in Amsterdam.[48] He judged that there was no occupation in the world that a man should be more disgusted with.

This scholar, moreover, who was a good man, had been robbed by his wife, beaten by his son and abandonded by his daughter, who had eloped with a Portuguese. He had just been deprived of a small job on which he lived, and the preachers of Surinam were persecuting him because they took him for a Socinian.[49] It

---

[48]   Because of French censorship, Dutch freedom of the press, and the lack of international copyright laws, many French books were published piratically in Holland. Voltaire, among others, had suffered much from this pirating. [Frame]

[49]   A religious rationalist, denying the Trinity and the personality of Christ. [Frame]

must be admitted that the others were at least as unfortunate as he; but Candide hoped that the scholar would allay his boredom on the voyage. All his other rivals considered that Candide was doing them a great injustice but he appeased them by giving them each a hundred piastres.

20
What happened to Candide and Martin at sea

So the old scholar, whose name was Martin, embarked with Candide for Bordeaux. Both had seen much, and suffered much; and if the ship had been scheduled to set sail from Surinam to Japan by the Cape of Good Hope, they would have had enough to say about moral and physical evil to last the whole voyage.

However, Candide had one great adventure over Martin; he still hoped to see Mademoiselle Cunégonde again, and Martin had nothing to hope for; furthermore, he had gold and diamonds; and though he had lost a hundred big red sheep laden with the greatest treasures on earth, though he still had the knavery of the Dutch captain on his mind, nevertheless, when he thought about what he had left in his pockets, and when he talked about Cunégonde, especially toward the end of a meal, he still leaned toward the system of Pangloss.

'But you, Monsieur Martin,' he said to the scholar, 'what do you think of all that? What is your idea about moral and physical evil?'

'Sir,' replied Martin, 'my priests accused me of being a Socinian; but the truth of the matter is that I am a Manichean.'[50]

'You are making fun of me,' said Candide, 'there are no more Manicheans in the world.'

'There's me,' said Martin; 'I don't know what to do about it, but I cannot think any other way.'

'You must be full of the devil,' said Candide.

'He takes so much part in the affairs of this world,' said Martin, 'that I might well be full of him, just like everything else; but I must admit that when I cast my eyes over this globe, or rather over this globule, I think that God has abandoned it to some maleficent being – always excepting Eldorado. I have hardly seen a town that did not desire the ruin of the neighbouring town, never a family that did not want to exterminate some other family. Everywhere the weak loathe the powerful before whom they crawl, and the powerful treat them like flocks whose wool and flesh are for sale. A million regimented assassins, ranging from one end of Europe to the other, practise murder and brigandage with discipline to earn their bread, because there is no more honest occupation; and in the towns that seem to enjoy peace and where the arts flourish, men are devoured with more envy, cares, and anxieties than the scourges suffered by a town besieged. Secret griefs are even more cruel than public miseries. In a word, I have seen so much, and undergone so much, that I am a Manichean.'

'Yet there is some good,' said Candide.

'That may be,' said Martin, 'but I do not know it.'

In the midst of this dispute they heard the sound of cannon. The noise redoubles each moment. Everyone takes his spyglass. They see two ships fighting about three miles away. The wind brought them both so near the French ship that they had the pleasure of seeing the combat quite at their ease. Finally one of the two ships sent the other a broadside so low and so accurate as to sink it. Candide and Martin distinctly saw a hundred men on the main deck of the sinking ship; they all raised their hands to heaven and uttered frightul screams; in a moment all was swallowed up.

'Well,' said Martin, 'that is how men treat each other.' 'It is true,' said Candide, 'that there is something diabolical in this affair.'

So saying, he spied, something, bright red swimming near his ship. They launched the ship's boat to see what it could be; it was one of his sheep. Candide felt more joy on finding this sheep again than he had felt grief on losing a hundred all laden with big diamonds from Eldorado.

The French captain soon perceived that the captain of the ship that sank the other was a Spaniard and that the captain of the ship that

---

[50] A follower of Mani or Manicheus, a third-century Persian who believed in two nearly equal forces, of good and of evil. The sect flourished in St Augustine's time. [Frame]

sank was a Dutch pirate; he was the very one who had robbed Candide. The immense riches that this scoundrel had stolen were buried with him in the sea, and nothing but one sheep was saved.

'You see,' said Candide to Martin, 'that crime is sometimes punished; that rascal of a Dutch captain met the fate he deserved.'

'Yes,' said Martin, 'but was it necessary that the passengers on his ship should perish also? God punished that knave, the devil drowned the others.'

Meanwhile the French ship and the Spaniard continued on their way and Candide continued his conversations with Martin. They argued for two weeks without stopping, and after two weeks they were as far advanced as the first day. But after all they were talking, they were exchanging ideas, they were consoling each other. Candide kept stroking his sheep 'Since I have found you again,'he said, 'I may well find Cunégonde again.'

21
Candide and Martin approach the coast of France, reasoning

At last they sighted the coast of France.

'Have you ever been in France, Monsieur Martin?' said Candide.

'Yes,' said Martin, 'I have been through several provinces. There are some where half the inhabitants are crazy, some where they are too tricky, others where they are usually rather gentle and rather stupid; others where they try to be witty; and in all of them the principal occupation is making love, the second talking slander, and the third talking nonsense.'

'But, Monsieur Martin have you seen Paris?'

'Yes, I have seen Paris; it is like all those kinds, it's a chaos, it's a crowd in which everyone seeks pleasure and in which almost no one finds it, at least so it appeared to me. I did not stay there long; on arrival I was robbed of all I had by pickpockets at the Saint-German fair. I was taken

for a thief myself and I was in prison for a week; after which I became a printer's proof-reader to earn enough to return on foot to Holland. I came to know the writing rabble, the intriguing rabble, and the convulsionary[51] rabble. They say there are some very polite persons in that city; I am willing to believe it.'

'For my part, I have no curiosity to see France,' said Candide. 'You can easily guess that when a man has spent a month in Eldorado, he does not care about seeing anything else on earth, except Mademoiselle Cunégonde; I am going to wait for her in Venice; we will cross France on our way to Italy; won't you come along with me?'

'Very gladly,' said Martin. 'They say that Venice is good only for Venetian nobles, but that nevertheless they receive foreigners very well when they have a lot of money; I have none, you have, I will follow you anywhere.'

'By the way,' said Candide, 'do you think that the earth was originally a sea, as we are assured in that big book[52] that belongs to the ship's captain?'

'I believe nothing of the sort,' said Martin, 'any more than all the daydreams that people have been trying to sell us for some time now.'

'But then to what end was this world formed?' said Candide.

'To drive us mad,' replied Martin.

'Aren't you quite astonished,' Candide continued, 'at the love of those two girls in the country of the Oreillons for those two monkeys, the adventure with whom I told you?'

'Not at all,' said Martin 'I don't see what is strange about that passion; I have seen so many extraordinary things that there is nothing extraordinary left.'

'Do you think,' said Candide, 'that men have always massacred each other as they do today, always been liars, cheats, faithbreakers, ingrates, brigands, weaklings, rovers, cowards, enviers, gluttons, drunkards, misers, self-seekers, carnivores, calumniators, debauchees, fanatics, hypocrites, and fools?'

'Do you think,' said Martin, 'that sparrow hawks have always eaten pigeons when they found any?'

---

[51] Convulsion(s) (convulsionary, convulsionaries): manifestations of religious ecstasy or mania, like those of the Holy Rollers today. The Jansenists were noted for them. [Frame]

[52] The 'big book' presumably is the Bible; the theory had recently been advanced again in Buffon's *Théorie de la terre* (1749). [Frame]

'Yes, no doubt,' said Candide.

'Well,' said Martin, 'if sparrow hawks have always had the same character, why do you expect men to have changed theirs?'

'Oh!' said Candide, 'there's a big difference, for free will...'

Reasoning thus, they arrived at Bordeaux.

22
What happened to Candide and Martin in France

Candide stopped in Bordeaux only as long as it took to sell a few pebbles from Eldorado and to provide himself with a good two–seated chaise; for he now could not do without his philosopher Martin; only he was very sorry to part with his sheep, which he left to the Bordeaux Academy of Science, which proposed, as the subject of that year's competition, to find out why this sheep's wool was red; and the prize was awarded to a scholar from the north, who proved by A plus B, minus C, divided by Z, that the sheep must be red and die of sheep pox.

Meanwhile all the travellers that Candide met in the inns on the road said to him: 'We are going to Paris.' This general eagerness finally gave him a hankering to see this capital; it was not much of a detour off the road to Venice.

He entered by the Faubourg Saint-Marceau[53] and thought he was in the ugliest village in Westphalia.

Hardly was Candide in his inn when he was attacked by a slight illness caused by his fatigue. Since he had an enormous diamond on his finger and a prodigioulsy heavy strongbox had been observed in his baggage, he immediately had at his side two doctors he had not called, some intimate friends who did not leave him, and two pious ladies heating up his broths.

Martin said: 'I remember having been sick in Paris too on my first trip; I was very poor, so I had neither friends, nor pious ladies, nor doctors; and I got well.'

However, by dint of medicines and blood-lettings, Candide's illness became serious. A neighbourhood priest came and asked him gently for a note payable to the bearer in the next world.[54] Candide wanted no part of it; the pious ladies assured him that it was a new fashion. Candide replied that he was not a man of fashion. Martin wanted to throw the priest out the window. The cleric swore that Candide should not be buried.[55] Martin swore that he would bury the cleric if he continued to bother them. The quarrel grew heated: Martin took him by the shoulders and pushed him out roughly, which caused a great scandal which led in turn to a legal report.

Candide got well, and during his convalescence he had very good company to supper with him. They gambled for high stakes. Candide was quite amazed that he never got any aces, and Martin was not amazed at this at all.

Among those who did the honours of the town for him was a little abbé from Périgord, one of those eager people, always alert, always obliging, brazen, fawning, complaisant, who lie in wait for strangers passing through, tell them the history of the town's scandals, and offer them pleasures at any price. This man first took Candide and Martin to the theatre. They were playing a new tragedy. Candide found himself seated next to some wits. This did not keep him from weeping at certain perfectly played scenes. One of the reasoners beside him said to him during an intermission:

'You are very wrong to weep, for that actress is very bad, the actor playing opposite her even worse, the play is even worse than the actors: the author doesn't know a word of Arabic, and yet the scene is in Arabia; and besides he is a man who doesn't believe in innate ideas;[56] tomorrow I will bring you twenty pamphlets against him.'

---

[53] In Voltaire's time an ugly, dirty suburb. [Frame]

[54] A reference to the *billets de confession* required from 1746 on, on pain of refusal of absolution and the sacraments. [Frame]

[55] That is, buried in consecrated ground. See below, note 59. [Frame]

[56] Voltaire followed Locke's view of the mind at birth as a blank slate, rather than Descartes' theory of innate ideas. [Frame]

'Sir,[57] how many plays do you have in France?' said Candide to the abbé, who replied: 'Five or six thousand.'

'That's a lot,' said Candide. 'How many of them are good?'

'Fifteen or sixteen,' replied the other.

'That's a lot,' said Martin.

Candide was very pleased with an actress who played Queen Elizabeth in a rather dull tragedy that is sometimes performed.[58]

'I like this actress very much,' he said to Martin; 'she reminds me of Mademoiselle Cunégonde; I would very much like to pay her my respects.'

The abbé from Périgord offered to take him to meet her. Candide, brought up in Germany, asked what the proper etiquette was, how they treated queens of England in France.

'You have to make a distinction,' said the abbé. 'In the provinces they take them to a tavern, in Paris they respect them when they are beautiful and throw them on a dump when they are dead.'

'Queens on the dump!' said Candide.

'Yes, really,' said Martin; 'the abbé is right; I was in Paris when Mademoiselle Monime[59] passed on, as they say, from this life to the next; she was refused what those people call the honours of burial, that is to say, of rotting with all the beggars of the district in an ugly cemetery; alone of her troupe, she was buried at the corner of the Rue de Bourgogne; which must have pained her extremely, for she had a very noble mind.'

'That was very impolite,' said Candide.

'What do you expect?' said Martin. 'These people are made that way. Imagine all possible contradictions and incompatibilities, you will see them in the government, the tribunals, the churches, the entertainments of this queer nation.'

'Is it true that people are always laughing in Paris?' said Candide.

'Yes,' said the abbé, 'but it is with rage in their hearts; for here people complain about everything with great bursts of laughter, and they even perform the most detestable actions with a laugh.'

'Who,' said Candide, 'is that fat pig who was telling so many bad things about the play at which I wept so much and about the actors who gave me such pleasure?'

'He is a living disease,' replied the abbé, 'who makes his living by saying bad things about all plays and all books; he hates anyone who succeeds, as eunuchs hate those who can enjoy sex; he is one of those serpents of literature who feed on filth and venom; he is a foliferous pamphleteer…'

'What do you mean by a foliferous pamphleteer?' said Candide.

'A producer of scribbled leaves,' said the abbé, 'a Fréron.'[60]

That is how Candide, Martin, and the Perigordian were talking on the staircase as they watched people file out after the play.

'Although I am very eager to see Mademoiselle Cunégonde again,' said Candide, 'still I would like to have supper with Mademoiselle Clairon,[61] for she seemed admirable to me.'

The abbé was not the man to approach Mademoiselle Clarion, for she saw only good company. 'She is engaged for this evening,' he said, 'but I shall have the honour of taking you to the house of a lady of quality, and there you will come to know Paris as if you had been here four years.'

---

[57]   Here begins a long passage added by Voltaire in 1761, which ends below, at note 70. [Frame]

[58]   Presumably Thomas Corneille, *Le Comte d'Essex.* [Frame]

[59]   Adrienne Lecouvreur (1690–1730), a distinguished actress who made her debut at the Comédie Française as Monime in Racine's *Mithridate.* Being an actress at her death, she was refused burial in consecrated ground. (See also note 55 above.) [Frame]

[60]   Élie Fréron (1719–76), publisher of the *Année Littéraire,* enemy of Voltaire and the *philosophes* and a favourite target for Voltaire's wit. [Frame]

[61]   A celebrated actress who played leading roles in many of Voltaire's plays. [Frame]

Candide, who was naturally curious, let himself be taken to the lady's house, at the far end of the Faubourg Saint-Honoré;[62] they were busy playing faro; twelve sad punters[63] each held a small hand of cards, the foolish register of their misfortunes. A deep silence reigned, pallor sat on the punters' foreheads, anxiety on that of the banker; and the lady of the house, seated beside the pitiless banker, watched with a lynx's eyes all the underhand plays for double stakes or for three straight wins to pay seven times, for which each player turned up the corner of his cards;[64] she had them turned back down with severe but polite attention, and did not show any anger for fear of losing her customers; the lady called herself the Marquise de Parolignac.[65] Her daughter, aged fifteen, was one of the punters, and tipped her off with a wink to the cheating of those who were trying to repair the cruelties of fortune. The abbé from Périgord, Candide, and Martin entered, no one got up, greeted them, or looked at them; all were deeply preoccupied with their cards.

'My Lady the Baroness of Thunder-ten-tronckh was more civil,' said Candide.

However, the abbé got the ear of the Marquise, who half rose, honoured Candide with a gracious smile and Martin with a truly noble nod; she saw to it that a seat and a hand of cards were given to Candide, who lost fifty thousand francs in two deals; after which they had supper most gaily, and everyone was astounded that Candide was not moved by his loss; the lackeys said to one another in their lackey language: 'He must be some English Milord.'

The supper was like most suppers in Paris; first a silence; then a noise of undistinguishable words; then jokes, most of them insipid, false news, bad reasoning, a little politics, and a lot of slander; there was even some talk about new books.

'Have you seen,' said the abbé from Périgord, 'the novel by a certain Gauchat,[66] Doctor of Theology?'

'Yes,' replied one of the guests, 'but I could not finish it. We have a host of nonsensical writings, but all of them together do not approach the nonsensicality of Gauchat, Doctor of Theology; I am so surfeited with the immense number of detestable books that inundate us that I have taken to punting at faro...'

'What about the *Mélanges* by Archdeacon Trublet?[67] What do you say about them?' said the abbé.

'Oh!' said Madame de Parolignac, 'what a tedious mortal! How assiduosly he tells you what everybody knows! How ponderously he discusses what is not worth being noted lightly! With what absence of wit he appropriates the wit of others! How he spoils what he plunders! How he disgusts me! But he will not disgust me any more; it is enough to have read a few pages by the Archdeacon.'

There was a learned man of taste at table who supported what the Marquise said. They talked of tragedies next; the lady asked why there were tragedies that were sometimes played and that could not be read. The man of taste explained very well how a play could have some interest and almost no merit; he proved in a few words that it was not enough to bring on one or two of those situations that you find in all novels and that always beguile the spectators, but that you have to be new without being bizarre, often sublime, and always natural, know the human heart and make it speak, be a great poet without letting any character in the play appear to be a poet, know the langauge perfectly, speak it with purity, with continual harmony, without ever rhyming at the expense of the sense.

'Anyone,' he added, 'who does not observe all these rules may compose one or two tragedies

---

[62] An aristocratic quarter of Paris. [Frame]

[63] Faro is played by an unlimited number of punters against the banker. [Frame]

[64] To mark that he was making this bet – illegally, however. [Frame]

[65] From *paroli*; the doubled stakes alluded to above, and the *gnac* ending common in the south-west of France, a great source of impoverished and spurious nobility. [Frame]

[66] Gabriel Gauchat (1709–74 or 1779), enemy of Voltaire and the Encyclopedists. [Frame]

[67] Nicolas-Charles-Joseph Trublet (1677–1770), bitter critic of Voltaire and the *Encyclopédie*, author of *Essais de littérature*. [Frame]

that win applause at the theatre, but he will never be ranked among good writers; there are very few good tragedies; some are idylls in well-written and well-rhymed dialogue, others are political arguments that put you to sleep, or repulsive amplifications; still others are the dreams of enthusiasts, in a barbarous style; interrupted speeches, long apostrophes to the gods – because the author does not know how to speak to men – false maxims, bombastic commonplaces.'

Candide listened attentively to this speech and formed a fine impression of the speaker; and since the Marquise had taken care to place him next to her, he got her ear and took the liberty of asking her who was that man who spoke so well.

'He is a learned man,' said the lady, 'who does not play faro and whom the abbé sometimes brings to supper with me; he is a perfect connoisseur of tragedies and books, and he has written a tragedy that was hissed and a book of which only one copy, which he dedicated to me, was ever seen outside his publisher's store.'

'What a great man!' said Candide. 'He is another Pangloss.'

Then turning toward him, he said to him:

'Sir, no doubt you think that all is for the best in the physical world and in the moral, and that nothing could have been otherwise?'

'I, sir,' replied the scholar, 'I think nothing of the sort; I think that everything goes awry with us, that no one knows his rank or his job or what he is doing or what he should do, and that except for supper, which is rather gay and where there seems to be a good deal of agreement, all the rest of the time is spent in senseless quarrels: Jansenists[68] against Molinists,[69] lawyers against churchmen, men of letters against men of letters, courtiers, financiers against the people, wives against husbands, relatives against relatives – it's all eternal war.'

Candide replied: 'I have seen worse; but a sage, who has since had the misfortune to be hanged, taught me that all this is wonderful: these are shadows in a beautiful picture.'

'Your hanged man was making fun of everybody,' said Martin; 'your shadows are horrible stains.'

'It is men who make the stains,' said Candide, 'and they can't help it.'

'Then it isn't their fault,' said Martin.

Most of the gamblers, who understood nothing of this kind of talk, were drinking; and Martin talked theory with the scholar, and Candide told the lady of the house part of his adventures.

After supper the Marquise took Candide into her boudoir and sat him down on a sofa.

'Well,' she said to him, 'so you are still madly in love with Mademoiselle Cunégonde of Thunder-ten-tronckh!'

'Yes, Madame,' answered Candide.

The Marquise replied to him with a tender smile: 'You answer me like a young man from Westphalia; a Frenchman would have said to me; "It is true that I have been in love with Mademoiselle Cunégonde, but when I see you, Madame, I fear I no longer love her."'

'Alas! Madame,' said Candide, 'I will answer as you wish.'

'Your passion for her,' said the Marquise, 'began when you picked up her handkerchief; I want you to pick up my garter.'

'With all my heart,' said Candide and he picked it up.

'But I want you to put it back on me,' said the lady, and Candide put it back on her.

'You see,' said the lady, 'you are a foreigner; I sometimes make my Parisian lovers languish for two weeks, but I give myself to you on the very first night, because one must do the honours of one's country to a young man from Westphalia.'

---

[68]   Jansenism, Jansenists, Jansenius: Jansenism is a Christian sect stressing predestination and asceticism, founded by Cornelius Jansen or Jansenius (1585–1638), Dutch Bishop of Ypres, author of the *Augustinus* (1640). It spread rapidly and widely in France, notably through the efforts of Saint-Cyran and Arnauld, and established its centre near Paris in the religious community of Port-Royal. Opposed violently by the Sorbonne and the Jesuits, persecuted by Louis XIV, and condemned by Pope Clement XI in 1713, Jansenism still retained some strength in France until about the mid-eighteenth century. [Frame]

[69]   Molinism, Molinists: Jesuits, from the name of Luis Molina (1535–1600), Spanish Jesuit, author of a widely influential theory reconciling predestination with free will. [Frame]

The beauty, having perceived two enormous diamonds on her young foreigner's two hands, praised them so sincerely that they passed from Candide's fingers to the fingers of the Marquise.

When Candide went home with his Perigordian abbé, he felt some remorse at having been unfaithful to Mademoiselle Cunégonde; the abbé took part in his grief; he had got only a small share of the fifty thousand francs lost at gambling by Candide and of the value of the two brilliants half given, half extorted from him. His plan was to make all the profit he could from the advantages that his acquaintance with Candide might procure him. He talked to him a lot about Cunégonde, and Candide told him that he would certainly beg that fair lady's pardon for his infidelity when he saw her in Venice.

The Perigordian redoubled his courtesies and attentions, and took a tender interest in everything Candide said, everything he did, everything he wanted to do.[70]

'So you have a rendezvous in Venice, sir?' he said.

'Yes, Mr. Abbé,' said Candide; 'I absolutely must go and find Mademoiselle Cunégonde.'

Then, led on by pleasure of talking about the one he loved, he related, as was his custom, a part of his adventures with that illustrious lady of Westphalia.

'I suppose,' said the abbé, 'that Mademoiselle Cunégonde has a great deal of wit and writes charming letters?'

'I have never received any from her,' said Candide, 'for you must realize that having been expelled from the castle for love of her, I could not write to her; that soon afterward I learned that she was dead, then I found her again and then lost her; and that I have sent her a dispatch by special messenger two thousand five hundred leagues from here and am awaiting her reply.'

The abbé listened attentively and seemed a bit thoughful. He took leave of the two foreigners after embracing them tenderly. The next day Candide, on waking, received a letter couched in these terms:

'Sir, my very dear lover, I have been ill in this city for a week; now I learn that you are here. I would fly into your arms if I could move. I heard that you had passed through Bordeaux, I left the faithful Cacambo and the old woman there and they are to follow me soon. The Governor of Buenos Aires took everything, but I still have your heart. Come, your presence will restore me to life or make me die of pleasure.'

This charming letter, this unhoped-for letter, transported Candide with inexpressible joy; and the illness of his dear Cunégonde overwhelmed him with grief. Torn between these two feelings, he takes his gold and his diamonds and had himself driven with Martin to the hotel where Mademoiselle Cunégonde was staying. He enters, trembling with emotion; his heart beats, his voice sobs; he wants to open the bed curtains, he wants to have a light brought.

'Don't do anything of the sort,' says the waiting maid, 'light is the death of her'; and promptly she closes the curtains again.

'My dear Cunégonde,' says Candide, weeping, 'how are you feeling? If you cannot see me, at least speak to me.'

'She cannot speak,' says the maid.

The lady then stretches out of the bed a plump hand which Candide waters at length with the tears and which he then fills with diamonds, leaving a bag full of gold on the armchair.

In the midst of these transports a police officer arrives followed by the Perigordian abbé and a squad.

'So these are two suspicious foreigners?' he says.

He immediately had them arrested and orders his bravoes to drag them off to prison.

'This is not how they treat travellers in Eldorado,' says Candide.

'I am more of a Manichean than ever,' says Martin.

'But, sir, where are you taking us?' says Candide.

'To a deep dungeon,' says the police officer.

Martin, having regained his coolness, decided that the lady who claimed to be Cunégonde was a fraud, the abbé from Périgord a fraud who had taken advantage of Candide's innocence as fast as he could, and the police officer another fraud of whom they could easily get rid.

---

[70] Here ends the addition of 1761 that began on at note 57. [Frame]

Rather than expose himself to the processes of justice, Candide, enlightened by Martin's advice and moreover still impatient to see the real Mademoiselle Cunégonde again, suggests to the police officer three little diamonds worth about three thousand pistoles each.

'Ah, sir,' says the man with the ivory baton, 'even had you committed all the crimes imaginable, you are the finest man in the world. Three diamonds! Each worth three thousand pistoles! Sir, I would let myself be killed for you, instead of taking you to a dungeon. They arrest all foreigners here, but let me take care of things; I have a brother at Dieppe in Normandy, I'm going to take you there; and if you have an extra diamond to give him, he will take care of you just as I am doing myself.'

'And why do they arrest all foreigners?' said Candide.

The abbé from Périgord then spoke up and said: 'It is because a tramp from the region of Atrebatun[71] listened to foolish talk; this alone made him commit a parricade not like that of May, 1610, but like that of December, 1594,[72] and like many others committed in other years and other months by other tramps who had listened to foolish talk.'

The police officer then explained what it was all about.

'Oh, the monsters!' exclaimed Candide. 'What! Such horrors in a nation that dances and sings! Can I not depart at once out of this country where monkeys incite tigers? I have seen bears in my own country; I have seen men only in Eldorado. In the name of God, Mr Officer, take me to Venice, where I am to await Mademoiselle Cunégonde.'

'I can take you only to Lower Normandy,' said the officer.

Immediately he has his chains taken off, says he has made a mistake, sends his men away, and takes Candide and Martin to Dieppe and leaves them in the hands of his brother. There was a little Dutch ship in the roads. The Norman, having with the help of three other diamonds become the most obliging of men embarks Candide and his men on the ship, which was about to set sail for Portsmouth in England. It was not the way to Venice; but Candide thought he was delivered from hell, and fully intended to get back on the way to Venice at the first opportunity.

23

Candide and Martin go to the coast of France; what they see there

'O Pangloss, Pangloss! O Martin, Martin! O my dear Cunégonde! What sort of a world is this?' said Candide on the Dutch ship.

'Something very mad and very abominable,' replied Martin.

'You know England; are they as mad there as in France?'

'It's another kind of madness,' said Martin. 'You know that these two nations are at war over a few acres of snow round about Canada, and that they are spending on that fine war much more than all of Canada is worth. As for telling you precisely whether there are more people who need to be locked up in one country than another, that is something that my poor lights do not allow me to do. I only know that in general the people we are on our way to see are very gloomy.'

While chatting thus, they arrived at Portsmouth; a multitude of people covered the shore and looked attentively at a rather fat man who was on his knees, his eyes bandaged, on the main deck of one of the ships of the fleet; four soldiers posted facing this man shot three bullets each into his skull as peacefully as can be, and the whole assemblage went back home extremely satisfied.

'What in the world is all this?' said Candide. 'And what demon is exercising his domination everywhere?' He asked who was that fat man who had just been ceremoniously killed.

'An admiral,'[73] was the reply.

---

[71] Latin name for Arras, home of Damiens, who attempted to assassinate Louis XV in 1757. [Frame]

[72] Two attempts on the life of Henry IV – the unsuccessful one by Châtel in 1594 and the successful one by Ravaillac in 1610. [Frame]

[73] Admiral Byng of England was executed on March 14, 1757, after a court-martial, for losing a naval battle to the French the year before. Voltaire had tried in vain to intervene to save his life. [Frame]

'And why kill this admiral?'

'Because,' he was told, 'he did not get enough people killed; he gave battle to a French admiral, and they decided that he was not close enough to him.'

'But,' said Candide, 'the French admiral was as far from the English admiral as he was from him!'

'That is incontestable,' was the reply; 'but in this country it is a good thing to kill an admiral from time to time to encourage the others.'

Candide was so stunned and so shocked at what he saw and what he heard that he would not even set foot on land, and made his bargain with the Dutch captain (even if he were to rob him like the one on Surinam) to take him to Venice without delay.

Two days later the captain was ready. They sailed along the coast of France. They passed in sight of Lisbon and Candide shuddered. They entered the Strait[74] and the Mediterranean. Finally they landed in Venice. 'God be praised,' said Candide, embracing Martin, 'here is where I shall see the fair Cunégonde again. I count on Cacambo as on myself. All is well, and all goes as well as it possbly could.'

24
Paquette and Friar Giroflée

As soon as he was in Venice, he had a search made for Cacambo in all the taverns, all the cafés, and among all the ladies of pleasure, and did not find him. Every day he sent to investigate all the ships and boats: no news of Cacambo.

'What!' he said to Martin. 'I have had time to cross from Surinam to Bordeaux, to go to Bordeaux to Paris, from Paris to Dieppe, from Dieppe to Portsmouth, to skirt the coasts of Portugal and Spain, to cross the whole Mediterranean, to spend a few months in Venice, and the fair Cunégonde has not arrived! Instead of her I have met only a tricky wench and an abbé from Périgord! Cunégonde is beyond doubt dead, there is nothing left for me to do but die. Ah! it would have been better to remain in the paradise of Eldorado than to return to this accursed Europe. How right you

are, my dear Martin! All is but illusion and calamity.'

He fell into a black melancholy and took no part in the opera *à la mode* or the other diversions of the carnival; not one lady caused him the least temptation. Martin said to him:

'Truly you are very simple to imagine that a half-breed valet who has five or six millions in his pockets will go find your mistress at the end of the world and bring her to you in Venice.

He will take her for himself if he finds her. If he does not find her, he will take another. I advise you to forget your valet Cacambo and your mistress Cunégonde.'

Martin was not consoling. Candide's melancholy increased and Martin never stopped proving to him that there was little virtue and little happiness on earth, except perhaps in Eldorado, where no one could go.

While arguing about this important matter and waiting for Cunégonde, Candide noticed a young Theatine[75] monk in the Piazza San Marco arm-in-arm with a girl. The Theatine looked fresh, plump, vigorous; his eyes were brilliant, his manner assured, his head erect, his bearing proud. The girl was very pretty and was singing; she looked lovingly at her Theatine, and from time to time pinched his plump cheeks.

'You will admit to me at least,' said Candide to Martin, 'that these people are happy; up to now I have found, in all the habitable earth except Eldorado, nothing but unfortunates; but as for that girl and that Theatine, I wager they are very happy creatures.'

'I wager they're not,' said Martin.

'We have only to ask them to dinner,' said Candide, 'and you'll see whether I'm wrong.'

Immediately he accosts them, pays them his compliments, and invites them to come to his inn and eat macaroni, Lombardy partridges, and caviar, and drink Montepulciano, Lacryma Christi, Cyprus and Samos wine. The lady blushed, the Theatine accepted the invitation, and the girl followed him, looking at Candide with eyes full of surprise and confusion and dimmed with a few tears. Hardly had she entered Candide's room when she said to him: 'What! Monsieur Candide no longer recognizes Paquette!'

---

[74] Of Gibraltar. [Frame]

[75] A member of a Catholic order founded in 1524 to combat Protestantism. [Frame]

At these words Candide, who had not looked at her with any attention until then, because he was so preoccupied only with Cunégonde, said to her:

'Alas! my poor child, so it was you who put Doctor Pangloss in the fine state in which I saw him?'

'Alas! sir, I myself,' said Paquette; 'I see that you are informed about everything. I learned about the frightful misfortunes that happened to the whole household of My Lady the Baroness and to the fair Cunégonde. I swear to you that my destiny has been hardly less sad. I was very innocent when you knew me. A Franciscan who was my confessor easily seduced me. The consequences were frightful; I was obliged to leave the castle a little while after My Lord the Baron had sent you away with great kicks in the backside. If a famous doctor had not taken pity on my I would have died. For some time out of gratitude I was that doctor's mistress. His wife, who was madly jealous, used to beat me pitilessly every day; she was a fury. This doctor was the ugliest of all men, and I the unhappiest of all creatures at being beaten continually because of a man I did not love. You know, sir, how dangerous it is for a shrewish woman to be a doctor's wife. This man, outraged at his wife's ways, one day gave her, to cure her of a little cold, a medicine so efficacious that she died of it in two hours' time in horrible convulsions. My lady's relatives brought a criminal suit against the gentleman; he took flight, and I was put in prison. My innocence would not have saved me if I had not been rather pretty. The judge turned me loose on condition that he would succeed the doctor. I was soon supplemented by a rival, tossed out with no compensation, and obliged to continue this abominable occupation which seems so amusing to you men and which for us is but an abyss of misery. I went to Venice to practise the profession. Ah! sir, if you could imagine what it is to be obliged to caress indiscriminately an old merchant, a lawyer, a monk, a gondolier, an abbé; to be exposed to every insult, every outrage; to be often reduced to borrowing a skirt in order to have it lifted by some disgusting man; to be robbed by one of what you have earned with the other; to be forced by the officers of the law to buy protection, and to have in prospect nothing

but a frightful old age, a hospital, and a dunghill – you would conclude that I am one of the unhappiest creatures in the world.'

Thus Paquette opened her heart to the good Candide in a private room in the presence of Martin, who said to Candide:

'You see, I have already won half my wager.'

Friar Giroflée had remained in the dining-room and was having a drink while waiting for dinner.

'But,' said Candide to Paquette, 'you looked so gay, so happy, when I met you, you were singing, you were caressing the Theatine with natural complaisance; you seemed to me as happy as you claim to be unfortunate.'

'Ah! sir,' replied Paquette, 'that is still another of the miseries of the trade. Yesterday I was robbed and beaten by an officer, and today I have to appear in a good humour to please a monk.'

Candide had had enough, he admitted Martin was right. They sat down to table with Paquette and the Theatine; the meal was rather entertaining; and toward the end they talked to each other with some frankness.

'Father,' said Candide to the monk, 'you seem to me to enjoy a destiny that everyone must envy; the flower of health shines on your face,[76] your physiognomy bespeaks happiness, you have a very pretty girl for your recreation, and you seem very content with your condition as a Theatine.'

'Faith, sir,' said Friar Giroflée, 'I wish all Theatines were at the bottom of the sea. I have been tempted a hundred time to set fire to the monastery and then turn Turk. My parents forced me at the age of fifteen to put on this detestable robe, in order to leave a greater fortune to an accursed older brother whom God confound! Jealousy, discord, rage inhabit the monastery. It is true, I have preached a few bad sermons that have brought me in a little money, half of which the prior steals from me; the rest serves me to keep girls; but when I go back to the monastery in the evening I am ready to smash my head against the dormitory walls; and all my colleagues are in the same state.'

Martin, turning toward Candide with his customary coolness, said to him: 'Well! Haven't I won the whole wager?

---

[76] In French, the monk's name means *gillyflower* or *wallflower*, while that of Paquette means *daisy*. [Frame]

Candide gave two thousand piasters to Paquette and a thousand piasters to Friar Giroflée. 'I warrant you,' he said, 'with this they will be happy.'

'I don't believe it in the very least,' said Martin; 'perhaps with these piasters you will make them unhappier yet.'

'That will be as it may,' said Candide. 'But one thing consoles me: I see that we often find people again whom we never thought to find; it may well be that having met up with my red sheep and Paquette, I shall also meet Cunégonde again.'

'I hope,' said Martin, 'that she may someday be the making of your happiness; but that is something I strongly doubt.'

'You are very hard,' said Candide.

'That's because I have lived,' said Martin.

'But look at these gondoliers,' said Candide. 'Aren't they always singing?'

'You don't see them at home, with their wives and their brats of children' said Martin. 'The Doge has his troubles, the gondoliers have theirs. It is true that taken all in all the lot of a gondolier is preferable to that of a doge; but I think the difference is so slight that it is not worth examining.'

'They speak,' said Candide, 'of Senator Pococurante,[77] who lives in that handsome palace on the Brenta, and who receives foreigners rather well. They claim he is a man who has never known grief.'

'I would like to see so rare a species,' said Martin.

Candide immediately sent to ask Lord Pococurante for permission to come to see him the next day.

25
Visit to the Venetian Nobleman, Lord Pococurante

Candide and Martin took a gondola on to the Brenta and arrived at the palace of the noble Pococurante. The gardens were well conceived and adorned with handsome marble statues; the architecture of the palace was fine. The master of the house, a man of sixty, very rich, received the two sightseers very politely but with very little enthusiasm, which disconcerted Candide and did not displease Martin.

First two pretty, neatly dressed girls served chocolate, well prepared with whipped cream. Candide could not refrain from praising them for their beauty, their grace, and their skill.

'They are pretty, good creatures,' said Senator Pococurante; 'I sometimes take them to bed with me, for I am very tired of the town ladies, their coquetries, their jealousies, their quarrels, their humours, their pettinesses, their prides, their follies, and the sonnets one must compose on order for them; but after all, these two girls are beginning to bore me a lot.'

Candide, walking after breakfast in a long gallery, was surprised by the beauty of the pictures. He asked what master had painted the first two.

'They are by Raphael,' said the senator; 'I bought them a few years ago at a very high price out of vanity; they say they are the finest things in Italy, but I do not like them at all; their colour had become very dark; the figures are not rounded enough and do not stand out enough; the draperies are not at all like cloth. In a word, no matter what they say, I do not find in them a true imitation of nature. I will like a picture only when I think I am seeing nature itself; and there are none of that kind. I have many pictures, but I no longer look at them.'

While waiting for dinner, Pococurante had a concerto played for him. Candide found the music delightful.

'That noise,' said Pococurante, 'can be entertaining for half an hour, but if it lasts longer, it tires everyone, though no one dares admit it. Music today is merely the art of executing difficult things; and in the long run what is merely difficult is not pleasing. Perhaps I would like opera better, if they had not found the secret of making it a monster that revolts me. Let those who wish go to see bad tragedies set to music, where the scenes are composed only to bring in very clumsily two or three ridiculous songs which show off an actress's vocal cords. Let those who will, or who can, swoon with pleasure at seeing a eunuch hum the part of Caesar or Cato and tread the boards awkwardly. As for me, it has been a long time since I gave up these trivialities, which today are the glory of Italy and for which sovereigns pay so dear.'

---

[77] From the Italian: 'caring little.' [Frame]

Candide argued a little, but with discretion. Martin was entirely in agreement with the senator.

They sat down to table, and after an excellent dinner they went into the library. Candide, seeing a magnificently bound Homer, praised the Illustrissimo for his good taste.

'That,' he said, 'is a book that was the delight of the great Pangloss, the best philosopher in Germany.'

'It is no delight to me,' said Pococurante coldly. 'Once I was made to believe I took pleasure in reading it.[78] But that continual repetition of combats that are all alike, those gods that are always active and never do anything decisive, that Helen who is the subject of the war and who has hardly any part in the action, that Troy which is always besieged and never taken – all that caused me the most deadly boredom. I have sometimes asked learned men whether they were as bored as I was reading it. All the sincere ones admitted to me that the book fell out of their hands, but that you always had to have it in your library, like an ancient monument, or like those rusty coins which cannot be used in commerce.'

'Your Excellency does not think the same thing about Virgil?' said Candide.

'I admit,' said Pococurante, 'that the second, fourth, and sixth books of his *Aeneid* are excellent; but as for his pious Aeneas and strong Cloanthes and faithful Achates and little Ascanius and the imbecile King Latinus and middle-class Amata and insipid Lavinia, I do not believe there is anything so frigid or more disagreeable. I prefer Tasso and the fantastic fairy tales of Ariosto.'

'Might I venture to ask you, sir,' said Candide, 'if you do not take great pleasure in reading Horace?'

'There are some maxims in him,' said Pococurante, 'that can profit a man of the world, and which, being compressed into energetic verses, engrave themselves the more easily on the memory. But I care very little about his journey to Brundisium or his description of a bad dinner, or the ruffians' quarrel between someone named Pupilus,[79] whose words, he said, were full of pus, and another whose words were vinegar. I have read only with extreme disgust his gross verses against old women and against witches; and I do not see what merit there can be in telling his friend Maecenas that if he is placed by him among the lyric poets he will strike the stars with his lofty brow. Fools admire everything in a noted author. I read only for myself, I like only what I have use for.'

Candide, who had been brought up never to judge anything for himself, was greatly astonished at what he heard, and Martin considered Pococurante's way of thinking rather reasonable.

'Oh, here is a Cicero,' said Candide. 'Now as for that great man, I suppose you never tire of reading him?'

'I never read him,' replied the Venetian. 'What do I care whether he pleaded for Rabirius or for Cluentius? I have quite enough with the cases that I judge; I would have made out better with his philosophical works, but when I saw that he doubted everything, I concluded that I knew as much about it as he did, and that I did not need help from anyone in order to be ignorant.'

'Ah, there are eighty volumes of proceedings of an Academy of Sciences,' exclaimed Martin; 'there may be something good there.'

'There would be,' said Pococurante, 'if a single one of the authors of that rubbish had invented even the art of making pins; but in all those volumes there is nothing but empty systems and not a single useful thing.'

'What a lot of plays I see here,' said Candide, 'in Italian, Spanish and French!'

'Yes,' said the senator, 'there are three thousand of them and not three dozen good ones. As for these collections of sermons, which all together are not worth one page of Seneca, and all these great volumes of theology, you may well suppose that I never open them, not I nor anyone else.'

Martin noticed some shelves loaded with English books. 'I suppose,' he said, 'a republican must enjoy most of those works written with so much freedom.'

---

[78] Pococurante's opinions are not to be taken for Voltaire's, but they often express Voltaire's sense of the weaknesses of the great. Virgil was generally much preferred to Homer until the nineteenth century. Ariosto and Tasso were favourites of Voltaire's. [Frame]

[79] Should be Rupilius. See *Satires*, I, vii. [Frame]

[80] The Inquisition was in the hands of the Dominicans. [Frame]

'Yes,' replied Pococurante, 'it is fine to write what you think; that is the privilege of man. In all this Italy of ours people write only what they do not think; those who inhabit the land of the Caesars and the Antonines dare not have an idea without the permission of a Dominican.[80] I would be glad of the freedom that inspires English geniuses, if passion and factionalism did not corrupt all that is estimable in that precious freedom.'

Candide, noticing a Milton,[81] asked him if he did not regard that author as a great man.

'Who?' said Pococurante. 'That barbarian who writes a long commentary on the first chapter of Genesis in ten books of harsh verses? That crude imitator of the Greeks, who disfigures the Creation and who, whereas Moses represents the eternal Being as producing the world by the word, has the Messiah take a great compass from a cupboard in Heaven to trace out his work? I should esteem the man who spoiled Tasso's Hell and Devil, who disguises Lucifer now as a toad, now as a pygmy, who makes him repeat the same remarks a hundred times, who makes him argue about theology, who, imitating in all seriousness the comical invention of firearms in Ariosto, has the devils firing cannon in Heaven? Not I, nor anyone in Italy has been able to enjoy all these sad eccentricities; and the marriage of Sin and Death, and the snakes that Sin gives birth to, make any man vomit who has a little delicacy of taste; and his long description of a hospital is good only for a gravedigger. This obscure, bizarre, and disgusting poem was despised at its birth; I treat it today as it was treated in its own county by its contemporaries. Besides, I say what I think, and I worry very little whether others think as I do.'

Candide was distressed by these remarks. He respected Homer, and he rather liked Milton.

'Alas!' he whispered to Martin. 'I'm very much afraid that this man may have a sovereign contempt for our German poets.'

'There would be no great harm in that,' said Martin.

'Oh, what a superior man!' said Candide under his breath. 'What a great genius this Pococurante is! Nothing can please him.'

After they had thus passed all the books in review, they went down into the garden. Candide praised all its beauties.

'I know of nothing in such bad taste,' said the master; 'we have nothing but trifles here; but tomorrow I am going to have one planted on a nobler plan.'

When the two sight-seers had taken leave of His Excellency, Candide said to Martin: 'Well now, you will agree that there is the happiest of all men; for he is above everything he possesses.'

'Don't you see,' said Martin, 'that he is disgusted with everything he possesses? Plato said a long time ago that the best stomachs are not those which refuse all food.'

'But,' said Candide, 'isn't there pleasure in criticizing everything, in sensing defects where other men think they see beauties?'

'That is to say,' retorted Martin, 'that there is pleasure in taking no pleasure?'

'Oh well!' said Candide, 'then there is no one happy except me – when I see Mademoiselle Cunégonde again.'

'It is always a good thing to hope,' said Martin.

However, the days, the weeks passed by; Cacambo still did not come back, and Candide was so sunk in his sorrow that he did not even notice that Paquette and Friar Giroflée had not so much as come to thank him.

26

Of a supper that Candide and Martin had with six foreigners, and who these were

One evening when Candide, followed by Martin, was going to sit down to table with the foreigners who were staying in the same hotel, a man with a soot-coloured face came up to him from behind and, taking him by the arm, said: 'Be ready to leave with us, do not fail.'

He turns around and sees Cacambo. Only the sight of Cunégonde could have astounded and pleased him more. He was on the point of going mad with joy. He embraced his dear friend.

'Then doubtless Cunégonde is here? Where is she? Take me to her, let me die of joy with her.'

'Cunégonde is not here,' said Cacambo, 'she is in Constantinople.'

'Oh heavens! In Constantinople! But were she in China, I fly to her, let's go.'

---

[81]   Voltaire had much admiration for Milton, as he did for Shakespeare, but as time passed he became more and more critical of what he considered the barbarism of both. [Frame]

'We will leave after supper,' said Cacambo; 'I cannot tell you any more; I am a slave, my master is waiting for me, I must go and serve him at table. Don't say a word; have supper and be ready.'

Candide, torn between joy and sorrow, charmed to see his faithful agent again, astounded to see him a slave, full of the idea of recovering his mistress, his heart agitated and his mind topsy-turvy, sat down to table with Martin, who observed all these adventures imperturbably, and with six foreigners who had come to spend the Carnival in Venice.

Cacambo, who was pouring drink for one of these six foreigners, got his master's ear toward the end of the meal and said to him: 'Sire, your Majesty will leave when you wish, the vessel is ready.' Having said these words he went out.

The guests, astonished, looked at each other without uttering a single word, when another servant, coming up to his master, said to him 'Sire, Your Majesty's chaise is in Padua, and the boat is ready.' The master made a sign, and the servant left.

All the guests looked at each other again, and the general surprise redoubled. A third valet, also approaching a third foreigner, said to him: 'Sire, believe me, Your Majesty must not remain here any longer; I am going to prepare everything.' And immediately he disappeared.

By now Candide and Martin had no doubt that this was a Carnival masquerade. A fourth servant said to the fourth master: 'Your Majesty will leave when you please,' and went out like the others. The fifth valet said as much to the fifth master. But the sixth valet spoke differently to the sixth foreigner who was sitting with Candide; he said to him: 'Faith, Sire, they won't give Your Majesty credit any more, nor me either; and we could well be locked up tonight, you and me; I am going to see to my own affairs; farewell.'

All the servants having disappeared, the six foreigners, Candide, and Martin remained in deep silence. Finally Candide broke it:

'Gentlemen,' he said, 'this is a singular jest. Why are you all kings? For myself, I admit that neither Martin nor I am.'

Cacambo's master then spoke up gravely and said in Italian: 'I am not jesting, my name is Ahmed III.[82] I was Grand Sultan for several years; I dethroned my brother; my nephew dethroned me; my viziers[83] had their heads cut off; I am ending my days in the old seraglio. My nephew, the Grand Sultan Mahmud, allows me to travel sometimes for my health, and I have come to spend the Carnival in Venice.'

A young man who was next to Ahmed spoke after him and said: 'My name is Ivan; I was Emperor of all the Russias; I was dethroned in my cradle; my father and mother were locked up; I was brought up in prison; I sometimes have permission to travel, accompanied by those who guard me, and I have come to spend the Carnival in Venice.'

The third said: 'I am Charles Edward, King of England; my father ceded me his rights to the kingdom. I fought to maintain them; they tore the hearts out of eight hundred of my supporters and dashed them in their faces. I was put in prison; I am going to Rome to pay a visit to the King my father, who is dethroned like my grandfather and me; and I have come to spend the Carnival in Venice.'

The fourth then took the floor and said: 'I am King of the Poles; the fortunes of war have deprived me of my hereditary states; my father underwent the same reverses; I resign myself to Providence like Sultan Ahmed, Emperor Ivan, and King Charles Edward, whom God give long life; and I have come to spend the Carnival in Venice.'

The fifth said: 'I too am King of the Poles; I have lost my kingdom twice; but Providence has given me another state,[84] in which I have done more good than all the kings of the Sarmatians together have even been able to do on the banks of the Vistula; I too resign myself to Providence; and I have come to spend the Carnival in Venice.'

---

[82]   All these kings are real. [Frame]

[83]   A high Mohammedan executive or judicial officer. [Frame]

[84]   Stanislas Leszczynski (1677–1766), father of the Queen of France, abdicated the throne of Poland in 1736, was made Duke of Lorraine, and did much good in and around Lunéville. The Sarmatians are the Slavs. [Frame]

It remained for the sixth monarch to speak. 'Gentlemen,' said he, 'I am not as great a lord as you; but even so I have been a King like anyone else. I am Theodore; I was elected King of Corsica; I have been called Your Majesty, and at present I am hardly called Sir. I have coined money, and I do not have a penny; I have had two secretaries of state, and I have scarcely a valet. I was once on a throne, and I was in prison for a long time in London, on the straw. I am much afraid I shall be treated the same way here, although I have come, like Your Majesties, to spend the Carnival in Venice.'

The five other Kings listened to this speech with noble compassion. Each of them gave King Theodore twenty sequins[85] to get clothes and shirts; and Candide presented him with a diamond worth two thousand sequins. 'Who is this man,' said the five Kings, 'who is in a position to give a hundred times as much as each of us, and who gives it? Are you a King too, sir?'

'No, gentlemen, and I have no desire to be.'[86]

At the moment when they were leaving the table, there arrived in the same hotel four Most Serene Highnesses, who had also lost their states by the fortune of war, and who were coming to spend the rest of the Carnival in Venice. But Candide did not even take note of these newcomers; he was preoccupied only with going to find his dear Cunégonde in Constantinople.

27
Candide's voyage to Constantinople

The faithful Cacambo had already obtained an agreement with the Turkish captain who was about to take Sultan Ahmed back to Constantinople that he would take Candide and Martin on his ship. Both came on board after having

prostrated themselves before his miserable Highness. On the way, Candide said to Martin:

'But those were six dethroned Kings that we had supper with, and besides, among those six Kings there was one to whom I gave alms. Maybe there are many other princes still more unfortunate. As for me, I have lost only a hundred sheep, and I am flying to Cunégonde's arms. My dear Martin once again, Pangloss was right, all is well.'

'I hope so,' said Martin.

'But,' said Candide, 'that was a most implausible adventure we had in Venice. No one ever saw or heard of six dethroned Kings having supper together in an inn.'

'That is no more extraordinary,' said Martin, 'than most of the things that have happened to us. It is very common for Kings to be dethroned; and as for the honour we had in having supper with them, it is a thing that does not deserve our attention. What does it matter whom you sup with, provided you make good cheer?'[87]

Scarcely was Candide in the ship when he threw his arms around the neck of his former valet, his friend Cacambo.

'Well,' he said, 'what is Cunégonde doing? Is she still a prodigy of beauty? Does she still love me? How is she? No doubt you bought her a palace in Constantinople.'

'My dear master,' replied Cacambo, 'Cunégonde is washing dishes on the banks of Propontis[88] for a prince who has very few dishes; she is a slave in the household of a former sovereign named Ragotsky,[89] to whom the Grand Turk gives three crowns a day in his refuge; but what is much sadder is that she has lost her beauty and become horribly ugly.'

'Ah! beautiful or ugly,' said Candide, 'I am an honourable man, and my duty is to love her always. But how can she be reduced to so abject a state with the six millions you brought her?'

---

[85] A Venetian gold coin. [Frame]

[86] These three sentences (from '"Who is this man"' on) are the final form that Voltaire intended, replacing the following:
'"Who is this ordinary citizen," said the five Kings, "who is in a position to give a hundred times as much as each of us, and who gives it?"' [Frame]

[87] This passage, from 'it is a thing' on, is another change intended by Voltaire (cf. note 86 above) to replace this: '"it is a trifle that does not deserve our attention"'. [Frame]

[88] The Sea of Marmora, between the Bosporus and the Dardanelles. [Frame]

[89] A former prince of Transylvania. [Frame]

'Well,' said Cacambo, 'did I not have to give two millions to Señor Don Fernando d'Ibaraa y Figueora y Mascarenes y Lampourdos y Souz, Governor of Buenos Aires, for permission to take Mademoiselle Cunégonde back? And did not a pirate bravely despoil us of all the rest? And did not that pirate take us to Cape Matapan, to Milo, to Nicaria, to Samos, to Petra, to the Dardanelles, to Marmora, to Scutari? Cunégonde and the old woman are servants with that prince I spoke to you about, and I am a slave of the dethroned Sultan.'

'What a chain of frightful calamities one after another!' said Candide. 'But after all, I still have a few diamonds. I shall easily deliver Cunégonde. It is a great pity that she has become so ugly.'

Then, turning to Martin, he said: 'Which one do you think is the most to be pitied, Emperor Ahmed, Emperor Ivan, King Charles Edward, or I?'

'I know nothing about that,' said Martin; 'I would have to be inside your hearts to know.'

'Ah!' said Candide, 'if Pangloss were here, he would know and would tell us.'

'I do not know,' said Martin, 'with what scales your Pangloss could have weighed the misfortunes of men and estimate their sorrows. All I presume is that there are millions of men on earth a hundred times more to be pitied than King Charles Edward, Emperor Ivan, and Sultan Ahmed.'

'That might well be,' said Candide.

They arrived in a few days in the Bosporus. Candide began by buying back Cacambo at a very high price; and without wasting time he flung himself into a galley with his companions to go to the shores of Propontis and find Cunégonde, however ugly she might be.

In the convict crew there were two galley slaves who rowed very badly, and from time to time the Levantine captain applied a few strokes of a bull's pizzle to their bare shoulders; Candide, from a natural impulse, looked at them more attentively than at the other galley slaves and went up to them in pity. Some features of their disfigured faces seemed to him to have some resemblance to Pangloss and to that hapless Jesuit, the Baron, Mademoiselle Cunégonde's brother. This idea touched him and saddened him. He looked at them even more attentively. 'Truly,' he said to Cacambo, 'if I had not seen Doctor Pangloss hanged, and if I had not had the misfortune to kill the Baron, I would think it is they that are rowing in this galley.'

At the names 'Baron' and 'Pangloss' the two convicts uttered a loud cry, sat still on their bench, and dropped their oars. The Levantine captain ran up to them, and the lashes with the bull's pizzle redoubled.

'Stop, stop, my lord,' cried Candide, 'I will give you as much money as you want.'

'What! It's Candide!' said one of the convicts.

'What! It's Candide!' said the other.

'Is this a dream?' said Candide. 'Am I really awake? Am I in this galley? Is that My Lord the Baron, whom I killed? Is that Doctor Pangloss, whom I saw hanged?'

'It is indeed, it is indeed,' they replied.

'What! Is this that great philosopher?' said Martin.

'Oh! Master Levantine Captain,' said Candide, 'how much money do you want for the ransom of My Lord of Thunder-ten-tronckh, one of the first barons of the Empire, and for Monsieur Pangloss, the most profound metaphysician of Germany?'

'Dog of a Christian,' replied the Levantine captain, 'since these two dogs of Christian convicts are barons and metaphysicians, which is no doubt a great dignity in their country, you shall give me fifty thousand sequins for them.'

'You shall have them, sir; take me back like a flash to Constantinople, and you shall be paid on the spot. But no, take me to Mademoiselle Cunégonde.'

The Levantine captain, at Candide's first offer, had already turned his prow toward the city, and he was making the oarsmen row faster than a bird cleaves the air.

Candide embraced the Baron and Pangloss a hundred times. 'And how is it that I did not kill you, my dear Baron? And my dear Pangloss, how is it that you are alive after being hanged? And why are you both in the galleys in Turkey?'

'Is it really true that my dear sister is in this country?' said the Baron.

'Yes,' replied Cacambo.

'So I see my dear Candide again,' exclaimed Pangloss.

Candide introduced Martin and Cacambo to them. They all embraced, they all talked at once. The galley flew, they were already in the port. They sent for a Jew, to whom Candide sold for fifty thousand sequins a diamond of the value of a hundred thousand, and who swore to him by Abraham that he could not give any more. Candide immediately paid the ransom of the Baron and Pangloss. The latter threw himself at the feet of his liberator and bathed them with tears; the other thanked him with a nod and promised to repay him the money at the first opportunity. 'But is it really possible that my sister is in Turkey?' he said.

'Nothing is so possible,' retorted Cacambo, 'since she is scouring dishes for a prince of Transylvania.'

Immediately they sent for two Jews; Candide sold some more diamonds; and they all set out again in another galley to go and deliver Cunégonde.

28
What happened to Candide, Cunégonde, Pangloss, Martin, et al.

'Once again, pardon,' said Candide to the Baron, 'pardon me, Reverend Father, for having given you a great sword-thrust through the body.'

'Let's say no more about it,' said the Baron; 'I was a little too hasty, I admit; but since you want to know by what chance you saw me in the galleys, I will tell you. After being cured of my wound by the brother apothecary of the College, I was attacked and carried off by a party of Spaniards; they put me in prison in Buenos Aires at the time when my sister had just left. I asked to return to the Father General in Rome. I was named to go to Constantinople and serve as almoner with My Lord the Ambassador of France. Not a week after I had taken up my duties, I met, toward evening, a very attractive ichoglan.[90] It was very hot; the young man wanted to bathe; I took the opportunity to bathe too. I did not know that it was a capital crime for a Christian to be found stark naked with a young Moslem. A cadi[91] had me given a hundred strokes on the soles of my feet and condemned me to the galleys. I do not think a more horrible injustice has ever been done. But I would certainly like to know why my sister is in the kitchen of a sovereign of Transylvania who is a refugee among the Turks.'

'But you, my dear Pangloss,' said Candide, 'how can it be that I see you again?'

'It is true,' said Pangloss, 'that you saw me hanged; naturally I was supposed to be burned; but you remember there was a heavy downpour just when they were going to cook me; the storm was so violent that they despaired of lighting the fire; I was hanged because they could do no better; a surgeon bought my body, took me home, and dissected me. First he made a cross-shaped incision in me from the navel to the clavicle. No one could have been worse hanged than I had been. The Holy Inquisition's Executor of High Operations, who was a subdeacon, did indeed burn people marvellously, but he was not accustomed to hanging them; the rope was wet and slipped badly, it became knotted; in short, I was still breathing. The cross-shaped incision made me utter such a loud scream that my surgeon fell over backward and, thinking that he was dissecting the devil, he fled, half-dead from fear, and he fell again on the staircase as he fled. His wife came running from a nearby room at the noise; she saw me stretched out on the table with my cross-shaped incision; she was even more afraid than her husband, fled, and fell over him. When they had recovered a little, I heard the surgeon's wife say to the surgeon: "My dear, what are you thinking of, dissecting a heretic? Don't you know that the devil is always in those people? I am going quickly to get a priest to exorcise him."

'I shuddered at these words and collected the little strength I had left to call out: "Have pity on me?" Finally the Portuguese barber[92] grew bolder; he sewed up my skin; his wife even took care of me; in two weeks I was on my feet. The barber found me a job and made me lackey to a knight of Malta who was going to Venice; but as this master had no money to pay me, I entered the service of a Venetian merchant and followed him to Constantinople.

[90] Page to the Sultan. [Frame]

[91] A minor Mohammedan judge or magistrate. [Frame]

[92] The surgeon. [Frame]

'One day I took a notion to enter a mosque; there was no one there but an old imam and a very pretty young devotee who was saying her prayers. Her bosom was fully uncovered; between her breasts she had a beautiful bouquet of tulips, roses, anemones, buttercups, hyacinths, and yellow primroses; she dropped her bouquet; I picked it up, and I replaced it for her with the most respectful eagerness. I was so long in replacing it for her that the imam grew angry, and, seeing that I was a Christian, called for help. I was taken before the cadi, who had me given a hundred strokes on the soles of the feet and sent me to the galleys. I was chained precisely in the same galley and on the same bench as My Lord the Baron. In this galley there were four young men from Marseilles, five Neapolitan priests, and two monks from Corfu, who told us that similar adventures occurred every day. My Lord the Baron claimed that he had suffered a greater injustice than I; for my part I claimed that it was much more permissible to replace a bouquet on a woman's bosom than to be stark naked with an ichoglan. We were arguing unceasingly and receiving twenty stokes a day of the bull's pizzle, when the concatenation of the events of this universe brought you into our galley and you ransomed us.'

'Well, my dear Pangloss,' said Candide, 'when you were hanged, dissected, racked with blows, and rowing in the galleys, did you still think that all was for the very best?'

'I am still of my first opinion,' replied Pangloss; 'for after all I am a philosopher, it is not fitting for me to recant, for Leibniz cannot be wrong, and besides, pre-established harmony is the finest thing in the world, like the plenum and subtle matter.'

29
How Candide found Cunégonde and the old woman again

While Candide, the Baron, Pangloss, Martin, and Cacambo were relating their adventure, reasoning on the contingent or non-contingent events of this universe, arguing about effects and causes, moral and physical evil, free will and necessity, and the consolation that may be experienced when one is in the galleys in Turkey, they landed on the shore of Propontis at the house of the prince of Transylvania. The first objects that met their eyes were Cunégonde and the old woman, who were spreading out towels on lines to dry.

The Baron paled at this sight. The tender lover Candide, on seeing his fair Cunégonde dark-skinned, eyes bloodshot, flat-bosomed, cheeks wrinkled, arms red and rough, recoiled three steps in horror, and then advanced out of good manners. She embraced Candide and her brother; they embraced the old woman; Candide ransomed them both.

There was a little farm in the neighbourhood; the old woman proposed to Candide that he buy it while waiting for the entire group to enjoy a better destiny. Cunégonde did not know that she had grown ugly, no one had told her so; she reminded Candide of his promises in so positive a tone that the good Candide did not refuse her. So he notified the Baron that he was going to marry his sister.

'I shall never endure,' said the Baron, 'such baseness on her part and such insolence on yours; no one shall ever reproach me with that infamy; my sister's children would not be able to enter the chapters[93] of Germany. No, never shall my sister marry anyone but a baron of the Empire.'

Cunégonde threw herself at his feet and bathed them with tears; he was inflexible.

'You are the maddest of madmen,' said Candide, 'I rescued you from the galleys, I paid your ransom, I paid your sister's too; she was washing dishes here, she is ugly, I am kind enough to make her my wife, and you still presume to oppose it; I would kill you again if I heeded my anger.'

'You may kill me again,' said the Baron, 'but you shall not marry my sister while I am alive.'

30
Conclusion

At the bottom of his heart, Candide had no desire to marry Cunégonde. But the Baron's extreme impertinence determined him to clinch the marriage, and Cunégonde urged him on so

---

[93]   Knightly assemblies. [Frame]

eagerly that he could not retreat. He consulted Pangloss, Martin and the faithful Cacambo. Pangloss composed a fine memoir by which he proved that the Baron had no rights over his sister, and that according to all the laws of the Empire she could make a left-handed marriage[94] with Candide. Martin's judgement was to throw the Baron in the sea; Cacambo decided that he should be returned to the Levantine captain and put back in the galleys, after which he would be sent by the first ship to the Father General in Rome. The plan was considered very good; the old woman approved it; they said nothing about it to his sister; for a little money the thing was carried out, and they had the pleasure of trapping a Jesuit and punishing the pride of a German Baron.

It was quite natural to imagine that after so many disasters Candide, married to his mistress and living with the philosopher Pangloss, the philosopher Martin, the prudent Cacambo, and the old woman, moreover having brought back so many diamonds from the land of the ancient Incas, would lead the most pleasant life in the world. But he was cheated by the Jews[95] so that he had nothing left but his little farm; his wife, becoming uglier every day, became shrewish and intolerable; the old woman was an invalid and was even more bad-humoured than Cunégonde. Cacambo, who worked in the garden and who went and sold vegetables at Constantinople, was worn out with work and cursed his destiny. Pangloss was in despair at not shining in some university in Germany. As for Martin, he was firmly persuaded that a man is equally badly off anywhere; he took things patiently.

Candide, Martin, and Pangloss sometimes argued about metaphysics and morality. They often saw passing under the windows of the farm boats loaded with effendis,[96] pashas,[97] and cadis who were being sent into exile at Lemnos,

Mitylene, and Erzerum. They saw other cadis arriving, other pashas, other effendis, who took the place of the exiles and were exiled in their turn. They saw properly impaled heads on their way to be presented to the Sublime Porte.[98] These sights redoubled their discourses; and when they were not arguing, the boredom was so excessive that one day the old woman to say to them:

'I would like to know which is worse – to be raped a hundred times by Negro pirates, have a buttock cut off, run the gauntlet among the Bulgarians, be flogged and hanged in an auto-da-fé, be dissected, row in the galleys, in short to undergo all the miseries we have all been through – or to stay here doing nothing?'

'It's a great question,' said Candide.

These remarks engendered new reflections, and Martin above all concluded that man was born to live in the convulsions of anxiety or the lethargy of boredom. Candide did not agree, but he asserted nothing. Pangloss admitted that he had always suffered horribly; but having once maintained that everything was wonderful, he still maintained it and believed not a bit of it.

One thing completely confirmed Martin in his detestable principles, made Candide hesitate more than ever, and embarrassed Pangloss: one day they saw coming to their farm Paquette and Friar Giroflée, who were in the utmost misery; they had very quickly gone through their three thousand piasters, had parted, made it up, quarrelled, been put in prison, escaped, and finally Friar Giroflée had turned Turk. Paquette continued to ply her trade everywhere, and no longer earned anything at it.

'I had quite foreseen,' said Martin to Candide, 'that your presents would be soon dissipated and would only make them more miserable. You and Cacambo were once glutted with millions of piastres, and you are no happier than Friar Giroflée and Paquette.'

---

[94] A morganatic marriage, giving no equality to the party of lower rank. [Frame]

[95] Voltaire had suffered financial losses from the bankruptcies of Jewish bankers. [Frame]

[96] Turkish title of respect used especially of state officials. [Frame]

[97] A Turkish governor or military leader. [Frame]

[98] Originally, the gate of the Sultan's palace, where justice was once administered; hence, his government. [Frame]

'Aha!' said Pangloss to Paquette, 'so heaven brings you back among us here, my poor child! Do you realize that you cost me the end of my nose, an eye, and an ear? Look at you now! Ah! What a world is this!'

This new adventure led them to philosophize more than ever.

In the neighbourhood there was a very famous dervish[99] who was considered the best philosopher in Turkey; they went to consult him; Pangloss was the spokesman and said to him: 'Master, we have come to ask you to tell us why such a strange animal as man was ever created.'

'What are you meddling in?' said the dervish. 'Is that your business?'

'But, Reverend Father,' said Candide, 'there is a horrible amount of evil on earth.'

'What does it matter,' said the dervish, 'whether there is evil or good? When His Highness sends a ship to Egypt, is he bothered about whether the mice in the ship are comfortable or not?'

'Then what should we do?' said Pangloss.

'Hold your tongue,' said the dervish.

'I flattered myself,' said Pangloss, 'that you and I would reason a bit together about effects and causes, the best of all possible worlds, the origin of evil, the nature of the soul, and pre-established harmony.' At these words the dervish shut the door in their faces.

During this conversation the news had gone round that in Constantinople they had just strangled two viziers of the Divan[100] and the mufti[101] and impaled several of their friends. This catastrophe caused a great stir everywhere for a few hours. Pangloss, Candide, and Martin, returning to the little farm, came upon a good old man enjoying the fresh air by his door under a bower of orange trees. Pangloss, whose curiosity was as great as his love of reasoning, asked him the name of the mufti who had just been strangled.

'I know nothing about it,' replied the good man, 'and I have never known the name of any mufti or any vizier. I am entirely ignorant of the adventure that you are telling me about; I presume that in general those who meddle with public affairs sometimes perish miserably, and that they deserve it; but I never inquire what is going on in Constantinople; I content myself with sending there for sale the fruits of the garden that I cultivate.'

Having said these words, he made the strangers come into his house; his two daughters and his two sons presented them with several kinds of sherbets which they made themselves, Turkish cream flavoured with candied citron peel, oranges, lemons, limes, pineapples, pistachios, and Mocha coffee that had not been mixed with the bad coffee from Batavia and the West Indies. After which the two daughters of this good Moslem perfumed the beards of Candide, Pangloss, and Martin.

'You must have a vast and magnificent estate?' said Candide to the Turk.

'I have only twenty acres,' replied the Turk; 'I cultivate them with my children; work keeps away three great evils: boredom, vice, and need.'

As Candide went back to his farm, he reflected deeply on the Turk's remarks. He said to Pangloss and Martin: 'That good old man seems to me to have made himself a life far preferable to that of the six Kings with whom we had the honour of having supper.'

'Great eminence,' said Pangloss, 'is very dangerous, according to the report of all philosophers. For after all Eglon,[102] King of the Moabites, was assassinated by Ehud; Absalom was hanged by his hair and pierced with three darts; King Nadab son of Jeroboam was killed by Baasha, King Elah by Zimri, Ahaziah by Jehu, Athaliah by Jehoiada; Kings Jehoiakim, Jeconiah, and Zedekiah became slaves. You know how Croesus perished, Astyages, Darius, Dionysius of

---

[99]   A member of a Mohammedan religious order. [Frame]

[100]   Turkish council of state. [Frame]

[101]   An official expounder of Mohammedan law. [Frame]

[102]   For this first group of Old Testament rulers, see Judges 3, II Samuel 18, and I and II Kings. [Frame]

Syracuse, Pyrrhus, Perseus, Hannibal, Jugurtha, Ariovistus, Caesar, Pompey, Nero, Otho, Vitellius, Domitian, Richard II of England, Edward II, Henry VI, Richard III, Mary Stuart, Charles I, the three Henrys of France, the Emperor Henry IV? You know ... '

'I also know,' said Candide, 'that we must cultivate our garden.'

'You are right,' said Pangloss, 'for when man was put in the Garden of Eden, he was put there *ut operaretur eum*, to work; which proves that man was not born for rest.'

'Let us work without reasoning,' said Martin, 'it is the only way to make life endurable.'

All the little society entered into this laudable plan; each one began to exercise his talents. The little piece of land produced much. True, Cunégonde was very ugly; but she became an excellent pastry cook; Paquette embroidered; the old woman took care of the linen. No one, not even Friar Giroflée, failed to perform some service; he was a very good carpenter, and even became an honourable man; and Pangloss sometimes said to Candide: 'All events are linked together in the best of all possible worlds; for after all, if you had not been expelled from a fine castle with great kicks in the backside for love of Mademoiselle Cunégonde, if you had not been subjected to the Inquisition, if you had not travelled about America on foot, if you had not given the Baron a great blow with your sword, if you had not lost all your sheep from the good country of Eldorado, you would not be here eating candied citrons and pistachios.'

'That is well said,' replied Candide, 'but we must cultivate our garden.'

Notes and Glossary

Anabapist: member of the Christian sect that rejected infant baptism in favour of baptism on confession of faith.

Année Littéraire: see Fréron.

auto-da-fé: from the Portuguese, 'act of the faith': the ceremony attendant to a judgement by the Inquisition: hence the burning of heretics as a result of such a judgement.

Barbados water: a cordial flavoured with orange peel and lemon peel.

berlin: a four-wheeled, two-seated, covered carriage.

Berruyer: Isaac-Joseph Berruyer (1681–1758), author of *L'Histoire du peuple de Dieu* (1728, 7 vols).

Berthier: Guillaume-François Berthier (1704–82), editor of the Jesuit *Journal de Trévoux*, opponent of Voltaire, the *Encyclopédie*, and the *philosophes* in general.

Bossuet: Jacques-Bénigne Bossuet (1627–1704), outstanding preacher, writer, and spokesman for the religious policy of Louis XIV.

Bougeant: Guillaume-Hyacinthe Bougeant (1690–1743), who argues in his *Amusement philosophique sur le language des bêtes* (1736) that fallen angels live in the bodies of animals.

cadi: a minor Mohammedan judge or magistrate.

Castel: Louis-Bertrand Castel (1688–1757), anti-Newtonian scientist, whose works include a *Traité de physique sur la pesanteur universelle* (1724, 2 vols) and *L'Optique des couleurs* (1750).

Christian Pedagogue: Pédagogue chrétien (1634 or earlier), French translation of a popular Latin work by Father Philippe d'Outreman (1585–1652).

Clélie: a tremendously popular novel (1654–61, 10 vols) by Mlle Madeleine de Scudéry, famous for its 'Carte de Tendre', an allegorical map of the country of love.

Clodion the Hairy: a fifth-century Frankish chief.

convulsion(s) (convulsionary, convulsionaries): manifestations of religious ecstasy or mania, like those of the Holy Rollers today. The Jansenists were noted for them.

Corneille: Pierre Corneille (1606–84), the first great French tragedian, author of *Le Cid, Horace, Cinna, Polyeucte, Rodogune,* many other tragedies, and a few comedies.

Croiset: Father Jean Croiset (died 1738), author of many collections of *Méditations (Retraite spirituelle pour un jour de chaque mois)* published from 1694 on.

Curious and Edifying Letters: Lettres édifiantes et curieuses, a collection of reports by Jesuit missionaries published from 1792 on.

daric: a gold coin of ancient Persia.

Derham: William Derham (1657–1735), author of *Astrotheology* (1715).

dervish: a member of a Mohammedan religious order.

Desterham: Voltaire's version of *defterdar,* a Turkish superintendent of finance.

Divan: Turkish council of state.

drachma: a Greek coin, once used also in Egypt.

Du Cerceau: Jean-Antoine Du Cerceau (1670–1730), Jesuit poet and dramatist.

effendi: Turkish title of respect used especially of state officials.

Encyclopédie: or *Dictionnaire raisonné des sciences, des arts, et des métiers*, a vast secular *summa* published (1751–65) despite many obstacles, edited by Diderot with the collaboration of most of the *philosophes*, including Voltaire.

English cordial: a cordial containing spirits of ammonia.

Erythrean Sea: the Red Sea.

Flower of the Saints: Flos Sanctorum, o Libro de las vida de los Santos (1599, 2 vols) by the Spanish Jesuit Pedro de Ribadeneira (1526–1611), popular in French translation.

Fréron: Élie Fréron (1719–76), publisher of the *Année Littéraire*, enemy of Voltaire and the *philosophes* and a favourite target for Voltaire's wit.

Gaeta: an Italian port north-west of Naples.

Gauchat: Gabriel Gauchat (1709–74 or 1779), enemy of Voltaire and the Encyclopedists.

Harlay (Archbishop de): François de Harlay de Champvallon (1625–95), Archbishop of Paris from 1670, a leader in the persecution of Protestants and Jansenists.

imam: a Mohammedan priest.

Imaus, Mount: ancient name for an Asian mountain range, probably the Himalayas.

Jansenism, Jansenists, Jansenius: Jansenism is a Christian sect stressing predestination and asceticism, founded by Cornelius Jansen or Jansenius (1585–1638), Dutch Bishop of Ypres, author of the *Augustinus* (1640). It spread rapidly and widely in France, notably through the efforts of Saint-Cyran and Arnauld, and established its centre near Paris in the religious community of Port-Royal. Opposed violently by the Sorbonne and the Jesuits, persecuted by Louis XIV, and condemned by Pope Clement XI in 1713, Jansenism still retained some strength in France until about the mid-eighteenth century.

Japan: To discourage trade with the Christians, the Japanese required European merchants to stamp on the cross as a sign of rejection of Christianity.

Journal de Trévoux: the Jesuit journal, founded in 1701 and edited for many years by Guillaume-François Berthier.

Kroust: Father Antoine Kroust, Jesuit, rector at Colmar from 1753 to 1763, hostile to Voltaire and the *philosophes*.

La Chaise: François de La Chaise (1624–1709), Jesuit father, from 1675 on the very influential confessor to Louis XIV.

lettre(s) de cachet: letters bearing the King's seal; in Voltaire's time, arbitrary warrants of imprisonment.

Lettre(s) provinciale(s): see Pascal.

Louisiade: an epic poem formally entitled *Saint Louis, ou le héros chrétien* (1653) by Father Pierre Le Moyne (1602–71).

Maeotian Marsh: ancient name for the Sea of Azov.

Malagrida: Gabriel Malagrida (1689–1761), Portuguese Jesuit, who pronounced it no sin to kill his King, Joseph I, was compromised in a plot against the King's life which led to the expulsion of the Jesuits from Portugal in 1759, and was executed in 1761.

Manichean: a follower of Mani or Manicheus, a third-century Persian who believed in two nearly equal forces, of good and of evil. The sect flourished in St Augustine's time.

maravedi: a small Spanish copper coin.

Marillac: Louis de Marillac (1573–1632), Marshal of France, who conspired against Richelieu and was executed by his orders.

Meknes: a town in Morocco.

moidore: a gold coin of Portugal and Brazil.

Molinism, Molinists: Jesuits, from the name of Luis Molina (1535–1600), Spanish Jesuit, author of a widely influential theory reconciling predestination with free will.

mufti: an official expounder of Mohammedan law.

Oratory: a preaching order (Oratorians, or Fathers of the Oratory) founded in Italy in 1564 and established in France in 1611.

Pascal: Blaise Pascal (1623–62), eminent French mathematician, physicist, and religious writer, spokesman for the Jansenists against the Jesuits in his *Lettres provinciales* (1656–57), Christian apologist in his unfinished *Pensées* (1670). His sister Gilberte told of his rediscovery of the first thirty-two propositions of Euclid at the age of twelve. Voltaire enjoyed his satire of the Jesuits but criticized his view of the misery of fallen man in his *Remarques sur les Pensées de M. Pascal* (1734).

pasha: a Turkish governor or military leader.

patacón (or pataca): a Portuguese and Brazilian silver coin.

piaster: a coin, usually silver, or Turkey and Egypt; also used to signify the Spanish peso.

pistole: a Spanish gold coin.

Port-Royal: *see* Jansenism.

Propontis: the Sea of Marmora, between the Bosporus and the Dardanelles.

Prosper, St: Prosper of Aquitaine or Prosper Tiro (*c*.390–*c*.465), a disciple of St Augustine.

Racine: Jean Racine (1639–99), great French tragedian, Voltaire's model in that genre, whose tragedies include *Andromaque, Britannicus, Bérénice, Bajazet, Mithridate, Iphigénie, Phédre, Esther,* and *Athalie.*

Recollects (*Récollets*): a strict branch of the Franciscans, rivals of the Jesuits.

Rohault: Jacques Rohault (1620–75), author of a *Traité de physique* (1671).

Sadder: an extract from the Zend-Avesta, the sacred book of Zoroastrianism.

Saint-Cyran: *see* Jansenism.

Saint-Pouange: a name probably representing Louis Phélypeaux, Count of Saint-Florentin (1705–77), minister under Louis XVI, who dismissed him in 1775. He was criticized for prodigality, loose morality, and over-use of *lettres de cachet* (q.v.).

Salé: a Moroccan port on the Atlantic near Rabat, once a headquarters for pirates.

sanbenito: a yellow robe worn by heretics condemned to the stake by the Inquisition.

sequin: a Venetian gold coin.

Socinian: a religious rationalist, denying the Trinity and the personality of Christ.

Sorbonne: a college of the University of Paris whose name is now used for the university itself and was used in Voltaire's day for the university's Faculty of Theology, a stronghold of conservative opposition to the new philosophical ideas.

Tetuan: a town in Morocco.

Theatine: a member of a Catholic order founded in 1524 to combat Protestantism.

Think Well on It: Pensez-y bien, a popular religious work by the Jesuit Father Paul de Barry (1585–1661).

Trublet: Nicolas-Charles-Joseph Trublet (1677–1770), bitter critic of Voltaire and the *Encyclopédie*, author of *Essais de littérature.*

Tucuman: a province in northern Argentina.

vizier: a high Mohammedan executive or judicial officer.

Source: Donald M. Frame (ed.), *Candide, Zadig and Selected Stories*, Cassell, London, 1962. (First edn New American Library, New York, 1961.)

James Lind
Extracts from A Treatise of the Scurvy

Prepared for the Course Team by
Michael Bartholomew

Contents

James Lind
Extracts from A Treatise of the Scurvy

These extracts come from A Treatise of the Scurvy *by James Lind M.D., published in Edinburgh in 1753. Lind (1716–94), was a product of Edinburgh's influential medical tradition. He worked as a surgeon in the Royal Navy, and rose to the post of Physician to the Haslar Naval Hospital at Portsmouth. The extracts printed here are divided into three sections. Each of these sections is intended to transmit the full sense of the arguments of the chapters from which they are derived, but substantial cuts have been made. As a whole, the extracts printed here represent about ten per cent of the total length of the* Treatise. *Modern equivalents of eighteenth-century terms, and a few explanatory glosses, have been given as notes at the foot of the page.*

The Dedication

To the Right Honourable GEORGE LORD ANSON &c &c &c, who, as a just reward for the great and signal services done to the BRITISH NATION, does now preside over her NAVAL AFFAIRS, the following *Treatise* is INSCRIBED, with the greatest respect, by his LORDSHIP'S *Most devoted, and Most obedient humble servant,* JAMES LIND.

Section 1: 'The true causes of the disease, from observations made upon it, both at sea and land' (from Treatise Part II, ch.I)

The scorbutic[1] taint is induced chiefly by the agency of certain external and remote causes; which, according as their existence is permanent or casual, and in proportion to the different degrees of violence with which they act, give rise to a disease more or less epidemic, and of various degrees of malignity.

Now, by considering the peculiarity of the circumstances, situation, and way of life of these people [i.e. victims of scurvy], and by attentively observing, what at any time gives rise to this disease, what is seen to remove it, and what to increase or mitigate its malignity, we shall be able to form a judgement, not only of the principal causes productive of it, but likewise of the subordinate, or those that in a less degree may contribute their influence. It is indeed a matter of the utmost consequence, to investigate the true sources of this evil; as, upon the removing or correcting of these, the preservation of the body from its first attacks, as well as its consequences, in a great measure depends. And we shall begin with considering the situation of those at sea, among whom it is said to be so often an epidemic calamity.

Many have ascribed this disease to the great quantity of sea-salt, necessarily made use of by seamen in their diet. But to put it beyond all doubt that sea-salt is not the occasion of the scurvy, I took two patients (in order to make trial of the effects of different medicines in this disease to be more fully related afterwards), with very putrid gums, swelled legs, and contracted knees, to whom I gave half a pint of salt water, and sometimes more, every day for a fortnight: at the expiration of which time, I was not sensible of their being in the least worse; but found them in the same condition as those who had taken no medicine whatever. From which I am convinced, that sea-salt, at least the drinking of salt water, by no means disposes the constitution to this disease.

But I would not be understood here to mean, nor does it follow from what has been said, that although sea-water, which is a composition in which this salt is a principal ingredient, has no bad influence upon the scurvy, that a diet of salt flesh and fish is equally innocent. The contrary of which will appear in the sequel. The brine of meats, in particular, is of a different quality from either purified sea-salt or salt-water;

---

[1] 'Scorbutic' means 'pertaining to, or afflicted by, scurvy', from the Latin name – 'scorbutus' – for the disease. 'Scorbutic taint' means 'symptoms of scurvy'.[eds]

for we find that this salt may be so intangled by the animal oils, especially in salt pork, that it is with great difficulty disengaged from them after many washings, and the most plentiful dilution. So that as this saline quality is inextricable from such food, it is rendered improper in many cases to afford that soft, mild nourishment, which is required to repair the body.

Others, again, have supposed such to be the constitution of the human body, that health and life cannot be preserved long, without the use of green herbage, vegetables, and fruits; and that a long abstinence from these, is alone the cause of the disease.

But if this were truly the case, we must have had the scurvy very accurately described by the ancients; whose chief study seems to have been the art of war; and whose manner of besieging towns was generally by a blockade, till they had forced a surrender by famine. Now, as they held out many months, sometimes years, without a supply of vegetables; we should, no doubt, have heard of many dying of the scurvy, long before the magazines of dry provisions were exhausted. It would likewise be a much more frequent disease in every country, than it really is: for there are persons every where, who, from choice, eat few or no green vegetables; and some countries are deprived of the use of them for five or six months of the year; as is the case of many parts in the highlands of Scotland, Newfoundland, &c., where, however, the scurvy is not a usual malady.

It would be tedious to give many instances, they being notorious, of ships' crews continuing several months at sea, upon their ordinary diet, without any approach of the scurvy. I have been three months on a cruise, during which time none of the seamen tasted vegetables or greens of any sort; and although for a great part of that time, from want of fresh water, their beef and pork were boiled in the sea-water, yet we returned into port without one scorbutical complaint. I have known messes, as they are called, of seamen, who have lived, during a whole voyage of three years, on the ship's provisions, for want of money to purchase better fare, especially greens: and who were so regardless of health, as to expend what little money they could procure, in brandy and spirits; so that a few onions, or the like, was their whole sea-store; and a meal with vegetables was seldom eat by them, above twice or thrice in a month, during the whole voyage.

Notwithstanding which, they have kept free from the scurvy.

But it was remarkable, in the two cruises afterwards to be mentioned, in his Majesty's ship the *Salisbury*, where I had an opportunity of making observations on this disease, that it began to rage on board that ship, and indeed all the Channel squadron, upon being less than six weeks at sea; and after having left Plymouth, where plenty of all sorts of greens were to be had; by which, as one would have thought, the sailors had sufficiently prepared their bodies against the attack of this malady. Yet here, in so short a time as two months, out of 4000 men in that fleet, 400 at least became more highly scorbutic than could reasonably have been expected had they all been debarred the use of vegetables for six months on shore, like our highlanders, and many others. And what puts it beyond all doubt, that the disease was not occasioned solely by the want of vegetables for so short a time, is, that the same ship's company of the *Salisbury*, in much longer cruises, kept quite free from the distemper, where their circumstances as to want of fresh vegetables were similar. It was observable, that in the longest cruise she performed, while I was surgeon, there was but one scorbutical patient on board, who fell into the disease after having had an intermitting fever. We were out at that time from the 10th of August to the 28th of October; which was a twelve weeks continuance at sea, and consequently as long an abstinence from vegetables.

So that although it is a certain and experienced truth, that the use of greens and vegetables is effectual in preventing the disease, and extremely beneficial in the cure; and thus we shall say, that abstinence from them, in certain circumstances, proves the *occasional cause* of the evil; yet there are unquestionably to be found at sea, other strong sources of it; which, with respect to the former (or want of vegetables) we shall hereafter distinguish by the name of the *predisposing causes* to it.

Some have alleged [scurvy] to proceed from something peculiar in the confined and polluted air of a ship; and the stagnation of the bilge-water in the hold has been accused as a main cause of the distress. But had this last the effects presumed, they would be most sensibly felt by those who are most exposed to it, *viz.* the carpenters; who at sea are often obliged to measure, every four hours, the quantity of bilge-water;

and do then, and at other times in mending the pumps, suffer very great inconveniences, being almost suffocated by it; nay instances are not wanting where they have been killed at once with this noxious vapour, to which they lie the nearest when in bed. Yet it does not appear from my own experience, nor from the accounts which I have been able to collect, that they are more liable to the scurvy than others on board.

As to any other inconveniences from filth, or want of cleanliness, in a close place, and where the cutaneous and pulmonary perspiration of a multitude is pent up and confined; they are not peculiar to ships, but common to all crowded jails, hospitals, &c; and whatever bad effects such a vitiated air may have on this disease, yet it is certain the scurvy is not the usual and natural consequence of it.

The truth really is, a putrid air, though never observed solely to be productive of this disease, has a pernicious influence in aggravating its several symptoms: and where an epidemic scorbutical constitution at the same time subsists, they give rise to a complicated, scorbutical and malignant fever; which I shall have occasion to mention among the symptoms of this malady.

From what has been said, it appears, that the strong predisposing causes to this calamity at sea, are not constant, but casual, upon that element. For though it should be granted, that the sea-air gives always a tendency to the scorbutic diathesis,[2] yet the evil proves often highly epidemic and fatal in very short voyages, or upon a very short continuance at sea, to crews of ships who, at other times, have continued out much longer, cruising in the same place, and in parallel circumstances of water and provisions, and yet have kept entirely free from it. Thus, the great Lord Anson cruised for four months, waiting for the Acapulco ship,[3] in the Pacific ocean; during which time, we are told, his crews continued in perfect health; when, at another time, after leaving the coast of Mexico, in less than seven weeks at sea, the scurvy became highly epidemic, notwithstanding plenty of fresh provisions and sweet water on board. And when it

raged with such uncommon malignity in passing Cape Horn, it destroyed above one half of his crew, in less time than he kept the seas in perfect health, in the before mentioned cruise.

I had an opportunity in two Channel cruises, the one of ten weeks, the other of eleven, *ann.* 1746 and 1747, in his Majesty's ship the *Salisbury*, a fourth rate,[4] to see this disease rage with great violence. And here it was remarkable, that though I was on board in several other long Channel cruises; one of twelve weeks particularly, from the 10th of August to the 28th of October; yet we had but one scorbutic patient; nor in any other that I remember, had we the least scorbutic appearance. But in those two I have mentioned, the scurvy began to rage after being a month or six weeks at sea; when the water on board, as I took particular notice, was uncommonly sweet and good; and the state of provisions such as could afford no suspicion of occasioning so general a sickness, being the same in quality as in former cruises. And though the scorbutic people were, by the generous liberality of that great and humane commander, the Hon. Captain George Edgcumbe, daily supplied with fresh provisions, such as mutton-broth and fowls, and even meat from his own table; yet, at the expiration of ten weeks, we brought into Plymouth 80 men, out of a complement of 350, more or less afflicted with this disease.

Now, it was observable, that both these cruises were in the months of April, May, and June; when we had, especially in the beginning of them, a continuance of cold, rainy and thick Channel weather, as it is called: whereas in our other cruises, we had generally very fine weather; except in winter, when, during the time I was surgeon, the cruises were but short. Nor could I assign any other reason for the frequency of this disease in these two cruises, and our exemption from it at other times, but the influence of the weather; the circumstances of the men, ship, and provisions, being in all other respects alike. I have more than once remarked, that after great rains, or a continuance of close foggy weather, especially after storms with rain, the scorbutic

---

[2] i.e. constitutional susceptibility to the disease. [eds]

[3] Acapulco ship: a Spanish treasure ship. [eds]

[4] Naval ships were classed into six 'rates'. [eds]

people generally grew worse; but found a mitigation of their symptoms and complaints, upon the weather becoming drier and warmer for a few days. And I am certain it will be allowed, by all who have had an opportunity of making observations on this disease at sea, or will attentively consider the situation of seamen there, that the *principal and main predisposing cause* to it, is a manifest and obvious quality of the air, *viz.* its *moisture.* The effects of this are perceived to be more immediately hurtful and pernicious in certain constitutions, in those who are much weakened by preceeding sickness; in those, who, from a lazy inactive disposition, neglect to use proper exercise; and in those who indulge a discontented melancholy humour: all which may be reckoned the *secondary disposing causes* to this foul and fatal mischief.

As the atmosphere at sea may always be supposed moister than that of the land; hence there is always a greater disposition to the scorbutic diathesis at sea, than in a pure dry land-air. But, supposing the like constitution of air in both places, the inconveniences which persons suffer in a ship during a damp wet season, are infinitely greater than people who live at land are exposed to; these latter having many ways of guarding against its pernicious effects, by warm dry cloaths, fires, good lodging, &c., whereas the sailors are obliged not only to breathe in this air all day, but sleep in it all night, and frequently in wet bed-clothes, the ship's hatches being necessarily kept open. And indeed one reason of the frequency of the scurvy in the above cruises, was no doubt the often carrying up the bedding of the ship's company to quarters; where it was sometimes wet quite through, and continued so for many days together, when, for want of fair weather, there was no opportunity of drying it.

No persons sensible of the bad effects of sleeping in wet apartments, or in damp bedcloaths, and almost in the open air, without any thing sufficiently dry or warm to put on, will be surprised at the havock the scurvy made in Lord Anson's crew in passing Cape Horn, if their situation in such uncommon and tempestuous weather be properly considered.

During such furious storms, the spray of the sea raised by the violence of the wind, is dispersed over the whole ship; so that the people breathe, as it were, in water for many weeks together. The tumultuous waves incessantly breaking in upon the decks, and wetting those who are upon duty as if they had been ducked in the sea; are also continually sending down great quantities of water below; which makes it the most uncomfortable wet lodging imaginable: and, from the labouring of the ship, it generally leaks down, in many places, directly upon their beds. There being here no fire or sun to dry or exhale the moisture, and the hatches necessarily kept shut, this moist, stagnating, confined air below, becomes most offensive and intolerable. When such weather continues long, attended with sleet and rain, as it generally is, we may easily figure to ourselves the condition of the poor men; who are obliged to sleep in wet cloaths and damp beds, the decks swimming with water below them; and there to remain only four hours at a time; till they are again called up to fresh fatigue, and hard labour, and again exposed to the washing of the sea, and rains. The long continuance of this weather seldom fails to produce the scurvy at sea.

As to its breaking out so immediately in those ships [of Anson's], upon their leaving the coast of Mexico, it was not only owing to their finding so few refreshments, especially fruits and vegetables fit to be carried to sea, at the harbour of Chequetan; but also to the incessant rains they had in their passage to Asia, and the great inconveniencies that necessarily must attend so long a continuance of such weather at sea. To which it may be added that, by observations made on this disease, it appears that those who are once infected with it, especially in so deep a degree as that squadron was, are more subject to it afterwards than others. I remember, that many of them who returned to England with Lord Anson, and afterwards went to sea in other ships, were much more liable to the scurvy than others.

It was however remarkable here, that though the calamity began so very soon after their leaving land; yet, in so tedious a passage as four months, it did not rage with that mortality as in passing Cape Horn: nor did it acquire so great virulence, as appears by its being so quickly removed upon their landing. And this was owing to the absence of another cause, which is found greatly to inforce and increase the distress, *viz.* cold; the combination of which with moisture is, upon all occasions, experienced to be the most powerful predisposing cause to this malady;

though indeed the latter of itself is found sufficient to produce it.

Now, any person who has sufficiently considered the situation of a ship's crew, exposed for many weeks to stormy, rainy, or perpetual foggy close weather at sea, will not by this time be surprised at our assigning dampness or moisture, as a principal cause of the frequency and virulency of this disease upon the watery element. And this is not only agreeable to my own experience, but is confirmed by all just observations that were ever made on this distemper. Accordingly we find, that petty officers, who sleep in close births, as they are called, with canvas hung round, by which they are sheltered from the inclemency of the weather; as also seamen who go well clothed, dry, and clean, though using the same diet with the rest of the crew, are not so soon infected. This is the principal reason why officers obliged to live on the ship's provisions, as the warrant-officers often do, (with this difference, that they drink a greater quantity of brandy and spirits, which, as shall be mentioned afterwards, should in a particular manner dispose them to this disease), by lying in warm dry cabins, and going better clothed, are seldom attacked by the scurvy; unless upon its most virulent rage, and when the common sailors have been previously almost destroyed by it.

It is observable, that such a situation as has been described, together with the use of such improper diet as shall hereafter be mentioned, produces the scurvy in any climate: but its virulence will always be greatly augmented by the addition of cold. Thus we find it a much more frequent disease in winter than in summer, and in colder than in warmer climates. Ships that go to the North, as to Greenland, and up the Baltic, are peculiarly subject to it; whereas it is generally owing, in southern latitudes, to the continual rains which fall there at certain seasons, and more particularly to the great length of these voyages. But a combination of moisture with cold, is the most frequent and genuine source of this disease: and a very intense degree of cold, as in Greenland &c. is experienced to have a more pernicious influence in heightening its malignity.

Moisture is the parent of corruption or putrefaction in nature; and, by the observation of all physicians from the days of Hippocrates, a moist warm air begets the most malignant putrid diseases, even the plague itself. But moisture

concurring with other peculiar circumstances, as a gross diet, cold, &c. disposes in a particular manner to the scorbutic corruption.

The qualities of the moist sea-air will certainly be rendered still more noxious, by being confined in a ship without due circulation; as air at all times in this state loses its elasticity, and is found highly prejudicial to the health and life of animals; but becomes much more so where stagnating water is pent up along with it, as it is from thence more speedily disposed to putrefaction. It is likewise heated in ships by passing through the lungs of many people, and impregnated with various putrid effluvia. Hence the eagerness and longings of scorbutic people in such circumstances for the land-air, and the high refreshment to their senses upon being put on shore, are very natural; but no more than what the vapour of fresh earth would afford to a person after being long confined in a close, damp, unwholesome air; as that of a prison, dungeon, or damp apartment at land; and what we all feel, upon taking in the fresh country-air, perfumed with the various odours of nature, after having been obliged to breathe in a crowded, dirty, populous city.

I come, in the next place, to an additional, and extremely powerful cause, observed at sea to occasion this disease, and which concurring with the former, in progress of time, seldom fails to breed it. And this is, the want of fresh vegetables and greens; either, as may be supposed, to counteract the bad effects of their before mentioned situation; or rather, and more truly, to correct the quality of such hard and dry food as they are obliged to make use of. Experience indeed sufficiently shows, that as greens or fresh vegetables, with ripe fruits, are the best remedies for it, so they prove the most effectual preservatives against it. And the difficulty of obtaining them at sea, together with a long continuance in the moist sea-air, are the true causes of its so general and fatal malignity, upon that element.

The diet which people are necessarily obliged to live upon while at sea, was before assigned as the *occasional cause of the disease*, as in a particular manner it determines the effects of the before mentioned predisposing causes to the production of it. And there will be no difficulty to conceive the propriety of this distinction, or understand how the most innocent and wholesome food, at times, and in peculiar situations, will with great certainty form a disease.

All rules and precepts of diet, as well as the distinction of aliment[5] into wholesome and unwholesome, are to be understood only as relative to the constitution or state of the body. We find a child and a grown person, a valetudinarian and a man in health, require aliment of different kinds; as does even the same person in the heat of summer and in the depth of winter, during a dry or rainy season. Betwixt the tropics, the natives live chiefly on fruits, seeds, and vegetables; whereas northern nations find a flesh and solid diet more suitable to their climate. In like manner it appears, I think, very plainly, that such hard dry food as a ship's provisions, or the sea-diet, is extremely wholesome; and that no better nourishment could be well contrived for labouring people, or any person in perfect health, using proper exercise in a dry pure air; and that, in such circumstances, seamen will live upon it for several years, without any inconvenience. But where the constitution is predisposed to the scorbutic taint, by the causes before assigned, (the effects of which, as shall be shown in a proper place, are a weakening of the animal powers of digestion), the influence of such diet in bringing on this disease, sooner or later, according to the state and constitution of the body, becomes extremely visible.

The first, generally, who feel its effects, are those who are recovering from other disease, or some preceeding fit of sickness, by which the whole body, and the digestive faculties, have been greatly weakened; and are in this condition obliged to use the ship's fare. Thus, in May 1747, when there prevailed several inflammatory disorders, particularly peripneumonic fevers,[6] all who were recovering from them became highly scorbutic. The next who complained, were the indolent and lazy; such as are commonly called *sculkers*, and use little or no exercise; a principal help to digestion. As the disease gathered strength, it attacked those who had formerly laboured under it, and had been our patients in May 1746; where the constitution had acquired

a tendency to it from being formerly deeply infected. It afterwards became more universal; but was confined to the common seamen, particularly to the rawest and newest sailors. Imprest men [i.e. men forced into the Navy by press gangs] are extremely liable to its attack, by reason of their discontented state of mind; and the marines, by not being accustomed to the sea.

I observed it increased in frequency and virulence, upon the ship's small beer being exhausted, and having brandy served in its place; and this last observation I made in both cruises.

But it will be now proper to inquire into the diet which mariners are necessarily obliged to live upon at sea. And as it appears to be the principal occasional cause of their malady, it may be worthwhile to consider sea-provisions in their best state; it being found by experience that, notwithstanding the soundness and goodness of both water and provisions, the calamity often rages with great fury, and can be removed only by change of diet. Now, if in this case they appear to have so great an influence in forming the distemper, what ill consequences may not reasonably be expected from a much worse state of them; as from putrid beef, rancid pork, mouldy biscuit and flour, or bad water, which are misfortunes common at sea? all which must infallibly have bad effects in so putrid a disease.

It must be remarked in general, that the sea-diet is extremely gross,[7] viscid,[8] and hard of digestion. It consists of two articles, *viz.* the sweet farinaceous substances unfermented; and salted, or dried flesh and fish.

But more particularly, in our Royal navy, whose provisions, for goodness and plenty, exceed those of any other ships or fleets in the world, every man has an allowance of a pound of biscuit a-day; which, in the manner it is baked, will be found more solid and substantial food, than two pounds of ordinary well-baked bread at land. And this is a principal article of their diet. But the sea-biscuit undergoes little or no fermentation in baking, and is consequently of

---

[5]   i.e. food. [eds]

[6]   Fevers associated with the lungs. [eds]

[7]   i.e. hard to digest. [eds]

[8]   i.e. sticky. [eds]

much harder and more difficult digestion, than well-leavened and properly-fermented bread. For it must be here understood, that the meally parts of vegetable seeds, dissolved only in water, are by experience found to make too viscid an aliment, to be constantly used by the generality of mankind, whereas, by fermentation, and the acid in leaven, the glutinous viscidity and tenacious oils of these meally substances are broken and subdued; and they become easily dissolvable afterwards in water, with which before they would only make a paste or glue; and are now miscible[9] with all the humours of the body. Well-baked bread, which has undergone a sufficient degree of fermentation, is of light and easy digestion; and indeed the most proper nourishment for man, as it is adapted by its acescency[10] to correct a flesh-diet: whereas, on the contrary, sea-biscuit, not being thus duly fermented, will in many cases afford too tenacious and viscid a chyle,[11] improper for the nourishment of the body, where the vital digestive faculties are weakened and impaired.

The next article in their allowance of what is called *fresh provisions*, is one pound and a half of wheat-flour in the week, which is made into pudding with water, and a certain proportion of pickled sewet. This last does not keep long at sea, so that they have often raisins or currants in its place. But flour and water boiled thus together form a tenacious glutinous paste; requiring the utmost strength and integrity of the powers of digestion, to subdue and assimilate it into nourishment. We find, that weak, inactive, valetudinary people, cannot long bear such food.

There remain two other articles of fresh provisions, of which the allowance to each man is more than they generally can use. The first is ground oats, boiled to a consistence with water, commonly called *burgow.* Of this the English sailors eat but little; though in their circumstances it would seem to be wholesome enough,

as being the most acescent part of their diet. The other is boiled peas; which are of a mild and softening quality; but having hardly any aromatic parts, they are apt in weak stomaches to breed flatulencies, and occasion indigestion; and, like all other farinaceous substances, give a *lentor* or viscidity to water in which they are boiled. It is evident, that in some cases they must afford gross and improper nourishment.

This is the allowance of fresh provisions; and they have, besides, a proper quantity given them of salt, butter and cheese.

Lastly, Of flesh each man has for allowance two pounds of salt beef, and two pounds of salt pork, per week. But these are found by every one's experience to be much harder, and more difficult to digest, than fresh meats; and, after all, to afford a much more improper chyle and nourishment. No person can long bear a diet of such salt flesh-meats, unless it is corrected by bread, vinegar, or vegetables.

To the above articles, which are the provisions with which our navy is usually supplied, may be added, stock fish, salt fish, dried or jerked beef,[12] with whatever is of the like gross, viscid, and indigestible nature; all which will have still more noxious qualities when unsound, or in a corrupted state.

For drink, the government allows, where it can be procured, good sound small beer; at other times wine, brandy, rum, or arrack,[13] according to the produce of the country where ships are stationed. Beer and fermented liquors of any sort will be found the best antiscorbutics, and most proper to correct the ill effects of their sea-diet and situation; whereas distilled spirits have a most pernicious influence on this disease.

As I shall have occasion elsewhere to show the natural consequences of such diet, it will be sufficient here to observe, that though the long continuance and constant use of any one particular sort of food, without variety, has its

---

[9]   i.e. able to be mixed with other substances. [eds]

[10]   i.e. sourness. [eds]

[11]   Food was believed to have been converted in the stomach, into a substance named *chyle*, which was, in turn, converted into blood. [eds]

[12]   i.e. cured or dried beef. [eds]

[13]   Any native liquor. [eds]

inconveniencies, and is justly condemned by physicians, nature having supplied us with an ample variety, designed no doubt for our use; yet the fact here truly is, that such food as has been mentioned, is at particular times, and in certain circumstances, not properly adapted to the state of the body, and the condition of the digestive powers. Our appetites, if they are not depraved, are upon this and many other occasions, the most faithful monitors, and point out that quality of such food as is suited to our digestive organs and to the state and condition of the body. For where there is a disposition to the scorbutic corruption from a long continuance in the moist sea-air, concurring with the viscous, glutinous and too solid diet used there, nature points out the remedy. In such a situation, the ignorant sailor, and the learned physician, will equally long, with the most craving anxiety, for green vegetables, and the fresh fruits of the earth; from whose healing, attenuating, and saponaceous [soapy] virtues, relief only can be had. And such people, in the height of the malady, not only employ their thoughts all day long on satisfying this importunate demand of nature, but are apt to have their deluded fancies tantalised in sleep with the agreeable ideas of feasting upon them at land. What nature, from an inward feeling, makes them thus strongly desire, constant experience confirms to be the most certain prevention and best cure of their disease.

[*Lind goes on to argue that, on land, scurvy is endemic in cold, damp, places. He then returns to his general list of causes.*]

Different ways of life have likewise a different influence on this disease. The lazy and indolent, and those of a sedentary life, as shoemakers, tailors, especially weavers, by reason of their working in damp places, are most subject to it; while hard labourers, and those who use much exercise, though living on the same, or even grosser food, keep entirely free. Fishermen, from their way of life, gross food, and habitual use of spirituous liquors, are often scorbutic.

The passions of the mind are experienced here to have a great effect. Those that are of a cheerful and contented disposition, are less liable to it, than others of a discontented and melancholy mind.

Lastly, it has always been remarked, that, in such circumstances as have been described, the present state of the body has a powerful influence in disposing to this affliction. They who are much exhausted and weakened by preceding fevers, and other tedious fits of sickness, or they who have unsound and obstructed viscera[14] (as after agues[15] of the autumnal kind), are apt, by the use of improper diet, to become scorbutic. Others that labour under a suppression of any natural and necessary evacuation, as women who have their menses [periods] suppressed, especially if the obstruction is occasioned by fear or grief, are more subject than others in similar circumstances to this disease; as they are likewise at the time that these naturally leave them.

Section 2: 'The prophylaxis, or means of preventing this disease, especially at sea' (from Treatise Part II, ch. IV)

It being of the utmost consequence to guard against the first approaches of so dreadful an enemy [i.e. scurvy], I shall here endeavour to lay down the measures proper to be taken for this end, with that minuteness and accuracy which the importance of the subject, and the preservation of so many valuable and useful lives, justly demand; and at the same time shall, as much as possible, avoid offering any thing that may be judged impracticable, or liable to exception, on account of the difficulty or disagreeableness of complying with it. And, *lastly,* I shall propose nothing dictated merely from theory; but shall confirm all by experience and facts, the surest and most unerring guides.

What I propose is, first, to relate the effects of several medicines tried at sea in this disease, on purpose to discover what might promise the most certain protection against it upon that element.[16]

---

[14]   i.e. interior organs. [eds]

[15]   i.e. shivering fit associated with fever. [eds]

[16]   i.e. when at sea. [eds]

The medicine which succeeded upon trial, I shall afterwards confirm to be the surest preservative, and most efficacious remedy, by the experience of others.

I shall then endeavour to give it the most convenient portable form, and show the method of preserving its virtues entire for years, so that it may be carried to the most distant parts of the world in small bulk, and at any time be prepared by the sailors themselves: adding some farther directions, given chiefly with a view to inform the captains and commanders of ships and fleets, of methods proper both to preserve their own health, and that of their crews.

The following are the experiments.

On the 20th of May 1747, I took twelve patients in the scurvy, on board the *Salisbury* at sea. Their cases were as similar as I could have them. They all in general had putrid gums, the spots and lassitude, with weakness of their knees. They lay together in one place, being a proper apartment for the sick in the fore-hold; and had one diet common to all, *viz.* water-gruel sweetened with sugar in the morning; fresh mutton-broth often times for dinner; at other times puddings, boiled biscuit with sugar, &c; and for supper, barley and raisins, rice and currants, sago and wine, or the like. Two of these were ordered each a quart of cyder a-day. Two others took twenty-five gutts [drops] of *elixir vitriol* [dilute sulphuric acid] three times a-day, upon an empty stomach; using a gargle strongly acidulated with it for their mouths. Two others took two spoonfuls of vinegar three times a-day, upon an empty stomach; having their gruels and their other food well acidulated with it, as also the gargle for their mouth. Two of the worst patients, with the tendons in the ham rigid, (a symptom none of the rest had), were put under a course of sea-water. Of this they drank half a pint every day, and sometimes more or less as it operated, by way of gentle physic. Two others had each two oranges and one lemon given them every day. These they eat with greediness, at different times, upon an empty stomach. They continued but six days under this course, having consumed

the quantity that could be spared. The two remaining patients, took the bigness of a nutmeg three times a-day, of an electuary [paste] recommended by a hospital-surgeon, made of garlic, mustard-seed, *rad. raphan.*[17] balsam of Peru, and gum myrrh; using for common drink, barley-water well acidulated with tamarinds; by a decoction of which, with the addition of *cremor tartar,* they were gently purged[18] three or four times during the course.

The consequence was, that the most sudden and visible good effects were perceived from the use of the oranges and lemons; one of those who had taken them, being at the end of six days fit for duty. The spots were not indeed at that time quite off his body, nor his gums sound; but without any other medicine, than a gargarism [gargle] of *elixir vitriol,* he became quite healthy before we came into Plymouth, which was on the 16th of June. The other was the best recovered of any in his condition; and being now deemed pretty well, was appointed nurse to the rest of the sick.

Next to the oranges, I thought the cyder had the best effects. It was indeed not very sound, being inclinable to be aigre [sour] or pricked.[19] However, those who had taken it, were in a fairer way of recovery than the others at the end of the fortnight, which was the length of time all these different courses were continued, except the oranges. The putrefaction of their gums, but especially their lassitude and weakness, were somewhat abated, and their appetite increased by it.

As to the *elixir of vitriol,* I observed that the mouths of those who had used it by way of gargarism, were in a much cleaner and better condition than many of the rest, especially those who used the vinegar; but perceived otherwise no good effects from its internal use upon the other symptoms. I indeed never had a great opinion of the efficacy of this medicine in the scurvy, since our longest cruise in the *Salisbury,* from the 10th of August to the 28th October 1746; when we had but one scurvy in the ship. The patient was a marine (one Walsh); who,

---

17   i.e. the botanical name for the plant. [eds]

18   i.e. had their stomachs/bowels emptied. [eds]

19   i.e. 'turned', 'gone off'. [eds]

after recovering from a quotidian ague in the latter end of September, had taken the *elixir vitriol* by way of restorative for three weeks; and yet at length contracted the disease, while under a course of a medicine recommended for its prevention.

There was no remarkable alteration upon those who took the electuary and tamarind decoction, the sea-water, or vinegar, upon comparing their condition, at the end of the fortnight, with others who had taken nothing but a little lenitive electuary and *cremor tartar,* at times, in order to keep their belly open; or a gentle pectoral in the evening, for relief of their breast. Only one of them, while taking the vinegar, fell into a gentle flux[20] at the end of ten days. This I attributed to the genius and course of the disease, rather than to the use of the medicine. As I shall have occasion elsewhere to take notice of the effects of other medicines in this disease, I shall here only observe, that the result of all my experiments was, that oranges and lemons were the most effectual remedies for this distemper at sea. I am apt to think oranges preferable to lemons, though perhaps both given together will be found most serviceable.

It may be now proper to confirm the efficacy of these fruits by the experience of others. The first proof that I shall produce, is borrowed from the learned Dr Mead.

'One year when that brave Admiral Sir Charles Wager commanded our fleet in the Baltic, his sailors were terribly afflicted with the scurvy: but he observed, that the Dutch ships then in company were much more free from this disease. He could impute this to nothing but their different food, which was stock-fish and gort; whereas ours was salt fish and oat-meal. He was then come last from the Mediterranean, and had at Leghorn taken in a great quantity of lemons and oranges. Recollecting, from what he had often heard, how effectual these fruits were in the cure of this distemper, he ordered a chest of each to be brought upon deck, and opened every day. The men, besides eating what they would, mixed the juice in their beer. It was also their constant diversion to pelt one another with the rinds, so that the deck was always strewed and wet with the fragrant liquor. The happy effect was, that he brought his sailors home in good health.'

[Oranges and lemons] have this peculiar advantage above any thing than can be proposed for trial, that their experienced virtues have stood the test of near 200 years. They were providentially discovered, even before the disease was well known, or at least had been described by physicians. Ronsseus, the first writer on this subject, mentions them; and observes, that in all probability the Dutch sailors had by accident fallen upon this remedy, when afflicted with the scurvy, in their return from Spain loaded with these fruits, especially oranges. Experience soon taught them, that by thus eating part of their cargo, they might be restored to health. And if people had been less assiduous in finding out new remedies, and trusted more to the efficacy of these fruits, for preventing this fatal pestilence to seamen, the lives of many thousand sailors, and others, (especially during the last war), might in all probability have been preserved.

[*Lind goes on to give five more examples of scurvy-ridden crews being cured by eating oranges and lemons. He then turns to the problem of preserving these fruits on long voyages.*]

As oranges and lemons are liable to spoil, and cannot be procured at every port, nor at all seasons in equal plenty; and it may be inconvenient to take on board such large quantities as are necessary in ships for their preservation from this and other diseases; the next thing to be proposed, is the method of preserving their virtues entire for years in a convenient and small bulk. It is done in the following easy manner.

Let the squeezed juice of these fruits be well cleared from the pulp, and depurated [purified] by standing for some time; then poured off from the gross sediment: or, to have it still purer, it may be filtrated. Let it then be put into any clean open earthen vessel, well glazed; which should be wider at the top than bottom, so that there may be the largest surface above to favour the evaporation. For this purpose a china bason or punch-bowl is proper; or a common earthen bason used for washing, if well glazed, will be sufficient, as it is generally made in the form required. Into this pour the

---

[20]   i.e. experienced mild diarrhoea. [eds]

purified juice; and put it into a pan of water, upon a clear fire. Let the water come almost to boil, and continue nearly in a state of boiling (with the bason containing the juice in the middle of it) for several hours, until the juice is found to be of the consistence of oil when warm, or of a syrup when cold. It is then to be corked up in a bottle for us. Two dozen of good oranges, weighing five pounds four ounces, will yield one pound nine ounces and a half of depurated juice; and when evaporated, there will remain about five ounces of the extract; which in bulk will be equal to less than three ounces of water. So that thus the acid, and virtues of twelve dozen of lemons or oranges, may be put into a quart-bottle, and preserved for several years.

I have some of the extract of lemons now by me, which was made four years ago. And when this is mixed with water, or made into punch, few are able to distinguish it from the fresh squeezed juice mixed up in like manner; except when both are present, and their different tastes compared at the same time; when the fresh fruits discover a greater degree of smartness and fragrancy.

In this manner prepared, it must be kept in bottles, where it will remain good for several years. When made in a proper place and season, it will come very cheap; and our navy may be supplied with it at a much easier rate than any thing as yet proposed. It will be found extremely wholesome on all occasions, but especially to correct bad brandy, and other noxious spirits, often drank by sailors in immoderate quantity. Rum in the West Indies, arrack or brandy, when served them by way of allowance, should always be first mixed up with the extract. This will not only make them more palatable, but, what is a matter of much greater moment, will convert these poisonous pernicious draughts into a sovereign remedy, and a preservative against a scorbutic habit, the bane of seafaring people.

I proceed to some farther directions given for the information of commanders of ships, and those who have proper conveniencies, who may relieve the sick, upon occasion, with their stores. And it may be proper to acquaint them, that most berries, and several fruits, when gathered two-thirds ripe on a dry day, while the sun shines,

if put into earthen pots, or rather in dry bottles, well corked, and sealed up, so that no air or moisture can enter, will keep a long time, and, at the end of a year; be as fresh as when new pulled. These the captains may supply themselves with at every port in England, from the pastry-cooks shops, with proper directions for their preservation. Green gooseberries will keep for years, if, after being put into dry bottles, their moisture is exhaled, by putting the bottles slightly corked into a pot of water, which is allowed to come nearly to boil, and continue so for a little; when a very small quantity of juice yielded by them is to be thrown away, and they are afterwards kept close stopt. These would prove a sovereign remedy for the sick; and, by such methods, ships in long voyages, when touching at any place for water and provisions, may likewise lay up a sea-store of berries and fruits.

Various wholesome herbs and roots may likewise be preserved at sea, according to the different directions given for that purpose in books of confectionery; such as small onions in a pickle of vinegar, &c. Most green vegetables, as cabbage, French beans, and others, are preserved, if put when very dry in clean dry stone-jars, with a layer of salt at bottom; then a thin layer of the vegetable covered with salt, and so alternately, till the jar is full; when the whole is to be covered with salt, and well pressed down with a weight, and its mouth close stopt, that no air or moisture may enter. At using, the salt is to be washed off by warm water; when the vegetable, after keeping a year, will be found fresh and green. I have been told, that in this manner that sovereign, never-failing remedy, the Greenland scurvy-grass, may be preserved, and that pots of it have been brought over quite fresh and green.

Every common sailor ought to lay in a stock of onions. I never observed any that used them fall into the scurvy at sea. When this stock is exhausted, the captains may have recourse to their pickled small onions; and with fowls, mutton, or portable soup,[21] and the pickled cabbage before mentioned, of which the Dutch sell great quantities, they will be able to make a broth at sea, almost the same with what is used in our naval hospitals for recovery of scorbutic people.

---

[21] An early version of the present-day stock cube. [eds]

I have known several captains, who, by carrying out boxes filled with earth, which stood in their quarter-galleries, were supplied with wholesome salads, after being some months out of harbour. A cask of rich garden-mould put occasionally in boxes on the poop; and sown with the seed of garden-cresses, would furnish these at any time. Such seeds will likewise grow in wet cotton.

Besides fresh and preserved fruits and vegetables, fermented liquors of all sorts are found beneficial in this disease. Some of them however are more antiscorbutic than others. By my own experience, I found cyder the best of any I have had occasion to try. And it would seem an excellent method of preserving other vegetable juice, (gooseberries, blackberriers, currants, elderberries, or even Seville oranges), to ferment them into made wines or beer. These I am persuaded will be found preferable to many medicated antiscorbutic ales and wines by infusion, that might here be recommended.

A simple decoction of the tops, cones, leaves, or even bark and wood of these [spruce] trees, is antiscorbutic: but it becomes much more so when fermented, as in making spruce beer; where the molosses [molasses sugar] contributes, by its diaphoretic [sweat-producing] quality, to make it a more suitable medicine. By carrying a few bags of spruce to sea, this wholesome drink may be prepared at any time. But where it cannot be had, the common fir-tops used for fuel in the ship, should be first boiled in water, and the decoction afterwards fermented with molosses, in the common method of making spruce beer; which will be found the most efficacious antiscorbutic perhaps of any fermented liquor, as being of a diuretic and diaphoretic quality. In extremity tar-water may be tried, fermented in like manner; by which it will certainly become much more antiscorbutic.

I proceed now to point out the means of correcting or removing many inconveniencies which occur at sea, especially those which are observed to be productive of this malady. A most powerful and principal cause of which, and indeed of many others at sea, is the moisture of the air, and consequently the dampness of their lodging; especially during a long continuance of thick close weather, or a stormy and rainy season. As this is found to be the most frequent cause of this fatal disease, whose effects are rendered still more pernicious when combined with cold; these require in a particular manner to be guarded against. And they are either immediately to be corrected, or their effects and consequences prevented.

As to the first: Although we cannot at once remove a person into another climate, or into the land-air; yet we can easily give to the air he breathes, a more salutary quality, by rendering it at any time warmer or colder, moister or drier, as the exigency of the case and circumstances may require. I observed elsewhere, that the noxious qualities of the moist air at sea were greatly heightened by being confined in so close a place as a ship, without a succession, or fresh supply of it. But as that inconvenience is sufficiently guarded against by the excellent invention of Sutton's machine,[22] which extracts all such foul and putrid air, and thus will prevent many infectious malignant fevers caused from thence; so there seems nothing wanting to make it likewise an excellent preservative against the scurvy, but that it should correct the moisture of the sea-air, and dry or warm it betwixt decks when needful.

This I conjecture it might be made to do by some additional contrivances, which may invert its operation; that is, instead of drawing up the air from below, the air warmed by the fire in the galley or fire-place, may be forced betwixt decks through its pipes when requisite. I mention it only (for experiments alone must make this improvement, and with such caution as to prevent detriment by it) to induce something of this kind to be thought of by proper judges. If the additional machinery were but small, and not incommodious in the ship, the advantages derived from it would be very great. These are evident from what has been said in discoursing on the causes of the scurvy. It must prove highly serviceable in cold climates, and in northern voyages in the winter, (where the sailors not only become terribly scorbutic, but are often chilled to death with the cold, and at other times have their limbs mortified), if, by a simple contrivance of this sort, the fire used for dressing their victuals, could be made to warm them even when in bed.

---

[22] A machine for ventilating ships. [eds]

Fire made with any of the aromatic woods, or even with common fir or pine, juniper, and the like, effectually corrects this disposition of the air, and at the same time renders it more salutary in other respects. It is observable, that betwixt the tropics, the rainy seasons prove the most unhealthy and dangerous, not only at land, but in ships; giving rise to malignant fevers, scurvies, &c. In this case, without any inconvenience or danger, a clear open fire, properly secured, might be lighted betwixt decks, to stand upon the hatchways in a stove; which would greatly purify the air, and destroy its hurtful moisture, without much increasing the heat, if burnt in an open hatchway.

Here I would [also] recommend a most simple and easy operation, to be performed in such damp seasons in a ship; which is, putting a red-hot loggerhead[23] in a bucket of tar, which should be moved about, so that all the ship, once or twice a-day, may be filled with this wholesome antiseptic vapour.

Persons for proper security, during a scorbutic and moist constitution of air, should go well clothed, and shift often with dry linen. Driness and cleanliness of body are excellent preservatives against this malady. They should use the flesh-brush, or frictions with a dry cloth on their skin; eat a bit of raw onion, or a head of garlic, in a morning before they are exposed to the rains and washings of the sea. Whatever promotes perspiration is useful; and perhaps nothing will do it more effectually at this time than a raw onion. Nor ought these farther precautions to be omitted, of using proper exercise in the day, and having their bedding kept always dry, not binding it up close together till sufficiently aired and dried.

When they are threatened with the approach of this disease, they ought, at going to bed, to promote a gentle *diaphoresis* [perspiration], by draughts of water-gruel and vinegar, with the addition of lemon-juice, or the extract. They should use plenty of mustard and onions with their victuals; and may then indulge more freely in the use of fermented vinous liquors, *viz.* cyder, beer, and wine; but when of necessity obliged to drink spirits, they ought always to acidulate them with the acid of oranges or lemons. These directions will preserve seamen not only from the scurvy, but from many other diseases, as coughs, catarrhs, &c. arising from an obstructed perspiration in a moist air.

Section 3: 'The theory of the disease' (from Treatise Part II, ch. VI)

An animal body is composed of solid and fluid parts; and these consist of such various and heterogeneous principles, as render it, of all substances, the most liable to corruption and putrefaction. Such indeed is the state and condition of every living animal, as to be threatened with this, from the mechanism of its own frame, and the necessary laws of circulation by which it subsists. For by the uninterrupted circulation of its fluids, their violent attrition, and mutual actions on each other, and their containing vessels, the whole mass of humours [bodily fluids] is apt to degenerate from its sweet, mild, and healthful condition, into various degrees of acrimony and corruption. Parts of the solids themselves, continually abraded by the repeated force of the circulating fluids, are again returned into their channels. Hence the necessity of throwing out of the body, by different outlets, these acrimonious and putrescent juices, rendered thus unfit for the animal uses and functions, together with the abraded particles of the solids. And a daily supply of food, or fresh nourishment, is required to recruit this constant waste, both of the solid and fluid parts. Thus the bodies of all animals are in a constant state of change and renovation, by which they are preserved from death and putrefaction.

There are two evacuations chiefly by which the blood is freed from these putrescent noxious humours, *viz.* urine, and insensible perspiration. Not but that there are many other secretions necessary to health: yet they are rather more properly adapted to other singular and peculiar uses; except that of stool, which in some cases may be substituted as a vent to these corrupted humours, upon the defect of either of the other two.

---

[23] i.e. a long-handled iron instrument with a bulb end, used to heat liquids, especially tar and pitch. [eds]

But the most considerable of all the evacuations, is that by insensible perspiration; which Sanctorius[24] found in Italy to be equal to five eighths of the meat and drink taken into the body. [Perspiration] is indeed, beyond doubt, the most copious evacuation of the whole body: and though it is sometimes in greater or lesser quantities, as influenced by various causes; yet it can never be partially suppressed long, much less can it be entirely obstructed, without the greatest detriment to health.

It may be proper farther to remark, that this being the last and most elaborated action of animal digestion, the body is hereby freed from what is consequently the most subtle and putrescent of the animal humours. And it is certain these excrementitious humours naturally destined for this evacuation, when retained long in the body, are capable of acquiring the most poisonous and noxious qualities, and a very high degree of putrefaction; becoming extremely acrid and corrosive: and do then give rise to various diseases, according to the habit or constitution of the person, *viz.* the state of the solids and fluids at that time, or the influence and determination of other causes.

Moreover, not only due and constant evacuations of what may be rendered thus so extremely pernicious to the body, are requisite towards the health and life of animals; but a fresh and daily supply of a soft and mild liquor, such as the chyle, is farther necessary to correct and prevent the constant natural putrescent tendency of the humours, and to sweeten and dilute the acrimony which they daily and hourly contract from the action of the body, and by life itself.

The obvious effect of cold on the human body is to constringe[25] the whole external habit, to dry and corrugate the skin; and all statical [statistical] experiments prove that cold obstructs or diminishes insensible perspiration. But it must be remarked, that cold joined with driness and purity in the air, by keeping up a due degree of tension in the solids, is not naturally productive of this disease.

By all faithful and accurate observations made on this disease, moisture is experienced to be the principal and main predisposing cause to it. This indeed of itself is sufficient to dispose the constitution to the scurvy in any climate, even the warmest. It is observable that, in warm climates, the crews of ships at sea are liable to this malady, when the hot weather, by which the fibres of the body are much relaxed, is succeeded by great and incessant rains usual in these latitudes, or when the season proves very unconstant. The disease is there likewise much owing to the great length of these southern voyages. But, otherwise, it is not near so frequent a calamity as in colder climates; the bad effects of moisture being rendered much more pernicious when combined with cold. A cold and moist constitution of the atmosphere, together with wet lodgings, damp beds, cloaths, and other inconveniencies which poor people necessarily suffer at such seasons, is the most frequent and strongest disposing cause to it. And, upon the whole, it is to be remarked, that whatever shuts up the pores of the skin, and impedes or lessens perspiration, which moisture or dampness effectually does, and that more strongly with the addition of cold, is chiefly productive of this disease.

Too moist an air not only stops up the pores of the skin, but weakens and relaxes the whole system of solids. Hence, during a rainy cloudy season, all the members of the body feel heavy, the appetite is diminished, the pulse of the heart and arteries is more feeble, and every one is sensible of a languor of strength, and a lowness of spirits. Farther, moisture, by weakening the spring and elasticity of the air, renders it unfit for the many salutary purposes obtained by respiration. Such an air not being able to overcome sufficiently the contractile force of the pulmonary fibres resisting the dilatation of the lungs, the blood is not here sufficiently comminuted[26] and broken, nor that lentor [viscidity] removed which it had contracted in its slow returning motion through the veins. From the impaired action also of this viscus, the last and most important office

---

[24]   Sanctorius of Padua (1561–1636); Italian physician, inventor of the clinical thermometer and researcher into the effects of 'insensible perspiration'. [eds]

[25]   i.e. to cause organic tissue to shrink. [eds]

[26]   i.e. divided minutely. [eds]

of animal digestion upon the chyle, that of sanguification[27] is not duly performed.

I come next to observe the other concurring causes which have so great an influence in disposing to this disease; such as laziness and indolence of disposition, and from thence a neglect of using proper exercise, or a sedentary and inactive life.

Every one, from experience, must be sensible how much exercise contributes to the health of the body, as well as to cheerfulness of mind. It is necessary to keep up that due degree of firmness and tension in the solids, upon which the strength and soundness of a constitution depend; and which is acquired by such motions as increase the mutual action of the vessels on their contents, and each other. But the whole process of animal digestion, as well as all the secretions, depend upon this strength and firmness of the vessels and viscera. Whenever the tone of these is relaxed and weakened, which is most effectually done by keeping the body long at rest, or by neglect of due exercise, there must follow a deficiency in the vigour and strength of the powers of digestion; so that they will not be sufficient to concoct and elaborate the aliment, especially if it is of a too crude and viscid nature. And the whole system of solids being thus relaxed, by reason of a deficiency of their action and efficacy, the chyle cannot be properly assimilated, nor the heterogeneous mass of fluids intimately mixed and blended: so that the body here is not duly nourished, nor the secretions rightly performed; especially that of perspiration, which exercise powerfully promotes. Hence the scorbutic diathesis, want of proper digestion, weak and relaxed fibres, with a stoppage of perspiration.

I proceed to observe what farther effects are produced by what has been assigned as the occasional cause of this disease, *viz.* a gross and viscid diet in such circumstances as have been described, and the want of fresh greens or vegetables, which are found so effectually to check the scorbutic virulence.

In order to understand the effects of [diet], it may be proper to premise some observations on the nature of digestion in general, and the different changes our aliment must necessarily undergo, in order to fit it for the various purposes of life.

By the first process of digestion in the mouth, stomach, and intestines, the food must be rendered quite fluid; otherwise it can never pass into the blood, through the exceeding fine, and almost imperceptible lacteal vessels.[28] For which purpose it is broken and divided by the teeth; farther subdued, macerated, and dissolved, by the heat, moisture, and various actions of the stomach, intestines, viscera, &c; diluted by watery liquors, dissolved by others that are saponaceous, till, in the nature of a fluid chyle, it is received into the lacteals. What is unconquerable by these first powers of digestion, is thrown out of the body by *stool*. After it has in this liquid form entered the blood, it seems but little changed; retaining still a vegetable character, and resembling the nature of milk, in colour as well as other qualities; all animals being thus nourished, as it were, with their own milk. It therefore requires a still farther and more perfect elaboration, in order to animalize it, and fit it for the important uses of nutrition and perspiration.

To nourish the fluids, is to replace a liquor of the same kind and quality with that which is gone. And as they are the thinnest parts of the fluids which are continually lost, so the aliment must be reduced extremely thin and fine to restore them. It must likewise be greatly attenuated, so as to pass through the most minute canals of the body, in order to adhere to, and repair the wasted solids. Lastly, It must still be more subtilized, before it can pass off, in the form of a volatile and insensible steam, by perspiration.

I proceed to apply this doctrine, and to consider more particularly the nature and qualities of such food as is truly the occasional cause of the scurvy, *viz.* a diet of dried or salt flesh or fish, together with the grosser farinaceous substances unfermented.

It is observable, that the tenderer or softer flesh is made by keeping for some time without

---

[27] i.e. the process whereby chyle is converted into blood. [eds]

[28] i.e. ultra-fine vessels thought to carry the refined chyle. [eds]

salt, it is found to be the easier of digestion: but by being long hardened and dried with salt, its most fine, subtle, and nutritious parts, either fly off, or are fixed. Experience shows, that flesh long salted is of very difficult digestion. It requires perfect health, together with exercise, plenty of diluting liquors, vinegar, and many other correctors, to subdue it in the first passages.

Few can live altogether on ship-puddings, dumplings, or the like, without being sensible of an oppression and uneasiness. But especially weak and exhausted people cannot well receive the necessary nourishment from such species of the mealy substances, until their lentor or mucosity is subdued by fermentation, or by some other method, by which they become lighter food. It is plain, that such a glutinous and viscid chyle as is afforded by hard sea biscuit, dumplings, ship-puddings, &c. requires the most perfect state of organs in the subsequent concoctions for its farther elaboration.

Hence the effects of the above diet constantly used, are twofold.

1st, Chyle is by this means wanting of a proper quality to dilute and sweeten the acrimonious animal juices, to correct the putrescent tendency of the humours, and to repair the decay of the body.

2dly, The tenacity of such aliment concurs in scorbutic cases; where the perspiration is already lessened, in a manner altogether to stop it. Indeed such a diet naturally lessens it, without the concurrence of other causes: for a laudable perspiration can only proceed from a duly-prepared and well-concocted humour, obtained from such aliment as is thin, light, and easy of digestion. The matter of perspiration is the last and most elaborated humour of the body: the perfection of which depends upon its being reduced to the most imperceptible tenuity, by a complete and thorough elaboration in all the different concoctions it undergoes. Hence all gross indigestible aliment is found to be imperspirable.

This leads me to inquire into the virtues of fresh green vegetables, which seem so necessary to correct the bad qualities of other dry and hard food, and are experienced so effectually to prevent, and often cure this distemper.

Recent vegetables, fresh plants and fruits, are of a more tender texture than animals; and their parts being more easily separable, by reason of the less force of their cohesion, and lesser tenacity of their cementing gluten, they yield more easily to the dividing powers of our organs. They also contain less oil than either flesh or the farines. But gross[29] oils (especially of the animal kind) seem not only to be the most unconquerable part of aliment; but, where there is already a corruption in the human body, may be apt, by becoming rancid, to acquire the highest and worst degree of it.

As these are the most necessary and requisite qualities in the present case, so perhaps by no other can all green fresh vegetables be characterized. There is no other particular virtue in which they all agree; a greater diversity of qualities being found in vegetable than in animal substances. But, besides what has been mentioned, vegetables have great and peculiar virtues in this disease, arising from a combination of various qualities; of which all vegetables possess one or more, in a higher or lesser degree; and do from thence accordingly become more or less antiscorbutic. The best remedies are furnished from a composition of different plants, most eminent for the properties required; and whatever simple possesses the most of these qualities, is, of all such, the most serviceable and efficacious for preventing and curing the malady.

If it be said, That scurvy-grass, cresses, and other acrid alcalescent plants, are found highly antiscorbutic; it must likewise be remembered, that they are not perhaps altogether so efficacious as the acescent fruits; or at least become much more so by the addition of lemon-juice, oranges, or a little sorrel; which last the Greenlanders are taught by experience to join with them for their cure: *the chief and most essentially requisite quality* in the antiscorbutic composition, *viz. a saponaceous attenuating, and resolving virtue* [i.e. both easily broken down in digestion, and excreted by perspiration], possessed by such acrid vegetables in the most eminent degree, being thereby heightened, improved, and exerted in its full force.

---

[29] i.e. indigestible. [eds]

Lastly, There is another property peculiar to many green vegetables, and especially to the riper fruits, which are found so beneficial here; and it is, that fermentative quality, by which they are preserved longer from corruption, both without and within the body. For whereas flesh and animal substances, without any other intermediate state, tend directly to putrefaction; vegetables are preserved longer from it by a fermentative tendency, which many vegetable juices naturally have, or may acquire by the addition of a proper ferment. We evidently see in this disease the good effects of spruce beer, cyder, ale, wine, and other vinous liquors, prone to fall into this state in the stomach; on the contrary, the pernicious effects of distilled spirits, which check such a fermentation. And I am of opinion, for several reasons, that this is somehow necessary to the perfection of animal digestion.

In a situation similar to that of the stomach, with regard to heat, moisture, and air, many substances must naturally fall into a fermentation. We are certain by their effects, that ripe fruits and some vegetables cannot well be prevented from it, and actually do often ferment in the stomach: and observing, that, in the scurvy, and some other disease, food of this tendency is requisite, and that abstinence from it is prejudicial; hence we conclude, that this operation, and food which tends to promote it, is necessary to digestion, and to prevent the scorbutic corruption.

Upon the whole, it follows, and will be found true in fact, that the more any food, drink, herbs, or medicine, partake of any of the aforesaid qualities, the more antiscorbutic they become; but that the most perfect and effectual remedies are found in a composition of different ingredients, each possessing in a high degree one or other of those virtues, from the combination of which, a vegetable, saponaceous, fermentable acid may result. Such an acid, ready prepared, is to be had in a certain degree in oranges, and most ripening sub-acid fruits; from whence they become the most effectual preservatives against this distemper.

Source: J. Lind, *A Treatise of the Scurvy in Three Parts*, Edinburgh, 1753.

James Cook
Extracts from A Voyage Towards the South Pole (1777)

Prepared for the Course Team by
Angus Calder

Contents

James Cook
Extracts from A Voyage Towards the South Pole

Captain James Cook (1728–79) was by common consent the greatest European navigator of his age. He commanded long expeditions to the Pacific Ocean, from 1768–71, then from 1771 to 1775, dying on the third which left Britain in 1776 and returned in 1780. These served the aims of British Imperialism, but also increased vastly the fund of accurate knowledge about the world, its peoples, its fauna and flora, available to eighteenth-century humankind.

The chapters which follow are extracted from an account of his second Voyage written by Cook with the help of a clergyman. Cook was the son of a Scottish farmworker who had migrated to Yorkshire. He himself had worked on a farm, and in a grocer's shop, before he went to sea at the age of eighteen. He studied mathematics and navigation in his spare time and developed his great power of observation.

This account of his visit to the island of Tanna, in the New Hebrides, in August 1774, after an unfortunate skirmish with the natives of nearby Eromanga, reveals his generally humane and sympathetic attitude to Pacific peoples – in this case, Melanesians – and the combination of scientific with commercial aims characteristic of the second voyage. Cook's greatest feat on this voyage was to prove that there was no 'Great Southern Continent' in Southern waters available for British colonization and exploitation. The detailed navigational record with which our extract begins displays Cook's pre-eminence as a calm and accurate captain in unknown waters. Some internal cuts have been made, mostly small.

Chapter IV
An Account of the Discovery of several Islands, an Interview and Skirmish with the inhabitants upon one of them. The Arrival of the ship at Tanna, and the Reception we met with there.

Soon after we got to sea, we had a breeze at E.S.E., with which we stood over for Ambrym till three o'clock in the afternoon [1774 July Saturday 23], when the wind veering to E.N.E., we tacked and stretched to the S.E., and weathered the S.E. end of Mallicollo, off which we discovered three or four small islands, that before appeared to be connected. At sun-set the point bore S. 77° West, distant three leagues, from which the coast seemed to trend away West. At this time, the isle of Ambrym extended from N. 3° E to N. 65° E. The isle of Paoom from N. 76° E. to S. 88° E.; and the isle of Apee from S. 83° E. to S. 43° East. We stood for this last isle, which we reached by midnight, and then brought to till day-break on the 24th [Sunday], when we made sail to the S.E., with a view of plying up to the eastward on the south side of Apee. At sun-rise, we discovered several more islands, extending from the S.E. point of Apee to the South as far as S.E. by S. The nearest to us we reached by ten o'clock, and not being able to weather it, we tacked a mile from its shore in fourteen fathoms water. This island is about four leagues in circuit, is remarkable by having three high peaked hills upon it, by which it has obtained that name. In the P. M. the wind veering more to the North, we resumed our course to the East; and having weathered Threehills, stood for the group of small isles which lie off the S.E. point of Apee. These I called Shepherd's Isles, in honour of my worthy friend Dr Shepherd, Plumian professor of astronomy at Cambridge. Having a fine breeze, I had thoughts of going through between them; but the channels being narrow, and seeing broken water in the one we were steering for, I gave up the design, and bore up, in order to go without, or to the South of them. Before this could be accomplished, it fell calm, and we were left to the mercy of the current, close to the isles, where we could find no soundings with a line of an hundred and eighty fathoms. We had now land or islands in every direction, and were not able to count the number which lay round us. The mountain on Paoom was seen over the east end of Apee, bearing N.N.W. at eight o'clock. A breeze at S.E. relieved us from the anxiety the calm had occasioned.

The night before we came out of Port Sandwich, two reddish fish, about the size of large bream, and not unlike them, were caught with hook and line. On these fish most of the officers, and some of the petty officers, dined the next day. The night following, every one who had eaten of them was seized with violent pains in the head and bones, attended with a scorching heat all over the skin, and numbness in the joints. There remained no doubt that this was occasioned by the fish being of a poisonous nature; and having communicated its bad effects to all who partook of them; even to the hogs and dogs. One of the former died about sixteen hours after; it was not long, before one of the latter shared the same fate; and it was a week or ten days, before all the gentlemen recovered.

At day-break on 25th [Monday], we made a short stretch to the East of Shepherd's Isles till after sun-rise, when, seeing no more land in that direction, we tacked and stood for the island we had seen in the South, having a gentle breeze at S.E. We passed to the East of Threehills, and likewise of a low isle, which lies on the S.E. side of it, between a remarkable peaked rock which obtained the name of Monument, and a small island named Twohills, on account of two peaked hills upon it, disjoined by a low and narrow isthmus. The channel between this island and the Monument is near a mile broad, and twenty-four fathoms deep. Except this rock, which is only accessible to birds, we did not find an island on which people were not seen. At noon, we observed, in latitude 17° 18' 30"; longitude, made from Port Sandwich, 45' East.

Continuing our course to the South, at five P.M. we drew near the southern lands, which we found to consist of one large island, whose southern and western extremities extended beyond our sight, and three or four smaller ones, lying off its North side. The two northernmost are much the largest, have a good height, and lie in the direction of E. by S. and W. by N. from each other, distant two leagues. I named the one Montagu, and the other Hinchinbrook, and the large island Sandwich, in honour of my noble patron the Earl of Sandwich.[1] Seeing broken water ahead, between Montagu and Hinchinbrook

isles, we tacked; and soon after it fell calm. The calm continued till seven o'clock the next morning [Tuesday 26th], when it was succeeded by a breeze from the westward. During the calm, having been carried by the currents and a S.E. swell, four leagues to the W.N.W., we passed Hinchinbrook Isle, saw the western extremity of Sandwich Island, bearing S.S.W., about five leagues distant, and at the same time discovered a small island to the West of this direction. After getting the westerly breeze, I steered S.E., in order to pass between Montagu Isle and the north end of Sandwich Island.

As we passed Montagu Isle several people came down to the sea-side, and, by signs, seemed to invite us ashore. Some were also seen on Sandwich Island, which exhibited a most delightful prospect, being spotted with woods and lawns, agreeably diversified, over the whole surface. It hath a gentle slope from the hills, which are of a moderate height, down to the sea-coast. This is low and guarded by a chain of breakers, so that there is no approaching it at this part. But more to the West, beyond Hinchinbrook Island, there seemed to run in a bay sheltered from the reigning winds. The examining it not being so much an object with me as the getting to the South, in order to find the southern extremity of the Archipelago, with this view I steered S.S.E., being the direction of the coast of Sandwich Island. We had but just got through the passage, before the west wind left us to variable light airs and calms; so that we were apprehensive of being carried back again by the currents, or rather of being obliged to return in order to avoid being driven on the shoals, as there was no anchorage, a line of an hundred and sixty fathoms not reaching to the bottom. At length a breeze springing up at S.W. we stood to S.E.

We continued to stand to S.E. till four A.M. on the 27th [Wednesday], when we tacked to the West. At sun-rise having discovered a new land bearing South, and making in three hills, this occasioned us to tack and stand towards it. At this time Montagu Isle bore N. 52° West, distant thirteen leagues; at noon it was nearly in the same direction, and the new land extended from

---

[1] John Montagu, Earl of Sandwich, formerly Lord Hinchinbrook. 'Sandwich Island' is now known as Efate. [eds]

$5^1/_2$ E. by W., and the three hills seemed to be connected. We continued to stand to the S.E., with a gentle breeze at S.W. and S.S.W., till the 28th [Thursday] at sun-rise, when, the wind veering to the South, we tacked and stood to the West. The three hills mentioned above, we now saw, belonged to one island, which extended from S. 35° to 71° West, distant about ten or twelve leagues.

Retarded by contrary winds, calms, and the currents, that set to N.W., we were three days in gaining this space; in which time we discovered an elevated land to the South of this. It first appeared in detached hummocks, but we judged it to be connected. At length on the 1st of August [Monday], about ten A.M. we got a fine breeze at E.S.E., which soon after veered to N.E., and we steered for the N.W. side of the island. Reaching it about two P.M., we ranged the west coast at one mile from shore, on which the inhabitants appeared in several parts, and by signs invited us to land. We continued to sound without finding bottom, till we came before a small bay, or bending of the coast, where, near a mile from shore, we found thirty and twenty-two fathoms water, a sandy bottom. I had thoughts of anchoring here, but the wind almost instantly veered to N.W.; which being nearly on shore, I laid this design aside. Besides, I was unwilling to lose the opportunity that now offered of getting to the South-east, in order first to explore the lands which lay there. I therefore continued to range the coast to the South, at about the same distance from shore; but we soon got out of soundings. About a league to the South of this bay, which hath about two miles extent, is another more extensive. Towards the evening, the breeze began to abate, so that it was sun-set before we got the length of it. I intended not to stop here, and to stand to the South under an easy sail all night, but at eight o'clock, as we were steering S.S.E., we saw a light ahead. Not knowing but it might be on some low detached Isle, dangerous to approach while dark, we hauled the wind, and spent the night standing off and on, or rather driving to and fro; for we had but very little wind.

At sun-rise on the 2nd [Tuesday], we saw no more land than the coast we were upon; but found that the currents had carried us some miles to the North, and we attempted, to little purpose, to regain what we had lost. At noon we were about a league from the coast, which extended from S.S.E. to N.E. Latitude observed 18° 46' S. In the afternoon, finding the ship to drift, not only to the North, but in shore also, and being yet to the South of the bay we passed the day before, I had thoughts of getting to an anchor before night, while we had it in our power to make choice of a place.[2] With this view, having hoisted out two boats, one of them was sent ahead to tow the ship; in the other Mr Gilbert went, to sound for anchorage. Soon after, the towing boat was sent to assist him. So much time was spent in sounding this bay, that the ship drove past, which made it necessary to call the boats on board to tow her off from the northern point. But this service was performed by a breeze of wind, which, that moment, sprung up at S.W.; so that as the boats got on board, we hoisted them in, and then bore up for the North side of the island, intending once more to try to get round by the East. Mr Gilbert informed me, that, at the South part of the bay, he found no soundings till close to a steep stone beach, where he landed to taste a stream of water he saw there, which proved to be salt. Some people were seen there, but they kept at a distance. Farther down the coast, that is to the North, he found twenty, twenty-four, and thirty fathoms, three-fourths of a mile, or a mile, from shore, the bottom a fine dark sand.

On the 3rd [Wednesday] at sun-rise, we found ourselves abreast a lofty promontory on the S.E. side of the island, and about three leagues from it. Having but little wind, and that from the South, right in our teeth, and being in want of fire-wood, I sent Lieutenant Clerke with two boats to a small islot which lies off the promontory, to endeavour to get some. In the mean time we continued to ply up with the ship; but what we gained by our sails, we lost by the current. At length, towards noon, we got a breeze at E.S.E. and E., with which we could lie up for the

---

[2] Cook called this island, on which he eventually landed with such difficulty and with such disastrous results, 'Erromango': now, Eromanga. [eds]

head; and soon after Mr Clerke returned, having not been able to land, on account of a high surf on the shore. They met with no people on the isle; but saw a large bat, and some birds, and caught a water-snake. At six o'clock P.M. we got in with the land, under the N.W. side of the head, where we anchored in seventeen fathoms water, the bottom a fine dark sand, half a mile from shore. Many people appeared on the shore, and some attempted to swim off to us; but having occasion to send the boat ahead to sound, they retired as she drew near them. This, however, gave us a favourable idea of them.

On the 4th [Thursday], at day-break, I went with two boats to examine the coast, to look for a proper landing-place, wood, and water. At this time, the natives began to assemble on the shore, and by signs invited us to land. I went first to a small beach, which is towards the head, where I found no good landing, on account of some rocks which every where lined the coast. I, however, put the boat's bow to the shore, and gave cloth, medals, &c. to some people who were there. For this treatment they offered to haul the boats over the breakers to the sandy beach; which I thought a friendly offer, but had reason afterwards to alter my opinion. When they found I would not do as they desired, they made signs for us to go down into the bay, which we accordingly did, and they ran along shore abreast of us, their number increasing prodigiously. I put into the shore in two or three places, but, not liking the situation, did not land. By this time, I believe, the natives conceived what I wanted, as they directed me round a rocky point, where, on a fine sandy beach, I stepped out of the boat without wetting a foot, in the face of a vast multitude, with only a green branch in my hand, which I had before got from one of them. I took but one man out of the boat with me, and ordered the other boat to lie to a little distance off. They received me with great courtesy and politeness; and would retire back from the boat on my making the least motion with my hand. A man, whom I took to be a chief, seeing this, made them form a semicircle round the boat's bow, and beat such as attempted to break through this order. This man I loaded with presents, giving likewise to others, and asked by signs for fresh water, in hopes of seeing where they got it. The chief immediately sent a man for some, who ran to a house, and presently returned with a little in a

bamboo; so that I gained but little information by this. I next asked, by the same means, for something to eat; and they as readily brought me a yam, and some cocoa-nuts. In short, I was charmed with their behaviour; and the only thing which could give the least suspicion was, that most of them were armed with clubs, spears, darts, and bows and arrows. For this reason I kept my eye continually upon the chief, and watched his looks as well as his actions. He made many signs to me to haul the boat up upon the shore, and at last slipped into the crowd, where I observed him speak to several people, and then return to me, repeating signs to haul the boat up, and hesitating a good deal before he would receive some spike-nails which I then offered him. This made me suspect something was intended, and immediately I stepped into the boat, telling them by signs that I should soon return. But they were not for parting so soon, and now attempted, by force, what they could not obtain by gentler means. The gang-board happened unluckily to be laid out for me to come into the boat. I say unluckily, for if it had not been out, and if the crew had been a little quicker in getting the boat off, the natives might not have had time to put their design in execution, nor would the following disagreeable scene have happened. As we were putting off the boat, they laid hold of the gang-board, and unhooked it off the boat's stern. But as they did not take it away, I thought this had been done by accident, and ordered the boat in again to take it up. Then they themselves hooked it over the boat's stem, and attempted to haul her ashore; others, at the same time, snatched the oars out of the people's hands. On my pointing a musquet at them, they in some measure desisted, but returned in an instant seemingly determined to haul the boat ashore. At the head of this party was the chief; the others, who could not come at the boat, stood behind with darts, stones, and bows and arrows in hand, ready to support them. Signs and threats having no effect, our own safety became the only consideration; and yet I was unwilling to fire on the multitude, and resolved to make the chief alone fall a victim to his own treachery; but my musquet at this critical moment missed fire. Whatever idea they might have formed of the arms we held in our hands, they must now have looked upon them as childish weapons, and began to let us see how much better theirs were, by throwing stones and darts, and by shooting arrows. This made it absolutely necessary for me to give orders to fire. The first discharge threw them into confusion; but a second was hardly sufficient to drive them off the beach; and after all, they continued to throw stones from behind the trees and bushes, and, every now and then, to pop out and throw a dart. Four lay, to all appearance, dead on the shore; but two of them afterwards crawled into the bushes. Happy it was for these people, that not half our musquets would go off, otherwise many more must have fallen. We had one man wounded in the cheek with a dart, the point of which was as thick as my finger, and yet it entered above two inches; which shows that it must have come with great force, though indeed we were very near them. An arrow struck Mr Gilbert's naked breast, who was about thirty yard off; but probably it had struck something before; for it hardly penetrated the skin. The arrows were pointed with hard wood.

As soon as we got on board, I ordered the anchor to be weighed, with a view of anchoring near the landing-place. While this was doing, several people appeared on the low rocky point, displaying two oars we had lost in the scuffle. I looked on this as a sign of submission, and of their wanting to give us the oars. I was, nevertheless, prevailed on to fire a four point shot at them, to let them see the effect of our great guns. The ball fell short, but frightened them so much, that none were seen afterwards; and they left the oars standing up against the bushes.[3]

It was now calm; but the anchor was hardly at the bow before a breeze sprung up at North, of which we took the advantage, set our sails, and plyed out of the bay, as it did not seem capable of supplying our wants, with that conveniency I wished to have. Besides, I always had it in my power to return to this place, in case I should find none more convenient farther South.

At one o'clock the next morning [Friday 5th], drawing near the shore, we tacked. At sun-rise we discovered a high table land (an island) bearing E. by S. [which] extended from S. 7° West to S. 87° West, distant three or four miles. We then found that the light we had seen in the night, was occasioned by a volcano, which we observed to throw up vast quantities of fire and smoke, with a rumbling noise heard at a great distance. We now made sail for the island; and, presently after, discovered a small inlet which had the appearance of being a good harbour. In order to be better informed, I sent away two armed boats, under the command of Lieutenant Cooper, to sound it; and, in the mean while, we stood on and off with the ship, to be ready to follow, or give them any assisance they might want. On the East point of the entrance, we observed a number of people, and several houses and canoes; and when our boats entered the harbour they launched some, and followed them, but came not near. It was not long before Mr Cooper made the signal for anchorage; and we stood in with the ship. The wind being at West, and our course S.S.W., we borrowed close to the West point, and passed over some sunken rocks, which might have been avoided by keeping a little more to the East, or about one-third channel over. The wind left us as soon as we were within the entrance, and obliged us to drop an anchor in four fathoms water. After this, the boats were sent again to sound; and, in the mean time, the launch was hoisted out, in order to carry out anchors to warp in[4] by, as soon as we should be acquainted with the channel.

While we were thus employed, many of the natives got together in parties, on several parts of the shore, all armed with bows, spears, &c. Some swam off to us, others came in canoes. At first they were shy, and kept at the distance of a stone's throw; they grew insensibly bolder; and, at last, came under our stern, and made some exchanges. The people in one of the first canoes, after coming as near as they durst, threw towards us some cocoa-nuts. I went into a boat and picked them up, giving them in return some cloth and other articles. This induced others to come under the stern, and along-side, where

---

[3] Only speculative anthropology, for which we have no space, could interpret this incident in the light of Mclanscian beliefs and customs. According to Eromangan tradition only one man, the 'chief', was killed. [eds]

[4]   To haul in the ship. [eds]

their behaviour was insolent and daring. They wanted to carry off every thing within their reach; they got hold of the fly of the ensign, and would have torn it from the staff; others attempted to knock the rings off the rudder; but the greatest trouble they gave us was to look after the buoys of our anchors, which were no sooner thrown out of the boats, or let go from the ship, than they got hold of them. A few musquets fired in the air had no effect; but a four-pounder frightened them so much, that they quitted their canoes that instant, and took to the water. But as soon as they found themselves unhurt, they got again into their canoes; gave us some halloos; flourished their weapons; and returned once more to the buoys. This put us to the expense of a few musquetoon[5] shot, which had the desired effect. Although none were hurt, they were afterwards afraid to come near the buoys; very soon all retired on shore; and we were permitted to sit down to dinner undisturbed.

During these transactions, a friendly old man in a small canoe made several trips between us and the shore, bringing off each time a few cocoa-nuts, or a yam, and taking in exchange whatever we gave him. Another was on the gang-way when the great gun was fired, but I could not prevail on him to stay there long. Towards the evening, after the ship was moored, I landed at the head of the harbour, in the S.E. corner, with a strong party of men, without any opposition being made by a great number of natives who were assembled in two parties, the one on our right, the other on our left, armed with clubs, darts, spears, slings and stones, bows and arrows, &c. After distributing to the old people, (for we could distinguish no chief) and some others, presents of cloth, medals, &c. I ordered two casks to be filled with water out of a pond about twenty paces behind the landing-place; giving the natives to understand, that this was one of the articles we wanted. Besides water, we got from them a few cocoa-nuts, which seemed to be in plenty on the trees; but they could not be prevailed upon, to part with any of their weapons. These they held in constant readiness, and in the proper attitudes of offence and defence; so that little was wanting to make them attack us; at least we thought so, by their

pressing so much upon us, and in spite of our endeavours to keep them off. Our early re-embarking probably disconcerted their scheme; and after that, they all retired. The friendly old man before mentioned, was in one of these parties; and we judged, from his conduct, that his temper was pacific.

Chapter V
An Intercourse established with the Natives; some Account of the Island, and a Variety of Incidents that happened during our Stay at it.

As we wanted to take in a large quantity both of wood and water, and as, when I was on shore, I had found it practicable to lay the ship much nearer the landing-place then she now was, which would greatly facilitate that work, as well as over-awe the natives, and enable us better to cover and protect the working party on shore; with this view, on the 6th [Saturday], we went to work to transport the ship to the place I designed to moor her in. While we were about this, we observed the natives assembling from all parts, and forming themselves into two parties, as they did the preceding evening, one on each side the landing-place, to the amount of some thousands, armed as before. A canoe, sometimes conducted by one, and at other times by two or three men, now and then, came off, bringing a few cocoa-nuts or plantains. These they gave us without asking for any return; but I took care that they should always have something. Their chief design seemed to be to invite us on shore. One of those who came off was the old man, who had already ingratiated himself into our favour. I made him understand, by signs, that they were to lay aside their weapons, took those which were in the canoe and threw them over-board, and made him a present of a large piece of cloth. There was no doubt that he understood me, and made my request known to his country-men. For as soon as he landed, we observed him to go first to the one party, and then to the other; nor was he, ever after, seen by us with any thing like a weapon in his hand. After this, three fellows came in a canoe under the stern, one of them brandishing a club, with which he struck

---

[5]   A form of musket with a short barrel of large bore. [eds]

the ship's side, and committed other acts of defiance, but at last offered to exchange it for a string of beads, and some other trifles. These were sent down to him by a line; but the moment they were in his posseession, he and his companions paddled off in all haste, without giving the club or any thing else in return. This was what I expected, and indeed what I was not sorry for, as I wanted an opportunity to show the multitude on shore, the effect of our fire-arms, without materially hurting any of them. Having a fowling-piece loaded with small-shot (No. 3) I gave the fellow the contents; and, when they were above musquet-shot off, I ordered some of the musquetoons, or wall-pieces, to be fired, which made them leap out of the canoe, keep under her offside, and swim with her ashore. This transaction seemed to make little or no impression on the people there. On the contrary, they began to halloo, and to make sport of it.

After mooring the ship, by four anchors, with her broadside to the landing-place, hardly musquet-shot off, and placing our artillery in such a manner as to command the whole harbour, I embarked with the marines, and a party of seamen, in three boats, and rowed in for the shore. It hath been already mentioned, that the two divisions of the natives were drawn up on each side the landing-place. They had left a space between them of about thirty or forty yards, in which were laid, to the most advantage, a few small bunches of plantains, a yam, and two or three roots. Between these and the water were stuck upright in the sand, for what purpose I never could learn, four small reeds, about two feet from each other, in a line at right angles to the shore, where they remained for two or three days after. The old man before mentioned, and two more, stood by these things, inviting us, by signs, to land; but I had not forgot the trap I was so near being caught in at the last island; and this looked something like it. We answered, by making signs for the two divisions to retire farther back, and give us more room. The old man seemed to desire them so to do, but no more regard was paid to him than to us. More were continually joining them, and, except two or three old men, no one unarmed. In short, every thing conspired to make us believe they meant to attack us as soon as we should be on shore; the consequence of which was easily supposed;

many of them must have been killed and wounded, and we should hardly have escaped unhurt; two things I equally wished to prevent. Since, therefore, they would not give us the room we required, I thought it was better to frighten them into it, than to oblige them by the deadly effect of our fire-arms. I accordingly ordered a musquet to be fired over the party on our right, which was by far the strongest body; but the alarm it gave them was momentary. In an instant they recovered themselves, and began to display their weapons. One fellow showed us his backside, in a manner which plainly conveyed his meaning. After this I ordered three or four more musquets to be fired. This was the signal for the ship to fire a few great guns, which presently dispersed them; and then we landed, and marked out the limits, on the right and left, by a line. Our old friend stood his ground, though deserted by his two companions, and I rewarded his confidence with a present. The natives came gradually to us, seemingly in a more friendly manner; some even without their weapons, but by far the greatest part brought them; and when we made signs to lay them down, they gave us to understand that we must lay down ours first. Thus all parties stood armed. The presents I made to the old people, and to such as seemed to be of consequence, had little effect on their conduct. They indeed climbed the cocoa-nut trees, and threw us down the nuts, without requiring any thing for them; but I took care that they should always have somewhat in return. I observed that many were afraid to touch what belonged to us; and they seemed to have no notion of exchanging one thing for another. I took the old man (whose name we now found to be Paowang) to the woods, and made him understand, I wanted to cut down some trees to take on board the ship; cutting some down at the same time, which we put into one of our boats, together with a few small casks of water, with a view of letting the people see what it was we chiefly wanted. Paowang very readily gave his consent to cut wood; nor was there any one who made the least objection. He only desired the cocoa-nut trees might not be cut down. Matters being thus settled, we embarked and returned on board to dinner, and, immediately after, they all dispersed. I never learnt that any one was hurt by our shot, either on this or the preceding day; which was a very happy circumstance. In the afternoon having landed again, we loaded the launch with water, and having made three hauls with the seine,[6] caught upwards of three hundred pounds of mullet and other fish. It was some time before any of the natives appeared, and not above twenty or thirty at last, amongst whom was our trusty friend Paowang, who made us a present of a small pig, which was the only one we got at this isle, or that was offered us.

During the night, the volcano, which was about four miles to the West of us, vomitted up vast quantities of fire and smoke, as it had also done the night before; and the flames were seen to rise above the hill which lay between us and it. At every eruption, it made a long rumbling noise like that of thunder, or the blowing up of large mines. A heavy shower of rain, which fell at this time, seemed to increase it; and the wind blowing from the same quarter, the air was loaded with its ashes, which fell so thick that every thing was covered with the dust. It was a kind of fine sand, or stone, ground or burnt to powder, and was exceedingly troublesome to the eyes.

Early in the morning of the 7th [Sunday], the natives began again to assemble near the watering-place, armed as usual, but not in such numbers as at first. After breakfast, we landed, in order to cut wood and fill water. I found many of the islanders much inclined to be friends with us, especially the old people; on the other hand, most of the younger were daring and insolent, and obliged us to keep to our arms. I staid till I saw no disturbance was like to happen, and then returned to the ship, leaving the party under the command of Lieutenants Clerke and Edgcumbe. When they came on board to dinner, they informed me that the people continued to behave in the same inconsistent manner as in the morning; but more especially one man, whom Mr Edgcumbe was obliged to fire at, and believed he had struck with a swan-shot. After that the others behaved with more discretion; and as soon as our people embarked they all retired. While we were sitting at dinner an old man came on board, looked into many parts of the ship, and then went ashore again.

In the afternoon, only a few of those who lived in the neighbourhood, with whom we were now upon a tolerable footing, made their appearance at the watering-place. Paowang brought us an axe which had been left by our people, either in the woods or on the beach, and found by some of the natives. A few other articles were afterwards returned to us, which either they had stolen, or we had lost by our negligence. So careful were they now not to offend us in this respect.

Early the next morning [Monday 8th] I sent the launch, protected by a party of marines in another boat, to take in ballast, which we wanted. This work was done before breakfast; and after it, she was sent for wood and water, and with her the people employed in this service, under the protection of a serjeant's guard, which was now thought sufficient, as the natives seemed to be pretty well reconciled to us. I was told, that they asked our people to go home with them, on condition they stripped naked as they were. This shows that they had no design to rob them; whatever other they might have.

On the 9th [Tuesday], I sent the launch for more ballast, and the guard and wooders to the usual place. With these I went myself, and found a good many of the natives collected together, whose behaviour, though armed, was courteous and obliging; so that there was no longer any occasion to mark out the limits by a line: they observed them without this precaution. As it was necessary for Mr Wales's instruments[7] to remain on shore all the middle of the day, the guard did not return to dinner, as they had done before, till relieved by others. When I came off, I prevailed on a young man, whose name was Wha-a-gou, to accompany me. Before dinner I showed him every part of the ship; but did not observe that any one thing fixed his attention a moment, or caused in him the least surprise. He had no knowledge of goats, dogs, or cats, calling them all hogs (*Booga* or *Boogas*). I made him a present of a dog and a bitch, as he showed a liking to that kind of animal. Soon after he came on board, some of his friends followed in a canoe, and enquired for him, probably doubtful of his safety. He looked out of the quartergallery, and having spoken to them, they went ashore, and quickly returned with a cock, a little

---

[6]   A fishing net designed to hang vertically in the water. [eds]

[7]   Astronomical. [eds]

sugar-cane, and a few cocoa-nuts, as a present to me. Though he sat down with us, he did but just taste our salt pork, but eat pretty heartily of yam, and drank a glass of wine. After dinner I made him presents, and then conducted him ashore.

As soon as we landed, the youth and some of his friends took me by the hand, with a view, as I understood, to conduct me to their habitations. We had not gone far, before some of them, for what reason I know not, were unwilling I should proceed; in consequence of which the whole company stopped; and, if I was not mistaken, a person was dispatched for something or other to give me; for I was desired to sit down and wait, which I accordingly did. During this interval, several of our gentlemen passed us, at which they showed great uneasiness, and importuned me so much to order them back, that I was at last obliged to comply. They were jealous of our going up the country, or even along the shore of the harbour. While I was waiting here, our friend Paowang came with a present of fruit and roots, carried by about twenty men; in order, as I supposed, to make it appear the greater. One had a small bunch of plantains, another a yam, a third a cocoa-nut, &c.; but two men might have carried the whole with ease. This present was in return for something I had given him in the morning; however, I thought the least I could do now, was to pay the porters.

After I had dispatched Paowang, I returned to Wha-a-gou and his friends, who were still for detaining me. They seemed to wait with great impatience for something, and to be unwilling and ashamed to take away the two dogs, without making me a return. As night was approaching, I pressed to be gone; with which they complied, and so we parted.

The preceding day, Mr Forster learnt from the people the proper name of the island, which they call Tanna;[8] and this day I learnt from them the name of those in the neighbourhood. The one we touched at last is called Erromango; the small isle, which we discovered the morning we landed here, Immer; the Table Island to the East, discovered at the same time, Erronan or Footoona; and an island which lies to the S.E.

Annattom.[9] All these islands are to be seen from Tanna.

They gave us to understand, in a manner which I thought admitted of no doubt, that they eat human flesh, and that circumcision was practised amongst them. They began the subject of eating human flesh, of their own accord, by asking us if we did; otherwise I should never have thought of asking them such a question. I have heard people argue, that no nation could be cannibals, if they had other flesh to eat, or did not want food; thus deriving the custom from necessity. The people of this island can be under no such necessity; they have fine pork and fowls, and plenty of roots and fruits. But since we have not actually seen them eat human flesh, it will admit of doubt with some, whether they are cannibals.

When I got on board, I learnt that, when the launch was on the west side of the harbour taking in ballast, one of the men employed on this work, had scalded his fingers in taking a stone up out of some water. This circumstance produced the discovery of several hot springs, at the foot of the cliff, and rather below high-water mark.

This day Mr Wales, and two or three of the officers, advanced a little, for the first time, into the island. They met with a small straggling village, the inhabitants of which treated them with great civility; and the next morning [Wednesday 10th] Mr Forster and his party, and some others, made another excursion inland. They met with several fine plantations of plantains, sugar-canes, yams, &c.; and the natives were courteous and civil. Indeed, by this time, the people, especially those in our neighbourhood, were so well reconciled to us, that they showed not the least dislike at our rambling about in the skirts of the wood, shooting, &c. In the afternoon, some boys having got behind thickets, and having thrown two or three stones at our people who were cutting wood, they were fired at by the petty officers present on duty. Being ashore at the time, I was alarmed at hearing the report of the musquets, and seeing two or three boys run out of the wood. When I knew the cause, I was much

---

[8]   In fact, the word simply meant 'ground'. [eds]

[9]   These names stuck. Islands referred to in this extract are still named: Ambrim; Anyeltum; Epi; Eromanga; Futuna; Malekula. [eds]

displeased at so wanton a use being made of our fire-arms, and took measures to prevent it for the future. Wind southerly, with heavy showers of rain.

During the night, and also all the 11th [Tuesday], the volcano was exceedingly troublesome, and made a terrible noise, throwing up prodigious columns of fire and smoke at each explosion, which happened every three or four minutes; and, at one time, great stones were seen high in the air. Besides the necessary work of wooding and watering, we struck the main-top-mast to fix new trestle-trees and back-stays. Mr Forster and his party went up the hill on the west side of the harbour, where he found three places from whence smoke of a sulphureous smell issued, through cracks or fissures in the earth. The ground about these was exceedingly hot, and parched or burnt, and they seemed to keep pace with the volcano, for, at every explosion of the latter, the quantity of smoke or steam in these was greatly increased, and forced out so as to rise in small columns, which we saw from the ship, and had taken for common fires made by the natives. At the foot of this hill are the hot springs before mentioned.

In the afternoon, Mr Forster having begun his botanical researches[10] on the other side of the harbour, fell in with our friend Paowang's house, where he saw most of the articles I had given him, hanging on the adjoining trees and bushes, as if they were not worthy of being under his roof.

On the 12th [Friday], some of the officers accompanied Mr Forster to the hot places he had been at the preceding day. A thermometer placed in a little hole made in one of them, rose from 80, at which it stood in the open air, to 170. Several other parts of the hill emitted smoke or steam all the day, and the volcano was unusually furious, insomuch that the air was loaded with its ashes. The rain which fell at this time, was a compound of water, sand, and earth; so that it properly might be called showers of mire. Whichever way the wind was, we were plagued with the ashes; unless it blew very strong indeed from the opposite direction. Notwithstanding the natives seemed well enough satisfied with the few expeditions we had made in the neighbourhood,

they were unwilling we should extend them farther. As a proof of this, some undertook to guide the gentlemen when they were in the country, to a place where they might see the mouth of the volcano. They very readily embraced the offer; and were conducted down to the harbour, before they perceived the cheat.

The 13th [Saturday], wind at N.E., gloomy weather. The only thing worthy of note this day, was, that Paowang being at dinner with us on board, I took the opportunity to show him several parts of the ship, and various articles, in hopes of finding out something which they might value, and be induced to take from us in exchange for refreshments; for what we got of this kind was trifling. But he looked on every thing that was shown him with the utmost indifference; nor did he take notice of any one thing except a wooden sand-box, which he seemed to admire, and turned two or three times over in his hand.

Next morning [Sunday 14th], after breakfast, a party of us set out for the country, to try if we could not get a nearer and better view of the Volcano. We went by the way of one of those hot smoking places before mentioned, and dug a hole in the hottest part, into which a thermometer of Fahrenheit's construction was put; and the mercury presently rose to 100°. It remained in the hole two minutes and a half without either rising or falling. The earth about this place was a kind of white clay, had a sulphureous smell, and was soft and wet, the surface only excepted, over which was spread a thin dry crust, that had upon it some sulphur, and a vitriolic substance tasting like alum. The place affected by the heat was not above eight or ten yards square; and near it were some fig-trees, which spread their branches over a part of it, and seemed to like their situation. We thought that this extraordinary heat was caused by the steam of boiling water, strongly impregnated with sulphur. I was told that some of the other places were larger than this; though we did not go out of the road to look at them, but proceeded up the hill through a country so covered with trees, shrubs, and plants, that the bread-fruit and cocoa-nut trees, which seem to have been planted here by Nature, were in a manner choked up. Here and

---

[10]   Johann Reinhold Forster, a German, was the expedition's chief official scientist – botanist and all-purpose 'naturalist'. [eds]

there, we met with an house, some few people, and plantations. These latter we found in different states; some of long standing; others lately cleared; and some only clearing, and before any thing had been planted. The clearing a piece of ground for a plantation, seemed to be a work of much labour, considering the tools they had to work with, which, though much inferior to those at the Society Isles,[11] are of the same kind. Their method is, however, judicious, and as expeditious as it can well be. They lop off the small branches of the large trees, dig under the roots, and there burn the branches and small shrubs and plants which they root up. The soil, in some parts, is a rich black mould; in other parts, it seemed to be composed of decayed vegetables, and of the ashes the volcano sends forth throughout all its neighbourhood. Happening to turn out of the common path, we came into a plantation where we found a man at work, who, either out of good-nature, or to get us the sooner out of his territories, undertook to be our guide. We followed him accordingly; but had not gone far before we came to the junction of two roads, in one of which stood another man with a sling and a stone, which he thought proper to lay down when a musquet was pointed at him. The attitude in which we found him, the ferocity appearing in his looks, and his behaviour after, convinced us that he meant to defend the path he stood in. He, in some measure, gained his point; for our guide took the other road, and we followed; but not without suspecting he was leading us out of the common way. The other man went with us likewise, counting us several times over, and hallooing, as we judged, for assistance; for we were presently joined by two or three more, among whom was a young woman with a club in her hand. By these people we were conducted to the brow of a hill, and shewn a road, leading down to the harbour, which they wanted us to take. Not choosing to comply, we returned to that we had left, which we pursued alone, our guide refusing to go with us. After ascending another ridge, as thickly covered with wood as those we had come over, we saw yet other hills between us and the volcano, which seemed as far off as at our first setting out. This discouraged us from proceeding farther, especially as we could

get no one to be our guide. We, therefore, came to a resolution to return; and had but just put this in execution when we met between twenty and thirty people, whom, the fellow before mentioned had collected together, with a design, as we judged, to oppose our advancing into the country; but as they saw us returning they suffered us to pass unmolested. Some of them put us into the right road, accompanied us down the hill, made us stop by the way, to entertain us with cocoa-nuts, plantains, and sugar-cane; and what we did not eat on the spot, they brought down the hill with us. Thus we found these people hospitable, civil, and good-natured, when not prompted to a contrary conduct by jealousy; a conduct I cannot tell how to blame them for, especially when I consider the light in which they must view us. It was impossible for them to know our real design; we enter their ports without their daring to oppose; we endeavour to land in their country as friends, and it is well if this succeeds; we land, nevertheless, and maintain the footing we have got, by the superiority of our fire-arms. Under such circumstances, what opinion are they to form of us? Is it not as reasonable for them to think that we come to invade their country, as to pay them a friendly visit? Time, and some acquaintance with us, can only convince them of the latter. These people are yet in a rude state; and, if we may judge from circumstances and appearances, are frequently at war, not only with their neighbours, but among themselves; consequently must be jealous of every new face. I will allow there are some exceptions to this rule to be found in this sea; but there are few nations who would willingly suffer visiters like us to advance far into their country.

Before this excursion some of us had been of opinion, that these people were addicted to an unnatural passion, because they had endeavoured to entice some of our men into the woods; and, in particular, I was told, that one who had the care of Mr Forster's plant bag, had been, once or twice, attempted. As the carrying of bundles, &c. is the office of the women in this country, it had occurred to me, and I was not singular in this, that the natives might mistake him, and some others, for women. My conjecture was fully verified this day. For this man, who was one of

[11] Tahiti, etc: Polynesian islands by this time well known to Cook. [eds]

the party, and carried the bag as usual, following me down the hill, by the words which I understood of the conversation of the natives, and by their actions, I was well assured that they considered him as a female; till, by some means, they discovered their mistake, on which they cried out, *Erramange! Erramange!* It's a man! It's a man! The thing was so palpable that every one was obliged to acknowledge, that they had before mistaken his sex; and that, after they were undeceived, they seemed not to have the least notion of what we had suspected. This circumstance will show how liable we are to form wrong conjectures of things, among people whose language we are ignorant of. Had it not been for this discovery, I make no doubt that these people would have been charged with this vile custom.

In the evening I took a walk, with some of the gentlemen, into the country on the other side of the harbour, where we had very different treatment from what we had met with in the morning. The people we now visited, among whom was our friend Paowang, being better acquainted with us, showed a readiness to oblige us in every thing in their power. We came to the village which had been visited on the 9th. It consisted of about twenty houses, the most of which need no other description than comparing them to the roof of a thatched house in England, taken off the walls and placed on the ground. Some were open at both ends; others partly closed with reeds; and all were covered with palm thatch. A few of them were thirty or forty feet long, and fourteen or sixteen broad. Besides these, they have other mean hovels, which, I conceived, were only to sleep in. Some of these stood in a plantation, and I was given to understand, that in one of them lay a dead corpse. They made signs that described sleep, or death; and circumstances pointed out the latter. Curious to see all I could, I prevailed on an elderly man to go with me to the hut, which was separated from the others by a reed fence, built quite round it at the distance of four or five feet. The entrance was by a space in the fence made so low as to admit one to step over. The two sides and one end of the hut were closed, or built, up in the same manner, and with the same materials, as the roof. The other end had been open, but was now well closed up with mats, which I could

not prevail on the man to remove, or suffer me to do it. There hung at this end of the hut a matted bag or basket, in which was a piece of roasted yam, and some sort of leaves, all quite fresh. I had a strong desire to see the inside of the hut, but the man was peremptory in refusing this, and even showed an unwillingness to permit me to look into the basket. He wore round his neck, fastened to a string, two or three locks of human hair; and a woman present had several about her neck. I offered something in exchange for them; but they gave me to understand they could not part with them, as it was the hair of the person who lay in the hut. Thus I was led to believe that these people dispose of their dead in a manner similar to that of Otaheite.[12] The same custom of wearing the hair is observed by the people of that island, and also by the New Zealanders. The former make *Tamau* of the hair of their deceased friends, and the latter make ear-rings and necklaces of their teeth.

Near most of their large houses were fixed upright in the ground, the stems of four cocoa-nut trees, in a square position about three feet from each other. Some of our gentlemen, who first saw them, were inclined to believe they were thus placed on a religious account; but I was now satisfied that it was for no other purpose but to hang cocoa-nuts on to dry. For when I asked, as well as I could, the use of them, a man took me to one, loaded with cocoa-nuts from the bottom to the top; and no words could have informed me better. Their situation is well chosen for this use, as most of their large houses are built in an open airy place, or where the wind has carefree passage, from whatever direction it blows. Near most, if not all of them, is a large tree, or two, whose far spreading branches afford an agreeable retreat from the scorching sun. This part of the island was well cultivated, open and airy; the plantations were laid out by line, abounding with plantains, sugar-canes, yams, and other roots, and stocked with fruit trees. In our walk we met with our old friend Paowang, who, with some others, accompanied us to the water side, and brought with them, as a present, a few yams and cocoa-nuts.

On the 15th [Monday], having finished wooding and watering, a few hands only were on shore making brooms, the rest being employed

---

[12]   Tahiti. [eds]

on board, setting up the rigging, and putting the ship in a condition for sea. Mr Forster, in his botanical excursion this day, shot a pigeon, in the craw of which was a wild nutmeg.[13] He took some pains to find the tree, but his endeavours were without success. In the evening a party of us walked to the eastern sea-shore, in order to take the bearing of Annattom, and Erronan or Foottoona. The horizon proved so hazy that I could see neither; but one of the natives gave me, as I afterwards found, the true direction of them. We observed that in all, or most of their sugar plantations, were dug holes or pits, four feet deep, and five or six in diameter; and on our inquiring their use, we were given to understand, that they caught rats in them. These animals, which are very destructive to the canes, are here in great plenty. The canes, I observed, were planted as thick as possible round the edge of these pits, so that the rats in coming at them are the more liable to tumble in.

Next morning [Tuesday 16th], we found the tiller sprung in the rudder head, and, by some strange neglect, we had not a spare one on board, which we were ignorant of till now it was wanting. I knew but of one tree in the neighbourhood fit for this purpose, which I sent the carpenter on shore to look at, and an officer, with a party of men, to cut it down, provided he could obtain leave of the natives; if not, he was ordered to acquaint me. He understood that no one had any objection, and set the people to work accordingly. But as the tree was large, this required some time; and, before it was down, word was brought me that our friend Paowang was not pleased. Upon this I gave orders to desist, as we found that, by scarfing a piece to the inner end of the tiller, and letting it farther into the rudder head, it would still perform its office. But, as it was necessary to have a spare one on board, I went on shore, sent for Paowang, made him a present of a dog and a piece of cloth, and then explained to him that our great steering paddle was broken, and that

I wanted that tree to make a new one. It was easy to see how well pleased every one present was, with the means I took to obtain it. With one voice they gave their consent, Paowang joining his also, which he perhaps could not have done without the others; for I do not know that he had either more property, or more authority than the rest. This point being obtained, I took our friend on board to dinner, and after it was over, went with him ashore, to pay a visit to an old chief, who was said to be king of the island; which was a doubt with me.[14] Paowang took little or no notice of him. I made him a present, after which he immediately went away, as if he had got all he came for. His name was Geogy, and they gave him the title of *Areeke*. He was very old, but had a merry open countenance. He wore round his waist a broad red and white checquered belt, the materials and manufacture of which seemed the same as that of Otaheite cloth; but this was hardly a mark of distinction. He had with him a son, not less than forty-five or fifty years of age. A great number of people were at this time at the landing-place; most of them from distant parts. The behaviour of many was friendly; while others were daring and insolent, which I thought proper to put up with, as our stay was nearly at an end.

On the 17th [Wednesday], about ten o'clock, I went ashore, and found in the crowd old Geogy and his son, who soon made me understand that they wanted to dine with me; and accordingly I brought them, and two more, on board. They all called them *Areekees* (or kings); but I doubt if any of them had the least pretensions to that title over the whole island. It had been remarked, that one of these kings had not authority enough to order one of the people up into a cocoa-nut tree, to bring him down some nuts. Although he spoke to several, he was at last obliged to go himself, and, by way of revenge, as it was thought, left not a nut on the tree, taking what he wanted himself, and giving the rest to some of our people.

---

[13] This was of acute economic interest. The nutmeg gave a much prized spice. It was native to the Banda Islands in the East Indies, where the Dutch had stepped in to monopolize its production and trade. Efforts to grow it elsewhere had failed. If it were indigenous to Tanna, this might be sufficient motive for colonization. Several species of wild nutmeg do grow in the 'New Hebrides'. [eds]

[14] Cook was shrewd. This island had no one 'chief'. We know from Forster that the disputed tree was a casuarina – very scarce, and the natives made clubs of it. [eds]

When I got them on board, I went with them all over the ship, which they viewed with uncommon surprise and attention. We happened to have for their entertainment a kind of pie or pudding made of plantains, and some sort of greens which we had got from one of the natives. On this, and on yams, they made a hearty dinner; for, as to the salt beef and pork, they would hardly taste them. In the afternoon, having made each of them a present of a hatchet, a spike-nail, and some medals, I conducted them ashore.

Mr Forster and I then went over to the other side of the harbour, and, having tried, with Fahrenheit's thermometer, the head of one of the hot springs, we found that the mercury rose to 191°. At this time the tide was up within two or three feet of the spring, so that we judged it might, in some degree, be cooled by it. We were mistaken, however; for, on repeating the experiment next morning [Thursday 18th], when the tide was out, the mercury rose no higher than 187°; but, at another spring, where the water bubbled out of the sand from under the rock at the S.W. corner of the harbour, the mercury, in the same thermometer, rose to 202°, which is but little colder than boiling water. The hot places before mentioned are from about three to four hundred feet perpendicular above these springs, and on the slope of the same ridge with the volcano; that is, there are no valleys between them but such as are formed in the ridge itself; nor is the volcano on the highest part of the ridge, but on the S.E. side of it. That is, I have been told, contrary to the general opinion of philosophers, who say that volcanos must be on the summits of the highest hills. So far is this from being the case on this island, that some of its hills are more than double the height of that on which the volcano is, and close to it. To these remarks I must add, that, in wet or moist weather, the volcano was most violent. There seems to be room for some philosophical reasoning on these phenomena of nature; but not having any talent that way, I must content myself with stating facts as I found them, and leave the causes to men of more abilities.

The tiller was now finished; but, as the wind was unfavourable for sailing, the guard was sent on shore on the 19th [Friday], as before, and a party of men to cut up and bring off the remainder of the tree from which we had got the tiller. Having nothing else to do, I went on shore with them, and finding a good number of the natives collected about the landing-place as usual, I distributed among them all the articles I had with me, and then went on board for more. In less than an hour I returned, just as our people were getting some large logs into the boat. At the same time four or five of the natives stepped forward to see what we were about, and as we did not allow them to come within certain limits, unless to pass along the beach, the centry ordered them back, which they readily complied with. At this time, having my eyes fixed on them, I observed the centry present his piece (as I thought at these men) and was just going to reprove him for it, because I had observed that, whenever this was done, some of the natives would hold up their arms, to let us see they were equally ready. But I was astonished beyond measure when the centry fired, for I saw not the least cause.[15] At this outrage most of the people fled: it was only a few I could prevail on to remain. As they ran off, I observed one man to fall; and he was immediately lifted up by two others, who took him into the water, washed his wound, and then led him off. Presently after, some came and described to me the nature of his wound; and, as I found he was not carried far, I sent for the surgeon. As soon as he arrived, I went with him to the man, whom we found expiring. The ball had struck his left arm, which was much shattered, and then entered his body by the short-ribs, one of which was broken. The rascal who fired, pretended that a man had laid an arrow across his bow, and was going to shoot at him, so that he apprehended himself in danger. But this was no more than they had always done, and with no other view than to show they were armed as well as we; at least I have reason to think so, as they never went farther. What made this incident the more unfortunate, was, it not appearing to be the man who bent the bow, that was shot, but one who stood by him. This affair threw the natives into the utmost consternation; and the few that were prevailed on to stay, ran to the plantations and brought cocoa-nuts, &c. which they laid down at our feet. So soon were these daring people humbled! When I went on board

[15] Cook's reaction was fierce. He flung the sentry in irons, and intended to have him flogged, but his officers took the man's side and after a heated argument the flogging was remitted. [eds]

to dinner they all retired, and only a few appeared in the afternoon, amongst whom were Paowang and Whã-ã-gou. I had not seen this young man since the day he dined on board. Both he and Paowang promised to bring me fruit, &c. the next morning, but our early departure put it out of their power.

Chapter VI
Departure from Tanna; with some Account of its Inhabitants, their Manners and Arts

During the night [Saturday 20th] the wind had veered round to S.E. As this was favourable for getting out of the harbour, at four o'clock in the morning of the 20th, we began to unmoor, and at eight, having weighed our last anchor, put to sea. As soon as we were clear of the land, I brought to, waiting for the launch which was left behind to take up a kedge anchor and hawser we had out, to cast by. About day-break a noise was heard in the woods, nearly abreast of us, on the east side of the harbour, not unlike singing of psalms. I was told that the like had been heard at the same time every morning, but it never came to my knowledge till now, when it was too late to learn the occasion of it. Some were of opinion, that at the east point of the harbour (where we observed, in coming in, some houses, boats, &c.) was something sacred to religion, because some of our people had attempted to go to this point, and were prevented by the natives. I thought, and do still think, it was only owing to a desire they shewed, on every occasion, of fixing bounds to our excursions. So far as we had once been, we might go again; but not farther, with their consent. But by encroaching a little every time, our country expeditions were insensibly extended without giving the least umbrage. Besides, these morning ceremonies, whether religious or not, were not performed down at that point, but in a part where some of our people had been daily.

I cannot say what might be the true cause of these people shewing such dislike to our going up into their country. It might be owing to a naturally jealous disposition, or perhaps to their being accustomed to hostile visits from their neighbours, or quarrels among themselves. Circumstances seemed to shew that such must frequently happen; for we observed them very

expert in arms, and well accustomed to them; seldom or never travelling without them. It is possible all this might be on our account; but I hardly think it. We never gave them the least molestation, nor did we touch any part of their property, not even the wood and water, without first having obtained their consent. The very cocoa-nuts, hanging over the heads of the workmen, were as safe as those in the middle of the island. It happened rather fortunately, that there were so many cocoa-nut trees, near the skirts of the harbour, which seemed not to be private property; so that we could generally prevail on the natives to bring us some of these nuts, when nothing would induce them to bring any out of the country.

We were not wholly without refreshments; for besides the fish, which our seine now and then provided us with, we procured daily some fruits or roots from the natives, though but little in proportion to what we could consume. The reason why we got no more might be our having nothing to give them in exchange, which they thought valuable. They had not the least knowledge of iron; consequently, nails and iron tools, beads, &c. which had so great a run at the more eastern isles, were of no consideration here; and cloth can be of no use to people who go naked.

The produce of this island is bread-fruit, plantains, cocoa-nuts, a fruit like a nectarine, yams, tarra, a sort of potato, sugar-cane, wild figs, a fruit like an orange, which is not eatable, and some other fruit and nuts whose names I have not. Nor have I any doubt that the nutmeg before mentioned was the produce of this island. The bread-fruit, cocoa-nuts, and plantains are neither so plentiful nor so good as at Otaheite; on the other hand, sugar-canes and yams are not only in greater plenty, but of superior quality, and much larger. We got one of the latter which weighed fifty-six pounds, every ounce of which was good. Hogs did not seem to be scarce; but we saw not many fowls. These are the only domestic animals they have. Land birds are not more numerous than at Otaheite, and the other islands; but we met with some small birds, with a very beautiful plumage, which we had never seen before. There is as great a variety of trees and plants here, as at any island we touched at, where our botanists had time to examine. I believe these people live chiefly on the produce of the land, and that the sea contributes but little to their subsistence. Whether this arises from the coast not abounding with fish, or from their being bad fishermen, I know not; both causes perhaps concur. I never saw any sort of fishing-tackle amongst them, nor any one out fishing, except on the shoals, or along the shores of the harbour, where they would watch to strike with a dart such fish as came within their reach; and in this they were expert. They seemed much to admire our catching fish with the seine; and, I believe, were not well pleased with it at last. I doubt not, they have other methods of catching fish besides striking them.

We understood that the little isle of Junner was chiefly inhabited by fishermen, and that the canoes we frequently saw pass, to and from that isle and the east point of the harbour, were fishing canoes. These canoes were of unequal sizes; some thirty feet long, two broad, and three deep; and they are composed of several pieces of wood clumsily sewed together with bandages. The joints are covered on the outside by a thin batten champhered off at the edges, over which the bandages pass. They are navigated either by paddles or sails. The sail is latteen, extended to a yard and boom, and hoisted to a short mast. Some of the large canoes have two sails, and all of them outriggers.

At first we thought the people of this island, as well as those of Erromango, were a race between the natives of the Friendly Islands[16] and those of Mallicollo; but a little acquaintance with them convinced us that they had little or no affinity to either, except it be in their hair, which is much like what the people of the latter island have. The general colours of it are black and brown, growing to a tolerable length, and very crisp and curly. They separate it into small locks, which they woold or cue round with the rind of a slender plant, down to about an inch of the ends; and, as the hair grows, the woolding is continued. Each of these cues or locks is somewhat thicker than common whip-cord; and they look like a parcel of small strings hanging down from the crown of their heads. Their beards, which are strong and bushy, are generally short. The women do not wear their hair so, but cropped; nor do the boys, till they approach manhood. Some few men, women, and children, were seen,

who had hair like ours; but it was obvious that these were of another nation; and, I think, we understood they came from Erronan. It is to this island they ascribe one of the two languages which they speak, and which is nearly, if not exactly, the same as that spoken at the Friendly Islands. It is therefore more than probable that Erronan was peopled from that nation, and that, by long intercourse with Tanna and the other neighbouring islands, each hath learnt the other's language, which they use indiscriminately.

The other language which the people of Tanna speak, and, as we understood, those of Erromango and Annatom, is properly their own. It is different from any we had before met with, and bears no affinity to that of Mallicollo; so that, it should seem, the people of these islands are a distinct nation of themselves. Mallicollo, Apee, &c. were names entirely unknown to them; they even knew nothing of Sandwich Island, which is much the nearer. I took no small pains to know how far their geographical knowledge extended; and did not find that it exceeded the limits of their horizon.

These people are of the middle size, rather slender than otherwise; many are little, but few tall or stout; the most of them have good features, and agreeable countenances; are, like all the tropical race, active and nimble; and seem to excel in the use of arms, but not to be fond of labour. They never would put a hand to assist in any work we were carrying on, which the people of the other islands used to delight in. But what I judge most from, is their making the females do the most laborious work, as if they were pack-horses. I have seen a woman carrying a large bundle on her back, or a child on her back and a bundle under her arm, and a fellow strutting before her with nothing but a club or spear, or some such thing. We have frequently observed little troops of women pass, to and fro, along the beach, laden with fruit and roots, escorted by a party of men under arms; though, now and then, we have seen a man carry a burden at the same time, but not often. I know not on what account this was done, nor that an armed troop was necessary. At first, we thought they were moving out of the neighbourhood with their effects; but

---

[16]   Tonga, etc. [eds]

we afterwards saw them both carry out, and bring in, every day.

I cannot say the women are beauties; but I think them handsome enough for the men, and too handsome for the use that is made of them. Both sexes are of a very dark colour, but not black; nor have they the least characteristic of the negro about them. They make themselves blacker than they really are, by painting their faces with a pigment of the colour of black lead. They also use another sort which is red, and a third sort brown, or a colour between red and black. All these, but especially the first, they lay on, with a liberal hand, not only on the face, but on the neck, shoulders, and breast. The men wear nothing but a belt, and the wrapping leaf as at Mallicollo. The women have a kind of petticoat made of the filaments of the plantain tree, flags, or some such thing, which reaches below the knee. Both sexes wear ornaments, such as bracelets, ear-rings, necklaces, and amulets. The bracelets are chiefly worn by the men; some made of sea-shells, and others of those of the cocoa-nut. The men also wear amulets; and those of most value being made of a greenish stone, the green stone of New Zealand is valued by them for this purpose. Necklaces are chiefly used by the women, and made mostly of shells. Ear-rings are common to both sexes, and those valued most are made of tortoise-shell. Some of our people having got some at the Friendly Islands, brought it to a good market here, where it was of more value than any thing we had besides; from which I conclude that these people catch but few turtle, though I saw one in the harbour, just as we were getting under sail. I observed that, towards the latter end of our stay, they began to ask for hatchets, and large nails; so that it is likely they had found that iron is more serviceable than stone, bone, or shells, of which all their tools I have seen are made. Their stone hatchets, at least all those I saw, are not in the shape of adzes, as at the other islands, but more like an ax. In the helve, which is pretty thick, is made a hole into which the stone is fixed.

These people, besides the cultivation of ground, have few other arts worth mentioning. They know how to make a coarse kind of matting, and a coarse cloth of the bark of a tree, which is used chiefly for belts. The workmanship

of their canoes, I have before observed, is very rude; and their arms, with which they take the most pains in point of neatness, come far short of some others we had seen. Their weapons are clubs, spears or darts, bows and arrows, and stones. The clubs are of three or four kinds, and from three to five feet long. They seem to place most dependence on the darts, which are pointed with three bearded edges. In throwing them they make use of a becket, that is a piece of stiff plaited cord about six inches long, with an eye in one end and a knot at the other. The eye is fixed on the fore-finger of the right hand, and the other end is hitched round the dart, where it is nearly on an equipoise. They hold the dart between the thumb and remaining fingers, which serve only to give it direction, the velocity being communicated by the becket and fore-finger. The former flies off from the dart the instant its velocity becomes greater than that of the hand, but it remains on the finger ready to be used again. With darts they kill both birds and fish, and are sure of hitting a mark, within the compass of the crown of a hat, at the distance of eight or ten yards; but, at double that distance, it is chance if they hit a mark the size of a man's body, though they will throw the weapon sixty or seventy yards. They always throw with all their might, let the distance be what it will. Darts, bows and arrows are to them what musquets are to us. The arrows are made of reeds pointed with hard wood: some are bearded and some not, and those for shooting birds have two, three, and sometimes four points. The stones they use are, in general, the branches of coral rocks from eight to fourteen inches long, and from an inch to an inch-and-half in diameter. I know not if they employ them as missive weapons; almost every one of them carries a club, and besides that, either darts, or a bow and arrows, but never both: those who had stones kept them generally in their belts.

I cannot conclude this account of their arms without adding an entire passage out of Mr Wales's journal.[17] As this gentleman was continually on shore amongst them, he had a better opportunity of seeing what they could perform, than any of us. The passage is as follows 'I must confess I have been often led to think the feats which Homer represents his heroes as

[17]   William Wales, the expedition's astronomer. [eds]

performing with their spears, a little too much of the marvellous to be admitted into a heroic poem; I mean when confined within the streight stays of Aristotle. Nay, even so great an advocate for him as Mr Pope, acknowledges them to be *surprising*. But since I have seen what these people can do with their wooden spears, and them badly pointed, and not of a very hard nature, I have not the least exception to any one passage in that great poet on this account. But, if I see fewer exceptions, I can find infinitely more beauties in him; as he has, I think, scarce an action, circumstance, or description of any kind whatever, relating to a spear, which I have not seen and recognized among these people; as their whirling motion, and whistling noise, as they fly; their quivering motion, as they stick in the ground when they fall; their meditating their aim, when they are going to throw; and their shaking them in their hand as they go along, &c. &c.'

I know no more of their cookery, than that it consists of roasting and baking; for they have no vessel in which water can be boiled. Nor do I know that they have any other liquor but water and the juice of the cocoa-nut.[18]

We are utter strangers to their religion; and but little acquainted with their government. They seem to have chiefs among them; at least some were pointed out to us by that title; but, as I before observed, they appeared to have very little authority over the rest of the people. Old Geogy was the only one the people were ever seen to take the least notice of; but whether this was owing to high rank or old age, I cannot say. On several occasions I have seen the old men

respected and obeyed. Our friend Paowang was so; and yet I never heard him called chief, and have many reasons to believe that he had not a right to any more authority than many of his neighbours, and few, if any, were bound to obey him, or any other person in our neighbourhood; for if there had been such a one, we certainly should, by some means, have known it. I named the harbour Port Resolution, after the ship, she being the first which ever entered it. It is situated on the North side of the most eastern point of the island, and about E.N.E. from the volcano; in the latitude of 19° 32' 25$\frac{1}{2}$" South, and in the longitude of 169° 44' 35" East. It is no more than a little creek running in S. by W.$\frac{1}{2}$W. three quarters of a mile, and is about half that in breadth A shoal of sand and rocks, lying on the east side, makes it still narrower. The depth of water in the harbour is from six to three fathoms, and the bottom is sand and mud. No place can be more convenient for taking in wood and water; for both are close to the shore. The water stunk a little after it had been a few days on board, but it afterwards turned sweet; and, even when it was at the worst, the tin machine[19] would, in a few hours, recover a whole cask. This is an excellent contrivance for sweetening water at sea, and is well known in the navy.

Mr Wales, from whom I had the latitude and longitude, found the variation of the needle to be 7° 14' 12" East, and the dip of its South end 45° 2$\frac{1}{3}$'. He also observed the time of high water, on the full and change days, to be about 5' 45"; and the tide to rise and fall three feet.

Source: J. Cook, *A Voyage Towards The South Pole*, London, 1777, Vol. II, pp.38–84.

---

[18]   They did: the drinking of fermented *Kava* was of central importance in Tannese social organization. [eds]

[19]   Otherwise known as 'Lieutenant Osbridge's machine'. With the help of a pump, water was repeatedly filtered through holes in plated sheet-iron trays, one on top of the other, with spaces between. Wind cleared the stench, and also cooled the water. [eds]

Olaudah Equiano
Extracts from *The Life of Olaudah Equiano, or Gustavus Vassa the African*

Prepared for the Course Team by
Angus Calder

Contents

Olaudah Equiano
Extracts from The Life of Olaudah Equiano, or Gustavus Vassa the African

Olaudah Equiano (c.1745–97) was not the first African to publish work in English, but is by far the most interesting today of a number of eighteenth-century black writers. His Life, published in the year of the French Revolution, was much read and reprinted for half a century after its first appearance. Its neglect thereafter can be attributed partly to the success of the anti-slavery campaign in Britain (slavery within the British Empire was abolished in 1838) and partly to the increasingly dominant racism of the Western World which suppressed any achievements of Africans that might cut across stereotypes of their 'savagery'.

Rediscovered in the 1960s, Equiano is now seen as a pioneer of African writing, of Black British writing and even of African-American writing. Although his cool eighteenth-century prose may seem remote from the discourses of such writers as Wole Soyinka and James Baldwin, it is nevertheless true that his book foreshadowed the importance of autobiography and of protest in the recent development of Black writing.

As the following extract shows, Equiano was born in what is now Eastern Nigeria in the mid eighteenth century. His homeland had become a prime source of slaves for the plantations of the Caribbean and British North America. In the Ibo country kidnappers found slaves for sale via African middlemen in the city-states of the coast.

Equiano was relatively lucky in his white masters, not least during his service, while still a boy, in the Royal Navy, but saw at first-hand the appalling conditions endured by most New World slaves. After purchasing his own freedom, he enjoyed a varied life – a tour of the Mediterranean, voyages to the Arctic and Central America, and an important role in the anti-slave trade campaign by Quakers and Evangelical Christians, which had become significant in Britain by the 1780s. He travelled through Britain selling copies of his book and making speeches. In 1792 he married a white woman, Miss Cullen of Ely. He became a small landowner. Granville Sharp, the leader of British anti-slavery, thought him 'a sober, honest man'.

Paul Edwards has shown that Equiano's Life *was quite certainly his own work. He was educated in English while still a slave, and by his mid forties was fluent in it. His memory of Ibo customs seems to be generally accurate. For a vivid impression of pre-colonial Ibo life, see Chinua Achebe's novels* Things Fall Apart *and* Arrow of God.

The text reprinted here is taken from the first three chapters of Paul Edwards's facsimile edition (the Life *runs to twelve chapters in all). Some internal cuts have been made, and the editors' linking passages are denoted by square brackets and italics. Equiano's footnotes and those of the editors are signed 'Equiano' and 'eds' respectively.*

Chapter One

I BELIEVE it is difficult for those who publish their own memoirs to escape the imputation of vanity; nor is this the only disadvantage under which they labour: it is also their misfortune, that whatever is uncommon is rarely, if ever, believed, and what is obvious we are apt to turn from with disgust, and to charge the writer with impertinence.

People generally think those memoirs only worthy to be read or remembered which abound in great or striking events, those, in short, which in a high degree excite either admiration or pity: all others they consign to contempt and oblivion. It is therefore, I confess, not a little hazardous in a private and obscure individual, and a stranger too, thus to solicit the indulgent attention of the public; especially when I own I offer here the

history of neither a saint, a hero, nor a tyrant. I believe there are few events in my life, which have not happened to many: it is true the incidents of it are numerous; and, did I consider myself an European, I might say my sufferings were great: but when I compare my lot with that of most of my countrymen, I regard myself as a *particular favourite of Heaven*, and acknowledge the mercies of Providence in every occurrence of my life. If then the following narrative does not appear sufficiently interesting to engage general attention, let my motive be some excuse for its publication. I am not so foolishly vain as to expect from it either immortality or literary reputation. If it affords any satisfaction to my numerous friends, at whose request it has been written, or in the smallest degree promotes the interests of humanity, the ends for which it was undertaken will be fully attained, and every wish of my heart gratified. Let it therefore be remembered, that, in wishing to avoid censure, I do not aspire to praise.

That part of Africa, known by the name of Guinea, to which the trade for slaves is carried on, extends along the coast above 3400 miles, from the Senegal to Angola, and includes a variety of kingdoms. Of these the most considerable is the kingdom of Benen, both as to extent and wealth, the richness and cultivation of the soil, the power of its king, and the number and warlike disposition of the inhabitants. It is situated nearly under the line, and extends along the coast about 170 miles, but runs back into the interior part of Africa to a distance hitherto I believe unexplored by any traveller; and seems only terminated at length by the empire of Abyssinia, near 1500 miles from its beginning. This kingdom is divided into many provinces or districts: in one of the most remote and fertile of which, called Eboe, I was born, in the year 1745, in a charming fruitful vale, named Essaka. The distance of this province from the capital of Benin and the sea coast must be very considerable; for I had never heard of white men or Europeans, nor of the sea; and our subjection to the king of Benin was little more than nominal;[1] for every transaction of the government, as far as my slender observation extended, was conducted by the chiefs or elders of the place. The manners and government of a people who have little commerce with other countries are generally very simple; and the history of what passes in one family or village may serve as a specimen of a nation. My father was one of those elders or chiefs I have spoken of, and was styled Embrenche; a term, as I remember, importing the highest distinction, and signifying in our language a *mark* of grandeur. This mark is conferred on the person entitled to it, by cutting the skin across at the top of the forehead, and drawing it down to the eye-brows; and while it is in this situation applying a warm hand, and rubbing it until it shrinks up into a thick *weal*

across the lower part of the forehead. Most of the judges and senators were thus marked; my father had long born it: I had seen it conferred on one of my brothers, and I was also *destined* to receive it by my parents. Those Embrenche, or chief men, decided disputes and punished crimes; for which purpose they always assembled together. The proceedings were generally short; and in most cases the law of retaliation prevailed. I remember a man was brought before my father, and the other judges, for kidnapping a boy; and, although he was the son of a chief or senator, he was condemned to make recompense by a man or woman slave. Adultery, however, was sometimes punished with slavery or death; a punishment which I believe is inflicted on it throughout most of the nations of Africa:[2] so sacred among them is the honour of the marriage bed, and so jealous are they of the fidelity of their wives. Of this I recollect an instance:– a woman was convicted before the judges of adultery, and delivered over, as the custom was, to her husband to be punished. Accordingly he determined to put her to death: but it being found, just before her execution, that she had an infant at her breast; and no woman being prevailed on to perform the part of a nurse, she was spared on account of the child. The men, however, do not preserve the same constancy to their wives, which they expect from them; for they indulge in a plurality, though seldom in more than two. Their mode of marriage is thus:– both parties are usually betrothed when young by their parents, (though I have known the males to betroth themselves). On this occasion a feast is prepared, and the bride and bridegroom stand up in the midst of all their friends, who are assembled for the purpose, while he declares she is thenceforth to be looked upon as his wife, and that no other person is to pay any addresses to her. This is also immediately proclaimed in the vicinity, on which the bride retires from the assembly. Some time after she is brought home to her husband, and then another feast is made, to which the relations of both parties are invited: her parents then deliver her to the bridegroom,

---

[1] 'Nominal' indeed! Equiano, perhaps to impress us with the grandeur of an African state, greatly exaggerates the size of Benin, which never controlled his own country. [eds]

[2] See Benezet's *Account of Guinea* throughout. [Equiano]
Benezet was an American pioneer of anti-slave-trade agitation. His book appeared in 1788. [eds]

accompanied with a number of blessings, and at the same time they tie round her waist a cotton string of the thickness of a goose-quill, which none but married women are permitted to wear: she is now considered as completely his wife; and at this time the dowry is given to the new married pair, which generally consists of portions of land, slaves, and cattle, household goods, and implements of husbandry. These are offered by the friends of both parties; besides which the parents of the bridegroom present gifts to those of the bride, whose property she is looked upon before marriage; but after it she is esteemed the sole property of her husband. The ceremony being now ended the festival begins, which is celebrated with bonefires, and loud acclamations of joy, accompanied with music and dancing.

We are almost a nation of dancers, musicians, and poets. Thus every great event, such as a triumphant return from battle, or other cause of public rejoicing is celebrated in public dances, which are accompanied with songs and music suited to the occasion. The assembly is separated into four divisions, which dance either apart or in succession, and each with a character peculiar to itself. The first division contains the married men, who in their dances frequently exhibit feats of arms, and the representation of a battle. To these succeed the married women, who dance in the second division. The young men occupy the third; and the maidens the fourth. Each represents some interesting scene of real life, such as a great achievement, domestic employment, a pathetic story, or some rural sport; and as the subject is generally founded on some recent event, it is therefore ever new. This gives our dances a spirit and variety which I have scarcely seen elsewhere.[3] We have many musical instruments, particularly drums of different kinds, a piece of music which resembles a guitar, and another much like a stickado.[4] These last are chiefly used by betrothed virgins, who play on them on all grand festivals.

As our manners are simple, our luxuries are few. The dress of both sexes is nearly the same. It generally consists of a long piece of calico, or muslin, wrapped loosely round the body, somewhat in the form of a highland plaid. This is usually dyed blue, which is our favourite colour. It is extracted from a berry, and is brighter and richer than any I have seen in Europe. Besides this, our women of distinction wear golden ornaments; which they dispose with some profusion on their arms and legs. When our women are not employed with the men in tillage, their usual occupation is spinning and weaving cotton, which they afterwards dye, and make it into garments. They also manufacture earthen vessels, of which we have many kinds. Among the rest tobacco pipes, made after the same fashion, and used in the same manner, as those in Turkey.[5]

Our manner of living is entirely plain; for as yet the natives are unacquainted with those refinements in cookery which debauch the taste: bullocks, goats, and poultry, supply the greatest part of their food. These constitute likewise the principal wealth of the country, and the chief articles of its commerce. The flesh is usually stewed in a pan; to make it savoury we sometimes use also pepper, and other spices, and we have salt made of wood ashes. Our vegetables are mostly plantains, eadas,[6] yams, beans, and Indian corn. The head of the family usually eats alone; his wives and slaves have also their separate tables. Before we taste food we always wash our hands: indeed our cleanliness on all occasions is extreme; but on this it is an indispensable ceremony. After washing, libation is made, by pouring out a small portion of the food, in a certain place, for the spirits of departed relations, which the natives suppose to preside over their conduct, and guard them from evil. They are totally unacquainted with strong or spirituous liquours; and their principal beverage is palm wine. This is gotten from a tree of that name by tapping it on

---

[3] When I was in Smyrna I have frequently seen the Greeks dance after this manner. [Equiano]

[4] A kind of xylophone. [eds]

[5] The bowl is carthen, curiously figured, to which a long reed is fixed as a tube. This tube is sometimes so long as to be born by one, and frequently out of grandeur by two boys. [Equiano]

[6] i.e. eddoes, or coco-yams. [eds]

the top, and fastening a large gourd to it; and sometimes one tree will yield three or four gallons in a night. When just drawn it is of a most delicious sweetness; but in a few days it acquires a tartish and more spirituous flavour: though I never saw any one intoxicated by it.[7] The same tree also produces nuts and oil. Our principal luxury is in perfumes; one sort of these is an odoriferous wood of delicious fragrance: the other a kind of earth; a small portion of which thrown into the fire diffuses a most powerful odour.[8] We beat this wood into powder, and mix it with palm oil; with which both men and women perfume themselves.

In our buildings we study convenience rather than ornament. Each master of a family has a large square piece of ground, surrounded with a moat or fence, or enclosed with a wall made of red earth tempered; which, when dry, is as hard as brick. Within this are his houses to accommodate his family and slaves; which, if numerous, frequently present the appearance of a village. In the middle stands the principal building, appropriated to the sole use of the master, and consisting of two apartments; in one of which he sits in the day with his family, the other is left apart for the reception of his friends. He has besides these a distinct apartment in which he sleeps, together with his male children. On each side are the apartments of his wives, who have also their separate day and night houses. The habitations of the slaves and their families are distributed throughout the rest of the enclosure. These houses never exceed one story in height: they are always built of wood, or stakes driven into the ground, crossed with wattles, and neatly plastered within, and without. The roof is thatched with reeds. Our day-houses are left open at the sides; but those in which we sleep are always covered, and plastered in the inside, with a composition mixed with cow-dung, to keep off the different insects, which annoy us during the night. The walls and floors also of these are generally covered with mats. Our beds consist of a platform, raised three or four feet from the ground, on which are laid skins, and

different parts of a spungy tree called plaintain. Our covering is calico or muslin, the same as our dress. The usual seats are a few logs of wood; but we have benches, which are generally perfumed, to accommodate strangers: these compose the greater part of our household furniture. Houses so constructed and furnished require but little skill to erect them. Every man is a sufficient architect for the purpose. The whole neighbourhood afford their unanimous assistance in building them and in return receive, and expect no other recompense than a feast.

As we live in a country where nature is prodigal of her favours, our wants are few and easily supplied; of course we have few manufactures. They consist for the most part of calicoes, earthen ware, ornaments, and instruments of war and husbandry. But these make no part of our commerce, the principal articles of which, as I have observed, are provisions. In such a state money is of little use; however we have some small pieces of coin, if I may call them such. They are made something like an anchor; but I do not remember either their value or denomination. We have also markets, at which I have been frequently with my mother. These are sometimes visited by stout mahogany-coloured men from the south west of us: we call them Oye-Eboe, which term signifies red men living at a distance. They generally bring us fire-arms, gunpowder, hats, beads, and dried fish. The last we esteemed a great rarity, as our waters were only brooks and springs. These articles they barter with us for odoriferous woods and earth, and our salt of wood ashes. They always carry slaves through our land; but the strictest account is exacted of their manner of procuring them before they are suffered to pass. Sometimes indeed we sold slaves to them, but they were only prisoners of war, or such among us as had been convicted of kidnapping, or adultery, and some other crimes, which we esteemed heinous. This practice of kidnapping induces me to think, that, notwithstanding all our strictness, their principal business among us was to trepan our people. I remember too they carried great sacks along

---

[7] This is surprising! But it certainly was not and is not as potent as English gin. [eds]

[8] When I was in Smyrna I saw the same kind of earth, and brought some of it with me to England; it resembles musk in strength, but is more delicious in scent, and is not unlike the smell of a rose. [Equiano]
    The wood mentioned here is camwood. [eds]

with them, which not long after I had an opportunity of fatally seeing applied to that infamous purpose.

Our land is uncommonly rich and fruitful, and produces all kinds of vegetables in great abundance. We have plenty of Indian corn, and vast quantities of cotton and tobacco. Our pine apples grow without culture; they are about the size of the largest sugar-loaf, and finely flavoured. We have also spices of different kinds, particularly pepper; and a variety of delicious fruits which I have never seen in Europe; together with gums of various kinds, and honey in abundance. All our industry is exerted to improve those blessings of nature. Agriculture is our chief employment; and every one, even the children and women, are engaged in it. Thus we are all habituated to labour from our earliest years. Every one contributes something to the common stock; and as we are unacquainted with idleness, we have no beggars. The benefits of such a mode of living are obvious. The West India planters prefer the slaves of Benin or Eboe to those of any other part of Guinea, for their hardiness, intelligence, integrity, and zeal. Those benefits are felt by us in the general healthiness of the people, and in their vigour and activity; I might have added too in their comeliness. Deformity is indeed unknown amongst us, I mean that of shape. Numbers of the natives of Eboe now in London might be brought in support of this assertion: for, in regard to complexion, ideas of beauty are wholly relative. I remember while in Africa to have seen three negro children, who were tawny, and another quite white, who were universally regarded by myself, and the natives in general, as far as related to their complexions, as deformed. Our women, too were in my eyes at least uncommonly graceful, alert, and modest to a degree of bashfulness; nor do I remember to have ever heard of an instance of incontinence amongst them before marriage. They are also remarkably cheerful. Indeed cheerfulness and affability are two of the leading characteristics of our nation.

Our tillage is exercised in a large plain or common, some hours walk from our dwellings, and all the neighbours resort thither in a body. They use no beasts of husbandry; and their only instruments are hoes, axes, shovels, and beaks, or pointed iron to dig with. Sometimes we are visited by locusts, which come in large clouds, so as to darken the air, and destroy our harvest. This however happens rarely, but when it does, a famine is produced by it. I remember an instance or two wherein this happened. This common is often the theatre of war; and therefore when our people go out to till their land, they not only go in a body, but generally take their arms with them for fear of a surprise; and when they apprehend an invasion they guard the avenues to their dwellings, by driving sticks into the ground, which are so sharp at one end as to pierce the foot, and are generally dipt in poison. From what I can recollect of these battles, they appear to have been irruptions of one little state or district on the other, to obtain prisoners or booty. Perhaps they were incited to this by those traders who brought the European goods I mentioned amongst us. Such a mode of obtaining slaves in Africa is common; and I believe more are procured this way, and by kidnapping, than any other.[9] When a trader wants slaves, he applies to a chief for them, and tempts him with his wares. It is not extraordinary, if on this occasion he yields to the temptation with as little firmness, and accepts the price of his fellow creatures liberty with as little reluctance as the enlightened merchant. Accordingly he falls on his neighbours, and a desperate battle ensues. If he prevails and takes prisoners, he gratifies his avarice by selling them; but, if his party be vanquished, and he falls into the hands of the enemy, he is put to death: for, as he has been known to foment their quarrels, it is thought dangerous to let him survive, and no ransom can save him, though all other prisoners may be redeemed. We have firearms, bows and arrows, broad two-edged swords and javelins: we have shields also which cover a man from head to foot. All are taught the use of these weapons; even our women are warriors, and march boldly out to fight along with the men. Our whole district is a kind of militia: on a certain signal given, such as the firing of a gun at night, they all rise in arms and rush upon their enemy. It is perhaps something remarkable, that when our people march to the field a red flag or banner is borne

---

[9] See Benezet's *Account of Africa* throughout. [Equiano]

before them. I was once a witness to a battle in our common. We had been all at work in it one day as usual, when our people were suddenly attacked. I climbed a tree at some distance, from which I beheld the fight. There were many women as well as men on both sides; among others my mother was there, and armed with a broad sword. After fighting for a considerable time with great fury, and after many had been killed our people obtained the victory, and took their enemy's Chief prisoner. He was carried off in great triumph, and, though he offered a large ransom for his life, he was put to death. A virgin of note among our enemies had been slain in the battle, and her arm was exposed in our market-place, where our trophies were always exhibited. The spoils were divided according to the merit of the warriors. Those prisoners which were not sold or redeemed we kept as slaves: but how different was their condition from that of the slaves in the West Indies! With us they do no more work than other members of the community, even their masters; their food, clothing and lodging were nearly the same as theirs, (except that they were not permitted to eat with those who were free-born); and there was scarce any other difference between them, than a superior degree of importance which the head of a family possesses in our state, and that authority which, as such, he exercises over every part of his household. Some of these slaves have even slaves under them as their own property, and for their own use.[10]

As to religion, the natives believe that there is one Creator of all things, and that he lives in the sun, and is girted round with a belt that he may never eat or drink; but, according to some, he smokes a pipe, which is our own favourite luxury. They believe he governs events, especially our deaths or captivity; but, as for the doctrine of eternity, I do not remember to have ever heard of it: some however believe in the transmigration of souls in a certain degree. Those spirits, which are not transmigrated, such as our dear friends or relations, they believe always attend them, and guard them from the bad spirits or their foes. For this reason they always before eating, as I have observed, put some small portion of the meat, and pour some of their drink, on the ground for them; and they often make oblations of the blood of beasts or fowls at their graves. I was very fond of my mother, and almost constantly with her. When she went to make these oblations at her mother's tomb, which was a kind of small solitary thatched house, I sometimes attended her. There she made her libations, and spent most of the night in cries and lamentations. I have been often extremely terrified on these occasions. The loneliness of the place, the darkness of the night, and the ceremony of libation, naturally awful and gloomy, were heightened by my mother's lamentations; and these, concurring with the cries of doleful birds, by which these places were frequented, gave an inexpressible terror to the scene.

We compute the year from the day on which the sun crosses the line, and on its setting that evening there is a general shout throughout the land; at least I can speak from my own knowledge throughout our vicinity. The people at the same time make a great noise with rattles, not unlike the basket rattles used by children here, though much larger, and hold up their hands to heaven for a blessing. It is then the greatest offerings are made; and those children whom our wise men foretell will be fortunate are then presented to different people. I remember many used to come to see me, and I was carried about to others for that purpose. They have many offerings, particularly at full moons; generally two at harvest before the fruits are taken out of the ground: and when any young animals are killed, sometimes they offer up part of them as a sacrifice. These offerings, when made by one of the heads of a family, serve for the whole. I remember we often had them at my father's and my uncle's, and their families have been present. Some of our offerings are eaten with bitter herbs. We had a saying among us to anyone of a cross temper, 'That if they were to be eaten, they should be eaten with bitter herbs.'

We practised circumcision like the Jews, and made offerings and feasts on that occasion in the same manner as they did. Like them also, our children were named from some event, some circumstance, or fancied foreboding at the

---

[10] Modern historians are in general agreement with Equiano's view that slavery in West Africa was not necessarily harsh. [eds]

time of their birth. I was named *Olaudah*, which, in our language, signifies vicissitude or fortune also; one favoured, and having a loud voice and well spoken. I remember we never polluted the name of the object of our adoration; on the contrary, it was always mentioned with the greatest reverence; and we were totally unacquainted with swearing, and all those terms of abuse and reproach which find their way so readily and copiously into the languages of more civilized people. The only expressions of that kind I remember were 'May you rot, or may you swell, or may a beast take you.'

I have before remarked that the natives of this part of Africa are extremely cleanly. This necessary habit of decency was with us a part of religion, and therefore we had many purifications and washings; indeed almost as many, and used on the same occasions, if my recollection does not fail me, as the Jews. Those that touched the dead at any time were obliged to wash and purify themselves before they could enter a dwelling-house. Every woman too, at certain times, was forbidden to come into a dwelling-house, or touch any person, or any thing we ate. I was so fond of my mother I could not keep from her, or avoid touching her at some of those periods, in consequence of which I was obliged to be kept out with her, in a little house made for that purpose, till offering was made, and then we were purified.

Though we had no places of public worship, we had priests and magicians, or wise men. I do not remember whether they had different offices, or whether they were united in the same persons, but they were held in great reverence by the people. They calculated our time, and foretold events, as their name imported, for we called them Ah-affoe-way-cah, which signifies calculators or yearly men, our year being called Ah-affoe. They wore their beards, and when they died they were succeeded by their sons. Most of their implements and things of value were interred along with them. Pipes and tobacco were also put into the grave with the corpse, which was always perfumed and ornamented, and animals were offered in sacrifice to them. None accompanied their funerals but those of the same profession or tribe. These buried them after sunset, and always returned from the grave by a different way from that which they went.

These magicians were also our doctors or physicians. They practised bleeding by cupping; and were very successful in healing wounds and expelling poisons. They had likewise some extraordinary method of discovering jealousy, theft, and poisoning; the success of which no doubt they derived from their unbounded influence over the credulity and superstition of the people. I do not remember what those methods were, except that as to poisoning: I recollect an instance or two, which I hope it will not be deemed impertinent here to insert, as it may serve as a kind of specimen of the rest, and is still used by the negroes in the West Indies. A virgin had been poisoned, but it was not known by whom: the doctors ordered the corpse to be taken up by some persons, and carried to the grave. As soon as the bearers had raised it on their shoulders, they seemed seized with some sudden impulse, and ran to and fro unable to stop themselves. At last, after having passed through a number of thorns and prickly bushes unhurt, the corpse fell from them close to a house, and defaced it in the fall; and, the owner being taken up, he immediately confessed the poisoning.

The natives are extremely cautious about poison. When they buy any eatable the seller kisses it all round before the buyer, to show him it is not poisoned; and the same is done when any meat or drink is presented, particularly to a stranger. We have serpents of different kinds, some of which are esteemed ominous when they appear in our houses, and these we never molest. I remember two of those ominous snakes, each of which was as thick as the calf of a man's leg, and in colour resembling a dolphin in the water, crept at different times into my mother's night-house, where I always lay with her, and coiled themselves into folds, and each time they crowed like a cock. I was desired by some of our wise men to touch these, that I might be interested in the good omens, which I did, for they were quite harmless, and would tamely suffer themselves to be handled; and then they were put into a large open earthen pan, and set to one side of the highway.[11] Some of our snakes, however, were poisonous: one of them

---

[11] The python, sacred in Ibo culture, does not harm people. But the 'crowing snake', still heard of from Ibos, does. Equiano's memory betrays him. [eds]

crossed the road one day when I was standing on it, and passed between my feet without offering to touch me, to the great surprise of many who saw it; and these incidents were accounted by the wise men, and therefore by my mother and the rest of the people, as remarkable omens in my favour.

Such is the imperfect sketch my memory has furnished me with of the manners and customs of a people among whom I first drew my breath.

[*At this point Equiano draws a comparison between 'the manners and customs of my countrymen and those of the Jews, before they reached the Land of Promise, and particularly the patriarchs while they were yet in that pastoral state which is described in Genesis'. He believes that the Ibo are descended from Jews, dismissing the difference of skin colour.*]

These instances, and a great many more which might be adduced, while they shew how the complexions of the same persons vary in different climates, it is hoped may tend also to remove the prejudice that some conceive against the natives of Africa on account of their colour. Surely the minds of the Spaniards did not change with their complexions! Are there not causes enough to which the apparent inferiority of an African may be ascribed, without limiting the goodness of God, and supposing he forbore to stamp understanding on certainly his own image, because 'carved in ebony.' Might it not naturally be ascribed to their situation? When they come among Europeans, they are ignorant of their language, religion, manners, and customs. Are any pains taken to teach them these? Are they treated as men? Does not slavery itself depress the mind, and extinguish all its fire and every noble sentiment? But, above all, what advantages do not a refined people possess over those who are rude and uncultivated. Let the polished and haughty European recollect that his ancestors were once, like the Africans, uncivilized, and even barbarous. Did nature make *them* inferior to their sons? and should *they too* have been made slaves? Every rational mind answers, No. Let such reflections as these melt the pride of their superiority into sympathy for the wants and miseries of their sable brethren, and compel them to acknowledge, that understanding is not

confined to feature or colour. If, when they look round the world, they feel exultation, let it be tempered with benevolence to others, and gratitude to God, 'who hath made of one blood all nations of men for to dwell on all the face of the earth; and whose wisdom is not our wisdom, neither are our ways his ways.'[12]

Chapter Two

I HOPE the reader will not think I have trespassed on his patience in introducing myself to him with some account of the manners and customs of my country. They had been implanted in me with great care, and made an impression on my mind, which time could not erase, and which all the adversity and variety of fortune I have since experienced served only to rivet and record; for, whether the love of one's country be real or imaginary, or a lesson of reason, or an instinct of nature, I still look back with pleasure on the first scenes of my life, though that pleasure has been for the most part mingled with sorrow.

I have already acquainted the reader with the time and place of my birth. My father, besides many slaves, had a numerous family, of which seven lived to grow up, including myself and a sister, who was the only daughter. As I was the youngest of the sons, I became, of course, the greatest favourite with my mother, and was always with her; and she used to take particular pains to form my mind. I was trained up from my earliest years in the art of war; my daily exercise was shooting and throwing javelins; and my mother adorned me with emblems, after the manner of our greatest warriors. In this way I grew up till I was turned the age of eleven, when an end was put to my happiness in the following manner:– Generally when the grown people in the neighbourhood were gone far in the fields to labour, the children assembled together in some of the neighbours' premises to play; and commonly some of us used to get up a tree to look out for any assailant, or kidnapper, that might come upon us; for they sometimes took those opportunities of our parents' absence to attack and carry off as many as they could seize. One day, as I was watching at the top of a tree in our

---

[12] Acts, c. xvii, v.26. [Equiano]

yard, I saw one of those people come into the yard of our next neighbour but one, to kidnap, there being many stout young people in it. Immediately on this I gave the alarm of the rogue, and he was surrounded by the stoutest of them, who entangled him with cords, so that he could not escape till some of the grown people came and secured him. But alas! ere long it was my fate to be thus attacked, and to be carried off, when none of the grown people were nigh. One day, when all our people were gone out to their works as usual, and only I and my dear sister were left to mind the house, two men and a woman got over our walls, and in a moment seized us both, and, without giving us time to cry out, or make resistance, they stopped our mouths, and ran off with us into the nearest wood. Here they tied our hands, and continued to carry us as far as they could, till night came on, when we reached a small house, where the robbers halted for refreshment, and spent the night. We were then unbound, but were unable to take any food; and, being quite overpowered by fatigue and grief, our only relief was some sleep, which allayed our misfortune for a short time. The next morning we left the house, and continued travelling all the day. For a long time we had kept the woods, but at last we came into a road which I believed I knew. I had now some hopes of being delivered; for we had advanced but a little way before I discovered some people at a distance, on which I began to cry out for their assistance: but my cries had no other effect than to make them tie me faster and stop my mouth, and then they put me into a large sack. They also stopped my sister's mouth, and tied her hands; and in this manner we proceeded till we were out of the sight of these people. When we went to rest the following night they offered us some victuals; but we refused it; and the only comfort we had was in being in one another's arms all that night, and bathing each other with our tears. But alas! we were soon deprived of even the small comfort of weeping together. The next day proved a day of greater sorrow than I had yet experienced; for my sister and I were then separated, while we lay clasped in each other's arms. It was in vain that we besought them not to part us; she was torn from me, and immediately carried away, while I was left in a state of distraction not to be described. I cried and grieved continually; for several days I did

not eat anything but what they forced into my mouth. At length, after many days travelling, during which I had often changed masters, I got into the hands of a chieftain, in a very pleasant country. This man had two wives and some children, and they all used me extremely well, and did all they could to comfort me; particularly the first wife, who was something like my mother. Although I was a great many days journey from my father's house, yet these people spoke exactly the same language with us. This first master of mine, as I may call him, was a smith, and my principal employment was working his bellows, which were the same kind as I had seen in my vicinity. They were in some respects not unlike the stoves here in gentlemen's kitchens; and were covered over with leather; and in the middle of that leather a stick was fixed, and a person stood up, and worked it, in the same manner as is done to pump water out of a cask with a hand pump. I believe it was gold he worked, for it was of a lovely bright yellow colour, and was worn by the women on their wrists and ankles. I was there I suppose about a month, and they at last used to trust me some little distance from the house. This liberty I used in embracing every opportunity to inquire the way to my own home: and I also sometimes, for the same purpose, went with the maidens, in the cool of the evenings, to bring pitchers of water from the springs for the use of the house. I had also remarked where the sun rose in the morning, and set in the evening, as I had travelled along; and I had observed that my father's house was towards the rising of the sun. I therefore determined to seize the first opportunity of making my escape, and to shape my course for that quarter; for I was quite oppressed and weighed down by grief after my mother and friends; and my love of liberty, ever great, was strengthened by the mortifying circumstance of not daring to eat with the free-born children, although I was mostly their companion.

[*Equiano does in fact run off, in terror, after accidentally killing a chicken. He realizes, in the forest, that escape will be dangerous, and returns. His master forgives him.*]

Soon after this my master's only daughter, and child by his first wife, sickened and died, which affected him so much that for some time he was almost frantic, and really would have killed himself, had he not been watched and prevented. However, in a small time afterwards he recovered, and I was again sold. I was now carried to the left of the sun's rising, through many different countries, and a number of large woods. The people I was sold to used to carry me very often, when I was tired, either on their shoulders or on their backs. I saw many convenient well-built sheds along the roads, at proper distances, to accommodate the merchants and travellers, who lay in those buildings along with their wives, who often accompany them; and they always go well armed.

From the time I left my own nation I always found somebody that understood me till I came to the sea coast. The languages of different nations did not totally differ, nor were they so copious as those of the Europeans, particularly the English. They were therefore easily learned; and, while I was journeying thus through Africa, I acquired two or three different tongues. In this manner I had been travelling for a considerable time, when one evening, to my great surprise, whom should I see brought to the house where I was but my dear sister! As soon as she saw me she gave a loud shriek, and ran into my arms – I was quite overpowered: neither of us could speak; but, for a considerable time, clung to each other in mutual embraces, unable to do anything but weep. Our meeting affected all who saw us; and indeed I must acknowledge, in honour of those sable destroyers of human rights, that I never met with any ill treatment, or saw any offered to their slaves, except tying them, when necessary, to keep them from running away. When these people knew we were brother and sister they indulged us together; and the man, to whom I supposed we belonged, lay with us, he in the middle, while she and I held one another by the hands across his breast all night; and thus for a while we forgot our misfortunes in the joy of being together: but even this small comfort was soon to have an end; for scarcely had the fatal morning appeared, when she was again torn from me for ever! I was now more miserable, if possible, than before. The small relief which her presence gave me from pain was gone, and the wretchedness of my situation was redoubled by my anxiety after her fate, and my apprehensions lest her sufferings should be greater than mine, when I could not be with her to alleviate them. Yes, thou dear partner of all my childish sports! thou sharer of my joys and sorrows! happy should I have ever esteemed myself to encounter every misery for you, and to procure your freedom by the sacrifice of my own. Though you were early forced from my arms, your image has been always rivetted in my heart, from which neither *time nor fortune* have been able to remove it; so that, while the thoughts of your sufferings have damped my prosperity, they have mingled with adversity and increased its bitterness. To that Heaven which protects the weak from the strong, I commit the care of your innocence and virtues, if they have not already received their full reward, and if your youth and delicacy have not long fallen victims to the violence of the African trader, the pestilential stench of a Guinea ship, the seasoning in the European colonies, or the lash and lust of a brutal and unrelenting overseer.[13]

I did not long remain after my sister. I was again sold, and carried through a number of places, till, after travelling a considerable time, I came to a town called Tinmah, in the most beautiful country I had yet seen in Africa. It was extremely rich, and there were many rivulets which flowed through it, and supplied a large pond in the centre of the town, where the people washed. Here I first saw and tasted cocoanuts, which I thought superior to any nuts I had ever tasted before; and the trees which were loaded, were also interspersed amongst the houses, which had commodious shades adjoining, and were in the same manner as ours, the insides being neatly plastered and whitewashed. Here I also saw and tasted for the first time sugar-cane. Their money consisted of little white shells, the size of the finger nail.[14] I was sold here for one hundred and seventy-two of them by a merchant who lived and brought me there. I had been about two or three days at his house, when a wealthy widow, a neighbour of his, came there

---

[13] Equiano spoils the effect of his moving account of his meeting with his sister by lavishing on it stock rhetoric derived from the 'sentimental' vein in the literature of his day. [eds]

[14] i.e. cowries. [eds]

one evening, and brought with her an only son, a young gentleman about my own age and size. Here they saw me; and, having taken a fancy to me, I was bought of the merchant, and went home with them. Her house and premises were situated close to one of those rivulets I have mentioned, and were the finest I ever saw in Africa: they were very extensive, and she had a number of slaves to attend her. The next day I was washed and perfumed, and when meal-time came I was led into the presence of my mistress, and ate and drank before her with her son. This filled me with astonishment; and I could scarce help expressing my surprise that the young gentleman should suffer me, who was bound, to eat with him who was free; and not only so, but that he would not at any time either eat or drink till I had taken first, because I was the eldest, which was agreeable to our custom. Indeed every thing here, and all their treatment of me, made me forget that I was a slave. The language of these people resembled ours so nearly, that we understood each other perfectly. They had also the very same customs as we. There were likewise slaves daily to attend us, while my young master and I with other boys sported with our darts and bows and arrows, as I had been used to do at home. In this resemblance to my former happy state I passed about two months; and I now began to think I was to be adopted into the family, and was beginning to be reconciled to my situation, and to forget by degrees my misfortunes, when all at once the delusion vanished; for, without the least previous knowledge, one morning early, while my dear master and companion was still asleep, I was wakened out of my reverie to fresh sorrow, and hurried away even amongst the uncircumcised.

Thus, at the very moment I dreamed of the greatest happiness, I found myself most miserable; and it seemed as if fortune wished to give me this taste of joy, only to render the reverse more poignant. The change I now experienced was painful as it was sudden and unexpected. It was a change indeed from a state of bliss to a scene which is inexpressible by me, as it discovered to me an element I had never before beheld, and till then had no idea of, and wherein such instances of hardship and cruelty continually occurred as I can never reflect on but with horror.

All the nations and people I had hitherto passed through resembled our own in their manners, customs, and language: but I came at length to a country, the inhabitants of which differed from us in all those particulars. I was very much struck with this difference, especially when I came among a people who did not circumcise, and ate without washing their hands. They cooked also in iron pots, and had European cutlasses and cross bows, which were unknown to us, and fought with their fists amongst themselves. Their women were not so modest as ours, for they ate, and drank, and slept, with their men. But, above all, I was amazed to see no sacrifices or offerings among them. In some of those places the people ornamented themselves with scars, and likewise filed their teeth very sharp. They wanted sometimes to ornament me in the same manner, but I would not suffer them; hoping that I might some time be among a people who did not thus disfigure themselves, as I thought they did. At last I came to the banks of a large river, which was covered with canoes, in which the people appeared to live with their household utensils and provisions of all kinds. I was beyond measure astonished at this, as I had never before seen any water larger than a pond or a rivulet: and my surprise was mingled with no small fear when I was put into one of these canoes, and we began to paddle and move along the river. We continued going on thus till night; and when we came to land, and made fires on the banks, each family by themselves, some dragged their canoes on shore, others stayed and cooked in theirs, and laid in them all night. Those on the land had mats, of which they made tents, some in the shape of little houses: in these we slept; and after the morning meal we embarked again and proceeded as before. I was often very much astonished to see some of the women, as well as the men, jump into the water, dive to the bottom, come up again, and swim about. Thus I continued to travel, sometimes by land, sometimes by water, through different countries and various nations, till at the end of six or seven months after I had been kidnapped, I arrived at the sea coast. It would be tedious and uninteresting to relate all the incidents which befell me during this journey, and which I have not yet forgotten; of the various hands I passed through, and the manners and customs of all the different people among whom I lived: I shall therefore only observe, that in all the places where I was the soil was exceedingly rich; the pomkins, eadas, plantains, yams, &c. &c. were in a great abundance, and of incredible size. There were also vast quantities of different gums, though not used for any purpose; and everywhere a great deal of tobacco. The cotton even grew wild; and there was plenty of red-wood. I saw no mechanics whatever in all the way, except such as I have mentioned. The chief employment in all these countries was agriculture, and both the males and females, as with us, were brought up to it, and trained in the arts of war.

The first object which saluted my eyes when I arrived on the coast was the sea, and a slave ship, which was then riding at anchor, and waiting for its cargo. These filled me with astonishment, which was soon converted into terror when I was carried on board. I was immediately handled and tossed up to see if I were sound by some of the crew; and I was now persuaded that I had gotten into a world of bad spirits, and that they were going to kill me. Their complexions too differing so much from ours, their long hair, and the language they spoke, (which was very different from any I had ever heard) united to confirm me in this belief. Indeed such were the horrors of my views and fears at the moment, that, if ten thousand worlds had been my own, I would have freely parted with them all to have exchanged my condition with that of the meanest slave in my own country. When I looked round the ship too and saw a large furnace or copper boiling, and multitude of black people of every description chained together, every one of their countenances expressing dejection and sorrow, I no longer doubted of my fate; and, quite overpowered with horror and anguish, I fell motionless on the deck and fainted. When I recovered a little I found some black people about me, who I believe were some of those who brought me on board, and had been receiving their pay; they talked to me in order to cheer me, but all in vain. I asked them if we were not to be eaten by those white men with horrible looks, red faces, and loose hair. They told me I was not; and one of the crew brought me a small portion of spirituous liquor in a wine glass; but, being afraid of him, I would not take it out of his hand. One of the blacks therefore took it from him and gave it to me, and I took a little down my palate, which, instead of reviving me, as they thought it would, threw me into the greatest consternation at the strange feeling it produced, having never tasted any such liquor before. Soon after this the blacks who brought me on board went off, and left me abandoned to despair. I now saw myself deprived of all chance of returning to my native country, or even the least glimpse of hope of gaining the shore, which I now considered as friendly; and I even wished for my former slavery in preference to my present situation, which was filled with horrors of every kind, still heightened by my ignorance of what I was to undergo. I was not long suffered to indulge my grief; I was soon put down under the decks, and there I received such a salutation in my nostrils as I had never experienced in my life: so that, with the loathsomeness of the stench, and crying together, I became so sick and low that I was not able to eat, nor had I the least desire to taste any thing. I now wished for the last friend, death, to relieve me; but soon, to my grief, two of the white men offered me eatables; and, on my refusing to eat, one of them held me fast by the hands, and laid me across I think the windlass, and tied my feet, while the other flogged me severely. I had never experienced any thing of this kind before; and although, not being used to the water, I naturally feared that element the first time I saw it, yet nevertheless, could I have got over the nettings, I would have jumped over the side, but I could not; and, besides, the crew used to watch us very closely who were not chained down to the decks, lest we should leap into the water: and I have seen some of these poor African prisoners most severely cut for attempting to do so, and hourly whipped for not eating. This indeed was often the case with myself. In a little time after, amongst the poor chained men, I found some of my own nation, which in a small degree gave ease to my mind. I inquired of these what was to be done with us; they gave me to understand we were to be carried to these white people's country to work for them. I then was a little revived, and thought, if it were no worse than working, my situation was not so desperate: but still I feared I should be put to death, the white people looked and acted, as I thought, in so savage a manner, for I had never seen among any people such instances of brutal cruelty; and this not only shown towards us blacks, but also to some of the whites themselves. One white man in particular I saw, when we were permitted to be on deck, flogged so unmercifully with a large rope near the foremast, that he died in consequence of it; and they tossed him over the side as they would have done a brute. This made me fear these people the more; and I expected nothing less than to be treated in the same manner. I could not help expressing my fears and apprehensions to some of my countrymen: I asked them if these people had no country, but lived in this hollow place (the ship): they told me they did not, but came from a distant one. 'Then,' said I, 'how comes it in all our country we never heard of them?' They told me because they lived so very far off. I then asked where were their women? had they any like themselves? I was told they had: 'and why,' said I, 'do we not see them?' they answered, because they were left behind. I asked how the vessel could go? they told me they could not tell; but that there were cloths put upon the masts by the help of the ropes I saw, and then the vessel went on; and the white men had some spell or magic they put in the water when they liked in order to stop the vessel. I was exceedingly amazed at this account, and really thought they were spirits. I therefore wished much to be from amongst them, for I expected they would sacrifice me: but my wishes were vain; for we were so quartered that it was impossible for any of us to make our escape. While we stayed on the coast I was mostly on deck; and one day, to my great astonishment, I saw one of these vessels coming in with the sails up. As soon as the whites saw it, they gave a great shout, at which we were amazed; and the more so as the vessel appeared larger by approaching nearer. At last she came to an anchor in my sight, and when the anchor was let go I and my countrymen who saw it were lost in astonishment to observe the vessel stop; and were now convinced it was done by magic. Soon after this the other ship got her boats out, and they came on board to us, and the people of both ships seemed very glad to see each other. Several of the strangers also shook hands with us black people, and made motions with their hands, signifying I suppose we were to go to their country; but we did not understand them. At last, when the ship we were in had got in all her cargo, they made ready with many fearful noises, and we were all put under deck, so that we could not see how they managed the vessel. But this disappointment was the least of my sorrow. The stench of the hold while we were on the coast was so intolerably loathsome, that it was dangerous to remain there for any time, and some of us had been permitted to stay on the deck for the fresh air; but now that the whole ship's cargo were confined together, it became absolutely pestilential. The closeness of the place, and the heat of the climate, added to the number in the ship, which was so crowded that each had scarcely room to turn himself, almost suffocated us. This produced copious perspirations, so that the air soon became unfit for respiration, from a variety of loathsome smells, and brought on a sickness among the slaves, of which many died, thus falling victims to the improvident avarice, as I may call it, of their purchasers. This wretched situation was again aggravated by the galling of the chains, now become insupportable; and the filth of the necessary tubs, into which the children often fell, and were almost suffocated. The shrieks of the women, and the groans of the dying, rendered the whole a scene of horror almost inconceivable. Happily perhaps for myself I was soon reduced so low here that it was thought necessary to keep me almost always on deck; and from my extreme youth I was not put in fetters. In this situation I expected every hour to share the fate of my companions, some of whom were almost daily brought upon deck at the point of death, which I began to hope would soon put an end to my miseries. Often did I think many of the inhabitants of the deep much more happy than myself. I envied them the freedom they enjoyed, and as often wished I could change my condition for theirs. Every circumstance I met with served only to render my state more painful, and heighten my apprehensions, and my opinion of the cruelty of the whites. One day they had taken a number of fishes; and when they had killed and satisfied themselves with as many as they thought fit, to our astonishment who were on the deck, rather than give any of them to us to eat as we expected, they tossed the remaining fish into the sea again, although we begged and prayed for some as well as we could, but in vain; and some of my countrymen, being pressed by hunger, took an opportunity, when they thought no one saw them, of trying to get a little privately; but they were discovered, and the attempt procured them some very severe floggings. One day, when we had a smooth sea and moderate wind, two of my wearied countrymen who were chained together (I was near them at the time), preferring death to such a life of misery, somehow made through the nettings and jumped into the sea: immediately another quite dejected fellow, who, on account of his illness, was suffered to be out of irons, also followed their example; and I believe many more would very soon have done the same if they had not been prevented by the ship's crew, who were instantly alarmed. Those of us that were the most active were in a moment put down under the deck, and there was such a noise and confusion amongst the people of the ship as I never heard before, to stop her, and get the boat out to go after the slaves. However two of the wretches were drowned, but they got the other, and afterwards flogged him unmercifully for thus attempting to prefer death to slavery. In this manner we continued to undergo more hardships than I can now relate, hardships which are inseparable from this accursed trade. Many a time we were near suffocation from the want of fresh air, which we were often without for whole days together. This, and the stench of the necessary tubs, carried off many. During our passage I first saw flying fishes, which surprised me very much: they used frequently to fly across the ship, and many of them fell on the deck. I also now first saw the use of the quadrant; I had often with astonishment seen the mariners make observations with it, and I could not think what it meant. They at last took notice of my surprise; and one of them, willing to increase it, as well as to gratify my curiosity, made me one day look through it. The clouds appeared to me to be land, which disappeared as they passed along. This heightened my wonder; and I was now more persuaded than ever that I was in another world, and that every thing about me was magic. At last we came in sight of the island of Barbados, at which the whites on board gave a great shout, and made many signs of joy to us. We did not know what to think of this; but as the vessel drew nearer we plainly saw the harbour, and other ships of different kinds and sizes; and we soon anchored amongst them off Bridge Town. Many merchants and planters now came on board, though it was in the evening. They put us in separate parcels, and examined us attentively. They also made us jump, and pointed to the land, signifying we were to go there. We thought by this we should be eaten by these ugly men, as they appeared to us; and, when soon after we were all put down under the deck again, there was much dread and trembling among us, and nothing but bitter cries to be heard all the night from these

apprehensions, insomuch that at last the white people got some old slaves from the land to pacify us. They told us we were not eaten, but to work, and were soon to go on land, where we should see many of our country people. This report eased us much; and sure enough, soon after we were landed, there came to us Africans of all languages. We were conducted immediately to the merchant's yard, where we were all pent up altogether like so many sheep in a fold, without regard to sex or age. As every object was new to me every thing I saw filled me with surprise. What struck me first was that the houses were built with stories, and in every other respect different from those in Africa: but I was still more astonished on seeing people on horseback. I did not know what this could mean; and indeed I thought these people were full of nothing but magical arts. While I was in this astonishment one of my fellow prisoners spoke to a countryman of his about the horses, who said they were the same kind they had in their country. I understood them, though they were from a distant part of Africa, and I thought it odd I had not seen any horses there; but afterwards, when I came to converse with different Africans, I found they had many horses amongst them, and much larger than those I then saw. We were not many days in the merchant's custody before we were sold after their usual manner, which is this:– On a signal given, (as the beat of a drum) the buyers rush at once into the yard where the slaves are confined, and make a choice of that parcel they like best. The noise and clamour with which this is attended, and the eagerness visible in the countenances of the buyers, serve not a little to increase the apprehensions of the terrified Africans, who may well be supposed to consider them as the ministers of that destruction to which they think themselves devoted. In this manner, without scruple, are relations and friends separated, most of them never to see each other again. I remember in the vessel in which I was brought over, in the men's apartment, there were several brothers, who, in the sale, were sold in different lots; and it was very moving on this occasion to see and hear their cries at parting. O, ye nominal Christians! might not an African ask you, learned you this from your God, who says unto you, Do unto all men as you would men should do unto you? Is it not enough that we are torn from our country and friends to toil for your luxury and lust of gain? Must every tender feeling be likewise sacrificed to your avarice? Are the dearest friends and relations, now rendered more dear by their separation from their kindred, still to be parted from each other, and thus prevented from cheering the gloom of slavery with the small comfort of being together and mingling their sufferings and sorrows? Why are parents to lose their children, brothers their sisters, or husbands their wives? Surely this is a new refinement in cruelty, which, while it has no advantage to atone for it, thus aggravates distress, and adds fresh horrors even to the wretchedness of slavery.

Chapter Three

I NOW totally lost the small remains of comfort I had enjoyed in conversing with my countrymen; the women too, who used to wash and take care of me, were all gone different ways, and I never saw one of them afterwards.

I stayed in this island for a few days; I believe it could not be above a fortnight; when I and some few more slaves, that were not saleable amongst the rest, from very much fretting, were shipped off in a sloop for North America. On the passage we were better treated than when we were coming from Africa, and we had plenty of rice and fat pork. We were landed up a river a good way from the sea, about Virginia county, where we saw few or none of our native Africans, and not one soul who could talk to me. I was a few weeks weeding grass, and gathering stones in a plantation; and at last all my companions were distributed different ways, and only myself was left. I was now exceedingly miserable and thought myself worse off than any of the rest of my companions; for they could talk to each other, but I had no person to speak to that I could understand. In this state I was constantly grieving and pining, and wishing for death rather than any thing else. While I was in this plantation the gentleman, to whom I suppose the estate belonged, being unwell, I was one day sent for to his dwelling house to fan him; when I came into the room where he was I was very much affrighted at some things I saw, and the more so as I had seen a black woman slave as I came through the house, who was cooking the dinner, and the poor creature was cruelly loaded with various kinds of iron machines; she had one particularly on her head, which locked her mouth so fast that she could scarcely speak; and could not eat nor drink. I was much astonished and shocked at this contrivance, which I afterwards learned was called the iron muzzle. Soon after I had a fan put into my hand, to fan the gentleman while he slept; and so I did indeed with great fear. While he was fast asleep I indulged myself a great deal in looking about the room, which to me appeared very fine and curious. The first object that engaged my attention was a watch which hung on the chimney, and was going. I was quite surprised at the noise it made, and was afraid it would tell the gentleman any thing I might do amiss: and when I immediately after observed a picture hanging in the room, which appeared constantly to look at me, I was still more affrighted, having never seen such things as these before. At one time I thought it was something relative to magic; and not seeing it move I thought it might be some way the whites had to keep their great men when they died, and offer them libation as we used to do to our friendly spirits. In this state of anxiety I remained till my master awoke, when I was dismissed out of the room, to my no small satisfaction and relief; for I thought that these people were all made up of wonders. In this place I was called Jacob; but on board the African Snow I was called Michael. I had been some time in this miserable, forlorn, and much dejected state, without having any one to talk to, which made my life a burden, when the kind and unknown hand of the Creator (who in very deed leads the blind in a way they know not) now began to appear, to my comfort; for one day the captain of a merchant ship, called the Industrious Bee, came on some business to my master's house. This gentleman, whose name was Michael Henry Pascal, was a lieutenant in the royal navy, but now commanded this trading ship, which was somewhere in the confines of the county many miles off. While he was at my master's house it happened that he saw me, and liked me so well that he made a purchase of me. I think I have often heard him say he gave thirty or forty pounds sterling for me; but I do not now remember which. However, he meant me for a present to some of his friends in England: and I was sent accordingly from the house of my then master, one Mr. Campbell, to the place where the ship lay; I was conducted on horseback by an elderly black man, (a mode of travelling which appeared very odd to me). When I arrived I was carried on board a fine large ship, loaded with tobacco, &c. and just ready to sail for England. I now thought my condition much mended; I had sails to lie on, and plenty of good victuals to eat; and every body on board used me very kindly, quite contrary to what I had seen of any white people before; I therefore began to think that they were not all of the same disposition. A few days after I was on board we sailed for England. I was still at a loss to conjecture my destiny. By this time, however, I could smatter a little imperfect English; and I wanted to know as well as I could where we were going. Some of the people of the ship used to tell me they were going to carry me back to my own country, and this made me very happy. I was quite rejoiced at the sound of going back; and thought if I should get home what wonders I should have to tell. But I was reserved for another fate, and was soon undeceived when we came within sight of the English coast. While I was on board this ship, my captain and master named me *Gustavus Vasa.*[15] I at that time began to understand him a little, and refused to be called so, and told him as well as I could that I would be called Jacob; but he said I should not, and still called me Gustavus; and when I refused to answer to my new name, which at first I did, it gained me many a cuff; so at length I submitted, and was obliged to bear the present name, by which I have been known ever since. The ship had a very long passage; and on that account we had very short allowance of provisions. Towards the last we had only one pound and a half of bread per week, and about the same quantity of meat, and one quart of water a day. We spoke with only one vessel the whole time we were at sea, and but once we caught a few fishes. In our extremities the captain and people told me in jest they would kill and eat me; but I thought them in earnest, and was depressed beyond measure, expecting every moment to be my last. While I was in this situation one evening they caught, with a good deal of trouble, a large shark, and got it on board. This gladdened my poor heart exceedingly, as I thought it would serve the people to eat instead of their eating me; but very soon, to my astonishment, they cut

off a small part of the tail and tossed the rest over the side. This renewed my consternation; and I did not know what to think of these white people, though I very much feared they would kill and eat me. There was on board the ship a young lad who had never been at sea before, about four or five years older than myself: his name was Richard Baker. He was a native of America, had received an excellent education, and was of a most amiable temper. Soon after I went on board he shewed me a great deal of partiality and attention, and in return I grew extremely fond of him. We at length became inseparable; and, for the space of two years, he was of very great use to me, and was my constant companion and instructor. Although this dear youth had many slaves of his own, yet he and I have gone through many sufferings together on shipboard; and we have many nights lain in each other's bosoms when we were in great distress. Thus such a friendship was cemented between us as we cherished till his death, which, to my very great sorrow, happened in the year 1759, when he was up the Archipelago, on board his majesty's ship the Preston: an event which I have never ceased to regret, as I lost at once a kind interpreter, an agreeable companion, and a faithful friend; who, at the age of fifteen, discovered a mind superior to prejudice; and who was not ashamed to notice, to associate with, and to be the friend and instructor of one who was ignorant, a stranger, of a different complexion, and a slave! My master had lodged in his mother's house in America: he respected him very much, and made him always eat with him in the cabin. He used often to tell him jocularly that he would kill me to eat. Sometimes he would say to me – the black people were not good to eat, and would ask me if we did not eat people in my country. I said, No: then he said he would kill Dick (as he always called him) first, and afterwards me. Though this hearing relieved my mind a little as to myself, I was alarmed for Dick and whenever he was called I used to be very much afraid he was to be killed; and I would peep and watch to see if they were going to kill him: nor was I free from this consternation till we made the land. One night we lost a man overboard; and the cries and noise were so great

[15]   After a famous king of Sweden. Slaves were often named Scipio and Hannibal after famous figures in classical antiquity who had been born in Africa. [eds]

and confused, in stopping the ship, that I, who did not know what was the matter, began, as usual, to be very much afraid, and to think they were going to make an offering with me, and perform some magic; which I still believed they dealt in. As the waves were very high I thought the Ruler of the seas was angry, and I expected to be offered up to appease him. This filled my mind with agony, and I could not any more that night close my eyes again to rest. However, when daylight appeared I was a little eased in my mind; but still every time I was called I used to think it was to be killed. Some time after this we saw some very large fish, which I afterwards found were called grampusses. They looked to me extremely terrible, and made their appearance just at dusk; and were so near as to blow the water on the ship's deck. I believed them to be the rulers of the sea; and, as the white people did not make any offerings at any time, I thought they were angry with them: and, at last, what confirmed my belief was, the wind just then died away, and a calm ensued, and in consequence of it the ship stopped going. I supposed that the fish had performed this, and I hid myself in the fore part of the ship, through fear of being offered up to appease them, every minute peeping and quaking: but my good friend Dick came shortly towards me, and I took an opportunity to ask him, as well as I could, what these fish were. Not being able to talk much English, I could just make him understand my question; and not at all, when I asked him if any offerings were to be made to them: however, he told me these fish would swallow any body; which sufficiently alarmed me. Here he was called away by the captain, who was leaning over the quarter-deck railing and looking at the fish; and most of the people were busied in getting a barrel of pitch to light, for them to play with. The captain now called me to him, having learned some of my apprehensions from Dick; and having diverted himself and others for some time with my fears, which appeared ludicrous enough in my crying and trembling, he dismissed me. The barrel of pitch was now lighted and put over the side into the water: by this time it was just dark, and the fish went after it; and, to my great joy, I saw them no more.

However, all my alarms began to subside when we got sight of land; and at last the ship arrived at Falmouth, after a passage of thirteen weeks. Every heart on board seemed gladdened on our reaching the shore, and none more than mine. The captain immediately went on shore, and sent on board some fresh provisions, which we wanted very much: we made good use of them, and our famine was soon turned into feasting, almost without ending. It was about the beginning of the spring 1757 when I arrived in England, and I was near twelve years of age at that time. I was very much struck with the buildings and the pavement of the streets in Falmouth; and, indeed, any object I saw filled me with new surprise. One morning, when I got upon deck, I saw it covered all over with the snow that fell overnight: as I had never seen any thing of the kind before, I thought it was salt; so I immediately ran down to the mate and desired him, as well as I could, to come and see how somebody in the night had thrown salt all over the deck. He, knowing what it was, desired me to bring some of it down to him: accordingly I took up a handful of it, which I found very cold indeed; and when I brought it to him he desired me to taste it. I did so, and I was surprised beyond measure. I then asked him what it was; he told me it was snow: but I could not in anywise understand him. He asked me if we had no such thing in my country; and I told him, No. I then asked him the use of it, and who made it; he told me a great man in the heavens, called God: but here again I was to all intents and purposes at a loss to understand him; and the more so, when a little after I saw the air filled with it, in a heavy shower, which fell down on the same day. After this I went to church; and having never been at such a place before, I was again amazed at seeing and hearing the service. I asked all I could about it; and they gave me to understand it was worshipping God, who made us and all things. I was still at a great loss, and soon got into an endless field of inquiries, as well as I was able to speak and ask about things. However, my little friend Dick used to be my best interpreter; for I could make free with him, and he always instructed me with pleasure: and from what I could understand by him of this God, and in seeing these white people did not sell one another, as we did, I was much pleased; and in this I thought they were much happier than we Africans. I was astonished at the wisdom of the white people in all things I saw; but was amazed at their not sacrificing, or making any offerings, and eating with unwashed hands, and touching the dead. I likewise could not help remarking the particular slenderness of their women, which I did not at first like; and I thought they were not so modest and shamefaced as the African women.

I had often seen my master and Dick employed in reading; and I had a great curiosity to talk to the books, as I thought they did; and so to learn how all things had a beginning: for that purpose I have often taken up a book, and have talked to it, and then put my ears to it, when alone, in hopes it would answer me; and I have been very much concerned when I found it remained silent.

My master lodged at the house of a gentleman in Falmouth, who had a fine little daughter about six or seven years of age, and she grew prodigiously fond of me; insomuch that we used to eat together, and had servants to wait on us. I was so much caressed by this family that it often reminded me of the treatment I had received from my little noble African master. After I had been here a few days, I was sent on board of the ship; but the child cried so much after me that nothing could pacify her till I was sent for again. It is ludicrous enough, that I began to fear I should be betrothed to this young lady; and when my master asked me if I would stay there with her behind him, as he was going away with the ship, which had taken in the tobacco again, I cried immediately, and said I would not leave her. At last, by stealth, one night I was sent on board the ship again; and in a little time we sailed for Guernsey, where she was in part owned by a merchant, one Nicholas Doberry. As I was now amongst a people who had not their faces scarred, like some of the African nations where I had been, I was very glad I did not let them ornament me in that manner when I was with them. When we arrived at Guernsey, my master placed me to board and lodge with one of his mates, who had a wife and family there; and some months afterwards he went to England, and left me in care of this mate, together with my friend Dick: This mate had a little daughter, aged about five or six years, with whom I used to be much delighted. I had often observed that when her mother washed her face it looked very rosy; but when she washed mine it did not look so: I therefore tried oftentimes myself if I could not by washing make my face of the same colour as my little play-mate (Mary), but it was all in vain; and I now began to be mortified at the difference in our complexions. This woman behaved to me with great kindness and attention; and taught me every thing in the same manner as she did her own child, and indeed in every respect treated me as such. I remained here till the summer of the year 1757; when my master, being appointed first lieutenant of his majesty's ship the Roebuck, sent for Dick and me, and his old mate: on this we all left Guernsey.

Source: Olaudah Equiano, *The Life of Olaudah Equiano, or Gustavus Vassa the African*, London, 1789, reprinted from the facsimile edition introduced by Paul Edwards, Dawson UK Ltd, London, 1969.